In 1965, a group of economists at Harvard University established the Project for Quantitative Research in Economic Development in the Center for International Affairs. Brought together by a common background of fieldwork in developing countries and a desire to apply modern techniques of quantitative analysis to the policy problems of these countries, they produced this volume, which represents that part of their research devoted to formulating operational ways of thinking about development problems.

The seventeen essays are organized into four sections: General Planning Models, International Trade and External Resources, Sectoral Planning, and Empirical Bases for Development Programs. They raise some central questions: To what extent can capital and labor substitute for each other? Does development require fixed inputs of engineers and other specialists in each sector or are skills highly substitutable? Is the trade gap a structural phenomenon or merely evidence of an overvalued exchange rate? To what extent do consumers respond to changes in relative prices?

Harvard Economic Studies

Volume 136

The studies in this series are published under the direction of the Department of Economics of Harvard University. This study was written under the auspices of the Center for International Affairs of Harvard University. Neither the Department nor the Center assumes responsibility for the views expressed.

Studies
In
Development Planning

edited by Hollis B. Chenery

with
Samuel Bowles
Walter Falcon
Carl Gotsch
David Kendrick
Arthur MacEwan
Christopher Sims
Thomas Weisskopf

Harvard University Press, Cambridge, Massachusetts

Contributors

Irma Adelman
Professor of Economics
Northwestern University

Samuel Bowles
Associate Professor of Economics
Harvard University

Michael Bruno
Professor of Economics
Hebrew University
Jerusalem

Hollis B. Chenery
Professor of Economics
Harvard University

Christopher R. S. Dougherty
Fellow of Kings College
Cambridge University
Cambridge, England

Walter Falcon
Lecturer on Economics
Harvard University

Carl Gotsch
Lecturer on Economics
Harvard University

David Kendrick
Professor of Economics
University of Texas

Luis Landau
International Bank for Reconstruction and Development
Washington, D. C.

Arthur MacEwan
Assistant Professor of Economics
Harvard University

William Raduchel
Assistant Professor of Economics
Harvard University

Marcelo Selowsky
Professor of Economics
Catholic University
Santiago, Chile

Christopher Sims
Associate Professor of Economics
University of Minnesota

Lance Taylor
Assistant Professor of Economics
Harvard University

Suresh D. Tendulkar
Planning Unit
Indian Statistical Institute
New Delhi

Richard Weisskoff
Assistant Professor of Economics
Yale University

Thomas E. Weisskopf
Assistant Professor of Economics
Harvard University

Larry E. Westphal
Assistant Professor of Economics and International Affairs
Princeton University

Preface

The study of development policy requires a variety of analytical techniques, an understanding of the technology and institutional characteristics of different sectors of an economy, and some feel for the limitations to government action. The individual scholar in this field is limited both in the range of knowledge that he can acquire and by the time needed to study complex systems. Since academic economists are not yet persuaded of the value of group research, studies of development policy have typically been specialized by sector, technique, or country.

In an effort to secure some of the benefits of collaboration without the rigidity of a formal research program, a group of economists established the Project for Quantitative Research in Economic Development in the Center for International Affairs at Harvard in 1965.[1] We were brought together by a common background of field work in developing countries and by a desire to apply modern techniques of quantitative analysis to the policy problems of these countries. This volume contains a selection of research produced by the Quantitative Project[2] chosen, in part, to illustrate the benefits of this type of informal collaboration.

Most of these studies are an outgrowth of extensive field work in a variety of countries—Pakistan, India, Korea, Israel, Greece, Nigeria, Colombia, Chile, Brazil, and elsewhere. This empirical beginning has resulted in several common characteristics: the design of models to utilize available data, a focus on policy variables, and the inclusion of specific institutional limits. A number of studies were done in consultation with local planning organizations or research groups[3] and incorporate some of their perceptions about the relevant limitations to policy.

This policy orientation leads to a confrontation between the neoclassical assumptions that dominate the thinking of Western economists and the technical and behavioral rigidities that are commonly assumed by development planners. This

[1] Original members of the group were Samuel Bowles; Michael Bruno (Hebrew University, Jerusalem); Hollis Chenery; Walter Falcon; Carl Gotsch; Stephen Lewis (now at Williams College); and David Kendrick.

[2] All but one of the studies were done under the sponsorship of the Quantitative Project during the years 1965–1969 (except for Bruno's pioneering study in Chapter 8, which antedates his association with us). With the exception of Irma Adelman, the authors all held teaching or research appointments at Harvard during this period. We have also benefited from our close association with the Development Advisory Service at Harvard.

[3] Including the planning offices of Korea, Pakistan, India, and Colombia; the Pakistan Institute of Development Economics; the Indian Statistical Institute; the Greek Center of Economic Research; the Bank of Israel; and the Nigerian Institute of Economic and Social Research.

conflict is reflected in many of the central questions raised in our analyses. To what extent can capital and labor substitute for each other? Does development require fixed inputs of engineers and other specialists in each sector or are skills highly substitutable? Is the trade gap a structural phenomenon or merely evidence of an overvalued exchange rate? To what extent do consumers respond to changes in relative prices?

Every author has had to choose among such hypotheses and to explore their implications in a specific context. The choice of a theoretical framework is dictated largely by the available data and the computational methods available for solving planning models. It is in this area that informal collaboration and exposure to other approaches has been particularly valuable. Project members with special skills in econometrics (Taylor and Sims), mathematical programming (Kendrick and Bruno), and computer techniques (Taylor and Raduchel), have been of great value to the rest of us. The regional experts among us have reciprocated by suggesting countries and problems where particular techniques might be tested.

In the papers selected for this volume, there has been a convergence on four of the basic factors in development:

1. capital formation and its financing
2. skill formation and educational planning
3. reallocation of resources necessary to avoid bottlenecks in trade or in specific sectors, such as agriculture
4. role of external resources in supplying capital and imports

These topics have been analyzed in both econometric studies and planning models. However, there are two other important areas to which we feel insufficient attention has been given—the nature of technical change and the redistribution of income. Their neglect in this volume is due to the lack of quantitative information and perhaps to our too ready acceptance of the notion that the economist's role is to prescribe policies designed to maximize output, leaving questions of income distribution and technology to politicians and engineers.

Research on development policy depends on progress in several fields: development theory, mathematical programming, econometrics, and computer technology. Improvements in computer technology now make it possible to formulate large economic models and to use nonlinear relations that would not have been practical ten years ago. Much of our work can therefore be thought of as "research and development," designed to test the value of different approaches to policy problems. While the volume contains a few theoretical novelties and a certain number of practical conclusions for individual countries, our main purpose has been to formulate operational ways of thinking about development problems.

The seventeen papers in this volume are organized under four headings: I. General Planning Models; II. International Trade and External Resources; III. Sectoral Planning; IV. Empirical Bases for Development Programs. Two members of the project have undertaken the editorial responsibility for each area and have surveyed related research under each heading. In this way we have tried to put the conclusions of these studies in a broader perspective.

Our research has been supported by grants to the Center for International Affairs from the Agency for International Development, the National Science Foundation, and the Ford Foundation, to whom we express our gratitude. Our intellectual debts are too numerous to be enumerated. However, we want to pay tribute to two men who pioneered many of the areas in which we are working: Jan Tinbergen and Wassily Leontief.

Cambridge, Massachusetts
September 1970

Hollis B. Chenery
Samuel Bowles
Walter Falcon
Carl Gotsch
David Kendrick
Arthur MacEwan
Christopher Sims
Thomas Weisskopf

Contents

Part IV: Empirical Bases for Development Programs

Studies in Development Planning

General Introduction

Hollis B. Chenery

Responding to urgent demands for economic and social improvement, most poor countries have adopted development plans as a basis for governmental action. This response has been produced by a variety of forces: reactions against colonial policies, the political appeal of development, examples of rapid progress elsewhere, and the urging of foreign lenders. In the face of these pressures, countries have often adopted the forms of planned development before they acquire the technical and administrative competence to carry them out.

Although initial attempts at planning are usually little more than analytical exercises, they have helped to identify the limits to more rapid growth and to initiate a systematic consideration of government policy. Procedures and analytical techniques have been patterned on some of the advanced countries—notably France, the Netherlands, the USSR—or improvised to meet specific needs. In retrospect, the past decade can be seen as a period in which the major problems of development have been identified and intuitive forms of planning tried out. Out of this effort has come a large increase in information which makes the use of formal economic analysis more feasible in the future.

Experience with intuitive planning methods has stimulated attempts to make better use of available information and analytical techniques. The first requirement is to test and revise many of the assumptions on which development theories are based. The second is to formulate more comprehensive analyses of future development possibilities which bring out the indirect effects and interactions of separate government policies.

The theoretical background for these attempts derives from Tinbergen's classic formulation (1956) of the nature of policy analysis. Although short-term stabilization and full employment have been the main concern of policy in the advanced countries, long-term development and structural change have become the focus of attention in the poorer countries. Policy analysis in developing countries has therefore stimulated both new theoretical formulations and new applications of statistical methods.

The seventeen papers in this volume explore the usefulness of several kinds of economic models for these purposes. Our studies use two types of model: (1) *econometric models*, which serve to test hypotheses and estimate past economic relationships; and (2) *planning models*, which are used to establish relationships between social objectives and the instruments of policy. Taken together these studies illustrate the interaction

1

between empirical and theoretical aspects of planning and the need to strike a balance between them.

Six of the studies demonstrate applications of econometric analysis to developing countries. Such analyses contribute to development policy in several ways. First, they test and refine many basic assumptions about development, such as the relationships between savings and income levels, the effect of changes in income and prices on consumer demand, the response of agricultural producers to market conditions, and so on. These results can then replace general deductions from economic theory as a basis for designing policy measures. They also provide components of more comprehensive models of the whole economy.

The other eleven papers are concerned with the design and use of models for long-term policy. These planning models analyze the direct and indirect effects of specified combinations of policy instruments on important aspects of economic behavior. Since it is impractical to include all the relevant economic activities in a single analysis, models are specialized according to sector, region, time period, and economic function.

Planning models are used for a variety of purposes. More abstract formulations are designed to explore general economic phenomena or to test the application of certain analytical techniques. The empirical content of these studies is limited to the specification of realistic orders of magnitude for the main structural relationships. At the other extreme are detailed models designed to produce specific policy recommendations for a given sector.

Although planning models originated as numerical procedures for solving specific problems of resource allocation, they are increasingly being used as a means of theorizing about development phenomena. The dynamic properties of economic systems having a substantial empirical content are so complex that general analytical solutions are no longer feasible. Numerical analysis of the properties of planning models under alternative empirical assumptions provides a method of exploring theoretical phenomena which can otherwise be described only in general terms.

The studies in this volume therefore serve several purposes. Each was originally aimed toward determining the best resource allocation in a given country or testing a given analytical procedure. In most cases, however, the specification of the model led beyond the original problem to the consideration of the nature of the economic system in which it arises. In this way we have given a specific formulation to some general concepts of development theory, such as balanced growth, absorptive capacity, and dynamic comparative advantage.

One theme that runs through many of our studies is the importance of recognizing interdependence or "systems effects" in designing development policies. The framework of interindustry analysis that is common to most planning models brings out the indirect effects of policies designed to influence investment allocation or the balance of payments. Although the interindustry studies of Korea, India, Pakistan, and Israel, Chapters 4 through 8, were carried out independently, when taken together they lead to some useful generalizations. The nature of the trade limit to development—the "two gap problem"—can only be fully appreciated in this context, in which the optimal allocation of resources is determined with simultaneous constraints on savings, exports and external capital inflows. These phenomena are generalized in more abstract form by the use of nonlinear and dynamic models in Part I. The study of similar phenomena with different types of model shows the extent to which the results depend on a particular analytical formulation and thus contributes to the process of generalization.

The volume is divided into four parts with a separate introduction to each. This organization permits us to provide a general framework for our studies and to bring out some of their common features and conclusions. Most of our work can be thought of as "research and development," designed to test the value of different approaches to policy problems. While the volume contains a few theoretical novelties and a certain number of practical conclusions for individual countries, our main purpose has been to develop quantitative methods of analysis and operational ways of thinking about development problems.

Part I
General Planning Models

Introduction to Part I

David Kendrick
and Arthur MacEwan

Planning models are designed to study the long-term consequences of policies affecting the allocation of resources, particularly the division of investment among sectors. They draw on the results of theoretical growth models but differ from them in that they (1) contain empirical estimates and are solved with numerical methods, (2) are usually disaggregated into many sectors, and (3) involve more complex specification of development processes and specific policy constraints. The net effect of these differences is to make theoretical models more useful for studying the general character of growth in an abstract setting and to make planning models more useful for studying more disaggregated and complex systems which include the instruments and constraints of government policy.

The development of planning methodology involves the interplay of new theoretical formulations with empirical perceptions of problems of resource allocation. On the technical side, progress has consisted in developing increasingly powerful methods of solving problems of optimization subject to constraints. On the empirical side a more realistic description of the structural constraints within which the economy operates has affected the basic formulation of the planner's problems.

The four papers in this section all reflect this interaction between empirical perceptions and the improvement of optimizing procedures. The main theoretical innovations are the substitution of nonlinear functions for the linear relations commonly used in input-output analysis and linear programming. A major purpose of each of these studies is to design nonlinear optimizing procedures for particular planning situations, focusing in most cases on the effects of a multiperiod analysis.

On the empirical side, a number of technological and behavioral relations are explored: economies of scale, specific substitution possibilities in production and demand, and realistic limitations on instrument variables.

It is characteristic of planning models that different empirical specifications require different numerical methods of computation. And the development of methodology requires an investigation of the type of optimization that is best suited to each empirical formulation. Our introductory discussion is therefore organized in terms of the properties of the models used rather than the problems considered.

It should be kept in mind that present model formulation is well ahead of the accumulation of empirical estimates of underlying relationships. The papers in this section are accordingly designed to show the feasibility of the method as well as to obtain analytic insight into planning problems. Only the Westphal study (Chapter 4) is derived from an actual planning situation, and even there emphasis is on the method of analysis rather than on the specific results.

Linear Dynamic Models

If economic models are fully disaggregated both by sector and time period, they include such a large number of variables and constraints that they become computationally unwieldy; and it is necessary to compromise between the two types of disaggregation. Feasible linear programming models may have as many as 200 sectors with a single time period, 10 to 30 sectors with 5 to 10 time periods, or 1 or 2 sectors and 100 time periods. Up to now the basic linear programming models of development planning have treated many sectors and a single time period.

Several experiments have been made with models of 20 to 30 sectors and up to 10 time periods.[1] Examples are studies by Eckaus and Parikh (1968); Chakravarty and Lefeber (1965); Manne and Weisskopf (1969); and Bruno, Fraenkel, and Dougherty (1968). When a model is designed to cover 20 or more time periods, the number of sectors must be even more limited. Chenery and MacEwan (1966), for example, specify 23 time periods but distinguish only 2 producing sectors.[2]

The paper by Taylor (Chapter 3) is closely related to the Chenery-MacEwan study, which provides a prototype of the so-called two-gap models. That formulation is based on the assumption that the principal limits to development are the supplies of capital and foreign exchange. Two-gap planning models focus on the interrelation between those constraints and the structure of the economy. In the dynamic form they are primarily concerned with time phasing of foreign exchange saving investment, on the one hand, and capital saving investment, on the other hand.

Taylor applies control theory techniques to the solution of a two-gap linear dynamic model. The control theory procedures can be used for solving any dynamic linear model but are best adapted to models with few sectors and many time periods. The advantage of this approach is that an examination of the first-order conditions to the control theory solution may reveal generalizations about the solution to the problem as a function of the relative values of various parameters. It may thus be possible to describe solutions to such models without incurring the substantial computational expenses associated with solving large linear programming problems.

Taylor's approach is similar to the analytical methods used in most of the growth theory literature, namely, the papers in Shell (1967). Taylor is able to generalize previous findings that heavy investment and capital inflow in the early periods of a plan are optimal in linear two-gap models under a wide variety of assumptions about parameter values.

Convex Programming Models

Static Models

Like their linear antecedents, nonlinear convex programming models may be usefully separated into single-period (static) and multiperiod or dynamic models.

1. Sometimes two or three years are aggregated to a single time period, allowing consideration of a longer planning horizon without increasing the size of the model.
2. Stern (1970) uses a Chenery-MacEwan type optimizing model to study intertemporal paths of aggregate variables; and then he uses the aggregate results as the basis of a multisectoral consistency model exercise. In this way he is able to obtain both temporal and sectoral disaggregation, albeit at the cost of not having a complete optimizing model.

The first works on static nonlinear development planning models were those of Chenery and Kretschmer (1956) and Chenery and Uzawa (1958). These models employed linear production functions and assumed export earnings to be linear decreasing return functions of export levels.

The study of Chenery and Raduchel (Chapter 2) is an extension of that approach to problems with nonlinear production and welfare functions as well as nonlinear trade relationships. The nonlinear formulation permits the authors to specify continuous functions and thereby examine any number of substitution possibilities.[3] In examining substitution possibilities in demand, production, and trade relationships, Chenery and Raduchel conclude that direct substitution between capital and labor in production appears to be of greater significance in affecting levels of employment than does indirect substitution via changes in the composition of consumption and trade.

Dynamic Models

Several dynamic nonlinear convex programming models have been developed, some with nonlinearities in the welfare function and some with nonlinearities in the production relationships. Johansen (1960), for example, has used a dynamic model with a nonlinear welfare function and linear production relationships. Radner and Friedman (1965) were among the first to study dynamic models with nonlinear (and convex) production functions. They used Cobb-Douglas functions that were linear in logs and employed computational procedures that were specific to the log-linear production and welfare relationships.

In Chapter 1, Kendrick and Taylor use control theory to solve planning models with nonlinear production and welfare relations. In doing so they demonstrate the usefulness of numerical methods for problems that cannot be solved in closed form. Although the models could also have been solved with nonlinear programming algorithms, control theory methods seem particularly suited for problems with few sectors and many time periods. Kendrick and Taylor solve numerically the one-sector model that was studied analytically by Chakravarty (1962) and thereby establish a procedure for computing the solution to the class of models with a continuum of parameter values. The turnpike properties of the model are computed and displayed.

Nonconvex Programming Methods

While economies of scale in individual industries have been studied by economists for some years—Chenery (1952), Vietorisz and Manne (1963), Manne (1966b), and Kendrick (1967)—economy-wide models with increasing returns (economies of scale) have been largely ignored. Westphal's study (Chapter 4) represents a new interest in such models, the solution of which has been made possible by improvements in algorithms for solving linear mixed integer programming problems. This

3. A number of linear programming models have incorporated nonlinear functions by using piecewise linear approximation. For example, Carter (1967a), Adelman and Sparrow (1966), and the Westphal study (Chapter 4 in this volume) use linear approximations of nonlinear welfare functions. Haldi (1960) and Westphal employ linear approximations to nonlinear nonconvex production functions, using a procedure first suggested by Markowitz and Manne (1957); and MacEwan (1971) introduces a diminishing returns production function in agricultural sectors.

form results from including economies of scale in some sectors in models that otherwise include only linear functions.

Westphal illustrates that procedure by assuming increasing returns in the steel and petrochemicals industries in his model of the South Korean economy. He shows that the time-phasing of the large and lumpy investments that are required in such industries is quite important to planning decisions throughout the economy. Decisions to invest in large complexes in a relatively small economy may deprive other industries of capital or foreign exchange to such an extent that their growth is limited. This limitation on the growth of other industries may invalidate the assumptions that justified the original investment. Because one can only capture such indirect effects in dynamic nonconvex models, which are relatively difficult to compute, rigorous treatment of these problems has not been possible in the past.

Conclusions

The four studies in this section demonstrate the advantages of using computational methods that are adapted to the empirical features of the allocation problems being considered. While in some cases the nonlinear formulation confirms the results of earlier linear simplifications, in others the nature of the conclusions is fundamentally different. The advance of computer technology and optimizing procedures has greatly reduced the limiting effects of computational limitations and makes it feasible to include a large selection of functional forms.

1 Numerical Methods and Nonlinear Optimizing Models for Economic Planning*

David Kendrick
and Lance Taylor

I. Introduction

This paper is a report on some experimentation with numerical methods for solving dynamic nonlinear planning models. The methods employed were first developed by control theorists and are applied here to some simple economic planning models.

The models are based on ideas drawn from two recent lines of thought about aggregate growth over time. The first line is that of nonlinear theoretical models designed to analyze the characteristics of an economy in asymptotic optimal growth, for example, Samuelson and Solow (1956), Chakravarty (1965), and Bruno (1967a). The other line is the construction of empirical multisectoral linear programming models to study the development programs of particular countries, for instance, the model for Israel by Bruno (1966) and those for India by Eckaus and Parikh (1968) and Chakravarty and Lefeber (1965).

Our purpose is to develop and solve empirically based finite horizon optimizing models that permit the specification of the production, welfare, and foreign trade relationships in a nonlinear form, and thereby to analyze some of the properties of such growth models.

Much of the previous work in this field of finite horizon models had made either the foreign exchange constraint or the welfare function nonlinear; for example, Chenery and Uzawa (1958) did some of the first experimentation with nonlinear optimizing models by introducing nonlinearities in the foreign exchange constraint. Models with nonlinear welfare (or criterion or objective) functions have been studied by Frisch (1961), Chakravarty (1962), Johansen and Lindholt (1964), and Barr and Manne (1967).

Finite horizon optimizing models with nonlinearities in the production functions have also been analyzed by Frisch, and by Chakravarty (1962) and Radner (1963, 1966), Radner and Friedman (1965), and Friedman (1968). Chakravarty considered a one-sector model with a nonlinear welfare function and a nonlinear production function of the form

$$Q = aK^\beta$$

* This research has been financed in part by the Agency for International Development and in part by the Harvard Institute for Economic Research under a grant from the National Science Foundation. We are grateful to Alan Manne for a number of helpful comments on an earlier draft, to Robert Kierr for able programming and for helpful advice on solving control theory problems, and to Andy Szasz for programming assistance.

11

where Q is output, K is capital stock, and β and a are parameters. He showed that for the special case of $\beta = \frac{1}{2}$ it was possible to obtain a closed form solution for the capital stock path. The $\beta = \frac{1}{2}$ case was the only nonlinear case he discussed since he implied that it was not possible to obtain closed form solutions for any other cases.[1]

Radner and Friedman have experimented with multisectoral models usually, with log-linear (Cobb-Douglas) welfare and production relations. Friedman (1968) reports on applications of this method to problems with constant elasticity of substitution production functions replacing the Cobb-Douglas specification. Apparently no great computational problems arise in this type of nonlog-linear problem, although convergence is somewhat slower than in the Cobb-Douglas version.

We have reported elsewhere on experimentation with heterogeneous capital good models (Kendrick and Taylor 1969, 1970); here we confine ourselves to one-sector models, with and without a foreign exchange constraint. These two models, involving one and two control variables respectively, provided the opportunity to modify algorithms and programs obtained from others and to develop some of our own programs for solving this class of optimization problems. As a by-product of this work, and because we were using numerical analysis techniques to analyze the effects of parameter changes, insights were obtained into the operation of small nonlinear models—even though these cannot be derived by strictly analytical approaches.

In Section II we report on our results in solving two nonlinear planning models: (1) a closed economy model without foreign trade and (2) an open economy model with foreign trade.

Since the solution techniques used in this article and in subsequent work are relatively new to economics, we discuss the general structure of nonlinear control problems in Section III and the properties of some algorithms for solving this class of problems in Section IV.[2] Our conclusions are given in Section V.

II. Economic Results

Our results consist of a study of the effects in one-sector optimizing models of (1) nonlinear specification of the production and welfare functions, (2) turnpike properties of the simple model, and (3) inclusion of a foreign exchange constraint.

Drawing on the work of Chakravarty (1962) and Maneschi's comments (1966) on that work, we used the model:

maximize
$$J^* = \int_0^n e^{-rt} \frac{1}{1-\eta} c(t)^{1-\eta} \, dt \qquad (1.1)$$

where
- J^* is a performance index
- r is a time rate of welfare discount
- $c(t)$ is instantaneous consumption at time t
- n is the final time period
- η is the elasticity of marginal utility with respect to consumption

1. Chakravarty also obtained a closed form solution for the linear production case ($\beta = 1$) with the nonlinear welfare function (1.4).

2. Mathematical programming methods may also be used to solve these problems. A short discussion about the comparative advantage of control theory and mathematical programming methods is given in Kendrick and Taylor (1969).

subject to

$$\dot{k}(t) = f[k(t)] - c(t) - \delta k(t) \tag{1.2}$$

where

$\dot{k}(t)$ = net investment
$f[k(t)]$ = the production function
$k(t)$ = the capital stock
δ = the rate of depreciation

$$k(0) = \bar{k} \tag{1.3a}$$

where

$\bar{k}$ = initial capital stock

and

$$y_n = \bar{y} \tag{1.3b}$$

where

y_n is a terminal output level uniquely determined by k_n

In our analysis we have experimented with both discrete and continuous formulations of the model. For computational purposes we rewrite the model in the discrete form and use i as the time subscript.[3]

$$J = \sum_{i=0}^{n-1} \frac{1}{(1+\rho)^i} \frac{1}{1-\eta} c_i^{1-\eta} \tag{1.1a}$$

$$k_{i+1} = f[k_i] - c_i + (1-\delta)k_i \tag{1.2a}$$

$$k_0 = \bar{k} \tag{1.3a}$$

$$y_n = f(k_n) = \bar{y} \tag{1.3b}$$

We have chosen the particular form

$$u(c) = \frac{1}{1-\eta} c_i^{1-\eta} \qquad \eta \geq 0, \eta \neq 1 \tag{1.4}$$

for the welfare function because of the following properties:

$$u'(c_i) = c_i^{-\eta} \geq 0$$

$$\frac{u'(c_i)}{u(c_i)/c_i} = 1 - \eta = constant \text{ elasticity of utility} \tag{1.4a}$$

$$u''(c_i) = -\eta c_i^{-\eta-1} \leq 0 \tag{1.4b}$$

$$\lim_{\eta \to 0} u(c_i) = c_i \tag{1.4c}$$

Property (1.4b) gives us diminishing marginal welfare and property (1.4c) shows that the welfare function becomes linear as η approaches zero.

The form of the production function we have used is

$$\begin{aligned} f[k(t)] &= e^{zt}\gamma k(t)^\beta (l_0 e^{rt})^{1-\beta} \\ &= e^{[r(1-\beta)+z]t}\gamma l_0^{1-\beta} k(t)^\beta \\ &= e^{qt}a[k(t)]^\beta \end{aligned} \tag{1.5}$$

3. Nonnegativity conditions on the variables k_i and c_i should also be included for completeness. However, since interior solutions are typically obtained, these constraints need not be treated explicitly.

where

$$a = \gamma l_0^{1-\beta}$$

which can be approximated in discrete time with a one-period investment lag by

$$y_i = f[k_i] = (l + g)^i a k_i^\beta \tag{1.6}$$

where

z = the rate of neutral technical progress
γ = efficiency parameter
β = elasticity of output with respect to capital
l_0 = initial labor force
r = rate of growth of labor force
$g = r(1 - \beta) + z$

Using the model (1.1a), (1.2a), and (1.3a) with (1.6) we obtain—either by the Kuhn-Tucker conditions or by the discrete-time maximum principle (see the Appendix to this article and Section III)—the following first-order conditions for a constrained maximum:

$$k_{i+1} = (1 + g)^i a k_i^\beta - c_i + (1 - \delta)k_i \tag{1.7}$$

$$\lambda_{i+1} = [(1 + g)^i \beta a k_i^{\beta-1} + 1 - \delta]^{-1}\lambda_i \tag{1.8}$$

$$c_i = [(1 + \rho)^i \lambda_{i+1}]^{-1/\eta} \tag{1.9}$$

$$\lambda_n = \nu \tag{1.10}$$

$$k_0 = \bar{k} \tag{1.11}$$

where

λ_i = the adjoint variables for the constraints (1.2a); that is the "shadow price" of capital

and

ν = a "shadow price" on the terminal capital constraint[4]

With $\bar{k}$ given, the system (1.7), (1.8), (1.9), and (1.10) can be solved with a one-dimensional search on λ_0 as follows:

1. Choose an arbitrary λ_0.
2. Use k_0 and λ_0 in (1.8) to obtain λ_1.
3. Use λ_1 in (1.9) to obtain c_0.
4. Use c_0 and k_0 in (1.7) to obtain k_1.
5. Repeat steps 2 through 4, increasing the index by one on each repetition until k_n is obtained.

4. Observing that the welfare summation runs over the period zero to $n - 1$ while the capital stock is constrained by the income target in period n and examining the first-order conditions (1.7–1.11), we see that these conditions can be satisfied by either of the following computational methods:

a. choosing λ_0 such that $\lambda_n = \nu$, the terminal shadow price of capital
b. choosing λ_0 such that k_n is equal to some target level while permitting λ_n to take any value (or equivalently choosing λ_0 such that y_n is equal to some target level while permitting λ_n to take on any value)

Thus we either choose a terminal unit scrap value for capital and obtained the implied terminal capital stock, or we choose the terminal capital stock and obtain the implied unit scrap value for capital at terminal time. Arrow and Kurz (1970) utilize a scrap-value concept for the terminal capital in analyzing finite horizon models.

6. Compare y_n to $\bar{y}$; halt if they are sufficiently "close" to one another or, if not, choose a new λ_0 and return to step 2.

Since in our experience this algorithm converges with only a few iterations and each iteration for a 50-period version of the model requires only about one second of computation time on an IBM 7094, we have been able to study the behavior of the model with many different parameter settings.

For a number of the solutions, including those reported on here, side calculations of the implied savings rate were made.

Effects of Nonlinear Specification of Production and Welfare Functions

Most numerical planning models that have been constructed are of the linear programming type. Since it is relatively easy to use piecewise linear segments to approximate diminishing marginal welfare but more time-consuming to approximate nonlinear production functions, we have attempted to gain some insight into how nonlinear specification of these functions affects the qualitative behavior of such models. In order to do this we have first varied β (the elasticity of output with respect to capital) and then varied η (the elasticity of marginal utility with respect to consumption), in each case holding all but one parameter constant. In varying β we chose the parameter "a" in a complementary manner in order to maintain a constant initial output level with the different specifications of the production function. The parameters used in the model, except in cases where an explicit variation from these values is mentioned, are given below.

Parameters for the Growth Model
$\delta = $ 0.05
$k_0 = $ 15.0
$\rho = $ 0.03
$\beta = $ 0.75
$y_0 = $ 4.275
$\eta = $ 0.9
$a = $ 0.5609
$\bar{y}$ = 85.5 (This level of $\bar{y}$ represents an approximate 6 percent geometric growth in income over the planning period)
$r = $ 0.025
$z = $ 0.01

Complementary Values of a and β

$a = 2.1723$	$\beta = 0.25$
$= 0.8419$	$= 0.60$
$= 0.5609$	$= 0.75$
$= 0.4900$	$= 0.80$
$= 0.285$	$= 1.00$

Figure 1.1 shows the path of the savings rate that is optimal under various values of β (and the complementary value of a). The $\beta = 0.8$ case approaches the behavior observed by linear programmers in the absence of a savings constraint and of piecewise linear approximations to nonlinear welfare or production functions, that is, extremely high savings rates in the early years falling off sharply over time.

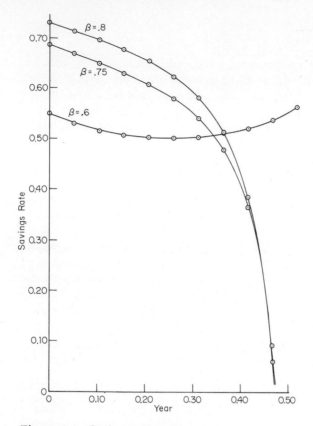

Figure 1.1 Savings-rate paths.

Then as β is changed to 0.75 and 0.60 the savings rate path exhibits qualitatively different behavior in leveling to an almost constant path in the $\beta = 0.60$ case.

This behavior corresponds with the expectation that, when attempting to hit certain target capital stocks, an economy with more productive capital should save more in the earlier years of the planning period.

Figure 1.2 shows changes in the savings rate path under variations in η.[5] Changes of η within reasonable ranges appear to have relatively less effect on the slope of the savings path than do changes in β.

A Turnpike Mapped

In another series of experiments, we chose $\beta = .25$ and set the rate of technical progress z equal to 0.03. These parameter specifications approximate those conventionally proposed for the United States. The behavior of the model with varying terminal income targets (calculated according to average growth rates over the

5. Mera (1968) has estimated the following values for η (with $\rho = .03$):

United States	η = .05 to .20
Canada	= .05 to .20
Japan	= .20 to .40

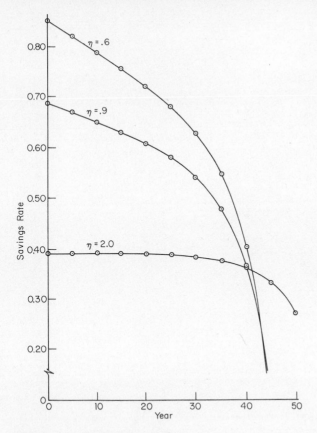

Figure 1.2   Savings-rate paths.

50-year period of 5, 6, and 6.5 percent) is shown in Figures 1.3 and 1.4. In both, the turnpike property implicit in all neoclassical closed economy models is strikingly apparent.[6] In Figure 1.3, the capital and consumption paths agree to three significant digits for the first 25 years of the 50-year planning horizon; in Figure 1.4, the savings rates are in close agreement for at least 20 years. We put no lower bound constraints on the rate of capital decumulation in the model, which explains the drop from the initial capital stock during the first years of the plan, while the economy brings its capital endowment into balance with the labor force growth rate and with the rate of technical progress, z. Capital decumulation shows up again at the end of the period under the 5 percent income growth target, which allows a big jump in the consumption level after year 40.

   Two stability characteristics of the model are worth explicit note. The first is simply that the initial almost identical behavior of the three plans is dependent on the long

---

   6. See Samuelson (1965) for a proof of the neoclassical turnpike theorem via the calculus of variations. As he points out, the actual turnpike growth rate can be discovered by putting our difference equations (7) and (8) in per capital terms and linearizing about the critical point where $k_{i+1} = k_i$, and $\lambda_{i+1} = \lambda_i$.
   The growth rate is then the largest characteristic value of the matrix of the linearized system, dependent on all parameters of the model. In the example presented here, simple graphical interpolation makes the turnpike rate approximately 5.8 percent.

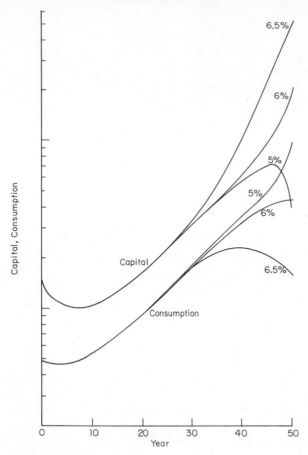

Figure 1.3

planning horizon used. A 20-year planning horizon would not have allowed the turn-pike behavior to manifest itself to the same extent as the 50-year horizon, with a consequent loss on the part of all generations—assuming no parameter changes, of course. Second, for growth rates near the turnpike rate computation of optimal paths via the one-dimensional search procedure sketched above is easy since for these paths small changes in λ_0 lead to small changes in the terminal income level. On the other hand, for growth rates far from the turnpike, the final capital stock is very sensitive to λ_0. Changes in the eighth significant digit of the initial shadow price can lead to changes of the order of a factor of 10 in terminal income. In other words, the closed model is relatively stable with respect to changes in boundary conditions on both capital stock and its shadow price, but only as long as one is operating within the vicinity of the turnpike.[7]

7. Note also that the turnpike property holds in simple form only in closed neoclassical models. When a number of "primary" resources (such as the exports of Section III) enter the model, it will show asymptotic exponential growth only if the primary resources are growing exponentially, and even then the growth rates in different sectors may differ. For nonexponentially growing primary resources, the situation becomes more complicated—we are aware of no straightforward analytic results. For a discussion of these problems, see Radner (1963).

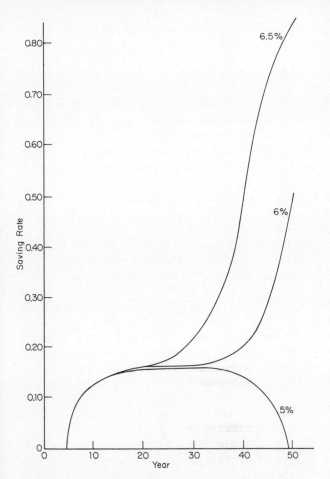

Figure 1.4

A Model for Primary Exporters

A second model with which we have conducted some experiments is one that has a foreign exchange constraint and includes two control variables.[8]

The model is motivated by the planning problem facing the oil exporting countries and some other natural resource exploiters. These countries have exceptionally high current foreign exchange revenues that may decline in the future. Their current foreign exchange earnings, to a first approximation, are generated at no domestic resource cost and can be used to supplement the relatively low domestic production and thereby allow fairly high consumption levels. This situation poses a difficult allocation-over-time problem for these countries. How much consumption should be allowed now? How much in the future? How much investment should be undertaken, at what times, and how should it be coordinated with the path of expected foreign exchange earnings?

8. We are grateful to Hossein Mahdavi for suggesting this problem and for supplying us with some of the parameters for the model.

To begin setting up a model for investigating these questions, we assume an unusual form of the national income identity,

$$y_t + m_t = c_t + \dot{k}_t + \delta k(t) \tag{1.12}$$

which states that aggregate supply (domestic production plus imports) equals consumption plus investment plus depreciation. Exports do not enter the accounting identity since they are assumed not to use domestic resources.

Using this income identity, and the production relations described earlier (1.6), and rewriting (1.12) in discrete form with a one-period investment lag, we obtain

$$k_{i+1} = (1 + g)^i a k_i^\beta + m_i - c_i + (1 - \delta)k_i \tag{1.13}$$

This is the capital stock accumulation equation for the model.

We now seek the maximum of the discounted sum of a stream of benefits from the utility function. However, this approach is modified somewhat to take account of two additional constraints imposed by opening the model to foreign trade:

1. foreign debt accumulations from period to period through interest payments on existing debt and through the difference between exports and imports
2. those times when imports must be "reasonably" close to exports, although equality need not be required (this restriction is imposed as an institutional constraint on the ground that most international lending agencies tie their loans to current and expected export performance)

The first constraint is stated as

$$h_{i+1} = h_i + m_i - x_i + \zeta h_i \tag{1.14}$$

where

h_i = foreign debt
x_i = exports (given exogenously)
ζ = rate of interest on foreign debt

The second constraint leads to a welfare function of the form

$$J = \sum_{i=0}^{n-1} \left[\frac{1}{(1 + \rho)^i} \frac{1}{1 - \eta} c_i^{1-\eta} - \gamma(m_i - x_i)^2 \right] - \tau h_n \tag{1.15}$$

The consumption utility function is the same as the one used in the Chakravarty model discounted at rate ρ, while $\gamma(m_i - x_i)^2$ is a "penalty function" on deviations of imports from exports. (Note that we could handle the problem of keeping imports "close" to exports by the use of inequality constraints on the variables. However, this is computationally tricky, as well as being somewhat inelegant. In practice, of course, the two approaches would tend to converge.) The final term in (1.15) is a penalty on terminal foreign debt. Variation of the parameter τ can be used from run to run to drive the terminal foreign debt to levels deemed "desirable."

With the export path predicted exogenously to the model, the problem is to maximize (1.15) subject to (1.13) and (1.14) and the initial values of the capital stock and foreign debt. This problem is solved in a manner that is completely analogous to the procedure used for the Chakravarty problem.

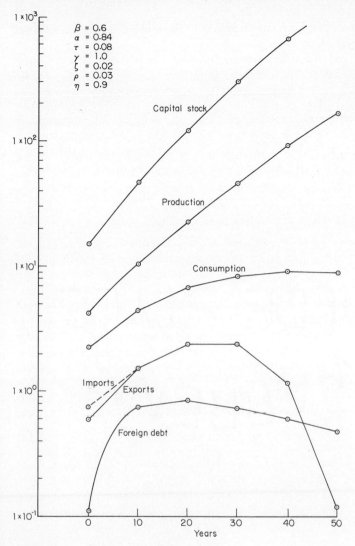

Figure 1.5 A model with foreign trade.

Figure 1.5 shows a solution to the problem and gives the values of the parameters. That solution embodies a rate of neutral technical change of about 1 percent, a target rate of growth of output of about 7.5 percent, and a nonlinear production function with $\beta = 0.60$. The exogenously computed export path assumes that oil exports will increase over the next 20 years and then level off and decline.

III. Formulation of Dynamic Nonlinear Optimization Problems in General Terms

There is a large literature, mainly in the engineering journals, on numerical methods for solving dynamic nonlinear optimizing models. In this and the next section we summarize some of the solution methods that control theorists have proposed, with some emphasis on their applicability to the kinds of problems that are likely to arise in economics.

An initial question in any study of dynamic problems is whether to work with discrete or continuous time. We formulated our models in discrete terms, largely for reasons of numerical convenience. One inevitably has to discretize problems for digital computer solution in any case, and an impressive body of oral tradition among numerical analysts has led us to use difference equations *before* going to the computer, rather than letting the machine chop up time in differential equations according to the whims of a Runge-Kutta integration routine. Since the mechanics of setting up the discrete-time optimal control problem are not as well known as the calculus-of-variations version, we review the problem here in general terms before discussing solution methods.[9]

Consider the problem of finding the minimum of a scalar function

$$J = \varphi(x_{N+1}) + \sum_{i=1}^{N} L^i(x_i, u_i) \tag{1.16}$$

of n-vectors[10] of state variables x_i and m-vectors of control variables u_i defined in each period $i = 1, 2, \ldots, N$ (and in period $N + 1$ for the state variables). The evolution of the state variables is described by the vector-valued *system equations*

$$x_{i+1} = f^i(x_i, u_i) \tag{1.17}$$

We assume *initial conditions*

$$x_1 \text{ specified} \tag{1.18}$$

and may require *terminal conditions*

$$(x_{N+1})_j = \bar{x}_j \tag{1.19}$$

to be met by some components (indexed by j) of the vector x_{N+1}. [The constrained terminal components of x_{N+1} will not enter into the function $\varphi(x_{N+1})$ in (1.16).]

In principle the problem as stated can be solved by standard methods of elementary calculus. We adjoin the system equations (1.17) to (1.16) with a sequence of multiplier vectors λ_{i+1},

$$J^* = \varphi(x_{N+1}) + \sum_{i=1}^{N} \{L^i(x_i, u_i) + \lambda_{i+1}^T[f^i(x_i, u_i) - x_{i+1}]\} \tag{1.20}$$

For convenience, we define a scalar sequence H^i (analogous to the Hamiltonian in the continuous formulation) as

$$H^i = L^i(x_i, u_i) + \lambda_{i+1}^T f^i(x_i, u_i) \tag{1.21}$$

and substitute into (1.20), also changing the indices of summation on the last term

$$J^* = \varphi(x_{N+1}) - \lambda_{N+1}^T x_{N+1} + \sum_{i=2}^{N} [H^i - \lambda_i^T x_i] + H^1 \tag{1.22}$$

---

9. Much of the remainder of this section is based on the control theory text of Bryson and Ho (1969).

10. As usual, we treat all vectors as columns, and write x^T for the transpose of x.

Taking differential changes in J^* due to differential changes in u_i, we get[11]

$$dJ^* = \left[\frac{\partial \varphi}{\partial x_{N+1}} - \lambda_{N+1}^T\right] dx_{N+1} + \sum_{i=2}^{N} \left\{\left[\frac{\partial H_i}{\partial x_i} - \lambda_i^T\right] dx_i \right.$$
$$\left. + \frac{\partial H_i}{\partial u_i} du_i\right\} + \frac{\partial H^1}{\partial x_1} dx_1 + \frac{\partial H^1}{\partial u_1} du_1 \tag{1.23}$$

Our aim is to find conditions on the x's, u's, and λ's that will guarantee that the standard first-order optimality condition $dJ^* = 0$ is satisfied. This task is considerably simplified if we choose the multiplier sequence λ_i so that

$$\lambda_i^T - \frac{\partial H^i}{\partial x_i} = 0 \qquad i = 2, \ldots, N$$

which implies that

$$\lambda_i^T = \frac{\partial L^i(x_i,u_i)}{\partial x_i} + \lambda_{i+1}^T \frac{\partial f^i(x_i,u_i)}{\partial x_i} \tag{1.24}$$

To simplify (1.23) further, we impose boundary conditions on the *costate equations* (1.24) as follows:

$$\lambda_{N+1}^T = \frac{\partial \varphi}{\partial x_{N+1}} \tag{1.25}$$

We have reduced equation (1.23) to the form

$$dJ^* = \sum_{i=1}^{N} \frac{\partial H^i}{\partial u_i} du_i + \frac{\partial H^1}{\partial x_1} dx_1$$

The vector x_1 is assumed given, so the second term vanishes. To set $dJ^* = 0$ and to satisfy the first-order necessary conditions for a minimum we finally specify *optimality conditions*[12]

$$\frac{\partial H^i}{\partial u_i} = 0 \tag{1.26}$$

Summarizing, to find the control sequence that gives a stationary value of the performance index J, we must choose at each step

a. the n state variables, x_i
b. the n adjoint variables, λ_i
c. the m control vectors, u_i

---

11. For a scalar function $f(x_1, \ldots, x_n)$, define $\partial f/\partial x$ as the row vector $[(\partial f/\partial x_1), \ldots (\partial f/\partial x_n)]$.

12. The discrete programming problem discussed here can be generalized by the addition of inequality constraints, in which case the Kuhn-Tucker conditions apply. For example, a minimum principle holds for the controls in a discrete system, that is, if the vector u_i is constrained to lie within some set Ω, and if the set $\{f^i(x_i,u_i): u_i \in \Omega\}$ is convex for all x_i, then simply minimizing H^i, $i = 1, \ldots, N$ for $u \in \Omega$ is a necessary condition for a minimum. (See Halkin 1966 for details.)

to satisfy, simultaneously,

1. the n system equations (1.17)
2. the n costate equations (1.24)
3. the m optimality conditions (1.26)
4. the initial and final boundary conditions and (1.18) and (1.25)[13]

IV. Solution Algorithms

Finding a set of variables which satisfies all of those equations is not an easy task in any nontrivial problem. Most solution methods, in fact, are based on *not* satisfying some of the first-order conditions. Rather, a nominal control history is chosen which satisfies some set of the four conditions. A system of difference equations linearized about this nominal is then formulated and solved in such a way as to indicate changes in the nominal solution that will bring it closer to satisfying the violated conditions. There are a number of possible sets of the four conditions that could be relaxed in these "successive linearization" algorithms. Three that have been used are shown in Table 1.1. We have experimented with the first two of these methods, and will sketch out both how they work and what we have learned about their applicability to economic optimization problems.

Neighboring Extremal Algorithms

The neighboring extremal class of algorithms is based on the most straightforward (perhaps naïve is a better word) method of solving optimal control problems. A typical recipe goes as follows:

1. Choose an initial λ_2. Use (1.18) to obtain x_1. Use x_1 and λ_2 in (1.26) to solve for u_1. Use x_1 and u_1 in (1.17) to obtain x_2. Set $i = 2$.
2. Use x_i and λ_i in (1.24) and (1.26) to solve for u_i and λ_{i+1}.[14]
3. Use u_i and x_i in (1.17) to obtain x_{i+1}. Set $i = i + 1$.
4. Repeat steps 2 and 3 until the final state variables and adjoint variables are obtained. Observe how far these values miss their respective boundary conditions (1.25)—or (1.19) and (1.25)—and use that information to modify the initial λ_2.
5. Repeat steps 1–4 until the final state and adjoint variables obtained in 4 are "close enough" to the boundary conditions.

As one might expect, this approach is a bit too simple to be of general applicability.[15] The problem is that state variables at the terminal time may be highly

---

13. If some of the terminal states are specified as in (1.19), the corresponding terminal costates satisfy the conditions

$$(\lambda_{N+1})_j = \nu_j \tag{1.25a}$$

where the ν_j can be interpreted as Lagrange multipliers on the constraints $(x_N)_j = x_j$.

14. In practice we found it useful to solve (1.24) and (1.26) separately, iterating between them until the λ_{i+1}'s converged. We did this by choosing λ_{i+1}'s, using these in (1.26) with an unconstrained minimization technique (see Fletcher and Powell 1963) to obtain u_i's, computing new λ_{i+1}'s with (1.24), and repeating the process until the λ_{i+1}'s converged.

15. However, we have observed that multisectoral programming models in which (1) all the distributional relations hold as equalities; (2) the production functions are linear; and (3) the welfare functions are nonlinear in the controls and do not include the state variables except at the terminal period, can be solved very quickly by naïve methods. With a terminal scrap value in each sector, we

sensitive to changes in the guesses of the initial costates. That sensitivity problem arises because equations (1.24) and (1.17), when linearized about the optimal path, are *adjoint*, with the property that solutions to the homogeneous parts of the two sets of equations may diverge from each other over time by many orders of magnitude. That divergence of fundamental solutions makes transmission of information about appropriate changes in λ_2 from the terminal time to the initial time very much subject to problems of numerical round-off error as indicated in Section II.

Those conditions may, but do not necessarily, occur; we found the neighborhood extremal method more efficient than the conjugate gradient method for solving the one-sector models discussed in this paper, but less efficient than gradient methods on our multisectoral models. Had we undertaken the extensive programming required to translate the effects of differential errors in missing boundary conditions into differential changes in λ_2, via the backward integration of quadratic Riccati matrix differential equations, this method might have surpassed the gradient approach.[16]

Gradient Methods[17]

As indicated in Table 1.1, most gradient algorithms work with a nominal solution that satisfies neither the optimality condition (1.26) nor terminal boundary conditions

Table 1.1

	Condition Satisfied			
Nominal solution	(1) System equations	(2) Costate equations	(3) Optimality conditions	(4) Boundary conditions
Neighboring extremal methods	Yes	Yes	Yes	No
Gradient methods	Yes	Yes	No	No
Quasilineari- zation methods	No	No	Yes	Yes

of the form (1.19) and (1.25a). The algorithms operate by iteratively improving the nominal control histories to meet these conditions. The boundary conditions may be approached by successive modification of estimates of the multipliers ν_j in (1.25a) or

---

obtain λ_{N+1}^T from (1.25) and sweep the equation (1.24) backward to provide the λ path for each sector. The linearity of the production functions and the fact that the capital stocks (that is, state variables) do not enter the performance index make it possible to sweep (1.25) backward without computing the control or state variables simultaneously. The λ's can then be used to compute the control variables using (1.26), and the control variables can be used to integrate (1.17) forward to obtain the state variables.

Even in the case when terminal capital stocks are specified instead of terminal unit scrap values, the procedure outlined above leads to a very effective iterative scheme for solving this class of optimizing planning models.

16. See Bryson and Ho (1969) for a discussion of such an algorithm.

17. We are grateful to Raman Mehra for giving us a copy of his conjugate gradient code and to Robert Kierr for excellent programming work in helping us to modify this code for our purposes. For more detailed comments on experience with these algorithms, see Kendrick and Taylor (1970).

else by adding to the performance index (1.16) quadratic penalty functions of the form $\frac{1}{2}a_j[(x_{N+1})_j - \bar{x}_j]^2$ on deviations of the final states $(x_{N+1})_j$ from their specified terminal values $\bar{x}_j$. Modifying the multipliers is a somewhat neater approach, since it does not distort the "true" shadow prices λ as do the penalty functions that substitute a condition of the form

$$(\lambda_{N+1}^T)_j = a_j[(x_{N+1})_j - \bar{x}_j] \tag{1.27}$$

for the condition (1.25a). However, penalty functions are useful since they are easy to apply and proved quite feasible in our planning model with five state variables specified at the terminal time (Kendrick and Taylor 1970).

Given a nominal control history u_i, the steps of the gradient algorithm we used go as follows:

1. Integrate the system equations (1.17) forward in time using the nominal u_i history.

2. At terminal time, evaluate λ_{N+1} using (1.27) for the constrained state variables and (1.25) for the unconstrained states.

3. Integrate the costate equations backward in time, and using the calculated λ_i and x_i histories, calculate the Hamiltonian (1.21) and its gradient with respect to the u_i.

4. Make a one-dimensional search in the gradient direction[18] until the Hamiltonian is minimized; more precisely, this means first choosing a parameter α to minimize

$$g(\alpha) = H[u - \alpha\nabla H^T(u)]$$

where

    u is the current control history vector
    H is the Hamiltonian
   ∇H is its gradient

and then calculating the new control history from the relationship

$$u_{\text{new}} = u - \alpha\nabla H(u)$$

We actually only approximated α, which is given by the condition

$$0 = \frac{dg(\alpha)}{d\alpha} = -\nabla H(u) \cdot [\nabla H(u - \alpha\nabla H(u))]^T \tag{1.28}$$

by varying u in the gradient direction until the quantity on the right of (1.28) changed signs, and then fitting an interpolating polynomial in α to the control vectors calculated just before and after the sign change.[19]

5. Return to step 1 with the new u history, after possible modifications to the penalty function constants a_j in (1.27).

---

18. In actual practice, it is often preferable to search in a modified gradient direction—the modifications attempting to take account of curvature properties of the Hamiltonian as a function of the u_i. We used a "conjugate gradient" procedure that, at each step, changes the u_i according to a weighted average of this step's gradient and last step's direction of movement. For details, see Lasdon, Mitter, and Warren (1967) and Fletcher and Reeves (1964).

19. We imposed nonnegativity constraints on some control variables, and when these applied, we simply set the negative controls equal to zero after fitting the polynomial. A more complete procedure would involve (a) minimizing the unconstrained discrete Hamiltonian; (b) checking for negative controls and setting them to zero; (c) reminimizing the unconstrained discrete Hamiltonian thus constrained. We did not go through those additional calculations largely because our problems seemed to converge well with the simpler procedure.

First-order gradient methods of this type typically show rapid convergence in the first few iterations but perform relatively poorly near the optimum. In addition, they have the drawback of not picking out with complete accuracy the optimal control histories. Both of those problems can be rectified near the optimum by using either neighboring extremal methods (if they converge) or second-order gradient methods that take account of curvature properties of the Hamiltonian. However, both second-order methods and neighboring extremal algorithms with modifications to counteract numerical instability require large inputs of programming logic and computation time. It is not clear in view of the high marginal costs of these inputs that the improvements that can be made on first-order solutions are economically justifiable. We have found that first-order methods will typically determine control histories to three significant digits in a score or so of iterations. Since the parameters in our problems are known at best to this degree of precision, better solutions seem somewhat extravagant.

V. Conclusions

Analytical techniques for studying the properties of growth models are sometimes limited to the examination of cases involving only particular values of parameters; for example, Chakravarty's (1965) study of a finite horizon model with a nonlinear Cobb-Douglas production was limited to a study of the case for $\beta = \frac{1}{2}$. We have discussed here some numerical procedures that may be used to permit the analysis of nonlinear growth models with a continuum of parameter values.

Those procedures are applied to two simple growth models, one for a closed economy and one for an open economy. The turnpike properties of the closed model are exhibited plainly with a set of numerical calculations. Also, a procedure for studying the relative effects of different degrees of nonlinearity in the welfare function and in the constraints (production functions) is demonstrated. Such procedures can lend insight into the question of the quality of linear approximations to nonlinear models when those approximations are made for the welfare function or for the production functions. Since models with nonlinear welfare functions and linear constraints are in general more simple to compute than models with linear (or nonlinear) welfare functions and nonlinear constraints, it would be good to find that the degree of nonlinearity of the production function has relatively little effect on the optimal policy. For the one-sector model studied here, that does not seem to be the case. However, the question remains open for other types of one-sector models and for multisectoral models.

Appendix to Chapter 1

For the problem (1.1a), (1.2a), and (1.3a) with (1.6), the discrete Hamiltonian is

$$H^i = \frac{1}{(1+\rho)^i} \frac{1}{1-\eta} c_i^{1-\eta} + \lambda_{i+1}[(1+g)^i a k_i^\beta - c_i + (1-\delta)k_i]$$

$$i = 1, \ldots, n-1$$

Thus using (1.17) (see Section III of this chapter), we obtain

$$k_{i+1} = (1 + g)^i a k_i^\beta - c_i + (1 - \delta)k_i \qquad (1.7)$$

using (1.18)

$$k_0 = \bar{k} \qquad (1.11)$$

using (1.24)

$$\lambda_i = \lambda_{i+1}[(1 + g)^i \beta a k^{\beta-1} + 1 - \delta]$$

or (1.28)

$$\lambda_{i+1} = [(1 + g)^i \beta a k^{\beta-1} + 1 - \delta]^{-1}\lambda_i$$

using (1.25)

$$\lambda_n = \nu \qquad (1.10)$$

and using (1.26)

$$\frac{\partial H^i}{\partial c_i} = \frac{1}{(1 + \rho)^i} c_i^{-\eta} - \lambda_{i+1} = 0$$

or

$$c_i = [(1 + \rho)^i \lambda_{i+1}]^{-1/\eta} \qquad (1.9)$$

2 Substitution in Planning Models*

Hollis B. Chenery
and William J. Raduchel

Development planning originates as a response to the immobility and specificity of economic resources. To the extent that production requires inputs in fairly fixed proportions, growth is likely to be impeded by shortages of specific factors rather than by a general scarcity of resources. On the other hand, if commodities and factors are highly substitutable in satisfying human wants, we need have no great concern for the supply of any particular one. The empirical analysis of substitution possibilities is therefore critical to the design of planning models and to the interpretation of their results.

Differing assumptions about substitution lie at the heart of some of the sharpest disagreements about economic policy. Neoclassical theory generally assumes high elasticities in both production and demand as well as mobility of productive factors in response to differential returns. However, students of underdeveloped economies are impressed with the inadequacy of the price mechanism to adjust the composition of supply to that of demand and to make full use of available resources. Development planning thus constitutes an attempt to improve on the allocation effects of market forces.

Planning models for less developed economies have concentrated mainly on avoiding bottlenecks in production by making better use of scarce resources of capital and foreign exchange.[1] Possibilities for increasing total welfare through varying the composition of consumer demand or through making greater use of surplus labor have been considered only in the context of partial analyses of individual projects. The problem of growing unemployment has acquired increased urgency in many developing countries because of that neglect of labor absorption in most development plans.

Econometric studies of intercountry data suggest that there are substantial possibilities for substitution between capital and labor in most types of production and that price elasticities of demand for commodities are significantly different from zero. Since computational methods for solving optimizing models that incorporate production functions and demand functions are now available, there is no reason to continue to ignore these possibilities in economy-wide planning.

* Our research has been supported by a grant from the National Science Foundation to the Project for Quantitative Research in Economic Development, Center for International Affairs, Harvard University. We are indebted to Kenneth Arrow and David Kendrick for valuable suggestions.
    1. This type of model is discussed in Chapters 5, 6, 7, and 8 in this volume.

The present paper attempts a preliminary exploration of this set of problems. We hope to demonstrate both the technical feasibility of more general planning models and the quantitative significance of introducing greater substitution. We first formulate a simplified general equilibrium model using empirically based functions that can be combined in a nonlinear programming model. We then test out a four-sector version of the model with illustrative data to show the relative importance of direct substitution in production compared to indirect substitution via demand and trade, concluding that the latter alone is unlikely to induce large changes in factor proportions. Finally we suggest some of the implications of the results for development policy.

I. The Role of Substitution in Planning

General equilibrium theory postulates a series of transformations by which factors of production are combined to produce social welfare. We can distinguish four types that are important to the empirical analysis of resource allocation:

1. transformation of generalized factors of production (capital, labor, natural resources) into specific factors (capital goods, skilled labor, irrigated land)[2]
2. transformation of specific factor services and raw materials (plus other commodities) into finished products
3. transformation of exported commodities into imports via international trade
4. transformation of finished goods and services into "social welfare" in accordance with consumer preferences

Each type of transformation allows for some degree of substitution among inputs in producing a given level of output. *Direct* substitution between labor and capital occurs in the first two types, which include all activities of physical production.[3] Types 3 and 4 constitute *indirect* means of substituting among capital, labor, and land by varying the composition of trade or final demand.

Planning models customarily allow for some substitution via trade but tend to exclude the other possibilities. Apart from trade, each transformation function is therefore stated in the form of a vector of inputs "required" to produce a given level of output—of skilled labor, steel, food, or "welfare." Linear programming models for planning are normally formulated on those assumptions. Substitution among commodities and factors takes place only through international trade. That type of substitution is limited by the range of variation in factor proportions available to produce tradable commodities and by the elasticity of demand for exports. Empirical studies using this type of model typically show a rather restricted scope for substituting labor for capital.[4]

The form and amount of substitution that should be included in a more realistic planning model depend to a large extent on the time period considered. Since the possible variation in output levels and input proportions is largely determined by the

2. In the case of capital this transformation into a specific form is the basis for the phenomenon of "embodiment." It is obvious that a similar process of specialization in a particular use and type of technology also applies to land and labor although the reconversion costs may be lower.

3. In the illustrative specifications of the model in Section II these two types of substitution are combined, but in a dynamic and less aggregated version they should be kept separate.

4. See Chenery and Kretschmer (1956), Eckaus and Parikh (1968), and Bruno (1966).

new equipment installed, changes in the structure of production are limited by the amount of new investment. Existing planning models are most appropriate to periods of up to 5 years, in which indirect substitution through changes in demand or trade may well outweigh the direct substitution possibilities.

In analyzing further possibilities for substitution, we will consider a "medium term" of, say, 10 years, in which the capital stock in a developing economy may be augmented by 50 to 100 percent and a "long term" in which only tastes and technology are specified.[5] Empirical evidence on production and demand functions comes largely from intercountry comparisons and is indicative of long-term substitution possibilities. The medium term is more important for policy purposes, however, and we will assume that here direct substitution possibilities are more limited.

The following questions are central to an assessment of the role of substitution in planning models:

1. How much difference in overall economic efficiency is there between the solutions to programming models with substitution in trade only and a more complete model?

2. How do the several types of substitution interact in an interdependent system?

3. What effect does greater substitution have on the policy conclusions of the model?

To explore these questions we formulate a computable version of a more complete model in Section II and use it as the basis for a series of experiments in Section III.

II. A Planning Model with Substitution

The evolution of planning models using the framework of linear programming is discussed in Part II of this book. Most commonly, imports are treated as perfect substitutes for groups of domestic products but no other substitution is permitted. Limits to the extent of substitution via trade are provided either by fixing exports exogenously or assuming that increased exports are possible only at declining prices.[6] It is also customary to limit arbitrarily the extent to which imports can replace domestic production.

The bases for a more general treatment of substitution in an empirical interindustry framework are suggested by Chenery and Uzawa (1958) and Johansen (1960). The former show how imports, exports, and final demand can be made functions of equilibrium prices in a computable programming model, while the latter demonstrates the use of Cobb-Douglas production functions in each sector. We will extend the Chenery-Uzawa model to include CES (constant elasticity of substitution) production functions for capital and labor as well as a more satisfactory set of demand relations of the type used by Johansen.

The Interindustry Model

The formulation of the model follows Chenery and Uzawa (1958). It consists of a conventional input-output core for commodity production to which have been added nonlinear demand functions, import and export functions, and production functions

5. It is only in the long term that the distinction between general and specific factors can be ignored.
6. This treatment of exports is discussed by Chenery and Kretschmer (1956) and Bruno (1966).

for direct factor use. We assume m desired commodities (final demands) and several primary factors—inputs available from outside the system. In the following illustration there are three primary inputs—labor, capital, and foreign exchange—and four commodities. The method of solution is affected only by the number of primary inputs. A summary of the notation follows.

Variables

X_j	output of sector j
V_j	value added in sector j
P_i	shadow prices of commodity i
P_K, P_L, P_f	shadow prices of capital, labor, foreign exchange, respectively; $\pi = P_K/P_L$
E_i	level of exports from sector i
M_i	level of imports of commodity i
K_j	use of capital in sector j
$\bar{L}$	total supply of labor
L_j	use of labor in sector j
Y_i	final demand for commodity i
R	total resource use
$\bar{D}$	maximum foreign trade deficit

Parameters for Each Sector

a_{ij}	input coefficient of commodity i into sector j
c	efficiency parameter in the production function
δ	distribution parameter in the production function
σ	elasticity of substitution between capital and labor
θ	price elasticity of final demand
k	capital coefficient (K/X)
ℓ	labor coefficient (L/X)
g_j	cost of unit import of commodity j in foreign exchange
h_j	price of unit export of commodity j in foreign exchange
α	slope of export demand function
ξ	slope of import substitution function

The general problem of development programming can be formulated as either the maximization of the welfare achievable from given resources or the attainment of a given level of welfare with a minimum input of scarce resources. The former corresponds to the planner's problem, but the latter is more convenient to analyze various forms of substitution. We therefore take as our objective function:

Minimize
$$R = P_K \Sigma K_j + P_L \Sigma L_j = \Sigma V_j \tag{2.1}$$
where

$$V_j = K_j P_K + L_j P_L = (P_K k_j + P_L \ell_j) X_j$$
$$= v_j X_j$$

and the valuation of capital (P_K) and labor (P_L) is given.[7] Only a single-period optimization will be discussed.

---

7. The value added per unit of output, v_j, is only a constant for a given set of factor prices.

We require that production plus imports in each sector be sufficient to meet final and intermediate demands plus exports:

$$X_i + M_i \geq Y_i + \Sigma a_{ij} X_j + E_i \tag{2.2}$$

Foreign trade is restricted by requiring that the trade deficit should not exceed a predetermined amount, $\bar{D}$:

$$\bar{D} + \sum_j h_j E_j \geq \sum_j g_j M_j \tag{2.3}$$

All quantities must, of course, be nonnegative.

Equations (2.1)–(2.3) are all familiar as standard elements of an economy-wide linear programming model.[8] We now introduce some new features. Although the sectors are linked by a fixed input-output matrix, we permit direct substitution between capital and labor in the production of value added for each sector.[9] This can be done without greatly complicating the computation if the production function specified is homogeneous and does not have increasing returns. So long as factor intensities depend only on relative factor prices, the several factors can be treated as one for a specified set of prices. This formulation permits us to utilize the substitution principle of Samuelson (1951) and others as a basis for the optimizing procedure.

Production Functions

In order to have a general production function for which some empirical estimates are available, we assume that output in each sector is related to capital and labor inputs according to a CES function:[10]

$$X = c[\delta K^{-\rho} + (1 - \delta)L^{-\rho}]^{-1/\rho} \tag{2.4}$$

For fixed relative factor prices we can derive the following cost-minimizing capital-output and labor-output ratios:

$$k = \frac{K}{X} = \frac{1}{c}[\delta + (1 - \delta)\nu]^{1/\rho} \tag{2.5}$$

$$l = \frac{L}{X} = \frac{1}{c}\left(\delta + 1 - \delta\right)^{1/\rho} \tag{2.6}$$

where

$$\nu = \left(\frac{P_K}{P_L}\frac{1 - \delta}{\delta}\right)^{\rho/1-\rho}$$

We emphasize that we are treating capital as one factor capable of use in all sectors, which is strictly valid only in the long run.

8. Such models are illustrated by Sandee (1960), Eckaus and Parikh (1968), and the chapters by Bruno (8), Weisskopf (5), and Tendulkar (6) in this volume.

9. This procedure was suggested by Johansen (1960), who used Cobb-Douglas functions for each sector. Note that the model can easily be generalized to permit alternative production activities in the linear programming manner. However, this would require engineering data that are generally unavailable.

10. This is the form given by Arrow, Chenery, Minhas, and Solow (1961). Specifications of this function used in our model are illustrated in Figure 2.1.

Foreign Trade

Domestic resources can be transformed into foreign exchange through either exports or substitution for imports. These possibilities will be described by an export revenue function and an import substitution function. Taken together they describe the net trading possibilities for each sector as a function of the cost of earning or saving foreign exchange.

Following Chenery and Kretschmer (1956) we assume that the average revenue in foreign exchange earned per unit of exports in sector j (h_j) is a declining function of the amount exported:

$$h_j = \gamma_j - \alpha_j E_j \tag{2.7}$$

As shown in equation (2.15) below, it will pay to expand exports in each sector until the marginal revenue earned is equal to the marginal cost of production valued in shadow prices (P_j/P_f).

An import substitution function can be constructed along similar lines, since the average amount of foreign exchange saved in each sector through domestic production depends on the level of imports. As illustrated in Weisskopf's detailed programming analysis of import substitution in India (Chapter 5), the rupee cost of replacing a dollar's worth of imports in the metal products industry varies according to the particular commodity produced. If only a small amount of foreign exchange is allocated to imports of metal products, it should be used for the commodity with the highest local production cost—that is, in which the import price at a given exchange rate is relatively the lowest. If imports of metal products are increased, the average foreign exchange cost (g_j) of replacing a rupee of domestic production will rise as we move up the scale of comparative advantage. The possibilities for import substitution in sector j can therefore be represented by assuming that g_j is an increasing function of M_j. Assuming a linear function gives:

$$g_j = \mu_j + \xi_j M_j \tag{2.8}$$

Equation (2.16) below gives a condition for an optional solution parallel to that for exports: imports of commodity j should be increased until the marginal savings of domestic resources are equal to the opportunity cost of imports (P_j/P_f).

In this formulation export expansion and import substitution are treated symmetrically. The overall substitution possibilities provided by foreign trade can therefore be shown by combining the solutions for the optimal levels of imports and exports into a composite net trade function which shows both E_j and M_j as a function of P_j/P_f. Such functions are derived in equations (2.15) and (2.16) and illustrated in Figure 2.2.

Final Demand

The other form of substitution included in this model is in the composition of final demand. Any set of demand functions can be used as long as the quantities consumed depend only upon prices and income. We assume that market prices are proportional to shadow prices and that the income and own-price elasticities of demand are constant. Our demand functions can be stated as:

$$Y_j = Y_j^0 (\lambda P_j)^{\theta_i} \tag{2.9}$$

where λ is a factor of proportionality relating market and shadow prices. Since we wish to hold some measure of welfare constant, λ will be defined as a price deflator such that a Lespeyre's index of welfare remains constant:

$$\Sigma P_j^0 Y_j = \text{constant}$$

where P_j^0 are the base year market prices for which $\lambda = 1$. That definition makes demands a function of all commodity prices.

Our programming problem can be restated as follows. For fixed P_K and P_L minimize $\Sigma v_j x_j$ subject to the following constraints:[11]

$$X_j + M_j - \sum_i a_{ji} X_i + E_j = 0 \tag{2.10}$$

$$\bar{D} + \sum h_j E_j - \sum g_j M_j = 0 \tag{2.11}$$

The solution is arrived at by minimizing the following Lagrangian form with respect to X, M, E, P, and P_f:

$$\Lambda(X,M,E,P,P_f) = \sum v_j X_j + \sum P_j \left(X_j + M_j - E_j - Y_j - \sum_i a_{ji} X_i \right)$$
$$+ P_f \left(\bar{D} - \sum g_j M_j + \sum h_j E_j \right) \tag{2.12}$$

A general exposition of this type of model is given in Chenery and Uzawa (1958). It is easy to see that the first-order conditions for an extremum of this form readily yield the following equations, which are familiar from linear programming solutions:

$$P = (I - A^t)^{-1} v \tag{2.13}$$

where $P = [P_j]$ and $v = [v_j]$ represents the inputs of the composite factor; and,

$$X = (I - A)^{-1}(Y + E - M) \tag{2.14}$$

Combined with the nonnegativity requirements $(E_j > 0, \; M_j > 0)$ and $(M_j < Y_j + E_j)$, the first-order conditions also yield equations for the determination of exports and imports:

$$E_j = \frac{\gamma_j - (P_j/P_f)}{2\alpha_j} \quad \text{if} > 0; \text{ otherwise } E_j = 0 \tag{2.15}$$

$$M_j = \frac{\mu_j - (P_j/P_f)}{-2\epsilon_j} \quad \text{if} > 0 \text{ and } < (Y_j + E_j) \tag{2.16}$$

$M_j = 0$ if the first condition is violated and $\gamma_j + E_j = 0$ if the second is.

We solve this constrained problem by using a theorem of Everett (1964). He shows that a constrained optimizing problem may be solved through converting it into an

---

11. The inequalities of equations (2.2) and (2.3) are replaced by equalities, since it is known in advance that both sets of constraints will be binding.

unconstrained problem by specifying the values of the Lagrangian multipliers (P_K, P_L, P_f) and then iterating on the multipliers.[12] For fixed P_K and P_L we need only specify the value of P_f, solve the resulting problem, and then adjust P_f in accordance with the indicated excess demand for foreign exchange. As explained in Raduchel (1970), we combined a Golden Section search procedure and a quadratic penalty function on foreign exchange to do that.

Estimation

Illustrative estimates of the parameters in this model are given in Table 2.1. Alternative specifications are given for low, medium, and high elasticities in trade, demand, and production.[13] In general, all elasticities are likely to be higher over longer periods as the capital stock, trade patterns, and tastes become adjusted to price changes. Our estimates are intended merely to illustrate realistic orders of magnitude. Wherever possible they are derived from econometric estimates of comparable functions, but no attempt has been made to determine consistent estimates of the model as a whole.

The starting point for our example is the illustrative four-sector model of Chenery and Uzawa (1958).[14] The sectors differ significantly in their demand and trade relations and in their role in the development process. Sector 1 includes most of the manufactured goods that are typically produced and exported at low levels of income, while sector 3 includes the basic industrial products (machinery, metals, chemicals) that are typically imported by underdeveloped countries. The parameters in the *production functions* (σ and δ) for the long-term case (2b) are based on the sector values given in Arrow, Chenery, Minhas, and Solow (1961: 240), which were derived from a comparison of capital and labor use in Japan and the United States. Lower values of the elasticity of substitution were set at arbitrary fractions of these long-term estimates to show the effects of lesser degrees of substitutability over shorter periods (the δ's are adjusted to maintain comparability in the basic solutions).

The parameters in the *demand functions* for the medium-term are based on Weisskoff's intercountry estimates in Chapter 14.[15] The "high" value of θ was arbitrarily set at -1.0 for all commodities to indicate an upper limit to this type of substitution.

The *trade parameters* were chosen to yield a realistic variation in the pattern of trade as P_K/P_L varies. Imports and exports are less than 10 percent of GNP in most cases, which is typical of larger countries. The import substitution functions are arbitrary although they could be derived for particular countries from a disaggregated model. Import and export functions for each sector can be combined as shown in Figure 2.2 to determine the net trade in each commodity group as a function of the ratio of its shadow price to the price of foreign exchange.

The production, demand, and trade functions are illustrated in Figures 2.1–2.3. They will be used in conjunction with the solutions in Tables 2.2 and 2.3 to show the variation in each sector that results from the three types of substitution.

---

12. Out computing algorithm generalizes the procedure suggested by Chenery and Uzawa for this problem. See Raduchel (1970).

13. These will be combined in different ways to analyze each type of substitution separately.

14. The sector classification and input structure for this model were in turn derived by aggregating the 14-sector programming model given in Chenery and Kretschmer (1956). We have kept the same commodity input coefficients and export functions but modified the remainder.

15. Johansen (1960) uses a similar formulation. His estimates of the own-price elasticities for Norway on a 20-sector basis also average about -0.5.

Table 2.1. Illustrative Estimates of Parameters

		Sector			
		(1) Finished goods	(2) Food and agric.	(3) Basic industry	(4) Services
All	a_{1j}	0.0	0.0	0.0	0.0
	a_{2j}	0.1	0.0	0.0	0.0
	a_{3j}	0.2	0.1	0.0	0.0
	a_{4j}	0.2	0.3	0.1	0.0
Low	P_0 σ	0	0	0	0.79
	δ	0.92	0.94	2.6	1.80
	c	3.83	3.24	4.0	0.05
Medium	P_{1a} σ	0.11	0.29	0.2	0.00798
	δ	0.3257	0.443	0.991	1.84
	c	3.97	3.33	1.67	0.1
	P_{1b} σ	0.22	0.58	0.4	0.08
	δ	0.41	0.47	0.92	1.89
	c	3.99	3.33	1.8	0.2
High	P_{2a} σ	0.45	1.15	0.4	0.23
	δ	0.456	0.483	0.917	1.92
	c	4.0	3.33	1.8	0.2
	P_{2b} σ	0.93	1.15	0.4	0.2
	δ	0.484	0.483	0.769	0.344
	c	4.0	3.33	1.96	1.96

Production Parameters: $[a_{ij}]$ = intermediate commodity requirements, σ = elasticity of substitution, δ = distribution parameter, c = efficiency parameter

Table 2.1 (*continued*)

			Sector			
			(1) Finished goods	(2) Food and agric.	(3) Baisc industry	(4) Services
Demand Parameters: Y^0 = final demand at base point, θ = price elasticity						
Low	D_0	Y^0	100	230	220	450
Medium	D_1	Y^0	100	230	220	450
		θ	-0.6736	-0.2462	-0.5869	-0.3520
High	D_2	Y^0	100	230	220	450
		θ	-1	-1	-1	-1
Trade Parameters: a = slope of export earnings function, γ = intercept, ξ = slope of import earnings function, μ = intercept = 1.0 for all						
Low	T_0		(no trade)			
Medium	T_1	a	-0.005	-0.001	-0.01	
		γ	1.0	1.1	1.0	
		ξ	0.005	0.0157	0.00178	
High	T_2	a	-0.0025	-0.0005	-0.00178	
		γ	1.0	1.1	1.0	
		ξ	0.005	0.0157	0.00178	

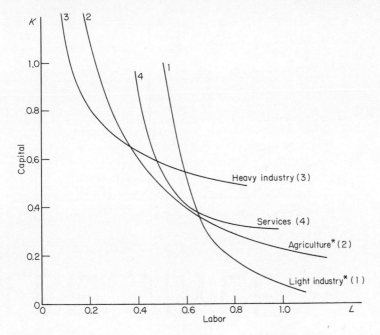

Figure 2.1 Production functions (P_{2b}')—unit value added.

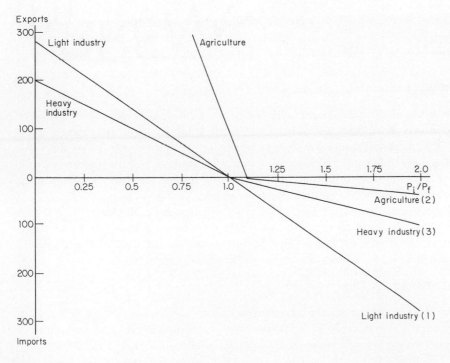

Figure 2.2 Net trade functions (T_2).

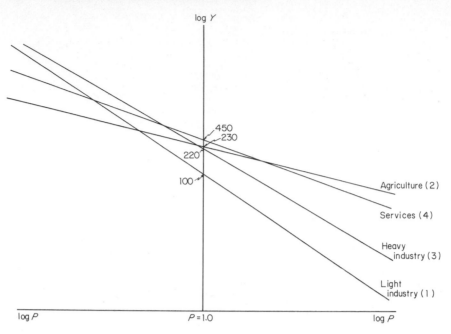

Figure 2.3   Demand functions (D_i)—unadjusted.

The model is calibrated so that all solutions are approximately the same for $P_K/P_L = 1.0$.

III. Substitution Between Capital and Labor

Several kinds of disequilibria arise in the course of development, which are variously attributed to limited possibilities for substitution or to inappropriate price policies. The most pervasive are foreign exchange scarcities and labor surpluses. Since rising unemployment has become a serious problem in many underdeveloped countries even with substantial rates of growth, we will focus our analysis on questions of labor-capital substitution and employment policy.[16]

Direct substitution between capital and labor appears to be of greater significance for employment than indirect substitution under most of our assumptions. We therefore illustrate the direct mechanism first and then take up the possibilities for substitution via demand and trade when direct substitution is restricted.

Direct Factor Substitution

The possibilities of substituting labor for capital are determined at a given level of GNP by varying the relative factor prices over a specified range and computing a series of optimal solutions.[17] Figure 2.4 gives a set of isoquants for the whole economy

16. A more disaggregated form of the present model would be necessary to discuss the effects of substitution on the trade bottleneck with any degree of realism.

17. In each case the price of foreign exchange is varied in such a way as to keep the capital inflow $\bar{D}$ at zero. The GNP is defined by equation (2.9) and set at 1000. All base prices $(P_i{}^0)$ are set equal to 1.0 by adjusting the efficiency parameters c_j.

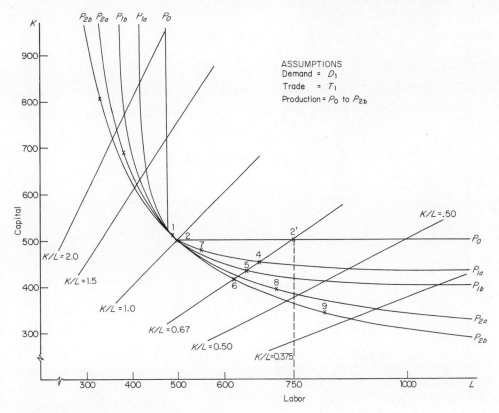

Figure 2.4   Isoquants for GNP = 1000.

that are derived for an increase in GNP of 1000. They show the extent of substitution that results from each of the five assumptions about the parameters in the production functions, assuming in each case the medium-term values for demand parameters (D_1) and trade parameters (T_1). Details of the solutions for points 1, 2, 4, and 6 are shown in Table 2.2.

The overall elasticity of substitution is shown more directly in Figure 2.5, in which factor proportions are plotted against relative factor prices for the same set of solutions. The slope of each curve at a given point gives the elasticity of substitution, which varies from .64 in the long-run case (2b) down to .21 in case 1a. The overall elasticity is a weighted average of the elasticities in the four sectors, but in the present example it is fairly constant.

To apply these results to a case of potential surplus labor, we assume that the economy will have an additional 500 units of capital and 750 units of labor over a planning period of 10 years. Solution to the programming model given by specification $T_1D_1P_0$ yields the results shown in solution 2 in Table 2.2: total output of 1000 and use of labor and capital of about 500 units each.[18] Figure 2.4 shows that under the other production assumptions 750 units of labor could be fully employed and capital reduced by between 10 percent and 28 percent at the same level of output.

18. Point 1 corresponding to $P_H/P_L = 1.0$ is taken as the basic or market solution. $P_H/P_L = 4.0$ was arbitrarily taken as the minimum labor cost to be considered, for reasons discussed below.

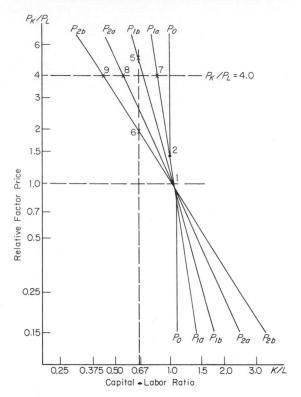

Figure 2.5 Variation in capital intensity with factor prices.

Alternatively, the appropriate factor proportions ($K/L = .67$) could be achieved at points 4, 5, or 6. Full use of capital and labor would then permit output to be expanded by 10 to 20 percent under the various assumptions.

Before these conclusions can be accepted as realistic, it is necessary to consider the implications of the factor prices that would be required to bring them about. The corresponding price ratios are shown by points 5 and 6 in Figure 2.5. At point 5, for example, P_K/P_L is 5, and capital would receive about 75 percent of the total product under market pricing, compared to 50 percent at point 1. Since there is a budgetary limit to the amount of income redistribution that might be carried out through taxes and subsidies, it is necessary to assume a corresponding limit to the extent to which effective labor costs to producers can be reduced.

The effect of assuming such a lower limit to the effective cost of labor is illustrated by imposing a maximum P_K/P_L ratio of 4.0 in Figures 2.4 and 2.5. The values of the solutions at this relative price show that K/L could be reduced from .98 at P_0 to .84 at point 7 and .42 at point 9. In practice the limits to a wage subsidy policy may be considerably more restrictive.

Indirect Factor Substitution

Indirect factor substitution takes place through the effects of changing commodity prices on both foreign trade and domestic demand. Detailed programming models for several countries suggest that a variation in overall capital-labor ratios of 10 to

Table 2.2. Effects of Direct Substitution in Production

Solution	Model	Factor prices	Sector	Capital coeff. K_i	Labor coeff. l_i	Final demand Y_i	Net trade T_i	Output X_i	Price P_i	Labor L_i	Capital K_i
				Basic Solutions							
1	$T_1D_1P_0$	$P_K/P_L = 1.0$	1	0.242	0.257	100	− 6	94	1.00	24	23
		$K/L = 1.04$	2	0.288	0.312	230	22	260	1.00	81	75
		$P_f = 0.948$	3	0.651	0.249	220	−15	249	1.00	62	162
			4	0.436	0.564	450		572	1.00	323	249
Total[a]										490	509
				Moderate Substitution in Demand and Trade							
2	$T_1D_1P_0$	$P_K/P_L = 4.0$	1	0.242	0.257	101	− 1	100	0.988	26	24
		$K/L = 0.98$	2	0.288	0.312	233	64	307	0.954	96	88
		$P_f = 0.982$	3	0.651	0.249	198	−60	189	1.194	47	123
			4	0.436	0.564	468		599	0.893	338	261
Total[a]										506	497
				Substitution in Production Only							
3	$T_0D_0P_{2b}$	$P_K/P_L = 2.15$	1	0.169	0.365	100		100	0.978	36	17
		$K/L = 0.67$	2	0.180	0.469	230		240	.949	113	43
			3	0.555	0.390	220		264	1.118	103	146
			4	0.373	0.656	450		568	1.943	373	212
Total[a]										625	419

Table 2.2 (*continued*)

Solution	Model	Factor prices		Sector	Capital coeff.	Labor coeff.	Final demand	Net trade	Output	Price	Labor	Capital
				Substitution in Production: Medium Demand and Trade								
4	$T_1D_1P_{1a}$	P_K/P_L	= 4.99	1	0.210	0.324	101	−2	99	0.980	32	21
		P_f	= 0.960	2	0.193	0.526	236	81	327	0.900	172	63
		K/L	= 0.67	3	0.575	0.411	197	−72	178	1.206	73	102
				4	0.411	0.617	466		612	0.908	371	247
Total[a]											648	434
6	$T_1D_1P_{2b}$	P_K/P_L	= 2.03	1	0.173	0.356	101	−3	99	0.989	35	17
		P_f	= 0.953	2	0.187	0.456	233	50	293	0.953	133	55
		K/L	= 0.67	3	0.561	0.738	207	−46	210	1.110	79	118
				4	0.377	0.648	459		587	0.945	381	221
Total[a]											629	419

[a] Totals may not add because of rounding.

Table 2.3. Effects of Indirect Substitution via Trade and Demand

Model	Factor prices	Sector	Capital coeff. k_i	Labor coeff. l_i	Final demand Y_i	Net trade T_i	Out-put X_i	Price P_i	Labor L_i	Cap-ital K_i
				Basic Solution						
$T_2 D_0 P'_0$	$P_K/P_L = 1.0$	1	0.108	0.392	100	- 7	93	1.000	37	10
	$K/L = 1.00$	2	0.305	0.295	230	29	268	1.000	79	82
	$P_f =$	3	0.651	0.249	220	-19	246	1.000	61	160
		4	0.436	0.564	450		574	1.000	324	249
Total[a]									501	501
				Trade Only						
$T_2 D_0 P'_0$	$P_K/P_L = 4.0$	1	0.108	0.392	100	22	122	0.871	48	13
	$K/L = 0.95$	2	0.305	0.295	230	59	301	1.017	89	92
	$P_f =$	3	0.651	0.249	220	-77	197	1.247	49	129
		4	0.436	0.564	450		584	0.933	329	255
Total[a]									516	488
				Demand and Trade						
$T_2 D_2 P'_0$	$P_K/P_L = 4.0$	1	0.108	0.392	115	22	137	0.871	54	15
	$K/L = 0.90$	2	0.305	0.295	226	59	299	1.017	88	91
	$P_f =$	3	0.651	0.249	176	-77	157	1.247	39	102
		4	0.436	0.564	482		615	0.933	347	268
Total[a]									528	476

[a] Totals may not add because of rounding.

20 percent might be achieved via trade alone through a fourfold variation in the relative price of capital and labor.[19] A good part of this variation is lost in our model through aggregation, which has the effect of reducing the range of variation in commodity prices and its resulting effects on trade. To secure a more realistic change in commodity prices as factor prices change, we have therefore altered the specification of the production function for sector 1 to make it less capital intensive.[20]

The effects of substitution via trade alone can be seen in Table 2.3 by comparing the trade-only solution to the basic solution. With trade only, both the capital and labor coefficients and the final demand are held constant, as in most linear programming models. Raising the relative price of capital from 1.0 to 4.0 has the effect of increasing the cost of producing the most capital intensive commodity (3) by 25 percent and lowering the price of commodity 1 by 13 percent. There is increasing

19. See, for example, Chenery and Kretschmer (1956); Bruno (1966); Weisskopf, Chapter 5 in this volume; and Tendulkar, Chapter 6 in this volume.
20. The alternative specification is illustrated in Figure 2.1. This change is shown in Tables 2.1 and 2.3 as specification P_0'. A small adjustment was also made in sector 2 to maintain the total use of both capital and labor at 500 in the basic solution. The overall effects of this change in the case of direct substitution are negligible.

trade and greater specialization as a result with a net reduction in the capital-labor ratio of 5 percent.[21]

The effects of allowing maximum substitution in demand (D_2) are shown in the demand-and-trade solution of Table 2.3, in which all other elements of the model remain the same as in trade only. There is a further drop of 40 units in production of commodity 3, which is almost as great as the reduction due to international trade. Demand and production rise by a corresponding amount for commodities 1 and 4 in response to their lower prices. The net effect of introducing demand elasticities is thus a further reduction in the capital-labor ratio from 0.95 to 0.90.

Although we have assumed relatively high elasticities for both demand and trade in this illustration, the total amount of indirect substitution between capital and labor is only 10 percent, somewhat less than the lowest assumption for direct substitution in production. Without further empirical evidence, it is impossible to say whether or not these results represent realistic orders of magnitude.

When all three types of substitution are included in the same model, the separate effect of each is reduced. This result can be seen in both Tables 2.2 and 2.3. A comparison of solutions 3 and 6 in Table 2.2 shows that when direct substitution effects are large, the effects on total factor use of adding substitution in trade and demand (by changing the specifications from $T_0 D_0$ to $T_1 D_1$) are quite small. This is true primarily because of the small variation in relative prices of commodities. When direct substitution is ruled out, as in Table 2.3, price variation and indirect substitution become much larger. The same effect is shown by comparing solutions 1 and 2 in Table 2.2.

IV. Implications for Development Policy

This paper illustrates the type of empirical study that is needed to resolve some of the basic issues between the neoclassical and structuralist approaches to development policy. The neoclassical assumptions of perfect markets and adequate substitution imply that an equilibrium growth process can take place regardless of the changes in factor supplies or the nature of demand functions. The structuralist assumptions of imperfect markets and low elasticities in production and trade imply that structural disequilibrium is likely to occur in a rapidly growing economy because the market mechanism will not necessarily produce equilibrium in both factor and commodity markets. The policy implications of the two systems are obviously quite different.

The present model contains most of the elements needed for an empirical test of these two approaches. A realistic analysis would have to specify the three sets of functions and change in factor supplies over time and be disaggregated to perhaps 20 sectors to deal adequately with differences in production and trade. Although this type of test has not yet been carried out, we can speculate on its outcome in the light of our preliminary results.[22] Since our model is neoclassical in virtually all of its assumptions, it brings out the nature of the changes in factor allocations and factor

---

21. The basic solution itself allows for some trade, which reduces the K/L ratio by 5 percent from the no-trade solution.

22. The closest approach to this type of empirical analysis is the study by Johansen, Alstadheim, and Langsether (1968) for Norway, in which virtually all the elements in a neoclassical model of similar type were projected for 20 years.

prices that would be needed to maintain equilibrium under varying conditions of factor supply.

The essence of neoclassical development policy is to make the actual economic system function as closely as possible like the idealized model. Our results suggest two important limitations to such a policy. In the first place, the possibilities for indirect factor substitution via demand and trade may not be extensive enough to accommodate very wide variations in factor proportions. Secondly, the feasible range of variation is made considerably narrower when we consider the implications of the equilibrium factor prices for the distribution of income between labor and capital.

Development policy in most countries has attempted to bring about equilibrium through variations in commodity prices but has not been systematically concerned with effective factor prices to the producer. Structural disequilibrium has frequently developed with that type of policy, which is in accord with our tentative finding that indirect substitution alone is unlikely to bring about large changes in factor proportions. This observation helps to explain the emergence of such disequilibrium phenomena as surplus labor and trade-limited growth and emphasizes the need to bring market prices closer to the equilibrium prices of labor, capital, and foreign exchange.

Although our results are likely to be extensively modified in more realistic applications, there remains the strong possibility of a second-best optimum in which limits to income transfers will prevent the economy from attaining the unconstrained equilibrium implied by rapid growth of the labor force.[23] Additional policy variables such as commodity prices and the exchange rate must therefore be utilized in order to approach full use of resources.[24]

The use of a nonlinear programming framework makes it possible to incorporate most of the structuralist qualifications into a model that retains the basic market assumptions of neoclassical theory. The solution to the model is more of a guide to planners than a description of how the economy works, since an ideal form of government policy is needed to bring it about.

This formulation offers the hope of shifting policy discussions from the ideological level to empirical questions of estimating structural relations and determining policy choices from them. In that context, there need be no inconsistency between the structuralist diagnoses of the causes of underdevelopment and the use of neoclassical guidelines for planners.

23. Several effects of surplus labor on optimal resource allocation are discussed by Lefeber (1968).

24. The introduction of a floor to the effective labor cost would make our model operate like a fixed coefficient system when the price of labor reaches this limit. Further reductions in the shadow price of labor would affect only commodity prices and the exchange rate. In such a labor surplus situation, the programming solution would produce a set of commodity prices that would correspond to the optimal degree of indirect substitution. Indirect adjustments in factor proportions via demand and trade increase in importance once the possibilities for direct substitution are exhausted. The technical feasibility of our nonlinear programming model is unimpaired by additional restrictions of this kind.

3 Investment Timing
in Two-Gap Models*

Lance Taylor

I. Introduction

Since their introduction in the early 1960s, two-gap models—although contro-versial—have served as the operational basis for a large number of empirical develop-ment policy studies. Given this continuing interest, more theoretical work on the properties of the models themselves seems appropriate, particularly in the little-explored field of dynamic welfare optimization.

In addition to the current general interest in this type of analysis, there is a pair of specific reasons for taking a look at optimal growth paths under two-gap assumptions. The first of these stems from the fact that the Chenery-MacEwan (1966) linear programming dynamic model (to my knowledge, the only explicit optimizing two-gap model in the literature) produced a certain sequence of investment paths, the rigidity of which has since evoked discussion (for example, Fei and Ranis 1968). One would like to know more precisely the conditions under which a Chenery-MacEwan invest-ment sequence will or will not be followed, and by extension, whether or not two-gap models have inherent in their very structure a lock-step sequence of economic development.

The second reason is somewhat more vague but nonetheless of great interest in the broader context of proper specification of the role of foreign exchange in empirically implemented planning models. The "obvious" way to open dynamic, multisectoral models to foreign trade follows the aggregate two-gap approach in specifying certain activities which generate import substitution or additional exports or both, and also in imposing some terminal conditions on the use of foreign capital inflows (the levels of which during the period of the model are treated as decision variables). If the analysis of the simple two-gap model of this paper carries over in a general way to that multisectoral specification (and there seems to be no obvious reason why it should not), there will be a strong bias in the solutions toward heavy investment (particularly investment in "trade creation") near the beginning of the planning period. In prac-tical terms, there are undoubtedly good reasons for recommending this sort of policy in many developing countries. However, under some conditions—for example, when

* This research was first undertaken when I was a graduate student in the Harvard Project for Quantitative Research in Economic Development, whose support is gratefully acknowledged. I have benefited greatly from comments by members of the Project, particularly Hollis Chenery and Arthur MacEwan.

foreign exchange is abundant and can be used for consumption imports or when the capital-output ratio of the economy is low—the opposite policy might be advisable. If two-gap models will never allow an investment postponing policy under these conditions, then there may be something wrong with the models.

This basic issue of model specification will be discussed again at the end of this paper. However, it is first necessary to analyze the two-sector, two-gap model in detail. This is done in the next three sections.

II. The Two-Gap Model of Interest

The main tool of analysis will be the "dual" solution to the linear optimal contro problem faced by a welfare-maximizing two-gap economy, as formulated in Section II. Through use of the dual, we will be able to specify quite easily the sequences of "bases" (sets of active linear inequality constraints) which can enter the optimal "primal" solution. These bases are of interest since each one carries with it an investment allocation (or phase of growth), and it is just the sequencing of investment decisions which we want to explore.

For convenience, the model has been set up with continuous time; however, many of the same results would emerge with careful scrutiny of the dual linear programming solution if the model were reformulated in discrete terms. To facilitate comparisons, I have made the model very similar to that of Chenery and MacEwan. The main differences involve the substitution of constraints relating minimum investment, absorptive capacity, and minimum consumption levels to GNP, instead of to growth rates of these respective variables as in the Chenery-MacEwan version. This was done to minimize the number of state variables in the model; I do not think it makes an essential difference in the characteristics of the solution.

To make the foregoing more precise, it is necessary to spell out the model in detail. I begin with the constraints, and then go on to the objective function. For more commentary on the economic meaning of the constraints, the reader is referred to Chenery-MacEwan (1966).

To begin, assume that GNP at any time t is the sum of the net outputs of two sectors: regular (traditional, domestic) production $V_1(t)$, and production for trade improvement $V_2(t)$:[1]

$$\text{GNP}(t) = V_1(t) + V_2(t) \qquad (3.1)$$

Production of both V_1 and V_2 is assumed to be related to capital stock via constant capital-output ratio production functions. This means that

$$\dot{V}_1 = \frac{I_1}{k_1}; \; I_1 \geq 0 \qquad (3.2)$$

$$\dot{V}_2 = \frac{I_2}{k_2}; \; I_2 \geq 0 \qquad (3.3)$$

---

1. As far as the model is concerned, "trade improvement" can take the form of either additional exports or import substitution. These two activities could be differentiated via the use of different cost structures; but, as we will see in Section V, this would not add much to the model.

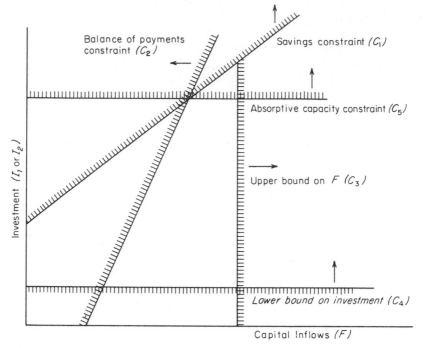

Figure 3.1 Problem constraints. Arrows indicate probable direction of movement of the constraints over time.

where the dot means differentiation with respect to time; and I_i and k_i are, respectively, investment and the capital-output ratio for production activity i. The usual supposition is that $k_2 > k_1$—that is, trade improvement is a more capital intensive activity than is ordinary production. As we will see below, this hypothesis will have some influence on the scheduling of investment within the model.

The distinguishing characteristics of two-gap analysis derive from the dual role of foreign capital inflows in both making possible additional imports and supplementing domestic savings. For the latter, we know that if maximum possible domestic savings are limited by a marginal savings rate,

$$\text{Savings } (t) \leq S_0 + \alpha \text{GNP}(t)$$

then investment can be undertaken up to the limit imposed by the sum of savings plus foreign capital inflows F:

$$C_1 = I_1 + I_2 - F - \alpha(V_1 + V_2) - S_0 \leq 0 \tag{3.4}$$

For any given value of F, the savings constraint C_1 puts an upper bound on total investment as indicated in Figure 3.1.[2]

2. Figure 3.1, to which we will refer with great frequency, shows a "typical" configuration of the nondifferential equation constraints of our problem, when one of the investment activities is operating at a zero level and the other operates at a positive level. (This pattern of use of the investment activities occurs frequently during the solution, as we shall see in Section II.) The constraints change position as V_1 and V_2 change. The arrows show their probable direction of motion over time.

The other limitation which capital inflows can ease is the balance of payments. Here we assume that exports of the "traditional" type $[E(t)]$ are given exogenously, while imports are assumed to depend on the levels of GNP in general and investment (with higher marginal import requirements) in particular:

$$\text{Imports } (t) \geq M_0 + \mu\text{GNP}(t) + \theta[I_1(t) + I_2(t)]$$

Imports can exceed the limitations imposed by exports to the extent that either capital inflows or production for trade improvement increases. This is expressed symbolically by the following constraint:

$$C_2 = \theta(I_1 + I_2) + \mu(V_1 + V_2) + M_0 - F - V_2 - E \leq 0 \tag{3.5}$$

Like the savings constraint, this constraint places an upper bound on investment for given levels of the other variables. Since $\theta < 1$, the constraint line relating I to F is steeper than in the savings constraint C_1, as indicated in Figure 3.1.

The other constraints are somewhat less essential to the workings of the model, and one can imagine a number of possible variations on them. It is realistic, for example, to put some sort of bound on capital inflows, but no one form of this constraint suggests itself as most appealing.[3] More for simplicity than anything else, F is limited as a share of GNP:

$$C_3 = F - \beta(V_1 + V_2) \leq 0 \tag{3.6}$$

The same sort of *ad hoc* approach is employed to allow for the nonshiftability of investment. It is sufficient to bound investment from below:

$$C_4 = -(I_1 + I_2) + \bar{I}(t) \leq 0 \tag{3.7}$$

where $\bar{I}(t)$ is some exogenously given function of time.

On the upper bound side, we already have investment limited by C_1 and C_2, but practical experience suggests a third type of constraint, for absorptive capacity. Such constraints ought ideally to be related to "real" limitations on growth of capacity such as shortage of skilled labor, increasing costs of rapid supply of key investment goods, and so on; but a more ad hoc specification is usually imposed by simple lack of knowledge. One often specifies an upper limit to the rate of growth of investment. Since this would be inconvenient for obtaining a model with only two state variables, a constraint relating absorptive capacity to total GNP will be used:

$$C_5 = I_1 + I_2 - \gamma(V_1 + V_2) \leq 0 \tag{3.8}$$

The joint effect of (3.7) and (3.8) is to place the rate of growth of GNP within certain bounds.

Turning to the specification of the objective function, note that the national income identity in this model is

$$V_1 + V_2 = TC + I_1 + I_2 + E + V_2 - TM$$

where

TC = total consumption
TM = total imports.

---

3. An incomplete list of possible specifications includes relating F to GNP, to investment, or to last period's F, or else restricting total foreign debt accumulation over the planning period.

By substitution of the amount of imports,

$$TM = E + F + V_2$$

and rearrangement, we find that consumption is given by

$$TC = V_1 + V_2 - I_1 - I_2 + F \tag{3.9}$$

Following Chenery-MacEwan, one can formulate a fairly general welfare function in the following way:[4]

$$\text{maximize} \int_0^T e^{-\rho t}(TC - \varphi F)\, dt + \bar{\lambda}_1 V_1(T) + \bar{\lambda}_2 V_2(T)$$

where

     ρ is the rate of discount

     φ is the shadow valuation of costly foreign capital

     T is the terminal time

$\bar{\lambda}_1$ and $\bar{\lambda}_2$ are weights applied to terminal levels of the two types of output.
For reasons of mathematical convenience, this will be converted into a minimization problem. Also, to suppress one parameter, let $\varphi = 2$. Hence, the problem is stated as

$$\text{Minimize} \int_0^T e^{-\rho t}[I_1 + I_2 + F - V_1 - V_2]\, dt - \bar{\lambda}_1 V_1(T) - \bar{\lambda}_2 V_2(T) \tag{3.10}$$

subject to the constraints (3.2)–(3.8). After an analysis of the characteristics of the solution to this problem in Sections III and IV, variants are discussed in Section V.

III. Solutions to the Model

There is a well-known recipe for solving the type of problem presented here.[5] One introduces multipliers (or "costate variables") λ_1 and λ_2 corresponding to the state variables V_1 and V_2 defined by the differential equations (3.2) and (3.3),[6] and uses them to define a Hamiltonian function H:

$$
\begin{aligned}
H &= e^{-\rho t}[I_1 + I_2 + F - V_1 - V_2] + \frac{\lambda_1 I_1}{k_1} + \frac{\lambda_2 I_2}{k_2} \\
&= \left[e^{-\rho t} + \frac{\lambda_1}{k_1} \right] I_1 + \left[e^{-\rho t} + \frac{\lambda_2}{k_2} \right] I_2 + e^{-\rho t} F - e^{-\rho t}(V_1 + V_2) \\
&= a_1 I_1 + a_2 I_2 + e^{-\rho t} F - e^{-\rho t}(V_1 + V_2) \tag{3.11}
\end{aligned}
$$

where in the last line the a_i are equal to $e^{-\rho t} + \lambda_i/k_i$. Necessary conditions for the minimization of (3.10) subject to (3.2)–(3.8) are, then, the following:

1. H should be minimized at each moment of time as a function of the control variables F, I_1, and I_2, subject to the constraints (3.4)–(3.8), which, in this model, amounts to a problem in linear programming. In the "usual" case when $a_1 \neq a_2$ in

---

4. It should be pointed out that the specification of the welfare functional follows most development programming models (but not most optimal savings models) in *not* assuming diminishing marginal utility of consumption.

5. The details of how to set up the necessary conditions for solution of an optimal control problem are given in a large number of textbooks. A good one is Bryson and Ho (1969).

6. The λ's at any time t are the derivatives of the minimized cost integral with respect to the state variables $V_1(t)$ and $V_2(t)$.

(3.11), the solution to this problem will involve nonzero values of only two control variables—F and either I_1 or I_2—since (with some malice aforethought) the constraints are all stated so that the I's enter them symmetrically.[7] Thus in the linear programming minimization, the investment activity with the algebraically smaller coefficient a_i takes on a positive value while the other investment activity is set to zero.[8] This implies in turn that only two constraints of the linear programming problem will be binding, with nonnegative shadow prices p_j and p_k, say.

2. The evolution of the costate variables λ_i over time is described by the differential equations[9]

$$\dot{\lambda}_1 = e^{-\rho t} + \alpha p_1 - \mu p_2 + \beta p_3 + \gamma p_5 \tag{3.12}$$

$$\dot{\lambda}_2 = e^{-\rho t} + \alpha p_1 + (1 - \mu)p_2 + \beta p_3 + \gamma p_5 \tag{3.13}$$

where the p_i are the shadow prices from the Hamiltonian-minimizing linear program. [Note that the two differential equations have the same form, except for the term multiplying p_2, which reflects the fact that production of more V_1 just uses up foreign exchange through generating imports, whereas V_2 adds to the effective supply of foreign exchange. Hence, when constraint C_2 is binding, $\lambda_1(t)$—the value of an additional unit of V_1 in terms of minimizing (3.10)—tends to decline while $\lambda_2(t)$ increases more rapidly.]

3. At terminal time T, the costate variables are

$$\lambda_1(T) = \bar{\lambda}_1 \tag{3.14}$$

$$\lambda_2(T) = \bar{\lambda}_2 \tag{3.15}$$

which simply restate that the valuation of terminal outputs in the welfare function is given by $\bar{\lambda}_1$ and $\bar{\lambda}_2$.

A *reference solution* to the model can be developed in the following way. We may impose a general condition on the solution that capital inflows F just fall to zero at the terminal time and, at the same time, require a certain level of terminal GNP. In general, there will be levels of $\bar{\lambda}_1$ and $\bar{\lambda}_2$ which will allow these conditions to be satisfied. [By looking at (3.10), it can be seen that these terminal multipliers will generally have negative values.] Given these multipliers, we can minimize the Hamiltonian (3.11) at time T, and use the shadow prices resulting from this minimization to evaluate the $\dot{\lambda}_i$ in preparation for a "step" backward in time.

---

7. Were the investment activities to enter some constraint nonsymmetrically (for example, in the foreign exchange constraint with different marginal import requirements), there would exist the possibility of all three control variables entering a "basis" with positive values even when $a_1 \neq a_2$, since the constraint set would then have corners outside the $I_1 - F$ and $I_2 - F$ planes in the three-dimensional space of control variables. Section V contains some analysis of this variant specification. Incidentally, the effects of the symmetric constraints on investment allocation justify the use of the "I_1 or I_2" label on the investment axis in Figure 3.1, and they also help explain the fact that Chenery and MacEwan (1966) observed a heavy preponderance of the use of one type of investment or the other for most periods of their linear program.

8. The case where $a_1 = a_2$ (so both investment activities can enter the basis) is discussed in Section IV.

9. The general equations for the evolution of the costate variables are

$$\dot{\lambda}_i = \frac{-\partial H}{\partial V_i} - \sum_j p_j \frac{\partial C_j}{\partial V_i} \qquad i = 1, 2$$

See Bryson and Ho (1969: sec. 3.10).

If we also assume that F falls to zero from a small positive value at time T, it is clear from Figure 3.1 that either constraints C_2 and C_4 (balance of payments and minimum investment restrictions) or C_1 and C_2 (savings and balance of payments) will have to be binding at this time. We consider these possibilities in turn.

Constraints C_2 and C_4

If constraints C_2 and C_4 are binding, the economy arrives at the end of the planning period with minimum investment levels (given by the investment floor C_4) just sufficient to provide the capacity needed to close the export-import gap at time T. Near the terminal time, foreign aid is used to cover the balance of payments deficit in constraint C_2, while there is excess potential savings. The economy is thus in a "trade limited" phase.

In general, constraints C_2 and C_4 can bind when a_i^*—the minimum of a_1 and a_2 in (3.11)—is positive or not sufficiently negative to make the level curve of the Hamiltonian in the I_i^*-F plane of Figure 3.1 less steep than the line C_2.[10] Under these conditions, the prices corresponding to the constraints are determined by the equations[11]

$$a_i^* + \theta p_2 - p_4 = 0$$
$$e^{-\rho t} - p_2 = 0$$

which have the solution

$$p_2 = e^{-\rho t}$$
$$p_4 = a_i^* + \theta e^{-\rho t}$$

Substituting these prices in the differential equations (3.12) and (3.13) for the costate variables, and noticing in general that

$$\dot{a}_i = -\rho e^{-\rho t} + \frac{\dot{\lambda}_i}{k_i} \quad i = 1, 2$$

we derive the following differential equations for the investment weights a_1 and a_2 in the Hamiltonian:

$$\dot{a}_1 = \left[-\rho + \frac{(1 - \mu)}{k_1} \right] e^{-\rho t} \tag{3.16}$$

$$\dot{a}_2 = \left[-\rho + \frac{(2 - \mu)}{k_2} \right] e^{-\rho t} \tag{3.17}$$

For empirically relevant values of the parameters, both $\dot{a}_1$ and $\dot{a}_2$ will be positive, meaning that they will decline as time flows backward from T. (In addition, a_2 will

---

10. Since much of the argument in Section III is devoted to working out the conditions under which minimizing the Hamiltonian implies arriving at various corners in the polygon in Figure 3.1, the following geometrical review should be useful: A level curve (or "isoquant") of the function $mI + F = $ constant, with $m > 0$, has a higher value the further we move northeast in the IF plane, as shown in Figure 3.2a. A big value of m gives a level curve like a, while a smaller value corresponds to b. If m is negative (Figure 3.2b), the function value increases in a southeasterly direction, and a value of m close to zero gives a line like c. A more negative m produces line d.

11. The general equations for the price equations when two constraints j and k are binding are

$$a_i^* + p_j \frac{\partial C_j}{\partial I_i^*} + p_k \frac{\partial C_k}{\partial I_i^*} = 0$$

$$e^{-\rho t} + p_j \frac{\partial C_j}{\partial F} + p_k \frac{\partial C_k}{\partial F} = 0$$

These are standard linear programming duality conditions which enter this problem via the minimization of a linear Hamiltonian subject to linear constraints.

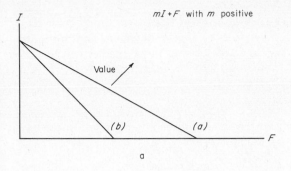

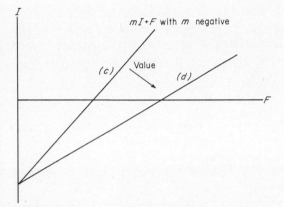

Figure 3.2 Sample level curves in the IF plane.

often decline more rapidly than a_1, indicating that investment will tend to shift from I_1 to I_2 as time grows earlier.)[12] The economy will either remain on basis C_2-C_4 until time zero is reached, or a_i^* will become sufficiently negative to allow a shift to another basis. Since the a_i decline smoothly, and since the balance of payments constraint C_2 will be "close" to the I-axis near the end of the planning period, the controls will jump to basis C_1 and C_2 or C_2 and C_5 (depending on the relative positions of lines C_1 and C_5 in Figure 3.1) when a_i^* is sufficiently negative to allow the level curves of the Hamiltonian to be less steep than the line C_2 in Figure 3.1.

Constraints C_1 and C_2

Constraints C_1 and C_2 (on, in order, savings and the balance of payments) can be binding either on transition with time running backward from C_2 and C_4, or else can bind at time T with no transitions. In either case, this constraint set holds when both savings and trade gaps are equal ex ante. However, additional capital inflows would permit more investment if additional savings were forthcoming, so the economy may be described as being in a "savings-limited" phase as far as its investment prospects are concerned.

12. This tendency is offset to the extent that trade improvement is more capital intensive than ordinary production, so $k_2 > k_1$.

Following the same sort of analysis as before, we find that

$$p_1 = e^{-\rho t} - \frac{a_i^* + e^{-\rho t}}{1 - \theta}$$

$$p_2 = \frac{a_i^* + e^{-\rho t}}{1 - \theta}$$

For the basis to be viable, we also require that p_1 and p_2 be nonnegative. In the case of p_1, this means that

$$a_i^* \leq -e^{-\rho t}\theta \quad \text{or} \quad \frac{\lambda_i^*!}{k_i} \leq -e^{-\rho t}(1 + \theta) \tag{3.18}$$

while the requirement on p_2 is equivalent to

$$a_i^* \geq -e^{-\rho t} \quad \text{or} \quad \frac{\lambda_i^*}{k_i} \geq -2e^{-\rho t} \tag{3.19}$$

Geometrically, these conditions mean that the slope of the level curves of the Hamiltonian function has to lie between the slopes of lines C_2 and C_1 in Figure 3.1.

The differential equations for the a_i on this basis are

$$\dot{a}_1 = e^{-\rho t}\left\{-\rho + \frac{1}{k_1}\left[1 + \alpha - \frac{2(\alpha + \mu)}{1 - \theta}\right]\right\} - \frac{(\alpha + \mu)}{k_1(1 - \theta)} \cdot \frac{\lambda_i^*}{k_i} \tag{3.20}$$

$$\dot{a}_2 = e^{-\rho t}\left\{-\rho + \frac{1}{k_2}\left[1 + \alpha + \frac{2(1 - \alpha - \mu)}{1 - \theta}\right]\right\} + \frac{(1 - \alpha - \mu)}{k_2(1 - \theta)} \cdot \frac{\lambda_i^*}{k_i} \tag{3.21}$$

Substituting the boundary values (3.18) and (3.19) for λ_i^*/k_1, we find that both $\dot{a}_1$ and $\dot{a}_2$ are positive,[13] indicating that they are positive for the whole range of the λ_i^*/k_i on the basis. Hence, we may conclude that as time flows backward, the a_i become more negative (again with a_2 decreasing more rapidly). Depending on the rate of decrease, the economy may stay on the basis C_1 and C_2, or else control may leave the constraint C_2—when condition (3.19) fails to be satisfied—and jump to either C_1 and C_3 or C_1 and C_5. The former of these alternatives seems empirically more probable, so we consider it next.

Constraints C_1 and C_5

On the set of constraints C_1 and C_5, the economy is limited by its savings potential according to C_1 and its limitations on absorbing investment, as specified in C_5. Trade problems are not relevant, since the savings gap dominates the trade gap ex ante. However, additional capital inflows could generate more investment through their savings-creating function if these additional resources could usefully be absorbed. For this reason, the economy can be said to be in an "absorption limited" phase.

The shadow prices of the constraints of this basis are given by

$$p_1 = e^{-\rho t} \tag{3.22}$$

$$p_5 = -(a_i^* + e^{-\rho t}) \tag{3.23}$$

13. The "tightest" condition for positivity is when λ_i^* is at its upper bound (3.18). In this case, $\dot{a}_1 > 0$ requires that $(1 - \mu)/k_1 > \rho$; that is, that one minus the marginal import propensity divided by the capital-output ratio in the first sector exceeds the discount rate. This condition seems likely to be satisfied in practice.

and nonnegativity of p_5 requires that the level curves of the Hamiltonian be less steep than C_1, or

$$a_i^* \leq -e^{-\rho t} \quad \text{or} \quad \frac{\lambda_i^*}{k_i} \leq -2e^{-\rho t} \tag{3.24}$$

When (3.22) and (3.23) are substituted into the general differential equations for the a_i, and (3.24) is applied, once again $\dot{a}_i > 0$. Hence, as time flows backward, the a_i grow increasingly negative, and the basis C_1 and C_5 stays active.

IV. Some Loose Ends

The general thrust of the foregoing analysis seems perfectly clear. On the three bases considered (and indeed on all bases), derivatives of the a_i are positive, implying that the optimal control sequence moves toward the northeast of the feasible area in Figure 3.1 as time flows backward. With forward time flow, this means that the optimal plan for the two-gap economy considered here will (1) pass through a phase where constraints such as the foreign aid upper bound or absorptive capacity constraint plus the savings limit are binding;[14] (2) pass through a phase where both balance of payments and savings constraints are binding; (3) finally coast into the terminal conditions with only the balance of payments and investment floor constraints binding.

Some variants on this sequence are possible—for example, an initial phase with absorptive capacity and balance of payments binding, or the omission of phase (2) or both.[15] However, positivity of the time derivatives of the a_i on all possible bases (which is easy but tedious to verify) rules out plans *beginning* with the investment floor binding and *ending* with a binding absorptive capacity constraint or foreign aid upper bound. Moreover, there is a general bias toward the use of investment activity I_2 early in the planning period, given that $\dot{a}_2$ is likely to exceed $\dot{a}_1$ on all bases in which the foreign trade constraint C_2 is binding. Exactly when the switch from I_2 to I_1 occurs is impossible to evaluate without numerical parameter values.

In addition to these conclusions, there are some specific caveats to be added to the foregoing analysis.

1. As any linear programmer could point out, the two types of investment could *both* enter the solution at positive intensity provided that both a_i stayed equal for a finite amount of time. This can happen only on bases in which the balance of payments constraint C_2 is not present, since there are unequal terms in p_2 in the differen-

14. Note that if the absorptive capacity constraint C_5 is binding at the beginning of the plan, the ad hoc upper limit C_3 on ofreign capital inflows will not enter the solution. It is excluded because he level curves of the Hamiltonian will always have some positive slope in the IF plane and are minimized toward the northwest. Hence, the intersection of C_3 and C_5 in Figure 3.1 can never be a minimizing point.

15. If domestic savings were large enough to finance any otherwise feasible investments, the only constraint on investment expenditure besides the lower and upper limits (3.7) and (3.8) would be the balance of payments restriction. Plentiful savings early in the planning period would therefore imply that the balance of payments and absorptive capacity constraint (or foreign aid limit) would bind. If savings were initially binding, but then became more plentiful, the sequence of bases

$$(C_1, C_5) \rightarrow (C_2, C_5) \rightarrow (C_2, C_4)$$

and

$$(C_1, C_5) \rightarrow (C_2, C_4)$$

would be possible. (See Figure 3.1.) In this case, phase (2) would not enter the solution.

tial equations (3.12) and (3.13) for the λ_i. An example would be the specification that foreign aid end *before* the end of the planning period, in which case total investment would be determined by the investment floor and the required mix of I_1 and I_2 necessary to keep the trade gap closed. The same phenomenon could occur at the beginning of the planning period, when two of the three constraints C_1, C_3, and C_5 would be binding.

2. F does not have to go smoothly to zero, as assumed in the previous section. In an economy without a binding trade constraint, there could be a shift in bases just at the end of the planning period from an absorption- or savings-limited phase with positive capital inflows to the point of intersection of the savings constraint C_1 and the vertical axis in Figure 3.1. This would imply a discontinuous fall of F from a positive level to zero at the end of the planning period, but would not affect investment timing in a significant way.

3. The above analysis could be modified by exogenous forces causing the constraints to move in directions opposite those indicated by the arrows in Figure 3.1 for significant periods of time. The qualitative effects of such perverse motions are fairly easy to work out and do not upset the general conclusions already reached.

V. Alternative Specifications

It is interesting to consider some variants to the model examined here, to see how robust the solution sequence would be with respect to changes in model specifications. Briefly, the following can be concluded:

1. The introduction of a distinction between exports and import substitution as different types of "trade creation" would have no important effects, provided that both these activities entered symmetrically with I_1 in all constraints. On the other hand, the use of, say, differential import coefficients for the investment activities in the foreign trade constraint C_2 could allow both investments to enter the solution simultaneously, bringing with them either the investment floor C_4 or ceiling C_5 to determine investment allocation. The general trend of the a_i to increase over time would not be changed by these specification changes.

2. One could introduce a lower bound on the share of consumption in GNP at any time. However, equation (3.9) indicates that this constraint would have the same form as the savings constraint C_1 (with unity substituting for α as the coefficient for GNP) and thus would add no essentially new festures to the solution.

3. It has been suggested (for example, by Millikan 1966) that foreign capital inflows depress potential domestic savings rates. If this were true, the coefficient of F in the savings constraint C_1 would presumably lie somewhere between minus one and zero. This would have no essential effect on the qualitative characteristics of the solution, although the $\dot{a}_i$ would be somewhat reduced and thus the period of heavy use of foreign aid in the early years of the model would be somewhat shortened.

4. The form of the absorptive capacity function used in this paper incorporates "learning" to the extent that it is reflected by the aggregate level of GNP. The more learning there is, the bigger is the coefficient γ in the absorptive capacity constraint C_5, and hence the less effective is the constraint in limiting the early concentration of investment. The most obvious change to the specification adopted here would be the introduction of differential learning effects from the two types of production. Once

again, this would influence the decision between the two types of investment but would not affect the time-phasing of total investment.

5. Some parameter variations in the welfare function might well be considered. As long as we stick to a linear specification, the Chenery-MacEwan function seems sufficiently general, but the roles of its various parameters are not completely clear. As it turns out, the most crucial parameter is φ, the shadow value of foreign aid.[16] When φ exceeds unity, changes in its value would not have qualitative effects on the characteristics of the solution, since the derivative of the Hamiltonian with respect to foreign capital inflows F would remain positive and the previous analysis in terms of level curves would apply. However, the specification $\varphi < 1$ would change the sign of F in the Hamiltonian, implying that minimizing constraint configurations would be on the eastern side of Figure 3.1. Thus, the savings and balance of payments restrictions would enter the problem in a much less important way, while the ad hoc restriction on foreign capital inflows would be very important. This alternative solution has not been considered in any detail, but given the way GNP enters the constraints C_3 and C_5, it seems obvious that the bias toward early investment also occurs in this formulation.[17]

VI. Conclusions

1. If we accept the hypothesis that the foreign exchange shadow price φ exceeds unity, the optimal policy is unshakable; heavy investment outlays early in the planning period. Fundamentally, this is due to the way that GNP enters the two "gap" constraints which set upper bounds on the control variables. If these constraints are binding toward the end of the plan (and the terminal conditions on V_1 and V_2 generally assure this), then an optimizing solution inevitably looks toward early investment as a means of easing these latter-day restrictions through the creation of constraint-relaxing capacity. The role of the state variables V_1 and V_2 in the constraints shows up clearly in the dual solution, where the costate variables λ_1 and (especially) λ_2 pick up their positive derivatives because the state variables create upper bounds on the controls. Since the costate variables govern the evolution of the solution over time, their positive derivatives guarantee the heavy emphasis on investment early in the planning period.

2. In more elaborate models (with more sectors and more intersectoral interaction), it is still true that the components of GNP would enter in defining upper bounds on investment and foreign aid through the two "gap" constraints. Since sector product levels (or closely related capacity levels) serve as state variables in the big models, their corresponding costates will have the same bias toward growth over time as the λ_i in the model of this paper. Although the conclusion is not so clearcut as in the present simple model, it seems a reasonable conjecture that the big models should have an implicit bias toward early investment, particularly in "trade improvement."

16. Increases in ρ, the discount rate (which might be expected to "spread out" investment over time), would not have a striking effect as long as the inequalities $(1 - \mu)/k_i > \rho$ were preserved. These guarantee the positivity of $\dot{a}_i$ in several bases and seem unlikely to be violated in the range of value for ρ usually assumed by economic programmers.

17. The case $\varphi = 1$ is very difficult to analyze, since minimization of the Hamiltonian fails to specify the value of F. The theory of "singular" problems of this type is not completely developed, and applications are correspondingly scarce.

4 An Intertemporal Planning Model Featuring Economies of Scale*

Larry E. Westphal

I. Introduction

The development literature has repeatedly questioned the market mechanism's efficiency as an instrument for allocating investment (see Scitovsky 1954, a classic in the area). Interdependencies between sectors that are not reflected in the structure of existing prices give rise to such questions. Multisector programming models have been constructed to provide an alternative source of the information necessary, but incompletely extant in the market, for making investment decisions. To date these models have successfully incorporated only a limited set of interdependencies between sectors—those arising from input-output relations, competition for scarce resources, and changes in relative factor scarcities over time.

Economies of scale in interdependent sectors constitute an empirically important case in which market signals are inefficient instruments of investment planning, but only recently has the numerical solution of nonconvex models become practical.[1] This study reports on a multisector, multiperiod optimizing model for South Korea in which economies of scale are specified in the petrochemicals and steel producing sectors. This Korean project evaluation model (KPEM) is applied to planning the timing and scale of investment in those sectors.

KPEM is similar to models constructed by Chenery and Kretschmer (1956), Bruno (1966), Eckaus and Parikh (1968), and Manne and Weisskopf (1969). Over a 10-year planning horizon, production and trade variables for 11 sectors encompassing all economic activity are endogenously determined along with investment by sector and aggregate consumption. The scarce resources in the model are foreign exchange and domestic savings. There are no labor constraints. KPEM spans 10 years using five 2-year periods; each variable represents an activity level summed over 2 years and yearly figures are assumed equal to period averages.

The model departs from those cited above in three major respects: the use of a

* The author is indebted to Hollis B. Chenery, David C. Cole, Charles R. Frank, Jr., David A. Kendrick, and Alan S. Manne for many valuable discussions during the course of this study. Mrs. Diane Sliney assisted with the computations. Grateful acknowledgment is also made for computer time and research assistance provided through a Ford Foundation grant (No. 690-0043) to the Development Research Project, Princeton University, and a National Science Foundation grant (No. GJ-34) to the Princeton University Computer Center. Of course, the conclusions in this paper are the sole responsibility of the author.

1. Chenery (1959) has exhibited the consequences of market "planning" when decreasing costs are found in interdependent sectors.

piece-wise linear approximation to a nonlinear objective function, the aggregation principles employed, and the inclusion of economies of scale.

Objective Function

The objective function in KPEM is a linear approximation to a constant elasticity of marginal utility welfare function (see Feldstein 1964). In any single period, welfare is equal to the natural logarithm of per capita consumption multiplied by a population factor which signifies policy-makers' concern with aggregate, in addition to per capita, consumption. Intertemporal welfare is the discounted *sum* of each period's welfare.[2] The welfare function to be maximized is

$$W = \sum_{t=1}^{\infty} (1 + \omega)^{-t} P_t^{\alpha} \log_e \frac{C_t}{P_t} \tag{4.1}$$

where P is population, C denotes total consumption, ω is the discount factor, and α is the exponent in the population weight.

A linear approximation to the nonlinear welfare function is required. The procedure employed in KPEM for approximating $y = f(x)$ by a linear function y^0 requires only two additional constraints regardless of the number of intervals (n) in the linear approximation. Variables w_i and values $\bar{x}_i$ are defined by the constraints

$$x = \sum_{i=1}^{n} w_i \bar{x}_i$$

$$1 = \sum_{i=1}^{n} w_i$$

and y is replaced by

$$y^0 = \sum_{i=1}^{n} w_i f(\bar{x}_i)$$

If $f(x)$ is a convex function of x then at most two w_i will be positive *and* these will be w_i and w_{i+1} such that $\bar{x}_i \leq x \leq \bar{x}_{i+1}$.[3]

Further approximation of (4.1) is needed to obtain KPEM'S objective function since only the first 10 years of the infinite horizon appear explicitly in the model. Investment in the terminal years spanned by KPEM will be artificially reduced unless postterminal consumption is valued in the objective function or investment in the terminal years is bounded from below. The amount of capacity available immediately after the plan is the principal determinant of the level and growth of postplan consumption. Thus, gross domestic product (GDP) in the postterminal year— determined as the value added coefficient weighted sum of the capacity available in each sector—is used in the objective function as a proxy for postterminal consumption.

With parameter symbols replaced by the numerical values used in the experiments, the objective function is

Maximize
$$W = \sum_{t=1}^{6} \sum_{i} \phi_{i,t} w_{i,t} \tag{4.2}$$

2. No philosophic content is ascribed to the use of a "pure time discount rate." It is simply required here to make the sum of utility over an infinite horizon finite.
3. The method is valid only for convex functions. See Dantzig (1963: 482–489).

where

$$\sum_i w_{i,t} = 1, \ t = 1, \ldots, 6 \tag{4.3}$$

In-plan welfare

$$\phi_{i,t} = (2.10)\left(\frac{P_t}{2}\right)^{\frac{1}{2}} (1.10)^{-2t} \log_e \bar{C}_{i,t}, \quad t = 1, \ldots, 5 \tag{4.4}$$

$$\sum_i \bar{C}_{i,t} w_{i,t} = \frac{1}{2} C_t, \quad t = 1, \ldots, 5 \tag{4.5}$$

Post-plan welfare

$$\phi_{i,6} = (1.95)\left(\frac{P_5}{2}\right)^{\frac{1}{2}} \log_e \overline{GDP}_{i,6} \tag{4.6}$$

$$\sum_i \overline{GDP}_{i,6} w_{i,6} = \sum_{i=1}^{12} V_i k_{i,6} \tag{4.7}$$

where V_i and $k_{i,6}$ are respectively the value added coefficient and postterminal capacity in the ith sector.[4] The value of the discount factor is 0.10 and the exponent of the population weight equals 0.5. Capacity is measured in yearly output whereas C_t is total consumption over 2 years, hence the one half in equation (4.5). $P_t/2$ is the average population during the period.

The discounted sum of consumption was rejected as an objective function since it results in the "flip-flop" property that the choice between consumption and investment is sensitive to the discount rate within only a narrow region. (See Tinbergen

---

4. The objective function is derived from equation (4.1) in the following manner: Let ρ be the postterminal (constant) rate of population growth ($= .02$); γ the postterminal (constant) growth rate of both consumption and gross domestic product; and β the ratio of consumption to GDP after the plan period. The first postterminal period is τ. There are n sectors. Using the assumptions that consumption and GDP grow at the same rate and that there is no excess capacity in period τ, the welfare from postterminal consumption is

$$P_\tau{}^\alpha \sum_{t=\tau}^{\infty} (1+\omega)^{-t}(1+\rho)^{\alpha(t-\tau)} \log_e \left[\beta P_\tau{}^{-1}\left(\frac{1+\gamma}{1+\rho}\right)^{(t-\tau)} \sum_{i=1}^{n} V_i k_{i,\tau}\right]$$

Re-expressed in these terms, the welfare function is (t designates single years)

$$W = \sum_{t=1}^{\tau-1} (1+\omega)^{-t} P_t{}^\alpha \log_e C_t + P_\tau{}^\alpha \sum_{t=\tau}^{\infty} \frac{(1+\rho)^{\alpha(t-\tau)}}{(1+\omega)^t} \log_e \sum_{i=1}^{n} V_i k_{i,\tau}$$

$$- \sum_{t=1}^{\tau-1} (1+\omega)^{-t} P_t{}^\alpha \log_e P_t$$

$$+ P_\tau{}^\alpha \sum_{t=\tau}^{\infty} \frac{(1+\rho)^{\alpha(t-\tau)}}{(1+\omega)^t} \log_e \left[\beta P^{1-}{}_\tau \left(\frac{1+\gamma}{1+\rho}\right)^{(t-\tau)}\right]$$

The last two terms in the above expression are composed of exogenous elements and are disregarded in the objective function.

An objective function weight on the value added weighted sum of capacity provided prior to and during the plan could have been derived from any welfare function based on consumption. The advantage of the log form is that the terms involving the postterminal growth rate and consumption propensity are additive and can be disregarded so that assumptions regarding these parameters are unnecessary. There is also the added convenience that some of the population terms can be neglected.

1960). For high discount rates consumption is at its upper bound in the initial periods; for low rates consumption is initially at its lower bound. Thus consumption growth "flips" from the terminal periods to the initial periods as the discount rate is increased over a very narrow region (see Eckaus and Parikh 1968: chap. 1).

The use of a piece-wise linear approximation to welfare function (4.1) yields a more gradual change in the investment-consumption choice as the discount rate is varied. There is less of a tendency to concentrate on consumption in some (connected) periods and on investment in the remaining (and connected) periods. Consumption exhibits a smoother path while the overall choice between consumption and investment during the plan is determined largely by the weight given postterminal capacities in the objective function. Furthermore, to the extent that use of the discounted sum of consumption may cause a "big push" early in the plan, use of (4.1) circumvents a possible bias in favor of lumpy investment in the decreasing cost industries.

Aggregation Scheme

KPEM is designed to determine the optimal timing and scale of capacity expansion in petrochemicals and steel, as well as to illustrate the implications of plant construction in these sectors for production, imports, and exports in related sectors. The model also provides insights into the broader issues of Korean development such as the timing of aid inflows, the trade-off between consumption and investment, and the aggregate implications of alternative growth rates.

Within each of the two sectors of principal interest the focus is on a single large project—an integrated steel mill of more than 1 million tons annual capacity and a petrochemicals complex. The need to evaluate these projects within a general equilibrium model arises from their "lumpiness." Either will alone require more than 1 percent of the total investment over 10 years.

With experience, it has become quite clear that disaggregation of input-output optimizing models into a large number of sectors is insufficient to assure operational policy prescriptions relating to capacity expansion at the project level. Here "project" refers to a single production facility such as a steel mill or a multipurpose dam. A "sector" is the aggregate of a number of projects. To yield operational results a multisectoral model must be explicitly structured around several concrete choices. This realization, along with a computational limit on the number of sectors that can be manageably handled within a multiperiod model, has led to an aggregation scheme that places the principal users of petrochemicals (or iron and steel) within the same sector, the principal suppliers of its intermediate products within another sector, and unrelated activities into sectors on the basis of common characteristics. The petrochemicals complex and the steel mill are each described by separate activities. The following list outlines the sectors and commodity classifications in the model.[5]

5. Fertilizer and petroleum production are distinguished so that the model can be used in part to assess Korea's comparative advantage in these lines. The aggregation to 11 sectors was also based on similar growth rates and responses to capacity expansion in petrochemicals and steel in a 17-sector, three-period model.

For traditional sectors and petrochemicals, the numbers appearing in the left-hand margin are the corresponding production activity and capacity subscripts.

For the steel mill, the production activity subscripts are given separately. The numbers in parentheses refer to the subscript of the commodity produced by the activity, and the numbers in brackets give the corresponding sectors in the 17-sector aggregation used in Westphal (1969b).

A. *Traditional Sectors.* Production competitive with imports in 1966
   1. Primary production—agriculture, forestry, fishing, coal and other mining, and coal products (1) [1,2]
   2. Processed primary and chemicals—processed foods, beverages, tobacco, forestry products, printing, publishing and chemicals (2) [3,7]
   3. Petrochemicals users—fiber spinning, textile fabrics and products, leather and rubber products, miscellaneous light manufacturing (including plastic products) (3) [4,5,6]
   4. Fertilizer (4) [8]
   5. Petroleum fuels and lubricants (5) [9]
   6. Cement and earthen products, construction (6) [10]
   7. Traditional iron and crude steel, steel products (7) [11,12]
   8. Engineering—finished metal products, nonferrous metals, machinery, and transport equipment (8) [13,14]
   9. Overhead and services—electricity, water, commerce, transport, and services (9) [15]
B. *Import Substituting Complexes*
   10. Petrochemicals complex—production of plastic resins, synthetic rubber polymers, and synthetic fiber intermediates from refinery off-streams (10) [16]
   11. Integrated iron and steel mill (includes two production activities)
      11. Iron, crude steel, and steel products, both traditionally and not traditionally produced in Korea (all output counted in 7) [17,18]
      12. Provision of nontraditional iron, crude steel, and steel products (11) [19]

It is important to distinguish between two means of expanding steel capacity. Pig iron, crude steel, and light steel sheets and bars (for use in construction) have been produced in Korea in small-scale mills for several decades. The proposed integrated steel mill uses the latest large-scale technology to produce a wider range of products. Thus KPEM distinguishes between capacity expansion along traditional lines or through construction of the integrated steel mill and between traditional and nontraditional forms of ferrous metal products. Only the integrated mill is capable of supplying both. Since there are alternative production techniques for traditional ferrous metals, the model has 12 production activities but only 11 commodity classes.

The petrochemicals complex is strictly a case of import substitution. The proposed complex will product synthetic fiber resins, plastic polymers, and synthetic rubber polymers, using naptha as the principal feed stock. The demand for these intermediate products comes principally from Korea's rapidly growing exports of textiles and light manufactures.

Economies of Scale

Economies of scale are found in a number of basic industries, typically in capacity construction and labor use. (See Haldi and Whitcomb 1967; Moore 1959 for surveys of the research.) The total cost of capacity is related to the size of the plant constructed through the equation Total Cost = ay^b where a is the constant of proportionality; b, the elasticity of total cost with respect to scale; and y, the capacity of the plant. Elasticity estimates for petrochemical complexes and integrated steel mills range between 0.6 and 0.8 (see Haldi and Whitcomb 1967; Ramseyer 1954).

To obtain a solvable model, the constant elasticity cost function has been replaced by the approximation Total Cost $= \bar{B}\delta + By$; $\bar{B}$ is a fixed requirement incurred only if capacity is built (that is, $\delta = 1$); B is the variable cost of constructing a unit of capacity; and δ is a zero-one variable equal to one if a plant is constructed, zero if not. This "fixed charge" cost function closely approximates the constant elasticity cost function over a wide range of plant sizes.

II. The Korean Project Evaluation Model

KPEM is a mixed integer programming problem in which some variables—the fixed requirement activities for the petrochemicals complex and integrated steel mill—are restricted to be either 0 or 1. With this exception, the individual elements of the model have appeared in other models so that its structure need only be quickly reviewed.

The constraints appearing in the model are conveniently summarized as follows (the constraints linking time periods have been starred):

Constraint group		Number of constraints
A	material balance equality constraints ($t = 1, \ldots , 5$; $i = 1, \ldots , 11$)	55
*B	foreign exchange balance ($t = 1, \ldots , 5$)	5
*C	capacity constraints ($t = 1, \ldots , 5$; $i = 1, \ldots , 11$)	55
*D	upper bound on marginal savings propensity ($t = 1, \ldots , 5$)	5
E	commodity export upper bounds ($t = 1, \ldots , 5$; $i = 1, \ldots , 8, 10, 11$)	50
F	total commodity exports upper bound ($t = 1, \ldots , 5$)	5
*G	primary production growth constraint ($t = 2, \ldots , 5$)	4
H	import substitution limit—nontraditional iron and steel ($t = 2, \ldots , 5$)	4
I	integer requirements on fixed charge variables ($t = 1, \ldots , 5$; $i = 10, 11$)	20
*J	upper bound on terminal debt	1
*K	terminal investment constraints ($t = 5$; $i = 1, \ldots , 11$)	11
L	objective function approximation ($t = 1, \ldots , 6$; equations 4.3, 4.5, and 4.7)	12
	Total	228

The endogenously determined variables include aggregate consumption; foreign exchange reserves accumulation; net foreign capital inflow; and, for each sector, production, imports, exports, and capacity expansion.[6] Consumption demands by commodity are related to total consumption by constant marginal consumption propensities. Government consumption demands are exogenously determined.

The endogenous variables in the model are listed below; each is defined to be a sum over 2 years. Also given are the exogenous and derived aggregate variables. All magnitudes are measured in 1965 prices in billions of Korean won ($\$1$ billion $= 270$

6. Imports and exports of services and overhead are excluded since these are not internationally traded.

billion won). The initial and terminal periods in KPEM are respectively 1967–68 and 1975–76.

Endogenous activity variables   *Number of variables*

$x_{i,t}$	gross production in sector "i" in period "t" ($i = 1, \ldots,$ 12; $t = 1, \ldots, 5$)	60
$y_{i,t}$	gross capacity increase in sector "i" in period "t" ($i = 1, \ldots, 11$; $t = 1, \ldots, 5$)	55
$\delta_{i,t}$	fixed construction requirement activity for capacity in sector "i", period "t" ($i = 10, 11$; $t = 1, \ldots, 5$)	10
$e_{i,t}$	exports of the "i^{th}" commodity in period "t" ($i = 1, \ldots, 8, 10, 11$; $t = 1, \ldots, 5$)	50
$m_{i,t}$	imports of the "i^{th}" commodity in period "t" ($i = 1, \ldots, 8, 10, 11$; $t = 1, \ldots, 5$)	50
C_t	aggregate consumption in period "t" ($t = 1, \ldots, 5$)	5
f_t	foreign exchange accumulated since 1966 ($t = 1, \ldots, 5$)	5
b_t	foreign capital inflow in period "t" ($t = 1, \ldots, 5$)	5
r_t	foreign debt repayment in period "t" ($t = 1, \ldots, 5$)	5
$w_{i,t}$	variables in objective function approximation ($i = 1, \ldots, 22$; $t = 1, \ldots, 6$)	132
$ek_{i,t}$	excess capacity in sector "i" in period "t"—measured with respect to 2-year production ($i = 1, \ldots, 11$; $t = 1, \ldots, 5$)	46
sl_i	slack variable (other than excess capacity) in equation "i"	84
	Total	507

Exogenous variables

$g_{i,t}$ government consumption demand for commodity "i" in period "t"

Derived aggregate economic variables

G total government consumption less product originating in government sector

$$= \sum_{i=1}^{11} g_i$$

I total investment expenditure

$$= \sum_{i=1}^{11} B_i y_i + \sum_{i=10}^{11} \bar{B}_i \delta_i + \sum_{s=10}^{11} s_i + HC_t$$

E total commodity exports valued at domestic prices

$$= \sum_{i=1}^{11} e_i$$

CM total competitive commodity imports

$$= \sum_{i=1}^{11} m_i$$

MM total noncompetitive imports of intermediate goods

$$= \sum_{i=1}^{12} M_i x_i$$

NM total noncompetitive imports of investment goods

$$= \sum_{i=1}^{11} N_i y_i + \sum_{i=10}^{11} \bar{N}_i \delta_i$$

M total imports
$$= CM + MM + NM$$

GDP^7 gross domestic product less product originating in household and government sectors

$$= \sum_{i=1}^{12} V_i x_i = \sum_{i=1}^{11} (c_i + g_i + e_i + z_i - m_i) - \sum_{i=1}^{12} M_i x_i$$
$$= C + I + G + E - M$$

where z_i (investment demand for the "i^{th}" commodity)

$$= \sum_{j=1}^{11} B_{ij} y_j + \sum_{j=10}^{11} \bar{B}_{ij} \delta_j + s_i \; (+ HC_t \text{ for } i = 6)$$

R net foreign capital inflow, measured at foreign exchange value

$$= M - \sum_{i=1}^{11} F_i e_i$$

Algebraic Statement of the Model

Time subscripts appear only when needed for clarity, and each parameter is defined immediately after its first appearance. The values of the "plan parameters" for the basic specification appear in the constraints.

Material Balances: Constraint A

$$m_i + x_i^* = \sum_{j=1}^{12} A_{ij} x_j + \sum_{j=1}^{11} B_{ij} y_j + \sum_{j=10}^{11} \bar{B}_{ij} \delta_j + c_i + e_i + g_i + s_i$$

where $x_i^* = x_i$ for $i = 1, \ldots, 6, 8, 9, 10$; $x_7 + x_{11}$ for $i = 7$; and x_{12} for $i = 11$

A_{ij} input of commodity "i" needed per unit of gross production in sector "j"
B_{ij} variable charge input—capacity coefficient for domestically produced goods
$\bar{B}_{ij}$ fixed charge input—capacity coefficient for domestically produced goods

---

7. The definition of GDP used here differs slightly from the national income accounting definition which values exports at f.o.b. prices. GDP in the national income accounts definition would be equal to

$$\sum_{i=1}^{12} V_i x_i - \sum_{i=1}^{11} (1 - F_i) e_i$$

Eleven constraints restrict the use of each commodity to the available supply. Since total saving is related to production through constraint D,[8] these must be *equality* constraints. Otherwise, if sufficiently valuable, savings might be obtained through excess production by using commodity disposal activities.[9]

Supply consists of imports (except for services and overhead) and production. Total use is the sum of (1) intermediate use to produce other commodities, (2) investment use for capacity expansion, (3) investment use to satisfy the fixed requirements for constructing capacity in the scale economy sectors, (4) private consumption, (5) government consumption (specified exogenously), (6) exports, and (7) stock accumulation.

Private Consumption Demand

The consumption of each commodity is determined from a linear approximation to the constant per capita income elasticity demand function.

$$c_i = \frac{P_t}{P_0} \bar{S}_i + S_i C_t$$

P_t sum of population estimates in years spanned by period "t"

$\bar{S}_i$ intercept coefficient in the consumption demand function for the "i^{th}" commodity

$$\left(\sum_{i=1}^{11} \bar{S}_i = 0 \right)$$

S_i marginal propensity to consume the "i^{th}" commodity (out of total consumption expenditure)

$$\left(\sum_{i=1}^{11} S_i = 1.0 \right)$$

By varying the parameters $\bar{S}_i$ and S_i any income elasticity of demand may be approximated for a given level of total consumption. The income elasticities were obtained from household budget surveys so the intercept term must be corrected for population changes.

Stock Accumulation

Inventory accumulation (s_i) is related to the producing sector. In the constant cost industries inventory accumulation is given by "$s_i = E_i y_i$" ($i = 1, \ldots, 9$)—inventories are built up when capacity is expanded.

E_i own output stock accumulation coefficient in producing sector "i"

In the decreasing cost industries inventory accumulation accompanies production growth: $s_i = E_i \Delta x_i$, $i = 10, 11, 12$.[10]

Housing Investment

Investment in residential housing is related to aggregate consumption through a parameter derived from the national income accounts. Investment in housing is HC_t, which must be added to the demand side of the construction equation ($i = 6$, not explicit in constraint A).

H requirement for housing construction to be met by the construction sector per unit of consumption

---

8. However, differential savings rates for each sector's value added are not used.

9. This does have the unfortunate consequence that a product price may be negative if the value of the saving generated by its production exceeds the production cost.

10. Δ is defined so that $\Delta u_t = u_t - u_{t-1}$.

Foreign Exchange Balance: Constraint B

$$\sum_{i=1}^{12} M_i x_i + \sum_{i=1}^{11} N_i y_i + \sum_{i=10}^{11} \bar{N}_i \delta_i + \sum_{i=1}^{11} m_i + f_t + r_t \leq \sum_{i=1}^{11} F_i e_i + f_{t-1} + b_t$$

M_i total noncompetitive imports—output coefficient for producing sector "i"
N_i variable charge noncompetitive imports—capacity coefficient
$\bar{N}_i$ fixed charge noncompetitive imports—capacity coefficient
F_i conversion factor for exports of commodity "i" from won value in domestic prices to won value of foreign exchange (roughly, f.o.b. price divided by c.i.f. price plus tariff—domestic prices are assumed equal to import prices)

The right-hand side of constraint B gives the supply of foreign exchange from (1) exports, (2) the reserves built up in preceding plan periods, and (3) the gross foreign capital inflow during the period. Net exports of invisibles and foreign exchange receipts from Koreans working abroad are assumed to be zero. The uses of foreign exchange are on the left-hand side: (1) purchases of noncompetitive imports of intermediate and capital goods, (2) purchases of competitive imports, (3) transfer of foreign exchange reserves into the future, and (4) the repayment of foreign debt incurred during the plan period.[11]

But for the treatment of foreign exchange reserves accumulated during the plan period, the equation is straightforward. The level of reserves available in period "t" due to accumulation in previous plan periods is f_{t-1}; reserve accumulation (or decumulation) during the period is $f_t - f_{t-1}$. Reserves built up prior to the planning period are not available for use during the plan.

Capacity Utilization: Constraint C

$$x_{i,t} \leq 2(1 - D_i)^{2(t-1)} k_{i,1} + 2 \sum_{s=1}^{t-1} y_{i,s}$$

D_i annual depreciation coefficient for the "i^{th}" sector's capacity

In all sectors a one-period gestation lag (2 years) is assumed between capacity construction and the capacity's availability for use. Since capacity is given on a yearly basis, it must be multiplied by 2 to obtain the upper bound on total production over 2 years. Only capacity initially available is depreciated, for it is highly unlikely that any capacity installed during the plan will disappear from use because of either physical deterioration or obsolescence.

Marginal Savings Propensity Upper Bound: Constraint D

$$\sum_{i=1}^{11} B_i \, \Delta y_{i,t} + \sum_{i=10}^{11} \bar{B}_i \, \Delta \delta_{i,t} + \sum_{i=1}^{11} \Delta s_{i,t} + H \, \Delta C_t + \Delta f_t - \Delta f_{t-1} + \Delta r_t - \Delta b_t$$

$$+ \Delta s l_{Bt} \leq .30 \sum_{i=1}^{12} V_i \, \Delta x_{i,t}$$

$$B_i = \sum_{j=1}^{11} B_{ji} + N_i, \, i = 1, \ldots, 11$$

$$\bar{B}_i = \sum_{j=1}^{11} \bar{B}_{ji} + \bar{N}_i, \, i = 10, 11$$

11. "Noncompetitive" here means the commodity was not produced in Korea in 1966.

V_i value added per unit of production in sector "i"

$$= 1 - \sum_{j=1}^{11} A_{ji} - M_i$$

Although the model is formulated as an "optimal accumulation model," we also require that the rate of capital accumulation be kept within politically and institutionally feasible bounds. This is achieved by using an upper bound on the marginal savings rate. On the left-hand side of constraint D the change in saving is determined from physical investment (first four terms), foreign exchange reserves accumulation, net foreign capital outflow, and the slack variable in constraint B. On the right, the maximum marginal savings rate, equal to 30 percent, is multiplied by the change in GDP.

Commodity Export Upper Bounds: Constraints E and F

(E) $e_i \leq \epsilon_i$

(F) $\displaystyle\sum_{i=1}^{11} e_i \leq 217.5 \prod_{s=1}^{t} (1 + \gamma_{e,s})^2; \ \gamma_{\epsilon,1} = 0$

ϵ_i upper bound on exports of commodity "i"[12]

$\gamma_{\epsilon,t}$ annual growth rate of aggregate exports between period t and $t - 1$ (= .31, .26, .16, and .12, respectively)

The world demand for Korea's exports is not unlimited. Thus the export of each commodity is not permitted to exceed an upper bound equal to 150 percent of the Korean government's Second Five-Year Plan (SFYP) export target for that commodity. The export demand functions are infinitely elastic over the feasible range.

An upper bound on total commodity exports less than the sum of the individual commodity export bounds is required to provide scope for comparative advantage in the *selection* of exports. In the absence of such a bound, and in the long run, every commodity would be exported in amount equal to its export upper bound so long as its foreign exchange cost per unit, both on current and capital account, is less than its foreign exchange price; in the opposite case it will not be exported. Misspecification of the resources required for production is responsible for this; were other resources (especially labor) present in the model, scope for comparative advantage would exist without constraint F. The upper bound on total commodity exports is the SFYP total commodity export target for the period.[13]

Primary Production Growth Limit: Constraint G

$$x_{1,t} \leq (1.06)^2 x_{1,t-1}$$

The application to agricultural activity of a capacity constraint based solely on past investments is, at best, tenuous. The major factors in agricultural production— the weather, input quality, techniques, organization, and the like—are difficult to treat adequately in an economy-wide planning model. G is a substitute for a more realistic specification of the production function in the primary sector. Somewhat optimistic anticipation of the growth of agricultural output is incorporated in KPEM by placing an upper bound on the growth rate of primary (including mining) output

12. Values available from the author on request.
13. Past 1972 the author's estimates are substituted for SFYP targets.

equal to 6 percent per annum. In the absence of the bound, agricultural growth is 8 to 10 percent per annum in representative solutions.

Import Substitution Limit: Constraint H (*Nontraditional Iron and Steel*)

$$A_{7,12}x_{12,t} \leq (1 - A_{7,11})x_{11,t}$$

The production of traditional and new ferrous metal products is not distinguished in the activity of the integrated mill—both are merged into a single activity, x_{11}. "Production" activity x_{12} uses the steel mill's output (not necessarily all) to meet the demand for nontraditional products. This activity has only two coefficients other than that in H: +1 on the right-hand side of the material balance for traditional iron and crude steel and steel products and +1 on the left of the nontraditional ferrous metal products material balance. To avoid the use of traditional products to meet the demand for new products, the amount of import substitution in the steel sector is restricted to be less than or equal to the supply of nontraditional ferrous metals.

Integer Requirements: Constraint I

$$y_i \leq Y_i\delta_i$$
$$\delta_i = 1 \text{ or } 0$$

Y_i scale of the largest plant that can be constructed in sector "i"

Two constraints are required for each decreasing cost function. The first links the variable and fixed charge activities, requiring the fixed charge activity to be at least as large as the fraction given by y_i/Y_i. The second forces the fixed charge to be fully incurred if it is incurred at all.[14]

Terminal Debt: Constraint J

$$\sum_{t=1}^{5} (1.10)^{2(5-t)}(b_t - r_t) = 726$$

The inelastic supply of foreign capital to Korea is reflected by imposing an upper bound on the accumulated debt in the terminal period. Interest charges are accumulated at an interest rate equal to 10 percent. This specification places no limits on the timing of capital inflows, although the timing affects the total net inflow over the plan through the accumulation of interest in constraint J. In retrospect, perhaps too much flexibility is allowed in this formulation.

Terminal Investment Constraint: K

$$(1.08)^2 \Delta x_{i,5} + \tfrac{1}{2}[1 - (1 - Di)^2]x_{i,5} \leq 2y_{i,5}, \ i = 1, \ldots, 9$$
$$(1.08)^2 \Delta x_{i,5} + \tfrac{1}{2}[1 - (1 - Di)^2]x_{i,5} - (1.08)^2m_{i,4} \leq 2y_{i,5} + ek_{i,5},$$
$$i = 10, 11$$

To insure sufficient *net* investment in the terminal period and, more importantly, in view of KPEM'S objective function, to insure that the sectoral composition of

14. The plant scale likely in Korea is far below the physical maximum—indeed for most plant types a maximum scale has not been empirically observed. Thus, the first constraint is really a fiction used to obtain the proper cost function and will never be binding. It is conjectured that it pays off in reduced solution times to set Y_i as small as possible without forcing the constraint to be binding.

terminal investment is appropriate, terminal capacity expansion in each sector is subject to a lower bound. If every lower bound is *just* met then the absolute growth in each production activity (and GDP, consumption, and so on) between 1973–74 and 1975–76 will be continued into the future at a compound growth rate of 8 percent. That is, a feasible growth path for the economy after the plan period is given by[15]

$$u_t = u_{t-1} + (u_5 - u_4)(1.08)^{2(t-5)}; \; t > 5$$

where u_t is any (and every) endogenous and derived macroeconomic variable in the postterminal future, as well as the foreign capital inflow per period and the variable upper bounds (where present). The *asymptotic* balanced growth is equal to 8 percent.[16]

To insure that production levels do not fall between the next to last and final periods (to avoid terminal investment), excess capacity is not allowed in the last period except in the complexes. Excess capacity is allowed in the increasing returns sectors and substitutes for terminal investment. The term "$(1.08)^2 m_{i,4}$" in the equations for the decreasing cost sectors is used to avoid forcing the construction of a plant in the terminal period if a plant is built in the next to last period.

The long-run determinants of comparative advantage are reflected in KPEM's terminal conditions. This is their principal attraction. The cost of production in the terminal period (in the dual problem) includes both a charge for constructing capacity during the plan (via constraint C for the terminal period) and the cost of expanding and replacing the capacity in the future (via the terminal conditions). The rate of interest implicit in the charge for postterminal capacity expansion and replacement is equal to the postterminal growth rate—the "golden rule" property of a maximal balanced growth path. But the same rate of terminal capacity growth is not forced on all sectors, as it often is in similar models; and there is ample empirical evidence that economic growth is not characterized by a balanced expansion of all sectors.[17]

15. Proof of postterminal feasibility requires the assumption that there is no excess capacity in period four. I am indebted to Alan Manne for pointing this out.

16. In the absence of *lower* bounds on investment in each sector, terminal investment (profitable due to the value of postterminal capacity in the objective function) would occur in only a few sectors due to the linear structure of the model. In the initial experiments with a "pure" discount rate of 10 percent, terminal investment in a single sector far exceeded its lower bound. Therefore an additional constraint on total terminal investment was included in KPEM:

$$(K')   -1.22 \sum_{i=1}^{9} y_{i,4} + \sum_{i=1}^{9} y_{i,5} \leq 0$$

This restricts the growth of total investment in the constant cost industries between 1973–74 and 1975–76 so that investment beyond the lower bounds will be minimal—since 1.22 is approximately equal to the weighted average of $(1.08)^2 + \frac{1}{2}[1 - (1 - D_i)^2]$ across sectors. This formulation was preferred to changing constraint K to equality constraints on the basis of the resulting dual equations. A more proper, but time-consuming, means of reducing the excessive terminal investment is to determine the "pure" time discount factor that just leads to the fulfillment of K as equalities. The discount rate would be a function of the technological parameters in the model, as well as the single-period welfare function.

17. See Chenery and Taylor (1968). KPEM's terminal conditions were suggested by Manne (1968) and Hopkins (1969). They obtain, with a different objective function and similar terminal constraints, sufficient conditions for the infinite horizon optimality of the optimal solution to the finite horizon model.

Nonnegativity Constraints

All variables are restricted to be greater than or equal to zero.

Solution Procedure

The model has been solved using the DKW (Davis, Kendrick, and Weitzman 1967) branch and bound algorithm. This is a more efficient solution procedure than complete enumeration, although a short description of the latter clarifies the meaning of the $0:1$ activities.

There are 2^{10} possible combinations for the values of the ten $0:1$ variables—each such variable is 1 if the plant is built in that period, 0 if not. Thus there are 1024 patterns of investment in the decreasing cost plants over the five periods. Solution by complete enumeration requires that the linear programming problem associated with each pattern be solved. Each linear programming problem is obtained by exogenously setting the appropriate fixed charge activities to 0 or 1—the optimal plant scales associated with a particular timing pattern are determined in the linear programming solution. This straightforward procedure enables one to compare the consequences of all capacity expansion timing decisions. The linear programming problem with the highest objective value yields the optimal investment pattern. A branch and bound algorithm precludes the necessity for complete enumeration by estimating upper bounds on the objective values for alternative investment patterns—the optimal solution has been found when a solution has been generated that has an objective value higher than the upper bounds (or actual values) for all other timing patterns.

The DKW algorithm appears to be an efficient branch and bound solution method (other algorithms were not tried, however), but it is expensive to use. A number of linear programming problems which do not satisfy constraint I are required to estimate the upper bounds; often as many as 30 were required in solutions for alternative specifications of the parameters. These solutions cannot be used directly to compare alternative investment patterns. An alternative to the DKW algorithm is incomplete enumeration in which the patterns most likely to be optimal are tried. The alternative is attractive after a few runs for parameter specification extremes with the DKW algorithm to get a good idea of the best candidates. The number of likely candidates for KPEM is not more than nine, which is far less than the number of solutions generally required when DKW is applied. Although incomplete enumeration does not guarantee that the optimal pattern has been found, its use is not as expensive. Several KPEM specifications were solved using incomplete enumeration.

Data

Table 4.1 gives selected parameter values along with the initial conditions. Korean statistical data appear more reliable than those usually encountered in developing countries. At least this is the judgment of those who have worked with data from Korea as well as from other countries. Furthermore, a wide range of statistical information is available—for example, input-output tables are compiled anew every 3 years.

Most of the data used here were generated in the process of formulating Korea's SFYP and are now somewhat out of date (relative to Korean standards at least). The input-output matrix is a modified matrix for 1963 that reflects structural changes identifiable through 1966. Government demands are SFYP projections (and appear

Table 4.1. Selected Parameter Values[a]

	Sector											
	1	2	3	4	5	6	7	8	9	10	11	12
Input-output coefficients: $1 - A_j$												
Commodity												
(1) Primary	0.90	-0.22	-0.10	-0.03		-0.06	-0.03	-0.03	-0.02	-0.01	-0.05	0
(2) Proc. pri.	-0.04	0.86	-0.03	-0.07	-0.01	-0.11	-0.01	-0.04	-0.05	-0.05	-0.01	0
(3) Textiles	-0.01	-0.02	0.69	-0.01				-0.02	-0.03			0
(4) Fertilizer	-0.05			0.99	0		0	0		0	0	0
(5) Petroleum			-0.01	-0.08	0.97	-0.02	-0.03	-0.01	-0.02	-0.06	-0.03	0
(6) Construction		-0.01				.87	-0.01	-0.02	-0.02	-0.01	-0.01	0
(7) Ferrous mts.						-0.06	0.65	-0.09		0	0.63	-1
(8) Fin. mt.	-0.01	-0.01	-0.02	-0.02		-0.07	-0.03	0.80	-0.02	-0.01	-0.02	0
(9) Overhead	-0.04	-0.13	-0.10	-0.16	-0.04	-0.13	-0.08	-0.12	0.87	-0.15	-0.12	0
(10) Petrochem.	0		-0.07	0	0		0			1.0	0	0
(11) New ferrous					0		-0.02	-0.07	-0.07		0	1
Noncompetitive intermediate imports: N_j												
	0.10	0.03	0.01	0.43	0.02	0.17	0.10	0.01	0.12	0.16	0	
Capacity cost coefficients												
Total $B_j^T + E_j$	1.13	0.41	0.41	1.89	0.93	0.80	0.66	0.54	1.54	1.66[b]	0.85[c]	
As percent of total												
Construction (6)	0.63	0.28	0.26	0.13	0.07	0.24	0.35	0.27	0.48	0.08	0.16	
Domestic equip.(8)	.09	.25	.11	.03	.09	.22	.15	.33	.20	.04	.02	
Imports	.17	.29	.43	.77	.73	.50	.37	.35	.25	.65	.79	
Value added coefficients: V_j												
	0.74	0.35	0.32	0.59	0.47	0.37	0.22	0.31	0.70	0.59	0.23	
Capital-output ratios: B_j^T/V_j												
	1.53	1.16	1.26	3.18	1.95	2.15	2.93	1.76	2.21	2.74	3.48	
Marginal consumption propensities: S_j												
	0.29	0.21	0.14		0.01			0.02	0.33	0	0	
Initial capacities, 1967-68												
	527	288	254	25	22	158	33	100	444	0	0	

Source: Westphal (1968: appendix C).

[a] All coefficients rounded to nearest hundredth. Totals may not add because of rounding error. Entries of nonzero elements that were less than 0.01 in absolute value are omitted from the table.

[b] Based on 50 billion-won capacity plant.

[c] Based on 66 billion-won capacity plant.

to be too low). The coefficients for the integrated steel mill and petrochemicals complex were derived from a number of project feasibility studies and engineering studies. The sectoral input-capacity coefficients are aggregated from data for a moderately large sample of projects undertaken during the SFYP. Further details can be found in Westphal (1970: append. C).

III. Behavior of a Model with Increasing Returns [18]

The determinants of optimal capacity expansion paths in decreasing cost industries are illustrated by comparing (1) optimal solutions for alternative patterns of investment in the complexes for a given specification of the parameters in KPEM, and (2) optimal patterns for alternative specifications of the "plan parameters" in KPEM. As noted above, all of the KPEM specifications discussed here use the same values for the parameters in the objective function and terminal constraint.

In the second mode of exploration (1) the terminal debt limit, (2) the limits on exports of products produced in the complexes, (3) the limit on total exports, and (4) the rate of interest charged on foreign borrowing are changed.

Table 4.2 gives the optimal investment pattern associated with each set of alternative parameter specifications. Regardless of specification, the growth rates of GDP, consumption, and investment are high—well above 9, 7, and 6 percent respectively. If the high export growth that has been achieved by Korea over the past decade (40 percent per annum compounded) is maintained or, more likely, only gradually reduced (as assumed in the basic specification of KPEM), these growth rates are not unreasonable. Furthermore, over the past 4 or 5 years Korean GDP has been growing at between 7 and 8 percent per annum, even during severe droughts that curtailed agricultural output. The basic specification leads to a net foreign capital inflow of 388 billion won ($1.4 billion) over the 10-year period. Given Korea's international credit-worthiness and aid prospects, this appears to be a reasonable figure.[19] Reductions in the terminal debt limit by 25 (model B-1) and 50 (B-2) percent reduce the growth rate of investment significantly and lead to greater exports, but only marginally influence the growth of GDP and consumption.

The optimal investment pattern for the basic model sees only the petrochemicals complex built, in 1967–68—the first period. Reducing the terminal debt does not result in a change in the optimal timing pattern, although it does lead to a larger scale plant which saves more foreign exchange through import substitution.

Exports of petrochemicals and nontraditional ferrous metals are not permitted in C-1. Optimal welfare is marginally less than for the basic solution. But the optimal scale of the petrochemicals facility falls by 10 percent to offset the absence of export demand. In addition, it becomes profitable to construct the steel mill simultaneously with the petrochemicals plant.[20]

In specification D-1 the maximum annual growth rate of total exports among successive periods is reduced to 18, 18, 12, and 9 percent respectively.[21] Both plants are constructed in the first period in the optimal solution.

18. A much less technical description of the model along with a discussion of project evaluation criteria based on an economic interpretation of mixed integer programming appears in Westphal (1969a).

19. Recall that, because interest is accumulated in the terminal debt constraint, the net foreign capital inflow over the plan period will be substantially less than the allowed terminal debt. Also note that the net foreign capital inflow over the plan period is not equal to the difference between the total export and import figures—the export figure is stated in domestic prices and must be converted to f.o.b. prices to determine foreign exchange receipts.

20. Too much importance should not be placed on the change in optimal pattern resulting from a small change in the *actual* amount of complex exports (in the basic solution, total petrochemicals and nontraditional ferrous metals exports are 15 billion won). Due to the linearity of the feasible space, small changes in parameters can lead to marked changes in the optimal basis which might not result in more realistic nonlinear models.

21. This is equivalent to reducing the absolute increment of the total export limit between successive periods by 50 percent.

Table 4.2. Optimal Investment Patterns for Alternative Parameter Specifications (billion won)[a]

	Model					
	Basic	B-1	B-2	C-1	D-1	E-1
Plan parameter specification						
Terminal debt limit	726	545	363	726	726	1,024
Limit on petrochemicals plus steel exports[b]	146	146	146	0	146	146
Limit on total exports[b]	2,979	2,979	2,979	2,979	2,034	2,979
Interest rate on foreign capital	0.10	0.10	0.10	0.10	0.10	0.2
Optimal growth rates						
Gross domestic product	9.7	9.5	9.3	9.8	9.1	9.3
Consumption	7.6	7.4	7.2	7.6	7.8	7.2
Investment	9.0	7.8	6.5	8.6	7.4	9.9
Optimal petrochemicals *capacity expansion*						
Plant timing (period)	1967–68	1967–68	1967–68	1967–68	1967–68	1967–6
Plant scale	44.4	47.3	47.6	40.1	44.6	29.9
Optimal Steel Capacity Expansion						
Plant timing (period)	n.c.[c]	n.c.[c]	n.c.[c]	1967–68	1967–68	n.c.[c]
Plant scale				46.1	41.3	
For the Optimal Pattern						
Welfare[d]	451.9	444.1	436.4	451.6	432.9	446.2
$\triangle$W(%)[e]		1.72	3.43	0.06	4.20	1.2
Total consumption during plan	10,872	10,840	10,800	10,984	10,726	10,430
Full capacity GDP in 1977	2,670	2,567	2,464	2,652	2,440	2,647

[a] Underline indicates element that has been changed from the basic model.
[b] Sum of upper bounds.
[c] n.c. indicates plant not constructed during plan, in this and other tables in Chapter 4.
[d] A linear transformation of the welfare function (4.1) is used so that (prior to approximation) welfare =

$$.02 \, (2.10) \, (1.10)^{-2t} \cdot \frac{P_t}{2} \log_e \frac{C_t}{20}.$$

[e] Percentage reduction in objective value from basic model's optimal objective value.

Finally, in E-1 the rate of interest on foreign debt is doubled.[22] Optimal timing is unchanged from that in the basic solution. However, a much smaller plant is built to eliminate overcapacity. By contrast, 20 percent of the petrochemicals capacity is unutilized immediately after construction in the basic solution.

In all specifications, it is optimal to construct plants in 1967–68, even if both complexes are thereby built simultaneously. The result is an average yearly foreign capital inflow in 1967–68 (168 billion won, or $622 million in C-1) that might appear excessive on the basis of criteria not incorporated in the model. The reasons for the early "big push" will become clear as alternative patterns are investigated. The

22. The maximal terminal debt was increased in E-1 to be compatible with some runs of a three-period model not reported here.

upper bound on the marginal savings rate is binding in all solutions. A higher "pure" time discount rate would lead to lower savings rates, but the low discount rate reflects the desire of Korean policy-makers for "growth now, consumption later."

Consequence of Alternative Patterns: The Complex Sectors

The KPEM specifications B-1 and D-1 were solved by partial enumeration.[23] In addition, the solutions for a number of patterns were individually obtained for the basic specification and C-1. Of greatest interest are patterns in which *at most* a single plant of either type is built between 1967 and 1971.[24] For these nine, the welfare value (relative to the optimal pattern) along with the optimal plant scales are given in Table 4.3.

Among those nine timing patterns enumerated, only the parameter specification D-1 results in suboptimal patterns yielding less than 99 percent of the welfare in the best pattern. Nonetheless, different phasings of capacity expansion lead to substantial differences in the path consumption and postterminal GDP (more meaningful measures). In Table 4.4 more detail is given on the patterns for the basic specification. Without exception, earlier complex construction results in greater total consumption during the plan. For example, building the petrochemicals complex in 1967–68 increases consumption by 286 billion won ($1.06 billion) as compared to the case in which neither complex is built. There is also a marked tendency for the postterminal capital stock in the economy (represented by full capacity postterminal GDP) to fall as plant construction is moved forward. Thus the optimal timing of a complex's construction is largely dependent on preferences for consumption within as opposed to after the plan.[25] In addition, earlier plant construction increases the foreign capital inflow in the initial periods and thereby reduces the total net inflow over the 10 years.

Looking across the rows under the heading "Percent change in welfare," one can determine the optimal phasing of the integrated steel mill (petrochemicals complex) given the timing of investment in the petrochemicals facility (steel mill). The best timing for the steel mill for each pattern of investment in petrochemicals is indicated by a "*c*"; in the case of petrochemicals a "*b*" is used. With only one exception, the optimal timing of either complex's construction is not affected by the investment pattern in the other sector. In large part this is because significant interdependence between the projects arises not from input-output relations but from the competition for scarce investment resources.

If both projects were constructed in the first period they would require 18.7 percent of that period's total investment. Given the availability of foreign capital, its cost,

23. Using the branch and bound algorithm, it required 25 linear programming solutions to find the optimal solution to the basic specification (representing 31 minutes of core time with an IBM 360/65 computer). And only one of these—the optimal solution—satisfied the integer requirements, I. The only specification that required fewer linear programming solutions was E-1 (four were needed). The enumeration of the patterns given in Table 4.3 never required more than 6 minutes of core time with the IBM 360/65.

24. It ought to be stressed that in using the branch and bound algorithm no a priori restrictions were placed on the possible investment patterns.

25. Experiments with a similar three-period model have shown that an increase in the "pure" time discount rate or the postterminal growth rate alone causes earlier plant construction to be associated with somewhat greater postterminal GDP but does not change the dependence of total consumption on plant construction (although the magnitude of change between patterns is less). Specifying both the high discount rate and the high growth rate produces a complete reversal—plant construction leads to less consumption and significantly greater postterminal GDP.

Table 4.3. Welfare and Plant Scales for Selected Investment Patterns

Timing of investment		Percent welfare change[a]				Petrochemicals plant scale[b]				Steel mill scale[b]			
Petrochemicals	Steel	Basic	B-1	C-1	D-1	Basic	B-1	C-1	D-1	Basic	B-1	C-1	D-1
n.c.	n.c.	0.490	0.470	0.431	2.632	64.0[c]	63.2[c]	64.0[c]	57.7[c]	118.7[c]	113.2[c]	118.7[c]	85.5[c]
1967–68	n.c.			0.007	0.757	44.4	47.3	39.6	43.7	n.c.	n.c.	n.c.	n.c.
1969–70	n.c.	0.138	0.109	0.122	1.266	48.9	49.0	41.0	47.1	n.c.	n.c.	n.c.	n.c.
n.c.	1967–68	0.487	0.485	0.431	1.870	n.c.	n.c.	n.c.	n.c.	52.6	52.7	44.5	41.5
n.c.	1969–70	0.488	0.485	0.440	2.100	n.c.	n.c.	n.c.	n.c.	58.2	54.8	51.7	41.2
1967–68	1967–68	0.024	0.009	0.110	0.564	47.8	48.1	40.1	44.6	52.7	52.8	46.1	41.3
1969–70	1967–68	0.121	0.103	0.128	0.818	50.6	55.1	41.5	48.2	56.1	53.1	47.6	41.6
1969–70	1969–70	0.133	0.119	0.016	0.281	50.5	55.0	41.5	48.3	56.2	53.2	51.5	41.3
1967–68	1969–70	0.026	0.016			47.9	48.1	40.1	44.9	56.3	53.3	51.5	41.8

[a] Percent reduction in objective value relative to specification's optimal objective value.

[b] Unit is annual output in billion won.

[c] Total demand for petrochemicals or steel in 1975–76 if a plant is not built in either sector during the plan.

Table 4.4. Summary Statistics for Alternative Investment Patterns: Basic Model

Period of petrochemicals plant's construction	Period of steel mill's construction			
	1967-68	1969-70	1971-72	n.c.
Percent change in welfare[a]				
1967-68	0.0238[b]	0.0263[b]	0.0870[b]	[b c]
1969-70	0.1214[c]	0.1329	0.1970	0.1382
1971-72	0.3180[c]	0.3253	0.3921	0.3351
n.c.	0.4870[c]	0.4877	0.5453	0.4903
Consumption growth rate during plan				
1967-68	7.7	7.7	7.7	7.6
1969-70	7.7	7.7	7.7	7.6
1971-72	7.7	7.7	7.7	7.6
n.c.	7.5	7.5	7.5	7.4
Full capacity GDP in 1977				
1967-68	2649	2651	2653	2670
1969-70	2650	2652	2654	2669
1971-72	2647	2649	2650	2667
n.c.	2660	2662	2664	2679
Plan incremental capital-output ratio				
1967-68	2.161	2.161	2.160	2.135
1969-70	2.161	2.161	2.158	2.137
1971-72	2.161	2.163	2.161	2.135
n.c.	2.131	2.131	2.131	2.108
Imports per unit of GDP over plan				
1967-68	0.1987	0.1996	0.1978	0.1992
1969-70	0.2008	0.2016	0.2017	0.2044
1971-72	0.2035	0.2044	0.2059	0.2073
n.c.	0.2062	0.2073	0.2055	0.2103

[a]Taken from Table 4.3.

[b]Optimal timing of single petrochemicals complex construction given timing of steel mill construction.

[c]Optimal timing of single steel mill's construction given timing of petrochemicals complex construction.

and the possibility for high export growth in the basic model, it is best to avoid building the complexes simultaneously. When the export growth rate is reduced (in D-1), however, both are built in the first period.[26]

The incremental capital-output ratio (ICOR) for the 10-year period roughly indicates the efficiency of investment resource allocation; similarly, the ratio of total imports to total GDP summarizes the effectiveness of foreign exchange use. The

26. But note that, on either the welfare criterion or on a comparison of consumption paths (and postterminal GDP), the construction of the petrochemicals plant alone in 1967–68 results in an optimal solution very similar to that when both plants are built simultaneously in 1967–68. Furthermore, when a much finer approximation to the welfare function is used (the distance between interpolation points was reduced by 80 percent), the optimal pattern turns out to be simultaneous construction in 1967–68. But the importance of the sensitivity of the optimal pattern to the fineness of the approximation is diminished by the fact that the optimal basis for each pattern is rather insensitive to the approximation.

ICOR is higher when a complex is constructed, since the complexes have high capital-output ratios. But since each represents substantial import substitution, the import requirement per unit of GDP is reduced. The efficiency of foreign exchange use is highest for early construction. The greater saving of foreign exchange resulting from earlier construction places the optimal timing of the petrochemicals complex in the first period; and it is responsible for the fact that *if* a steel mill is to be built, it should be built in the same period.

To reduce the average cost of a unit of capacity, it pays to overbuild where there are economies of scale. Associated with overbuilding are excess capacity and, where possible, exports. In addition, through imports, it is profitable to delay the construction of a plant beyond the time when currently existing capacity is fully utilized. (See Chenery 1952; Manne 1967; Chenery and Westphal 1967.) Figure 4.1 traces out alternative paths of petrochemicals capacity construction, production, and imports for the basic specification and for D-1, the limited export case.

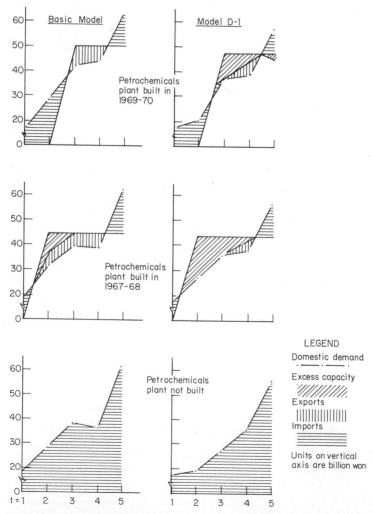

Figure 4.1 Capacity expansion paths in a decreasing cost sector: petrochemicals.

Excess capacity and exports are present for several periods following the building of a petrochemicals plant regardless of the investment pattern, although the amount of excess capacity is minimized through exports.[27] Furthermore, in the terminal period petrochemicals are imported although the constraints do not preclude the construction of a complex in the next to last period. It can also be seen in the figure that delaying a complex's construction increases its scale. The excess capacity that sometimes crops up in the terminal period in the petrochemicals complex is an aberration caused by the terminal conditions.

There is never excess capacity in the steel mill. Its market includes that previously supplied by traditional producers, and the growth in demand after the mill's construction can be satisfied by increasing the capacity of the traditional sector. Thus the existence of small-scale producers and the proper coordination of their capacity expansion with the construction of the steel mill permits large-scale construction without excess capacity. This does not require that traditional producers have excess capacity, although excess capacity among traditional producers is sometimes present immediately after the mill's construction in suboptimal solutions.

The importance of exports in permitting overbuilding can be seen by comparing plant scales for similar investment patterns in the basic specification and in C-1 (see Table 4.3). In C-1, where petrochemicals and nontraditional ferrous metals exports are not permitted, smaller scale complexes are built although a comparison of the first row figures shows the potential terminal domestic demand is equal in both cases.

The opportunity cost of excess capacity rises as the rate of return to investment rises. Though the definition of the latter is ambiguous in this type of model, it is conjectured that it is positively associated with the interest rate on foreign capital. Indeed, a doubling of the cost of borrowing leads to the construction of a much smaller petrochemicals complex (specification E-1).[28]

The construction of several small-scale plants in each sector is illustrated in two patterns in Table 4.5. Building several petrochemicals complexes leads to greater capacity by the terminal period (although imports are positive in 1975–76) and avoids excess capacity. The total capacity in the several integrated steel mills is very close to the optimal capacity of a single plant because, in every pattern, the scale of the mill is set just to substitute for nontraditional ferrous metal imports in the terminal period.

The *timing* of investment in petrochemicals substantially affects the *scale* of the steel mill and vice versa (see Table 4.2). This interdependence arises not from intermediate demands between the two but from changes in the growth of GDP and consumption resulting from plant construction. For a given timing of investment in petrochemicals, for example, there is a tendency for the scale of the petrochemicals complex to be larger the earlier the timing of the steel mill. This is due to the more rapid growth of GDP.

Consequences of Alternative Patterns: The Macrovariables

For the scales observed, the petrochemicals complex costs about 80 billion won ($296 million) and the steel mill roughly 45 billion won ($167 million); approxi-

27. Note, however, that in some patterns for D-1, including the optimal one, exports of petrochemicals are below the upper bound although excess capacity is present.

28. The comparison is somewhat obscured by the fact that the basic solution is not feasible for E-1 due to the terminal debt constraint's level.

Table 4.5. Some Multiple-Plant Investment Patterns in the Basic Model

	Solution I	Solution II
Scale of petrochemicals plant built in		
1967-68	47.9	37.2
1969-70	n.c.	10.8
1971-72	n.c.	8.3
1973-74	n.c.	n.c.
1975-76	n.c.	n.c.
Scale of steel mill built in		
1967-68	39.7	39.4
1969-70	n.c.	15.6
1971-72	16.2	a
1973-74	n.c.	n.c.
1975-76	n.c.	n.c.
Percent reduction in welfare from optimal pattern	0.1589	0.5287
Consumption growth rate during plan	7.6	7.6
Full capacity GDP in 1977	2615	2640
Plan incremental capital-output ratio	2.204	2.163
Imports per unit of GDP over plan	0.1989	0.1992

[a] Although the fixed charge for the plant's construction was incurred, the associated scale activity was optimally zero.

mately 70 percent of the cost is foreign exchange. By the terminal period, the import savings from the former plant is 44 billion won per annum; for the latter plant it is 33 billion won. It is clear that timing of capacity expansion will have a pronounced impact on the aggregate variables.

Table 4.6 gives the macrovariables over time for three investment patterns in the basic model. The gap between imports and exports displays the most interesting dependence on plant timing. Imports are higher in the period of a plant's construction and lower thereafter. The foreign capital inflow exhibits a similar reaction, made even more pronounced in the fourth period by increased exports. While the additional exports contribute to repaying the increased interest charges incurred when the complex is built, the major burden of repayment falls on the foreign exchange saved through import substitution. The composition of imports is also affected. The investment demands generated by building a complex are satisfied by increased competitive and noncompetitive imports of investment goods. After its construction, competitive imports of the complex's output fall off and noncompetitive intermediate imports rise (permitting more rapid GDP growth).

Construction of a complex produces greater changes in the macrovariables than can be attributed to the complex alone. After a complex is built, GDP increases by significantly more (relative to not building) than value added in the complex. Higher GDP leads to more saving during the plan, which yields greater investment (but only by a slight margin) and permits the payment of the higher interest charges incurred when a complex is built. An additional cause of the more rapid growth of

Table 4.6. Macrovariables for Alternative Investment Patterns: Basic Model (unit: billion won/year)

Solution	Period of plant construction		Period	GDP	C	I	E	M	CM	MM	NM	R
	Petrochemicals	Steel Mill										
A	n.c.	n.c.	1967–68	988	752	247	109	185	47	65	73	83
			1969–70	1207	891	254	188	201	45	89	67	24
			1971–72	1419	1025	268	297	254	67	110	76	– 26
			1973–74	1611	1159	451	283	365	112	131	122	99
			1975–76	2070	1466	550	497	529	201	179	149	61
B	1967–68	n.c.	1967–68	994	756	305	109	241	66	66	109	139
			1969–70	1251	922	261	188	196	30	97	70	19
			1971–72	1476	1064	275	297	244	47	119	77	– 36
			1973–74	1676	1204	425	290	327	72	141	114	54
			1975–76	2102	1489	517	497	486	163	185	138	18
C	1967–68	1967–68	1967–68	997	758	341	109	276	78	66	132	174
			1969–70	1273	939	271	188	201	23	105	74	24
			1971–72	1508	1087	281	297	240	32	128	80	– 39
			1973–74	1721	1232	402	347	344	89	151	104	18
			1975–76	2118	1499	487	497	451	131	194	126	– 17

GDP is increased imports of noncompetitive intermediate and capital goods. Though imports as a whole decline, imports outside the complex sectors rise.

Consequences of Alternative Patterns: The Related Sectors

The amount of overcapacity when a plant comes on-stream is a function of previous investment in its using and supplying facilities. Simultaneous complex construction and capacity expansion in related sectors is the pattern preferred in KPEM'S solutions, although others are possible—intermediate products could be imported for a time, capacity could be built ahead of demand in the related sectors, and so on. When investment in the complex and related sectors is simultaneous, either immediate capacity expansion in unrelated sectors is sacrificed, the scale of the complex is reduced, or the period's total investment rises by more than the cost of the complex.[29] It can be seen in Table 4.6 that the latter occurs in KPEM as a result of the flexible timing of foreign capital inflows.

Table 4.7 gives more detail on production, imports, and exports immediately after a complex is built and in the terminal period for two patterns in the basic specification and in D-1—limited export case. On comparing the figures for the basic specification, only a slight difference in the terminal composition of activity is seen between the two patterns. The most pronounced contrast is greater production in all sectors when both plants are built, which is associated with the more rapid growth of consumption.

By contrast to the basic specification, in D-1 there is a distinct change in the composition of activity toward related sectors immediately after the petrochemicals complex and steel mill are built. Building the former permits increased exports of light manufactures, but only through the middle of the plan period. Associated with the larger impact on the composition and level of activity of plant phasing in D-1 are the greatest observed differences in welfare values for alternative patterns. Although overcapacity is more pronounced in this specification, limiting the growth of exports clearly leads to greater returns from building the complexes. However, by the end of the plan, the *composition* of activity outside petrochemicals and steel is nearly the same regardless of the investment pattern or the specification.

A Caveat

It appears that the principal determinant of the timing of optimal capacity expansion in petrochemicals or steel is the structure of the model coupled with the absence of other major import substituting investments. Associated with the high rate of growth exhibited by the solutions is the virtual disappearance of competitive imports by 1975–76.[30] Investment and GDP are both rather rigidly related to the foreign exchange available for noncompetitive imports once competitive imports have disappeared.[31] This makes the return to import substitution very high. In fact, because of (1) the almost complete disappearance of competitive imports by the second period; (2) the flexible timing of foreign capital inflows; and (3) a rate of return to

29. The discussion of results using a similar three-period model in Westphal (1969b) is principally focused on these trade-offs. It is shown there that these trade-offs are far more significant when the foreign capital inflow is limited period by period rather than over the plan as a whole.
30. Except in the primary sector, the growth of which is limited.
31. This is largely due to the *fixed* marginal consumption propensities.

Table 4.7. Imports, Production, and Exports in 1969-70 and 1975-76 [a] (unit: billion won/year)

Sector	Period	Basic No plants M	X	E	Basic Both plants, 1967-68 M	X	E	D-1 No plants M	X	E	D-1 Both plants, 1967-68 M	X	E
Agriculture, forestry fishing and mining	1969-70	7	592	0	23	592	0	0	592	45	0	592	8
	1975-76	96	840	0	109	840	0	49	840	0	77	840	0
Processed food, wood [b] products and chemicals	1969-70	0	331	34	0	348	34	0	301	34	0	291	0
	1975-76	0	617	79	0	626	79	0	495	0	0	517	0
Textiles, light manufacturing [c]	1969-70	0	377	136	0	390	136	0	257	66	0	375	136
	1975-76	0	844	347	0	845	347	0	762	303	0	777	303
Fertilizer	1969-70	0	36	3	0	33	0	0	33	0	0	33	0
	1975-76	3	43	0	3	43	0	0	46	0	0	46	0
Petroleum	1969-70	0	39	0	0	45	0	0	35	0	0	41	0
	1975-76	0	70	0	0	75	0	0	65	0	0	71	0
Construction and cement	1969-70	0	179	3	0	185	4	0	145	3	0	170	0
	1975-76	0	348	0	0	323	0	0	300	0	0	305	0
Traditional iron and steel	1969-70	0	39	0	0	59	3	0	31	0	0	43	0
	1975-76	1	81	0	0	99	0	0	60	0	0	78	0
Engineering products [d]	1969-70	0	133	12	0	131	0	0	105	0	0	113	0
	1975-76	0	330	72	0	319	72	0	200	0	0	206	0
Overhead and services [e]	1969-70		535			571			480			534	
	1975-76		930			951			867			910	
Petrochemicals	1969-70	38	0	0	0	37	6	19	0	0	0	35	5
	1975-76	64	0	0	16	48	0	58	0	0	14	45	0
Nontraditional iron and steel	1969-70	21	0	0	0	24	6	13	0	0	0	15	0
	1975-76	37	0	0	2	33	0	25	0	0	0	26	0

Notation: M = imports, overhead and services are not internationally traded. X = production, the composition of its output changes. E = exports, where the same export figure is repeated for every solution, the upper bound constraint on that commodity's exports is binding.

[a] Traditional iron and steel refers to existing technology which produces light steel sheets and bars for construction from scrap and uses pig iron primarily in castings. The integrated steel mill will produce both traditional and nontraditional iron and steel, the latter comprising a wider product mix, directly from imported ore. Petrochemicals include synthetic fiber resins, plastic polymers, and synthetic rubber polymers (production to be based on naptha feed from refineries).

[b] Principally related to consumption.

[c] Principal user of petrochemicals.

[d] Principal user of nontraditional iron and steel.

[e] Principally related to gross domestic product.

investment that appears to approach 30 percent, either plant is optimally built (if built at all) in the first period.

In competition with other major import substituting investments, such as in new areas of the engineering sector, capacity expansion in petrochemicals and steel might best be delayed past 1976. The model does not reflect this competition because of a lack of data on other investments that might significantly alter the structure of Korean industry. However, the model's structure would easily permit the inclusion of a larger number of major investment projects were information available and were they of sufficient interest to policy-makers.[32]

IV. Conclusion: Policy Use

KPEM was built partly to investigate the claim that serious resource misallocation would result if either the petrochemicals complex or the steel mill were built. KPEM demonstrates that in competition with the expansion of traditional production neither would result in serious resource misallocation. But the principal defect of the model is that this is a *necessary* and not a *sufficient* condition for implementing either project.

KPEM can also make an important contribution in decisions on the scale of construction. The model includes most of the important determinants of optimal scale. Should either plant be built, on whatever grounds, the best scale for the plant will not be far from that estimated here. The use of a model in such "second best" decision-making is by no means a minor contribution and may often be the most that can be expected.

When evaluating projects characterized by economies of scale and high cost, evidence from the solutions discussed here suggests that the large number of trade-offs to be considered calls for a general equilibrium model. More exact criteria for identifying such projects have yet to be developed. In this light, the exceptional lumpiness—measured by the proportion of investment resources required over the plan—of the two projects in KPEM is a characteristic that appears not to be readily generalized.[33] The same projects would not be as lumpy in economies with higher GDP and investment.

32. It would also easily permit a more realistic description of capacity expansion in petrochemicals and steel. Three features which would thereby be included are (1) the existence of a period of lower capacity immediately after a plant comes on-stream during which bugs are worked out and the staff learns to operate the plant; (2) the possibility of phasing the construction of a large steel mill in several stages thereby spreading its cost out over a longer period; and (3) increased labor productivity over time due to various forms of learning. The latter would require putting labor into the model.

33. In the discussion of interdependence we have omitted the shadow prices (which *do* have meaning as marginal revenue products; see Westphal 1969a) associated with alternative patterns of investment. Relative prices change very little from pattern to pattern for a given specification. This result suggests that hueristic computing algorithms may lead to satisfactory results when applied to KPEM. Further information may be obtained from the author on request.

Part II
International Trade
and External Resources

Introduction to Part II

Hollis B. Chenery
and Thomas E. Weisskopf

One of the main reasons for the adoption of development plans has been the need to adjust the structure of the economy to the changing possibilities for trade. Less developed countries are much more dependent on international trade for essential commodities than are the more industrialized nations, and their possibilities for accelerated growth depend to a large degree on the successful reallocation of resources to avoid balance of payments difficulties. It is this characteristic that gives external resources a special role in the development process.

Scope and Methodology

Over the past decade input-output analysis has been widely used by planning agencies to test the feasibility of development plans in relation to projections of export earnings and import needs. It is generally recognized, however, that feasibility is only a first step in designing a development policy and that the problem of choice among alternatives can be handled much better in an optimizing framework. The prior development of input-output accounts in a number of countries makes possible the type of programming analysis that is developed in this section.

The five studies in Part II apply quantitative models to analyze the relations among trade, aid, and development policy in four countries: India, Pakistan, Israel, and Greece. Four of the five use an interindustry programming framework for this purpose.[1] While each model charts the growth of the entire economy over a finite period of time, particular attention is focused on the pattern of imports and exports characterizing alternative growth paths and the use of foreign aid as an element in the strategy of economic development.

In order to deal with trade limits and comparative advantage in a meaningful way, the studies are carried out with considerable empirical detail. Each model is characterized by a multisectoral description of an economy, with varying degrees of disaggregation depending upon data availability and particular objectives. While data limitations call for caution in the interpretation of the numerical results, the models are intended to provide some guidelines for the formulation of economic policy in the countries concerned.

Chapters 5 through 8 use interindustry models constructed in a linear programming framework. Their objective is to optimize a criterion function subject to linear con-

1. Chapter 4 on Korea also includes many of the same features.

straints that describe the technological and behavioral relationships of the economy. Each model is designed to allocate scarce resources optimally among alternative uses in a future target year. Particular attention is given to the choice between domestic production and imports in each sector when there are different opportunity costs of earning foreign exchange.

This type of multisectoral programming model has proved to be an efficient means of utilizing the considerable body of empirical data available on the structure of a developing economy. The input-output framework—with full detail on primary and intermediate input requirements for each productive process—is essential for a comprehensive examination of comparative advantage in international trade. The linear programming formulation is valuable not so much in pointing to a single optimal solution as in generating alternative feasible paths and thereby shedding light on the range of possibilities that should be considered.

Each study uses a somewhat different variant of this basic linear programming format. Weisskopf's analysis of import substitution in India (Chapter 5) has a relatively simple structure but a very high degree of disaggregation. He focuses on the trade-off between the use of domestic and foreign resources in a framework in which the cost of achieving target rates of development is to be minimized. The primary domestic resource is a combination of skilled and unskilled labor measured in rupees; the primary external resource is foreign exchange measured in dollars. By varying the effective exchange rate between rupees and dollars, Weisskopf generates alternative patterns of domestic production and imports that satisfy the given targets. The savings constraint is not specified in advance, but its value is derived from each solution.

A somewhat different view of the Indian economy is presented by Tendulkar in Chapter 6. He contrasts two linear programming formulations in which target year consumption is maximized subject to constraints upon the availability of primary resources. In his "open-loop" model, Tendulkar follows Weisskopf in taking the supply of foreign exchange as the factor limiting growth. In the alternative "closed-loop" model, Tendulkar adopts a two-gap formulation in which upper bounds are imposed on the rates of saving by two classes of income recipients. Tendulkar concentrates his attention upon the interplay of the trade and savings constraints on growth and the dual role of foreign aid in both financing imports and supplementing domestic savings.

In Chapter 7 MacEwan follows a similar approach in analysing regional resource allocation in Pakistan. Like Tendulkar, MacEwan incorporates both trade and savings constraints into a consumption-maximizing model and does not deal explicitly with labor requirements. MacEwan's study is unique in its treatment of distributional problems in a developing economy made up of two distinct regions—in this case, East and West Pakistan. Given different factor endowments, technologies, and demand structures in each region, he analyses the pattern of regional comparative advantage under alternative assumptions about the inflow of external resources and political preferences.

The most sophisticated of the four programming models is that developed by Bruno (Chapter 8) to analyze trade and growth in Israel.[2] Bruno summarizes his model in a convenient reduced form in which its primal and dual structure is clearly

2. Bruno's model was also the first of this group to be completed, and it provided some methodological guidance for the other studies.

exposed. In a consumption-maximizing framework he includes constraints on both skilled and unskilled labor as well as on the balance of payments and savings. He then proceeds to investigate the optimal patterns of production and trade implied by alternative resource endowments, paying particular attention to the skilled labor constraint and the relationship between the supply of human capital and comparative advantage.

In Chapter 9 Adelman and Chenery analyze both past and future effects of external resources on Greek development in order to determine the productivity of foreign assistance. To do so they estimate the aggregate relations in a simple general equilibrium model from time series data covering the period 1950–1961. Although Adelman and Chenery also focus on the dual import-financing and savings-supplementing role of aid, theirs is the only study that provides estimates of the actual effects of aid on the growth of the national product.

Results and Policy Implications

Although the conclusions of these studies are quite varied, it is possible to generalize about the *nature* of the results and to draw some conclusions of general applicability.

Three types of numerical results emerge directly from the solutions to the programming models. (1) A quantitative description of the performance of each economy at the macroeconomic level. (2) Values of output and trade that describe the performance of the economy at the sectoral level. (3) A valuation of scarce resources by means of the shadow prices associated with the constraints upon each economy's behavior. The first two are derived from the primal solution to the linear programming problems and the third is obtained from the dual solution.[3]

These three types of information can be used in different ways in planning development. The macroeconomic results are useful in predicting the growth of an economy under varying assumptions about resource availability and in determining the resource requirements of a target growth path. The interindustry detail provides more reliable projections than could be obtained from any extrapolation or simple macromodel, since planned development typically involves a substantial degree of structural change in the economy.

The linear programming framework is uniquely suited to the analysis of alternative strategies because it facilitates a systematic exploration of the macroeconomic transformation surface characterizing each economy. For example, Weisskopf derives the alternative combinations of domestic savings and foreign aid that can be used to meet any given target level of aggregate consumption. Tendulkar, MacEwan, and Bruno each show the relationship between the availability of foreign aid and the level of consumption in the target year under alternative assumptions about the level of domestic savings. Each study thus helps to focus on both the range of and limits to the choices open to planners in charting the development of an economy.

The numerical results at the sectoral level are particularly useful in generating a rank ordering of sectors according to their comparative advantage in international

3. Although the Adelman-Chenery study is not based on a programming model, similar quantitative information at the aggregate level is derivable in an indirect way through manipulation of the equations of their econometric model.

trade. Each programming model focuses on the "make-or-buy" choice between domestic production and imports, and two of them also involve a choice among export activities. Parametric programming techniques are used in each case to generate a ranking of sectors according to the desirability of import substitution or export promotion. The results of such exercises—and their sensitivity or invariance to changes in basic assumptions—provide important guide lines for the allocation of investment resources.

Of great interest to economists—and of at least as great potential use to planners—are the shadow prices that emerge from the solutions to programming models. Because models necessarily represent an economy in highly simplified terms and cannot include the myriad activities potentially relevant to the development process, one looks for results from the general equilibrium framework that can be applied in a partial equilibrium analysis of specific activities. Ideally, shadow prices can serve the purpose of decentralized planning when used to evaluate the benefits and costs of a particular project.

Especially important in this respect are the shadow prices of the primary resources, among which foreign exchange receives the greatest attention in the present studies. The increased value of foreign exchange can be measured by the increase in the level of aggregate consumption made possible by an extra unit of external resources, that is, the marginal productivity of foreign exchange in terms of current consumption. Tendulkar, MacEwan, and Bruno calculate this shadow price explicitly under alternative parametric assumptions. Weisskopf utilizes a similar measure—the shadow exchange rate between domestic and foreign currency—while Adelman and Chenery evaluate the marginal productivity of foreign capital inflow in terms of cumulative additions to gross national product.

In each of these studies the price of foreign exchange turns out to be significantly greater than its nominal value (at official exchange rates). Even in the absence of a binding savings constraint, the marginal productivity of foreign exchange is shown to be higher than its par value for levels of foreign aid that are within a politically feasible range. For a given foreign capital inflow, the imposition of a savings constraint may increase the scarcity value of foreign capital—since it then serves to relieve the pressure on the domestic savings potential as well as on the balance of payments.

All of the studies have a direct bearing on the two-gap problem: the dual role of foreign aid in helping to fill both the trade and the savings gaps. Unlike the aggregate two-gap models of Chenery and Bruno (1962), McKinnon (1964) and Chenery and Strout (1966), multisectoral models do not necessarily imply that only one of the two gaps can be closed in given circumstances. Rather, the substitution possibilities built into these models often allow for structural adjustment within the economy that enables foreign aid to close both gaps simultaneously. These studies show that with a well-planned change in the economic structure, growth should be limited simultaneously by a shortage of savings and by a shortage of specific imports. Only under more extreme conditions or with inefficient allocation mechanisms does one constraint completely dominate the other. These results help to clarify the nature of the two-gap problem and to identify it as a symptom of inefficient allocation policies in most cases. They also show the large change in the existing pattern of resource allocation that may be needed to secure the optimal use of resources.

These conclusions illustrate the kind of generalization that can be derived from sets of solutions to planning models. Although the primary motivation of each paper was to analyze resource allocation in a particular country, sensitivity analysis can be made a form of theorizing about developmental phenomena when it is extended to several countries. Since the deductions obtainable from analytical solutions to formal growth models are quite limited, empirically based programming models provide a better way of gaining insight into many development problems. The presence of multiple restraints affects the nature of comparative advantage, the value of external resources, and the optimal pattern of production in ways that could hardly be analyzed without the use of these tools.

5 Alternative Patterns of Import Substitution in India*

Thomas E. Weisskopf

I. Introduction

In recent years a great variety of interindustry programming models have been formulated and applied to developing countries in the context of the planning of their economic growth (See "Introduction to Part II" of this volume). India, in particular, has been favored in this respect: a long-standing commitment to economic planning, as well as a relatively plentiful supply of statistical data, has made it especially attractive to model-builders. This study reports on a detailed numerical application of an interindustry programming model to the Indian economy that concentrates particular attention on the structure of imports and the scope for import substitution in Indian industry. (See also Weisskopf 1967.)

The present model essentially distinguishes itself from alternative programming models that have been applied to the Indian economy in its high degree of sectoral disaggregation. One hundred and forty-seven sectors are distinguished within the industrial part of the economy, which forms the focus of the analysis.

In the earliest application of linear programming techniques to India, Sandee (1960) constructed a single-period "demonstration planning model" based upon a 13-sector classification. The more ambitious multiperiod models developed by Chakravarty and Lefeber (1965) and Eckaus and Parikh (1968) distinguished 11 and—in some cases—18 sectors. Manne and Weisskopf (1969) worked with 30 sectors in a later multiperiod model; and Tendulkar (Chapter 6, this volume) used a 32-sector single-period model in his recent study. Thus each of the alternative models has been carried out on the basis of a relatively aggregated interindustry description of the Indian economy. While such studies and their results are undoubtedly of interest, there are a number of respects in which a more disaggregated analysis can yield significant dividends.

In the first place, a high degree of disaggregation permits one to unearth specific commodity shortages or bottlenecks that would be disguised at a higher level of aggregation. Only if the input coefficients of a group of industries are identical, or

* This paper is a revised and edited version of an earlier one—"A Programming Model for Import Substitution in India," *Sankhya: The Indian Journal of Statistics*, December 1967, *29*, Series B, 257–306 —based upon the author's unpublished doctoral thesis, "A Programming Model for Import Substitution in India," submitted to the Department of Economics at M.I.T. in June 1966. In addition to the acknowledgments recorded in the thesis itself, the author would like to express his indebtedness to the Project for Quantitative Research in Economic Development, Harvard University, for supporting his continued research on interindustry programming models.

if the demand for the output of those industries remains always in fixed proportions, will no information be lost by aggregating all of them into a single sector. (See Chenery and Clark 1959: 34–39.) This is manifestly not the case for most sectors defined even at a 30-sector level of disaggregation. Sectors such as electrical machinery, metal products, chemicals, and so on, include a great variety of products differing radically both in their input structure and in their sources of demand.

This point assumes particular importance in the context of choice among alternative production, importing, and exporting activities in a linear programming framework. There is little sense in asking a model to choose between the alternatives of producing or importing the combined output of a "chemicals" sector, or in asking it to determine whether the export of "textiles" is profitable. Typically, model-builders either ignore the absurdity of the answers that are given to such questions or avoid them by imposing rather arbitrary limits on the range of choice of the model. If such choice elements are to be fruitfully approached in the context of a programming model, it is essential that the relevant sectors be defined in fairly precise terms rather than as broad aggregates.

Quite apart from the above considerations, it is helpful to set up interindustry planning models on the basis of sectors and industries in terms of which the actual plans are formulated. While the macroeconomic results of a 150-sector model may not differ significantly from the results of a 30-sector model, the sectoral detail that emerges from the former is far more meaningful than from the latter. Models which prescribe targets for "transport equipment" as a whole are of little use to a planner who is interested in the future demand for railway wagons or diesel engines.

The programming model used in this study pays for its high degree of disaggregation by being limited to a single period of time. Because of the size limitations on the computer programs available when the study was carried out, it was not possible to work simultaneously with extensive disaggregation and multiple time periods. The model has subsequently been extended by Manne and Weisskopf (1969) to five time periods. In order to accommodate the five periods, however, it was necessary to aggregate the sectors to a 30-sector classification and to introduce a number of additional modifications arising from the dynamic context.

Until the further development of computer technology permits much larger systems to be programmed, model-builders interested in numerical results will clearly have to choose between greater theoretical refinement and more empirical detail. Most interindustry programming models to date have inclined to the former. The present work represents an attempt to move in the direction of the latter.

II. The Nature and Scope of The Model

The programming model in this study is used to generate alternative patterns of domestic production and imports which satisfy a set of predetermined goals of final demand in 1975.[1] It differs from a straightforward consistent-requirements planning model only in that it allows explicitly for choice between production and importing activities, according to comparative cost criteria in a linear programming framework.

In contrast to the treatment of importing activities, estimates of exports are specified

---

1. All references to calendar years are understood to apply to the Indian fiscal year which runs from April 1 through March 31; thus 1975 denotes the fiscal year 1975–76.

exogenously on the basis of independent projections for the target year 1975. This asymmetry in the approach to foreign trade does not imply that export promotion is in any way less important than import substitution, but it reflects the more complicated nature of optimal choice among exporting activities. Unless both the internal supply of, and the external demand for, each sectoral type of export can be regarded as perfectly elastic at a given price, the treatment of exporting activities calls for an explicitly nonlinear formulation. In the absence of data which would permit a realistic nonlinear formulation, the effect of alternative export possibilities is examined in this study by parametric variation of exogenously given export levels rather than by allowance for an arbitrary range of choice among exporting activities.

Given the final demand targets, and a set of basic assumptions about export prospects and noncompetitive import requirements, the model is programmed to solve for that pattern of production and imports in the target year 1975 which would minimize a cost function made up of a weighted sum of domestic and foreign primary factor costs, measured respectively in rupees and dollars. By varying the weights—that is, by altering the rate of exchange between rupees and foreign currency—alternative solutions are generated which satisfy the predetermined final demand goals with (inversely) varying requirements of internal and external resources.

For the purposes of the analysis, the Indian economy as a whole is divided into two parts, which are treated differently in the application of the programming model. The industrial part of the economy is disaggregated into 147 distinct sectors whose levels of output, imports, and so on, are determined endogenously through the operation of the choice mechanism of the model. The remainder of the economy—consisting primarily of the agricultural and service sectors—is strictly exogenous to the model and affects it only as a source of demand for industrial sector products.

The endogenous industrial part of the economy—defined here to include all mining, power, and manufacturing industries, as well as road and rail transport—accounts at present for about one-fourth of India's net national product and one-sixth of the total labor force. These figures reflect the characteristic dependence upon agriculture of an economy as poor as India's. However, the endogenous sectors loom much larger in the analysis of the structure of imports with which this study is primarily concerned: they account for about four-fifths of current imports. In terms of gross domestic expenditure, one-half of total investment and one-third of total consumption is directed to the products of the endogenous sectors.

The dividing line between the endogenous and exogenous sectors was determined primarily by two considerations: (1) the relevance and stability of linear input-output coefficients and (2) the nature of the make-or-buy choice between domestic production and imports. The endogenous sectors of the model include those for which interindustry relations are readily quantifiable and can be assumed to be relatively constant—or predictably changing—over time. It is much less meaningful in theory—and often impossible in practice—to deal with the exogenous sectors in terms of stable input-output and capital-output coefficients. Furthermore, the production and trade of the-exogenous sectors products depend very much on factors not usefully analysed by interindustry techniques. Agricultural production functions are notoriously nonlinear and are likely to be especially strongly affected by such nonmaterial inputs as organization and education; the import of foodgrains is largely a matter of weather conditions and government policies. Services do not enter at all into foreign trade, and hence the question of import substitution does not even arise.

In contrast, most of the products of the endogenous sectors can and do enter into foreign trade, and some of the important aspects of the comparative cost of producing and importing can be illuminated with an interindustry approach.

The 147 endogenous sectors, which are classified into nine distinct groups, are listed below.

Code	Sector
100	*Mineral industries*
111	iron ore
112	manganese ore
113	chromite
114	bauxite
115	copper ore
116	lead concentrate
117	zinc concentrate
118	ilmenite
119	other metallic minerals
120	gold
131	limestone
132	dolomite
133	china clay
134	gypsum
135	salt
136	mica
137	other nonmetallic minerals
141	rock phosphates
142	sulphur
143	asbestos
144	cryolite and fluorspar
150	minor minerals
160	crude oil
200	*Fuel and power industries*
210	coal
220	coke
230	electricity
241	light distillates
242	kerosenes
243	diesel oils
244	fuel oils
245	bitumens
246	other petroleum products
250	lubricating oils
300	*Light industries*
311	sugar
312	tea
313	vegetable oils
314	hydrogenated oils
315	other food, beverages and tobacco

Code	Sector
320	jute textiles
331	cotton textiles
332	woollen textiles
333	art silk fabrics
334	other textile manufactures
340	leather and products
350	rubber products
361	wood products
362	glass
363	refractories
364	other nonmetallic mineral products
370	cement
381	paper and paperboard
382	newsprint
400	*Chemical industries*
411	nitrogeneous fertilizers
412	phosphatic fertilizers
413	potassic fertilizers
421	sulphuric acid
422	soda ash
423	caustic soda
424	other inorganic chemicals
430	organic chemicals
441	dyestuffs
442	plastic and synthetic resins
443	synthetic rubber
444	synthetic fibres
445	chemical pulp
446	soaps
450	paints
460	drugs and pharmaceuticals
470	other chemicals and products
500	*Metallurgical industries*
510	pig iron
521	finished steel
522	special steel
531	ferro-manganese
532	ferro-silicon
533	other ferro-alloys
541	aluminum
542	copper

Code	Sector
543	lead
544	zinc
545	tin
546	nickel
547	other base metals
551	cast iron pipes
552	steel pipes and tubes
553	iron castings
554	steel castings and forgings
555	heavy ferrous structurals
560	light metal fabrication
600	*Mechanical engineering industries*
611	machine tools
612	boilers
613	diesel engines
614	pumps
615	compressors
616	refrigeration equipment
617	material handling equipment
618	conveying and hoisting machinery
621	construction machinery
622	mining machinery
623	drilling machinery
624	agricultural machinery
631	textile machinery
632	jute mill machinery
633	sugar machinery
634	tea processing machinery
635	paper mill machinery
636	cement machinery
637	chemical equipment
640	ball bearings
650	instruments
661	sewing machines
662	typewriters
663	watches and clocks
670	other mechanical engineering products

Code	Sector
700	*Electrical engineering industries*
711	thermal turbo-generators
712	hydro turbo-generators
713	electric motors
714	transformers
715	switchgear and controlgear
720	cables, wires and flexes
731	refrigerators
732	air conditioners
733	water coolers
734	electric fans
735	electric lamps
736	dry cells
737	storage batteries
738	house service meters
739	radio receivers
740	communications equipment
750	other electrical eng. products
800	*Transport equipment industries*
811	steam locomotives
812	diesel locomotives
813	electric locomotives
821	railway wagons
822	railway coaching stock
831	automobiles
832	commercial vehicles
833	motorcycles and scooters
840	bicycles
850	other transport equipment
900	*Transport services*
910	rail goods transport
920	rail passenger transport
930	road goods transport
940	road passenger transport
951	automobile transport
952	motorcycle and scooter transport
953	bicycle transport

The greatest degree of disaggregation has been carried out in the metallurgical and engineering sectors, and among certain chemical industries; it is in these sectors that many of the most crucial problems in regard to import substitution arise. Among the older manufacturing industries, a broader classification has been adopted, reflecting their relative self-sufficiency in the Indian economy. The final breakdown of industries corresponds closely to the kind of classification adopted by most of the Indian statistical and planning agencies. This is due to both considerations of data availability and the desirability of working with sectors that are meaningful from the point of view of the Indian planners. In each broad group of industries a residual sector (for example, other chemicals and products, other transport equipment) was formed to complete the coverage after individual industries, for which data were adequate, were distinguished.

To each of the 147 endogenous sectors there corresponds a distribution equation balancing supply (from domestic production or imports) with demand (from final consumption, investment, intermediate uses, and so on). And, with few exceptions, to each of these sectors there corresponds a distinct domestic productive activity with which is associated a single sectoral output, a production function in the form of a vector in a current flow matrix, and an incremental fixed capital structure in the form of a vector in a capital matrix. The exceptions arise in the case of joint production, alternative techniques of production, and noncompetitive imports. While there are many instances of joint production in the economy, only in the case of petroleum refining does this study deal with more than a single major product. Seven varieties of petroleum products have been distinguished as sectors. But to these there correspond only two production activities: the basic refining process which yields light distillates, kerosenes, diesel oils, and so forth, in certain technologically determined fractions; and the further processing required for the production of lubricating oils. Alternative techniques of production were initially included for electricity generation, where the radically different hydro and thermal processes have to be separated; for rail transport, where coal, diesel, and electric power are distinguished; and for motor goods transport, which uses petrol or diesel oil. The choice between the alternative techniques, however, is predetermined for the purposes of the analysis, since many of the considerations on which it depends could not be incorporated into the model. Finally, several sectors such as tin, sulphur, and so on, are tied to raw materials unavailable in India—there can be no domestic production in these industries, whose products enter only as noncompetitive imports.

There are no overall distribution equations for the exogenous production activities of the economy; only their demand for the products of endogenous sectors and their impact on the balance of trade is considered. In the following list, the exogenous part of the economy is classified into a number of sectors, each of which forms a source of demand for current or for capital account inputs or for both from the endogenous sectors.[2]

Exogenous sectors

Sources of demand for current inputs
agriculture and irrigation
exogenous transport and other services
Sources of demand for capital inputs
agriculture
major irrigation
railway construction
road construction

2. The availability of data permitted a finer classification of exogenous sources of investment than of exogenous sources of current input demand. Although rail and road transport are included as endogenous sectors (910 to 940) in the model, their demand for construction capital inputs is treated exogenously.

other transport and communications
social services
private and commercial construction

For each choice of an overall consumption goal in the target year, a corresponding set of demand vectors must be specified for the exogenous sectors. While no mechanical set of relations can be employed, one would naturally want to balance in a general way the ambitiousness of the exogenously determined consumption target with the extent of the input demand from the exogenous sectors. These input-demand vectors can be treated as independent parameters, subject to variation according to different estimates of demand or different future goals.

Since the output of the exogenous part of the economy does not enter explicitly into the analysis, it is not included in the production and capital vectors of the endogenous industries. This means that the cost of agricultural and service inputs, other than rail and road transport, is omitted from the analysis. This omission results in an understatement of the domestic cost of production of sectors with significant inputs of agricultural commodities, notably the food and fiber industries; and it biases the model's choice mechanism against imports in these sectors. However, this bias is unlikely to affect the validity of the results since the case for such imports rather than domestic production is surely very weak. And since most of the output of these sectors is delivered directly to final consumption, the potential range of distortion through interindustry linkage is sufficiently limited to be negligible. The omitted cost of services—mostly trade and commerce—is also negligible, since it affects more or less equally the activities of production and importing.

Since the focus of the whole study is on import substitution, the structure of import requirements receives detailed empirical attention. Five separate sources of demand for imports are distinguished in the analysis.

First, there is the demand for the import of endogenous sector commodities as an alternative to domestic production. These are competitive imports which constitute separate activities of the programming model. In general, import substitution is allowed full scope at the margin; that is, there is a free choice between importing or expanding domestic productive capacity to satisfy whatever demand is generated in the target year over and above that which can be satisfied by capacity existing in the base year. In a few sectors whose products are relatively heterogeneous,[3] the scope for import substitution is exogenously restricted to reflect the fact that only some of the heterogeneous products may actually be profitably substitutable. In these sectors there is hence a fraction of the total demand which must be satisfied by noncompetitive imports. In addition, there are a few endogenous sectors whose products simply cannot be produced in India (for example, tin, sulphur, and so on); as noted earlier, the entire demand for these products must also be satisfied by noncompetitive imports.

A third type of import which is distinguished in the analysis arises from the demand for agricultural raw materials which cannot be made available from domestic agricultural production. These products belong to the exogenous part of the economy, but they are used in endogenous industries. Imports of noncompetitive agricultural raw materials are related via fixed coefficients to the endogenous production activities

3. These sectors include primarily the residual sectors defined earlier on page 100.

which use them as inputs. Thus they are treated as a separate category of noncompetititive imports, distinguished from the imports of noncompetitive industrial products.

The fourth source of demand for imports is for the remaining commodities which belong to the exogenous part of the economy. These include primarily food-grains for direct consumption and military supplies for government use.[4] While the demand for a few minor exogenous categories of imports can be projected into the future, it is very difficult to forecast in advance the requirements of food and military imports. In any case, the supply of foreign exchange for such purposes is often quite independent of the supply available for other imports. Since the analysis of this study cannot meaningfully take these imports into consideration, all references to the balance of trade will be understood to exclude them. To the extent that foreign exchange will be necessary in the target year for the supply of food or tanks, it will represent an additional requirement over and above what is generated by the runs of he model.

The final source of import demand is of considerable significance in the Indian context and has therefore been incorporated in a separate way into the interindustry framework. The products of the engineering sectors (included in the mechanical engineering, electrical engineering, and transport equipment groups in the list of sectors) differ from the products of almost all the other sectors in a basic way: they consist both of complete units and of parts. The demand for complete units arises either from fixed investment (in the case of capital equipment) or from direct consumption (in the case of consumer durables). The demand for parts, on the other hand, arises from two different sources: fabrication of new complete units and maintenance of old units. The domestic production of complete units is typically also subject to quite different factors from the domestic production of parts. Like the production of most of the other endogenous sector products, the production of complete units in the engineering sectors is limited primarily by the existing capacity of the capital stock, the availability of raw material inputs, and the supply of primary factors such as skilled labor. The production of many parts and components, however, is most critically limited by factors, such as an uneconomic scale of demand or an inadequate technical knowledge, which could not be incorporated explicitly into the analysis.

The most satisfactory way of dealing with the important different between complete units and parts would be to define a separate new sector for each type of component part. The existing availability of data, however, ruled out such an ambitious undertaking. The alternative adopted in this study was the following. Each of the nonresidual engineering sectors listed on page 99 is understood to represent complete units only. *All* engineering parts and components are divided into two groups: domestically produced and imported. Domestically produced parts are included in the output of the corresponding residual engineering sectors, while imported parts are treated as an additional category of noncompetitive imports.

Both the imports of complete units and the imports of parts are distinguished according to the classification of engineering sectors given in the list. The import of each type of complete unit enters into the corresponding distributional equation as an alternative source of supply, just as in the case of competitive imports in the other endogenous sectors. The import of each type of component part, on the other hand, is related via fixed coefficients to the production level of the corresponding domestic

4. Military supplies consist of industrial products, but they could not be included in any endogenous sector for lack of detailed statistics.

industry and to the existing stock of the corresponding type of equipment. These noncompetitive parts imports constitute the fifth and last source of import demand distinguished in the analysis.

III. The Algebraic Formulation of The Model

The model on which this study is based is a single-period linear programming model which focuses on the structure of the economy in a future target year. The corresponding structure in a base year, for which the relevant economic data have already been made available, is used as a point of reference from which the future growth possibilities are charted.

The basic set of constraints of any interindustry model relate to the distribution of the supply of products from each endogenous sector among the alternative sources of demand. In its simplest form, the typical distribution constraint in the present model is formulated as follows:

$$d_i + m_i \geq t_i + v_i + c_i + e_i \tag{5.1}$$

where d_i, m_i, c_i and e_i denote the level of domestic output, imports, consumption, and exports of sector i products, respectively; and t_i and v_i denote the total level of current and capital account deliveries of sector i products throughout the economy.[5] Constraint (5.1) simply requires that in the target year the total supply of each endogenous sector's output must be at least as great as the corresponding total demand. All of the sectoral supply and demand variables are expressed in terms of 1960 producers' prices.

In the formulation of the model, a distinction must be made between the products of the endogenous sectors and the domestic production activities which produce them. As discussed in Section II, there is not a complete one-to-one correspondence between sectors and productive activities. The domestic output d_i of sector i products is related algebraically to the activity levels x_j of the productive activities j as follows:

$$d_i = \sum_j u_{ij} x_j \tag{5.2}$$

where U is a matrix with n rows corresponding to the n endogenous sectors and m columns corresponding to the m domestic production activities. U is equivalent to an identity matrix, with the following exceptions: (1) rows representing sectors whose products cannot be domestically produced have no corresponding columns; and (2) the rows representing the joint products of the petroleum industry have positive elements u_{ij} denoting the fractions in which they are produced by the refining activity j.

The target year level of production x_j of each domestic production activity j is made up of two components:

$$x_j = \bar{x}_j^R + x_j^* \tag{5.3}$$

where $\bar{x}_j^R$ is defined as the output obtained from capacity existing already in the base year, and x_j^* represents the incremental output obtained from new capacity installed

---

5. All variables without a time superscript are understood to apply to the single target year of the model.

between the base year and the target year.[6] As a rather harmless simplification, it is assumed that in each sector the capacity remaining from the base year will be fully utilized in the target year; thus $\bar{x}_j^R$ applies both to the remaining capacity and to the corresponding production level in sector j. In the interval between the base and target years there will generally have been some retirement of the base year capital stock, so that $\bar{x}_j^R$ does not necessarily equal the base year productive capacity.

To all of the endogenous sectors whose products can be physically imported there corresponds an importing activity which provides an alternative source of supply to domestic production. Thus we may write for each such sector i:

$$m_i = \pi_i y_i \tag{5.4}$$

where y_i denotes the activity level (measured in c.i.f. dollars) of the activity for importing sector i products, and π_i is the equivalent domestic value (measured in 1960 producers' price rupees) of a dollar's worth of imports of sector i products. The export demand for sector i products is simply specified exogenously:

$$e_i = \bar{e}_i \tag{5.5}$$

The total demand t_i for intermediate deliveries from each endogenous sector i is made up of three components:

$$t_i = t_i^R + t_i^* + \sum_k t_i^k \tag{5.6}$$

The first two terms account for the demand on current account from the endogenous productive activities, and the last term accounts for the demand from the exogenous part of the economy. The former are related to endogenous production levels as follows:

$$t_i^R = \sum_j a_{ij}^0 \bar{x}_j^R \tag{5.7}$$

$$t_i^* = \sum_j a_{ij}^* x_j^* \tag{5.8}$$

Two separate current flow matrices are distinguished: A^0 is the base year matrix which reflects the input structure of production with "old" capacity, and $A*$ is the corresponding incremental matrix which applies to production with the "new" capacity installed between the base and the target year. The current input demand t_i^K for sector i products from each exogenous source k is related to an index T^k of total current input demand from exogenous source k by the following formula:

$$t_i^k = \tau_i^k T^k \tag{5.9}$$

where τ_i^k is an estimated coefficient of demand for product i per unit value of the total demand index for exogenous source k.

The total demand for capital good deliveries from each endogenous sector i is also made up of several components:

$$v_i = v_i^F + v_i^W + v_i^X + \sum_k v_i^k \tag{5.10}$$

---

6. Barred variables denote predetermined constants.

The first term refers to the demand for fixed capital investment in the endogenous production activities, which is determined as follows:

$$v_i^F = \eta^F \sum_j b_{ij}^* k_j^*$$ (5.11)

The coefficient b_{ij}^* is an element of the incremental fixed capital structure matrix B^*, which gives the rate at which the products of sector i are required per unit increment in the value of capital stock installed in activity j. k_j^* includes both the expansion of the capital stock from its base year to its target year level and the replacement of part of the base year capital stock which is retired during the period. It is related to the incremental production variable x_j^* of equation (5.2) as follows:

$$k_j^* = \beta_j^* x_j^*$$ (5.12)

where β_j^* is the incremental capital-capacity ratio defined in terms of value of capital stock per unit of productive capacity in activity j.[7]

The expression $\sum_j b_{ij}^* k_j^*$ in equation (5.11) represents the total amount of sector i products that must be added to fixed capital stock in the full period from the base year to the target year. To convert this stock variable into the flow variable required by the model—namely, the demand for investment goods in the single target year—the "stock-flow" conversion factor η^F is applied. η^F approximates—for the endogenous activities as a whole—the ratio of target year fixed capital investment demand to the addition to fixed capital stock between the base and target years.

The second term of equation (5.10) relates to the demand for inventory investment in the endogenous production activities, which is given by:

$$v_i^W = \eta^W \sum_j s_{ij}^* (x_j - \bar{x}_j^0)$$ (5.13)

Equation (5.13) is analogous to equation (5.11): s_{ij}^* is an element of an incremental stock coefficient matrix S^* which is applied to the corresponding change in the level of domestic production in activity j between the base and the target year. η^W is a working capital stock-flow conversion factor, which approximates the ratio of target year inventory investment demand to the addition to inventory stock between the base and target years.

The estimation of the numerical values assigned to η^F and η^W was carried out as follows. Denoting by V the level of fixed capital investment in the endogenous activities, and by K the corresponding capital stock, we may write

$$\eta^F = \frac{V^T}{K^T - K^0}$$ (5.14)

where the superscripts 0 and T refer to the base and target years of the model, respectively. A stock-flow conversion factor used for precisely this purpose was intro-

---

7. The use of an equality rather than an inequality constraint in equation (5.12) implies that target year capacities will be fully utilized in each activity. Since a single-period optimizing model would surely not build additional capacity unless it intended to use it, this does not represent any restriction on the operation of the model. If historical experience suggests that capacity is unlikely to be fully utilized in a rapidly growing economy, the same effect can be incorporated simply by raising the values of the β^* in the proportion that new capacity is likely to be underutilized.

duced by Manne (1966a; see also Manne and Rudra 1965; Srinivason, Saluja, and Sabherwal 1965). Manne's derivation of the numerical value to be given to the factor was based on the assumption of a constant exponential rate of growth of investment activity between the base and the target year. This rate of growth r had to be guessed at in advance of each programming run, but he showed that the numerical value of the stock-flow conversion factor was relatively insensitive to variation—within a "reasonable" range—of r (see Manne 1966a; Manne and Rudra 1965).

For the purposes of the present model, in its primal form, a slightly different method for estimating η^F is suggested. The difference lies primarily in the fact that investment activity in the target year is related explicitly to the growth of output *beyond* the target year, as—in principle—it should be. Assuming an annual rate of growth of capital stock of r^T after the target year, and an average lag of θ years between the production of investment goods and the corresponding increase in productive capacity, we may express V^T as

$$V^T = K^{T+\theta+\frac{1}{2}} - K^{T+\theta-\frac{1}{2}} = r^T K^T (1 + r^T)^{\theta-\frac{1}{2}} \qquad (5.15)$$

If we define the average annual rate of growth of capital stock between the base and target years as r^0, we may write

$$K^T = K^0 (1 + r^0)^T \qquad (5.16)$$

where T is the corresponding length of the period in years. Substituting equations (5.15) and (5.16) into equation (5.14), we get:

$$\eta^F = \frac{r^T (1 + r^T)^{\theta-\frac{1}{2}}}{1 - (1 + r^0)^{-T}} \qquad (5.17)$$

Thus η^F is a function of four variables: $\eta^F(T, \theta, r^0, r^T)$. T is determined by the formulation of the problem; θ can be estimated from empirical data; r^T must be specified in advance as one of the target parameters of the model (like the final demand variables C, T^k and V^k); and r^0 must be estimated prior to each programming run (like Manne's rate of growth of investment activity r). The working capital stock-flow conversion factor η^W is estimated in exactly the same way as η^F, with the single exception that the average lag θ is assumed to equal zero; thus

$$\eta^W(T, r^0, r^T) = \eta^F(T, \theta, r^0, r^T) \qquad (5.18)$$

Each of the stock-flow conversion factors η^F and η^W is applied uniformly to investment demand from all of the endogenous activities of the model. In principle, it would be more accurate to apply distinct stock-flow conversion factors to each of the domestic production activities j, since the variables on which the values of η^F and η^W depend (see equation 5.17) are likely to differ as between different activities. On the other hand, since the values of η^F and η^W are relatively insensitive to changes in the growth rates r^0 and r^T, and since the estimation of r^0 is in any case only approximative, the additional complexity would not appear to be justified. One might further suggest that the value of η^F be distinguished according to the sector of *origin* of the capital goods—since the gestation lag θ may well differ as between different types of goods i—but the lack of sufficiently detailed information, and the relatively small effect of changes of this kind, dictated the simplest course of a common η^F for use in the present study.

The third term of equation (5.10) refers to a part of the demand for replacement investment which arises from the retirement of capital stock between the base and the target years. Because retirement rates differ as between different types of capital equipment, the residual productive capacity $\bar{x}_j^R$ for each activity j can be sustained with capital stock remaining in the target year only if some of the less durable types of capital are kept in the right proportions by partial replacement. This partial replacement investment must be evaluated exogenously according to the age structure and retirement rates of the various types of capital equipment existing in the base year.[8]

$$v_i^X = \bar{v}_i^X \tag{5.19}$$

As noted above, the total demand for replacement investment in the endogenous production activities is not limited to the v_i^X terms but includes also a fraction of the v_i^F terms defined in equation (5.11).

The exogenous demand for endogenous capital inputs is summed in the last term of equation (5.10). Analogously to equation (5.9), the capital input demand v_i^k for sector i products from each exogenous source k is related to the total (market) value of investment V^k in exogenous sector k by the following equation:

$$v_i^k = \varphi_i^k V^k \tag{5.20}$$

where φ_i^k is a coefficient giving the capital input norm of the products of endogenous sector i per unit investment in exogenous sector k.

In the remaining equations relating to constraint (5.1), the final consumption demand c_i for the output of each individual endogenous sector i is related to the total (market) value of aggregate consumption C in the target year. The relationship is analogous to those of equations (5.9) and (5.20) but it is nonhomogeneous: incremental sectoral coefficients are introduced which differ from the corresponding base year ratios.

Each target year consumption demand c_i is expressed as the sum of two components:

$$c_i = c_i^B + c_i^* \tag{5.21}$$

The first term c_i^B represents a per capita level of consumption equivalent to that of the base year:

$$c_i^B = c_i^0 e^{nT} \tag{5.22}$$

where c_i^0 is the base year level of consumption of sector i products, and n is the expected annual rate of growth of population. The second term c_i^* includes that part of target year consumption which represents an increase above the base year per capita level:

$$c_i^* = \gamma_i^*(C - \bar{C}^0 e^{nT}) \tag{5.23}$$

The term in parentheses represents the amount by which target year consumption expenditure exceeds the expenditure required to maintain the base year per capita consumption levels, and the coefficient γ_i^* denotes the proportion of this excess consumption expenditure which is spent on the products of sector i. The γ_i^* are thus

---

8. It is assumed that none of the capital equipment installed between the base and the target year will have to be replaced before the target year.

equivalent to incremental per capita consumption coefficients; when divided by the corresponding average coefficients obtaining in the base year, they yield implied linear per capita expenditure elasticities.

This completes the presentation of the structural equations which underlie the initial set of distribution constraints (5.1). If all of the equations are directly substituted into the original constraints, these constraints can be expressed in reduced form in terms of the following independent variables:

x_j^* the endogenous incremental production activity levels
y_i the endogenous importing activity levels
T^k the indices of current input demand from each exogenous source
V^k the market value of investment in each exogenous sector
C the market value of aggregate consumption

The reduced form (P.1) of the typical distribution constraint is shown in the following enumeration of the primal constraints.

$$\sum_j (u_{ij} - w_{ij})x_j^* + \pi_i y_i - \sum_k \tau_i^k T^k - \sum_k \phi_i^k V^k - \gamma_i^* C \geq \bar{q}_i \qquad (i = 1, \ldots, n)$$

(P.1)

where

$$w_{ij} = a_{ij}^* + \eta^F b_{ij}^* \beta_j^* + \eta^W s_{ij}^*$$

$$\bar{q}_i = \sum_j (u_{ij} - a_{ij}^0)\bar{x}_j^R + \bar{e}_i + \eta^W \sum_j s_{ij}^*(\bar{x}_j^R - \bar{x}_j^0) + (\bar{c}_i^0 - \gamma_i^* \bar{C}^0)e^{nT}$$

$$-x_j^* \geq \bar{x}_j^R - \bar{x}_j^M \qquad (j \in XM)$$

(P.2)

$$-\sum_j \mu_i u_{ij} x_j^* + (1 - \mu_i)\pi_i y_i \geq \sum_j \mu_i u_{ij} \bar{x}_j^R \qquad (i \in MM)$$

(P.3)

$$T^k \geq \bar{T}^k \qquad (k = 1, \ldots, l^T)$$

(P.4)

$$V^k \geq \bar{V}^k \qquad (k = 1, \ldots, l^V)$$

(P.5)

$$C \geq \bar{C}$$

(P.6)

$$L - \sum_j \lambda_j^X x_j^* \geq \sum_j \lambda_j^0 \bar{x}_j^R$$

(P.7)

where

$$\lambda_j^X = \lambda_j^* + \eta^F \lambda_j^B \beta_j^*$$

$$M - \sum_j \mu_j^X x_j^* - \sum_i y_i - \sum_k \mu_k^V V^k - \mu^C C \geq \bar{q}^M$$

(P.8)

where

$$\mu_j^X = \underset{(j \in AM)}{\psi_j} + \underset{(j \in PM)}{\xi_j} + \sum_{(i \in PM)} (\xi_i/z)b_{ij}^* \beta_j^*$$

$$\mu_k^V = \sum_{(i \in PM)} (\xi_i/z)\sigma_i \phi_i^k$$

$$\mu^C = \sum_{(i \in PM)} (\xi_i/z)\sigma_i \gamma_i^*$$

$$\bar{q}^M = \sum_j \mu_j^X \bar{x}_j^R + \sum_{i \in PM} (\xi_i/z)\bar{s}_i^R + \sum_{i \in PM} (\xi_i/z)\sigma_i(\bar{c}_i^0 - \gamma_i^* \bar{C}^0)e^{nT}$$

The remaining constraints in the programming model are of three kinds. The first are inequalities which further constrain the basic activity variables x_j^* and v_i. The second are equalities which fix the exogenously specified values of the aggregate variables T^k, V^k, and C. The third are equalities which define additional activities measuring the requirements of domestic and foreign primary resources.

The additional inequality constraints are introduced as linear approximations to what are in fact likely to be nonlinear situations. For a few of the endogenous production activities of the model, upper bounds are imposed on the level of domestic production:

$$x_j \leq \bar{x}_j^M \qquad (j \epsilon XM) \tag{5.24}$$

Such bounds are required when production is restricted in actuality by a factor which is not incorporated into the interindustry framework of the model. This is notably the case in several mining activities, where the scope for (profitable) production is sharply limited by the availability of mineral resources. A second set of inequality constraints is applied to some activities in order to limit the scope for import substitution afforded by the linear structure of the model. As discussed in Section II, it is desirable to allow for the fact that in a few productive activities whose output is relatively heterogeneous some of the products may not be (profitably) substitutable. Thus the following type of constraint is introduced:

$$m_i \geq \mu_i(d_i + m_i) \qquad (i \epsilon MM) \tag{5.25}$$

where μ_i represents the minimum proportion of the supply of the products of sector i which must be imported.

The following three sets of constraints serve to introduce the target year goals, subject to the attainment of which the programming model minimizes costs. These goals are described by the aggregate variables T^k, V^k and C, for which values must be determined prior to each run of the model. Thus the constraints may be written as follows:

$$T^k = \bar{T}^k \qquad (k = 1, \ldots, l^T) \tag{5.26}$$
$$V^k = \bar{V}^k \qquad (k = 1, \ldots, l^V) \tag{5.27}$$
$$C = \bar{C} \tag{5.28}$$

where the barred variables represent the pre-determined target year values.

The last pair of constraints in the model measure the endogenous use of the primary resources in the system: labor and foreign exchange. These constraints are required to define the two terms which enter the cost function, representing the domestic and foreign primary resources respectively.

Labor resources are required by each of the domestic production activities of the model. These labor requirements are measured in terms of their total wage cost rather than the size of the working force. If different categories of labor cannot be adequately distinguished and independently treated, it is more meaningful to deal with an aggregate based on wages than on numbers. The total labor cost in rupees incurred by the endogenous production activities[9] is given by:

$$L = \sum_j (\lambda_j^0 \bar{x}_j^R + \lambda_j^* x_j^*) + \eta^F \sum_j (\lambda_j^B k_j^*) \tag{5.29}$$

9. Labor is of course also employed in the exogenous part of the economy, but this labor cost is extraneous to the model.

The first term measures the direct current costs of operating labor, where λ_j^0 denotes the labor cost per unit of residual capacity production and λ_j^*, the labor cost per unit of new capacity production, in 1975. The second term measures the indirect capital costs of construction labor required for the installation of the capital stock.[10] The coefficients λ_j^B may be regarded as the $(n + 1)^{\text{th}}$ row of the B^* matrix, giving the construction labor cost per unit increase in capacity for each activity j.

The foreign exchange cost (that is, the import requirements) generated by the model can be analyzed in terms of the five separate sources of import demand distinguished in Section II. Of these five, four are functionally related to the activities included in the model and are summed to yield the total value—measured in c.i.f. prices—of endogenous imports M:

$$M = \sum_{k=1}^{4} M^k \tag{5.30}$$

The first type are the competitive imports of endogenous sector products, whose total value is given by

$$M^1 = \sum_{i \epsilon CM} y_i \tag{5.31}$$

where CM is the set of endogenous sectors in which imports compete with domestic production. The second type are the noncompetitive imports of endogenous sector products, whose total value is given by

$$M^2 = \sum_{i \epsilon NM} y_i \tag{5.32}$$

where NM includes the set of sectors whose products cannot be produced domestically.[11] The third type are the imports of noncompetitive agricultural raw materials, with a total value of

$$M^3 = \sum_{j \epsilon AM} \psi_j x_j \tag{5.33}$$

where AM includes the set of endogenous production activities which use imported agricultural raw materials as inputs. To each activity j there corresponds at most one such input, which is required in the proportion ψ_j in terms of c.i.f. dollars per unit. A fourth category of imports was defined to cover the remaining imports of exogenous sector commodities, but since these are entirely exogenous to the model they are not included here.

The last source of imports was discussed in considerable detail in Section II; it involves the demand for imported engineering parts and components both for further fabrication and for the maintenance of existing stock. The total value of such imports is expressed as follows:

$$M^4 = \sum_{j \epsilon PM} \xi_j x_j + \sum_{i \epsilon PM} \left(\frac{\xi_i}{z}\right) s_i \tag{5.34}$$

where PM is the set of engineering activities (and corresponding sectors) in which parts are distinguished from complete units. The first and second terms of the equation cover the fabrication and the maintenance demands, respectively. ξ_j represents the total dollar value of imported parts required in the production of one unit of output x_j of activity j. The same coefficient ξ_i is applied to the existing stock s_i of equipment of sectoral type i in order to determine the total embodied value of parts which can only be replaced by noncompetitive imports. Assuming that the average life of engineering parts is z years, a fraction $1/z$ will have to be replaced every year: this leads to the maintenance demand described by the second term in the equation.

The stock of equipment s_i can be expressed as follows:

$$s_i = s_i^R + s_i^* + \sum_k \sigma_i v_i^k + \sigma_i c_i \tag{5.35}$$

The first two terms of the equation cover the stock of capital equipment in the endogenous productive activities of the economy. s_i^R is the residual in the target year which remains from the stock of type i existing in the base year, and s_i^* represents the addition to the endogenous stock of type i between the base and the target years given simply by

$$s_i^* = \sum_j b_{ij}^* k_j^* \tag{5.36}$$

The third term of equation (5.35) represents the stock of sector i output which is held as capital equipment in the exogenous sectors, and the fourth term applies when the products of sector i can be held as consumer durables. Since these stocks are exogenous to the interindustry framework of the model, it is necessary to approximate them independently. σ_i is a rule-of-thumb conversion factor which relates the stock of durable equipment of sectoral type i to the corresponding exogenous investment and consumption flows v_i^k and c_i in the target year.

It remains now only to define the objective function which is to be minimized subject to the attainment of the targets prescribed in constraints (5.26), (5.27), and (5.28).

$$\Omega = \theta^L L + \theta^M M \tag{5.37}$$

The function Ω consists of a weighted sum of the domestic (L) and foreign (M) primary resource costs. The relevant weights θ^L and θ^M must be preassigned for each run of the model; the corresponding weight ratio can be interpreted as the shadow rate of exchange between rupees and dollars, on the basis of which all other prices in the system are determined.

This completes the presentation of the primal constraints and objective function of the programming model (see Weisskopf 1967: sec. 4). All of the constraints entering into the model can be expressed in reduced form in terms of the independent variables x_j^*, y_i, T^k, V^k, and C (identified on page 108) along with the following additional independent variables:

L the total rupee c.i.f. dollar value of the wage bill in the endogenous, production activities

M the total c.i.f. dollar value of endogenous imports in the economy

Table 5.1. Identification of Alternative Cases

Case	Rate of growth of consumption (percentage)	Rate of growth of exports (percentage)	Noncompetitive import coefficients[a]
A-1	7.5	5	1/2
A-2	6.0	5	1/2
A-3	4.5	5	1/2
B-1	7.5	7	1/2
B-2	6.0	7	1/2
B-3	4.5	7	1/2
C-1	7.5	5	1/3
C-2	6.0	5	1/3
C-3	4.5	5	1/3

[a] 1975 values as compared with 1960 values, for a subset of noncompetitive imports.

The full set of constraints in the model are shown in reduced form on page 108. The constraints are arranged so that the independent variables and their coefficients appear on the left-hand side of the inequalities, and the constant terms appear on the right-hand side.[12]

IV. A Summary Analysis of the Numerical Results

The programming model described in the previous section was applied with the help of a detailed body of data on the present and future structure of the Indian economy.[13] Given the basic structural coefficients, and the initial conditions of the economy in 1965, the model was programmed under a variety of parametric assumptions about the future in order to provide a wide spectrum of alternative (optimal) solutions for 1975. The key parameters include:

1. the rate of growth of exports from 1965 to 1975
2. the anticipated levels of a subset of noncompetitive import coefficients (μ_i, ψ_i, and ξ_i) which might reasonably be expected to decline by 1975
3. the target rate of growth of aggregate consumption from 1965 to 1975
4. the ratio of weights (θ^M/θ^L) given to foreign and domestic costs in the objective function to be minimized

Table 5.1 displays the alternative values assigned to these key parameters. The various cases can be divided into three groups according to the basic assumptions made about exports and non-competitive imports. In group A, the rate of growth of exports was set equal to 5 percent per year, with an appropriate sector-wise breakdown, and the values of the relevant noncompetitive import coefficients (applying mainly to machinery and parts imports) were assumed to fall to one-half

12. Although some of the constraints are in fact equalities, they can be represented as inequalities in the appropriate direction, and they have been entered as such on page 108.
13. The sources and methodology used to compile the required data are described in Weisskopf (1967: appendix).

of their levels during the Third Plan period.[14] In group B, the rate of growth of exports was raised to 7 percent per year; and in group C, the noncompetitive import coefficients were lowered to one-third of their Third Plan levels.

In each group of cases, the target annual rate of growth of aggregate consumption between 1965 and 1975 was fixed successively at 7.5 percent, 6.0 percent, and 4.5 percent respectively. The population growth rate for this period has been estimated at 2.5 percent, so that these targets represent growth rates of 5.0 percent, 3.5 percent, and 2.0 percent in per capita consumption. From the corresponding aggregate consumption levels in 1975, related sets of values were derived for the final consumption demand, and also for the associated exogenous sector demands on both current and capital account, for the output of each individual sector. Finally, alternative solutions were generated in every case by varying the ratio of weights on foreign and domestic costs in the minimand from 4.75 to infinity.[15] Each weight ratio corresponds to an effective rate of exchange between rupees and dollars. When the ratio is equal to 4.75, it is assumed that the official exchange rate measures the relative scarcity of foreign exchange. As the ratio is raised above the initial level, a premium is placed upon foreign exchange, and when the ratio becomes infinite, foreign exchange costs alone enter into the minimand.

A similar qualitative pattern of choice characterized each set of solutions under the various assumptions considered. In the solutions for which the weight ratio θ^M/θ^L was set equal to 4.75, there were—in addition to essential noncompetitive imports—also competitive imports in approximately 30 of the endogenous sectors. These sectors consisted mainly of modern engineering industries but included also some base metals and heavy chemicals; they are listed in Table 5.2.[16] For the remaining 100-odd producing sectors—of which about 80 faced competitive imports—domestic production was cheaper than importing at the predevaluation exchange rate, and was hence preferred for every run of the model. As the weight ratio was raised to reflect an increasing premium on foreign exchange, there was a progressive substitution of domestic production activities for competitive imports. The sectors involved are listed in Table 5.2 in the order in which the substitution took place under the initial set of basic assumptions; in each case the exchange rate θ^M/θ^L at which the domestic production activity first became profitable is also listed. The rank ordering was relatively insensitive to the alternative assumptions considered. In all of the polar solutions for which foreign exchange costs alone were minimized, the model predictably replaced all competitive imports with domestic production activities and thereby reduced the import bill to the minimum of essential noncompetitive imports.[17]

14. To the extent that noncompetitive import coefficients are reduced in any given case, the corresponding coefficients for inputs of domestically produced goods are increased.

15. Since most of the work on this study was completed before the devaluation of the Indian rupee on June 5, 1966, the "official exchange rate" denotes the old rate of 4.75 rupees to the dollar.

16. Because of the great number of coefficients required for the numerical applications of the model (there were approximately 5000 matrix entries in the final form of the linear programming problem), it is quite possible that isolated numerical errors may have crept in at various stages of the study. Hence the precise results at the sectoral level presented in Tables 5.2 and 5.3 should be regarded as preliminary and interpreted with caution.

17. It is theoretically possible for the model to prefer imports to domestic production in foreign exchange minimizing solutions if the minimal foreign exchange content of domestic production actually exceeds the corresponding import price. That this was not the case here can be verified from Table 5.3.

Table 5.2. Import Substitution by Sector

Serial no.	Code no.	Sector	θ^M/θ^L
1	738	House service meters	4.79
2	611	Machine tools	4.93
3	662	Typewriters	5.10
4	624	Agricultural machinery	5.15
5	612	Boilers	5.57
6	613	Diesel engines	5.72
7	733	Water coolers	5.91
8	160	Crude oil	6.13
9	622	Mining machinery	6.32
10	522	Special steel	6.39
11	614	Pumps	6.61
12	637	Chemical equipment	7.02
13	821	Railway wagons	7.34
14	623	Drilling machinery	7.59
15	712	Hydro turbo-generators	8.21
16	732	Air conditioners	8.34
17	731	Refrigerators	8.39
18	711	Thermal turbo-generators	9.12
19	544	Zinc	9.57
20	542	Copper	9.84
21	532	Ferro-silicon	10.66
22	541	Aluminum	11.73
23	422	Soda ash	12.87
24	822	Railway coaching stock	13.16
25	543	Lead	13.78
26	833	Motorcycles and scooters	14.22
27	421	Sulphuric acid	14.81
28	445	Chemical Pulp	16.23
29	423	Caustic soda	17.12
30	813	Electric locomotives	20.13
31	812	Diesel locomotives	22.46
32	640	Ball bearings	31.25

In the solutions obtained by minimizing foreign exchange costs alone, the shadow prices for each sectoral distribution constraint reflect simply the (minimal) foreign exchange content of a unit of output from the corresponding domestic production activity. For each sector the ratio of the shadow price to the alternative import price then represents the relative foreign exchange content of domestic production vis-à-vis importing activities. The higher this ratio, the lower the net saving of foreign exchange afforded by import substitution. In Table 5.3, 41 endogenous production activities[18] are listed in the order of their relative foreign exchange content in 1975, as calculated from the shadow prices of an import-minimizing solution under the initial set of basic assumptions. There is naturally a fairly close correspondence between the rank orderings in Tables 5.2 and 5.3: sectors near the top of Table 5.3

18. The remaining domestic production activities that compete with imports all had percentages of less than 30 percent under the initial set of assumptions.

Table 5.3. Relative Foreign Exchange Content of Domestic Production Activities

Serial no.	Code no.	Activity	Group A, B	C
1	640	Ball bearings	95.8	81.4
2	812	Diesel locomotives	84.8	72.2
3	421	Sulphuric acid	81.8	77.7
4	423	Caustic soda	79.1	68.9
5	445	Chemical pulp	78.7	64.1
6	813	Electric locomotives	72.8	63.4
7	833	Motorcycles and scooters	58.6	50.6
8	711	Thermal turbo-generators	53.0	44.6
9	541	Aluminium	52.6	45.7
10	712	Hydro turbo-generators	52.0	44.6
11	532	Ferro-silicon	49.9	43.5
12	443	Synthetic rubber	47.1	38.3
13	822	Railway coaching stock	46.5	40.1
14	522	Special steel	46.1	43.1
15	623	Drilling machinery	46.0	39.2
16	613	Diesel engines	45.6	41.5
17	422	Soda ash	44.3	38.2
18	732	Air conditioners	42.9	37.9
19	731	Refrigerators	42.9	37.8
20	637	Chemical equipment	42.9	37.8
21	714	Transformers	41.3	38.5
22	424	Other inorganic chemicals	41.1	35.9
23	614	Pumps	40.8	35.7
24	412	Phosphatic fertilizers	39.5	37.9
25	622	Mining machinery	39.5	33.2
26	442	Plastics	39.4	32.3
27	137	Other nonmetallic minerals	38.2	32.1
28	670	Other mechanical engineering	36.3	30.6
29	444	Synthetic fibres	36.3	30.6
30	750	Other electrical engineering	33.6	30.6
31	612	Boilers	33.5	28.5
32	430	Organic chemicals	33.3	28.5
33	611	Machine tools	33.2	28.2
34	821	Railway wagons	32.9	28.9
35	662	Typewriters	32.5	27.7
36	733	Water coolers	32.1	27.8
37	617	Material handling equipment	31.6	26.8
38	720	Cables, wires and flexes	31.4	26.9
39	382	Newsprint	31.4	26.9
40	624	Agricultural machinery	31.3	27.3
41	832	Commercial vehicles	30.8	26.7

are found close to the bottom of 5.2. The sequential order of import substitution presented in Table 5.2 depends both on the relative foreign exchange contents shown in 5.3 and on the total domestic resource content of each production activity. Sectoral differences in the latter account for the differences in the ordering of the two tables: the higher the rupee content of a domestic production activity, the later it will substitute for imports as the premium on foreign exchange is increased.

The nature of the alternative solutions to the programming runs can be further illuminated by examining the macroeconomic implications of the sectoral results for 1975. Aggregate consumption C (at market prices) appears as a parameter in the model. Aggregate investment V (at market prices) can easily be obtained by summing (1) the fixed and working capital investment generated by the model in the endogenous sectors; (2) the exogenously given replacement investment in these sectors; and (3) the exogenously specified investments V^k in the exogenous parts of the economy. The aggregate value of exports E (in dollars) is exogenously specified together with the corresponding sectoral export demands; and the aggregate value of imports M (in dollars) can be derived by supplementing the endogenously generated import total with an estimate of the total value of imports of exogenous sector products.[19] Given the values of C, V, E, and M—and converting the dollar magnitudes into rupees at the official predevaluation exchange rate—the corresponding values of net foreign capital inflow (F),[20] gross savings (S), and gross national product (Y) can easily be calculated by means of the usual national income identities (see Weisskopf 1967: Table 9).

For the purposes of the analysis, it is most interesting to compare the alternative values of S—as a measure of internal resources—and F—as a measure of external resources—required to sustain a given targetted rate of growth g of aggregate consumption. The three parts of Figure 5.1 display the values of S and F (in billions of rupees at 1960 prices) obtained under the alternative sets of basic assumptions A, B, and C. For each of the nine cases of Table 5.1, the set of alternative required combinations of internal and external resources is shown in the appropriate diagram as a continuous contour.[21] For each group of basic assumptions, the three contours corresponding to the three different consumption targets can be interpreted as isoquants of an aggregative function relating the rate of growth of consumption to the inputs of savings and foreign capital. Additional isoquants of the same kind could be interpolated to represent different consumption targets. The left-hand end of the continuous part of each contour corresponds to the solution in which the weight ratio in the minimand conforms to the official predevaluation rate, while the right-hand end corresponds to the solution in which all the weight is placed on foreign exchange. The contours could also be extended further to the left (as indicated by the broken lines), where they would correspond to solutions based on weight ratios giving even greater emphasis to domestic vis-à-vis foreign costs.

19. The exogenous imports included here involve a few miscellaneous agricultural and industrial products which could not be classified in any of the 147 endogenous sectors of the model. As noted in Section II, foodgrains for direct consumption and military supplies for government use are excluded from this category.

20. The net inflow of foreign capital is defined in this exercise simply as the balance of trade deficit on merchandise account, excluding the import of foodgrains and military supplies. To the extent that foreign exchange is required for the latter items, or for any net payments under invisibles, an additional inflow of foreign capital would be called for.

21. Because they actually represent a series of discrete steps, these lines should not really be continuous but piece-wise linear.

Read from left to right, the isoquants of Figure 5.1 reflect the substitution of domestic production activities for competitive imports that takes place as the premium on foreign exchange is raised. The marginal rate of substitution between savings and foreign capital inflow—given by the slope of the isoquants—shows considerable invariance under the alternative assumptions considered. Up to an effective exchange rate of about twice the official predevaluation rate, the isoquants are almost straight lines[22] and are also reasonably parallel as between cases. Thus for a wide range of combinations there is a more or less constant trade-off between domestic and foreign effort which equates one rupee of net foreign capital inflow with roughly two rupees of gross domestic savings.

The marginal rate of substitution between savings and foreign exchange increases rapidly as the foreign exchange minimizing solution is approached at the right-hand end of each contour. This point defines the limit beyond which savings alone are of no avail in raising consumption possibilities. Further to the right, there is no more scope for import substitution, and the isoquants become straight lines parallel to the savings axis at a level representing the minimum net inflow of foreign capital required to sustain the given targetted rate of growth of consumption.

For each set of basic assumptions, a cut-off line joining the right-hand ends of the three different consumption isoquants divides the range of values where there are substitution possibilities (to the left) from the range of values where there is no further scope for import substitution (to the right). Each cut-off line can be used to determine the maximum amount of savings that can be translated into productive investment, and hence also the maximum sustainable rate of growth of consumption, corresponding to any given net inflow of foreign capital. Conversely, the cut-off line can be used to evaluate the minimum level of net foreign capital inflow consistent with any given rate of growth of consumption.

Under the initial set of basic assumptions, the maximum rate of growth of consumption that can be sustained without any net capital inflow appears from Figure 5.1A to be approximately 5.5 percent per year. This would call for gross savings of about 50 billion rupees in 1975, representing an average rate of saving of 15 percent in 1975, and an implied marginal rate of saving between 1965 and 1975 of close to 19 percent. To achieve a target rate of growth of consumption of 7.5 percent per year, the minimum net capital inflow in 1975 would appear to be between 4 and 5 billion rupees. This in turn would require gross savings of close to 75 billion rupees in 1975, which implies an average rate of $18\frac{1}{2}$ and a marginal rate of $23\frac{1}{2}$ percent. Alternative strategies with less emphasis on import substitution would allow the same consumption targets to be achieved with lower rates of saving and higher levels of foreign capital inflow.

To study the effect of changing the underlying assumptions about exports and noncompetitive imports, it is helpful to superimpose the isoquants of Figures 5.1B and 5.1C on those of Figure 5.1A; the result is shown in Figure 5.2. As compared with the initial set of assumptions A, it will be observed that the more optimistic export projections of B, or the lower values for noncompetitive import coefficients of C, have the effect of displacing the isoquants downward. Thus they allow the same consumption targets to be satisfied with less savings or less foreign capital inflow or both, and they allow higher consumption levels to be attained with any given combination of internal

22. The isoquants cannot be perfectly straight lines, for at each successive import substituting step the marginal rate of substitution necessarily changes.

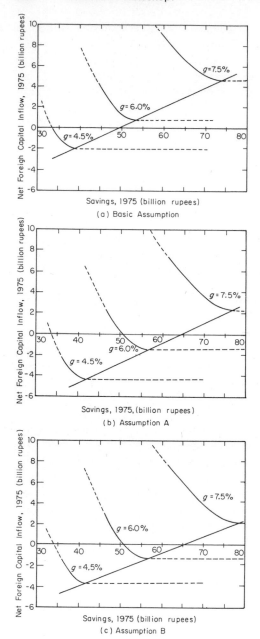

Figure 5.1

and external resources. Furthermore, the isoquants—and hence the cut-off lines—under B and C are also shifted to the right, relative to their position under A. This means that a greater amount of savings can be translated into productive investment for any given level of net foreign capital inflow.

At a zero trade deficit, either the higher export projections or the lower noncompetitive import coefficients allow for a maximum (productive) level of gross savings in 1975 of approximately 65 billion rupees, which in turn will sustain a maximum rate

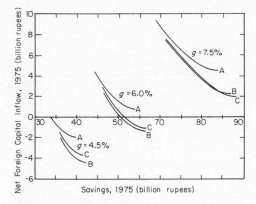

Figure 5.2

of growth of consumption of the order of 6.5 percent. As compared with the initial results, the more optimistic assumptions thus permit an increase of 1 percent in the rate of growth of consumption without any additional foreign capital inflow. The corresponding average and marginal savings rates are 18 percent and 23 percent, respectively, representing increases of 3 percent and 4 percent over the requirements of the initial case. These differences serve to emphasize the critical importance of the basic assumptions underlying each particular solution to the programming model.[23]

V. Conclusion

It may be useful, in conclusion, to compare the qualitative nature of the macro-economic results that emerge from the multisectoral model of this study with the results obtained from aggregate models of a similar kind. Chenery and Bruno (1962), McKinnon (1964), and Chenery and Strout (1966) have worked with aggregate models emphasizing the two independent constraints on growth imposed by savings, on the one hand, and by foreign exchange, on the other. The savings constraint is a familiar one: assuming a constant incremental capital-output ratio, the rate of growth of an economy is limited by the rate of investment which is equal to the sum of domestic savings and foreign savings (net capital inflow).

The phenomenon of an independent foreign exchange constraint has been more recently stressed in connection with the industrialization of underdeveloped econ-omies (see McKinnon 1964). When exports are limited exogenously (for example, by inelastic world demand), and when noncompetitive imports are required in fixed proportions for domestic production or investment or both, there is always a point beyond which potential domestic savings cannot be put to use, and the growth of domestic output cannot be increased, for lack of foreign exchange to purchase specific complementary imports. At this point, a higher growth rate can be attained only by working directly on the foreign exchange constraint—by increasing exports, reducing noncompetitive imports, or receiving additional foreign aid (net capital inflow).

23. It should be emphasized that the programming model employed in this study does not trace out the time path of the economy from the base to the target year. To arrive at any judgment about the overall feasibility of the alternative strategies described, it would be necessary to consider explicitly the dynamic implications of the static solutions.

Table 5.4. **Aggregate Coefficients (percent)**

g	θ^M/θ^L	Incremental capital-output ratio 1965-1975			Import-output ratio 1975[a] (percent)		
		A	B	C	A	B	C
7.5	4.75	2.03	2.03	2.04	5.82	5.95	5.34
	6.00	2.07	2.07	2.10	5.29	5.39	4.62
	7.50	2.12	2.11	2.13	4.87	4.94	4.27
	10.00	2.13	2.12	2.15	4.78	4.86	4.14
	15.00	2.18	2.18	2.21	4.51	4.57	3.85
	∞	2.25	2.26	2.28	4.41	4.46	3.73
6.0	4.75	2.10	2.18	2.19	5.34	5.49	4.87
	6.00	2.23	2.22	2.24	4.82	4.94	4.25
	7.50	2.26	2.26	2.27	4.50	4.62	3.96
	10.00	2.27	2.27	2.29	4.44	4.56	3.90
	15.00	2.32	2.32	2.35	4.23	4.32	3.61
	∞	2.39	2.39	2.41	4.13	4.25	3.52
4.5	4.75	2.50	2.47	2.48	4.67	4.82	4.18
	6.00	2.53	2.51	2.54	4.23	4.34	3.70
	7.50	2.54	2.52	2.55	4.18	4.30	3.67
	10.00	2.56	2.53	2.56	4.08	2.27	3.56
	15.00	2.59	2.58	2.62	3.96	4.07	3.37
	∞	2.66	2.64	2.67	3.89	3.97	3.28

[a] 1965 value equals 7.66.

The implications of a simple aggregative model embodying these two constraints could also be portrayed in the form of the graphs in Figure 5.1 With a single aggregate capital-output ratio, and a single aggregate ratio of imports to total output,[24] the result would be consumption isoquants consisting of two straight lines meeting at a cut-off line of the same kind as shown in the figure. To the right of the cut-off line, the isoquants would be paralel to the savings axis, reflecting the fact that the foreign exchange constraint was binding and additional savings alone were of no use in raising consumption possibilities. To the left, the isoquants would be straight parallel lines, reflecting the constant trade-off between savings and foreign capital inflow that prevails when the savings constraint is binding. Since, under these circumstances, foreign capital inflow plays only the role of foreign savings, the slope of the lines would be 45 degrees in the case of *output* isoquants. In the case of consumption isoquants of the kind shown in Figure 5.1, the slope of the line would be less than 45 degrees because, unlike domestic savings, foreign savings add to the total supply of savings without subtracting from total consumption.

By contrast with the results of an aggregative model, the results of the multisectoral model of this study—involving a wide range of substitution possibilities between domestic production and imports—show a relatively smooth approach to the foreign exchange bottleneck. There is still, to be sure, a cut-off line beyond which no further possibilities for substitution arise; however, this cut-off line is reached only after all

24. The assumptions of a single capital-output ratio and a single import coefficient could be relaxed to accommodate different coefficients associated with consumption and investment; the basic character of the aggregative model, as well as the conclusions, would remain unaffected.

possibilities for import substitution have been exhausted. In the process, the overall import-output ratio in the economy gets depressed to a minimum level well below its base year value, and the overall capital-output ratio rises above what it would have been with less import substitution. Thus the rigid implications of the aggregative model are tempered by the introduction of choice among linear activities at the sectoral level.

The element of choice in the programming model is brought into play by variation of the effective rate of exchange between the rupee and the dollar. The resulting reallocation of domestic and foreign resources is reflected by changes in the values of the aggregate capital-output and import-output ratios. Table 5.4 presents the alternative values[25] for those ratios implied by alternative solutions to the programming model. A, B, and C represent as before the three sets of basic assumptions about exports and noncompetitive imports; g denotes the target rate of growth of consumption; and θ^M/θ^L the effective rate of exchange (the rupee price of the dollar). It is clear from the table that the values of the two ratios vary not only with θ^M/θ^L, but also significantly with g and—in the case of the import ratio—with the alternative assumptions A, B, and C.

The multisectoral linear programming model of this study provides a more flexible —and presumably a more realistic—representation of the economy than any simple aggregative, or less disaggregated, model could. Largely because of considerations of data availability, however, the scope for optimization in the model was limited to the choice between domestic production and importing activities. In three important respects, a greater degree of realism could be achieved by widening the area of choice. First of all, export levels could be made a function of the effective rate of exchange in those sectors for which there is a significant price elasticity in the demand for—or supply of—exports.[26] Secondly, the sectoral composition of consumption— which was fixed (at the margin) in the present form of the model—could also be allowed to adjust to some extent to the relative scarcity of domestic and foreign resources.[27] Finally, alternative techniques of production for domestically produced goods and services could be introduced—where appropriate—in the form of additional linear production activities (see Chapter 2 in this volume).

Each of those extensions would increase the flexibility of the model. For any given variation in the effective rate of exchange, an even greater degree of reallocation of resources would be called for. The increased possibilities of substitution would further weaken the rigid conclusions of the simplest aggregative model, and push somewhat further back the spectre of a foreign exchange bottleneck. Whether this spectre can— in the Indian case—actually be wholly exorcised would depend on the extent to which export levels and consumption patterns are, or can be made, responsive to price changes. This is clearly a subject on which much more quantitative research will have to be carried out before any definitive judgments can be made.

25. The incremental capital-output ratios listed in Table 5.4 were calculated by relating the total cumulative gross investment requirements from 1963 to 1973 to the increase in aggregate production capacity from 1965 to 1975; thus a 2-year average investment output lag was assumed. The actual figures obtained depend on an estimate of the extent to which overall capacity exceeded actual output in the Indian economy in 1965. Since any such estimate is necessarily very uncertain, the absolute values given in the table should be interpreted with some caution. More reliance can be placed on *relative* values, which are in any case the more significant from the point of view of the analysis.

26. As noted in Section II, any such modifications would involve the approximation of nonlinear functions reflecting diminishing marginal net earnings from exporting activities.

27. I am indebted to S. Chakravarty for emphasizing this point.

6 Interaction Between Domestic and Foreign Resources in Economic Growth: Some Experiments for India*

Suresh D. Tendulkar

I. Introduction

The purpose of this chapter is to present a multisectoral, single-period, optimizing programming model that explicitly incorporates two primary bottleneck constraints on economic growth, namely, domestic savings and foreign exchange.[1] Most of the presently available multisectoral models (for example Chenery and Kretschmer 1956; Chenery and Uzawa 1958; Bruno 1966; Weisskopf, Chapter 5, this volume) introduce only the trade constraint bringing out the import financing role of foreign capital inflow. The justification for suggesting yet another model lies in introducing the savings constraint in order to focus also on the savings supplementing role of foreign assistance in a multisectoral framework.[2] It is contended that this construction is better suited to highlight the interaction between domestic and foreign resources and its effects on economic growth.

The problem posed by our model is comparative static in nature. It consists of making an optimal jump from the initial conditions in the base year to the target year of the planning horizon by maximizing the criterion function subject to the constraints operating on the system in the terminal year. Although intertemporal models are decidedly superior on theoretical grounds for analysing a dynamic process of economic development, the single-period analysis has been adopted in this study

* This is a revised version of parts of the doctoral dissertation submitted by the author to the Department of Economics, Harvard University, in April 1968. The original study was carried out under a generous scholarship from the Rockefeller Foundation with Professors H. S. Houthakker, H. B. Chenery, and D. A. Kendrick acting as dissertation committee members. The revision was made possible by support from the Project for Quantitative Research in Economic Development under AID Contract 1543. The author wishes to acknowledge the continuous encouragement and the detailed, penetrating, and constructive criticisms he received from Professor Chenery at various stages in writing this paper. Professor T. N. Srinivasan gave valuable comments and suggestions in preparing the final version. The author, however, retains sole responsibility for the views expressed and imperfections that may persist.

1. A pioneering study in this area was made by Chenery and Bruno (1962), who, in an aggregated 1-sector framework, formulated a single-period model for Israel which introduced both these bottleneck constraints simultaneously. Our model may be regarded as a multisectoral generalization of theirs.

2. Bruno (1966) mentions the savings constraint in his algebraic formulation but does not include it explicitly in his solutions. However, he works out the implicit savings rates in the solutions with varying capital inflow. Eckaus and Parikh (1968) add the constraint in their Guidepath II version in an intertemporal framework. Both the Bruno and the Eckaus-Parikh formulations approach the savings constraint as a lower limit on incremental consumption whereas our model imposes savings as an upper limit on investment.

by considering possible trade-offs between (1) intertemporal and intersectoral disaggregation with reference to computational costs: (2) methodological refinements and data requirements; and (3) analytical complexity and easy comprehensibility (for more detail, see Tendulkar 1968).

The central problem is to assess how important in practice the savings constraint is likely to be for the developing economies to which our model claims to be applicable. The current view appears to suggest that domestic savings are capable of being optimally adjusted to the investment requirements if the plan is "physically, technically and organizationally feasible and makes sense on the foreign exchange side."[3] In other words, domestic savings do not impose a binding constraint on economic growth. This approach is valid as long as no conflict appears between individual time preferences of the population and social time preference of the planning authority. However, possibilities of conflict arise from political, sociological, behavioral, and institutional considerations imposing a definite upper limit on the feasible rate of savings in the underdeveloped countries (see Sen 1961; United Nations 1967c: 7–50). Under these circumstances, the planned quantum of investment is unlikely to materialize because of infeasibilities involved in raising the domestic resources.[4] Successful planning requires an attempt to ensure a mutual consistency between the investment plan and its sectoral allocation on the one hand, and its internal and external resource requirements on the other. The model suggested here is well suited for this analysis. It incorporates both the balance of trade and savings as primary constraints. For a given availability of foreign assistance and specified institutional limits on savings rates, the model permits an empirical determination of whether the savings constraint is binding or nonbinding. Whenever the savings limit is not binding we get the usually available trade-limited multisectoral models as a special case.[5]

Consequently, two variants of the basic model are developed and empirically investigated with reference to India. First, an *open-loop variety* is considered where the domestic financing of consumption and investment is regarded as exogenous to the system and the optimization process is carried out unconstrained by the availability of domestic resources and subject only to the availability of the primary resource of foreign exchange.[6] This gives rise to the purely trade-limited (PTL) growth process. In terms of policy implications, this approach assumes that the government has sufficient fiscal and monetary control over the economy so that the mobilization of domestic savings does not pose a binding constraint. When, however, the PTL process involves raising the domestic savings well beyond the institutional and behavioral limits, the implied investment strategy is unlikely to be successful. It is in such situations that the second variant, a *closed-loop variety*, is relevant. In this case, the problem of domestic financing is made endogenous to the system through an explicit feedback from the process of production to the generation of incomes and

3. Lewis (1962: 35). This view is also implicit in the multisectoral models cited at the beginning.

4. It is assumed that foreign assistance is exogenously fixed and cannot be increased. As is well known, foreign aid can act as a substitute for domestic efforts in a limited range.

5. As an alternative possibility we may consider a purely savings limited growth process which may apply to oil-rich economies with nonscarce supplies of foreign exchange.

6. An "optimal growth" theorist would immediately detect that this is a comparative static analogue of the optimal savings models of the Ramsey type. In our model, foreign exchange is the primary resource, whereas in the Ramsey problem, labor is the autonomous factor limiting growth.

in turn back to the principal components of gross domestic expenditure. The feedback is accomplished by the introduction of the domestic savings constraint through the specification of the marginal savings propensities for wage and nonwage income earners. The criterion function is optimized subject to the availability of the two primary resources of foreign exchange and domestic savings.[7] Consequently, we get a simultaneous trade-and-savings limited (TSL) growth process.

In the standard terminology of two-gap analysis (see Chenery and Strout, 1966), the PTL variant implies that the trade gap is dominant at a given foreign aid availability so that the savings constraint becomes nonbinding in character. The TSL variant, on the other hand, may be taken to represent a situation where foreign aid is insufficient to bridge even the smaller of the two gaps. This case may be quite realistic for a country like India with a large population whose foreign assistance requirements may be too great to fit into the foreign aid budgets of the advanced countries. In both the variants, our model addresses itself to the problem of optimally adjusting to a given level of foreign aid. Instead of finding the foreign assistance requirements for attaining a prespecified growth rate with a fixed output mix on the lines of the standard two-gap analysis[8] we allow both the output mix and the growth rate to vary and the latter to be optimized in a multisectoral framework so that, in the optimal adjustment,[9] both the constraints (domestic savings and foreign exchange) may remain binding.

II. Formulation of the Model and Its Variants

We will start by first presenting the notation to be used.

Endogenous Variables

C_i — private consumption expenditure on commodities in the ith sector

C — total private consumption expenditure

X_i — gross output level in the ith sector

I_i — gross fixed investment originating in the ith fixed capital producing sector

I — total fixed investment

M_i — level of competitive imports in the ith sector

E_i — level of exports from the ith sector

W_1, W_2 — levels of wage and nonwage incomes, respectively, generated from domestic production

Exogenous Variables

$\bar{G}_i$ — public current consumption demand on the ith sector

$\bar{I}_i^{\text{exo}}$ — exogenous investment requirements in the ith fixed capital producing sector

$\underline{E}_i, \bar{E}_i$ — floor and ceiling requirements on exports in the ith sector

$\bar{\bar{M}}_i$ — import ceiling level in the ith sector

$\bar{S}_g, \bar{S}_g^0$ — public savings in the target and base years, respectively

7. For a dynamic analogue of this variant in the optimal growth theory, see Phelps and Pollak (1968).

8. That is, "model 1" or "disequilibrium model" in Chenery, and Strout (1966).

9. The problem of optimal adjustment has been studied in a 2-sector intertemporal framework by Chenery and MacEwan (1966). See also Chenery and Strout (1966), Chenery and Eckstein (1967), Cohen (1966), McKinnon (1966), and Vanek (1967) for possible adjustments in an intertemporal consistency model at the aggregate level.

$\bar{S}_c, \bar{S}_c^0$ corporate savings in the target and base years, respectively

$\bar{F}, \bar{F}^0$ maximum permissible import surpluses in the target and base years, respectively

$\bar{D}, \bar{D}^0$ depreciation provisions in the target and base years, respectively

$\bar{G}, \bar{G}^0$ total current government expenditure in the target and base years, respectively

$\bar{W}_1^0, \bar{W}_2^0$ base year levels of corresponding endogenous variables

Parameters

a_{ij} current input requirement from the ith sector per unit of output in the jth sector

η_j inventory investment per unit of output in the jth sector

k_{ij} marginal fixed capital requirement of the ith type per unit of output in the jth sector

θ stock-flow conversion factor

f_i noncompetitive imports per unit of output in the ith sector

d_i^M foreign exchange outlay per unit of imports from the ith sector

μ_i proportion of imports in the ith sector in relation to total supplies in that sector

d_i^E foreign exchange earning per unit of exports from the ith sector

v_{1j}, v_{2j} wage and nonwage income respectively generated per unit of gross output in the jth sector

s_1, s_2 Marginal propensities to save out of wage and nonwage incomes, respectively

γ Nominal rate of exchange (rupees per dollar)

Now we algebraically specify the constraint sets appearing in the model. Detailed comments are made on those relations which constitute a point of departure as compared to the already formulated multisectoral models. Other constraints are described only briefly. It may be observed at this point that all the constraints involve the flows of the endogenous and exogenous variables (denoted without and with bars) either in the final year or base year (distinguished by an absence or presence of a supercript o) of a given planning horizon. No time subscript appears because of the single-period nature of this study.

Constraint Sets

A $X_i + M_i \geqq C_i + \sum_j a_{ij}X_j + \eta_iX_i + \bar{G}_i + I_i + E_i \quad i = 1, 2, \ldots, 32$

B $C_i = \alpha_i C \text{ where } \sum_i \alpha_i = 1 \text{ and } \sum_i C_i = C$

C $I_i - \theta \sum_j k_{ij}X_j \geqq I_i^{\text{exo}} - \theta \sum_j k_{ij}\bar{X}_j^0 \quad i = 1, 2, \ldots, 5 \left(\text{also}, \sum_i I_i = I\right)$

D $\mu_iX_i - (1 - \mu_i)M_i \geqq 0 \quad i \in \text{subset of importable sectors}$

E $E_i' \geqq \underline{E}_i$

E′ $E_i \leqq \bar{E}_i \quad i \in \text{exportable sectors for both E and E}'$

F $\sum_i f_iX_i + \sum_i d_i^MM_i - \sum_i d_i^EE_i \leqq \bar{F}$

G $\sum_j v_{1j}X_j - W_1 = 0$

$$\text{G'} \quad \sum_j v_{2j} X_j - W_2 = 0$$

$$\text{H} \quad (I - \bar{I}^0) \leqq s_1(W_1 - \bar{W}_1^0) + s_2(W_2 - \bar{W}_2^0) + (\bar{S}_g - \bar{S}_g^0) + (\bar{S}_c - \bar{S}_c^0)$$
$$+ (\bar{D} - \bar{D}^0) + \gamma(\bar{F} - \bar{F}^0)$$

$$\text{I} \quad C + I - W_1 - W_2 \leqq \bar{S}_g + \bar{S}_c + \gamma\bar{F} + \bar{D}$$

The first set of inequalities, A, describes the familiar sectoral supply-demand relationship stating that the supplies from domestic production and imports in each sector be at least as great as the aggregate demand arising from current private. public, and intermediate consumption; fixed and inventory investment; and export.

The second set, B, specifies the composition of the private consumption basket.

The third set of relations, C, indicates that the output of the ith investment producing sector allocated for gross investment purposes must be as great as that required to meet the needs of exogenous investment (for education, health, and so on) and of capacity creation for the production of commodities in excess of the base year level. The parameter θ describes the stock-flow conversion coefficient[10] which is a device to transform the additions to capital stock over a given horizon into the investment flow of the target year of the plan. It provides a built-in rationale for investment activity in the final year of the finite planning horizon.

The fourth set, D, incorporates the import substitution target by stipulating that the competitive imports in a given sector be less than or equal to a prespecified proportion (μ_i) of supplies in that sector. μ_i is regarded as a policy parameter. It may be noted that if the economy has a comparative advantage in the domestic production of the ith sector, this constraint would not be binding. If the constraint operates with a strict equality, a forced import substitution policy would be indicated and the corresponding shadow price would provide the evidence of the cost involved in terms of the criterion function.

The constraint set E and E' makes a crude attempt to introduce the rigidities and nonlinearities in the export sector by imposing upper and lower bounds on the export earnings in individual sectors. The lower limits are meant to eliminate a sharp and unrealistic drop in the export earnings resulting from the specialization implicit in linear models (see, for example, Bruno 1966) whereas the upper limits are expected to reflect certain exogenous factors such as nonexpanding, inelastic demand conditions, as well as quota and tariff restrictions on imports in the industrialised countries.

The next constraint, F, describes the balance of trade or the familiar "trade gap." It states that the demand for foreign exchange from noncompetitive (first term on the left) and competitive imports must not exceed the supplies from exports and the net private and public inflow of capital. This constraint is formulated in terms of foreign currency (dollars). The shadow price would give the marginal productivity of foreign exchange within a given optimal structure.

The equations defining income generation are given in G and G'. The total net value added (after deductions are made for depreciation, undistributed profits, and direct taxes) per unit of gross output in each sector has two components: (1) wage

10. This has been derived under the following assumptions: (a) the length of the planning horizon is 15 years; (b) the average gestation lag between investment and output is two years; and (c) the gross investment grows at an exponential rate of 8.7 percent throughout the planning horizon. Assumptions (b) and (c) are numerically the same as those of Manne and Rudra (1965). For further details, see Manne (1963, 1966a) and Tendulkar (1968).

income plus income from self-employment in agriculture, and (2) nonwage income. These sectoral incomes are aggregated to derive total wage (W_1) and nonwage (W_2) income, which is connected in the next two relations to appropriate constraints.

The domestic savings constraint is described in H. It uses the well-known national accounting relationship that aggregate investment equals domestic savings plus net foreign capital inflow. Total domestic savings are divided into personal, corporate, and public savings. The public and corporate parts are treated exogenously whereas personal savings are related to the wage and nonwage income. Constraint H is formulated as an upper limit on aggregate investment and in marginal terms with reference to the base year initial conditions. It directly gives us the familiar "savings gap." Several advantages of this specification may be noted. In the first place, it explicitly takes into account the role of foreign aid as a supplement to domestic savings[11] in addition to its import financing aspect incorporated already in the trade gap constraint (F). Secondly, it helps reveal the interaction between the autonomous resource of foreign aid and the endogenous resource of domestic savings in bringing about the optimal solution and their often repeated complementary relationship. Thirdly, with its origins in the income generation equations G and G′, it discloses the interdependent links between output mix, income creation, feasible ranges of savings and investment (consistent with the foreign aid availability), and the resulting components of gross domestic expenditure. Fourthly, by incorporating savings propensities by income type, the income distribution and the significance of its components in generating domestic savings have been brought into the picture. The empirical analysis also comes closer to the theoretical growth models where different savings propensities for wage and nonwage income earners have been recognized and their effects on growth investigated. Constraint H may be taken to reflect the institutional, behavioral, and policy limitations on financing additional capital formation, and its shadow price would indicate the extent of scarcity of this domestic resource.

The final constraint, I is required to ensure consistency between income generation and its uses. We have closed the model from the savings side in H. We have to close it also from the consumption side by establishing a definitional equality between the aggregate disposable income and consumption plus savings. Some computational difficulties, however, arise in this connection. Note that the exogenously specified $\bar{D}$, $\bar{S}_g$, and $\bar{S}_c$ (on the right-hand side of I) in the target year have to be fixed independently of the related prior adjustments necessary in the sectoral gross values added per unit of output for depreciation, direct taxes, and undistributed corporate profits while deriving the disposable income components W_1 and W_2 (on the left-hand side of I). Mutual consistency between these related quantities cannot be guaranteed in advance because W_1 and W_2 are endogenously determined from the solution of the model, whereas $\bar{D}$, $\bar{S}_g$, and $\bar{S}_c$ are determined outside the system. Consequently, we have to be content with a less elegant alternative of the inequality constraint stating that private consumption plus savings be less than or equal to the aggregate disposable income generated. Whenever private consumption plus savings tend to exceed

11. The alternative formulation (see Bruno 1966: 331, constraints b.4 and h.1) of savings constraint as an upper limit on incremental consumption does this only implicitly through GNP. Moreover, it has two other drawbacks. First, it does not highlight the domestic savings as a primary resource and its connection to the income generated from production. Second, the shadow price of the equation determining GNP (Bruno's eq. h.1) creates difficulties of interpretation. Our formulation appears to be better on all three counts.

disposable income, the model adjusts the output mix through constraint I by satisfying it with a strict equality; and no conceptual problem arises. When, however, it is satisfied with a strict inequality, we have to assume transfer payments (such as taxes) from within the system to the exogenous sectors. Theoretically it is uncomfortable indeed. In actual solutions, however, its nature turns out to be quantitatively unimportant in most of the cases.

This completes the description of the various components of the model. Except for the last three constraints G and G', H, and I, the model is similar to the earlier programming models of Chenery and Kretschmer (1956), Chenery and Uzawa (1958), Bruno (1966), and Weisskopf (Chapter 5, this volume).

The model is solved by finding the maximum value of aggregate private consumption, C, in the target year of the planning horizon, subject to the constraints listed above. The open-loop or PTL variant concentrates only on the foreign exchange bottleneck to economic growth and assumes a priori that the savings constraint is nonbinding by hypothesizing that the mobilization of domestic savings may be taken care of exogenously. This implies that constraint H is satisfied either with a strict inequality or drops off altogether. Consequently the related constraints G, G', and I also become redundant, and the open-loop system contains constraint A to F only.

The closed-loop or TSL variant, on the other hand, explicitly introduces the feedback between gross output and its uses through the income generation equations G and G' and the savings and closing constraints H and I. As a result, the optimization problem incorporates all of the constraint sets A to I.

III. Comparison of Closed- and Open-Loop Versions on the 15-Year Horizon

The two variants of the model are empirically investigated in a 32-sectoral breakdown for the Indian economy with a 15-year planning horizon starting from the base year 1960–61 and ending with 1975–76. This section seeks to bring out the structural differences between the open- and the closed-loop versions and their policy implications.

The reference point of net foreign aid has been fixed at $0.50 billion in the target year 1975–76 for both versions. It conforms closely to that projected by India's Perspective Planning Division (1966). This was done in order to keep some contact with the official thinking and to explore its implications. With the same purpose, projections of government and corporate savings were taken from the Perspective Planning Division (1964).[12] (See Table B.1.) For personal savings, two parameters require specification: the marginal savings propensity for (1) wage income *plus* income from self-employment in agriculture, and (2) residual nonwage income. (These two propensities are denoted respectively by s_1 and s_2.) In the absence of any detailed empirical studies that would enable us to estimate more accurately the numerical values for these two critical parameters, we have adopted for the purposes of this analysis

12. The outbreak of war with Pakistan in late 1965, the devaluation of the Indian rupee in June 1966, the two successive droughts of 1965–66 and 1966–67, the subsequent recession, and the postponement of the starting date of the fourth Five-Year Plan from April 1966 to April 1969 have made these projections obsolete and also make impossible the comparison of our results with the official targets. For these reasons and others connected with weaknesses in data, the present calculations are regarded as experimental in character. They do, however, serve to highlight the differential policy implications of the two variants of the basic model suggested in this study.

the values $s_1 = .05$ and $s_2 = .45$ suggested by Houthakker (1965b). With these particulars, the two reference solutions here investigated in detail may be conveniently summarized with reference to primary resources. On the 15-year horizon,

open-loop (PTL) variant
    F = $0.50 billion; no savings limitation
closed-loop (TSL) variant
    F = $0.50 billion; $s_1 = 0.05$, $s_2 = 0.45$

Macroeconomic Results

The optimal level of aggregate private consumption of Rs32,485 crores, in the open-loop reference solution, turns out to be 7 percent higher than the corresponding projected value for 1975–76 worked out by Srinivasan, Saluja, and Sabherwal (1965) in collaboration with the Perspective Planning Division (see Table B.5, which summarizes the relevant macroeconomic results).

When the savings constraint is introduced in a closed-loop framework (for the same level of foreign assistance as in the open-loop solution), the immediate impact is reflected in a decline in the average rate of growth of private consumption from 6.5 percent to 4.5 percent per annum and that of gross national product from 8.2 percent to 6.2 percent per annum in comparison with the open-loop solution. This sharp reduction is brought about by a limited availability of domestic savings reducing the gross capital formation over the 15-year planning horizon[13] from 109 thousand crores in the open-loop version to 71 thousand crores, or about 35 percent. Not only is there a severe cutback in the gross capital formation, but the importance of new capacity creation in the aggregate investment is also reduced. This is indicated by a fall in the ratio of induced fixed investment to aggregate gross investment[14] in the target year from 67 percent in the PTL version to 57 percent in the TSL system.

The sectoral output mix is so adjusted as to produce a somewhat higher aggregate gross incremental capital-output ratio (ICOR)[15] at 3.4 in a closed-loop system as against 3.0 in the open-loop solution. On the other hand, the ratio of aggregate gross investment to gross national product in the target year is lower at 25.6 percent in the closed-loop model as compared to 28.3 percent in the open-loop variant. It can thus be seen through the Harrod-Domar mechanism that the lower growth rate in the closed-loop system has resulted from both the reduction in the proportion of GNP diverted to gross investment and the rise in the aggregate ICOR. This rise can be shown to be a consequence of a shift in the underlying curves relating investment and GNP. The shift, in turn, can be traced to the binding or nonbinding nature of the institutional savings constraint in passing from one version to another. This argument can be explained intuitively with the help of Figure 6.1. It describes the relationship between aggregate gross investment, I, and GNP, V, in the target year of the planning horizon under the two systems for varying levels of the autonomous resource of foreign assistance. The linear form is postulated for convenience. D_1

13. The gross capital formation over a given planning horizon is obtained by dividing the target year levels of gross induced fixed investment (with a gestation lag of 2 years) and inventory plus exogenous investment (with no lags) by appropriate stock-flow conversion factors and adding them together.

14. The difference between the quantities in the denominator and numerator of this ratio is accounted for by inventory plus exogenous investment components.

15. This is given by a ratio of gross capital formation over a planning horizon (see note 11) to the incremental GNP in the target year.

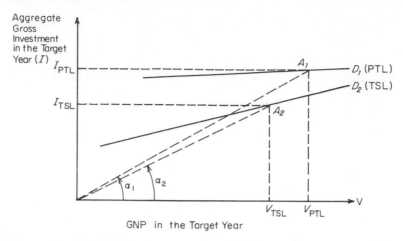

Figure 6.1   Relationship between aggregate gross investment and GNP in the target year under two systems for varying levels of the autonomous resource of foreign assistance.

represents the relationship under the PTL system assuming nonscarcity of domestic resources, the only limit to growth being varying availabilities of foreign assistance. When, however, there are institutional and behavioral limits to raising the domestic resources, this constraint puts an upper bound on feasible levels of gross investment by introducing a downward shift in the curve to D_2 appropriate to the closed-loop system.[16] Consequently, the optimal equilibrium shifts from A_1 to A_2 in the I-V plane, going from the PTL to the TSL system. Notice that in the absence of the shift factor in the form of endogenous personal savings limit, the target year ratio of gross investment to GNP would *increase* at a lower level of GNP in the savings constrained solution.

Let us now turn to the investigation of domestic resources. Only the personal savings component is endogenous to the model. Other sources of savings have been treated as exogenous. In the closed-loop solution, we directly get the aggregate personal savings consistent with the trade and the savings constraints. In the open-loop solution we can compute the comparable implied personal savings (S_i) by the following formula, in the notation of Section II:

$$S_i = I - \bar{S}_g - \bar{S}_c - \gamma \bar{F} - \bar{D}$$

16. The construction of the curves implies that the same level of GNP can be produced by a lower level of gross investment in the TSL system than in the PTL system. Strange though this result may appear prima facie, it can be explained in the following manner. Whenever the savings constraint is binding, the same level of GNP as in the open-loop system is possible only through higher availabilities of foreign aid, which also contribute to lowering the aggregate gross ICOR by enabling higher imports of formerly domestically produced capital-intensive commodities. These two factors together enable the closed-loop system to reach that level of GNP which the open-loop system produces with higher gross investment but lower supplies of foreign assistance. Two more brief observations may be made about the nature of these curves. First, the flatter shape of D_1 relative to D_2 is warranted by the investment being at the domestic resource saturation level in the open-loop system. Additional foreign assistance may not be expected to add as much to gross investment as to consumption. Second, since foreign exchange is the primary limit to growth and the only one operating in the PTL system, D_1 would always lie above or at the same level as D_2 where savings are an additional limiting factor to growth. These hypotheses will be verified in the next section where we trace the shape of these curves empirically by varying foreign capital inflow.

Table 6.1. Personal Savings Ratios and Their Contribution to Gross Investment: Reference Solutions

	Open-loop system	Closed-loop system
Target year personal savings-ratio (S/W)	23.09	15.28
Marginal personal savings-ratio (ΔS/ΔW)	31.33	20.73
Ratio of personal savings to gross investment (S/I)	62.27	44.25

as a difference between gross investment and exogenous components of savings plus replacement requirements. It is assumed that the investment program is carried out by sacrificing consumption. It is instructive to compare the relevant savings ratios in the alternative systems. These are presented in Table 6.1.

The comparison between the ratios in the alternative systems indicates at once the nature of the conflict between the social judgment of the planning authority (given by the open-loop solution) and the private preferences of the population consistent with its savings propensities (incorporated in the closed-loop solution). It is also interesting to note that personal savings are expected to contribute as much as 62 percent of the aggregate gross investment in the target year in the open-loop system whereas they contribute only 44 percent in a closed-loop solution optimal with respect to both foreign assistance and domestic savings constraints.

Productivity of Foreign Assistance and Domestic Savings

Having examined the quantity solutions in the form of macroeconomic results, it is appropriate to turn to the price solutions and the important question of assessing the relative effectiveness of the primary resources under the two systems we have been considering.

The shadow price on the balance-of-trade constraint of the model, (P_F), reflects the marginal addition to the criterion function resulting from an additional unit of foreign exchange. It is calculated under the assumption that all other constraints remain unchanged, and therefore takes account of the effect of additional foreign exchange *only* in financing additional imports and *not* in supplementing domestic savings. In the present context, the key characteristic of foreign assistance is that it does both: it finances additional imports and it adds to the supply of savings. Since savings is not a binding constraint in the open-loop model, the shadow price of foreign exchange (P_F) in this case fully measures the marginal productivity of foreign assistance, P_A. In the case of the closed-loop model, however, the marginal productivity foreign assistance (P_A) must be measured by the sum of the shadow price foreign exchange (P_F) *and* the shadow price on the savings constraint, P_S.

On a priori grounds, one would expect the shadow price P_F to be higher in the open- than in the closed-loop system. In the open-loop system, foreign exchange is the only primary resource bottleneck. In the closed-loop system, domestic savings is also a bottleneck. By restricting the feasible level of gross investment and, hence, the rate of growth of economic activity, the limitation on domestic savings introduces a downward shift in the demand for and consequently in the marginal productivity of foreign exchange. This can be verified in the reference solutions (see Table B.5) by observing that the shadow price of the balance-of-trade constraint (P_F) turns out to be very high at Rs23.64 per dollar in the open-loop system and declines by about 58 percent to Rs10.00 per dollar in the closed-loop framework.

The shadow price P_S reveals how scarce the domestic 'resources are—both endogenously generated personal savings and exogenous components of government and corporate savings. The marginal productivity of domestic savings is zero under the assumptions of the open-loop system. For the closed-loop system, Table B.5 shows that a rupee worth of domestic savings adds 3.6 times its value to the criterion function.

Since the marginal productivity of foreign assistance, P_A, is given by

$$P_A = P_F + P_S$$

we can now get the idea of its relative magnitude in the two systems. Converting P_F at the nominal rate of exchange, we find that a rupee worth of foreign aid makes a marginal contribution of Rs 3.14 in the open-loop system and of Rs4.93 in the closed-loop framework. The dual role of an additional unit of foreign capital inflow in the TSL version thus results in larger absolute additions to the criterion function than in the case of the PTL variant, when the level of foreign assistance remains the same in each case.

Trade Structure, Comparative Advantage, and Import Substitution

We have studied the basic features of the open- and the closed-loop reference solutions connected with macroeconomic aggregates and resource productivities. It is relevant now to carry the analysis to the disaggregated sectoral level. Since foreign exchange, as the primary bottleneck to growth, governs the composition of the domestic output mix through the trade structure, it is necessary to investigate the pattern of the trade structure and how it is affected by the savings limitation in the closed-loop in comparison with the open-loop system.

The trade structure in the optimal models is determined by the principle of comparative costs. A tradable sector is importable if the unit domestic cost at the margin exceeds c.i.f. foreign exchange outlay on imports and exportable, if the unit domestic cost at the margin is less than f.o.b. export price in the international market.

The basic cost elements in the trade-constrained open-loop system consist of direct and indirect current outlays on fixed capital requirements and direct and indirect foreign exchange costs necessitated by imported inputs. Since the system is domestic-resource saturated, the cost of investment turns out to be equal to that of sectoral domestic production.

The joint scarcity of foreign exchange and domestic savings is the major determinant of the comparative cost structure in a closed-loop system. The nonzero scarcity price of domestic savings has a twofold consequence. First, the system now differentiates between a unit of output going into investment and one going into non-investment. The former has a higher cost associated with it because investment involves raising the scarce domestic resources. Second, current primary factor payments enter the system as legitimate cost elements and are determined by the capacity of various sectors to contribute to the endogenous resource of personal savings (see Tendulkar 1968). The criteria just outlined for both the systems are subject to modifications introduced by import restrictions and export-ceiling constraints.

Having presented the general principles determining the trade structure, we may examine how they operate empirically by starting with the import structure in the two systems, summarized in Table 6.2. Since sectoral direct and indirect fixed capital requirements form a major cost element in both the systems, they are presented in the table along with the ranking of sectors resulting from them.

It may be noted that the aggregate import outlays did not change significantly in the two versions. Since net foreign capital inflow remained fixed, this implies that the structure of exports was virtually invariant under the alternative assumptions about limitations on saving.

An obvious inference from the open-loop import structure is that it is not entirely governed by the domestic fixed capital costs. The other cost elements of noncompetitive import outlays and import restrictions play a predominant role, not surprising in view of a very high accounting price of foreign exchange in the open-loop system. This phenomenon explains why transport equipment (4), petroleum products (23), and rubber products (25), with relatively low domestic fixed capital costs but higher foreign exchange input costs, are imported, whereas the high capital cost outputs like iron and steel (6) and chemical fertilizers (19) are domestically produced.

In contrast to the open-loop system, the additional domestic resource costs involved in the closed-loop system, combined with a lower accounting price of foreign exchange (resulting from a downward shift in its demand curve because of the savings limitation), restore the ranking of comparative advantage consistent with the domestic (direct and indirect) unit fixed capital costs. It is interesting to note that in this case, competitive imports take place in industries with the six largest fixed capital cost elements. The import activity in foodgrains (15) with the lowest domestic capital requirements enters the structure because it is intensive in chemical fertilizers (19), whose cost is high due to import restrictions. The nature and importance of these restrictions will be discussed shortly.

Table 6.2. Import Structure in the Reference Solutions (rupees crores unless otherwise indicated)

Competitive imports sector[a]	Unit fixed capital costs		Open-loop system		Closed-loop system	
	Direct and indirect	Rank	Imports	Distribution (percent)	Imports	Distribution (percent)
Transport Equipment (4)	2.23	8	409	25.00		
Iron and Steel (6)	4.86	3			339	33.25
Other metals (9)	6.90	2	332	35.98	488	26.99
Foodgrains (15)	2.06	9			242	15.44
Chemical fertilizers (19)	4.01	4			85	19.51
Petroleum products (23)	2.35	6	190	17.48		
Crude oil (24)	7.57	1	240	6.27	179	1.55
Rubber products (25)	2.27	7	19	13.21		
Plantation rubber (26)	3.31	5	40	1.70	23	3.26
Total competitive imports			1,230	100.00	1,356	100.00
Noncompetitive imports			536		406	
Total import outlay			1,766		1,762	

[a] A complete list of sectors by number is in Appendix A to this chapter.

In order to reflect the import substitution drive, we constrained the competitive imports in iron and steel (6) as well as in chemical fertilizers (19) to be less than or equal to 15 percent of the total supplies in each sector. It is instructive to observe that these import restrictions are not binding in the open-loop system, whereas they are in the closed-loop variant. This means that the average annual growth rates of domestic output of 18 percent and 27 percent, respectively, for iron and steel and chemical fertilizers (see Table B6.7) in the open-loop variant reflect the efficient working of comparative advantage, whereas the growth rates of 14 percent and 22 percent for the same two sectors in the closed-loop system highlight the effects of the forced import substitution strategy. In order to assess the cost of import substitution, the closed loop reference solution was recomputed after removing import restrictions in sectors (6) and (19). The new solution indicated the optimal level of consumption in the target year to be Rs24,547 crores or a little over 1 percent higher than the level reached in the reference solution. The relative magnitude of the cost does not appear to be quantitatively significant.[17]

The final feature of the trade structure relates to exports. As we have observed in Section II, we have imposed upper limits on export expansion to take into account exogenous limitations on demand. In certain traditional exporting sectors like iron ore (7), plantations (11), cotton and other textiles (16), and jute textiles (17), we also added lower limits to avoid an unrealistically sharp drop in export earnings possible in linear models.　Since foreign exchange is a primary bottleneck to growth under both systems, export expansion, in general, would always remain profitable. However, in view of a downward shift in the demand for foreign exchange in the closed-loop as compared to the open-loop system, we may expect some reshuffling in the composition of exports at a disaggregated level. From Table B6.6 we observe that in passing from the open-loop to the closed-loop version, the exports of iron ore (7) have been reduced to the lower limit, those in cement (8) and coal (30) disappear, and transport equipment (4) changes from an importable sector to an exportable one. The quantitative significance of these shifts is quite small. The upper limits on exports are binding in all the other exporting sectors—traditional as well as non-traditional—and in both versions. The importance of the limitations on export expansion highlights a realistic though disturbing phenomenon faced by most of the underdeveloped countries[18] (see, for example, Lewis 1962: 38–45, 233–247; Vanek 1967: 119–124).

IV. Implications of Variations in Foreign Assistance

Section III concentrated on bringing out detailed structural differences between the open- and the closed-loop systems for the two reference solutions. This section seeks to explore the differential response mechanisms of the system to variations in foreign assistance. Every change in the optimal combination of domestic and foreign

17. The new solution brings about an increase in consumption by lowering competitive imports of iron and steel (6) and expanding them in chemical fertilizers (19), domestic production of which turns out to be inefficient. This makes profitable the fertilizer intensive process of foodgrains (15), with the elimination thereby of competitive imports in that sector altogether. This produces the import structure strictly according to the direct and indirect fixed capital requirements.

18. The disaggregated average annual sectoral growth rates as well as sectoral levels of induced fixed investment are presented in Tables B6.7 and B6.8 for interested readers. They do not bring out any important points of general interest and, hence, their discussion is skipped.

trade activities may be regarded as a structural change emerging at that particular level of net foreign capital inflow. We would thus be tracing successive structural adjustments in the two systems. The analysis is confined only to the aggregate level. The macroeconomic results for the two systems are presented in Tables B6.9 and B6.10 whereas the analysis of savings in the open-loop solutions appears in Table B6.11.

It is appropriate to start by tracing the nature of relationships between the aggregate target year variables like gross investment, personal consumption, and savings on the one hand and the aggregate GNP on the other. This provides an overall picture of the differences between the structural adjustments in the two systems. Figure 6.2 and 6.3 present the relevant curves for the two systems with the level of foreign assistance indicated at each point, and they illustrate the broad features that are discussed below.

The aggregate private consumption curve in the open-loop system is steeper than that for the closed-loop, for a given level of foreign capital inflow and also for a given level of GNP. This implies that foreign aid increases private consumption faster in the PTL than in the TSL variant. The PTL system, with the nonscarcity of domestic resources, reacts to additional foreign capital inflow by adding maximally to consumption more than to investment. The situation is reversed in the savings limited closed-loop system. This is clear from observing the aggregate gross investment curves in the two versions. The open-loop model produces a flatter gross investment curve than the closed-loop. In fact, the aggregate gross investment, being already at a

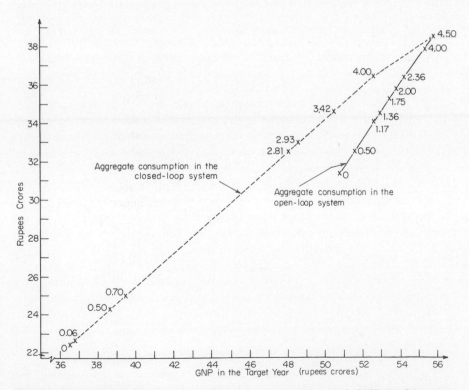

Figure 6.2 Relationship between aggregate consumption and GNP in the target year for variations in foreign assistance.

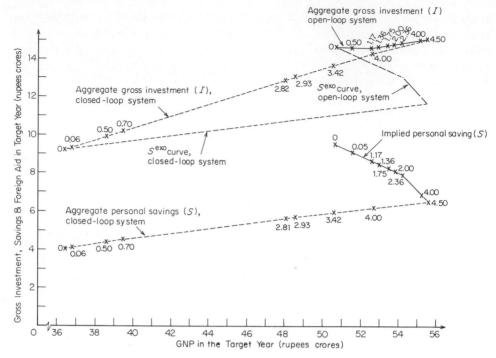

Figure 6.3 Relationship between gross investment, its financing elements, and GNP in the target year for variations in foreign assistance. Numbers at each point on the curve indicate foreign assistance in billion dollars. S^{exo} curve indicating fixed amount of exogenous savings is superimposed for convenience on personal savings curve for each system so that vertical distance between gross investment curve and S^{exo} curve represents level of foreign assistance at any given point.

high level in the absence of savings limitation in the open-loop system, declines slightly as foreign assistance is increased from zero to $1.17 billion and then slopes slightly upward.[19] In contrast to this, the savings supplementing character of foreign aid in a domestic-resource scarce closed-loop version gives a continually upward and steeper slope to the gross investment curve. The major factors behind this differential behavior of the gross investment curves may be spotted by investigating the financing elements of gross investment, namely, exogenous and personal savings and foreign assistance. Exogenous savings remain fixed between the two systems. In the savings limited closed-loop system, the additional foreign aid may be seen from Figure 6.3 to increase the absolute availability of personal savings and, hence, investment. On the other hand, a downward sloping, implied personal savings curve is indicated by the open-loop version. At the level of foreign aid amounting to $4.5 billion, the savings constraint becomes nonbinding at the GNP of Rs55,600 crores,[20] and thereafter the closed-loop system merges into the open-loop system. Before this point is reached, and most of the feasible ranges of foreign aid in practice would be in this

19. This virtual constancy of the aggregate gross investment in the open-loop system is due to the fact that post-terminal capital-stock is neither specified in the terminal conditions nor is it given any weight in the objective function. The system, therefore, does not discriminate between domestic capacity creation and imports in satisfying demand for any particular use within a given planning horizon. The absence of savings constraint is also a contributing factor.

20. This solution was found too late for inclusion in the tables in Appendix B.

region, our discussion has shown that the macroeconomic variables respond differently to variations in the foreign capital inflow in the two systems. This necessitates a detailed inquiry into the impact of foreign assistance on the two systems under investigation.

An additional dollar of foreign aid in the open-loop version breaks the trade bottleneck only and raises the aggregate growth rate by maximally contributing to the composite private consumption basket. As we go from one extreme with no foreign aid to the other extreme, the resources may be expected to be released from exports and the least profitable domestically produced importables and allocated to more profitable uses with a view to maximizing aggregate consumption. The previously unprofitable import processes, because of a very high scarcity value of foreign exchange at low levels of foreign assistance, enter the optimal structure as this scarcity is relaxed gradually with the expansion of foreign capital inflow. This would be reflected in a steady decline in the aggregate incremental capital-output ratio (ICOR). The confirmation of this phenomenon is available in Figure 6.6 for the open-loop model in a downward sloping curve of ICOR. The increasing availability of foreign resources also enables the economy to devote a continually declining proportion of GNP to gross investment while raising the aggregate growth rate (see Figures 6.4 and 6.5 for the open-loop solution).

We now turn to the solutions of the closed-loop model for the impact of foreign aid. A marginal dollar, by breaking the trade bottleneck, raises the disposable income and

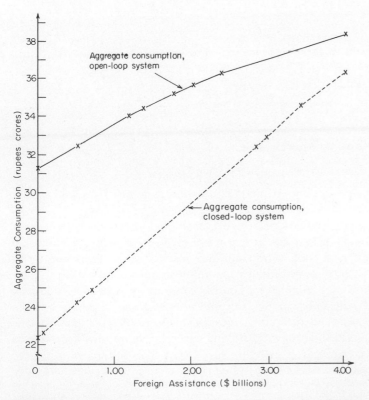

Figure 6.4 Aggregate consumption for varying levels of foreign assistance.

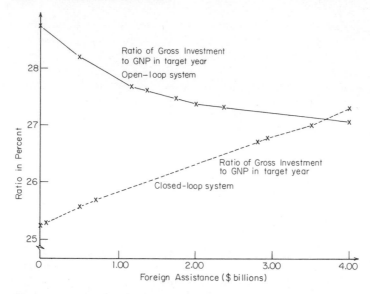

Figure 6.5   Ratio of gross investment to GNP in the target year for varying levels of foreign assistance in the two systems.

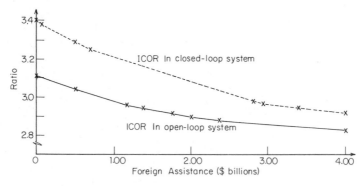

Figure 6.6   Aggregate incremental capital-output ratio (ICOR) for varying levels of foreign assistance in the two systems.

consequently the aggregate savings performance to finance the higher level gross investment. Simultaneously, it also acts as a supplement to the domestic savings and breaks the savings bottleneck itself. The combined interaction of these two forces results in an additional dollar contributing more than proportionately to the aggregate gross investment. (It may be noted for comparison that the additional domestic savings effort, by itself, adds only as much to gross investment as to savings because only the savings bottleneck is affected.) This multiplier effect of foreign assistance on gross investment is revealed in an upward sloping curve for the ratio of gross investment to GNP in the target year (see Figure 6.5, closed-loop solutions). Thus the dual effect of foreign aid in a closed-loop system of breaking the savings and trade bottlenecks simultaneously enables the economy to attain higher growth rates by devoting a higher proportion of GNP to the domestic capacity creation. This is in sharp contrast to the open-loop growth process, where this rate has been observed to be downward sloping; although it must be remembered that for the same amount of foreign assistance, the PTL process achieves a higher growth rate than the TSL version. As in the case of the open-loop model, the aggregate ICOR in the closed-loop model also exhibits an expected steadily declining tendency as foreign aid is expanded. From Figure 6.6 it is also clear that for a given level of foreign assistance, the aggregate ICOR in a closed-loop system remains consistently higher than that in the open-loop system. This is because in a closed-loop system, the capital intensive industries are also major savings contributing sectors by virtue of their relatively larger generation of nonwage income with an associated higher marginal savings propensity.[21] Thus the reduction in the aggregate growth rate that takes place because of the savings bottleneck results not only from a lower ratio of gross investment to GNP but also from changes in the output mix leading to an increase in the aggregate ICOR.

How do variations in foreign aid affect the other primary resource of domestic savings? By construction, this resource is nonscarce in the open-loop system. We have already seen in this case, from Figure 6.3, that the absolute availability of personal savings goes on declining with an expansion in foreign aid. It is, therefore, no surprise to find, in Figure 6.7, that the marginal and target year (personal) savings ratios for the open-loop variant exhibit a continuously downward sloping tendency. On the other hand, foreign aid has been shown to increase the absolute availability of personal savings in a closed-loop framework because it breaks the trade and the savings bottlenecks simultaneously. It is interesting to note that its relative burden in the form of an aggregate marginal (personal) savings ratio may be seen from Figure 6.7 to be gradually declining. This result follows from the fact that increasing foreign assistance enables a continuous reduction in the aggregate ICOR; and lower capital-intensity implies a larger generation of wage-income with an associated very low marginal savings propensity and, correspondingly, a smaller generation of non-wage income with an associated high marginal savings propensity. The net effect of this change in the output mix is reflected in a decline in the aggregate marginal (personal) savings ratio. A similar downward sloping movement, though in a much less pronounced form, may also be observed in the same figure for the target year (personal) savings ratio. Thus, twofold influences of foreign aid on personal savings in a closed-loop version may be detected. A given increase in foreign aid brings about an improvement in the absolute personal savings performance, but it raises the aggregate disposable income and private consumption more than proportionately so that the marginal (personal) savings-income ratio is steadily reduced. Secondly, it also makes possible a reduction in the target year (personal) savings ratio while enabling a gradual stepping up in the target year ratio of gross investment to GNP. This brings out explicitly the savings supplementing role of foreign assistance in all its aspects.

Comparison of the (personal) savings ratios between two systems indicates that the open-loop ratios remain consistently higher and decline faster than their closed-loop counterparts for expanding levels of foreign assistance. This implies that the conflict between the social and the individual preferences goes on narrowing with higher availabilities of foreign capital inflow.

Our analysis so far indicates that shapes of the curves for certain important macro-economic variables as well as key ratios in adjusting to varying levels of foreign

21. I am indebted to Kirit S. Parikh for suggesting this explanation.

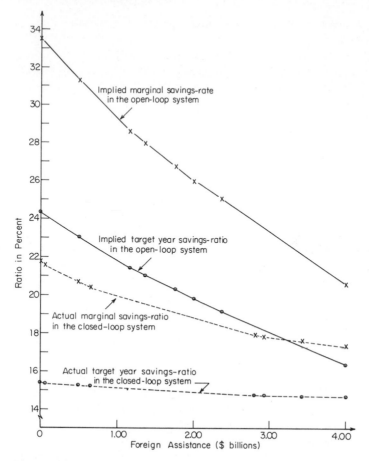

Figure 6.7

capital inflow differ very significantly. It is obvious, therefore, that the corresponding policy prescriptions for optimal adjustment to changes in foreign aid availability (because of uncertainty in aid prospects, and so on) would also change radically as between the two systems. Consequently, in the event of misspecification in representing a system, the resulting misallocation of resources due to wrong policies would be correspondingly great. This emphasizes the importance of correctly specifying a given situation as belonging to either of the two systems.

With this survey of the features of the adjustment mechanisms involved in the two growth systems, let us examine the marginal productivity of foreign assistance in each given by the numerical value of the slope of the aggregate consumption curve in Figure 6.4. As we have observed in the Section III, this is given by the shadow price (P_F) of the balance-of-trade constraint in the open-loop system and by the sum of P_F and the shadow price (P_S) of the savings constraint in the closed-loop framework. The figures are presented in Table 6.3 in the appropriate common intervals to facilitate the comparison of the relative impact of the same amount of foreign aid on the two systems. Note that for a given level of foreign aid, the marginal productivity of foreign assistance is higher in a closed-loop framework than in the open-loop solution (except at a high point of $4.5 billion when the closed-loop system

**Table 6.3. Marginal Productivities of Foreign Aid in Terms of
Aggregate Consumption**

Foreign aid interval ($ crores)	Open-loop model (rupees)	Closed-loop model (rupees)
0-5	3.1446	5.6565
6-135	3.1446	4.9302
136-174	2.9800	4.9302
175-235	2.5368	4.9302
236-280	2.0547	4.9302
281-292	2.0547	4.5657
293-341	2.0547	4.5429
342-399	2.0547	4.4033
400-449	1.7321	3.9655
450	1.6900	1.6900

merges into the open-loop variant). Moreover, it may be observed to decline faster
in the PTL system where foreign exchange is the only scarce primary factor than
in the TSL system in which two scarce resources—domestic and foreign—interact
in a complementary manner to bring about the final marginal effect of foreign
assistance.

V. Conclusions and Suggestions for Improvement

An attempt has been made to bring out the interaction between domestic and
foreign resources in the economic growth of an underdeveloped economy by suggesting an appropriate multisectoral closed-loop model for analysis and carrying out
some experiments with Indian data.

Most of the presently available models provide an upper limit to the aggregate
growth rate with foreign exchange as the only scarce factor. Domestic savings are
usually assumed to be optimally adjusted to the gross investment requirements. If,
however, they pose a binding constraint because of institutional and behavioral
limitations, the closed-loop model becomes relevant. The main impact of the savings
limitation is reflected in a downward adjustment in the aggregate growth rate. This
immediately indicates that if the target year growth rate is regarded as fixed, the
closed-loop system would reveal higher foreign aid requirements than the open-loop
variant.

In analyzing the effects of variations in net capital inflow, it is observed that a
marginal dollar releases only the trade bottleneck in the open-loop system, whereas
it directly and simultaneously breaks the savings and the trade bottlenecks in the
closed-loop system. This reveals a multiplier effect of foreign assistance on gross
investment in the closed-loop version and consequently results in higher marginal
productivity of foreign assistance than in the open-loop system.

The additional foreign aid with unchanged domestic savings specifications has
been shown to make possible for the closed-loop system, in addition to higher growth
rates, inter alia, (1) a higher level of aggregate personal savings; (2) a declining
marginal savings ratio; and (3) a downward sloping savings ratio in the target year
despite a rising target year ratio of gross investment to GNP. This reveals the savings
supplementing role of foreign assistance in all its aspects.

The two alternative systems considered in this study have been found to lead to two different sets of policy prescriptions in optimally adjusting to varying levels of foreign aid. The importance of a correct representation of an actual situation as belonging to either of the two systems is, therefore, obvious.

Conceptually, the single-period comparative static framework adopted in this study is restrictive in investigating the consequences of a given assumption about savings which involve intertemporal decisions in giving up immediate consumption in favour of higher future increments in the same. From this point of view, an explicitly dynamic framework is preferable. However, our result from a comparative static model about the greater effectiveness of foreign assistance in the presence of a savings constraint is general and not confined only to the particular framework adopted here. Of course, in a general dynamic framework, this result does not hold time-point by time-point[22] and there appears to be no plausible reason why it should. But this does not invalidate the generality of the result. In a dynamic model, it is necessary to assess the effect of a *given time-stream* of foreign assistance *as a whole*. The revelant criterion would be the evaluation of alternative time-streams of foreign assistance in terms of changes in the corresponding discounted present values of consumption over a given horizon under closed and open-loop versions. The result would hold under this criterion.

Finally, brief mention should be made of the areas in which this study requires further improvements. First, the treatment of the final consumption basket in a proportional form is obviously a drastic simplification of the real world, especially when incomes are undergoing structural changes. The introduction of Engel elasticities and variations around them along the lines of Bruno (1966; Chapter 8, this volume) would provide a better alternative.

Second, step demand functions for the major exporting sectors of plantations and jute textiles where India supplies a major share of the world market would be useful in assessing the costs and benefits of pushing up exports in these traditional sectors. A more detailed disaggregation of the exporting sectors would also be helpful.

Third, since the growth rate of the Indian economy is inextricably bound with the vicissitudes of agriculture, this sector needs more attention than is given in this study. The technological transformation of such a decentralized sector dependent upon the vagaries of the monsoons may be handled with incremental production processes along the lines of Sandee (1960), with appropriate bounds to incorporate the limitations imposed by institutional and time factors.

Fourth, the recent unprecedented droughts and their aftereffects have dislocated the process of economic development in India. In this situation a more recent base year would better reflect the possibilities for future growth.

Finally, there has been a mixture of pricing procedures in the data used for these experiments. It would be desirable to have all the information uniformly in market prices.

Despite all these limitations, however, it is hoped that the experiments have served the suggestive purpose of highlighting the structural differences between open-loop models and the closed-loop system developed in this paper. The closed-loop system is clearly the more relevant for economic planning when the central government

---

22. I am indebted to C. R. Blitzer of Stanford University for raising this point in a private communication and providing examples from the results of his model for Turkey in collaboration with H. Cetin and A. S. Manne.

does not have full control over the rate of saving but is obliged to operate within the framework of institutionally given savings constraints.[23]

Appendix A to Chapter 6
List of Sectors and List of Notation

Sectors

(1)   Construction, urban and industrial
(2)   Construction, rural
(3)   Electrical equipment
(4)   Transport equipment
(5)   Nonelectrical equipment
(6)   Iron and steel
(7)   Iron ore
(8)   Cement
(9)   Other metals
(10) Other minerals
(11) Plantations
(12) Leather and leather products
(13) Animal husbandry
(14) Food industries
(15) Foodgrains
(16) Cotton and other textiles
(17) Jute textiles
(18) Other agriculture
(19) Chemical fertilizers
(20) Glass, wooden, and nonmetallic mineral products
(21) Forestry products
(22) Motor transport
(23) Petroleum products
(24) Crude oil
(25) Rubber products
(26) Plantation rubber
(27) Chemicals
(28) Railway transport
(29) Electricity
(30) Coal
(31) Housing (residential)
(32) Others

Notation to Tables

1. C optimal level of consumption in target year (rupees crores)
2. I level of total gross investment in target year (rupees crores)

23. For an analysis of the same kind of problem within the context of an aggregate model, see Marglin (1967) and Sen (1960).

3. ΔI incremental gross investment over the base year (rupees crores)
4. I_I level of induced fixed investment in the target year (rupees crores) obtained by subtracting inventory and exogenous investment from total gross investment
5. S personal savings in target year (rupees crores)
6. ΔS incremental personal savings over the base year (rupees crores)
7. V level of GNP in target year (rupees crores)
8. ΔV incremental GNP over the base year (rupees crores)
9. W level of disposable income in target year ($= C + S$) (rupees crores)
10. ΔW incremental disposable income over the base year (rupees crores)
11. T level of transfer payments in target year (rupees crores) obtained as an excess of wage plus nonwage income over the disposable income
12. I/V ratio of (2) to (7) in percent
13. $\Delta K/\Delta V$ aggregate incremental capital-output ratio
14. S/W ratio of (5) to (9) in percent
15. $\Delta S/\Delta W$ ratio of (6) to (10) in percent
16. S/I ratio of (5) to (3) in percent
17. $\Delta S/\Delta I$ ratio of (6) to (3) in percent
18. I_I/I ratio of (4) to (2) in percent
19. P_F shadow price of foreign exchange (rupees per dollar)
20. P_S shadow price of savings constraint (rupees)
21. γ_1 annual rate of growth of consumption, in percent
22. γ_2 annual rate of growth of GNP in percent
23. F level of maximum permissible import surplus ($ crores)
24. F/V ratio of (23) to (7) in percent
25. F/I ratio of (23) to (2) in percent

Appendix B to Chapter 6
Detailed Tables Giving Empirical Results

Table B6.1. Aggregate Exogenous Variables and Initial Conditions (rupees crores)

	1960-61	1975-76
Government expenditures	1,380	4,900
Government savings	135	3,540
Corporate savings	90	500
Foreign aid	520	381
Depreciation allowances	460	1,090
Aggregate private consumption	12,604	
Aggregate gross national product	15,700	
Aggregate gross investment	2,232	
Aggregate wage income	10,769	
Aggregate nonwage income	2,863	

Sources: Manne and Rudra (1965); Srinivasan, Saluja, and Sabherwal (1965); Perspective Planning Division (1964); Perspective Planning Division (1966).

Table B6.2. Private Consumption Expenditure

Sector	Expenditure elasticity[a]	Proportional basket[b]
(3)	2.5000	0.0036
(4)	2.7520	0.0048
(5)	3.0000	0.0146
(11)	1.2558	0.0063
(12)	2.4000	0.0110
(13)	0.8000	0.0787
(14)	1.0799	0.0791
(15)	0.6148	0.2458
(16)	1.3076	0.0612
(18)	0.9546	0.0597
(20)	2.0000	0.0066
(22)	1.2000	0.0082
(23)	1.6808	0.0078
(25)	2.4000	0.0046
(27)	1.6729	0.0172
(28)	1.2000	0.0075
(29)	2.2000	0.0012
(30)	1.5000	0.0006
(31)	1.0000	0.0452
(32)	1.1132	0.3363

[a] Engel Elasticities are taken from Perspective Planning Division (1966).
[b] The proportional basket is derived on the basis of the annual rate of growth of consumption of 3.8 percent over 1960-61.

Table B6.3. Floor and Ceiling Limits on Exports, 1975-76

Sector	Floor	Ceiling[a]
(3)		58
(4)		28
(5)		158
(7)	15	38
(8)		8
(11)	200	276
(12)		55
(13)		49
(14)		228
(16)	80	120
(17)	175	274
(18)		137
(20)		13
(21)		36
(30)		1

[a] Ceiling limits 1975-76 are derived from Srinivasan, Saluja, and Sabherwal (1965) with appropriate adjustments for the postdevaluation change in the nominal exchange rate.

Table B6.4. Import Ceilings

Sector	1975-76
Proportional form (specified as a maximum percentage of total supply in a sector)	
(6)	0.15
(15)	0.05
(19)	0.15
(23)	0.10
(25)	0.05
(27)	0.10
Absolute ceilings (rupees crores)	
(24)	240.0
(26)	40.0

Table B6.5. Basic Reference Solutions: Macroeconomic Results
(rupees crores in 1959-60 prices unless otherwise mentioned)

	15-Year horizon	
	Open-loop model	Closed-loop model
C	32,485	24,259
I	14,593	9,886
ΔI	12,360	7,654
I_I	9,821	5,654
S		4,375
ΔS		3,348
V	51,603	38,670
ΔV	35,803	22,870
W	39,355	28,633
ΔW	25,723	16,149
T	- 2,168	213
$I/V(\%)$	27.67	25.57
$\Delta K/\Delta V$	3.0466	3.3770
$S/W(\%)$		15.28
$\Delta S/\Delta W(\%)$		20.73
$S/I(\%)$		44.25
$\Delta S/\Delta I(\%)$		43.74
$I_I/I(\%)$	67.09	56.89
P_F	23.6440	9.9828
P_S		3.6025
$\gamma_1(\%\text{ p.a.})$	6.50	4.50
$\gamma_2(\%\text{ p.a.})$	8.20	6.15
F	50.00	50.00
$F/V(\%)$	0.73	0.97
$F/I(\%)$	2.57	3.79

Table B6.6. Reference Solutions, Primal: Sectoral Gross Outputs, Consumption, Investment, and Import-Export Levels; 15-Year Horizon (rupees crores in 1959-60 prices)

| Sector | Gross output levels | | Import (M) and export (E) levels | | | | 15-year horizon | |
| | Open-loop model | Closed-loop model | Open-loop model | | Closed-loop model | | Open-loop model | Closed-loop model |
			M	E	M	E		
(1)	7,789	5,441						
(2)	1,347	942						
(3)	1,333	917		58		58		
(4)	1,370	1,340	409			28		
(5)	4,403	3,021		158		158		
(6)	3,288	1,918			339			
(7)	103	53		38		15		
(8)	369	252		8				
(9)	594	32	332		488			
(10)	322	149						
(11)	504	450		276		276		
(12)	592	461		55		55		
(13)	2,889	2,178		49		49		
(14)	3,582	2,829		228		228		
(15)	10,347	7,446						
(16)	2,322	1,779		120	242	120		
(17)	420	364		214		214		
(18)	6,144	4,788		137	85	137		
(19)	769	483						
(20)	2,355	1,666		13		13		
(21)	1,023	756		36		36		
(22)	2,523	1,738						
(23)	1,707	1,378	190					
(24)	80	80	240		179			
(25)	356	287	19					
(26)	51	51	40		23			
(27)	1,724	1,252						

Table B6.6. (*continued*)

| | Gross output levels | | Import (M) and export (E) levels | | | | 15-year horizon | |
| | Open-loop model | Closed-loop model | Open-loop model | | Closed-loop model | | Open-loop model | Closed-loop model |
			M	E	M	E		
(28)	2,268	1,564						
(29)	1,094	681						
(30)	582	380		1				
(31)	1,468	1,096						
(32)	17,868	14,184						
Optimal consumption							32,485	24,259
Induced investment levels								
Sector (1)							4,613	2,551
(2)							873	500
(3)							830	490
(4)							1,014	616
(5)							2,490	1,467
Inventory investment							1,888	1,378

Table B6.7. Basic Reference Solutions: Annual Rates of Growth of
Sectoral Gross Output Levels, Consumption, and GNP;
15-Year Planning Horizon

	Open-loop model	Closed-loop model
Sector		
(1)	13.3	10.7
(2)	8.1	5.6
(3)	17.0	14.0
(4)	13.6	13.5
(5)	18.5	15.6
(6)	18.2	14.1
(7)	18.6	13.4
(8)	13.8	11.0
(9)	17.7	0
(10)	14.0	8.3
(11)	6.5	5.7
(12)	7.9	6.1
(13)	6.5	4.5
(14)	6.9	5.3
(15)	6.6	4.3
(16)	7.4	5.5
(17)	7.9	7.1
(18)	7.4	5.7
(19)	27.1	21.7
(20)	12.6	9.9
(21)	12.3	9.9
(22)	14.6	11.8
(23)	14.1	12.5
(25)	15.4	10.1
(27)	12.8	10.4
(28)	11.3	8.6
(29)	17.1	13.4
(30)	11.8	8.7
(31)	5.1	3.0
(32)	5.2	3.6
Consumption	6.50	4.50
GNP	8.20	6.15

Table B6.8. Reference Solutions: Sectoral Induced Fixed Investment[a] Levels; 15-Year Horizon (rupees crores in 1959-60 prices)

Sector	Induced investment open-loop model (A)	Percentage distribution of (A) (B)	Induced investment open-loop model (C)	Percentage distribution of (C) (D)	(C) as percent of (A) (E)
(1)	922	1.43	594	1.56	64.43
(2)					
(3)	785	1.22	514	1.35	65.48
(4)	818	1.27	797	2.09	97.43
(5)	4,059	6.30	2,677	6.91	65.95
(6)	4,076	6.33	2,226	5.84	54.61
(7)	314	0.50	149	0.39	47.45
(8)	727	1.13	458	1.20	63.00
(9)	1,686	2.62			0
(10)	457	0.72	172	0.45	37.64
(11)	277	0.44	229	0.60	82.67
(12)	141	0.23	95	0.25	67.38
(13)	2,639	4.10	1,572	4.12	59.57
(14)	858	1.33	572	1.50	66.67
(15)	9,560	14.85	5,208	13.67	54.48
(16)	1,111	1.73	715	1.88	64.36
(17)	183	0.28	147	0.39	80.33
(18)	6,071	9.43	4,037	10.59	66.50
(19)	1,122	1.74	693	1.82	61.76
(20)	1,272	1.98	824	2.16	64.78
(21)	1,236	1.92	864	2.27	69.90
(22)	3,297	5.12	2,120	5.56	64.30

Table B6.8 (*continued*)

Sector	Induced investment open-loop model (A)	Percentage distribution of (A) (B)	Induced investment open-loop model (C)	Percentage distribution of (C) (D)	(C) as percent of (A) (E)
(23)	735	1.14	571	1.50	77.68
(24)	529	0.82	529	1.39	100.00
(25)	144	0.23	110	0.29	76.39
(26)	94	0.15	94	0.25	100.00
(27)	1,498	2.33	1,007	2.64	67.22
(28)	4,172	6.48	2,553	6.70	61.19
(29)	6,075	9.43	3,543	9.30	58.32
(30)	946	1.47	542	1.42	57.29
(31)	7,680	11.93	3,960	10.39	51.56
(32)	867	1.35	532	1.40	93.83
Total	64,351	100	38,104	100	59.21

[a] Induced fixed investment in each sector is derived by multiplying sectoral incremental gross capital-output ratio by the corresponding incremental gross output over the base year level.

Table B6.9. **Parametric Programming with Foreign Aid on 15-Year Horizon, Open-Loop Model, Macroeconomic Results (rupees crores in 1959–60 prices)**

	F ($ crores)							
	0	50	117	136	175	200	236	400
C	31,303	32,485	34,085	34,486	35,239	35,715	36,308	38,438
I	14,604	14,593	14,579	14,636	14,698	14,736	14,818	14,957
ΔI	12,372	12,360	12,345	12,404	12,466	12,504	12,585	12,725
I_I	9,851	9,821	9,781	9,833	9,881	9,910	9,983	10,128
V	50,807	51,603	52,686	53,022	53,524	53,851	54,256	55,295
ΔV	35,007	35,803	36,886	37,202	37,724	38,051	38,456	39,495
I/V (%)	28.74	28.27	27.67	27.60	27.46	27.36	27.31	27.04
$\Delta K/\Delta V$	3.1173	3.0466	2.9554	2.9413	2.9126	2.8950	2.8797	2.8286
I_I/I (%)	67.45	67.30	67.09	67.18	67.23	67.25	67.37	67.71
P_F	23.6440	23.6440	23.6440	22.4064	19.0740	19.0740	15.4495	13.0239
γ_1 (% p.a.)	6.3	6.5	6.9	7.0	7.1	7.2	7.3	7.7
γ_2 (% p.a.)	8.1	8.2	8.4	8.4	8.5	8.5	8.6	8.7
F/V (%)		0.73	1.67	1.92	2.45	2.79	3.26	5.43
F/I (%)		2.57	6.02	6.97	8.93	10.18	11.95	20.06 -

Table B6.10. Parametric Programming with Foreign Aid on 15-Year Horizon, Closed-Loop Model, Macroeconomic Results (rupees crores in 1959-60 prices)

	F ($ crores)							
	0	6	50	70	281	293	342	400
C	22,387	22,623	24,259	24,986	32,463	32,902	34,595	36,388
I	9,215	9,268	9,886	10,151	12,846	13,010	13,649	14,382
ΔI	6,983	7,056	7,654	7,913	10,614	10,778	11,417	12,150
I_I	5,028	5,091	5,624	5,860	8,242	8,387	8,955	9,603
S	4,079	4,109	4,375	4,493	5,606	5,677	5,946	6,246
ΔS	3,052	3,082	3,348	3,466	4,579	4,650	4,918	5,219
V	36,502	36,768	38,670	39,512	48,101	48,614	50,579	52,670
ΔV	20,702	20,968	22,870	23,712	32,301	32,814	34,779	36,870
W	26,467	26,732	28,633	29,478	38,068	38,577	40,544	42,636
Δw	13,983	14,248	16,149	16,994	25,584	26,093	28,060	30,151
T	758	691	213	0				
$I/V(\%)$	25.25	25.26	25.57	25.69	26.70	26.76	26.98	27.30
$\Delta K/\Delta V$	3.4030	3.3770	3.2913	3.2547	2.9893	2.9786	2.9423	2.9184
$S/W(\%)$	15.41	15.37	15.28	15.24	14.73	14.73	14.67	14.65
$\Delta S/\Delta w(\%)$	21.83	21.63	20.73	20.40	17.90	17.82	17.53	17.31
$S/I(\%)$	44.26	44.23	44.25	44.26	43.69	43.64	43.56	43.43
$\Delta S/\Delta I(\%)$	43.66	43.67	43.74	43.80	43.14	43.14	43.08	42.95
$I_I/I(\%)$	54.56	54.81	56.89	57.73	64.16	64.47	65.60	66.77
P_F	17.2567	9.9828	9.9828	9.9828	8.6377	8.6377	8.6840	8.7256
P_S	3.3614	3.6025	3.6025	3.6025	3.4169	3.3941	3.2484	2.8050
γ_1 (% p.a.)	3.9	4.0	4.5	4.7	6.5	6.6	7.0	7.4
γ_2 (% p.a.)	5.8	5.8	6.2	6.3	7.8	7.8	8.1	8.4
$F/V(\%)$		0.12	0.97	1.33	4.38	4.52	5.07	5.70
$F/I(\%)$		0.48	3.79	5.17	16.41	19.50	18.79	20.86

Table B6.11. Analysis of Implied Personal Savings on the Open-Loop System (rupees crores in 1959-60 prices)

	F ($ crores)							
	0	50	117	136	175	200	236	400
W	38,822	39,355	40,076	40,291	40,660	40,894	41,172	41,890
ΔW	25,190	25,723	26,444	26,659	27,028	27,262	27,540	28,258
I	14,604	14,593	14,579	14,636	14,698	14,736	14,818	14,957
S^{exo}	5,130	5,505	6,008	6,150	6,443	6,630	6,900	8,130
S_i	9,474	9,088	8,571	8,486	8,255	8,106	7,918	6,827
ΔS_i	8,447	8,061	7,544	7,459	7,228	7,079	6,891	5,800
$S_i/W(\%)$	24.40	23.09	21.38	21.06	20.30	19.82	19.23	16.29
$\Delta S_i/\Delta W(\%)$	33.53	31.33	28.52	27.97	26.74	25.96	25.02	20.52
$S_i/I(\%)$	64.87	62.27	58.82	57.98	56.16	55.00	53.43	45.64
$\Delta S_i/\Delta I(\%)$	68.27	65.21	61.10	60.13	57.98	56.61	54.75	45.57

NOTATION: $S^{exo} = \bar{S}_g + \bar{S}_c + \gamma \bar{F}_c + \bar{D}$; $S_i = I - S^{exo}$; W = aggregate wage plus nonwage income; ΔW and ΔS_i are increments with respect to the base year actual values.

7 Problems of Interregional and Intersectoral Allocation: The Case of Pakistan*

Arthur MacEwan

I. The Regional Problem

Many countries have "regional problems." Income and political power are allocated unequally among regions with no significant change over time, and these inequities are a source of political tension. The regional problem in Pakistan is especially severe because the peculiar geographic nature of Pakistan makes the issue so visible.[1]

Economic planners in Pakistan and other poor countries are often assigned the task of designing programs to bring about income parity among regions. In doing so, planners confront several analytic and technical problems. The principal difficulty is how to allocate resources in order to conform best to political preferences of policy-makers. In this context it is desirable to discover and exploit the comparative advantages of the regions. Regional comparative advantages, in turn, are dependent upon the regional distribution of resources and upon political preferences as to the regional allocation of welfare.

In this study a multisectoral regional linear programming planning model is used to investigate various aspects of Pakistan's "regional problem." First, the model will serve to illustrate the dependence of the average productivity of a region upon the structure of demand in that region. Usually one conceives of productivity as being a function of primarily supply conditions. When trade limitations exist, however, the composition of supply and hence the average productivity are also dependent upon the structure of demand.

Second, the model will aid in an examination of the dependence of regional comparative advantage on political preferences regarding the regional allocation of welfare. The decision to favor the development of one region necessarily implies a

* Reprinted from *Pakistan Development Review*, Spring 1970. The author is Assistant Professor of Economics at Harvard University and former Research Associate at the Pakistan Institute of Development Economics (PIDE). Research for this study was begun at PIDE and completed at the Harvard Economic Research Project and the Project for Quantitative Research in Economic Development, Harvard University. Portions of this research were supported by the Project for Quantitative Research in Economic Development through funds provided by the Agency for International Development under Contract CSD-1543. The views expressed in this do not, however, necessarily reflect the views of AID. The author is grateful to Dr. A. R. Khan and Professors H. B. Chenery and W. W. Leontief for advice along the way.

1. Pakistan is unique in its regional division into two districts sharing population on a 55:45 basis and separated from one another by 1000 miles of foreign territory (for trade purposes the relevant distance is the 3000 miles that separate the major ports of the two regions).

shift of resources to that region and away from the other. The change in resource availabilities in the two regions affects relative prices and hence affects comparative advantage in each region.

Third, the model will be used to isolate the economic factors which are most important in determining relative regional advantages. It will be seen that regional differences in the ability to generate resources that can be transferred between the regions do not seriously affect regional comparative advantages. However, regional comparative advantages can be affected either by changes in national resource availabilities—for example, the increase of capital availability relative to foreign exchange availability—or by regional differences in the ability to generate non-transferable resources.

Before a full discussion of these aspects of regional planning can be undertaken, it is first necessary to lay out the model. In Section II, following a brief discussion of the assumptions and principles of design behind the model, the basic equations are laid out. Section III discusses the analytic results obtained from various solutions to the problem embodied in the model. In Section IV the general conclusions are summarized.

II. The Regional Planning Model[2]

The planning problem for Pakistan examined here may be stated as follows: Find a resource allocation program—among sectors and between regions—for the period 1964–65 to 1974–75. The program should lead the economy to the highest feasible consumption path by the latter date. The program is constrained by the shortages of investment funds and foreign exchange earning possibility and by limited agricultural growth possibilities.[3]

Before laying out the equations which define the linear programming problem, it will be useful to state some of the features of the model.

1. The model is regional. Production processes and demand in the two regions of Pakistan are considered separately, while tied together by tariff-free trade, a common supply of certain resources, and a common central planning authority. (All parameter values have been estimated separately for the two regions.)

2. The model is a multisectoral or an input-output type of model. That is, explicit account is taken of the deliveries of goods and services between producing sectors as well as to final demand categories.[4] The technical coefficients embody an attempt to estimate important technical change. Sector Classifications follow.

(1) *Rice* * growing and processing
(2) *Wheat* growing and processing
(3) *Jute* growing and baling
(4) *Cotton* growing and ginning
(5) *Tea* growing and processing

(6) All *other agriculture*, forestry and fishery
(7) *Sugar* refining
(8) *Edible oils*
(9) *Tobacco* products

2. For a more complete description of the model and its uses, see MacEwan (1971). There the reader will also find the complete set of parameter values and exogenous variable values.

3. Labor is assumed to be in surplus. Skilled labor is taken into account only indirectly: export limitations, noncompetitive import requirements, and agricultural growth limitations are, at least in part, based on consideration of skilled labor shortages (see MacEwan 1971).

4. The general input-output framework is Leontief's dynamic model.

* Abbreviated names will usually be used, indicated by italics.

(10) *Other food* and drink	(24) *Wood, cork, and furniture*
(11) *Cotton textiles*	(25) *Construction* of residential *houses*
(12) *Jute textiles*	(26) *Construction* of nonresidential *build-*
(13) *Other textiles*	*ings*
(14) *Paper* and printing	(27) All *other constructions*
(15) *Leather* and leather products	(28) *Miscellaneous manufacture*
(16) *Rubber* and rubber products	(29) *Coal and petroleum* products
(17) *Fertilizer*	(30) *Electricity and gas*
(18) *Other chemicals*	(31) *Transport*
(19) *Cement*, concrete, and bricks	(32) *Trade*
(20) *Basic metals*	(33) Ownership of dwellings (*housing*)
(21) *Metal products*	(34) *Government* †
(22) *Machinery*	(35) *Services*, n.e.s.
(23) *Transport equipment*	

† That is, public administration and defense.

3. Special attention has been given to technical change in the agricultural sectors, especially in foodgrains. The large foodgrain production program being undertaken in Pakistan should substantially reduce the cost of producing rice and wheat. The cost of rice and wheat will be shown to have a substantial effect upon regional issues (see MacEwan 1971: Chap. 6).

4. The model is comparative static. That is, variables are defined as changes taking place between 1964–65—the base year of Pakistan's Third Five-Year Plan—and 1974–75—the terminal year of Pakistan's Fourth Five-Year Plan. The solution of the model problem, therefore, yields a comparison of 1974–75 with 1964–65, but it does not reveal anything about the time pattern of change between those years.

5. The explicit choice variables of the linear programming problem are plan period increments to: (1) the level of consumption in each region; (2) the quantity of capital flowing between the regions; (3) and the source of supply of each commodity—that is, production in East Pakistan, production in West Pakistan, or importing from abroad.[5]

Algebraic Statement of the Problem

In algebraic terms the skeleton structure of the problem may be stated as follows:

$$\textit{Maximize} \qquad\qquad W = \delta^e \omega^e C^e + \delta^w \omega^w C^w \qquad\qquad (7.1)$$

subject to

A. Supply and demand balances

for goods and services, for each region

$$x_i + m_i + r_i^1 = c_i + \sum_j x_{ij} + \sum_j h_{ij} + \text{rep}_i + w_i + e_i + r_i^2 + \text{gov}_i \qquad (7.2)$$

for foreign exchange, for each region

$$\sum_i p_i e_i + \sum_i p_i' r_i^2 + f = \sum_i q_i m_i + \sum_i q_i' r_i^1 \qquad (7.3)$$

5. It should be evident that the problem can be viewed as a three-country trade problem and is analogous to many custom-union type problems.

for capital, for each region

$$S + f + \sum_i \text{tar}_i = \sum_i \sum_j h_{ij} + \sum_i w_i + \sum_i \text{rep}_i + \sum_i \text{gov}_i \qquad (7.4)$$

overall supply of funds, for the nation

$$f^e + f^w = F \qquad (7.5)$$

B. Export limits, for each region

$$p_i e_i \leq \bar{e}_i \qquad (7.6)$$

$$\sum_i p_i e_i \leq \bar{E} \qquad (7.7)$$

where

$$\bar{E} < \sum_i \bar{e}_i \qquad (7.8)$$

C. Savings limits, for each region

$$S = \sum_{i=1}^{6} s_1 v_i + \sum_{i=7}^{35} s_2 v_i \qquad (7.9)$$

$$v_i = \nu_i x_i \qquad (7.10)$$

where

$$\nu_i = 1 - \sum_j a_{ji} \qquad (7.11)$$

D. Availability of foreign funds, for the nation

$$F = \bar{F} \qquad (7.12)$$

E. Agricultural growth limits, for each region

$$x_i \leq x_1^*[(1.05)^{10} - 1] \qquad (7.13)$$

for i, a nonfoodgrain agricultural sector.

The variables and parameters specified separately for each region are defined as follows:

Endogenous Variables in Increments Over 1964–65

C^e, C^w per capita consumption in East Pakistan and West Pakistan, respectively

x_i regional gross output of sector i

m_i imports to the region from abroad of goods classified under sector i

r_i^1 imports to the region from the other region of goods classified under sector i

c_i regional consumption of the products of sector i

x_{ij} current deliveries to sector j of goods classified under sector i

h_{ij} net fixed capital deliveries to sector j of goods classified under sector i

rep_i deliveries of goods classified under sector i for replacement investment

w_i working capital deliveries of goods classified under sector i

e_i exports of goods of sector i from the region to abroad

r^2 exports of goods of sector i from the region to the other region

gov_i government public administration and defense expenditure on the products of the ith sector (zero except for $i = 34$)

f net regional inflow of funds

S aggregate regional savings

tar_i total tariff earned on imports of goods classified under sector i

F net inflow of funds to the nation from abroad

v_i value added in sector i

Predetermined Base Year Variables and Exogenous Variables

$\bar{e}_i$ upper limit on the increment to foreign exchange earned from the increment to exports abroad of type i

$\bar{E}_i$ upper limit on the increment to foreign exchange earned from total increment to exports abroad

$\bar{F}$ exogenously specified increment over the plan to net inflow of funds to other nations from abroad

x_i^* peak output attained up to 1964–65 in nonfoodgrain agricultural sectors

Parameters

δ^e, δ^w weights, representing the political valuation of increments to consumption in East Pakistan and West Pakistan, respectively

ω^e, ω^w population shares of East Pakistan and West Pakistan

p_i f.o.b. price of foreign exports of type i

p_i' f.o.b. price of regional exports of type i

q_i c.i.f. price of foreign imports of type i

q_i' c.i.f. price of regional imports of type i

v_i ratio of value added to output in sector i

s_1, s_2 marginal savings rates for agricultural and nonagricultural sectors, respectively

Welfare Function

The welfare function consists of the maximization of the weighted sum of 1964–65 to 1974–75 increments to regional per capita consumption. The weights are population shares (ω^e, ω^w) and political valuations (δ^e, δ^w). When political valuations are taken as unity for both regions, that is, $\delta^e = \delta^w = 1$, this is equivalent to maximization of the increment to total national consumption. Because of the manner in which the economy is constrained to continue growing, maximization of this welfare function puts the economy on the highest feasible consumption growth path. The structure of consumption is determined by a linear relationship between consumption of each type in a region and aggregate consumption in the region.

Supply and Demand Balance for Goods and Services

The supply and demand balance for goods and services states that demand for each commodity in each region cannot exceed supply in each region. The supply variables (all in increments)—production (x_i), foreign import (m_i), and regional import (r_i^1)—are explicit choice variables.[6] Consumption demand (c_i), as stated in the previous paragraph, is linearly related to aggregate consumption in the region. Intermediate deliveries on current account (x_{ij}) are proportionally related to output. Net fixed capital deliveries (h_{ij}) and working capital deliveries (w_i) are linearly related to output increments in the receiving sectors by using the stock-flow con-

---

6. Some imports, foreign and regional, are taken as noncompetitive and proportionally related to output increment in certain sectors.

version factor technique.[7] Replacement (rep_i) and government consumption expenditure (gov_i) are determined exogenously. Foreign exports (e_i) and regional exports (r_i^2) are explicit choice variables, the latter being regional imports of the other region.

Supply and Demand Balances for Foreign Exchange and Capital

The supply and demand balances for foreign exchange and for capital are accounting identities. It should be noted that tariffs are included as a source of capital, and government consumption expenditures are included as a demand for capital. These terms are included because, from the point of view of the central planner trying to determine how to raise a surplus and decide how to allocate it, these terms need to enter into the savings-investment relationship.

Overall Supply of Funds

The overall supply of funds specifies that foreign funds (F), which are exogenously specified ($\bar{F}$), can be allocated in any manner between the regions. In particular, the region can have capital outflows as well as capital inflows; that is, f^e and f^w can take on negative values.[8]

Export Limits

The export limits or foreign exchange earning limits are specified so as to allow some choice in the specification of an export program. It is assumed that the limits to exporting are primarily marketing problems, and to a certain degree marketing "effort and ability" may be shifted among sectors.

Savings Limit

The savings limit specifies saving in each sector as proportional to value added in that sector—at base year prices. Separate savings rates are specified for agriculture and nonagriculture, but no distinction is made between profits and wage income. Savings includes all forms of savings out of domestic income, whether "voluntary" or "forced" by one or another forms of fiscal or monetary policy (including taxation).

Agricultural Growth Limits

The agricultural growth limits are based on the reasoning that there are "institutional" limits—the structure of human capital and the social relations of peasant agriculture, for example—which inhibit the expansion of agricultural output. Although ideally such limits should be specified by rising costs, for nonfoodgrain agricultural sectors an absolute upper limit has been placed on the average growth rate of output over the 10-year planning period, namely, 5 percent per annum based on projections for the Third Five-Year Plan. While these limits play an important

7. The stock-flow conversion factor technique is explained by Manne (1963, 1966). Briefly, an assumption is made about the growth rate for the plan period. Further, it is assumed that the growth rate is constant over the period. These assumptions make it possible to determine the ratio between investment in the terminal year and the stock of investment accumulated over the plan period. This ratio is the stock-flow conversion factor. Output in the terminal period is related to the stock and, using the conversion factor, output is directly related to the flow of investment. The stock-flow conversion factor technique is one way of dealing with the so-called terminal conditions problem in planning models. It is this technique, referred to above, which puts the economy on the highest consumption path and provides for future growth. Working capital is treated in the same manner as fixed capital. Working capital deliveries, however, go not only to producing sectors but also to final demand categories.

8. The nonnegativity constraints of linear programming provide no obstacle in this respect. Extra variables, the negatives of f^e and f^w, can be included.

role in some cases, they represent a relatively optimistic appraisal of the situation. In foodgrain sectors, rising cost functions have been used. But for purposes of this essay, it is sufficient to note that overall costs of foodgrain production should be substantially reduced, as compared to the base year, by the new foodgrain program.

The first step in investigating the regional problem is to obtain a solution based upon a "best guess" at the values of behavioral and structural parameters and upon the assumption of political neutrality with regard to the regional origin of increments to national per capita consumption (that is, the δ's in equation 7.1 both have the value of unity). This original solution will be referred to as the basic solution. Table 7.1

Table 7.1. Key Parameters of the Basic Solution

	East Pakistan	West Pakistan	All Pakistan
Political valuation of consumption increments (δ)	1.0	1.0	
Marginal savings rate agricultural sectors (s_1)	0.14	0.14	
Nonagricultural sectors (s_2)	0.24	0.24	
Export growth rate	7.5(percent)	7.5(percent)	
Increment to foreign funds inflow (F)			0

presents the most important aggregate parameters upon which the basic solution is obtained. These include the δ's, the savings rates, the export growth rates, and the increment to foreign funds inflow.

A single solution to the model yields the value of the increment to per capita consumption in each region, an incremental production-trade program for each region, and the value of the interregional flow of resources. Thus associated with any regional consumption program there is a production-trade program, that is, a comparative advantage program. It is by varying the principal assumptions about the economy and about political preferences that alternative solutions may be obtained and compared.

III. Economic and Political Determinants of Regional Allocation

Disparity and Regional Productivity

The basic solution serves two functions in addition to providing a best guess at an overall resource allocation plan. First, it serves as a reference point. By comparing alternative solutions to the model with the basic solution, an analysis of interregional and intersectoral allocation can be developed. Second, a direct examination of the basic solution reveals information about the relationship between regional productivity and the structure of demand. This latter issue is dealt with first.

In Table 7.2 the main macrovariables of the basic solution are presented: per capita consumption, per capita income, population, the incremental aggregate savings ratio, the incremental gross and net capital-output ratios, and the average annual rate of growth. In the table the values of the macrovariables are also shown

Table 7.2. **Macrovariables of the Basic Solution**

	Per capita private consumption (rupees)	Per capita income (rupees)	Population (millions)	Incremental gross aggregate domestic savings rate[a]	Incremental capital-income ratio net/gross	Average annual rate of growth of GNP
Basic solution increment						
East Pakistan	144.9	197.3	21.5	22.3	2.17/2.66	7.5
West Pakistan	146.4	203.5	15.9	22.3	2.54/3.63	6.0
All Pakistan	144.4[b]	198.6	37.4	22.3	2.35/3.13	6.7
Base year 1964-65						
East Pakistan	309.5	377.1	60.5	14.8		
West Pakistan	423.1	547.9	51.7	16.9		
All Pakistan	361.8	455.8	112.2	16.0		
Terminal year 1974-75						
East Pakistan	454.0	574.2	82.0	18.7		
West Pakistan	569.5	751.4	67.6	19.3		
All Pakistan	506.2	654.4	149.6	18.9		
Plan assumption for 1975						
East Pakistan	n.a.[c]	565.9[d]	81.1	n.a.	n.a./n.a.	7.7[e]
West Pakistan	n.a.	662.1[d]	66.3	n.a.	n.a./n.a.	6.2[e]
All Pakistan	n.a.	609.3[d]	147.4	23.5[e]	n.a./2.90	7.0

Source: Plan Assumptions for 1975 are from Pakistan Planning Commission (1965). Population estimates for the model computations are from a study by the Demographic Section of the Pakistan Institute for Development Economics (1967). All other entries can be derived from these and Table 7.1.

[a] These are average rates for the base and the terminal years. Savings include government savings.

[b] That the increment to national per capita consumption is less than either of the regional increments is due to the faster rate of population growth in East Pakistan.

[c] Not allowed.

[d] The Plan document gives per capita income figures inconsistent with its aggregate GNP and population estimates. The estimate given here is based on the aggregate GNP data and population with the same regional breakdown as given by the plan per capita figures.

[e] Arithmetic average of third and fourth plan rates.

for the base year, the terminal year, and for the situation envisioned in the Plan document (Pakistan Planning Commission 1965). (The terminal year variables are simply the base year values plus the increments obtained in the basic solution.)

It can be noted from the data in Table 7.2 that on an aggregate level the basic solution (for a sector-by-sector description, see MacEwan 1971) is roughly in accord with the projections contained in Pakistan's Third Five-Year Plan. With regard to reduction of disparity between East and West Pakistan, the basic solution and the Plan are also in general agreement. The disparity ratios of the two programs are shown in Table 7.3

Table 7.3. Disparity Ratios from the Plan and the Basic Solution[a]

	1964-65	1974-75
Plan		
in terms of per capita income	1.34	1.17
Basic solution		
in terms of per capita income	1.45	1.31
in terms of per capita private consumption	1.37	1.25

[a] The disparity ratio is defined as the ratio of the West Pakistan value to the East Pakistan value.

Although the Plan and the basic solution begin with different estimates of base year disparity, both prescribe large reductions of disparity over the plan period. However, while the disparity reduction of the Plan is a matter of policy, no politically based restrictions on regional distribution have been employed in the basic solution. The disparity reduction of the basic solution is an optimal economic program where national per capita consumption is the welfare criterion.

This result—that it is economically optimal to move toward parity between East Pakistan and West Pakistan—requires some explanation.[9] It might be expected that the economically more advanced region (in this case, West Pakistan) would be more efficient in its use of scarce resources and, hence, that increased disparity would result from purely economic considerations (see, for example, Hirschman 1958).

When trade opportunities are limited, the productivity of a region cannot be defined independently of what must be provided for final demand in that region. Because East Pakistan is the poorer of the two regions, it has a larger share of agricultural goods in its marginal consumption bundle. These agricultural goods, especially rice, are relatively cheap to provide when the rate of growth is not high; that is, when the limits on agricultural production are not reached. Thus, until a level of consumption is reached which requires East Pakistan to import agricultural products—and therefore undertake costly import substitution in nonagricultural sectors—supplying additional consumption is "cheaper" in East than in West Pakistan. This is due to large part to the very low cost of increasing rice production that is expected to result from the use of new seed varieties.

When East Pakistan needs to import agricultural goods in order to expand consumption further, it cannot do so simply by expanding low cost exports. Because of trade limitations the East must engage in costly import substitution; and at that

9. Somewhat contrary results have been obtained by Khan (1967) and by J. Stern (1970).

point, provision of consumption in the West becomes cheaper. It is trade limitations that prevent either region from expanding consumption simply by concentrating production in the highest productivity sectors, exporting goods from these sectors, and importing higher cost items.

East Pakistan's ex post production advantage can be seen from the capital-income ratios in Table 7.2. The incremental net capital-income ratio in East Pakistan is 2.16 and in West Pakistan, 2.54. The higher productivity of capital in East Pakistan is explained primarily by the very high capital costs of agricultural expansion in the West. While those costs in the East have been taken as much higher than average costs of agricultural production, costs in the West are still a good deal more.[10] The point is that the productivity of either region can be derived only in terms of what must be provided for consumption.

Alternative Regional Allocation Programs

The optimality of disparity reduction, as stated above, holds under the condition of political neutrality; that is, increments to national per capita consumption are weighted equally regardless of region. By varying the relative political valuations of regional consumption (the δ's in the welfare function), alternative political situations can be simulated, and a regional incremental consumption frontier can be generated.

In addition to the basic solution, five solutions have been obtained, each with a different relative valuation of increments to national per capita consumption originating in the East and in the West. With δ^w as unity, the values of δ^e in the six solutions are (a) 2.00, (b) 1.22, (c) 1.00 (the basic solution), (d) 0.79, (e) 0.68, and (f) 0.60. The segment of the incremental regional consumption frontier which these solutions imply is shown in Figure 7.1; values of increments to per capita consumption obtained are shown in Table 7.4.

The segment of the regional consumption frontier in Figure 7.1 is obtained by linear interpolation between the six points obtained by the solutions. The slope of the frontier is the quantity of per capita consumption which must be given up in the West in order to expand consumption in the East by one unit, that is, the marginal rate of transformation of per capita consumption in the West for per capita consumption in the East. It is an interesting result that the marginal rate of transformation is close to unity over a wide range. Consequently, in terms of national per capita consumption, no great loss would result from placing strong emphasis on the development of one of the regions.[11]

Movement along the consumption frontier involves a transfer of resources from one region to the other. There are two ways such a transfer can take place. First, there can be a direct transfer of resources by a change in the net flow of capital between the regions. The capital serves to finance investment in and imports to the receiving region. Second, a transfer of foreign exchange between the regions can be effected by adjustment of trade patterns. That is, the region which is favored runs a regional trade surplus in order to finance a foreign trade deficit. The other region, accordingly, must run a foreign trade surplus and a regional trade deficit. The foreign trade surplus region is forced to produce commodities that it would otherwise

10. Whether East Pakistan really does have an overall production advantage may be subject to some question; in particular if skilled labor requirements and supplies were taken into account, the situation might be significantly modified.

11. A similar result was obtained by Khan (1967).

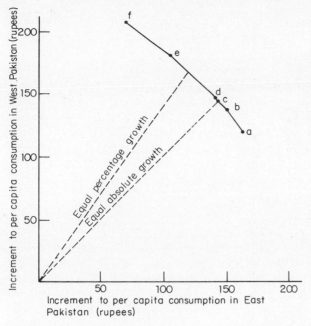

Figure 7.1   Incremental regional consumption frontier.

Table 7.4. Increment to Per Capita Consumption Under Alternative Relative Valuations of Consumption in the Two Regions

| Solution | Valuation of increments to national per capita consumption | | Increments to per capita consumption (rupees) | | |
	East (δ^e)	West (δ^w)	East Pakistan	West Pakistan	All Pakistan
(a)	2.00	1.00	162.3	120.3	142.3
(b)	1.22	1.00	150.4	138.3	143.9
(c)	1.00	1.00	144.9	146.6	144.4
(d)	0.79	1.00	143.8	147.2	144.3
(e)	0.68	1.00	105.9	181.5	139.0
(f)	0.60	1.00	70.4	208.3	131.6

import and to regionally import commodities that it would otherwise produce. That is, one region saves foreign exchange which is then used by the other region.

Both processes of resource transfer are exhibited in the movement between the solution points on the consumption frontier in Figure 7.1. In Table 7.5, the regional, foreign, and total trade deficits of each region are shown. In moving from the basic solution (c), toward a greater emphasis on development in East Pakistan, solution (b), resources are shifted to the East by a direct transfer of capital and by a decline in the East's net regional trade deficit. The next shift toward the East—from (b) to (a)—is accomplished completely by adjustment of the trade patterns. In fact, in the solution that favors the East more, the capital inflow to the East is less. At the extreme solution (a), the expansion of East is very intesive in foreign imports. To finance the increase of foreign imports in the East, capital is transferred to the West and used for import

Table 7.5. Trade Deficits and Surpluses Under Alternative Valuations of Consumption in the Two Regions[a]

Solution	Valuations of increments to national per capita consumption (δ^e and δ^w)		Total incremental capital inflow to East = total incremental capital outflow from West	Incremental foreign and regional trade deficits for East = incremental foreign and regional trade surplus for West	
	East (1)	West (2)	(3)	Foreign (4)	Regional (5)
(a)	2.00	1.00	38.5	868.4	-829.9
(b)	1.22	1.00	142.7	153.5	- 10.8
(c)	1.00	1.00	101.6	- 7.9	109.5
(d)	0.79	1.00	91.1	- 18.4	109.5
(e)	0.68	1.00	-458.2	-322.0	-136.2
(f)	0.60	1.00	-890.0	-693.6	-196.4

[a] Column (3) equals (4) plus (5).

substitution there. The foreign exchange thus saved in the West is transferred to the East by East's running a large regional trade surplus.

Moving in the other direction from the basic solution—that is, toward programs favoring the West—resources are transferred to the West by direct capital transfer. In fact, as the West is favored more, both the West's net regional trade deficit and its net foreign trade deficit rise. Emphasis on the development of either region brings about a rise in that region's foreign trade deficit and a rise in the other region's foreign trade surplus. However, the alternative solutions illustrate that the way in which the deficit for the favored region is financed can be by capital transfers from the other region or by import substitution in and foreign exchange transfers from the other region.

In Table 7.6 the production and trade programs of the two regions are shown for the basic solution. The programs serve as a reference point for the changes which occur when alternative political assumptions are employed.

Table 7.6. Source of Supply in the Basic Solution[a]

Sector	Producing in East	Producing in West	Importing from abroad
(1) Rice	x	x	
(2) Wheat		x	
(3) Jute	x		
(4) Cotton	x	x	
(5) Tea	x	x	x
(6) Other agriculture	x	x	
(7) Sugar		x	x
(8) Edible oils	x	x	x
(9) Tobacco			x
(10) Other food		x	x
(11) Cotton textiles	x		
(12) Jute textiles	x		
(13) Other textiles	x	x	x
(14) Paper		x	x
(15) Leather	x	x	
(16) Rubber	x	x	
(17) Fertilizer	x		
(18) Other chemicals	x	x	
(19) Cement	x	x	
(20) Basic metals	x	x	
(21) Metal products	x	x	
(22) Machinery	x	x	
(23) Transport equipment	x	x	
(24) Wood, cork, and furniture			x
(25) Miscellaneous manufacturing	x	x	
(26) Coal and Petroleum products	x	x	

[a] There are several products for which there is more than one source of supply. In agricultural sectors this results from limits on the quantity of production or from limits on trade. Some of these agricultural production limits carry over to effect the need for additional sources of supply for agriculture-based manufactures, for example, edible oils. For several manufacturing sectors the difference between the cost of production in the two regions is not sufficient to warrant interregional trade.

The nonparallel nature of resource transfers can be explained by the difference in the requirements of the two regions as output expands. Starting from the basic solution, expansion of the East tends to require more foreign exchange than expansion of the West. Thus when emphasis on development in the East is increased, the economy is forced upon a more import intensive path. Since foreign exchange earnings and capital inflow are fixed, the increase in the requirement for (agriculture-based) imports must be accompanied by import substitution in some other sectors. Industries importing in the basic solution in which import substitution is most efficient are West Pakistan industries—cotton textiles and wood, cork, and furniture. Therefore, substitution for foreign imports takes place in the West. Simultaneously, production in certain East Pakistan industries—rubber, transport equipment, metal products—is expanded to replace either production in the West or regional imports to the East from the West or both. By this process, the foreign exchange saved by the West is transferred to the East.

When West Pakistan expands, the need for additional imports is offset by the contraction of the East Pakistan economy and the consequent release of foreign exchange. The expansion in the West does not carry with it the need for elimination of some foreign imports, so that expansion is effected by a direct transfer of resources from the East.

The movement from the basic solution toward greater emphasis on West Pakistan development does, however, result in some changes in interregional trade patterns and the change of the location of expansion for some industries. The expansion of the West cannot be accomplished by a balanced expansion because of the limits on the production of agricultural goods. West Pakistan is forced to import other agriculture products and edible oils from the East. To offset the increased requirement for these imports, West Pakistan substitutes its own production for the regional import of rubber and fertilizer. Furthermore, West Pakistan production of cement, machinery, miscellaneous manufacturing, and coal and petroleum products is expanded to replace production of these products in the East by regional trade (although in the case of machinery the elimination of production in the East is only partial).

The switches that take place when the relative weights on consumption in the two regions are changed illustrate the changes in comparative advantage that result from variation of the regional emphasis of a national development program. Although some of the solutions considered may not be politically reasonable, the tendency of comparative advantage to shift will not be eliminated when only the less extreme solutions are considered. The switching seems to be a clear illustration of the interdependence between regional and sectoral allocation programs.

Economic Determinants of Regional Development

Although the degree of emphasis placed on development in each of the regions is primarily a political decision, that decision is influenced and constrained by economic circumstances. A regional allocation program may, therefore, be viewed as the result of an interaction between political and economic forces. When decision-makers have no preference for one region relative to the other—as in the basic solution—economic circumstances will determine regional allocation.

In the preceding discussion, economic circumstances were taken as given, and the implications of alternative political decisions were examined. Now attention is given to the relation between the shape of the consumption frontier and specific economic factors.

The basic solution calls for a development program which brings about a significant reduction in disparity, the resulting increment to per capita consumption being about the same in each of the regions. As pointed out above, the disparity reduction program was a result of economic circumstances rather than of any political allocation decisions. That is, in the basic solution, increments to national per capita consumption are weighted equally regardless of the region of origin.

Reduction of the savings rate in the East relative to that in the West would raise the relative cost of producing consumption in the East. However, the differential between the savings rate in the two regions would have to be large before a shift toward the West is effected. A solution to the model was obtained with a 12/22 savings rate for East and a 15/25 savings rate for the West.[12] The resulting change from the basic solution was a decline in total resource availability and in consumption in the West. In some East Pakistan sectors the fall in the savings rate was sufficient to eliminate production, and in some West Pakistan sectors the rise in the savings rate led to some import substitution. However, on balance resources are shifted to the East by a rise in the net capital flow from West to East.

Differential assumptions about the export possibilities of the two regions will not effect a change in regional allocation of consumption. It is possible, of course, that a decline in the assumed level of export expansion for the East would reduce or eliminate certain exports. However, because foreign funds can be transferred between the regions, the decline in export possibilities would have no more effect on overall costs in the East than would a decline in export earnings in the West or a general decline in export opportunities. A solution to the model was obtained in which the export growth rate for the East was reduced to 6.5 percent per annum while the export growth rate in the West was maintained at 7.5 percent. As compared to the basic solution, consumption in the West was reduced and consumption in the East was unaffected.[13]

Although the shift of consumption away from the East is not effected by a decline in the savings rate (of the magnitude considered) or export growth rate in the East, such a change in distribution is effected by a resouce change which raises the availability of capital relative to the availability of foreign exchange. Consumption in the East is relatively less capital intensive, and therefore a relative increase in capital availability favors the West, that is, shifts the regional consumption frontier so that the politically neutral assumptions of the basic solution lead to more development in the West. Although a complete consumption frontier has not been obtained under such economic assumptions, it is easy to show how the new consumption frontier would differ from that obtained with the assumptions of the Basic solution.

In Figure 7.2, the theoretical relationship between the two consumption frontiers is illustrated. The curve AA' represents the consumption frontier under conditions of relative capital scarcity. The curve BB' represents the consumption frontier under conditions of relative foreign exchange scarcity. As capital becomes less scarce, the

---

12. That is, the rates of savings on value added in agriculture were set at 12 percent in the East and 15 percent in the West, and the rates of savings on value added in other sectors were set at 22 percent and 25 percent, respectively.

13. The result is generally the same when exports for both regions are lowered.

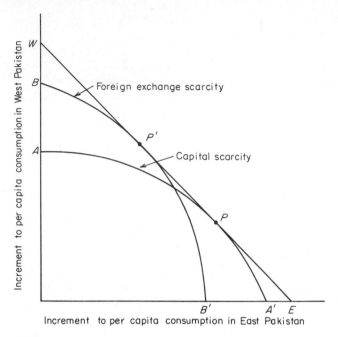

Figure 7.2 Illustration of different consumption frontier positions under alternative relative capital and foreign exchange availabilities.

consumption space shifts upward and to the left, *WE* represents the line with slope of minus unity, and the optimal solution shifts from *P* to *P'*.

A shift in the consumption frontier that will lead to a shift in the allocation of consumption toward the West would also result from an assumption of relatively poor performance in East Pakistan agriculture. Solutions were obtained which show that less success (as compared to the basic solution) of the new foodgrains production techniques would force the East to import rice and thereby raise the cost of consumption there. Under these circumstances a large shift of consumption toward the West results. Also, if the performance of the nonfoodgrains agricultural sectors is less than that assumed in the basic solution, the point on the frontier at which the marginal rate of transformation rises above unity is moved upward to the left. A solution was obtained in which the growth of other agriculture in East Pakistan was limited to 4.5 percent per annum over the plan (rather than the 5 percent of the basic solution). The result was to change the per capita consumption increment in the East from Rs144.9 to Rs118.9 and the per capita consumption increment in the West from Rs 146.4 to Rs160.3.

On the basis of these observations (and the points made in the discussion on "Disparity and Regional Productivity"), it can be seen why the macroeconomic results of this study differ in their regional aspect from the results obtained in other regional studies of Pakistan development.

A. R. Khan (1967), using a 7-sector regional programming model to investigate problems of development during Pakistan's Third Plan (1965–1970), obtained results which imply that a reduction of income disparity between the regions is not optimal when the political objective is to maximize national income (that is, increments to per capita income in the two regions are weighted by population shares). Although

Khan's model does not include a savings constraint, it does include agricultural growth limits and operates like the model used in this study. The difference between the two studies arises because Khan does not specify rice production as a sector separate from other agricultural sectors, and he does not consider the cost reductions in rice production resulting from the introduction of the new techniques.[14] When the agricultural growth limits are binding in both regions and agricultural goods must be imported, the Khan model chooses to expand further in that region where industrial development costs are less. According to his data, that region is West Pakistan. In this study, however, because rice can still be produced within East Pakistan, even when the nonfoodgrain agricultural growth limits are binding, some further expansion of the region is warranted.

A study by Stern (1970) also shows that an optimal national growth policy will lead to an increase of regional disparity. Stern's optimizing model, however, distinguishes only 2 sectors, and it thereby obscures the differences in the relative costs of consumption bundles in the two regions.[15] Furthermore, Stern assumes a generally more optimistic set of resource use and resource generation parameters for the West than for the East. With East's advantage on the consumption side eliminated by aggregation, and with the assumption of a more favorable set of production possibilities in the West, the regional allocation results which Stern obtains follow automatically.

Comparison with the Khan and Stern studies brings out one important aspect of disaggregation. When working with more sectors, it is possible to take account of more differences between the regions. The differences revealed by disaggregation can have important implications for regional allocation decisions.

IV. Conclusions

The regional allocation of welfare (consumption or income) is a function of the interplay between economic circumstances and political motives. The purpose of this study has been (1) to investigate the relationships between regional productivity and the structure of regional demand; (2) to determine the implications of alternative sets of political decisions regarding the relative emphasis to be placed upon development in each region; and (3) to examine the economic factors most important in determining the range of possibilities within which decisionmakers must act. Several conclusions can be drawn.

1. When trade opportunities are limited, regional productivity is a function of the structure of final demand. Therefore, the combination of the facts that East Pakistan, being the poorer region, consumes more foodgrains (rice) and that significant advances in foodgrain production are expected give East Pakistan a productivity advantage. Under such circumstances, disparity reduction becomes an economically optimal program.

2. The comparative advantage of each region is a function of the relative emphasis placed upon development in the two regions. That is, the set of industries that should be active within each region cannot be determined independently of the inter-

14. Khan deals only with the Third Plan period. The reduction in rice production costs will be more important in the Fourth Plan period.
15. Stern used a 2-sector optimizing model because he was concerned with long-run dynamic phenomena. He thus gave up the sectoral distinctions in favor of the temporal distinctions.

regional consumption allocation program. One interesting aspect of the changing comparative advantage associated with changing regional consumption allocation programs is the possibility of import substitution taking place in one region to finance increased requirements for imports in the other region.

3. The relative costs of expanding production in the two regions are not significantly affected by differences between the two regions in savings or foreign exchange earning abilities. Regardless of where capital and foreign exchange resources are generated, they are transferable between the regions and will be used to expand consumption in the region where the consumption bundle is cheaper.

4. Although differential savings and export performance in the two regions have little effect upon the relative costs of supplying consumption, major changes in the national supplies of capital and foreign exchange will effect changes in the relative costs of the consumption bundles. In particular, if the availability of capital rises relative to foreign exchange, the cost of consumption in the West will drop relative to the cost of consumption in the East.

5. The ability to expand agricultural production can be viewed as a resource that cannot be transferred between the regions. Therefore, changes in the performance in agricultural sectors significantly affect the relative costs of consumption expansion in the two regions. If the performance of the rice sector or of the other agriculture sector or of both in the East do not meet the expectations implicit in the basic solution, the reduction in disparity will not be as great as in the basic solution.

6. The differences between the regions in terms of costs of consumption can be seriously obscured by aggregation of the agriculture sectors. Were the rice sector in East Pakistan not specified as an individual sector, the lower costs of East Pakistan consumption would probably be overlooked.

These conclusions give a realistic description of some of the problems related to interregional development in Pakistan, and they yield some insight into regional problems elsewhere. The particular regional allocation program in the basic solution may be subject to question. It should be clear, however, which assumptions are most important in determining the basic solution and how changes of these assumptions change the regional and sectoral allocation programs.

8 Optimal Patterns of Trade and Development*

Michael Bruno

I. Introduction: The Model

This paper is a discussion of a general equilibrium framework for optimal resource allocation in an open and growing economy in which simultaneous decisions have to be made both on consumption, investment, and on the future levels and composition of foreign trade, in view of changing factor proportions and productivity. Our main emphasis is on the problem of incorporating the foreign exchange constraint together with limitations on both physical and *human* capital in rational decisions on the planning of trade in a way that would be analytically satisfactory but at the same time *practically feasible*. Practical applicability does, of course, entail some cost in terms of theoretical refinement.

Our analysis is closely linked to, and much inspired by, two main streams of theoretical and empirical work related to the above question. On the side of international trade theory,[1] it is associated with the attempts to give the Heckscher-Ohlin theory empirical content in a world in which there are intermediate as well as final goods, in which there are more than two factors of production, and where dynamic elements in the form of changing factor proportions and technical progress play an important role. The tools and the literature associated with the celebrated Leontief Paradox (1954, 1956) come most to mind in the present context.

The other and most obvious source is the growing literature on resource allocation planning models based on activity analysis, begun by Chenery and Kretchmer (1956), with more recent examples by Sandee (1960), Manne (1963), and Eckaus and Parikh (1968). The framework discussed here is essentially based on the reduced form of one such model (Bruno, 1966). One feature that may differentiate this product is the special consideration of the demand for skills. Otherwise, what we do here mainly is to bring explicitly to the surface the general trade-theoretical aspects

* Reprinted from *The Review of Economics and Statistics*, November 1967, *49*, 545–554 by permission of the publisher. This paper is based on research carried out at the Bank of Israel and the Hebrew University in Jerusalem in 1965 and supported by the Project for Quantitative Research in Economic Development, Center for International Affairs, Harvard University, during a 1966 visit to Massachusetts Institute of Technology and Harvard.

For high-powered research assistance and helpful discussions I am indebted to Mordecai Fraenkel and Christopher Dougherty, I also wish to thank Clopper Almon and Hollis B. Chenery for helpful comments on an earlier version of this paper.

1. For two excellent articles which survey some of these questions see Bhagwati (1964) and Chenery (1961).

that are usually implicit in one form or another in most of these models, in particular by making heavy use of the underlying concept of shadow pricing for the primary factors of production.

Consider an open economy, operating under the constraints imposed by four primary factors of production: foreign exchange (F), overall labor supply (L_0), the supply of a specific labor "skill" (L_1), and "capital." It produces composite private consumption good (C). It can operate m foreign trade activities $(T_s; s = 1, 2, \ldots, m)$, in addition to the production of public consumption goods, which are taken as exogenously fixed, and the necessary investment goods required for the construction of "capital." The definition and role of these factors and commodities will be made clear as we go along.

Next, assume that the economy's productive system can be described by means of a dynamic Leontief technology consisting of an intermediate input-output matrix $A = (a_{ij})$, a capital-output matrix $K = (k_{ij})$ and a primary input matrix

$$Q = (q_{rj}) = \begin{pmatrix} m_j \\ l_{0j} \\ l_{1j} \end{pmatrix}$$

where $i, j = 1, 2, \ldots, n$; $r = 1, 2, 3$; and m_j, l_{0j}, and l_{1j} represent, respectively, the input coefficients (in the jth sector) of imports, total labor, and "skilled" labor.[2]

Now suppose that the economy plans to allocate its resources over a planning horizon by looking at alternative resource allocation patterns at the *end* of the planning period, with three additional types of constraint in mind: (1) The growth rates of the various capital stocks at the end of the planning horizon are stipulated in advance $(h_i; i = 1, 2, \ldots, n)$. (2) The level of operation for each of the trade activities is bound by institutional and by supply and demand conditions. (3) There is an overall domestic savings constraint.

If we set up the detailed constraint system implied by all of these relationships and perform the necessary substitutions and eliminations, we can finally end up by reducing the system to $(2m + 4)$ basic constraints for $(m + 1)$ activities C, T_i:

Foreign exchange constraint

$$\mu_0 C - \sum_{i=1}^{m} (v_i - \mu_i) T_i \leq F - F_d \tag{8.1}$$

Labor constraint

$$\lambda_{00} C + \sum_{i=1}^{m} \lambda_{0i} T_i \leq L_0 - L_{0d} \tag{8.2}$$

Skill constraint

$$\lambda_{10} C + \sum_{i=1}^{m} \lambda_{1i} T_i \leq L_1 - L_{1d} \tag{8.3}$$

2m trade activity constraints

$$\underline{T}_i \leq T_i \leq \bar{T}_i \qquad (i = 1, 2, \ldots, m) \tag{8.4}$$

2. Skilled labor is also included in the total labor input, thus $l_{0i} \geq l_{1i}$ and $L_0 \geq L_1$. Because of this formulation the price attached to this factor will be the net price of skill (excluding the basic unskilled wage). It will be clear from what follows how the model could be generalized to take account of heterogenous types of "skill."

Savings constraint

$$-\beta_0 C + \sum_{i=1}^{m} \beta_i T_i \leq B \qquad (8.5)$$

μ_i, λ_{0i}, and λ_{1i} are the "total" (direct and indirect) import, labor, and skill coefficients, respectively (see discussion below). v_i is the marginal foreign exchange revenue per unit of the ith trade activity. F, L_0, and L_1 are the given endowments of foreign aid, labor, and skilled labor, respectively, and F_d, L_{0d}, and L_{1d} are fixed exogenous demands thereof.

The trade activities include both exports (E_i) and import substitutes (R_i) which are here treated symmetrically. Different T_i may refer to physically different commodities, in which case the lower and upper bounds may reflect both supply and demand constraints as well as institutional limitations, vested interests and the like.[3] These activities may, however, also relate to segments in step-function approximations to the downward sloping demand or upward sloping supply curve of any one commodity.[4]

Next we turn to explain briefly how the input of "capital" is suppressed in the coefficients of primary inputs appearing in equations (8.1) to (8.5).

Suppose our original Leontief model produces a vector of outputs X, let us denote the domestic net investment vector by J, and all other final goods by D.[5]

If the Leontief domestic input-output matrix is denoted by A, we have:

$$AX + J + D = X, \qquad (8.6)$$

Since we assume the capital stock growth rates h_i to be given, we can write:

$$J = HKX \qquad (8.7)$$

where H is a diagonal matrix with h_i in the ith row and column, and K is the capital-output matrix. Substituting into equation (8.6) we get:

$$X = \Omega D \qquad (8.8)$$

where $\Omega = (I - A - HK)^{-1}$ is an "enlarged" Leontief inverse matrix, which includes both raw materials and capital goods.

Next consider the $3 \times n$ matrix of direct primary input coefficients Q. We have:

$$QX = Q(\Omega D) = (Q\Omega)D \qquad (8.9)$$

---

3. For import substitutes R_i are allowed to become negative up to a limit to allow for future alleviation of present overprotective policies. To prevent negative variables from entering a linear programming model, a suitable transformation of coordinates is introduced (Bruno 1966).

4. In our empirical model for Israel a downward sloping demand curve for citrus exports is introduced (see Section III). For the introduction of upward sloping supply curves see Chenery and Kretschmer (1956).

There is one *analytical* limitation of this formulation which will not be dealt with here but may be of great importance in some cases: the phenomenon of increasing returns. Falling demand curves and rising supply schedules are consistent with convexity required by a linear programming formulation. Falling supply schedules are not. A partial solution is mentioned in Bruno (1966), but the problem can really be adequately dealt with only in an integer programming model.

5. D includes domestic consumption, foreign trade goods, and replacements of capital.

where ΩQ is a $3 \times n$ matrix of *total* primary input coefficients and we can write

$$Q\Omega = \begin{pmatrix} \mu_i \\ \lambda_{0i} \\ \lambda_{1i} \end{pmatrix}$$

This explains the meaning of the respective total input coefficients in equations (8.1) to (8.5). They incorporate both direct and indirect primary inputs, including an allowance for the future of growth of capital.[6]

The particular form in which we choose to take care of the capital coefficients has some clear analytical drawbacks, as it ignores problems of excess capacity and of intertemporal choice within the planning horizon. At the same time, if we take a pragmatic view, with a long enough planning period (5 years at least), problems of excess capacity become relatively unimportant. Also successive approximation can be used to make a sensible choice of the terminal growth rates h_i so that they are not too far off from the implied intraperiod exponential growth rates. It thus is a more realistic procedure than may seem at first sight.[7]

Let us now denote the prices of foreign exchange, unskilled labor, and skill by $p_\$$, w_0, and w_1 respectively, and the corresponding 1×3 price vector by $W = (p_\$ \; w_0 \; w_1)$. Similarly denote the commodity $1 \times n$ price vector by P. The dual price system[8] will be given by

$$WQ + P(A + HK) = P \tag{8.10}$$

therefore

$$P = W(Q\Omega) \tag{8.11}$$

where $\Omega = (I - A - HK)^{-1}$, sa before.

The price structure thus corresponds to that of a dynamic Leontief model in competitive equilibrium with a given *rate of return* h_i for the ith capital good.[9] This is another way of looking at the role of capital in the present model. It is as if capital stocks of the various kinds are in perfectly elastic supply at given specified interest rates h_i.[10] We shall make use of this underlying price structure in what follows.

A word must be said on the aggregate form in which consumption appears in the reduced form equations (1) to (5). In our original model, consumption appears as a vector C_i.[11] If we assume that there are fixed expenditure elasticities for each consumption good, and we write these down in linearized form, the result will be to impose fixed proportions on the marginal consumption basket, which is tantamount to having only one composite consumption good in the system.

---

6. It should be stressed that since our analysis refers to a future point in time, namely the end of a planning period, all coefficients are also assumed to incorporate projected technical progress (see Bruno 1966).

7. A dynamic version of our model is now being constructed. See also Eckaus and Parikh (1968).

8. See, for example, Dorfman, Samuelson, and Solow (1958).

9. In our present empirical model we have taken all h_i to be the same and equal to 10 percent. (See Bruno 1966.) In this case equation (10) corresponds exactly to the price relationship obtained by Solow (1959). For the duality between growth rates and interest rates in the case of unbalanced growth, see also Bruno (1969).

10. Another way of looking at the same thing is to remember that by specifying the terminal growth rates of the capital goods and looking for efficient solutions, we are implicitly imposing a kind of golden rule (Phelps 1965) behavior on our model. Strictly speaking, this is so only as long as the savings constraint is not effective (see below).

11. In Bruno (1966), like Sandee (1960), we allow for some variation around the Engel curves, and there is some choice involved in the composition of ΣC_i. In such cases μ_0, λ_{00}, λ_{10} will not be constants but rather endogenously determined in the optimization process.

Finally, the savings constraint in equation (5) can be derived from an underlying relation of the form

$$S \leq S_0 + s(V - V_0) \tag{8.12}$$

where S denotes gross domestic savings and V stands for GNP. S_0 and V_0 are base year constants. The marginal savings propensity (s) can be thought of either as a behavioral parameter or a policy variable.[12]

If we write an equality sign in equation (5) we can use the implied relationship to compute s for alternative values of C and T_i.[13]

II. Efficient Development and the Optimal Composition of Trade

Aggregate Transformation Curves

Consider the system of constraints in equations (1) to (4), assuming for the moment that savings in equation (5) is made to adjust by suitable policy measures. For any given values of L_0 and L_1 we can draw an efficient transformation curve which gives maximal levels of C for any value of F.[14]

Such curve is represented by a hypothetical broken line $G_1 G_2 G_3 \ldots G_m$ in Figure 8.1. The individual linear segments $G_1 G_2$, $G_2 G_3$, and so on, correspond to the introduction of the various trade activities T_i into the "basis" of the linear programming solution and changing them from $\underline{T}_i$ to $\bar{T}_i$.

The slope of the segments equals the marginal productivity of foreign aid in terms of consumption goods. Strictly speaking this is the *gross* marginal productivity, not including an allowance for the cost of borrowing, which is ignored in the present formulation. An alternative procedure would be to incorporate the cost of borrowing in the welfare function. Theoretically, if what the economy is planning to maximize is some function of C and F (and not only C) we would expect this to be a function which is convex to the origin and of positive slope, as is represented by the curve U in Figure 8.1 with maximization at X.[15] It is very likely that what society attempts to maximize is not only a function of C and F but incorporates some other factors, for example, security, regional dispersion, employment, and so on, in which case

---

12. It is, in fact, a combination of both since S includes both private and public savings. In $S = V - (C + G)$, G is given public consumption, and V can be written as

$$V = V_d + \alpha_0 C + \sum_{i=1}^{m} \alpha_i T_i \tag{8.13}$$

where V_d is an exogenous part and α_i are the total value added components in the various commodities. From equations (8.12) and (8.13) we get equation (8.5) by relabeling coefficients.

13. In most of the analytical discussion that follows, equation (8.5) will, in fact, not be considered as an effective constraint but rather as a determinant of public savings policy. In practical use of the model it must be a constraint in the sense that policy solutions that suggest values of s that are too high must be discarded (in the case of Israel, for example, s at present is 0.19 and socially acceptable upper limits are considered to be 0.25 for 1970 and 0.30 for 1975. (See Bruno 1966. This, of course, is a matter of judgment.)

14. Computationally what is involved is solving the parametric linear programming problem maximizing C subject to equations (8.1) through (8.4) for alternative values of the parameter F (see Bruno 1966).

15. $U(C,F)$ should incorporate all the factors that go into the social trade-off between C and F, both pecuniary and nonpecuniary. See also Chenery and Bruno (1962). In the case of flexibility in the choice of C_i, we would have $U = U(C_i,F)$.

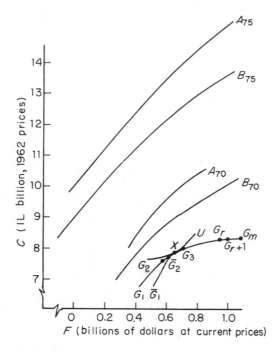

Figure 8.1

maximization, in terms of the CF plane, need not take place on the transformation frontier $G_1 G_m$ at all. Lacking knowledge of the structure and shape of U, we can still proceed to look at solutions along the $G_1 G_m$ frontier and pretend that what the system is attempting to maximize is C (subject to all the given constraints). We should remember, however, that what we obtain thereby may be "efficient" patterns and not necessarily "optimal" ones.[16]

Human Capital and Comparative Advantage

Suppose that the segment $G_r G_{r+1}$ in Figure 8.1 corresponds to a change in the rth trade activity T_r from its lower bound $\underline{T}_r$ (at G_{r+1}) to its upper bound $\bar{T}_r$ (at G_r). For F values anywhere along this segment the operation of this activity must be *just* profitable. In terms of the price solution described in Section I we must have

$$p_\$ v_r = p_\$ \mu_r + w_0 \lambda_{0r} + w_1 \lambda_{1r}$$

or

$$\Psi_r = \frac{w_0 \lambda_{0r} + w_1 \lambda_{1r}}{v_r - \mu_r} = p_\$ \tag{8.14}$$

16. This is in part like the distinction between dynamic efficiency and optimality in optimal growth theory (see Phelps 1965). Note that by specifying the interest rate through the terminal growth rate and assuming automatic savings adjustment, we already sweep part of the problem under the rug. See, however, the discussion of the savings constraint below.

The expression appearing in equation (8.14) we can term the *exchange cost* (ψ_r) of the commodity in question; it measures the domestic resource cost incurred, both directly and indirectly, per marginal unit of net foreign exchange, earned (in case of an export), or saved (in case of an import substitute). By the simplex criterion for linear programming, for all trade activities represented by linear segments to the left of $G_r G_{r+1}$ we have $\psi_r > p_\$$ (that is, they are unprofitable at the prices corresponding to the segment $G_r G_{r+1}$), whereas all trade activities to the right of $G_r G_{r+1}$ are intramarginal and $\psi_r < p_\$$.[17] Another paper (Bruno 1967b) analyses in great detail the closely related "exchange cost" investment criterion that has been used in Israel for the allocation of public development funds to investment in the foreign trade sector. It is based on an attempt to measure something like ψ_r for the various projects even in the absence of a comprehensive model and is an obvious application of the comparative cost principle to the planning of international trade.[18]

If the number of discrete activities is sufficiently large the transformation curve may give the appearance of a fairly "smooth" curve (at least to the naked eye). While the curve $G_1 G_m$ of Figure 8.1 was drawn only for purpose of exposition, the curve B_{70}, for example, is based on an actual empirical study, to be discussed in the next section. Next we note that ψ_r and the ordering of T_i along such a curve are functions of the given factor endowments L_0 and L_1 (through the prices w_0 and w_1). Consider, for example, a situation in which there is more human capital embodied in the given labor force, that is, a higher ratio L_1/L_0. The result is another curve A_{70} (Figure 8.1) which is above B_{70}. The ordering of segments along this curve need not correspond to the ordering along B_{70} and in general will not be the same. The difference in ranking will in fact reveal the importance of skill and education in determining the optimal pattern of trade.[19] Note that, strictly speaking, there are four factors in our model and we cannot in general rank activities by factor intensity independently of given factor endowments.[20]

Consider the ratio $\psi_r/(w_0 + w_1)$, where $(w_0 + w_1)$ can be looked upon as the compound wage of a skilled worker. Given the rate of interest (or rates of interest) there are two extreme cases in which this expression becomes independent of the relative human capital endowment and this is when either L_0 or L_1 become redundant, that is, either w_0 or w_1 are equal to zero. Only in such case can we speak of a "pure" ranking of activities. These two extreme form a convenient reference scheme for assessing the practical importance of the problem.[21]

Dynamic Comparative Advantage

Next, suppose we apply our model to a different point in time, that is, to the end of another 5-year planning period. We now have to recompute all input coefficients

17. In terms of the trade constraints given in equation (8.4), for all $i < r$ $T_i = \underline{T}_i$, and for $i > r$ $T_i = \bar{T}_i$.

18. See also Chenery (1961).

19. If we know the cost of training we can use the model to determine whether it pays to perform such shifts. See also Bruno (1966).

20. Note that we can also change the price of "capital" by varying the value of the implicit rate of interest in the model.

21. When $w_0 = 0$,

$$\frac{\psi_r}{w_1} = \frac{\lambda_{1r}}{v_r - \mu_r}$$

and for $w_1 = 0$,

$$\frac{\psi_r}{w_0} = \frac{\lambda_{0r}}{v_r - \mu_r}$$

μ_i, λ_{0i}, λ_{1i} to take account of changes in productivity and of other technical coefficients. Possibly the marginal revenue coefficients v_i might also change over time as a result of changes in world prices. Similarly the relative supply of factors (L_0 and L_1) may be changing.[22] An example in terms of Figure 8.1 is a shift from A_{70} to A_{75}. The ranking of activities along the transformation frontier may be changing, thus giving a quantitative representation of the importance of *dynamic* comparative advantage. We shall return to a numerical illustration in the next section.

The Role of the Savings Constraint

So far we have assumed that savings behavior was adjusting optimally (that is, s implicit in equations 8.5 and 8.12 was flexible). What will happen to our system if the savings rate becomes an effective constraint?

The result is shown by the modified transformation curve $\bar{G}_1\bar{G}_2G_3 \cdots G_m$ in Figure 8.1. To the left of the point $\bar{G}_2$ the savings constraint becomes an effective bottleneck for growth, whereas to the right of $\bar{G}_2$ it is redundant and the solutions are the same as before. There are a number of points to note:

1. The savings constraint need not slice off the curve G_1G_m in the particular way that is shown here. It may become effective for a range of F that is higher, rather than lower, than a certain critical value. It all depends on the parameters of a particular economy or point in time.

2. The curve $\bar{G}_1G_m$ brings to mind again the dual nature of the balance of payments constraint in economic development, as has been pointed out by Chenery and Bruno,[23] McKinnon (1964) and elsewhere, the role of foreign aid being both foreign exchange supplying and savings supplementing. The particular role depends on the range of F and the phase of development in which the economy happens to be. The experience of a number of developing economies, so far, seems to place the bottleneck mainly on the foreign exchange supplying side; for example, see Manne (1963) and Little (1960).

3. When the savings constraint becomes effective, a modified price formula has to be applied. Suppose q is the shadow price attached to the savings constraint in equation (8.5). For a trade activity T_r that is just profitable we would now have:[24]

$$p_\$ v_r = p_\$ \mu_r + w_0\lambda_{0r} + w_1\lambda_{1r} + q\beta_r$$

or

$$\Psi'_r = \frac{w_0\lambda_{0r} + w_1\lambda_{1r} + q\beta_r}{v_r - \mu_r} = p_\$ \tag{8.15}$$

III. Some Empirical Results

We now turn to consider briefly some empirical results obtained from application of the model to Israeli data.[25]

22. Through a training process, learning by doing, and so on.

23. In Chenery and Bruno (1962) the aggregate transformation curve has three linear segments, two corresponding to the savings and export constraints respectively, the third being the limit on the "capacity to absorb." The latter is here taken care of by the "skill" constraint, and our present disaggregated formulation makes for a smoother "curve."

24. This formulation suggests a possible further generalization of the treatment of savings whereby incomes from different sectors may have different savings coefficients attached to them (due to different wage-profit distribution or varying degrees of taxability). Such differences could be incorporated in the β_i coefficients. I am indebted to Paul G. Clark for this suggestion.

25. The usual disclaimer on the tentative nature of these results and the care with which these have to be interpreted is quite appropriate here.

The model includes 30 trade activities (T_i) of which 5 are different import substitutes (R_i) and 25 are export activities (E_i). The latter, in turn, relate to 24 different export activities of which one, Citrus (E_3), appears in the form of two activities, Citrus (E_3'), and Marginal Citrus (E_3''), a very rough approximation to a downward sloping demand curve.[26] The original model (Bruno 1966) which, in full form, numbers about 160 activities and 190 constraints, was run for the year 1970 and 1975, each time with a different set of coefficients to take account of technical change, and changes in supply of the various factors.

The curves B_{70} and B_{75} of Figure 8.1 provide a parametric programming experiment of the kind described in Section II. The supply of skilled labor (L_1) was set at its forecast level. This essentially assumes that the proportions of skilled and unskilled manpower supplied will remain roughly the same as in the recent past. This provides us with one extreme solution in which unskilled labor turns out to be in excess supply ($w_0 = 0$ throughout).

The curves A_{70} and A_{75} give another extreme set of solutions in which complete adjustment in the labor force is assumed, in the course of the planning horizon, so that the only effective bottleneck becomes the total projected labor force ($w_1 = 0$). The "truth," if such a thing exists, probably lies somewhere between these two extremes. Here, however, we are not particularly interested in giving answers to specific policy problems but rather to characterize the nature of such different sets of solutions in the light of our previous discussion. They form a convenient illustrative reference scheme for the general points made in Section II.[27]

Figure 8.2 gives the implied values of the marginal savings rate (s) for B_{70} and A_{75}, respectively. The other two curves would give very similar results (obtained from equations 8.5 and 8.12). To introduce some degree of realism, we point out that the total foreign capital inflow (F) in recent years came to approximately 500 to 550 million dollars per annum and can reasonably be expected to remain around that level till 1970, and then go down at a rate of approximately 20 million dollars per annum, reaching something like 400 to 450 million dollars in 1975. This would suggest a shadow price $(p_\$)$ of around Israeli pound (IL) 4.50 to 5.00 per dollar[28] as compared to the present market or effective rate of around IL 3.00 to 3.50 per dollar. Consumption figures can be compared with a 1962 base year figure of IL 4364 million (see Bruno 1966).

Table 8.1 provides a full ranking of the trade activities for the curves B_{70}, A_{70} and A_{75}, respectively, together with F values for the right-hand corners of the relevant linear segments. Table 8.1 lists only the changes of "basis" that occur in the trade sector.[29]

---

26. Table A8.1 gives a list of all trade activities together with their upper and lower bounds. Table A8.2 gives their "total" input structure under the assumption $h_i = 10$ percent. Skilled labor is defined as requiring at least 2 years of extra training in addition to ordinary schooling, obviously a very heterogenous group.

27. The results in Figure 8.1 are a somewhat modified version of those presented in figure 2 of Bruno (1966). Import substitutes were not included in the earlier analysis and the flexible consumption pattern was not allowed for. Also the full parametric programming solution with corner points was not given. Otherwise the structure of the model and the general feature of the solutions are very similar.

28. This can be read off in Figure 8.1 by looking at the slopes of the curves at the relevant points.

29. The other changes are shifts in the composition of the consumption vector and are not relevant to our present discussion. We have nonetheless marked those points on the curves.

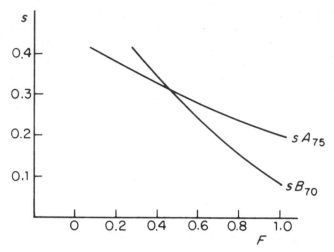

Figure 8.2

A comparison of the first two rankings (B_{70} and A_{70}) illustrates the point made earlier about the importance of taking the skill composition into account in discussing comparative advantage in a development context. Human capital is as much a limiting factor as foreign exchange, physical capital, or savings. Leaving it out of the analysis can considerably distort our estimates of the optimal development and trade pattern. If we divide the ranked list of activities into three groups of ten activities each, then one can roughly say that in the first and third group there are relatively few shifts in ranking, whereas the middle group has very many such shifts.[30]

If we look at Table A8.2 we can rationalize this result in terms of total input coefficients. The most productive trade activities are productive in both skilled and unskilled labor, and similarly for the least productive ones.[31]

A comparison of curves A_{70} and A_{75} and the corresponding rankings in Table 8.1 provides a hypothetical experiment comparing two situations in which skill provides no effective limit and the only difference between the two sets of solutions is a change in overall labor productivity in the different sectors. It is somewhat surprising to find that these two rankings are almost the same, despite the fact that considerable differences in productivity growth are assumed in the different industries.[32] A possible reason for this result is the fact that what matters for comparative advantage is the "total" labor input coefficient, and that the indirect productivity effects (through the intermediate and capital inputs) cancel the differences in direct productivity growth. Also, a 5-year period may not be long enough for such differences to show up, and the base year static differences may dominate.

30. This group also happens to be concentrated around our "reasonable" estimate of F. See, for example, the importance of skilled labor for such sectors as equipment (20), vehicles (21), and paper (10).
31. In this connection we can point out that the ranking of activities along the two curves could also be read from comparison of columns 5_{70} and 6_{70} of Table A8.2, in which ψ_r for these cases has been worked out explicitly. The input of unskilled labor can be worked out as the difference $(\lambda_{0i} - \lambda_{1i})$.
32. These *direct* labor input coefficients are not reproduced here.

If we want to use our results for statements about *dynamic* comparative advantage, a more legitimate comparison may be that of B_{70} and A_{75}, that is, comparing a "medium" run limited skill situation with what is likely to be the case in the "longer" run after the economy has managed to upgrade its labor force, thus combining a change in productivity with a change in factor endowment (see first and third columns of Table 8.1).

Table 8.1. Ranking of Trade Activities Under Different Factor Endowments

Activities	B_{70} Skill shortage $(1970)(w_0=0, w_1\neq0)$		A_{70} Free skill $(1970)(w_0\neq0, w_1=0)$		A_{75} Free skill $(1975)(w_0\neq0, w_1=0)$	
E_{29} Services	E_{29}	(1055)	E_{14}	(*)	E_{14}	(*)
E_4 Misc. agriculture	E_4	(730)	E_5	(*)	E_5	(*)
E_{14} Fuel	E_{14}	(723)	E_{29}	(*)	E_{29}	(*)
E_{12} Rubber and Plastics	E_{12}	(710)	E_{18}	(799)	E_{18}	(1112)
E_2 Livestock	E_2	(699)	E_{12}	(763)	E_{12}	(1007)
E_5 Mining	E_5	(691)	E_{15}	(752)	E_4	(968)
E_3 Citrus	E_3'	(642)	E_4	(744)	E_{15}	(947)
E_{18} Metal products	E_{18}	(631)	E_2	(735)	E_2	(930)
E_{15} Cement	E_{15}	(594)	E_{17}	(727)	E_{17}	(911)
E_{17} Basic metals	E_{17}	(585)	E_{19}	(719)	E_3'	(890)
E_6 Meat and dairy products	E_6	(577)	E_{10}	(702)	E_{19}	(862)
E_{28} Misc. transport	E_{28}	(577)	E_{20}	(686)	E_{20}	(818)
R_6 Meat and dairy products	R_6	(575)	E_{16}	(669)	E_{10}	(768)
E_7 Other food products	E_7	(569)	E_3'	(644)	R_{19}	(728)
E_1 Field crops	E_1	(539)	R_{19}	(632)	E_{16}	(678)
E_{19} Machinery	E_{19}	(538)	E_{21}	(607)	E_7	(633)
E_{10} Paper and printing	E_{10}	(519)	E_7	(597)	E_6	(547)
E_{20} Household equipment	E_{20}	(502)	E_6	(565)	E_{21}	(546)
E_3'' Marginal citrus	E_3'	(482)	R_6	(564)	R_6	(515)
R_{19} Machinery	R_{19}	(470)	E_8	(557)	E_{28}	(501)
E_8 Textiles	E_8	(439)	E_1	(479)	E_1	(495)
E_{21} Vehicles	E_{21}	(355)	E_{28}	(478)	E_8	(492)
R_2 Livestock	R_2	(344)	E_9	(475)	E_3''	(234)
E_{16} Polished diamonds	E_{16}	(338)	E_{27}	(467)	E_9	(220)
R_{13} Chemicals	R_{13}	(301)	E_3''	(439)	R_{13}	(198)
E_9 Wood products	E_9	(293)	R_{13}	(431)	E_{27}	(183)
E_{13} Chemicals	E_{13}	(283)	E_{13}	(419)	E_{13}	(123)
E_{27} Shipping and aviation	E_{27}	(265)	E_{11}	(402)	R_2	(63)
E_{11} Leather goods	E_{11}	(*)	R_2	(396)	E_{11}	(49)
R_{17} Basic metals	R_{17}	(*)	R_{17}	(389)	R_{17}	(23)

Having only one type of skilled labor in the model is clearly a gross oversimplification of reality. This is best borne out by looking at the relative position of the diamond polishing industry (E_{16}) on the curve B_{70} (see Table 8.1). The amount of training required for a worker in that industry is relatively small and it is traditionally considered one of Israel's export successes. The fact that it comes out so low in priority in the limited skill situation is only the result of aggregating semiskilled with highly skilled workers, engineers and scientists.

It is interesting that for the one trade-good for which a quasinonlinear demand curve has been introduced, namely, Citrus, the basic activity (E_3') turns out to be relatively profitable, whereas the next "step," the falling marginal productivity activity (E_3''), is relatively unprofitable. This illustrates the importance of such formulation, and at the same time points out another weakness of our specific industry results. Had we incorporated rising supply curves and more sloping demand curves where applicable, we could not rank goods, but only portions of expansion curves for such goods. After all, economies need not specialize in a small group of commodities, but often the question is to what *extent* to expand existing or new activities. Moreover, in a fully fledged realistic model, marginal revenues (v_i) need not be given and known constants, but might be subject to stochastic influences. This would only strengthen the argument for a balanced export portfolio and be against overspecialization. But now, not only will the remaining kinks in our curves be rounded off, but instead of neat transformation curves we shall be left with a set of fuzzy "milky ways." At this point we hasten to leave the scene.

Appendix to Chapter 8

Table A8.1. Lower and Upper Bounds on Trade Activities

Exports	Value of exports in 1964 ($ millions)	Bounds on annual rates of growth			
		1964-70		1970-75	
		Min.	Max.	Min.	Max.
(1) Field crops	3.1		5		5
(2) Livestock	7.2		11		8
(3) Citrus	52.9		a		a
(4) Misc. agriculture	3.9		18		14
(5) Mining	18.7		25		10
(6) Meat and dairy products	0.4		10		10
(7) Other food products	23.5	15	25	10.0	15
(8) Textiles	39.8	15	26	15.0	20
(9) Wood products	7.1	8	17	8.0	13
(10) Paper and printing	5.1		23		15
(11) Leather goods	0.8		25		23
(12) Rubber and plastics	10.3	9	18	9.0	18
(13) Chemicals	17.3	15	28	10.0	20
(14) Fuel	9.6	10	30	5.0	10
(15) Cement	4.1		18		11
(16) Polished diamonds	118.2	10	16	2.5	5
(17) Basic metals	3.5		30		18
(18) Metal products	10.6		30		20
(19) Machinery	1.5		50		20
(20) Household equipment	6.3		30		20
(21) Vehicles	7.2		22		20
(27) Shipping and aviation	116.6	7	15	7	10
(28) Misc. transport	2.2	7	15	7	10
(29) Services	155.6		20		15
(V_E) Interest and dividends	27.8				
Total exports	633.3		18		

Import Substitutes	Bounds on change from projected base year (1962); structure (IL million)			
	1970		1975	
	Min.	Max.	Min.	Max.
(2) Livestock	-22	10	- 44	20
(6) Meat and dairy products	-25	0	- 50	0
(13) Chemicals	-30	30	- 60	60
(17) Basic metals	-50	50	-100	100
(19) Machinery	-20	50	- 40	100

a Maximum: first step (E_3') 70 - 289.3   75 - 358.3
            marginal (E_3'') 70 - 42.7   75 - 53.7

Table A8.2. Total Primary Input Components and Foreign Exchange Revenue

	(1)	(2)	(3)		(4)		$(5) = \dfrac{(3)}{(2)-(1)}$		$(6) = \dfrac{(4)}{(2)-(1)}$	
	Total imports	Marginal revenue	Skilled labor λ_{1i}		Total labor λ_{0i}		Exchange-cost $\lambda_{1i}/(v_i-\mu_i)$		Per unit (ψ_i) $\lambda_{0i}/(v_i-\mu_i)$	
Industry code definition [a]	μ_i	v_i	70	75	70	75	70	75	70	75
Exports (E_i)										
(1) Field crops	0.097	0.356	49.15	39.61	164.31	133.24	189.8	153.0	636.1	514.5
(2) Livestock	0.111	0.338	25.77	19.06	84.22	62.16	133.5	84.0	371.0	273.9
(3′) Citrus	0.080	0.282	27.05	19.61	89.39	63.63	133.9	97.1	442.5	315.0
(3″) Marginal citrus	0.080	0.196	27.05	19.61	89.39	63.63	233.2	169.1	770.6	548.6
(4) Misc. agriculture	0.073	0.404	32.06	23.67	106.12	77.27	96.8	71.5	320.6	233.4
(5) Mining	0.081	0.279	24.34	16.02	45.58	31.03	122.9	80.8	230.2	156.7
(6) Meat and dairy products	0.102	0.250	24.50	18.62	78.03	59.51	165.5	125.8	527.2	402.1
(7) Other food products	0.142	0.275	24.27	18.71	69.40	53.18	182.5	140.7	521.8	399.9
(8) Textiles	0.112	0.248	39.85	32.52	82.02	66.73	293.0	239.1	603.1	490.6
(9) Wood products	0.089	0.172	32.55	26.36	57.68	46.20	382.2	317.6	695.0	556.6
(10) Paper and printing	0.091	0.272	41.46	34.10	73.99	60.53	229.1	188.4	408.8	339.4
(11) Leather goods	0.114	0.237	82.07	80.01	123.39	118.29	667.2	650.5	1003.1	961.7
(12) Rubber and Plastics	0.171	0.322	16.36	12.84	42.11	32.78	108.3	85.0	218.8	217.1
(13) Chemicals	0.206	0.253	20.17	14.76	44.04	32.54	429.1	314.0	937.0	692.3
(14) Fuel	0.281	0.377	9.20	6.65	20.51	14.93	95.8	69.3	213.7	155.6
(15) Cement	0.090	0.278	26.97	20.60	56.69	43.37	142.7	108.0	299.9	232.1
(16) Polished diamonds	0.271	0.337	22.63	18.79	25.78	21.33	342.9	284.7	390.8	323.2
(17) Basic metals	0.172	0.287	16.57	12.29	42.21	31.53	144.1	106.8	367.1	279.3
(18) Metal products	0.137	0.344	27.53	21.14	56.93	43.66	133.0	102.1	275.0	210.9
(19) Machinery	0.127	0.343	46.40	35.47	87.37	66.72	214.8	164.2	404.4	308.9
(20) Equipment	0.111	0.267	35.05	27.23	63.63	49.33	224.7	174.6	407.8	316.6
(21) Vehicles	0.135	0.282	47.67	37.99	74.57	59.15	324.3	258.4	507.3	402.
(27) Shipping and aviation	0.287	0.330	18.37	15.44	30.45	25.23	427.2	359.1	708.1	586.8
(28) Misc. transport	0.055	0.146	15.44	11.53	60.89	44.56	160.7	126.7	619.2	489.
(29) Services and tourism	0.077	0.327	23.48	17.97	62.78	47.79	93.9	71.9	251.1	191.
Import substitutes (R_i)										
(2) Livestock	0.111	0.185	25.77	19.06	84.22	62.16	348.2	257.6	1138.1	840.
(6) Meat and dairy products	0.102	0.238	24.50	18.62	78.03	59.51	180.1	136.9	573.8	437.
(13) Chemicals	0.206	0.256	20.17	14.76	44.04	32.54	403.4	295.2	880.8	650.
(17) Basic metals	0.172	0.222	16.57	12.29	42.21	31.53	331.4	245.8	884.2	630.
(19) Machinery	0.127	0.317	46.40	35.47	87.37	66.72	224.2	186.7	459.8	351.

[a] The code and definition relate to a 30-branch input-output aggregation. An import substitute and an export of the same code are usually not the same product. Because of aggregation they have the same input structure but their v_i's are different (for example, R_{17} is mainly construction steel whereas E_{17} is mainly steel pipes).

Units: Column (1) and (2), $ per IL; (3) and (4), man years per IL million; (5) and (6), man years per $ million.

9 Foreign Aid and Economic Development: The Case of Greece*

Irma Adelman
and Hollis B. Chenery

I. Introduction

Although advanced countries are now providing public grants and loans to less developed countries at a rate in excess of six billion dollars per year, there is as yet no scientific basis for determining the effects of this resource transfer on the recipient's economic development. In the absence of a valid quantitative analysis, intuitive judgments are made as to the importance of foreign aid, ranging from "vital" to "negligible."

Suggestions for a strategy for more rapid development utilizing substantial amounts of external assistance have been set out in several recent papers (Chenery and Bruno 1962; Chenery 1963; McKinnon 1964). These studies suggest that a moderate volume of external resources may make possible a substantial increase in the rate of growth of an underdeveloped economy through financing additional investment as well as through providing the additional imports required to sustain a higher level of income. The key elements in this process are the response of the country to the availability of additional resources and its ability to replace these resources over time by changes in the structure of its production and its use of income.

Although these papers establish some of the criteria for effective programs of foreign assistance, the extent to which aid recipients are able to carry out the required policies can only be determined from a study of actual cases. Since the time span required for a successful process of development-through-aid may be from 10 to 30 years or more, there are few less developed countries which have received substantial external assistance for a long enough period to make possible an evaluation of its effectiveness. There are, however, several countries in which successful programs of economic development have originated from postwar recovery programs—notably Greece, Taiwan, Israel, and the Philippines. All of these have received substantial amounts of assistance, have had an accelerated growth of national income, and have steadily reduced their dependence on external assistance for continued growth. We have selected Greece from this group as best suited for an econometric investigation

* Reprinted from *The Review of Economics and Statistics*, February 1966, *48*, 1–19 by permission of the publisher. The authors are indebted to C. F. Christ, A. Goldberger, Z. Griliches, and J. Vanek for comments, and to J. Bergsman, A. Strout, and L. Yap for assistance with some of the computations. The basic research was supported by the Agency for International Development, but that agency has no responsibility for the analysis.

of (1) the effects of aid on growth, and (2) the policy problems presented by dependence on external assistance.[1]

II. Foreign Aid and Development Policy

A transfer of external resources enables the recipient to raise the level of investment and to increase the supply of commodities that are not domestically produced. The first requirement of development policy under these circumstances is to allocate a sufficient portion of the import surplus to increased investment and to the import of commodities needed to prevent bottlenecks in production. Continuation of a substantial resource transfer implies adjustments in the structure of domestic production and income use to accommodate this element in total supply. Once a growth process is established, changes in the economic structure in the direction of increased savings, import substitution, and increased exports are required in order to reduce the dependence on external resources. The development policies which were appropriate to the earlier period of maximizing growth with a large volume of foreign aid will then have to be modified in order to bring about the structural changes required.[2]

These problems have been particularly acute in Greece over the past 15 years, since her dependence on external assistance at the beginning of the period was abnormally high. In 1950, the Greek import surplus was equivalent to 24 percent of GNP, 78 percent of imports, and nearly 100 percent of gross investment. While a comparable degree of dependence in the recent past can be found in Taiwan, Israel, Korea, Jordan, and a few other countries, an upper limit of 5 percent of GNP and 30 percent of investment is typical of underdeveloped countries as a whole. Greece has had, therefore, both the advantages and the adjustment problems of reliance on external resources to an extreme degree.

Over the period covered by this study (1950–1961) Greece's dependence on external resources was reduced by more than 50 percent while a growth rate of 6 percent was maintained with relatively stable prices. This performance implies a set of development policies which were consistent with the supply of external resources, her export possibilities, and other limitations. The results of these policies are reflected in the quantitative estimates of the model developed in the next section. Changes in these structural relations will be required to maintain the growth process, however, since our tests show that a continuation of the existing relations is inconsistent with the policy objectives and limitations likely to prevail in the future. We shall therefore make alternative projections for the next decade to indicate the magnitude of the structural changes needed to complete the transition to self-sufficient growth.

III. Description of the Model

In analyzing the role of external resources in development policy, it is necessary to distinguish between their functions as (a) a supplement to local savings and (b) a net addition to foreign exchange resources. Development policy must be such as to equate the resource transfer to both the investment-savings gap and the import-

1. Some of these problems were investigated for Israel in Chenery and Bruno (1962), but the Israeli data were not adequate for time series estimation of the type attempted here.
2. A fuller statement of these requirements is given in Chenery and Strout (1966).

export gap. While these two are of necessity equal in the past, since savings are defined as a residual, one or the other may be the limiting factor in determining the need for a capital inflow in the future.[3] The present model is designed to bring out the determinants of the two gaps and to suggest the types of policy change that may be needed to bring them into equilibrium.

Elements of the Mode

To analyze the need for external assistance and its effects on the performance of the economy, a number of elements of a general equilibrium system should be considered. The most important of these are the structural determinants of imports and investment, the tax and savings functions, and factors affecting exports. Starting from a rather general model of this sort, we have simplified the relations to adapt them to the data available for the Greek economy. Only this specialized version is given here.[4]

After a number of preliminary tests, the model chosen for this study consists of a set of disaggregated functions which describe economic behavior in the following spheres of activity: (1) consumption by households and government; (2) private and public gross capital formation; (3) imports of goods and services; and (4) exports of goods and services. The statistical portion of the model also incorporates a depreciation function and two tax-transfer functions. These are supplemented by a set of nonstatistical accounting definitions, a balance of payments equilibrium condition, and, implicitly, a savings-investment equilibrium condition.

No production function has been included in the initial estimation of the model since, in the absence of data on the rate of utilization of capital stock and of continuous employment or wage series, no meaningful production relationship could be obtained. Similarly, while it would have been desirable to incorporate a description of price-wage interactions into the model, this was precluded by the absence of continuous statistics on Greek wage rates.

The Consumption Functions

The dependence of consumer expenditures upon the level of disposable income has been well established in both budget surveys and cross-country analyses. It is therefore assumed in this investigation that private consumer expenditures are a linear function of after-tax income. For the purposes of this analysis, private consumption expenditures are disaggregated into (a) consumption expenditures on food plus beverages and tobacco; (b) consumption expenditures on clothing and other personal effects; (c) consumption expenditures on rent, water, fuel, light, furniture, and household operations; and (d) consumption of services. In the case of government consumption it is assumed that, by analogy with private consumption, government expenditures are linearly related to the gross national product.

The Investment Functions

The behavior pattern of producers in making capital expenditures is represented by separate investment functions for residential construction, nonresidential con-

---

3. This problem is treated in Chenery and Bruno (1962) and McKinnon (1964).

4. Further work has been done by the present authors at the Agency for International Development and Johns Hopkins to test the usefulness of more general models. Tests on Greece and other less developed countries suggest that it will not be possible to secure satisfactory statistical estimates for more complicated models until there has been a greater accumulation of data.

struction, and plant and equipment. Several types of explanation were tested for each component.

Residential Construction

Since Keynesian theory stresses the importance of the difference between the marginal efficiency of capital and the rate of interest as a determinant of investment behavior, an indicator of rates of return on capital was incorporated into the investment equation for housing. An interest variable (the bank discount rate) was tried but dropped, as its coefficient was not statistically significant. Similarly, initial experimentation with investment functions which relate construction investments to changes in capacity requirements by an accelerator model yielded unsatisfactory results. Construction investment was therefore assumed to be related to a profitability variable and to time. The latter variable may be considered to be a proxy variable for population growth.

Nonresidential Construction

Attempts to relate gross investment in plant and other nonresidential construction to profit rates, interest rates, or to changes in income, or both, yielded generally unsatisfactory results. Capital formation in these forms of construction was therefore related to the value of nonresidential construction investment in the previous year[5] and to time.

Machinery and Transport Equipment

Since the domestic production of heavy capital goods is very low in Greece, gross domestic investment in transport equipment and in machinery and other equipment was assumed to be a linear function of the supply of imports of goods and services during this period. Attempts to introduce profitability, interest, and accelerator variables into this investment function did not substantially improve the fit.[6] These variables were therefore dropped from the time series analysis, although an estimate of the effect of investment on productive capacity will have to be added in considering policy alternatives.

Inventories

No successful explanatory relationship for investments in inventory was found. For this reason, investments in inventory were taken to be exogenously determined.

The Import Functions

Total imports are divided into five main components: (1) imports of foods, beverages, and animal and vegetable oils; (2) imports of crude materials plus mineral fuels and chemicals; (3) imports of manufactured goods; (4) imports of machinery and transport equipment; and (5) imports of services. Each category of imports is assumed to be a linear function of the gross national product and of the relative price of imports.

The Export Functions

Four categories of exports are distinguished: (1) exports of food, beverages, and tobacco, and animal and vegetable oils; (2) exports of crude materials plus mineral

---

5. The latter variable can be interpreted to represent the effect of expectations. See Nerlove (1958: 141).

6. The investment functions obtained by D. Suits (1964: chap. 4) for the various categories of investment are equally unsatisfactory.

fuels and chemicals; (3) exports of manufactured goods and of machinery and transport equipment;[7] and (4) exports of services. Each of these types of Greek export is expressed simply as a function of time. A proxy variable for world income (world exports) was tried but deleted since it yielded poorer fits. In the preliminary analysis a relative price variable was also considered but dropped, since it resulted in positive price elasticities.

Other Statistical Functions

Since both gross investment and net capital formation appear as endogenous variables in the model, it becomes necessary to treat depreciation as a separate endogenous variable. It is assumed that depreciation charges depend in a linear manner upon the size of the capital stock at the beginning of the period. Two additional endogenous variables—direct taxes and transfer payments, and indirect taxes minus subsidies—are taken, for simplicity, to be linearly related to the gross national product.

Definitions and Identities

In addition to the usual accounting identities which express consumption, investment, imports, and exports as the sum of their component parts, the model includes definitions of the gross national product, national income, and disposable income. Two equilibrium conditions are also incorporated into the system: (1) a balance of payments condition, which states that the difference between imports and exports of goods and services is represented by net foreign capital inflows; and (2) a definition of capital stock, which expresses the capital stock at the end of a period as the sum of the capital stock at the end of the previous period plus the net capital formation during the period. A savings-investment equilibrium condition is implicit in the definitions of savings and gross national product.

IV. The Data

The basic data required for the analysis come mostly from the U. N. *Yearbook of National Account Statistics*, although collateral sources, such as the *National Accounts of Greece*, were used as well. The time period chosen was 1950–1961, as it was felt that the degree of the postwar dislocation of the Greek economy would vitiate attempts to extend the time span to include earlier years. The detailed data and the sources appear as Appendix B. All values are in millions of drachmas at 1954 prices unless otherwise noted.

V. The Statistical Results

List of Variables
C_f^* consumption expenditures on food, beverages, and tobacco
C_c^* consumption expenditures on clothing and other personal effects
C_h^* consumption expenditures on rent, water, fuel, light, furniture, and household operations

7. These two categories were combined because each, individually, is rather small.

C_s^* consumption of services

G^* government consumption expenditures

C^* total private consumption expenditures

I_d^* gross domestic investment in residential construction

I_c^* gross domestic investment in nonresidential and other construction

I_m^* gross domestic investment in transport equipment and in machinery and other equipment

I_s increase in stocks

I^* gross capital formation

P/K index of average rate of return on capital, 1954 = 100

M^* imports of goods and services

M_f^* imports of food, beverages, and tobacco, and animal and vegetable oils

M_i^* imports of crude materials, mineral fuels, and chemicals

M_m^* imports of manufactured goods

M_t^* imports of machinery and transport equipment

M_s^* imports of services

X^* exports of goods and services

X_f^* exports of food, beverages, and tobacco, and animal and vegetable oils

X_i^* exports of crude materials, mineral fuels and chemicals

X_{mt}^* exports of manufactured goods and of machinery and transport equipment

S^* gross savings

X_s^* exports of services

F^* net foreign capital inflow

V^* gross national product

Y_d^* disposable income

T_d^* direct taxes and transfer payments

T_i^* indirect taxes minus subsidies

P_m index of the relative price of imports, 1954 = 100

K^* end of year capital stock

D^* depreciation

t time in years measured from 1950 = 1

Endogenous variables in this list are marked with an asterisk. The exogenous variables which appear in the model are inventory investment, I_s; the index of the average rate of return on capital, P/K; the index of the relative price of imports, P_m; and time, t. The predetermined variables are K_{-1}, and $I_{c_{-1}}$.

Estimated Equations for 1950–1961

The sample consists of yearly observations for the period 1950–1961. The method of estimation used for those equations which contain more than one endogenous variable, (9.1)–(9.6), (9.9)–(9.13), and (9.18)–(9.19), was Theil's two-stage least squares.[8] Equations (9.7), (9.8), (9.14)–(9.17), and (9.20), which contain only a single endogenous variable, were estimated by ordinary least squares.[9] The pre-

---

8. See Theil (1961: chap. 6). Actually, there was remarkably little difference between single stage least squares, limited information, and two-stage least squares estimates of these equations. The single stage, two-stage, and limited information estimates of the relevant equations are reproduced in Appendix A for purposes of comparison.

9. This is, of course, equivalent to two-stage least squares.

determined and exogenous variables used in the first stage of the two-stage least squares procedures were K_{-1}, I_{c-1}, I_s, P/K, P_m, and t.

As usual, the standard errors of the coefficients are listed in parentheses below each coefficient, and $\bar{R}^2$ denotes the value of the coefficient of multiple determination adjusted for degrees of freedom. In addition, for each equation, one of two measures of serial correlation in the residuals is listed.[10]

Stochastic Equations

$$C_c = \begin{array}{c} 1024 \\ (510) \end{array} + \begin{array}{c} .1318Y \\ (.0082) \end{array} \qquad R^2 = .966 \qquad \delta^2/S^2 = 2.24 \qquad (9.1)$$

$$C_h = \begin{array}{c} -1522 \\ (714) \end{array} + \begin{array}{c} .2121Y \\ (.0116) \end{array} \qquad R^2 = .974 \qquad \delta^2/S^2 = 1.18 \qquad (9.2)$$

$$C_s = \begin{array}{c} -3171 \\ (949) \end{array} + \begin{array}{c} .2182Y \\ (.0153) \end{array} \qquad R^2 = .958 \qquad \delta^2/S^2 = 2.21 \qquad (9.3)$$

$$C_f = \begin{array}{c} +11540 \\ (1048) \end{array} + \begin{array}{c} .3151Y \\ (.0169) \end{array} \qquad R^2 = .975 \qquad \delta^2/S^2 = 1.63 \qquad (9.4)$$

$$G = \begin{array}{c} 1459 \\ (780) \end{array} + \begin{array}{c} .1046V \\ (.0095) \end{array} \qquad R^2 = .931 \qquad \delta^2/S^2 = 1.80 \qquad (9.5)$$

$$I_m = \begin{array}{c} -4776 \\ (1432) \end{array} + \begin{array}{c} .6714M \\ (.060) \end{array} \qquad R^2 = .934 \qquad \delta^2/S^2 = .78 \qquad (9.6)$$

$$I_d = \begin{array}{c} -2049 \\ (1485) \end{array} + \begin{array}{c} 36.3P/K \\ (17.3) \end{array} + \begin{array}{c} 264t \\ (50.9) \end{array} \quad R^2 = .907 \qquad d = 2.33 \qquad (9.7)$$

$$I_c = \begin{array}{c} -413 \\ (310) \end{array} + \begin{array}{c} 208t \\ (93.0) \end{array} + \begin{array}{c} .84I_{c-1} \\ (.19) \end{array} \quad R^2 = .959 \qquad d = 2.44 \qquad (9.8)$$

$$M_s = \begin{array}{c} -732 \\ (128) \end{array} + \begin{array}{c} .0653V \\ (.011) \end{array} - \begin{array}{c} 21.1P_m \\ (13) \end{array} \quad R^2 = .826 \qquad \delta^2/S^2 = 2.04 \qquad (9.9)$$

$$M_f = \begin{array}{c} 1695 \\ (964) \end{array} + \begin{array}{c} .0190V \\ (.008) \end{array} - \begin{array}{c} 7.2P_m \\ (9.7) \end{array} \quad R^2 = .419 \qquad \delta^2/S^2 = 1.22 \qquad (9.10)$$

$$M_i = \begin{array}{c} 2301 \\ (874) \end{array} + \begin{array}{c} .0505V \\ (.066) \end{array} - \begin{array}{c} 17.7P_m \\ (8.1) \end{array} \quad R^2 = .880 \qquad \delta^2/S^2 = 2.85 \qquad (9.11)$$

$$M_m = \begin{array}{c} -428 \\ (584) \end{array} + \begin{array}{c} .0643V \\ (.0048) \end{array} - \begin{array}{c} 9.7P_m \\ (5.9) \end{array} \quad R^2 = .957 \qquad \delta^2/S^2 = 3.15 \qquad (9.12)$$

$$M_t = \begin{array}{c} -1801 \\ (2987) \end{array} + \begin{array}{c} .1836V \\ (.0247) \end{array} - \begin{array}{c} 76.1P_m \\ (30.0) \end{array} \quad R^2 = .876 \qquad \delta^2/S^2 = 1.90 \qquad (9.13)$$

$$X_f = \begin{array}{c} 2181 \\ (283) \end{array} + \begin{array}{c} 198t \\ (46) \end{array} \qquad R^2 = .665 \qquad d = 1.65 \qquad (9.14)$$

$$X_i = \begin{array}{c} 314 \\ (113) \end{array} + \begin{array}{c} 146t \\ (18) \end{array} \qquad R^2 = .875 \qquad d = 2.44 \qquad (9.15)$$

$$X_{mt} = \begin{array}{c} 146 \\ (39) \end{array} + \begin{array}{c} 18t \\ (6) \end{array} \qquad R^2 = .448 \qquad d = 1.12 \qquad (9.16)$$

10. For equations estimated by means of two-stage least squares, the measure used is the Von Neumann statistic δ^2/S^2. The Durbin-Watson statistic, d, is computed for equations estimated by ordinary least squares procedures. With our sample size, a value of δ^2/S^2 below 0.90 indicates significant, serial correlation at the 1 percent level of significance. Similarly, for equations with a single dependent variable, a value of d below 0.81 indicates significant autocorrelation at the 1 percent level of significance; a value of d above 1.07 indicates serial independence, while a value of d between 0.81 and 1.07 yields inconclusive results. For equations with two dependent variables, the corresponding limits for d are 0.70 and 1.25, respectively.

$$X_s = \begin{matrix} 70 \\ (227) \end{matrix} \quad \begin{matrix} + 321t \\ (37) \end{matrix} \qquad R^2 = .894 \qquad d = 1.50 \qquad (9.17)$$

$$T_d = \begin{matrix} -757 \\ (480) \end{matrix} \quad \begin{matrix} + .0921V \\ (.0058) \end{matrix} \qquad R^2 = .965 \qquad d = 1.56 \qquad (9.18)$$

$$T_i = \begin{matrix} -1284 \\ (298) \end{matrix} \quad \begin{matrix} + .1317V \\ (.0036) \end{matrix} \qquad R^2 = .993 \qquad d = 2.28 \qquad (9.19)$$

$$D = \begin{matrix} -88 \\ (163) \end{matrix} \quad \begin{matrix} + .0213K_{-1} \\ (.0010) \end{matrix} \qquad R = .979 \qquad \delta^2/S^2 = 1.37 \qquad (9.20)$$

Identities

$$C = C_h + C_f + C_s + C_c \qquad (9.21)$$
$$I = I_c + I_m + I_s + I_d \qquad (9.22)$$
$$M = M_s + M_c + M_i + M_m + M_t \qquad (9.23)$$
$$X = X_f + X_i + X_{mt} + X_s \qquad (9.24)$$
$$M = X + F \qquad (9.25)$$
$$V = C + G + I - F \qquad (9.26)$$
$$Y = V - D - T_i - T_d \qquad (9.27)$$
$$K_t = (I - D)_t + K_{t-1} \qquad (9.28)$$
$$S = V - C - G = I - F \qquad (9.29)$$

VI. The Performance of the Model, 1951–1961

One test of the descriptive validity of an econometric model[11] may be obtained by comparing the predicted values of the endogenous variables with the values actually observed during a sample period. In Table 9.1, the estimated and actual values of the endogenous variables of the system are listed side by side. The estimated values were obtained by solving the system of simultaneous equations under the assumption that all disturbances (other than those which arise due to fluctuations of the exogenous variables) are zero. The only data additional to those summarized in equations (9.1) through (9.29) which were used in these computations were the actual values of the exogenous variables I_s, P_m, and K and the initial values of $I_{c_{-1}}$ and K_{-1}, which were appropriate in 1950. A comparison of the estimated and the actual values indicates that the model economy reproduces remarkably faithfully the time paths of all endogenous variables. There is little evidence of any systematic bias in the model.

This test differs from the more usual one, in which one-examines the residuals of each individual estimated equation using only the observed values of the explanatory variables. In the present computations, the estimated values of the current and lagged endogenous variables were substituted for their observed values in the solution of the simultaneous equations and the resulting estimates were compared with the observed values. This procedure provides a more stringent test of the performance of the model economy, inasmuch as it tends to reveal systematic biases which may arise because of the cumulative effects of estimation errors introduced by the nature of the simultaneous and dynamic structure inherent in the model.

We shall, therefore, proceed to use the model to investigate the effects of the external capital inflow and to project the future evolution of the Greek economy

11. For a discussion of other tests see, for example, Christ (1956), and Adelman and Adelman (1959).

Table 9.1. Actual and Estimated Values of the Most Important Endogenous Variables, 1951-1961[a] (millions of 1954 drachmas)

Year	V Estimated	V Actual	C Estimated	C Actual	G Estimated	G Actual	S Estimated	S Actual
1951	49,050	47,819	40,987	40,090	6,590	7,018	1,474	3,111
1952	46,712	47,358	39,257	40,091	6,345	6,922	1,110	2,897
1953	54,967	54,315	44,802	44,181	7,208	6,347	2,957	6,179
1954	55,482	58,690	45,059	47,239	7,262	7,396	3,161	4,475
1955	62,331	63,318	49,658	49,573	7,978	7,657	4,964	8,019
1956	67,822	67,753	53,263	53,584	8,553	8,526	6,006	8,144
1957	78,331	73,914	58,194	57,551	9,339	9,132	7,801	9,596
1958	74,508	76,352	57,388	59,446	9,252	9,171	7,869	1,417
1959	79,274	79,366	60,389	60,585	9,751	10,151	9,136	9,214
1960	79,464	83,076	60,236	63,350	9,771	10,494	9,007	6,794
1961	89,469	92,656	66,767	68,178	10,817	11,125	11,884	13,160

Year	I Estimated	I Actual	X Estimated	X Actual	M Estimated	M Actual	F Estimated	F Actual
1951	9,554	9,502	4,077	3,127	12,154	13,396	8,077	7,727
1952	5,633	7,333	4,760	3,948	9,279	9,775	4,519	5,079
1953	7,056	8,137	5,443	5,422	9,535	9,003	4,092	2,934
1954	6,114	7,745	6,126	6,227	9,072	11,441	2,946	4,341
1955	10,245	10,083	6,809	7,731	12,354	12,318	5,545	3,635
1956	13,503	12,107	7,492	7,488	14,984	14,586	7,492	5,644
1957	16,916	13,450	8,175	8,759	17,330	16,032	9,155	5,321
1958	17,218	16,170	8,858	8,987	18,203	17,892	9,345	7,064
1959	19,495	18,670	9,541	9,156	19,896	19,478	10,355	8,289
1960	19,866	24,715	10,224	9,583	20,628	25,698	10,404	13,578
1961	25,837	26,130	10,907	11,054	24,854	24,716	13,947	10,462

[a] For notation, see Section III.

under varying conditions. In interpreting the results of such studies, especially in the context of "what might have happened," it must be recognized that the present model of the Greek economy has been, in a sense, normalized to actual events during the period 1951–1961. Therefore, while a certain amount of validity may be ascribed to the interpretation of relatively small changes from the actual conditions of the period, one must be extremely cautious in judging the implications of larger departures from actual events. This is due partly to certain economic pecularities of the period in question. In particular, the period 1951–1961 was characterized by an intensive effort to rebuild the capital stock of Greece in the aftermath of World War II and the internal fighting which followed the expulsion of the German army. Therefore, the rate of investment in residential and other construction is significantly higher than that which would normally have been justified by the actual or anticipated growth in GNP. Furthermore, the combination of the devaluation of the drachma in 1953 and the subsequent relaxation of import controls tended to increase the marginal propensity to import above its normal long-term equilibrium level.

VII. Past Effects of Foreign Aid

To make an assessment of the past effects of foreign assistance, we propose to use this model to get an approximate indication of the rate of growth and the behavior of the major aggregates that might have occurred with less capital inflow. The estimates can only be approximate, since they do not allow for possible adjustments in the economic structure to a reduction in F. Since the equation system is a consistent and determinate one, the level of capital inflow can only be varied on the assumption that one of the behavioral equations is not binding.

Limits to Growth

The effect of variation in the capital inflow will depend on which of the two functions of foreign assistance sets the limit to growth in given circumstances. The two possibilities are: (1) *savings limited growth*, for which it is assumed that the investment determined by the model is essential to sustain the level of GNP; and (2) *import limited growth*, for which it is assumed that the amount of imports determined by the system are required by the structure of demand at any given level of GNP.

Import Limited Growth

When import requirements are the limiting factor, the corresponding level of GNP is determined by substituting equations (9.9)–(9.13) into equation (9.23) and solving for V:

$$V = 2.61M + 344.9P_m - 2704 \qquad (9.30)$$

Imports are in turn limited to the sum of export earnings and capital inflow. Substituting for M from (9.14)–(9.17) and (9.25) gives the following expression for import-limited GNP (V^m) as a function of external capital and time:

$$V_t^m = 2.61F_t + 344.9P_{mt} + 1782t + 9780 \qquad (9.31)$$

In this situation—when savings and investment are not a limitation on growth—the productivity of an additional unit of external assistance in a given year is given by:

$$\frac{\Delta V^m}{\Delta F} = 2.61 \tag{9.32}$$

Savings Limited Growth

As indicated earlier, the role of investment is only partially described by the investment functions which we have estimated so far. An equation analogous to (9.31) can be obtained by combining (9.1)–(9.5), (9.18)–(9.20), and (9.26)–(9.29) and solving for V:

$$V = 52,210 - .087K_{-1} + 4.662(I - F) \tag{9.33}$$

The omission of productive capacity from our model makes this function unsuitable for the present purpose, since investment in equation (9.33) performs only the Keynesian function of generating aggregate demand. Without also considering the capital stock required to permit an expansion of output, it would appear that GNP could be increased by reducing F, even if account is taken of the fact that the supply of investment goods depends on the level of imports.[12]

To supply the required link between investment and capacity, we postulate a conventional linear function of the form:

$$I_t = k(V_t - V_{t-1}) + I_s \tag{9.34}$$

where the first term represents gross fixed capital formation requirements and the second is investment in inventories. For the whole period 1951–1961, the value of k may be estimated at about 3.0 from the data in Appendix B.[13] This estimate agrees with the aggregate value of $k = 2.975$ that can be derived from Papandreou's estimates (1962–65) of sectoral capital requirements.[14] We shall use the latter for planning purposes. We then replace the investment equations (9.6)–(9.8) in the original model with the alternative relation between gross investment and output:

$$I_t = 2.975(V_t - V_{t-1} + 1076 \tag{9.35}$$

Equations (9.1)–(9.5), (9.18)–(9.21), and (9.29) yield an estimate of investment as the total of domestic savings and capital inflow. Together with (9.35) they therefore

12. This can be seen by substituting (9.6)–(9.8) and (9.25) in (9.33) and solving for V as a function of F. The partial multiplier $(\Delta V)/(\Delta F)$ is then -1.55.

13. Using a 1-year lag gives:

$$R = \frac{\sum\limits_{t=50}^{t=60} I_t}{V_{61} - V_{51}} = 3.08$$

14. The incremental capital-output ratios derived by Papandreou represent ratios of gross fixed capital formation to gross domestic product. For computational convenience, these ratios were adjusted so that the gross national product is placed in the denominator by multiplying the capital-output ratios cited by Papandreou by the average ratio of gross domestic product to gross national product during 1951–1961. It may be worthwhile explaining the basis on which the Papandreou ratios were derived. In his words, "The sectorial capital/output ratios used for our projections are not statistical estimates. Qualitative information (including expert opinion) was used side by side with quantitative information drawn from the experience of the fifties."

describe the growth of GNP over time when productive capacity and its financing are the factors limiting growth. The equation for V_t^s is:

$$V_t^s = 1.078V_{t-1} + .3622Ft + .0067K_{-1} - 4390 \tag{9.36}$$

External Capital Requirements

Equations (9.31) and (9.36) give two separate estimates of the amount of external capital required to sustain any given rate of growth. To illustrate this result, the requirements for 6 percent growth over the period 1951–1961 (the rate actually achieved) are plotted in Figure 9.1, together with the required levels of imports,

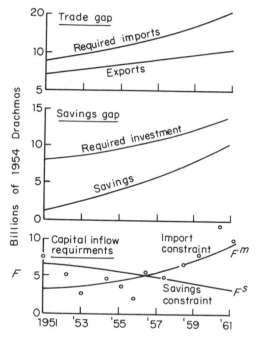

Figure 9.1 Trade and savings gaps with 6 percent growth (1951–1961).

investment, and savings. This analysis suggests that up to 1957 the principal function of external assistance was to make up the gap between savings and required investment, while, since then, the import-export gap has become increasingly dominant.[15] The actual levels of capital inflow shown are roughly consistent with the pattern of decreasing an then increasing requirements implied by this analysis. Even though the investment-capacity relationship which we have used to arrive at this result is approximate, almost any plausible substitute for equation (35) would lead to a similar conclusion.[16]

15. This interpretation is strengthened by the findings of Ellis (1964: chap. 1), that in recent years the supply of funds for investment has tended to exceed the demand.
16. We make no attempt to determine the way in which the two gaps are equalized, since we are interested only in the maximum GNP achievable under various assumptions. As indicated in Chenery and Strout (1966), the mechanisms by which the lesser gap is increased to equal the dominant one include changes in reserves, excess imports, less productive investment, reduced pressure for exports, and so on.

The Productivity of Aid

To determine the effects that would have resulted from different levels of external capital, we can make alternative assumptions about the ways in which the economy would have adjusted to a reduction in external resources. At one extreme, it can be assumed that the structural relations of the model indicate the best performance of the economy. In this case, the effect of a reduction in external assistance would have been to reduce the level of GNP to that indicated by the smaller of the two values, V^s or V^m. For example, the effect on external capital needs of reducing the growth rate to 2 percent over this period is shown in Figure 9.2. Since export growth

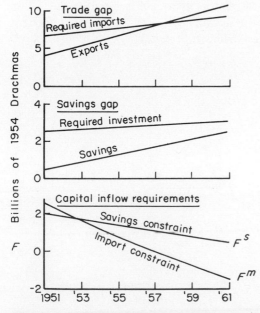

Figure 9.2 Effect of lower growth rate (2 percent) on capital inflow (1951–1961).

is assumed to be unaffected, the export-import gap falls below the savings investment gap after 1952 and the latter becomes the dominant restriction. On this assumption, a reduction in the external capital inflow over the period 1951–1961 from 75 billion to 16 billion drachmas could have been achieved by reducing the growth rate from 6 percent to 2 percent. Alternatively, the gain from the additional capital inflow that was actually forthcoming may be measured by the difference in GNP that results from raising the rate from 2 percent to 6 percent. Cumulating the effects over the decade gives a marginal productivity of this additional capital inflow[17]; $(\Sigma\Delta V)/(\Sigma\Delta F)$, of 2.49.

17. For consistency, the capital requirement is computed from the dominant constraint in the model in each year. The actual capital inflow over 1951–1961 (74,074) is not very different from the theoretical requirement (74,862). The basis for the productivity calculation is as follows:

	2 percent growth	6 percent growth	Increase	$(\Sigma\Delta V)/(\Sigma\Delta F)$
ΣV	531,108	679,069	147,961	2.49
ΣF	15,544	74,862	59,318	

The productivity of aid increases with the time period considered when the savings limitation is dominant, but it declines when the import limit is controlling. See Chenery and Strout (1966: sec. IB).

A generalization of this analysis is given in Figure 9.3, which shows the mean capital inflow that would have been required to sustain any rate of growth between 2 percent and 12 percent on the assumption that the larger of the two gaps provides the limit to growth in each year. As shown by the comparison between Figures 9.1 and 9.2, the import gap becomes increasingly important as the growth rate is raised and, in the aggregate, it is the larger of the two for growth rates above 6 percent.

We next consider the possibility that if aid had been reduced during the previous decade the Greek economy would have been able to economize on its use by improved internal performance. In this case, the smaller of the two gaps may be taken as a measure of the minimum aid required to sustain a given level of GNP. For growth rates less than 6 percent, this assumption implies that savings rates would have had to be higher than the model estimates (or the use of capital more efficient) in order to reduce the savings gap to the smaller import gap.

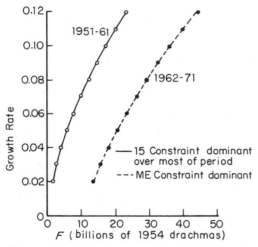

Figure 9.3 Effects of growth rate upon mean net foreign capital requirements.

To estimate the performance of the economy under this more optimistic assumption, we have calculated the achievable levels of GNP for amounts of capital inflow varying from the observed level to zero by equal increments. For each assumed level of F_t, the corresponding V_t calculated from equation (9.32) is shown in Table 9.2. While this procedure is overly rigid, since it rules out the possibility of short-term borrowing to achieve a more even growth rate, the cumulative GNP for the period is not affected. Since the import limit is controlling, the marginal productivity of assistance of 2.61, as determined from equation (9.32), applies to each increment of assistance in a given year.[18] Although the total aid required to sustain any given level of GNP under the minimum-gap assumption is less, the marginal productivity of assistance is not very different from that computed for the maximum-gap assumption.[19]

18. If the import equations overestimate the imports required to sustain a given level of GNP, there could be some further reduction in capital inflow without any drop in V. The marginal import coefficient of .38 would probably be lowered by this correction, however, and hence the *marginal* productivity of external capital for further reductions would be higher.

19. There would be little difference in the productivity calculation if the alternative procedure of fixing the growth of GNP and determining the corresponding F^m had been followed in Table 9.2 as in Figures 9.1 and 9.2.

Table 9.2. GNP Levels Permitted with Reduced Amounts of Foreign Aid Under the Import Constraint, 1951-1961[a]

Year	$F = 0$	$F = 1/4$ Actual	$F = 1/2$ Actual	$F = 3/4$ Actual	$F =$ Actual	Actual F	Actual GNP
1951	28.0	33.0	38.1	43.1	48.1	7.7	47.8
1952	34.9	38.2	41.5	44.9	48.2	5.1	47.4
1953	44.3	46.2	48.1	50.0	52.0	2.9	54.3
1954	47.8	50.6	53.5	56.3	59.1	4.3	58.7
1955	47.9	50.2	52.6	55.0	57.4	3.6	63.3
1956	48.3	51.9	55.6	59.3	63.0	5.6	67.7
1957	51.4	54.9	58.4	61.9	65.3	5.3	73.9
1958	50.1	54.7	59.3	63.9	68.6	7.1	76.4
1959	52.2	57.6	63.1	68.5	73.9	8.3	79.4
1960	52.3	61.2	70.0	78.9	87.8	13.6	83.1
1961	53.0	59.9	66.7	73.5	80.4	10.5	92.7
Total	509.2	558.1	606.9	655.3	703.7		744.7

[a] In billions of 1954 drachmas calculated from equation (32).

Although these alternative measurements can only suggest the benefits that have been achieved by providing external capital to Greece over the decade of the 1950s, it would be hard to devise a plausible set of assumptions which would not indicate that this had been a highly productive use of resources. The benefits to the Greek economy greatly exceed the costs of the capital imported, even if the opportunity cost of this capital is taken to be considerably higher than the actual cost to Greece of interest and amortization.

The principal source of the high productivity of external resources in this situation has been the great increase in domestic savings that has been made possible by more rapid growth. The savings achieved by 1960 out of the actual 6 percent growth rate were nearly three times as high as the amount that would have been produced with the same savings function at 2 percent growth. This increased savings potential is the main source of the high productivity of external resources in a country which is able to capture a substantial fraction of the increase in GNP for further investment as Greece has done.[20]

VIII. *Progress toward Self-Sustaining Growth*

Over the past 15 years, Greece has demonstrated its ability to maintain a high rate of growth and to finance an increasing share of the investment needed to sustain it from internal sources. Despite this impressive accomplishment, Greece continues to depend for its further development on a large inflow of capital. We therefore conclude our study by analyzing the magnitude and feasibility of structural changes designed to reduce this inflow to more manageable proportions over the next decade.

20. The marginal ratio of gross savings to GNP in our model is .22 for the decade 1950–1961. It seems to have been even higher in 1962–1964, since gross savings now have reached 21 percent of GNP. Ellis shows that private savings have been the dominant element in this increase. He gives an estimate of the (gross) marginal propensity to save out of personal disposable income of about .20.

The Need for Structural Change

Contries relying heavily on external capital for their development do not typically experience balance of payments pressures until they try to reduce the extent of their external dependence. The resulting shift from the savings limit to the import limit in the development process which we have found in Greece is characteristic of many underdeveloped countries (see Chenery and Strout 1966: part II). This phenomenon results from the fact that the market mechanism reflects current rather than future supplies of foreign exchange. It is therefore unlikely to produce the redirection of investment needed to reduce the payments deficit as fast as the rise in savings would allow.

Since our model of the Greek economy describes its economic structure in the 1950s, it does not permit a separation between feasible short-run changes with the existing productive structure and those that would necessitate a redirection of investment. We shall therefore characterize any change in the equation system of Section V as a "structural change" and qualify our results accordingly in translating them into policy conclusions.

To show the need for structural change, we have first projected the volume of external capital required to sustain continued growth at 6 percent with the economic structure of the 1950s.[21] The results of these projections for 1962–1971 are given in Figure 9.4. They show that although the investment-savings gap could be closed by 1970, the import gap would continue to widen. The experience of 1961–1964.[22] suggests that potential export growth may be understated by our projected 5 percent. To reduce the present large capital inflow will also require substantial import substitution, however, since export growth of 10 percent per year would be needed just to prevent the import-export gap from increasing by 1971.

The tendency for the savings gap to decline while the balance of payments gap rises is a clear indication that new investment has not been sufficiently directed into sectors that earn or save foreign exchange. This conclusion is amply borne out by the sectoral analyses of Papandreou (1962), Coutsoumaris (1963), and Ellis (1964), which point to the falling share of investment in industry, excessive amounts of construction, and other weaknesses in the current allocation pattern. Although our model is a highly aggregated one, it can be used to show the extent of the prospective imbalance with the present structure and to assess the consistency of sectoral analyses with general objectives and limitations.

The extent to which investment needs to be redirected—or other measures taken to reduce the growing structural imbalance—is shown by the projected difference

---

21. In making these projections, we have used the two-gap form of the model, in which the capacity-investment equation (9.36) replaces the investment equations (9.6)–(9.8). The exogenous variable P_m was projected from the following least squares fit for 1951–1961:

$$P_m = 81.5 + .80t$$

I_s was taken as a constant at its average value: $I_s = 1076$.

A projection of the original model to 1971 was also made, based on an extrapolation of the historical trend of profits: $P/K = 84.6 + 2.14t$. This projection showed a fall in the rate of growth to 4 percent, because of the balance of payments limitation, despite unrealistically large amounts of investment due to the extrapolation of the past trend of rising profits. The two-gap version of the model is more useful for the analysis of structural change, since it permits us to consider the costs and benefits of alternative policy changes, including capital requirements to raise output.

22. Export earnings have been growing at over 10 percent for the past 3 years, largely due to tourism and other service items.

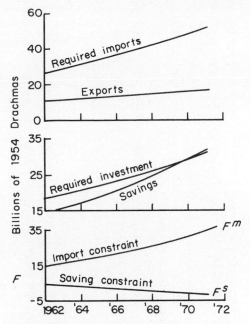

Figure 9.4 Projection of present structure to 1972 (growth rate = 6 percent).

between the two resource gaps. By 1970, the projected level of domestic saving would be more than sufficient to finance a growth rate of 6 percent with a capital-output ratio of 3.0. To make this possible, however, import requirements will have to be reduced or export growth increased. It will be necessary to devote an increasing share of investment to this purpose, since otherwise the attempt to transform additional savings into productive investment will be thwarted by lack of foreign exchange to purchase investment goods and raw materials.

Possibilities for Self-Sustaining Growth

The only comprehensive sectoral projections that have been published for Greece are those of Papandreou (1962: chaps. 3–5). We shall start by assessing the most optimistic of these, which assumes that the share of manufacturing in GNP will rise from 20 percent in 1960 to 28 percent in 1972 with a slight reduction in the aggregate capital-output ratio. On the most optimistic assumption, all of this increase in the share of manufacturing output would go toward reducing the trade deficit, either through increased exports or reduced imports.

Projections to 1971 with the original structure (Program A) and with the maximum structural change suggested by Papandreou (Program B) are given in Table 9.3. Program B would reduce the balance of payments deficit in 1971 shown by Program A by a third, but F would still be rising almost as fast as GNP. Furthermore, there would still be a substantial excess of potential savings over investment needs if foreign capital covered the larger gap. This excess of the trade gap over the savings gap suggests that further import substitution or export expansion would be economical— even if larger amounts of capital are required per unit of foreign exchange saved— since otherwise there will be a waste of potential savings.

Table 9.3. Requirements for External Capital Under Three Development Programs[a]

	Program A[b]			Program B[c]			Program C[d]		
	1962	1971	Total 1962-1971	1962	1971	Total 1962-1971	1962	1971	Total 1962-1971
1. Gross national product (V)	98.2	165.9	1294.5	98.2	165.9	1294.5	98.2	165.9	1294.5
2. Gross investment (I)	16.3	26.8	211.6	16.3	26.8	211.6	23.2	29.1	242.5
3. Gross savings (S)	14.0	31.0	218.8	14.0	31.0	218.8	14.0	31.0	218.8
4. Savings gap (F^s)	2.3	- 4.2	- 7.2	2.3	- 4.2	- 7.2	9.1	- 1.9	23.9
5. Imports (M)[d]	26.5	51.5	379.7	25.7	38.2	317.8	25.7	38.2	317.8
6. Exports (E)[d]	11.6	17.7	146.6	11.6	17.7	146.6	16.6	40.1	293.9
7. Import gap (F^m)[d]	14.9	33.7	233.1	14.1	20.4	171.1	9.1	- 1.9	23.9
8. Reduction in import gap from program A				0.8	13.3	62.0	5.8	35.6	209.2
9. Total investment in import gap reduction						36.8			129.5
10. Share of investment in structural change (9 ÷ 2)						17.4%			53.4%

[a] The reduction in the trade gap in Program B is arbitrarily assigned to import reduction and the additional reduction under Program C to export expansion. These divisions do not affect the final import gap under our assumptions.

[b] Program A: Projection of model of section V with growth of V of 6 percent per year and gross investment estimates of Program B.

[c] Program B: Investment requirements of 6 percent growth from Papandreou, chapter 3, "program 22/28." We have translated his assumptions to $k = 2.773$, declining by .008 per year. All the increase in manufacturing output above 20 percent of GNP is assumed to replace imports.

[d] Program C is based on the following assumptions and their implications:

1. Import substitution or export expansion beyond the amount permitted in Program B will require a marginal capital-output ratio of $km = 1.5$ $k = 1.5 \times 2.77 = 4.155$.
2. Additional investment is therefore required by Program C to the extent of $.333\, I\, m$, where $I\, m$ is extra investment in import substitution or exports.
3. The annual reduction in the import gap due to each year's investment is equal to $I\, m/km = .241\, I\, m$.
4. The amount of import substitution that can take place in each period is determined from (2) and (3) and the initial difference between F_0^m and F_0^s:

$$F_0^m - F_0^s = \Delta F_{-1} = \Delta F_1^m + \Delta F_1^s = .241\, I\, m + .333\, I\, m = .574\, I\, m$$

$$\Delta F_1^m = .42\ \Delta F_1$$
$$\Delta F_1^s = .58\ \Delta F_1$$

The calculation is repeated each year, starting from the export and import levels and resulting values of F^m and F^s of the previous period. The rationale of this process is elaborated in Chenery and Strout (1966, section IC).

To get an idea of the maximum investment that might be devoted to reducing the import gap, we have devised a hypothetical Program C in which it is assumed that export-increasing (or import-substituting) investment beyond Program B can be undertaken with a marginal capital coefficient of 4.15, which is 50 percent higher than the average value of k used in Program B. This high value of k is assumed to allow for the import content of increased exports and for the need to reduce the price of additional exports or import substitutes. Further investment to reduce the import-export gap will therefore increase the savings gap. To minimize the requirement for external capital, however, it is efficient to continue this process until the two gaps are equal ex ante.[23] Program C therefore assumes that export expansion will continue until the two resource gaps are equal. This reduces the cumulative import gap for the period 1962–1971 from 171 to 24, while the additional investment required would increase the savings gap from −7 to 24. On aggregate resource grounds, it therefore appears that Greece could maintain a growth rate of 6 percent and eliminate its requirement for additional external capital by 1970 if the structure of output could be changed as rapidly as is assumed here.

The feasibility of such a massive change in the composition of investment can only be tested adequately in a sectoral analysis. One indication of the magnitude of the effort required by Program C is the fact that more than half of the total investment over this decade would have to be devoted to import substitution or export expansion in order to change from the existing structure—indicated in Program A—to the "optimum" structure of Program C, in which the trade gap would not exceed the savings gap.

Another indication of the magnitude of the structural change required between Programs A and C is the reduction in the imported component of GNP and expansion of exports. The illustrative figures of Table 9.3 result in a rate of growth of 12 percent in exports from 1961–1971 and a reduction in the import ratio to GNP from .27 to .23. In marginal terms, the increase in imports would be only 16 percent of the increase in GNP in Programs B and C as compared to the marginal ratio of .38 estimated in the equations for the 1950s.

While both this degree of import substitution and of export expansion seem very optimistic, structural changes of this magnitude are not unprecedented in rapidly developing countries. They would, however, require a substantial reorientation of development policy in Greece.

IX. Conclusions

We have reached some conclusions as to the success of Greece in developing with heavy reliance on external assistance and some conclusions of more general significance. As to the Greek experience of the past decade, our results indicate that:

a. Measured by benefits achieved (in increased GNP, consumption, and capital formation) in relation to the cost of external resources, the Greek experience has been quite successful on almost any interpretation of the measures used.

b. Quite substantial changes are needed in the economic structure of the past decade to enable Greece to finance a larger share of its required investment from domestic savings without having growth inhibited by balance of payments limitations.

23. This proposition is demonstrated in Chenery and Strout (1966: sec. IC).

The problem has been shown to be one of allocating investment resources rather than of domestic finance for investment.

From a broader methodological standpoint, the use of an econometric model with fairly limited and aggregated data has been shown to have some definite advantages as well as some pitfalls.[24] The main virtue demonstrated by the formal model is its ability to make consistent projections of the performance of an economy under alternative policy assumptions. The effects of uncertainty or errors in some of the key parameters and of limitations of the model can be tested by assuming alternative values. Our principal conclusions do not appear to be very sensitive to moderate errors in estimating the values of the principal parameters.

24. While it is difficult to generalize about pitfalls, the difficulties in Greece and in other countries of securing explanations of investment behavior are indicative of the type of problem encountered. The policy uses of the model must be considered as well as the goodness of fit in choosing among alternative forms of equations.

Appendix A to Chapter 9:
Alternative Estimates
of the Statistical Functions

The symbols used to identify the variables in each equation are the same as those listed in Section V. Different estimates are identified as:

SSLS   single-stage least squares
TSLS   two-stage least squares
LI   limited information

Table A9.1. Consumption Functions

Dependent variable	Type of estimate	Y_d	Constant	$\bar{R}^2$
C_c	SSLS	+ 0.1318 (0.0082)	+ 1020 (432)	0.966
C_c	LI	+ 0.1317 (0.0082)	+ 1027 (434)	0.966
C_c	TSLS	+ 0.1318 (0.0082)	+ 1024 (510)	0.966
C_h	SSLS	+ 0.2120 (0.0115)	- 1517 (606)	0.974
C_h	LI	+ 0.2163 (0.0117)	- 1742 (618)	0.974
C_h	TSLS	+ 0.2121 (0.0116)	- 1522 (714)	0.974
C_s	SSLS	+ 0.2190 (0.0153)	- 3213 (805)	0.958
C_s	LI	+ 0.2175 (0.0153)	- 3135 (809)	0.958
C_s	TSLS	+ 0.2182 (0.0153)	- 3171 (949)	0.958
C_f	SSLS	+ 0.3146 (0.0169)	+ 11564 (889)	0.975
C_f	LI	+ 0.3177 (p.0170)	+ 11400 (897)	0.975
C_f	TSLS	+ 0.3151) (0.0169)	+ 11540 (1048)	0.975
G	SSLS	+ 0.1043[a] (0.0095)	+ 1479 (654)	0.931
G	LI	+ 0.1054[a] (0.0095)	+ 1405 (659)	0.931
G	TSLS	+ 0.1046[a] (0.0095	+ 1459 (780)	0.931

[a] Independent variable is V.

Table A9.2. Investment Functions

Dependent variable	Estimate type	Constant term	M	P/K	Dependent variable lagged	Time	$\bar{R}^2$
I_m	SSLS	- 4799 (987)	+ 0.6729 (0.0594)	a	a	a	0.934
I_m	LI	- 4469 (1023)	+ 0.6518 (0.0611)	a	a	a	0.934
I_m	TSLS	- 4776 (1432)	+ 0.6714 (0.0601)	a	a	a	0.934
I_d	SSLS	- 2049 (1485)	a	+ 36.3 (17.3)	a	+ 264 (50.9)	0.907
I_c	SSLS	- 413 (310)	a	a	+ 0.84 (0.19)	+ 208 (93.0)	0.959

a Not applicable.

Table A9.3. Import Functions

Dependent variable	Type of estimate	V	P_m	Constant term	$\bar{R}^2$
M_s	SSLS	+ 0.0652 (0.011)	- 21 (13)	- 727 (119)	0.826
M_s	LI	+ 0.0654 (0.011)	- 21 (13)	- 742 (120)	0.826
M_S	TSLS	+ 0.0653 (0.011)	- 21 (13)	- 732 (128)	0.826
M_f	SSLS	+ 0.0190 (0.008)	- 7.16 (9.71)	1693 (900)	0.419
M_f	LI	+ 0.0187 (0.008)	- 7.07 (9.71)	1710 (903)	0.419
M_f	TSLS	+ 0.0190 (0.008)	- 7.15 (9.71)	1695 (964)	0.419
M_i	SSLS	+ 0.0508 (0.066)	- 17.8 (8.11)	2289 (753)	0.880
M_i	LI	+ 0.0502 (0.067)	- 17.6 (8.12)	2315 (755)	0.880
M_i	TSLS	+ 0.0505 (0.066	- 17.7 (8.12)	2301 (874)	0.880
M_m	SSLS	+ 0.0645 (0.0048)	- 9.75 (5.87)	- 433 (544)	0.957
M_m	LI	+ 0.0641 (0.0048)	- 9.66 (5.88)	- 415 (546)	0.957
M_m	TSLS	+ 0.0643 (0.0048)	- 9.73 (5.87)	- 428 (584)	0.957
M_t	SSLS	+ 0.1832 (0.0246)	- 76.02 (30.04)	+ 1784 (2786)	0.876
M_t	LI	+ 0.1845 (0.0247)	- 76.34 (30.05)	- 1844 (2795)	0.876
M_t	TSLS	+ 0.1836 (0.0247)	- 76.12 (30.05)	- 1801 (2987)	0.876

Table A9.4. Export Functions

Dependent variable	Type of estimate	t	Constant term	$\bar{R}^2$
X_t	SSLS	+198 (45.6)	+2181 (283)	0.665
X_i	SSLS	+146 (18.2)	+ 314 (113)	0.875
X_{mt}	SSLS	+ 18 (6.3)	+ 146 (39)	0.448
X_s	SSLS	+321 (36.7)	+ 70 (227)	0.894

Table A9.5. Tax Functions and Depreciation Function

Dependent variable	Type of estimate	V	Constant term	$\bar{R}^2$
T_d	SSLS	+ 0.0921 (0.0058)	- 757 (403)	0.965
T_d	LI	+ 0.0921 (0.0058)	- 755 (405)	0.965
T_d	TSLS	+ 0.0921 (0.0058)	- 757 (480)	0.965[
T_i	SSLS	+ 0.1318 (0.0036)	-1294 (248)	0.993
T_i	LI	+ 0.1312 (0.0036)	-1252 (250)	0.993
T_i	TSLS	+ 0.1317 (0.0036)	-1284 (298)	0.993
D	SSLS	+ 0.0213[a] (0.0010)	- 88 (163)	0.979

[a] The independent variable is capital stock at the beginning of the year.

Appendix B to Chapter 9:
The Data

The major source of our data is United Nations (1957–1962). Because of the occasional revisions of data, the most recent annual data have been selected: for 1950, the 1957 edition was used; for 1951, the 1958 edition; for 1952, the 1959 edition; 1953, the 1960 edition; 1954, the 1961 edition; and 1955–1961, the 1962 edition.

Table B9.1. Greece: GNP, National Income, and Income Shares (millions of 1954 drachmas)

Year	GNP (1)	National income factor cost (2ª)	Agricultural income (3ª)	Nonfarm wage and salary income (4ª)	Profits (residual) (5)	Price deflator GNP (6)
1950	42,790	37,030	12,927	13,330	10,772	0.672
1951	47,819	40,889	15,275	14,883	10,730	0.720
1952	47,358	39,734	14,694	14,622	10,417	0.762
1953	54,315	45,892	18,091	17,072	10,730	0.893
1954	58,690	49,696	17,445	18,704	13,547	1.000
1955	63,318	53,538	18,827	20,118	14,594	1.051
1956	67,753	57,447	19,547	21,816	16,083	1.147
1957	73,914	62,337	21,726	24,004	16,608	1.134
1958	76,352	63,977	20,434	25,667	17,876	1.145
1959	79,366	66,656	20,360	27,399	18,897	1.146
1960	83,076	69,543	19,746	29,572	20,224	1.172
1961	92,656	77,520	23,467	32,264	21,790	1.184

Sources: Column (1) 1950–1961: U.N., *National Accounts Statistics*, 1957–1962. (2) Ibid. (3) National Accounts of Greece, 1948–1959; 1960; 1961 (Greek ed.). Agricultural, animal breeding, forestry, fishing. (4) 1954–1961: U.N., *National Accounts Statistics*, 1960–1962. 1950–1953: extrapolated, on basis of .04 decrease per annum in the ratio of wage and salary income. (5) Residual: National income *less* agricultural income *less* nonfarm wage and salary income. (6) U.N., *National Accounts Statistics*, 1957–1962. Implicit deflator obtained by dividing current price by 1954 constant price series.

ª Data originally in current prices, converted by implicit GNP deflator.

Table B9.2. Greece: Composition of Private Consumption Expenditure
(millions of 1954 drachmas)

Year	Food etc.[a]	Clothing[b]	Household operations[c]	Net services[d]	Total
1950	20,890	6,000	6,170	5,114	38,174
1951	22,080	5,890	6,440	5,680	40,090
1952	23,270	6,040	6,680	4,101	40,091
1953	24,510	6,480	7,200	5,991	44,181
1954	26,010	7,140	7,950	6,139	47,239
1955	27,050	7,150	8,390	6,983	49,573
1956	28,330	7,650	9,110	8,494	53,584
1957	29,580	8,030	9,940	10,001	57,551
1958	30,240	8,960	10,740	9,506	59,446
1959	30,770	9,000	11,380	9,435	60,585
1960	31,190	9,130	12,210	10,820	63,350
1961	32,540	10,500	13,450	11,688	68,178

Source: 1950-1953: National Accounts of Greece, 1948-1959. 1954-1961: U.N.,
National Accounts Statistics, 1961, 1962.

[a] corresponds to U.N. category food, beverages, and tobacco.
[b] corresponds to U.N. category clothing and other personal effects.
[c] corresponds to U.N. category rent, water; fuel, light; furniture; and household operations.
[d] corresponds to U.N. category all others.

Table B9.3. Greece: Gross Capital Formation (millions of 1954 drachmas)

Year	Residential construction (1)	Nonresidential construction (2)	Machinery and transport equipment (3)	Increase in stocks (4)	Gross capital formation (5)	Depreciation (6)	Net capital formation (7)
1950	2062	2125	3999	1895	10081	1892	8189
1951	1547	1708	3630	2618	9502	2037	2456
1952	1677	1930	3008	718	7333	2624	4709
1953	2264	2326	1970	1577	8137	2777	5360
1954	2498	2577	2950	− 290	7745	2788	4957
1955	3939	2482	2915	747	10083	2808	7275
1956	4074	3221	3640	1172	12107	2949	9158
1957	3683	3582	4018	2167	13450	3122	10328
1958	4252	4394	6814	710	16170	3414	12756
1959	4075	5195	8670	750	18670	3629	15061
1960	4466	7095	13704	− 550	24715	3784	20931
1961	5090	7789	11851	1400	26130	4262	21868

Sources: Columns(1) – (6): U.N., *National Accounts Statistics 1957-1962.* (7) = (5) minus (6).

Table B9.4. Greece: Net Foreign Capital Inflow, Composition of Exports and Price Deflator (millions of 1954 drachmas)

Year	Net foreign capital inflow (1)	Exports goods and services[a] (2)	Exports goods (3)	Food, etc.[b] (4)	Industrial[c] (5)	Manufacturing and machinery[d] exports (6)	Price deflator exports 1954=100 (7)
1950	10,268	2797	2154	1568	440	146	0.608
1951	7,727	3127	2408	1753	491	164	0.590
1952	5,079	3948	3240	2307	701	32	0.555
1953	2,934	5422	4117	2991	896	30	0.825
1954	4,341	6227	4556	3392	868	96	1.000
1955	3,635	7731	5159	3582	1355	22	1.063
1956	5,644	7488	5015	3122	1651	242	1.036
1957	5,321	8759	5850	4351	1268	231	1.126
1958	7,064	8987	6444	4540	1622	282	1.079
1959	8,289	9156	6128	4043	1827	258	1.000
1960	13,578	9583	6195	4015	1817	363	0.984
1961	10,462	11054	6872	4326	2082	464	0.975

Sources: Column (1): Imports of goods and services (Table B9.5) *less* exports of goods and services (Column 2) *plus* income from abroad. (2) U.N., *National Accounts Statistics*, 1957-1962. (3) - (6): U.N., *Yearbook of International Trade Statistics*, 1955, 1957, 1961. Data in current prices; converted to 1954 prices with GNP deflator (see Table B9.1). Data for 1950 and 1951 extended by using average percent of total in 1952-1954. (7): U.N., *National Accounts Statistics*, 1957-1962. Implicit deflators obtained from dividing current price series by the 1954 constant price series.

a Does not include income from ocean-going ships under Greek flag or ownership.
b Corresponds to U.N. category food (0); beverages and tobacco (1); animal, vegetable oils (4).
c Corresponds to U.N. category crude materials (2); mineral fuels, etc. (3); chemicals (5).
d Corresponds to U.N. category manufactured goods by material (6); miscellaneous manufactured articles (8); other commodities and transactions, n.e.c. (9); machinery, transport equipment (7).

Table B9.5. Greece: Composition of Imports (millions of 1954 drachmas)

Year	Imports goods and services (1)	Imports goods (2)	Imports food, etc. (3)	Imports industrial (4)	Imports manufacturing (5)	Imports machinery (6)	Imports services (7)	Price deflator imports 1954 = 100 (8)
1950	13,383	12,133	2,722	4,469	2,569	2,373	1,250	0.520
1951	11,396	10,317	2,315	3,801	2,185	2,016	1,079	0.570
1952	9,775	8,892	1,923	3,346	1,818	1,805	883	0.584
1953	9,003	8,160	1,897	2,939	1,788	1,536	843	0.811
1954	11,441	9,901	1,644	3,701	2,674	1,882	1,540	1.000
1955	12,318	11,151	2,351	3,795	2,670	2,335	1,167	1.028
1956	14,586	13,163	3,010	3,973	3,104	3,076	1,423	1.057
1957	16,032	14,343	2,802	4,734	3,455	3,352	1,689	1.097
1958	17,892	15,921	2,596	4,906	3,709	4,701	1,971	1.065
1959	19,478	16,792	2,308	4,480	3,716	6,288	2,686	1.009
1960	25,698	21,756	2,366	5,338	4,402	9,650	3,942	0.968
1961	24,716	21,294	2,858	5,262	4,536	8,638	3,422	1.006

Sources: Column (1): U.N., National Accounts Statistics, 1957–1962. For 1950–1951, estimates are derived by applying 1952–1953 percentages to total goods and services imports. (2) - (6): U.N., Yearbook of International Trade Statistics, 1955, 1957, 1961. Data in current prices; converted to 1954 prices with GNP deflator; see Table B9.1, col. (6); see Table B9.4, col. (3) for a description of categories. (7): (2) minus (3). (8): U.N., National Accounts Statistics, 1957–1962; obtained by dividing current price series by the 1954 constant price series.

Table B9.6. Greece: **Export, Import Price Indices; Exchange Rate**

Year	Export price index 1954 = 100 (1)	Import price index 1954 = 100 (2)	Exchange rate Dr./US $ (3)	Relative price of imports (4)
1950			15	
1951	59	55	15	58
1952	55	56	30	73
1953	83	85	30	95
1954	100	100	30	100
1955	110	100	30	95
1956	118	105	30	91
1957	116	108	30	95
1958	113	99	30	86
1959	103	100	30	87
1960	101	96	30	82
1961	102	94	30	79

Sources: Columns (1) and (2): 1953-1961: IMF, *International Financial Statistics*, July 1963; 1949-1953, *IFS* Supplement. Adjusted to 1954 = 100; 1954 weights. (3): *Ibid.* (4): Import price index divided by GNP deflator and multiplied by index of exchange rate (1954 = 100).

Table B9.7. Greece: **Savings, Capital Stock, Profit Rate, and Deflators** (millions of 1954 drachmas)

Year	Saving gross (1)	Capital stock (2)	Index of profit rate 1954 = 100 (3)	Deflator gross capital formation 1954 = 100 (4)	Deflator depreciation 1954 = 100 (5)
1950	1597	115065	97.25	596	586
1951	3111	123254	90.50	678	667
1952	2897	130710	82.8	702	707
1953	6179	135419	82.3	910	821
1954	4475	140879	100.0	1000	1000
1955	8019	145836	103.9	1045	1059
1956	8144	153111	109.1	1107	1104
1957	9596	162269	106.3	1133	1152
1958	1417	172597	107.6	1039	1100
1959	9214	185353	106.0	1035	1150
1960	6794	200414	104.8	1008	1167
1961	13160	221345	102.2	1042	1156

Sources: Column (1): U.N., *National Accounts Statistics*, 1957-1962. Sum of depreciation and net savings, deflated by implicit gross capital formation deflator (see Table B9.3). (2): 1950 figure equals three times the Gross Domestic Product. Subsequent figures derived by cumulating net capital formation (Table B9.3). (3): Profit (see Table B9.1) divided by column (2) and converted into an index. (4): U.N., *National Accounts Statistics*, 1957-1962. Obtained by dividing current price series by 1954 constant price series. (5): Depreciation deflator from Greek Ministry of Coordination, *National Accounts of Greece* 1948-1958, 1960, 1961 (Greek edition). Obtained by dividing current price series by 1954 constant price series.

Table B9.8. Greece: Taxes, and Government Expenditures
(millions of 1954 drachmas)

Year	Direct taxes and transfer payments (1)	Indirect taxes *less* subsidies (2)	Government consumption expenditures (3)
1950	2689	4124	5559
1951	3656	5036	7018
1952	4154	5173	6922
1953	4113	5870	6347
1954	4587	6206	7396
1955	4945	6959	7657
1956	5177	7481	8526
1957	5846	8413	9132
1958	6184	9070	9171
1959	6540	9034	10151
1960	6991	9732	10494
1961	8149	10946	11125

Sources: Column (1): 1950-1953: U.N., *National Accounts Statistics,* 1957;
1954: *National Accounts Statistics,* 1961; 1955-1961; *National Accounts Statistics,*
1962. Current price series deflated by 1954 GNP price deflator, (see Table B9.4).
Includes direct tax on corporations, household and private nonprofit organizations,
and other transfers. (2) and (3): U.N., *National Accounts Statistics,* 1957-1962.

Part III
Sectoral Planning

Introduction to Part III

Samuel Bowles
and Walter Falcon

The three studies in Part III present planning models for particular sectors in the economy—agriculture and education. Both sectors have recently received increased attention from economists interested less in developed countries. This is because of the predominant role that agriculture plays in the economic life of poor nations and the conviction that, through its contribution to the quality of the labor force, education is one of the major sources of economic growth. A brief discussion of sectoral models and their applications to agriculture and education will serve as a preface for these studies.

The Nature of Sectoral Models

The choice of a sectoral, as opposed to an economy-wide, model for planning is dictated by the need for a more detailed representation of policy alternatives than is feasible in an analysis of the whole economy. Highly disaggregated economy-wide models are costly to estimate and use. Indeed, they are often so complex that the essential functions of model building—simplification and the clarification of alternatives—are lost. Moreover, if a particular set of decisions involves policies and projects largely internal to a given sector, there may be little gain from using a model of the whole economy. Finally the appropriate time framework for decision-making often varies greatly between sectors, making it very difficult to aggregate various portions of the economy in a meaningful way. For all these reasons, sectoral models are used extensively in the analysis of water resources, power, transport, and industry, as well as education and agriculture.

Problems in Model Formulation

In spite of their merits, sectoral formulations also present a series of special problems. The first set of difficulties involves the various linkages to the national models that are necessary to assure consistency of results. These difficulties arise because the economy is a general equilibrium system, and decisions taken in one sector cannot be easily separated from decisions taken elsewhere. Thus, for example, the opportunity costs of inputs used in the sector but supplied from other parts of the economy cannot be known precisely without a full specification of conditions in the entire economy. And these conditions depend, in part, on the decisions taken in the sector under consideration. Similarly, the demand for the output of the sector may depend in important ways on external developments, which may themselves be influenced by choices within the sector. Because of these features, a sectoral model should be thought of as being complementary to, rather than a substitute for, an aggregated model.

When used in this manner, the detailed results given by a sectoral model can provide a basis for revisions in the estimated parameters of the more comprehensive analysis. For example, a detailed study of agricultural cropping patterns may well reveal that the choice of crops does not have a significant effect on the growth of GNP; on the other hand, this choice may have a profound influence on the growth of exports. Similarly, the quantity solution and shadow prices in a national model may often allow a more accurate specification of the economic parameters in which a sectoral model must operate. An obvious example of this type is the real price of foreign exchange which should be used in the calculation of costs and benefits to various sectoral projects or programs.

Another set of linkage problems in model construction centers on the nature of the demand for products of certain sectors. Education is a prime example, since one of the central problems in constructing an educational planning model arises from the fact that the product of the schools—educated labor—has a derived demand based on the levels of output and technologies used throughout the economy. Specifying the relationship between the production of educated labor and the future growth of the economy is probably the most difficult task facing the educational planner. In fact, the method for solving this problem provides the basis for classifying planning approaches in the field. They range from the manpower requirements approach, based on the assumption of zero price elasticity demand for educated labor; to the rate of return approach and Bowles' linear programming model, which operate on the assumption of an infinite long-run price elasticity of demand for all types of labor; to Dougherty's formulation, which avoids both extremes through the use of estimated demand functions for labor. Bowles (1970) has attempted a test of the empirical validity of these alternative assumptions concerning the demand for labor with various levels of schooling. Regardless of the approach taken, the researcher is handicapped by another problem, the multidimensional nature of the output, which defies adequate measurement by simple monetary indices of purely economic benefits.

Yet another aspect of the linkage difficulty concerns the supply and demand functions for various sectors. Adequate specification of these relationships is particularly important when linear programming techniques are applied. (More than one agricultural researcher has found—much to his dismay—that his models suggest that the entire world should be planted in vegetables!) Special care must therefore be taken to build into these models falling demand prices and rising supply prices when these functions are less than infinitely elastic.

A second general set of problems concerns the dynamic properties of various sectors and the importance of a correct specification of the role of time in the production process. This feature is illustrated well in both Gotsch, Chapter 10, and Bowles, Chapter 11. In the former, for example, the availability of water is dated not by year, but by month. Bowles' model takes into account the very long time horizon required to evaluate the returns to investments in schooling, as well as the extended periods of production in the actual production of schooling itself. Accommodating the time factor, which is but one dimension of disaggregation, can be very demanding of data as both these studies show. Moreover, even within a given sector there may be two or more competing dynamic dimensions that must be considered in formulating the model. In a model involving multipurpose water development, for example, dams may have a 10-year construction period and may provide live storage over a period of 50 to 75 years; irrigation benefits may be related critically to monthly spill patterns; navigation benefits may also have a strong seasonal aspect; and in the case of power, the critical benefit calculations may involve the ability to serve peak loads between, say, 5 and 7 P.M. each day. Incorporating these dynamic features and determining the optimal degree of time disaggregation, is often one of the most difficult practical problem in sectoral formulations.

The final category of applied problems involves the special constraints that are invariably needed in sectoral models, particularly when they involve programming formulations. These are of many types, but particularly important is the need to introduce explicitly various social, political, and institutional features of the sector. In agriculture, for example, the evaluation of a new technology may depend in large measure on whether its associated inputs are to be privately or publicly distributed. No matter how the inputs are distributed, the technology may have important consequences for the distribution of income in the villages and the perpetuation of a peasant, as opposed to a plantation, society.

Another important characteristic of the agricultural sector that may require explicit recognition is the large number of decision-makers and the dubious validity of the assumption—crucial to linear programming models—that the elasticity of substitution in production is zero. (In industrial planning, by contrast, the number of key decision-makers, even in a thoroughgoing market economy, may be less than 100.) In most of agriculture, the independent farmer is the prime decision-making unit. With the number of decision-makers characteristically in the millions, agricultural planners are forced to specify the way in which the "optimal" plan will be implemented. Since simple fiat is usually very inadequate, price policy, lags in response, and the other dimensions of the incentive structure must often be incorporated into the analysis. Similarly, in education, one must take into account the direct impact of resource decisions in the schools on the distribution of income and opportunity. There is no reason to expect, for example, that economically efficient solutions will increase the capacity to earn higher incomes of those who most deserve increases in welfare. While these troublesome issues are present in any planning problem, they are particularly acute in the cases of agriculture and education.

Applications of Sectoral Models

No single set of three articles can hope to cover definitively the planning techniques relevant for agriculture and education. Hence it is useful to place these particular analyses in a slightly broader perspective.

Beginning first with methodological considerations, there are several features of the Gotsch model on agriculture which should be noted. One of the major dilemmas facing rural planners involves the treatment of technological change. Since most agricultural development programs have as their major objectives changing input-output relationships or relaxing the major constraints on production or both, historic data are of limited value in analyzing potential outcomes. Gotsch, drawing upon empirical work which indicated a positive farmer response to economic stimuli, was able to use the normative framework of a programming model to simulate a series of important emerging policy problems in West Pakistan. In the case of the normative supply curves, for example, his conclusions on elasticities are quite different from those derived from more traditional econometric techniques. The fact that Gotsch addresses specific *policy* issues is also significant. Although programming models have often been used as a technique in farm planning, rarely have they been carried forward into a policy context. Here too, the Gotsch essay breaks new ground.

An important feature of all three essays is the way each overcomes the linkage problems mentioned in the preceding section. In his paper on Colombia, Dougherty adopts an imaginative solution to the demand problem by using explicit estimates of the demand functions for educated labor. In Bowles' paper on education in Nigeria, the rising supply price of inputs supplied from outside the educational sector is introduced by the use of "recruiting activities," which hire incremental amounts of factors from the rest of the economy and from abroad at progressively higher opportunity costs. Generally speaking, these formulations indicate that when care is taken in model construction, it *is* possible to assure consistency of results between sectoral and national formulations.

More specifically, they indicate that in spite of the paucity of data and other problems, the gains from decentralization in model construction may be very considerable. For example, Bowles is able to state quite unequivocally that even if several basic parameters were off by as much as 20 percent, his major conclusions for Northern Nigeria would not be altered. He attributes this fact to the nature of educational decision-making and to the general difficulty of viewing the educational system as one involving significant interactions. As a result, he concludes that educational systems tend to be far from efficient, and that simple economic models which can take account of the sector's internal intertemporal relations will often yield substantial gains in system efficiency.

A final remark should be offered about the actual use of the models presented here. One of the most difficult, yet useful, roles of the sectoral planner in practice is his liaison function between particular ministries or firms and the macroplanners. Those who think that this role is impossible (or at least completely frustrating) will be interested to know that both the Gotsch and Dougherty essays were developed when the authors were acting as planning advisors. In both cases, their results had a substantial impact on actual decision-making.

10 A Programming Approach to Some Agriculture Policy Problems in West Pakistan*

Carl H. Gotsch

I. Introduction

Planners attempting to influence the course of a country's agricultural develop-ment can expect to confront a wide variety of problems which are difficult, perhaps impossible, to formalize. Many of these will involve the most significant decisions in determining an effective sectoral growth strategy. Examples that come readily to mind for agriculture include the assessment of the optimal level of resources to be devoted to research and extension activities, the development of viable credit and marketing institutions, provisions for productive land tenure arrangements, and so on.

There is, in addition, however, an important class of problems for which formal computational tools can be a significant aid to policy planning. As one might expect, these have to do primarily with problems of pricing and resource allocation. In the field of agriculture, for example, most developing countries engage in the manipu-lation of commodity prices. What is the proper relative price structure for securing the desired crop mix? Or, in the same vein, what are the effects of subsidies on the optimal level of input use? Such allocation models can also be used to assess the impact of changed input-output coefficients on optimal resource use. It is to issues of this type that the present essay on programming as a policy tool is addressed.

The Linear Programming Approach

Optimal solutions are undoubtedly of interest to planners. In recent years, how-ever, it has become rather widely appreciated that the usefulness of economic models in analyzing policy issues lies more often in the systematic exploration of alternative parameter assumptions than in the results obtained with any particular set of param-eters. This attitude is desired from two reasons: (1) decision-makers are not about to take seriously results that are not supported by a thorough understanding of the sensitivity of a particular solution to small changes in the parameters, and (2) by varying the parameters over wide ranges, schedules and curves can be constructed

* Reprinted from the *Pakistan Development Review*, Summer 1968, *8*, 192–225 by permission of the publisher. The author is currently Lecturer, Department of Economics, and Development Advisor in the Development Advisory Service of Harvard University. This paper was presented at the Development Advisory Service Sorrento Conference in September 1967. In addition to the general discussion at the conference, acknowledgments are due to Walter Falcon, Gustav Papanek, and Bart Duff for specific comments. Remaining errors are the author's alone.

Portions of this research were supported by the Project for Quantitative Research in Economic Development and the Development Advisory Service through funds provided by the Agency for International Development under Contract CSD-1543.

that permit policy makers to engage in a number of revealing, yet much less demanding, partial analyses.

The opportunity to derive interesting and useful information by varying parameter values systematically is clearly demonstrated in the variable price and variable resource programming potential of the standard linear programming format (Heady and Chandler 1958). Variable price programming, sometimes called "price-mapping," involves the derivation of a series of price-quantity relationships for a particular activity by parametrically varying the weight of that activity in the objective function of the model. Where the activity represents, say, a crop, the price-quantity curve may be interpreted as a normative, static supply curve for that crop. In the case of activities denoting inputs of one kind or another, systematic variation of the cost of operating the activity produces a normative demand curve for the input.

Other useful parametric programming exercises can be carried out by varying the availability of the fixed resources. As is well known, the implicit prices associated with each constraint represent the value of the marginal product of that particular "resource." Hence, systematically changing the magnitude of an element in the constraint vector can be used to produce a VMP curve (demand curve) for that resource.

II. The Model

The programming model presented in the following section was developed for the north central part of the Former Punjab. This area is one of the more rapidly growing agricultural areas in West Pakistan, averaging, since 1957–58, a 5.5 percent per annum increase in the gross value of production.[1] Most of the increased output was due to an expansion in rice acreage and a shift from low-quality coarse rice to a type of high-valued fine rice suitable for export. The rapid increase in the value of rice output has been due primarily to increased availability of irrigation water supplies. For although it receives more rain than most parts of the Punjab, the fortunes of the Gujranwala-Sheikhupura area are still dependent on surface canal flows and the amount of water withdrawn from the underground aquifer. With regard to the latter alternative, it is significant that over the 1957–58 to 1965–66 period, over 6000 tubewells were installed by local individuals in Gujranwala district alone (Ghulam Mohammad 1965). Assuming a one-cusec discharge and approximately 2000 working hours per year, these tubewells by 1965–66 added nearly 95 percent to the district's previously available water supply.[2] In view of this unusually rapid increase in irrigation supplies and the role of water in promoting agricultural growth in the area, the tract is particularly appropriate for a study whose emphasis is on problems of changing technology, water pricing, and water allocation.

Structure of the Model

The objective of the following programming model is to maximize:

$$R = \sum_{i=1}^{k} c_i X_i - \sum_{i=k+1}^{m} d_i X_i - \sum_{i=m+1}^{n} e_i X_i \qquad (10.1)$$

1. This includes a correction for the shift from coarse rice to high-valued fine rice which is not accounted for in a constant price growth calculation.
2. Calculations based on West Pakistan Water and Power Development Authority (1965) and Gotsch (1966a).

where
   c_i = the per acre net revenue obtained from the ith crop activity (gross revenue minus seed, fertilizer, pesticides, and so on)
   d_i = the variable cost of the ith water pumping activity
   e_i = the wages paid to the ith labor-hiring activity
Equation (1) is maximized subject to a series of constraints

$$\sum_{i=1}^{n} a_{ij}X_i \leq b_j \quad j = 1, \ldots, z \tag{10.2}$$

where
   a_{ij} = the input-output coefficient of the jth resource for one unit of the ith activity[3]
   b_j = a vector of resource availability.

Water Constraints
   In the Pakistan model, the first group of restrictions describes the role of irrigation. Water use and water availability are divided into 12 time periods assumed to be one month in length. Such a breakdown of the annual water usage is important since the extent to which the moisture needs of plants are met through time is, within bounds, as important to plant growth as the degree to which they receive their total water requirements. An obvious example is the limited usefulness of a downpour that provides one-tenth of the season's precipitation within a 24 hour period. (As the water a_{ij}'s are at the heart of the model, their estimation is discussed in some detail in the appendix to this chapter.)

Land Constraints
   In addition to the water needs, land requirements were estimated by crop. The resulting coefficients are simply a description of the periods during which a particular crop "occupies" the land. They are not strictly synonymous with the plant's growing season, however, since some time must be allotted for seedbed preparation and the removal of crop residues. Total land availability is assumed to be ten acres—about the size of an average farm worked by one pair of bullocks.

Bullock Constraints
   A third group of constraints describes the animal power needed in the production of various crops, again by month. Bullock services are treated as a fixed resource because they represent a highly indivisible input for which virtually no rental market exists. As a consequence, nearly all farmers own at least one pair of bullocks regardless of the size of the farm. From several farm management studies, it appears that the animals can be worked about six hours per day for a 24-day month. This gives a limit of 144 hours of bullock pair labor as the appropriate monthly animal power constraint. No provision is made in the model for the possibility that the animals could work for longer days during peak periods.

Human Labor Constraints
   Human labor requirements were also calculated by crop for each month of the growing season. The fixed nature of this resource stems from its interpretation as the labor of the tenant or owner and his family. Again based on farm management data collected in the Punjab, it appears that a farm of 10 acres would have about

---

3. All a_{ij}'s have been standardized to reflect requirements per acre of crop.

one and one-half man-days of family labor associated with it. Assuming an eight-hour day for 25 days per month, a total of about 300 hours per month would normally be available for use on the typical 10-acre farm.

Resource-Augmenting Constraints-Activities

In addition to the processes that use resources, two types of resource-augmenting activities are included. The first of these makes it possible to add to the fixed amount of available surface water. Physically, these activities represent the operation of tubewells that tap the underground water reservoir of the Indus Plain. The second set of augmenting activities permits the hiring of additional labor beyond that supplied by the family.

Activities that supply inputs may also be constrained to operate within certain limits. In the case of a tubewell, if capacity is given, the amount of additional water that can be produced by it is limited by the number of hours it can run per day. An absolute maximum, of course, would be 24, but when maintenance requirements and down time are considered, available running time may be considerably less.

Capacity constraints for the model were developed from farm management data in the Gujranwala area.[4] In that region, the average one-cusec tubewell commands approximately 80 acres. Assuming a maximum operating time of 23 hours, the well could deliver a total of about 690 inches per month or 86 inches to the 10-acre farm assumed in the model.

In the case of hired labor, it was assumed that the farmer could hire as much additional labor as necessary at the going wage rate. There is no provision in the model—even in its regional version—for the documented phenomena that the wages of labor do vary by season.

Special Constraints

Lastly, the model contains a set of inequalities that restrict the range of feasible cropping patterns to ones that (1) provide sufficient fodder for the farmer's bullocks and (2) do not permit "unreasonably" large acreages for "unusually" high-valued perishable crops such as fruits and vegetables. As long as it is assumed that small farmers do not think of their own effort on the market, there is little theoretical justification for the latter constraints. Failure to include them, however, results in an optimal solution in which virtually the entire farm is devoted to vegetables. Without knowing a great deal more about the difficulties of marketing perishables under primitive conditions—not to mention problems of risk aversion, and so on, that appear to be among the real determinants of limited fruit and vegetable production—there is little more that one can do.

A Schematic Representation of the Model

The structure of the programming model discussed above can perhaps be best appreciated schematically. Table 10.1 shows that there are 35 crops activities plus 12 water-producing activities plus 12 labor-hiring activities for 59 activities in all. There are 5 sets of 12 monthly constraints plus 5 special constraints for a total of 65 constraints.

---

4. A more complete treatment of the subject could have included capacity as a variable by expanding the model to include capital as an input into tubewells and limiting its availability or charging a price for its use.

Table 10.1. Schematic Representation of the Model

Constraints	Activities (Number)	Crops (35)	Water pumping (12)	Labor hiring (12)	Resource availabilities
Water	(12)	Water (irrigation) requirements (acre-inches/month)	Additional pumped water (acre-inches/month)		Canal water available (acre-inches/month)
Land	(12)	Land requirements (1)			Land available (acres/month)
Animal power	(12)	Animal power requirements (hours/acre/month)			Animal power available (hours/month)
Labor	(12)	Labor requirements (hours/acre/month)		Additional hired labor (hours/month)	Operator's labor available (hours/month)
Tubewell capacity	(12)		Tubewell capacity requirements (1)		Tubewell capacity available (acre-inches/month)
Special	(5)	Land requirements for specific crops (1)			Land available for specific crops (acres)
Objective function		Rs. (net) revenue/acre	Rs/acre-inch	Rs/hour	

The Basic Solution

As indicated earlier, the empirical estimates for the model's parameters were derived by constructing budgets for representative farms in the northern part of the Punjab. Material for these calculations was obtained from a variety of sources including the Indus Basin Special Survey undertaken by the World Bank (International Bank for Reconstruction and Development 1966), feasibility studies by Tipton and Kalmbach (West Pakistan Water and Power Development Authority 1965), a comparative study of tubewell and nontubewell cultivators by Ghulam Mohammad (1965), and a farm management survey by Harza Engineering and the author (1967).

Table 10.2 shows the optimal solution of the model when water availability is limited to perennial canal supplies. As can be seen from a comparison with relevant empirical data in Table 10.3, the model reproduced the historical situation in perennial areas with reasonable accuracy. Although the cropping intensity is somewhat less than that reported by Ghulam Mohammad, this can be explained in part by his definition of nontubewell farmers as those receiving (purchasing) up to 25 percent of their water from supplementary sources. Moreover, the Ghulam Mohammad study was done in the heart of the fine rice area which explains the somewhat greater proportion of rice in the cropping pattern.

Table 10.2. Cropping Patterns and Cropping Intensities, Rechna Doab, Perennial Canal only[a] (based on 10 cultivated acres)

	Model	District data (Central Rechna)	Ghulam Mohammad (Upper Rechna)
Winter Crops (acres)			
Wheat	2.80	3.70	3.23
Barley		0.14	
Oilseeds	0.86	0.10	0.21
Gram	0.82	0.70	0.35
Fodder	1.44	0.91	1.41
Fruits, vegetables, and misc.	0.16		0.35
Total	6.08	5.55	5.44
Summer Crops (acres)			
Rice	1.78	1.73	3.60
Cotton		0.72	0.27
Maize	0.64	0.29	0.25
Fodder	0.64	0.66	1.07
Sugarcane	0.80	0.26	0.58
Fruits, vegetables, and misc.	0.24		0.27
Total	4.10	3.66	6.04
Grand total	10.10 acres	9.21 acres	11.48 acres
Cropping intensity[b]	101.00 percent	92.10 percent	114.80 percent

[a] The model approximates most closely data from the central part of the Punjab (Rechna Doab). Column (2) shows the cropping pattern of Sheikhupura district in 1950-51 before the implementation of SCARP I. The lower intensity is due in part to the nonperennial areas located in the northern part of the district.

[b] Cropping intensity is defined as the ratio of cropped to cultivated acreage.

Table 10.3. Cropping Patterns and Cropping Intensities for Areas in Rechna Doab Receiving Supplementary Tubewell Water (based on 10 cultivated acres)

	Model	SCARP I[a] (Central Rechna)	Ghulam Mohammad (Upper Rechna)	Bureau of Statistics[b]
Winter Crops (acres)				
Wheat	5.04	3.44	3.17	3.96
Barley		0.07		
Oilseeds	0.80	0.40	0.12	0.20
Gram		0.33	0.22	0.59
Fodder	1.28	1.68	1.38	1.48
Fruits, vegetables, and misc.	0.40	0.61	0.51	0.18
Total	7.52	6.53	5.40	6.41
Summer Crops (acres)				
Rice	5.10	1.66	6.22	4.12
Cotton		0.89		0.21
Maize		0.59	0.08	0.74
Fodder	0.64	1.33	1.08	0.94
Sugarcane	0.80	0.83	0.65	1.34
Fruits, vegetables, and misc.	0.32	0.74	0.49	0.18
Total	6.86	6.01	8.52	7.53
Grand total / (Cropping intensity)[c]	14.38	12.54	13.92	13.94

[a]Salinity and Reclamation Project No. 1 cultivated acreage assumed to equal 1 million acres. (Total project area is slightly larger.)
[b]Calculated from Bureau of Statistics compilations on acreage by type of irrigation.
[c]Cropping intensity is defined as the ratio of cropped to cultivated acreage.

The purpose in presenting the above solution is to show that the optimal solution of the programming model is consistent with what farmers have been doing in the area from which the parameters have been drawn. As such, it has not been a rigorous attempt to show that farmers allocate resources efficiently although the evidence clearly points in that direction. Rather it has been an attempt, in some sense, to "calibrate" the model. Needless to say, the demonstration that the model behaves reasonably well when faced with expected prices lends confidence to the results of the following sections in which the analysis is based on a parametric variation of prices.

III. Experiments with the Programming Model and Their Policy Implications

Groundwater Development and the Supply Response of Crops

Much has been written in recent years about the extent to which farmers respond to changes in the relative prices of crops. The results of various attempts to estimate "positive" supply models have provided convincing evidence that, by and large, farmers in developing countries employ the same economic logic as their brothers in more highly developed areas.[5]

5. For estimates of supply elasticities in the Punjab, see Falcon (1964), Falcon and Gotsch (1966), Krishna (1963), and Ghulam Mohammad (1963).

What is frequently overlooked, however, is that insofar as farmers employ a calculus of profit maximization, their response is not to relative prices but to relative net revenues. This distinction is of some significance in a number of developing countries where a major effort to promote growth by introducing rapid technological change has had significant differential effects on crop costs. In the section that follows, an attempt is made to show, using the model developed in Section II, that many of the previous calculations on supply elasticities in West Pakistan may be irrelevant as a result of the widespread groundwater development being undertaken there. This issue is of some importance since commodity price elasticities enter into a number of policy calculations including support prices and buffer stock operations, the utilization of surplus U. S. commodities under P.L. 480, and so on. In the following section, static supply curves are developed for "with" and "without" tubewell conditions to examine the effect of an increased, highly flexible water source on the likely reactions of farmers to changing price-quantity relationships. They can easily be derived from the programming model by varying the price for a given crop, computing the net revenue associated with each price and then re-solving the model for each variation. The linear programming model is, of course, an optimizing model, and hence, the supply curves derived by parametrically varying prices are normative in nature. That is, they describe what farmers *should do* at varying prices in order to maximize profits, and thus they differ conceptually from the supply response estimated from time series data which show what farmers *have done*. Nevertheless, the conclusion that the new tubewell technology can be expected to exert a profound influence on (1) the optimal *level* of output at current prices (shifts in the supply curve) and (2) the *elasticity* of farmer price responses appears unmistakable.

The two effects described above are readily discernible in Figure 10.1. The equilibrium level of sugarcane output at current prices has more than doubled under the impact of a flexible supply of supplementary water. Moreover, over the relevant range, Curve II is much more elastic than Curve I. This comparative increase in price elasticity is significant in that Curve I is in some sense analogous to the long-run supply elasticities derived from time series estimates.[6] The link is that the latter estimates assume a time lapse sufficient for farmers to have made all the adjustments implied in the normative curve.

The choice of sugarcane as an example is not without reason. Present cane prices to growers are substantially above world market prices and are held there by factory price guarantees and a restrictive government import policy.

Historically, the distortion of cane prices has been minimized by the extremely high water requirements of sugarcane. In fact, many areas served by non-perennial canals grow virtually no cane at all. As Figure 10.1 indicates, however, and as evidence from SCARP I and other high tubewell density areas corroborates, large-scale groundwater development has substantially altered the relative profitability of the cane crop. Hence, if the government does not want further inroads into land which might be devoted to export crops such as rice and cotton, or into food crops, some adjustment will be required in its present sugar policy. A failure to make these alterations may prove quite costly, both in terms of budget expenditure and national income foregone. Quantitatively, it would appear that maintenance of the status quo

---

6. Indeed, for sugarcane, the relationship is remarkable. A crude calculation of the elasticity of Curve I gives a value of approximately 2.7. The long-run estimate based on time series data is slightly greater than 3 (see Falcon and Gotsch 1966).

in sugarcane output in the face of a widespread increase in water availability would require a decrease in the guaranteed mill price (2.0 rupees per maund) of 25–30 percent—or at least in the Central Rechna area for which the tableau is apropos.

Additional experiments along these lines for other crops have been reported elsewhere (Falcon and Gotsch 1966) and will not be repeated here. However, the general conclusion appears to be that the degree to which farmers can be expected to respond to changes in the relative profitability has increased considerably upon the installation of tubewells. Such a finding suggests, of course, that agricultural prices will become an increasingly powerful policy tool as the water development program accelerates.

The next subsection shifts the focus of the investigation from agricultural outputs to inputs—in this case, water. Although the approach is again that of parametric price variation, the policy issues raised are substantially different from those discussed in the preceding paragraphs.

Water Pricing, the Demand for Supplementary Water, and Groundwater Development Policy

As indicated in Section II and the foregoing section of Section III, a separate set of activities was included in the model to simulate the introduction of a new technology whose function was to provide additional water deliveries to the water using rows. Operation of these pumping activities, of course, entailed a penalty, namely the variable cost of operating a tubewell. In this section, pumping costs were varied parametrically to trace out seasonal and annual demand curves for supplementary water. The derived schedules are used, in turn, as the basis for a discussion of certain aspects of groundwater development policy in West Pakistan.

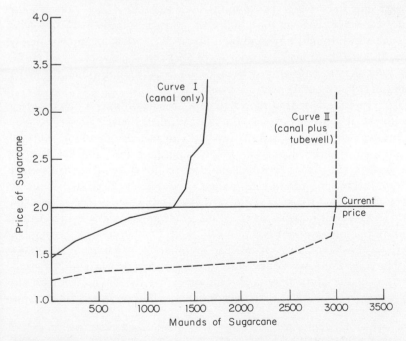

Figure 10.1 Normative supply curves for sugarcane (10.0 acre farm, Central Rechna area).

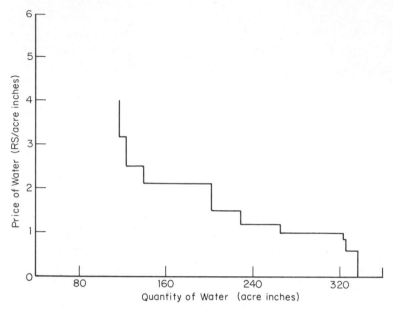

Figure 10.2   Annual demand for supplementary water at various pumping costs.

Figure 10.2 shows the demand curve for supplementary water on a representative farm of 10 cultivated acres. According to the schedule, diesel tubewell owners with costs of approximately 1.2 rupees per acre-inch should have pumped of the order of 230 inches of supplementary water per annum if they equated the value of the marginal product of water with its marginal cost. Electric tubewell owners with variable costs of 0.8 rupee should have pumped about 320 inches or approximately 40 percent more. If a weighted average price were assumed ($\frac{2}{3}$ diesel, $\frac{1}{3}$ electric), Figure 10.2 indicates that private entrepreneurs should have pumped of the order of 270 acre-inches of supplementary water per annum.

The results of the exercise based on representative farms can be compared, albeit a bit crudely, with the actual withdrawals of a large public tubewell project located in the area from which the model's parameters were drawn. By invoking the proportionality assumption of linear models and multiplying the entire vector of resource constraints (b_j's) by 10^5, the 10-acre farm becomes a 1 million-acre farm with surface water availability measured in million acre-inches, animal power in million bullock-hours, and so on. Solutions to the problem must then also be multiplied by 10^5. (For example, the demand for supplementary water at 0.8 rupee per acre-inch would be interpreted as 32 million acre-inches.)

Multiplying the "right-hand side" of the representative farm model by 10 results in an area roughly equivalent in size to Salinity Control and Reclamation Project No. I.[7] Comparison of the optimal withdrawals suggested by the model with the current pumping rate in SCARP I (28 million acre-inches) indicates that if the

---

7. Lee (1967) shows that there is probably no more bias in this approach to aggregation than in one in which programming models are developed for a series of different farm sizes and then aggregated. Nevertheless, the assumption that all crops are planted as though on a single farm clearly violates reality and is responsible for part of the peaking in Figure 10.4.

same area were covered with private diesel tubewells, profit-maximizing cultivators would probably pump less than is presently being withdrawn; if all farmers owned electric wells, they would probably pump more.

Comparison of quantity alone, however, is of little direct value since actual farmer payments for water from public projects are considerably less than the cost to private tubewell owners of operating their own pumps. Although several difficulties arise in attempting to assess the cost of supplementary water in SCARP I in a way that is compatible with the assumptions underlying Figure 10.2, a crude estimate of the cost of water can be obtained by comparing the revenue obtained by the government before and after the installation of tubewells and dividing the difference by the total water pumped.[8] Harza Engineering, in their evaluation of SCARP I (1966), supply the numerator for the above computation. In 1959–60, the government recovered from the project area 14.5 million rupees from water rates, land revenue, and other taxes assessed on a cropped-acre basis; in 1964–65, this figure had risen to 29.4 million rupees. Dividing the difference by the water pumped yields a figure of 0.5 rupee per acre-inch as payment, direct and indirect, for the supplementary groundwater. Substitution of this result in Figure 10.2 gives an estimate of water demanded of 34 million acre-inches, an amount significantly above the 28 million acre-inches actually being pumped. One source of the discrepancy between the cost of water and the withdrawals and cropping intensities predicted by the model seems to be related to the installed tubewell capacity.

The per acre pumping capacity assumed in the model was based on the findings of the farm management studies alluded to earlier. For the central part of Rechna Doab, this proved to be approximately 1 cusec for 80 acres. For SCARP I, on the other hand, there is an installed capacity of only 1 cusec per 150 acres. Consequently, there are substantial limitations on the ability of the operating organization of the project to respond to the seasonality of water demands. This restriction in turn leads to a *lower* overall application rate than would be desirable given the extremely low-water rates but probably a *higher* rate than is optimal for meeting the requirements of the current cropping intensity.

Figures 10.3 and 10.4 illustrate monthly water demands at different pumping costs and the difference between current pumping practices and the optimal pattern suggested by the model under comparable monthly surface water flow constraints. Caution should be used in interpreting these results since it must be kept in mind that in the case of the model, SCARP I has been treated as a gigantic farm subject to a single decision-maker.[9] Nevertheless, when the comparisons of pumping patterns in Figure 10.4 are considered in conjunction with the attained intensities in Table 10.3 (SCARP I = 125; model = 143), the evidence points strongly to the conclusion that flexibility is an extremely important element in efficient water use.

To reiterate, under present conditions in SCARP I, farmers do not have the opportunity of pumping as much water as the price of water would warrant since tubewell

8. The problem arises primarily because water charges are currently on an acreage-irrigated and not on a volumetric basis. Operationally, this means that farmers decide once and for all at the beginning of the growing season how much of a crop they are going to plant and, hence, what their water costs are going to be. Once this decision has been made, water may quite legitimately be treated by them as a fixed cost and used to the point where the value of its marginal product is zero.

9. This undoubtedly has the effect of overstating the variance in the optimal time distribution of supplementary water. The fact that farmers typically spread their planting dates as a result of labor constraints tends to mitigate the extremes shown in Figure 10.4.

capacities are too low to meet seasonal demands. At the same time, much water is wasted because once the acres that can be planted have been sown, additional water may be applied to the point where the marginal product is zero. For certain plants, such as rice and berseem (Egyptian clover), this can lead to unusually high applications per acre.[10]

It could be argued in rebuttal to the implied case for individually owned tubewells made by this finding, that the result is simply a function of a poorly designed public project. If water were sold on a volumetric basis and sufficient capacity were installed, the needed flexibility could be attained.[11] Unfortunately, the regime-type distribution system in West Pakistan allocates water to farmers in rotation. Since groundwater and surface water are mixed at the head of the water course, both are subject to the same rotational scheme. It is difficult to see how this system can be modified to provide the flexibility of individual water control implied in Figure 10.4.

The foregoing paragraphs offer a number of comments on water pricing and the demand for supplementary water. This discussion suggests a further use of the experiment in clarifying certain aspects of the current debate over an appropriate groundwater development strategy for West Pakistan.

Some participants in the discussions over groundwater policy allege that the development program must be in public hands. This is the only way, it is held, that the surface and groundwater resources of the province can be used most effectively. Specific arguments include the need to coordinate surface flows and groundwater withdrawals, the importance of overall control of the aquifer, the necessity of evening out interseasonal variation in groundwater availability, the need to insure applications of water sufficient to insure that the tendency of harmful salts to collect in the root zone is reversed, and the importance of equity in distributing the benefits of groundwater development.

Private development proponents counter by pointing out that another, and possibly overriding, set of considerations has been ignored, namely, that investments in tubewells by private farmers add net resources to the country's development program. Moreover, individual farmers, controlling their own water supplies, will use scarce water resources more efficiently. Lastly, profit-motivated cultivators, spurred by the returns on private tubewells, have become a modernizing segment within the agricultural sector that is impossible to value.

In some cases, the arguments hinge on differences in opinion regarding the appropriate time horizon to use in evaluating development proposals. If the long-run, aggregate water management problems are deemed to be of overwhelming importance, then a predominantly public program appears to be attractive. If, on the other hand, one feels that growth in a developing country has a very high rate of

10. Corroboration of this explanation is given in the Indus Basin Special Study (IBRD, 1966). On the watercourse studied in SCARP I, the following amounts of water were applied per acre (consumptive use requirements at the same point of measurement are given in parentheses): rice 72.6 (46.1); fodder 92.8 (38.3); cotton 30.8 (34.5); wheat 22.8 (23.9). Cultivator awareness of water response curves is implied by the deltas they have used. Rice grows in standing water, and hence there is no negative marginal product for water. Berseem is also tremendously tolerant of high applications. On the other hand, both wheat and cotton can be drowned by overirrigation. Moreover, one could argue that the deltas supplied on rice and berseem had some greater than zero value which compensated for the labor involved in irrigation in that the leaching process was accelerated by the additional water.

11. Additional capacity in public projects also has, of course, a cost. But this diminishes sharply as tubewell sizes increase.

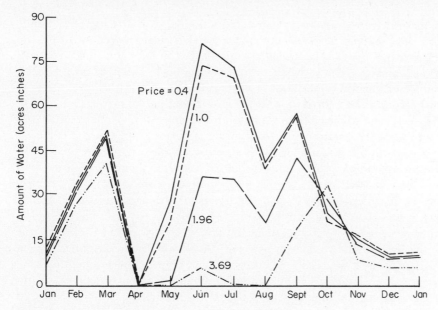

Figure 10.3 Effect of pumping costs on ground water usage.

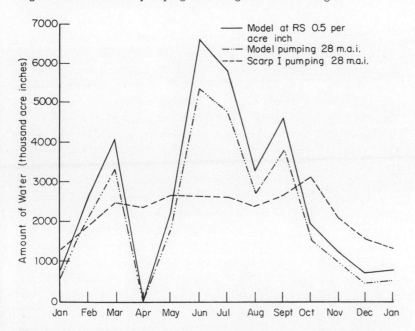

Figure 10.4 Seasonal distribution of pumping.

discount, the unavoidable conclusion is that, with present resource availabilities, everything possible must be done to encourage private development.

The nature of the conflicting objectives between public and private development outlined in the paragraph above leads naturally to a search for policies which might alter certain aspects of either one or the other. In particular, since the resource constraint appears to be the most significant constraint currently operating in Pakistan, policies that would make private development an acceptable long-run alternative to public projects need careful exploration. As the analysis makes clear, objections to private development can by no means be removed entirely, but at least the choice between alternatives can subsequently be based on differences that cannot be remedied by relatively simple changes in public policy.

The basic question to be addressed is the allegation that public projects are needed for proper management of the underground aquifer. Concern on this point originates as much from the rather disastrous United States experience as anything else. Developments in the southwestern part of the United States have confirmed that individuals trying to maximize profits will (1) expand irrigated agricultural areas well beyond the long-run yield of the aquifer on which they are dependent, and (2) permit even the destruction of an aquifer by seawater through the failure to deal adequately with the commonality problem.

The commonality problem as it exists in the United States and as it exists in the Indus Basin has important differences, however. Perhaps of greatest significance for this study is the fact that the pricing of energy is largely under government control. Electricity generation is almost wholly under the semiautonomous provincial Water and Power Development Authority. Currently, farmers are being supplied power at 0.08 rupee per KWH which is approximately half its real cost. On the other hand, excise taxes on diesel oil have also set a precedent that could easily be used as a tool of public policy.

Given the power to control energy costs—and hence the cost of pumping water— it appears that the government could, by *indirect* means, influence substantially groundwater withdrawals. For example, suppose that the recharge of the aquifer in SCARP I were approximately 26 m.a.i. From Figure 10.2, this would mean a price per acre-inch of about 1.0 rupee. Using Ghulam Mohammad's figure for variable costs of private tubewells, this could be achieved by setting the cost of electricity at 0.09 rupee per KWH; diesel at 53 rupees per barrel. In other words, by increasing electricity prices by 15 percent if pumping were done with electricity, and subsidizing the price of diesel by 30 percent if pumping were done with diesel, withdrawals could be brought into balance with recharge.[12]

Conversely, the pricing mechanism might be used to increase withdrawals in the interest of promoting reclamation and salinity control. The principal cause of soil salinity is inadequate "deltas" to leach the accumulated salts through the root zone. However, as cropping intensities approach 125–130, land becomes a binding constraint and applications per acre can be expected to rise. The extent to which such increases will occur is, of course, a function of the price of the additional water.[13]

It might be argued that the policy suggested above would be less sensitive in year-to-year fluctuations than direct government operation. While this is true, it is unlikely

12. This is not to argue that such a balance is an appropriate public policy. For an interesting discussion of the complexity of determining optimum rates of groundwater withdrawal, see Burt (1966).

13. Some consultants have suggested that a 10 to 15 percent increase in application above the evapotranspiration (maximum yield) requirement is needed for leaching purposes. If the production function in Figure 10.1 is generally valid, this would prove difficult to bring about without a direct acreage control system. One could envisage payments for the use of water beyond the point where short-run $MC = VMP$, but it would appear that a more convincing solution would be a program of cultivator education about the long-run gains from applying the additional 10 to 15 percent. Unfortunately, this area of investigation is still clouded by a lack of agreement among irrigation engineers regarding the physical requirements of the leaching process.

that highly sensitive annual adjustments between surface water inputs and ground-water withdrawals are necessary. What is needed is a long-run equilibrium between inflow and outflow and for this, an appropriate energy pricing system would appear to be valid.

The foregoing argument has been centred on countering objections to private water development put forth on water management grounds. It has not tried to add yet another variant to the proposals for an optimal public-private strategy, but has shown that certain technical arguments, thought by many to be central to the problem, are amenable to public policy. Hopefully, greater attention can now be focused on the opportunity cost of the resources involved, on the rapidity with which water resources can be developed, and on considerations of equity, which appear to be more fruitful focal points for the public-private debate.

Tubewell Technology, the Demand for Agricultural Labor, and Alternative Uses of the Rural Labor Force

In developing countries with high birth rates and large agrarian populations, there is little doubt that the agricultural sector must continue to provide a large amount of incremental employment. Recognition of this problem has led to suggestions by a number of economists and administrators that off-season labor be used to create rural infrastructure such as roads, drainage works, schools, minor irrigation channels, and so on. Successful efforts to implement such a program for underemployed labor have, in fact, been carried out under the Rural Works Programme in both East and West Pakistan (see especially Gilbert 1964).

While the instruments suggested above have an important place in creating additional employment, it is likely that a more massive impact on the demand for labor will come from the water development program mentioned earlier. In the following section, an attempt is made to estimate quantitatively the magnitude of the increase. In addition, an integration of the two alternatives is suggested as a goal for provincial employment policy.

As Figures 10.5 and 10.6 make clear, the demand for labor generated by the model was indeed altered significantly by a simulated water resource development program. Total labor use was increased by over 40 percent; of this increase, nearly 28 percent was due to the hiring of additional workers on a monthly basis.

The seasonal distribution of agricultural employment, particularly of hired workers, was also altered rather significantly. As Figure 10.6 shows, not only is there the usual peak in labor demand for the harvesting of winter crops and the planting of summer crops, but a second peak has arisen because of the opposite phenomena. The latter case, in which rice is being harvested and the land preparation and seeding of winter crops is under way, is not of the magnitude of the spring peak, but it is a singular departure from the historical pattern.

These findings provide some guide to the planning of public expenditures aimed at increasing employment in agriculture. First of all, it is obvious that the most massive increase can be brought about by developing water resources. The 40 percent increase mentioned earlier is undoubtedly a substantial understatement since it results only from increased acreage and changed cropping patterns. The increase in labor required for intensifying agriculture, that is, increasing yields, has not been included. As the Indus Basin Special Studies have shown, this may be substantial, particularly in the fodder crops, and in rice and cotton.

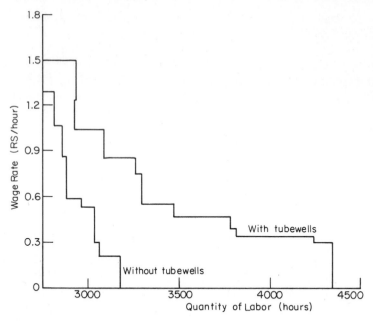

Figure 10.5   Total labor used in tubewell and nontubewell farms.

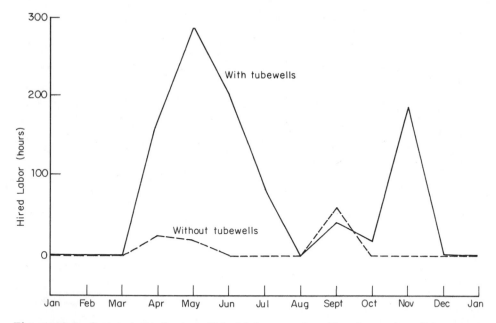

Figure 10.6   Seasonal distribution of hired labor on tubewell and nontubewell farms.

A second important factor not included in the 40 percent is the increased activity in the livestock sector, especially dairying, which is often associated with areas where extensive water development has taken place.

Addition of the omissions mentioned would probably place the increased demand for labor in irrigated areas at closer to 55 percent, some 30 to 35 percent of which is likely to be hired.

The increased demand for labor in areas where water resources are being developed suggests that a substantial migration of laborers from less fortunate areas can be expected. While this labor transfer should be welcomed, past experience teaches that such population movements are sometimes carried out under trying conditions which could be mitigated through appropriate relocation policies. Obviously such policies are double-edged in that they relieve the pressure of unemployment in areas where additional water supplies are unavailable, as well as add to the labor force in areas experiencing rapid agricultural growth.

One of the serious obstacles that such a relocation policy would encounter is that bane of all temporarily hired labor, namely, the seasonality of labor requirements. The result of incorporating tubewells into the model suggests that seasonal fluctuations may even be accentuated with additional water supplies as farmers tend to increase their specialization (Figure 10.6). Obviously, if this is true, then the seasonal underemployment about which so much has been written could be increased rather than diminished with labor migration.

It is at this point that additional government policies designed to absorb seasonally available labor could be brought into play. This is particularly feasible in irrigated areas where there are a significant number of small irrigation and drainage works that could undoubtedly be carried out economically using labor-intensive methods. Much needed renovation of silted irrigation distributaries and minors comes immediately to mind. Moreover, the increased output in agricultural areas where rapid growth is anticipated will require a proportionate, perhaps exponential, increase in rural infrastructure. More and better roads will be required to bring the additional commodities to market, communications systems will need to be improved, schools built, and so on.

A policy of providing substantial off-season employment as part of an overall employment policy will require a good deal of planning. For example methods for supervising and administering labor-intensive methods must be revived, appropriate wage rates must be set by season in order to minimize the interference with agricultural employment, and so on. But without some supplementary program the unfortunate circumstances surrounding migrant laborers that have been experienced in so many parts of the world are likely to be repeated in Pakistan.

Devising a Strategy for Agricultural Research

As indicated earlier, the levels of the primal activities are often of less interest in a programming model than various by-products of the optimal solution. This is particularly true of the so-called dual solution from which can be read the implicit "shadow prices" of the various constraints imposed upon the model. In the following section, use is made of the implicit values of several constraints to suggest what might be termed a "bottleneck-breaking" approach to agricultural strategy.

Table 10.4 gives the dual of the optimal solution whose primal values are shown in Column (1) of Table 10.3. In addition to shadow prices for various constraints, total availability of resources plus amounts used in the solution are shown.

The inclusion of tubewell or water-pumping activities has virtually removed the constraint imposed by insufficient water supplies. (The remaining shadow prices are merely the opportunity cost of pumping water.) Instead, land, at least during the months of September and October, is the principal binding resource. This results from the competition between the dominant summer crops that are not yet harvested

Table 10.4. Dual of the Primal Model Solution Given in Table 10.3 for Rechna Doab

Resource	Amount available	Amount used	Shadow price (rupees)
Water (acre-inches)			
April	16.2	15.8	0
May	19.3	19.3	1.0
June	21.4	21.4	1.0
July	21.0	21.0	1.0
August	20.7	20.7	1.0
September	21.4	21.4	1.0
October	16.9	16.9	1.0
November	11.5	11.5	1.0
December	10.3	10.3	1.0
January	10.7	10.7	1.0
February	13.8	13.8	1.0
March	16.6	16.6	1.0
Land (acres)			
April	10.0	8.9	0
May	10.0	5.6	0
June	10.0	7.7	0
July	10.0	7.7	0
August	10.0	7.7	0
September	10.0	9.7	0
October	10.0	10.0	78.1
November	10.0	10.0	20.8
December	10.0	8.35	0
January	10.0	7.96	0
February	10.0	7.96	0
March	10.0	8.36	0
Family labor (hours)			
April	300.0	300.0	0.3
May	300.0	300.0	0.3
June	300.0	300.0	0.3
July	300.0	300.0	0.3
August	300.0	276.76	0
September	300.0	300.0	0.3
October	300.0	300.0	0.3
November	300.0	300.0	0.3
December	300.0	239.4	0
January	300.0	226.9	0
February	300.0	273.9	0
March	300.0	203.1	0
Hired labor (hours)			
April	Unlimited	165.0	0
May	Unlimited	0	0
June	Unlimited	201.0	0
July	Unlimited	132.8	0
August	Unlimited	0	0
September	Unlimited	44.6	0
October	Unlimited	17.7	0
November	Unlimited	185.7	0
December	Unlimited	0	0
January	Unlimited	0	0
February	Unlimited	0	0
March	Unlimited	52.7	0

Table 10.4 (*Continued*)

Resource	Amount available	Amount used	Shadow price (rupees)
Animal power (hours)			
April	144.0	40.6	0
May	144.0	144.0	0.92
June	144.0	144.0	0.30
July	144.0	107.2	0
August	144.0	47.8	0
September	144.0	55.8	0
October	144.0	42.5	0
November	144.0	82.9	0
December	144.0	77.4	0
January	144.0	38.0	0
February	144.0	43.5	0
March	144.0	54.6	0
Tubewell capacity (hours)			
April	88.0	0	0
May	88.0	16.8	0
June	88.0	59.1	0
July	88.0	55.4	0
August	88.0	31.5	0
September	88.0	45.5	0
October	88.0	17.2	0
November	88.0	13.0	0
December	88.0	8.2	0
January	88.0	8.1	0
February	88.0	26.8	0
March	88.0	42.2	0
Crop constraints (acres)			
Sugarcane	1.0	1.0	356.6
Fruit	0.3	0.3	350.2
Winter vegetables	0.2	0.2	396.1
Summer vegetables	0.1	0.1	247.8
Winter fodder	1.6	1.6	161.6
Summer fodder	0.8	0.8	95.0

and the demands of winter food crops for seedbed preparation and sowing. If it were possible to move summer crops ahead slightly in their planting dates—or, alternatively, shorten the growing season—and if it were possible to move the winter planting dates slightly further into the year, substantial increases in cropping intensity could be achieved.

Armed with the results of the model which show the high returns to relaxing the land constraints in September and October, it is possible to begin a systematic exploration of means by which such "bottlenecks" could be relaxed. For example, upon inquiry, one finds that much of the rice crop is delayed in planting because of the infestation by the rice stem borer. It was discovered historically that, without modern plant control measures, about the only effective means of holding down infestations of this extremely damaging pest was to deny it the residues of rice plants for a period sufficiently long to break its life cycle. The result was an ordinance forbidding the planting of rice before June 15. This in turn means a harvesting date which makes it extremely difficult to prepare the seedbed and plant winter crops.

Entomologists, examining the rice pest problem, have suggested that there are now plant protection measures, such as systemics, which can virtually assure control of rice pests. Widespread adoption of these new techniques would seem to pave the way for a revision in harvesting and planting dates so that winter crops might be planted after rice.

Conversations with plant breeders indicate, however, that still other means are possible for opening up a gap between summer and winter crops. Work at the International Rice Research Institute is progressing on rice varieties that mature two to three weeks earlier than the present improved varieties. The initial impetus behind the work was to develop plants that would be less vulnerable to lack of moisture in shortened monsoon seasons, but their applicability to the situation in West Pakistan is obvious.

The possibilities suggested above, coupled perhaps with some improvement in seedbed preparation, could be used to decrease the amount of overlap between the two seasons. This can easily be expressed in the programming model by modifying the land requirements for the crops involved. In the following example, rice and wheat were assumed to be the principal crops to be affected. Rice planting dates were moved forward by one week and the growing season reduced from 5½ months to 5 months. It was also postulated that some improvements in bullock implements or some degree of mechanization had made it possible to delay the time of starting normal seedbed preparation for wheat and grain by one week. The new solution of the model is shown in Table 10.5.

Table 10.5. Primal Solution to the Model with Revised Land Constraints (based on 10 cultivated acres)

	Activity level (acres)	Yield (maunds/acre)	Delta (inches/acre)
Winter Crops			
Wheat	6.21	1.25	2.39
Fodder	1.28	45.00	3.40
Vegetables	0.16		1.93
Fruits	0.24		3.20
Total	7.89		
Summer Crops			
Rice	3.68	1.80	4.61
Fodder	0.64	25.00	2.06
Maize	3.28	1.50	2.96
Sugarcane	0.80	50.00	9.51
Vegetables	0.08		1.93
Fruit	0.24		3.20
Total	8.72		
Grand total	16.61 acres		
Cropping intensity[a]	166.1 percent		

[a] Cropping intensity is defined as the ratio of cropped to cultivated acreage.

It is apparent from the results of the exercise that the modification of planting and harvesting dates had an improvement impact on cultivator productivity. Cropping intensities rose from 143 percent to 166 percent and net revenue increased by nearly 10 percent. The magnitude of the benefits corroborates comments made earlier about the pay-off of research directed at bottlenecks in the agricultural production process.

IV. Summary

The preceding exercises provide an example of the way in which a relatively simple linear programming model can be manipulated to yield quantitative policy prescriptions that are useful in certain types of agricultural situations. The basic approach is one of varying parametrically the objective function weights and resource constraints to generate a series of curves and schedules that can, in turn, be used as inputs into some broader policy discussion involving cropping patterns, groundwater control, employment, and so on.

The first experiment, in which normative supply curves were generated with and without a new technology for providing supplementary groundwater, illustrated the significant impact that changes in the nature of resource constraints could have on price responsiveness. The provision of additional irrigation water is not unique in this respect; there are many other innovations in West Pakistan agriculture which act, not only to increase output per acre, but to change the configuration of binding constraints. For example, the use of pesticides makes it possible to change crop planting and harvesting dates and, with that, the seasonal competition of crops for land. New varieties that have shorter growing seasons have the same effect. Each of these cases underscores the general point that despite the amount of research that has been devoted to the topic, measures of historical price response are likely to be of little use to planners where technical change destroys the fundamental *ceteris paribus* assumption.

The second experiment demonstrated the means by which an important groundwater regulation problem could be handled with an appropriate price policy for energy. The approach was similar to the notion, popularized by Lange and Taylor (1969), that centrally calculated prices could be used to direct the workings of decentralized decision-making units in a socialist economy. In the Pakistan case, the issue is how to limit the withdrawal of groundwater by private tubewell owners, a limitation that is required in order to prevent salt water incursion in those parts of the acquifer that produce water fit for irrigation. It was estimated that increasing the pumping costs on electric tubewells by increasing the price of electricity by 15 percent and, in the case of diesel wells, providing a subsidy of 30 percent on diesel oil, would result in a water table that was consistent with the hydrological requirements. While this approach does not remove a number of objections to the private tubewell program (for example, equity), it does question the validity of frequently expressed opinions regarding the need for direct public control of the acquifer.

The third example deals with the increase in employment that could be expected as a result of groundwater development. In West Pakistan, as in almost every other developing country, both unemployment and underemployment plague the agricultural sector. There is little reason for optimism that this problem can be alleviated within the traditional framework, since the rate of industrialization is insufficient to permit net migration from agriculture to be positive. Consequently, any kind of productivity increases based on a technology that is labor-absorbing are highly desirable. An estimate made of the increase in labor requirements resulting from the provision of supplementary wages suggested that the additional irrigation supplies were likely to produce an increase of over 50 percent in labor utilized. Nearly 35 percent of this increase could be identified as incremental hired labor.

While water development would have a positive effect on total employment, the model also suggests that it would affect underemployment inversely. Reduction in the number of sharply binding water constraints results in a high degree of specialization among crops, a finding which is consistent with practices developing among large farmers. Since substantial labor migrations can be expected into areas in which water resources are being developed, it would be highly desirable for policy makers to anticipate the seasonality problems of migrant labor by planning and providing for nonseasonal construction jobs in fields of irrigation, education, health, and so on.

The last section of the paper demonstrated the use of the dual of the programming model in defining strategic areas for agricultural research. For example, the shadow price that exists for land in September and October due to the competition between summer crops not yet harvested and seedbed preparation for winter crops, indicated the value of research programs which would create a time gap between the two crops and hence permit double cropping.

Since the correct setting of research priorities is particularly important in countries where scientific manpower is critically short, returns to such a bottleneck-breaking approach would appear to be quite high.

As indicated earlier, the models presented here are simple and there is much room for improvement in both their structure and the estimation of parameters. It would be useful, for example, to know more about the effects of drought at different points in a plant's growth curve. It would also be desirable to incorporate the demand side of the economy into the model. In spite of their relatively simple nature, however, the foregoing exercises demonstrate that the programming approach can incorporate a variety of complicated relationships among water, animal power, land, and output—relationships that would have been difficult to analyze using ordinary budgeting techniques. Since a significant number of agricultural planning problems *do* involve price and resource allocation problems, it seems reasonable to assume that the techniques employed in this study can be expanded and multiplied to serve an ever-widening audience of policy makers.

Appendix to Chapter 10:
Diminishing Returns to Water

Methods of estimating most of the parameters of the model may be found elsewhere (Gotsch 1966b; IBRD 1966). However, the central role of the water coefficients in the constraint matrix suggests that at least a brief description of their derivation be given in this paper.

Although the model described above is a straightforward application of the linear programming technique, an attempt was made in the case of water to permit some deviations from fixed input proportions. Such a modification was felt to be necessary

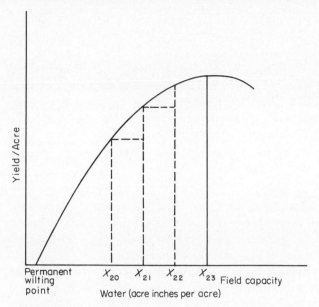

Figure A10.1   Approximated water response curve for wheat.

in view of the widely demonstrated diminishing response of plant growth to increments in water availability. For example, a large number of field experiments have shown that the water response curve for wheat has the shape indicated in Figure A10.1.

For inclusion in the model, the curve in Figure A10.1 was *approximated by* a step function.[14] The linear segments so derived became the basis for the wheat activities in the program. (For example, X_{20} through X_{23} all refer to wheat.) A similar procedure was applied to the remaining crops.

Since one of the primary objectives of the model was to take into account the importance of intraseasonal competition for resources in a climate where continuous cropping is possible, the second step in developing the water coefficients for wheat activities was to break down the total "delta" reported in the agronomic experiments into monthly requirements.[15] This was done by assuming that, for a given amount of water, the time distribution that would maximize the output of wheat was proportional to the monthly net consumptive use requirements.[16] That is, if the net consumptive use requirements of the month of October was 20 percent of the total requirement, water supplies which were less than the full requirements were also distributed so that 20 percent of the available water was used in October.

The approach outlined above for obtaining monthly water coefficients for the constraint matrix, A, is clearly crude and does not include the recognition that

14. For a discussion of the methodology involved in developing suitable curves from a large number of experiments, see Gotsch (1966b). Further justification of the methodology can be found in the highly competent study by Yaron (1966).

15. "Delta" is the usual engineering shorthand for the amount of water applied per acre.

16. Net consumptive use refers to the total calculated requirements of the plant (closely related to the evapotranspiration on the area) minus the effective precipitation. Meeting consumptive use requirements insures that the plant is not hindered in its growth by moisture deficiencies.

optimal irrigation practices are essentially a sequential decision-making problem. The use of evapotranspiration estimates at point X_{23} in Figure A10.1 can be justified unambiguously. By definition there is no appreciable water shortage in any period and hence, the timing of water application is of marginal significance. But it is well known that in cases where the quantity of water available is less than that required for maximum yield, its distribution over the growing period of the plant is a significant determinant of the effect of moisture shortages. Nevertheless, until more empirical material on the effects of drought at various points on the plant's growth stage curve becomes available, the approximation suggested above permitted the inclusion in the model of a good deal of information on the timing of water requirements and water availability.

11 Efficient Allocation of Resources in Education*

Samuel Bowles

I. Introduction

Recognition of the important contribution of education to economic growth has heightened the interest of economists and economic planners in the development of an economically rational basis for the allocation of resources in the educational sector. A number of recent models of the entire economy have explicitly incorporated inputs of labor of various skill or educational levels (Bruno 1966b; Brown et al. 1964). In addition, economists have directed their attention toward the educational sector itself and have attempted to develop methods which yield economically rational patterns of resource allocation and enrollments within the educational system (see Stone 1965).

The model described below is addressed to four major questions concerning the efficiency of the educational system as a producer of educated labor, namely:

1. What amount of society's resources should be devoted to education?

2. How should the total resource use be distributed among various types of education?

3. What educational technologies should be chosen?

4. What is the optimal level and composition of the importation of labor for use within the educational system?

This model differs from most existing approaches to educational planning in the following ways:

1. It is based on the principle of constrained maximization and involves the explicit consideration of both the costs and benefits of various educational programs.

2. Use of the model allows the simultaneous computation of optimal enrollment levels in each type of education, an optimal pattern of importation (or exportation) of educated labor, and the choice of efficient educational technologies.

3. The model is based on the assumption that each category of educated labor is highly substitutable both vis-à-vis other types of labor and vis-à-vis capital. In this

* Reprinted with minor revisions from the *Quarterly Journal of Economics*, May 1967, *87*, 189–219, by permission of the publisher. An earlier version of this paper was awarded the Selma A. Goldsmith Prize for the best economics seminar paper at Harvard University in the year 1963–64. An earlier version was also read at the joint meeting of the Econometric Society and the American Economic Association in December 1965. I have benefited greatly from advice and criticism from my colleagues and friends, especially Hollis B. Chenery, Hendrick Houthakker, and Arthur MacEwan. I am grateful to James Huntsberger for computational and other assistance. The shortcomings remaining in the paper are, of course, my own responsibility.

respect the model differs significantly from most other planning approaches, which assume that the production functions in the economy are characterized by fixed input coefficients for labor classified by occupational group or educational level.

4. It deals directly with labor classified by educational level.[1] This feature of the model avoids the problem of translating demands for labor classified by occupational group into demands for the outputs of specific educational levels.[2]

Although this paper is devoted primarily to a discussion of the model, a number of observations on its application to Northern Nigeria will be made (based on Bowles 1965). Section II contains a brief outline of the model and a sketch of the structure of the educational system of Northern Nigeria. Sections III and IV present the objective function and the constraint equations, respectively, along with some related data. Sections V through VIII contain a discussion of the application of the model to actual policy problems.

Some of the more important results based on the operation of the model with Nigeria data may be summarized as follows:

1. The educational sector has an extremely strong claim on economic resources.

2. Efficient allocation of resources within the educational system requires a rapid expansion of primary education and a reduction in enrollments in technical and secondary schools.

3. The introduction of new educational technologies allows for major increases in the efficiency of the system.

4. The productivity of foreigners imported to teach in the system is very high at the present levels of importation.

The optimal enrollments in various types of schools based on solutions of this model appear to differ considerably from Nigerian educational plans based on the manpower requirements approach.

II. An Outline of the Model

We seek to maximize a weighted function of enrollments in various types of educational institutions over time, subject to constraints based on an educational production technology and given resource availabilities. The constraint equations define what can be called an intertemporal production possibility set for the educational system. The objective function is the contribution of the educational system to future national income, measured by the increment in discounted lifetime earnings attributable to additional years of education.

The educational system is represented in this model as an aggregation of production activities. In the application of the model to Northern Nigeria, the educational activities included primary education, secondary education, higher education, various types of teacher training, and technical and vocational education (see Table 11.1). Each of these processes used a variety of inputs (both human and otherwise) to transform raw materials (the uneducated) or intermediate goods (continuing students) into a producer's good.[3] Relationships between educational activities are presented

---

1. In this respect it is similar to the model presented by Tinbergen and Correa (1962) and the more recent versions of the original model.

2. The conversion of occupational into educational classifications is generally accomplished on the basis of the concept of an educational "requirement" (or a distribution of "requirements") for the average performance of each occupation. See Eckaus (1964).

3. The system concurrently produces a consumer's good "education."

Table 11.1. The Educational System of Northern Nigeria[a]

Producing sectors	Usual age of entry	Duration of course in years	1	2	3	4	5	6	7	8	9	Labor market
(1) Primary school	6	7		S	S	S		S				L
(2) Craft school	13	3										
(3) Grade III Teacher's course (teacher training college)	13	3	T	T	T							
(4) Secondary school	13	5				S	S		S	S		L
(5) Grade II Teacher's course (teacher training college)	16	2	T	T	T	T	T		S	S		
(6) Technical training school	16	3								S		L
(7) Form VI	18+	2					T	T			S	L
(8) Northern Secondary Teacher's College (NSTC)	18+	3	T	T	T	T	T	T				
(9) University study	18+	3	T	T	T	T	T		T			L

Notation: T indicates a flow of teachers; S indicates a flow of students; L indicates a flow of school-leavers to the labor market.
[a] Some insignificant flows which have not been represented in the model have been excluded from this table.

as a system of intertemporal flows of students and teachers. The output of a given educational institution can be allocated to one of three tasks:

1. continuation of his education at a higher level
2. employment as a teacher at a lower level
3. employment in the labor force outside the educational system[4]

The structure of flows of teachers and students within the educational system is best described in the usual input-output format, as in Table 11.1, which presents the intra-educational flows among the nine major types of formal education in Northern Nigeria.[5]

The constraints relate to the use by the educational system of inputs supplied from outside the educational system (for example, expenditure on education, total population in the school-going age group), as well as endogenously produced inputs (teachers of various types, student outputs from one educational process who appear as inputs into higher educational processes). In addition, boundary conditions limit the policy instruments to values which are judged to be politically and administratively feasible.

The method described here is a sectoral model of the educational system. Production processes in the rest of the economy are not included explicitly. Thus the demand functions for the outputs of the educational system and the supply functions for the exogenously supplied educational inputs are specified prior to the operation of the model.

The instrument variables in the model include enrollments and resource use at the various educational levels, and additional instruments which require discontinuous or institutional changes. Examples of the latter are choices involving new educational technologies (for example, increased use of audio-visual equipment) or changes in the structure of the system (for example, extending university education to a four-year course). The instrument variables have been defined so as to correspond to the actual policy instruments available to most governments. In addition to the instrument variables relating to the production of specific types of education, the system is allowed to import a number of types of educated labor, and to send students abroad for their education. Thus for some types of labor, the system is presented with a three-way choice: the production of labor with a given level of educational attainment either within the country or in foreign educational institutions, or the importation of foreign labor possessing the educational attainments in question. Additional activities allow the system to recruit back into the educational sector personnel trained as teachers but who are presently working in nonteaching positions.

The model encompasses a number of time periods, so as to allow consideration of the intertemporal relationships within the educational system. Educational decisions involving enrollments, resource use, and hiring of staff are generally incorporated in annual budgets or similar documents, and are made prior to the beginning of the school year to be implemented in the course of the year. It is thus appropriate to select the year as the time unit used in the model.

4. Some of the outputs will either not seek employment or will for some period of time be involuntarily unemployed.
5. Note that the table has been arranged so that all of the flows of students (intermediate goods) lie above the diagonal, while flows of teachers (capital goods) lie below the diagonal. Lack of data prevented the inclusion of various educational activities outside of the formal educational system, for example, on-the-job training and adult education.

In actual application the model should probably be operated on a year-by-year sequential basis. If the planning period is n years, the model can be operated in year 0 (the base year) and the results for the years 1, . . . , n computed. Only the enrollments and resource allocation for the year 1 must be acted on at that time, so that at the end of year 1 the model can be operated once more, incorporating new information on either the production processes or the present values of the educational output. The results for years 2, . . . , $n + 1$ can then be calculated, the values of the instrument variables for year 2 acted upon, and the process continued.[6]

Solutions of the model yield optimal values of the instrument variables in each year of the planning period, namely:

1. a time pattern of enrollments and resource use in each type of education

2. levels of recruitment of new inputs (for example, foreign teachers and domestic ex-teachers) to the system

3. an efficient choice of educational techniques including such choices ss foreign as opposed to domestic university study. The solutions also generate shadow prices for resources used in the production of education

While the values of the instrument variables for any given solution are interesting in themselves, results to be gained through parametrically programming some of the crucial elements in the model are probably more useful from the standpoint of policymaking. The model not only allows us to explore the production possibility set for the educational system, but also to measure the trade-off between the availability of particular inputs, on the one hand, and the values of the instrument variables, the objective function, and the shadow prices on the other.

III. The Objective Function

The objective function used in this model represents the net economic benefits associated with the educational activities, namely, the present value of the economic benefits associated with the output of all level of the educational system over a number of years minus the present value of the associated costs.

As the social welfare function presumably contains many components which have some functional relation to education, it is useful to distinguish between those educational benefits which operate via the income or income-related terms of the welfare function, and those which operate on other components.

We will call the former "economic" and the latter "noneconomic," although any dichotomous distinction of this type is bound to be somewhat arbitrary. This classification excludes from the category of "economic" benefits those consequences of education generally called "consumption benefits," namely, those which accrue to the student in the form of pleasure in studying or later in being an educated man and having access to the style of life open to those with education.

Any consequence of the educational system's output which results in an increase in the value of present or future national income is thus defined as an economic benefit

6. Operation of the model in this manner is probably a good reflection of the actual policy-making process, which proceeds from year to year rather than on a once-for-all basis for an entire n-year period. In addition, it allows the efficient use of new data. A further advantage is that it avoids the necessity of acting on the values of the instrument variables in the later years in the planning period, which are presumably sensitive to the somewhat arbitrary terminal conditions.

of education. If we confine attention to the level of income rather than its distribution the maximization of net economic benefits corresponds to the maximization of the contribution of the educational system to the future (discounted) national income.[7]

Ideally, we would like to measure the economic benefits by the increase in an individual's social marginal productivity resulting from his education. The social marginal productivity of an educational output can be described as the total effect on future national income attributable to the individual's education, taking into account his direct contribution to output, as well as any external effects (Weisbrod 1964) which may exist. In the application of this model to the educational planning problems of Northern Nigeria, earnings were used as an estimate of the marginal productivity of each category of labor. While this measure is subject to a number of objections, it was thought to be a rough indication of the private marginal productivity of the worker.

In view of the fact that each educational output has a working life extending over a number of time periods, future increases in labor productivity generated by the educational system are discounted at an appropriate rate of time preference.

The direct social costs associated with each activity are the present value of the annual per student costs summed over the duration of the educational course. The cost of one student year is the sum of the required inputs valued at their opportunity cost, that is, their social marginal productivity in their next best use, or at their social marginal cost.[8] The cost of education to the educational institution is not the relevant cost figure, as it includes items of private as well as social cost, such as feeding the students and perhaps housing and clothing them, services which if not undertaken at the school would have to be undertaken in the home.[9]

The indirect cost element relates to the withdrawal of students from the labor force (or their retention in the educational system) for the continuation of the education. Students' time should be valued at its opportunity cost, namely, the social marginal productivity of the student if he were on the labor market. Measurement of the social marginal productivity of the student must include consideration of his prospects for being employed were he to leave school.

The net benefits coefficient associated with each activity is the present value of the estimated stream of lifetime earnings corresponding to the type of labor produced, (Y_j),

7. The exclusion of the noneconomic benefits is not intended to suggest that these should be ignored in the construction of the educational plan. The economically efficient patterns of allocation yielded by the model presented here are intended to be one input into the planning process, in competition with other allocation plans based on noneconomic considerations. The function of this approach is not to specify one socially desirable pattern of allocation but, rather, to clarify the economic benefits and costs of the educational choices facing a society. An alternative approach, based on a simple hypothetical planner's preference function, has been used in the application of a similar model (Bowles 1964).

8. While the relevant cost concept is marginal rather than average cost, in most educational activities studied in Nigeria there were good grounds for assuming that the two quantities coincided. The expansion of primary education, for example, requires a nearly proportional duplication of the existing processes through the addition of production units (schools) of the same scale and input structure as those presently existing. In the field of university education, however, there are significant indivisibilities and fixed costs and, consequently, a major divergence between average and marginal costs. In the case of university education it was judged likely that additional enrollments would be accommodated in existing institutions with less than proportional changes in existing plant and equipment. In these cases marginal costs (over the relevant range) were estimated and used in the operation of the model.

9. Naturally, if the marginal cost of these services when provided by the school differs from their marginal cost when provided at home, the difference (positive or negative) should be attributed to education.

minus the present value of the foregone stream of lifetime earnings corresponding to the type of labor used as a student input into the production process, $(Y_{j'})$, and minus also the present value of the direct costs, (C_j). Thus net benefits for education j are

$$Z_j = Y_j - Y_{j'} - C_j \tag{11.1}$$

and, using the p superscript to indicate the year of the planning period in which a student is admitted to the given level j, we may define the objective function as

$$Z^* = \sum_j \sum_p Z_j^p X_j^p \tag{11.2}$$

The earnings data were based on a sample survey of employment in private firms in Northern Nigeria in 1965. Costs were estimated on the basis of school by school financial records with expenditures grouped in a number of functional categories. Standard architectural plans and associated cost data were used to estimate the annual capital costs. The resulting net benefits coefficients and some of the underlying data are presented in Table 11.2.

IV. The Constraints

The education production technology is represented by a set of fixed input coefficients production functions. The choice of educational production functions embodying fixed input coefficients is justified on the grounds that while a considerable amount of input substitution may in fact be possible from a pedagogical standpoint, many educational administrators appear to believe that at any given time the appropriate teacher-student ratios and other input coefficients are roughly fixed, and insist on a common educational process in all schools of the same type.[10]

For any level of education, j, in period P the production function can be written:

$$X_j^p = \min_{i,t} \left[\frac{X_{ij}^t}{a_{ij}^t} \right] \text{ for all } j \text{ and } p \quad \begin{array}{l} i = 1, \ldots, m + q \\ t = p, \ldots, p + s_j - 1 \\ j = 1, \ldots, m \\ p = 1, \ldots, n \end{array} \tag{11.3}$$

where

X_j^P = the number of students admitted at level j in period p

X_{ij}^t = the amount of input i devoted to activity j, in period t

a_{ij}^t = the minimum amount of input i required to accommodate one student in activity j in year t[11]

m = the number of types of education considered in the model

n = the number of years in the planning period

q = the number of factors supplied from outside the educational system

s_j = the duration of course j in years

Equation (11.3) states that admissions, X_j^P, cannot exceed the value of the smallest ratio of total inputs (X_{ij}^t) to the relevant input coefficient (a_{ij}^t).

The a_{ij}^t coefficients referring to inputs produced by the education system itself represent teacher student ratios for each of the types of teachers used in the model and student input ratios. The latter refer to the minimum number of leavers from level i

10. The available school-by-school data on teacher-student ratios and other input coefficients for Northern Nigeria exhibit a remarkably small dispersion around the mean value.

11. Many of the $a_{ij}{}^t$ coefficients are zero.

Table 11.2. The Present Value of the Net Benefits Associated with Various Educational Activities in 1964[a] (adjusted for wastage, failures, labor force participation, and unemployment)

Activity[b] (1)	Present value of lifetime earnings Y_j (2)	Present value of lifetime earnings foregone[c] Y_j' (3)	Increment in present value of earnings (2)-(3) (4)	Present value of direct social costs C_j (5)	Present value of net benefits (2)-(3)-(5) Z_j (6)	Ratio of present values of increment in earnings to direct costs[d] (4)/(5) (7)
Primary school	1659	611	1048	62	986	16.9
Secondary school	4592	2910	1682	476	1206	3.5
Technical training school	4337	2713	1624	785	839	2.1
Form VI	7460	7356	104	326	- 222	0.3
University studies	20559	9130	11429	1350	10079	8.5
University studies abroad	20559	9130	11429	1730	9699	6.6

Source: See text. The basic data are reported in Bowles (1965: chaps. 5 and 6).

[a] All figures are in pounds and are based on a 5 percent discount rate.

[b] Net benefits coefficients for activities making no direct deliveries to the labor market (that is, craft school, which serves as a feeder for technical training school plus the three types of teacher training) do not appear in this table. The demand for the outputs of these activities is derived endogenously from the admissions levels in the optimal solution. The objective function coefficients for these activities are based on the direct costs plus earnings foregone during the process of education. The net benefits coefficients in this table refer only to activities in the base year, 1964.

[c] The present value of income foregone is the discounted lifetime earnings of an individual who enters the labor force with the prerequisites for admission to level j. Thus the alternative earnings stream from Form VI is the stream accruing to those who had passed the West African School Certificate, not the composite secondary school stream adjusted for failures, dropouts, etc.

[d] The ratios in Column (7) are not used in the operation of the model. They are presented here merely for reference.

required to admit one student to level j in time t. If level i is the "feeder" for level j then the relevant input coefficient is one.[12] The a_{ij}^t coefficients for inputs supplied from outside the system represent the marginal per student resource requirements.

Outputs appear in the system of constraint equations as negative inputs, and are computed on the basis of the total original student input multiplied by the fraction of the original students who can be expected to fall into each output category, namely, dropouts, failures, and successful leavers.

The matrix of a_{ij}^t's, along with the output coefficients, is an intertemporal input-output system representing the intra-educational flow of teachers and continuing students along with the inputs of exogenous (primary) factors. It closely resembles an intertemporal input-output system for an entire economy with the major exception that the educational production processes are extremely time-consuming, some

12. In one case (Northern Secondary Teachers College) the student inputs are of two different types, secondary-school leavers and grade II teachers. In this case the student input coefficients relating to these types of students have been set at fractional values representing the student input structure of this particular institution.

requiring as much as seven years between original input of a student and the eventual output of a graduate from that activity.

The input coefficients relating to Northern Nigeria were estimated on the basis of historical and present data on teacher student ratios (for a number of different types of teachers) and other input data. Time series of teacher student ratios were used as the basis for the projection of future changes in the teacher input coefficients. In most cases the movement of the coefficients indicates a significant improvement in the quality of the teaching staff, namely, a substitution over time of relatively well trained for less well trained teachers. An illustration of this process of technological change can be seen in Figure 11.1, which presents the estimated values of the primary school teacher input coefficients over the years 1964 to 1971.

The resource constraints relate to three types of use:

1. use of inputs generated by the educational system itself which are defined in stock terms (that is, teachers)
2. use of the endogenously generated inputs which are defined as flows (that is, continuing students)
3. use of inputs supplied from outside of the educational system

Considering the two types of constraints relating to resources produced by the educational system, recall that there are three possible uses for the output of any activity: pursuit of further education in the system, employment as a teacher in the system, or employment in the labor force outside of the educational system. These three uses can be referred to as use as an intermediate good, use for capacity creation, and deliveries for final demand. The total requirements within the educational system for labor of a given type thus depends on the levels of the activities which use it as a student input, and the required capacity creation in the activities which use it as a teacher. The total availability of individuals with each qualification is given by the numbers surviving from the base period plus the amount produced within the

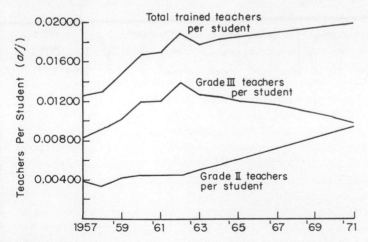

Figure 11.1 Historical and projected technological change in the production of primary education.

NOTES: Values for 1957–1964 are actual; values for 1965–1971 are projected; grade III and grade II teachers have completed 3 and 5 years of postprimary education, respectively.

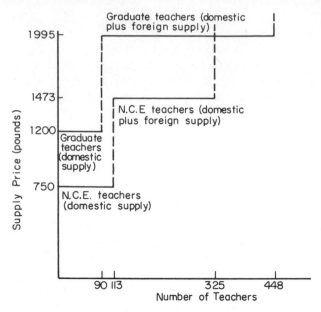

Figure 11.2   Supply functions for graduate teachers and Nigerian Certificates of Education (N.C.E.) teachers in 1965.

NOTES: The height of the first segment of each function reflects the cost of hiring domestic teachers (salaries plus other payments). The difference between the first and second segments reflects the cost of importation of the teacher (travel costs, salary, additions, and so on).

The lengths of the segments are determined by the available domestic supply and the maximum limit on importation.

Graduate teachers refer to those holding a university degree. N.C.E. teachers and their foreign equivalents have completed 8 years of postprimary education.

system or recruited from outside the system.[13] The constraint equations insure that the amount of teachers and continuing students required by a solution does not exceed the number available.

The constraints on the use of exogenously supplied resources refer to such inputs as primary school age population and total social expenditure on education, and require that the total use of each resource not exceed the exogenously specified supply.

In addition to the resource constraints, boundary conditions are imposed on the instrument variables. The main considerations here were the political difficulties involved in any drastic reductions in enrollments, and the administrative obstacles to any very rapid increase.[14] The complete set of equations and a glossary of notation appear in the appendix.

Thus far we have made the usual linear programming assumption that inputs are available at constant cost up to some level beyond which they are not available at any price. An attempt has been made to modify this somewhat extreme requirement by constructing supply functions which reflect the rising supply price of the factor. The supply functions for two types of teachers, each of which may be hired locally or

13. We have assumed that while teachers can be recruited or imported from outside the system, continuing students must be produced endogenously.

14. In the Nigerian application of the model admissions in any year were restricted to a value between 1.3 and 0.7 of the previous year's admissions.

imported, are depicted in Figure 11.2. The vertical distance between the first and second segment of each function is the cost of importing the teacher, namely, transport and other payments additional to the salary. The step is built into the function by allowing the system to use a new activity which imports the teacher at the indicated cost.[15] Similarly, in some runs activities allowing the recruitment of ex-teachers back into the school system have been introduced. These activities are operated at a cost based on the foregone productivity of the teacher in his nonteaching occupation; the output is the availability of additional teachers within the educational system. The introduction of these activities for the recruitment of grade II and grade III teachers (used largely in primary school) has the effect of adding a step to the present supply functions and thus reflecting the rising supply price of these inputs.

For those years immediately preceding the end of the plan period, terminal conditions must be developed so that some allowance will be made for intraeducational demand for educational outputs during the years immediately following the end of the plan period. Were this not done the system would undertake what may be called capital consumption; it would cease producing teachers and students for pursuit of further studies in the last few years of the period. A number of methods of dealing with the terminal conditions is available.[16] The method adopted here is to insure that for teacher training or the production of continuing students the activity levels immediately prior to the end of the plan period will be sufficient to support post terminal rates of growth similar to those established during the planning period.[17]

V. The Pattern of Enrollments and Resource Use Within the Educational Sector

Only a small portion of the body of results generated with the model will be discussed below;[18] emphasis will be directed to the types of insights into concrete policy problems which can be gained with the aid of this approach to educational planning.

Before considering the actual solutions, it should be pointed out that the production side of the model alone is sufficient to generate alternative patterns of enrollments which are both internally consistent and which do not violate the exogenously specified resource constraints. Moreover, the inverse of the matrix of input and output coefficients is a convenient summary of the available educational technologies, and allows the computation of the direct and indirect input requirements for a unit of final delivery of each type of labor to the labor force. Thus we can solve a number of planning problems without reference to the discounted future earnings stream attributable to education. The objective function provides one (but not by any means the only) method of selecting a desirable solution from the multitude of feasible solutions.

15. The cost of using the teacher (salary) is charged directly to the using activity.

16. Two possible methods were considered but not used. First, one might have required a minimum terminal year stock of teachers of each type capable of supporting some desired (exogenously specified) rate of post terminal enrollments. A second possibility would have been first to value the terminal year stock of teachers (presumably using shadow prices from previous runs in an iterative process) and then maximize some function incorporating the present maximand and the value of the terminal year stock of teachers.

17. The choice of terminal conditions is somewhat arbitrary. It should be pointed out, however, that while the values of the instrument variables for the last few years in the planning period may be sensitive to the choice, the relevant years are those on which immediate action must be taken. The sequential application of the model suggested in Section II obviates the need for taking action on any but the first, or the first and second, year of the plan period.

18. Well over 100 solutions of the model have been computed using alternative assumptions concerning policy, technology, and the future demand for educated labor. A more complete description of the results appears in Bowles (1969).

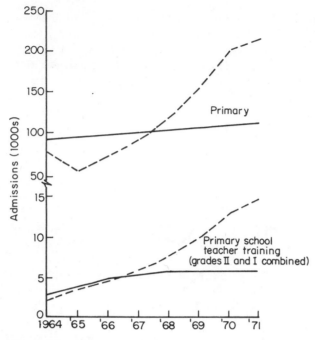

Figure 11.3 Primary school and teacher training admissions, 1964–1971.

NOTES: Dotted lines indicate admissions levels specified by the model; solid lines indicate admissions levels in current Northern Nigerian plans.

This section will present some of the results concerning enrollments in the various types of schools. The following three sections will deal with the choice of techniques, the optimal total resource use by the educational system, and the pattern of importation of educated labor.

Solutions to the model yield values for each of the instrument variables relating to the admission of students to each type of school in each year of the planning period. We shall confine our attention here to primary education and related activities.

The present Northern Nigerian educational plans call for a very gradual increase in primary school enrollments accompanied by gradual increases in the associated teacher training institutions, as indicated in Figure 11.3.[19] The model, using much of the same data, yields a radically different pattern of growth, shown also in Figure 11.3.[20] The rapid rate of growth of primary education over the entire 8 year period reflects the high ratio of net benefits to both social cost per student and inputs of teachers in the primary school activity. More explicitly one can say that the strong claim on resources exerted by primary education is due to a great extent to the low opportunity cost of its major inputs; the opportunity cost of student time is zero and

19. Given the planned upgrading of the primary school teaching staffs, the admissions levels in current government plans (Figure 11.3) are inconsistent. The demands for grade II and grade III teachers derived from the planned primary school admission in the early years of the plan appear to be considerably in excess of current availabilities plus planned outputs. Only a major program of recruitment of ex-teachers could render the existing plans feasible.

20. The planned admissions figures represent the outcome of a comprehensive planning process which took into account a number of noneconomic aspects of the problem not considered in this model. Thus the figures are not strictly comparable.

the opportunity cost of grade II and grade III teachers in the economy is minute compared with the opportunity cost of university graduates, who form the bulk of teaching staffs at the postprimary institutions.

The initial decline in primary school admissions indicated in Figure 11.3 is explained largely by the required upgrading of the primary school teaching staffs and the rather complicated interrelations between primary schools and teacher training. We have found that there are a number of activities within the educational system which are particularly closely intertwined, and that the reciprocal and even multi-lateral trading of continuing students and teachers often results in a somewhat unexpected pattern of optimal educational growth. The connection between primary education and the two major types of primary school teacher training (grade II and grade III) is a good example of this problem.[21] Primary-school leavers are an input into grade III teacher training courses (see Table 11.1). The outputs of the grade III course are delivered back to the primary school as teachers, or to the grade II training course for further training. Those who successfully complete the grade II course serve as teachers in the primary schools or as student inputs into the higher teacher training institutions (NSTC). Thus, while it is not exactly true that everything depends on everything else (this particular whirlpool of interdependence appears to be relatively self-contained), each activity level depends on a number of others, often in a rather complicated way.

Recall that as part of the program of quality improvement in primary school teaching the relatively well trained grade II teachers are being substituted for un-trained and grade III teachers. The upward movement of the grade II teacher input coefficient over time requires that in addition to training teachers to accommodate the increment in total enrollments, the grade II teacher course must train a sufficient number to effect an increase in the grade II teacher coefficient, not only for the increment in enrollments but for the entire stock of primary students currently in the process of being educated.

The educational system is given the choice of four alternative methods of acquiring the necessary grade II teachers:

1. admit primary-school leavers into the (3-year) grade III course and admit those who successfully complete the course to the grade II course
2. withdraw grade III teachers from teaching in primary school and admit them to the grade II course
3. recruit ex-grade III teachers from the nonteaching labor force, and admit them to the grade II course
4. recruit ex-grade II teachers from the nonteaching labor force

All four methods are used. However, it is the withdrawal of grade III teachers from primary school for further training which is largely responsible for the early fall in primary school admissions. The process is analogous to a temporary cutback of production to allow retooling of the existing capital stock, followed by a rapid expansion with a new technology. Were the system restricted to channeling school leavers through the usual grade III and grade II sequence, a total of 5 years would elapse before an increased volume of grade II output could be made available to the primary schools. In this case either admissions would have to be significantly

---

21. Grade III teachers have 3 years of postprimary education and are the lowest category of trained teachers in the primary schools. Grade II teachers have a total of 5 years of postprimary training.

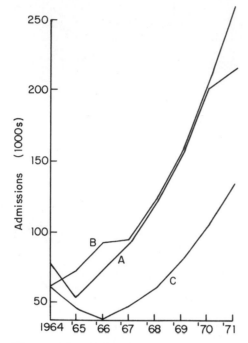

Figure 11.4 Primary school admissions with various policy assumptions.

NOTES: A refers to the basic run presented in Figure 11.3; B refers to a run in which there is no upgrading in the qualifications of the primary school staff; C refers to a run in which the recruitment of ex-teachers from the nonteaching labor force was not allowed.

reduced, or the upgrading of the primary school teaching staff would have to be postponed, or both. A number of runs in which recruiting ex-teachers from the nonteaching labor force was not allowed resulted in a much more pronounced and more prolonged reduction in primary school admissions. On the other hand, a run incorporating no temporal change in the teacher/student ratio (no upgrading of the primary school staffs) resulted in a monotonically increasing admissions level for primary education (see Figure 11.4).

VI. The Choice of Educational Techniques

Many of the policy decisions facing planners in the field of education concern changes in educational technologies. In this section we shall explore the economic implications of a number of technological changes in primary education.

The Ministry of Education in Northern Nigeria has recently given consideration to a proposal which would reduce the number of years in the primary school course. The proposal for a shorter course offers the same number of classroom hours as are presently offered over the 7 year course. This is possible because of the relatively short school year in the present system. The optimality of a similar proposal has been considered with the model. Primary school activities of 5 years duration have been introduced. The *annual* costs are somewhat higher (to allow for the opportunity cost of withdrawing the teaching staff from possible vacation time employment) but given the reduction of the course from 7 to 5 years, the total discounted cost is not increased. The teacher/student ratios are unchanged, except that the elimination of the sixth and seventh year obviously releases a significant portion of the teaching staff. Once the system is in operation, overall teacher requirements are reduced to five-sevenths of the previous level.[22] In addition, the availability of the primary school output 2 years earlier increases the present value of the benefits stream.

The effect of the introduction of the new primary school course can now be outlined. The optimal primary school admissions levels are significantly increased. Moreover, the net benefits generated by the optimal solution are more than 10 percent higher at the present level of expenditure on education (see Figure 11.6). Despite the increase in primary school admissions, the teacher training activities are run at virtually the same levels as in the solution with the 7-year primary school course. Both the increase in total net benefits and the increase in optimal primary school admissions can be explained by:

1. the reduction in overall teacher requirements which, among other things, facilitates the "retooling" process
2. the increase in the present value of net benefits per student

A number of other runs have tested the implications of the following types of structural or technological change in the production of education; all resulted in significant increases in the value of the objective function:

1. an increase in the university course from 3 to 4 years, accompanied by the elimination of the present Sixth Form, the 2-year university preparatory course
2. a reduction of the failure rates in various teacher training activities
3. a less rapid quality improvement in the teaching staffs in primary schools
4. various changes in the productive techniques at the primary school level

A particularly interesting experiment in the fourth category was to allow the model to substitute equipment (texts and audiovisual materials) for the lowest grade of teachers in primary school (grade III), and to allow some substitutability between different types of teachers in the production of primary education. Using constant marginal rates of substitution between grade II and grade III teachers and between grade III teachers and equipment, over a limited range, an optimum pattern of enrollments and substitution was generated. Some factor substitution was optimal in all years of the planning period.

VII. Optimal Total Resource Use by Education

We turn now to the question of the total resource use by the educational system. We have two related types of measures of the optimality of the division of resources between education and the rest of the economy:

1. the amount of additional resources recruited into the educational system in the optimal solution
2. the shadow prices of resources

22. If one took account of the effect of wastage on the teacher/student ratios, the reduction in overall requirements would be somewhat less. It should be pointed out that the impact of the change is not felt in the model until the sixth year of the plan, because it is assumed that primary school students already in school at the beginning of the plan will remain for the usual 7 years.

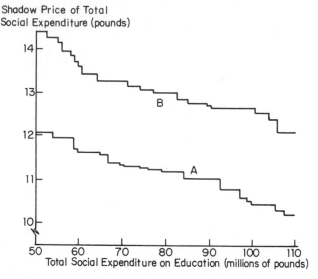

Figure 11.5 Shadow prices as a function of total social expenditure on education.

NOTES: Present value of total social expenditure is based on a 5 percent discount rate. The function indicated by B refers to the run using a shortened (5 year) primary school course. The function indicated by A refers to the run using the existing (7 year) primary school course. Current planned expenditure is in the neighborhood of £80 million.

The activities which recruit new factors (for example, recruiting exteachers back into the educational system) will be run at positive levels whenever the indirect effect of an additional unit of resource on the discounted value of future GNP is greater than the estimate of the resource's unit cost.[23]

In all solutions of the model it has been optimal to augment the existing factor supplies with recruits both from the Nigerian labor force outside of education, and from abroad. Thus, for example, the high level of recruitment of grade III teachers reflects the fact that the marginal productivity (in terms of discounted future GNP) of grade III teachers when used in the production of primary education is considerably higher than the direct productivity of these personnel when employed in the rest of the economy. The high levels of importation of foreign teachers indicate that during most years of the planning period the value of the marginal product of these teachers within the Nigerian educational system exceeded the rather substantial importation costs.

The shadow prices of each resource provide some indication of the optimal total resource use by the educational system. If the shadow price of the resource within the educational system, measuring the direct and indirect contribution of a unit

23. The unit cost of imported teachers is the additional salary and other associated costs; the unit cost of additional factors recruited from other sectors in the economy is the factor's marginal productivity in its alternative use.

Where z is a row vector of the objective function coefficients, B is the basis of included activities, a_k is the vector representing the recruiting activity, and c_k is the estimated opportunity cost of recruitment, the simplex criterion insures that the recruiting activity will be run at positive levels whenever:

$$c_k \leq zB^{-1}a_k$$

The right-hand term of the inequality is the direct and indirect effect of the availability of an additional unit of the resource on the objective function.

of the resource to discounted future GNP exceeds the marginal productivity of the resource in its next best use, then we can conclude that the allocation of more of the resource in question to the educational system would increase the present value of future GNP.

Total resource use in the model is measured in money terms and referred to as total social expenditure on education. This quantity includes the direct social costs of education along with the opportunity costs of students' time incurred during the process of education. In all solutions of the model the shadow price referring to total social expenditure on education is high relative to any plausible estimate of the marginal productivity of resources in alternative uses. At first glance one would conclude that a major increase in the availabilities of resources for the educational system is called for. However, the skeptic and the planner may wish to investigate how the shadow price is affected by changes in the availability of resources to the system.

Parametric programming has been used to estimate the marginal productivity function for expenditures on education. The element in the constraint vector referring to the maximum total expenditure has been first set at a low level and then increased. At the point where each change in the optimal basis occurs, an entire new optimal solution, including the total benefits, the shadow prices and the optimal activity

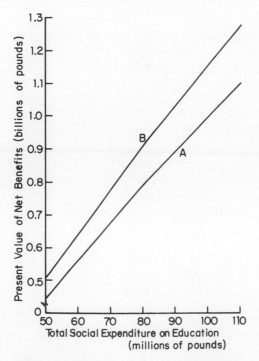

Figure 11.6   Present value of net benefits as a function of total social expenditure on education.

NOTES: Present value of net benefits and total social expenditures are based on a 5 percent discount rate. A refers to the present system with a 7-year primary school course. B refers to the revised system with a 5-year primary school course.

levels has been recorded. This technique allows us to trace out both the marginal productivity function for expenditure on education, and a function relating the total benefits to total expenditure. The two functions appear in Figures 11.5 and 11.6. The shadow prices appearing in the step functions in Figure 11.5 are clearly the slopes of the minute line segments which make up the total benefits function in Figure 11.6.[24] The range of variation of the total social expenditure on education presented here is centered on £80 million, which is about what present government plans imply. Variations beyond the range presented in the tables were thought to be of dubious value because the linearity of the relationships in the model is open to serious question when very major changes in allocation are being considered.

Two aspects of Figures 11.5 and 11.6 are particularly striking: the high level of the shadow prices over a wide range of expenditure on education and the very favorable ratio of net benefits to total costs. These results seem to confirm the earlier impression that a revision of the present division of resources between education and and the rest of the economy in favor of education would significantly increase the present value of future GNP.

VIII. The Importation of Educated Labor

The number of foreigners involved in teaching a nation's youth is naturally a question of political as well as economic importance. The replacement of foreign by indigenous teachers is a major policy goal in a number of countries; others have explicit or implicit limits on the proportion of teaching positions which may be held by aliens. Yet foreigners are often a crucial element in expanding the supply of teachers, particularly as a temporary measure to break bottlenecks in teacher training itself. The optimal importation of foreign teachers thus depends on a trade-off between income (and perhaps other) gains made possible through a more rapid expansion in educational facilities and welfare losses occasioned by an increased dependence on foreigners.

We may expect the social welfare function to contain a negative term relating to the number of imported teachers in the school system. We may write:

$$W = W(Y, F, \ldots) \quad \frac{\partial W}{\partial Y} > 0$$
$$\frac{\partial W}{\partial F} < 0 \tag{11.4}$$

where

W = the social welfare function

F = total number of teachers imported

Y = the present value of future national income

In view of the fact that over some ranges of importation foreign teachers contribute to the expansion of educational output and hence of future national income, we can further write:

$$Y = g(F) \quad \text{(all other inputs constant)} \tag{11.5}$$

and therefore,

$$W = W[g(F), F] \tag{11.6}$$

24. Although difficult to detect visually the functions in Figure 11.6 are concave from below; the implied diminishing marginal productivity is clearly shown in the negative inclination of the step functions in Figure 11.5.

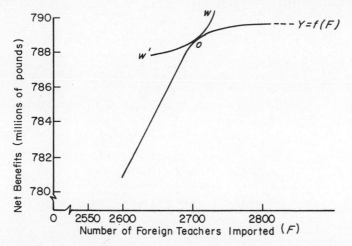

Figure 11.7 Net benefits as a function of the number of foreign teachers imported.

NOTES: ww' represents the (hypothetical) social welfare function. For $F > 2812$ the shadow price of foreign teachers is zero. For $F < 2597$ no feasible solution exists.

First-order conditions for the maximum W requires that

$$\frac{-\partial W/\partial F}{\partial W/\partial Y} = \frac{\partial Y}{\partial F} \tag{11.7}$$

or that the negative of the marginal rate of substitution in the social welfare function between income and foreigners must equal the marginal product of foreigners or the rate of transformation of foreigners into income.[25]

We can estimate the relation (11.5) using the parametric programming technique described in the previous section. The term $\partial Y/\partial F$ is the shadow price of foreign teachers in the model or the slope of the function appearing in Figure 11.7. The shape of the function and the limited range of variation of F between the point of redundancy and the point at which no feasible solution exists suggests that, given the present structure of the system, the productivity of foreigners is high at present levels of use, but that any major increase in importation would quickly depress their marginal product to zero. Nonetheless, the high shadow price of foreigners over the relevant range is suggestive of a rather major opportunity cost of pursuing nationalistic educational policies. The dotted line WW' in that figure represents a hypothetical social welfare function which yields an optimum as described in (11.7) at point a.

IX. Conclusions

Because the model employs linear constraints and a linear maximand, there are relatively few computational problems involved in solving and using the model.

25. For simplicity of presentation, we have here ignored the term $(\partial W/\partial E)(\partial E/\partial F)$ which would take account of the fact that increased importation of foreigners allows an expansion of enrollment (E) which may be valued directly in the social welfare function, apart from the associated income gains.

However, computational simplicity has been gained at the cost of a number of assumptions which do not strictly correspond to the reality of any concrete planning situation. The following limitations of the model arising from the use of these simplifying assumptions are particularly important.

First, the maximand is a linear function of the activity levels; thus the net benefits coefficients must not be a function of the level of output of any of the activities. Strictly speaking, this requires that the elasticity of demand for labor is infinite and the cross derivatives (with respect to the various labor inputs) of the production functions in the economy are zero.[26] This assumption is at the opposite extreme from that made or implied by the manpower requirements school of educational planning, namely, that the price elasticity of demand for labor is zero. The problems mentioned here are attributable to the fact that we are dealing with a sectoral model rather than with a model of the entire economy. Ideally we would use a model of the educational system and the economy in which the demand for educated labor and the supply of inputs to education are generated endogenously.

Second, in the empirical implementation of the model it has been necessary to use estimated future earnings streams as the basis for the objective function. This approach relies on the assumption that workers are paid according to their marginal productivity. In addition, the use of observed earnings as a basis for the estimation of future earnings streams rests on the assumption that the real absolute differences in the earnings accruing to labor educated to different levels and with a given number of years of experience will remain constant over time.[27]

Third, it is assumed that the observed income differentials can be attributed entirely to differences in education. This is clearly not the case if intellectual and physical aptitudes, parental wealth, or various sociopsychological attributes which are positively correlated with an individual's future earnings are also positively correlated with the likelihood of his getting an education.

Fourth, even if the first three assumptions were close approximations of reality, it should be pointed out that the observed earnings measure the private marginal productivity to the individual or to the firm rather than his social marginal productivity. The external effects of an individual's education have been omitted.

Fifth, the objective function measures only those effects which result in higher earnings. The benefits which have been defined above as noneconomic, namely, those which affect the nonincome terms in the social welfare function, are not included in the objective function.

The usefulness of a linear model of the type proposed here depends on how closely the assumptions and structure of the model approximate reality in any given planning situation and on how sensitive the results of the model are to a likely degree of error. On the basis of sensitivity analysis of the model with respect to each of the above assumptions it can be said that the results for Northern Nigeria are not significantly affected by plausible alternative assumptions. The same general conclusion applies to reasonable changes in the data underlying the parameters of the model. Similarly favorable results were yielded by sensitivity analysis of the choice of a time discount rate and the estimated rate of unemployment among the outputs of the educational

26. In the absence of strict conformity with the requirement, approximate constancy of the present value of the outputs may result from the interaction of a number of influences, for example, the expansion of the supply of educated labor accompanied by a rightward movement of the demand curve for educated labor as a result of economic growth or technological change.

27. It should be pointed out that in the presence of general increases in output per worker, constancy of the absolute differences in earnings is consistent with a narrowing of relative earnings.

system.[28] A run in which only 60 percent of the earnings differentials by educational level were attributed to education produced no major qualitative changes, although net benefits were naturally reduced.

Despite the very real nature of the above shortcomings of the model, this approach to the economics of educational planning does yield a wealth of insights into the question of optimal resource allocation in education. By making explicit the complicated interrelations within the educational system it allows the investigation of the direct and indirect effects of a multiplicity of concrete policy choices. The model facilitates the consideration of the efficiency of alternative educational production processes simultaneously with the choice of levels of production. The shadow prices generated by the model are useful in identifying major resource scarcities and in suggesting the relative importance of policy measures to alter educational technologies or the structure of the educational system. Lastly, the model has been constructed so as to rely on data which are either available in most countries or can be easily generated.

Appendix to Chapter 11
Outline of the Structure
of the Model as Applied
to Northern Nigeria

   I. The planning period: Eight years extending from 1964 through 1971.
  II. Activities: In most runs, a total of 120 activities, or one per year for the following:
  A. Activities making deliveries to the labor force
    1. primary school
    2. secondary school
    3. technical training school
    4. form VI (college preparatory)
    5. university education in Nigeria
    6. university education abroad
  B. Activities devoted exclusively to teaching training or to the preparation of students for further courses
    1. craft school (preparation for technical training school)
    2. grade III teacher training
    3. grade II teacher training
    4. Nigerian Certificate of Education teacher training
  C. Activities importing and recruiting teachers
    1. importing foreign teachers holding university degrees
    2. importing foreign teachers holding the equivalent of a Nigerian Certificate of Education
    3. recruiting ex-grade II teachers from the labor force
    4. recruiting ex-grade III teachers from the labor force
    5. recruiting additional senior university teachers from abroad

28. The sensitivity tests and a more complete discussion of the empirical importance of the limitations of the model are found in Bowles (1965: appendix 6.4 and appendix 7.1). Some of the insensitivity to plausible parametric variations may be explained by the upper and lower bounds on activity levels.

III. The objective Function: The terms in the objective function measure the net contribution of each activity to the present value of future national income, as defined in Section III.

Using the notation as defined in the glossary (below), the maximand is:

$$Z^* = \sum_{j=1}^{m} \sum_{p=1}^{n} X_j^p (Y_j^p - Y_{j'}^p - C_j^p)$$

IV. Constraints

A. Constraints on the use of inputs which are defined as stock and which are generated within the educational system, namely, teachers:

$$\sum_{j=1}^{m} \sum_{p=t+1-s_j}^{t} a_{ij}^t X_j^p - \sum_{p=1}^{t-s_j} g_i X_i^p - X_{i*}^t \leq B_i^t$$

The first term of the expression is the total enrollments in activity X_j at time t, multiplied by the required input of teachers of type i per student in activity j, summed over all of the m activities. The second term is the total output since the beginning of the planning period of the teacher training activity producing resource i (adjusted for failures and dropouts). The third term is the total importation or recruitment of teachers of type i from outside the educational system in time t. The right-hand term is the total stock of the type i teachers in the system in the first year of the planning period who have remained in the system (that is, who have not retired) up to year t. Thus the above set of equations requires that total use of type i teachers not exceed the available supply for each type of teacher in each year of the planning period.

These constraints are 32 in number corresponding to one per year for the following inputs:

1. grade III teachers
2. grade II teachers
3. Nigerian Certificate of Education teachers
4. university graduate teachers

B. Constraints on the use of inputs which are defined in flow terms and which are generated within the educational system, namely, students.

$$\sum_{j=1}^{m} a_{ij} X_j^t - g_i X_i^{t-s_i} \leq 0.$$

The first term of this constraint is the total students with qualifications i required as inputs into educational processes in time t, while the second term is the total output of the activity producing these students at the end of the previous year. This set of equations thus requires that the intake of students into a given type of school in time t must not exceed the previous year's output of students with the prerequisite qualifications for entry.

These constraints are 32 in number corresponding to one per year for the following inputs:

1. primary school-leavers
2. craft school-leavers
3. secondary school-leavers
4. form VI leavers

C. Constraints on the use of exogenously supplied inputs:

$$\sum_{j=1}^{m} \sum_{p=t+1-s_j}^{t} a_{ij}^t X_j^p \le B_i^t.$$

The first term is the total enrollments in time t in type j schools, multiplied by the per student input requirement, summed over the m types of education. The right-hand term is the exogenously specified total availability of resource i in time t.

These constraints are 17 in number and refer to the following inputs:

1. present value of total social expenditure on education (only one constraint for all 8 years)
2. senior university teachers
3. children in the 6 year age group

D. Boundary conditions for admissions levels:

$$X_j^p \ge .7 X_j^{p-1}$$
$$X_j^p \le 1.3 X_j^{p-1}$$

for recruiting and importing activities:

$$X_{i*}^p \le R_{i*}^p$$

Glossary of Notation

Notation Relating to the Instrument Variables

X_j^p = the number of students admitted to level j in period p: $j = 1, \ldots, m$, $p = 1, \ldots, n$

m = the number of activities

n = the number of years in the planning period

X_{i*}^t = the imports or recruitment of resource of type i in period t

Notation Relating Primarily to the Constraint Equations

a_{ij}^t = the minimum input of resource i in period t required to accommodate one student in activity j: $t = 1, \ldots n$, $j = 1, \ldots, m$, $i = 1, \ldots, m + q$

q = number of exogenously supplied inputs

B_i^t = the amount of resource i available to the system in time t

s_j = the length of course j in years (similarly defined for s_i)

X_{ij}^t = the amount of input i devoted to activity j in period t

R_{i*}^p = upper limit on the recruitment or importation of teachers with qualification i in period p

Notation Relating Primarily to the Objective Function

Z_j^p = the net benefits function coefficient associated with activity X_j^p

z = the row vector $(1 \times nm)$ of net benefits coefficients Z_j^p

Y_j^p = the present value (discounted to year 1) of the earnings accruing to an output of activity X_j^p

$\bar{Y}_j^p$ = the present value (discounted to year 1) of the alternative earnings stream; namely, that which would have accrued to the individual had he not received education at activity j

C_j^p = the present value (discounted to year 1) of the per student cost of operating activity X_j^p for the entire course of s_j years

g_j = the fraction of the total admissions to activity X_j which is expected to complete successfully the course

12 Optimal Allocation
of Investment in Education*

C. R. S. Dougherty

I. Introduction

In recent years recognition of the fact that education has many of the character-istics of an investment process has led to its formal treatment as a capital good and to attempts to measure its marginal efficiency. The rate-of-return approach to edu-cational planning that has thus evolved is faced by the same difficulty that confronts the technique when applied to investment problems in general, that it is valid only as long as the investment under consideration is sufficiently marginal so that it does not affect the structure of prices. Unless one extends the analysis to take into account the effect of an investment, especially the effect of the increase in output due to the investment, on the relevant markets, its usefulness is confined to making quali-tative but not quantitative assessments of desirable investment. And it cannot be used at all for determining the distribution of such investment over time. For this reason the approach has generally been employed as an indicator of immediate priorities rather than as a planning tool, and for the latter purpose it has been dis-placed by relatively primitive techniques like the manpower requirements approach.

The purpose of this chapter is to extend the approach so that it may be used for estimating the return to nonmarginal investments in education. As in the classical variation of the approach, wage differentials are used to measure the benefits of education. However, instead of taking wage differentials to be exogenous quantities, the effect on them of the growth of the educational system is estimated. This is achieved by calculating the impact of the growth of the educational system on the supplies of different types of labor and then estimating how changes in the structure of the supply of labor will affect the structure of wage rates. One thus obtains a feed-back relationship between the growth of a level of education and its own profita-bility. The faster the growth of a level of education, the greater will be the supply of graduates from it and therefore the lower their wage; meanwhile, the smaller will be the supply of persons who enter the labor force immediately instead of receiving

* Economic Development Report No. 129, presented at the Development Advisory Service Conference, Sorrento, Italy, September 5–12, 1968 (revised April 1969).

Portions of this research were supported by the Development Advisory Service and the Project for Quantitative Research on Economic Development through funds provided by the Agency for Inter-national Development under AID Contract CSD 1543. The views expressed in this paper do not, however, necessarily reflect the views of AID.

I am indebted to Marcelo Selowsky for many helpful discussions and suggestions and to Samuel Bowles for numerous comments on earlier drafts.

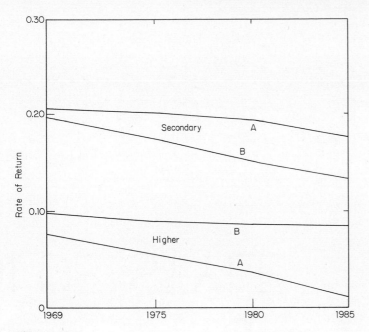

Figure 12.1

the education, and the higher will be their wage; hence the lower will be the wage differential and thus the rate of return to that type of education.

Figure 12.1 illustrates this point. The lines marked *A* show the course of the rate of return over time to secondary education and higher education in Colombia on the assumption that those levels of education maintain their historical growth rates of 10 percent and 11 percent per year, respectively. The lines marked *B* show what happens if the growth rates are changed to 15 percent and 5 percent per year, respectively.[1]

If one believes that investment in education should be carried to the point where the marginal rate of return is equal to a given social rate of discount, the feedback relationship can be used to estimate the amount of investment required and also to determine its timing. In Figure 12.1 when higher education grows at 11 percent, its rate of return falls from just over 7 percent in 1969 to less than 1 percent by 1985. For a social discount rate of 10 percent this growth rate would be much too high. Cutting the growth rate back to 5 percent per year brings the trajectory of the rate of return close to the 10 percent line, and thus it is shown that the optimal growth rate for that discount rate is near 5 percent. In principle by making finer, year-to-year adjustments in the enrollment growth rate one could bring the rate of return trajectory to lie exactly on the 10 percent line. It should be noted, however, that the growth of one level of education will affect the profitability of another, and so such adjustments should be made simultaneously for all levels.

The key part of the analysis is the relationship between the supplies of different types of labor and wage levels. Studies of the rate of return to education have gen-

1. In this figure, the elasticity of substitution, σ, $= 6$ and the rate of growth of GDP due to non-labor factors of production, λ, $= 0.04$. The significance of these parameters is explained in Sections IV and V.

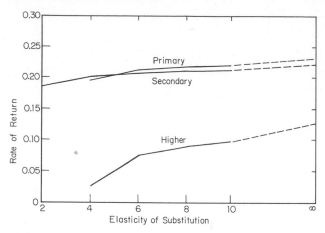

Figure 12.2   1969.

erally made the somewhat ingenuous assumption that relative wage levels will not change over time.[2] Given that in most countries the educational quality of those joining the labor force for the first time is appreciably superior to that of the existing stock and that therefore the labor force is being secularly, but in the long run, substantially, upgraded, this assumption implies that the elasticity of substitution between different types of labor is infinite.[3] However, casual observation of cross-section data and time series data shows that the greater are the relative supplies of the more highly skilled types of labor, the lower are their relative wages, implying a less than infinite elasticity of substitution. This impression has been confirmed by Samuel Bowles (1968), who found an elasticity of substitution of between six and eight using two categories of labor and international cross-section data, a result corroborated by an experiment of my own in which time series data for the United States yielded an estimate of 3.6 for the elasticity (Dougherty, 1969: appendix 2).

The projection of wage rates is important because the estimate of the rate of return to a level of education may be sensitive to yearly earnings far into the future, unless the estimate of the rate of return itself is high. (For a discussion of this point, see Section VI.) This is true for estimates of the current rate of return to education, and especially true for estimates of the rate of return in future years. Figure 12.2 shows the sensitivity of estimates of the current rates of return to Colombian education using alternative assumptions about the elasticity of substitution. The lower the elasticity, the faster the relative wage levels are expected to contract. It can be seen that the estimate of the current rates of return to primary and secondary education, both high, are not influenced much by the elasticity; but that of higher education, which is low, is severely affected. Figure 12.3 shows the effect of the elasticity of substitution on the estimates of the rates of return in 1980. In this case the estimates of both primary and secondary education are significantly affected by the elasticity, and the estimate for higher education is very sensitive to it. Table 12.1 shows base year (1964) wage

2. Some are downright naïve and assume that absolute wage levels will remain unchanged.
3. Providing that there do not exist relative complementarities between some types of labor and other factors of production, for example, between highly skilled workers and capital. If such relative complementarities do exist, it would be possible for relative wage levels to remain constant with less than infinite elasticities of substitution.

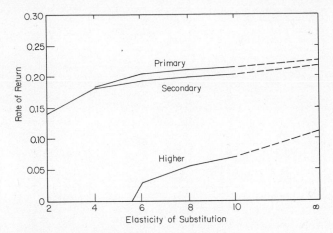

Figure 12.3   1980.

Table 12.1. Projected Wage Levels in Colombia[a] (thousand 1958 pesos per year)

	Illiterates	Primary 1-3	Primary 4-5	Secondary 1-4	Secondary 5-6	Higher 1-3	Higher 4-6
1964 (base year)	1.50	2.26	3.27	5.61	12.65	17.07	21.61
1980							
$\sigma = 4$	2.45	2.98	4.56	6.15	18.83	17.32	23.04
6	2.27	2.96	4.46	6.51	17.99	18.81	24.61
8	2.19	2.95	4.40	6.69	17.57	19.58	25.41
10	2.14	2.95	4.37	6.80	17.32	20.06	25.90
∞	1.94	2.92	4.22	7.24	16.33	22.03	27.89

[a] All the parameters except σ were set at their reference values. See Section VII below.

levels and projected 1980 wage levels corresponding to alternative hypotheses about the elasticity of substitution, in constant 1958 pesos per year.

The calculations required by the analysis are executed in six stages. Exogenously given projections of the number of students entering the first year of each educational level are used to estimate the additions to the different categories of workers and to calculate the demand for teachers and for investment in fixed capital in schools. This information is used to project the number of workers in each of the different categories by which the labor force is classified. A constant elasticity of substitution function is then used to aggregate these projections into a single measure of the labor force which takes into account not only the increase in the total number of workers but also the improvement in its quality. This index is used together with an estimate of growth due to factors of production other than labor in order to estimate the rate of growth of GDP for the country. This enables the marginal product of each different category of worker to be calculated, and, hence, one obtains projections of the wage rate for each category. The wage-rate projections can then be used to evaluate the present discounted values of the benefits and the costs of each level of education, and one arrives at an estimate of their rates of return. If it is desired that the rate of return to each level of education should be equal to some predetermined social dis-

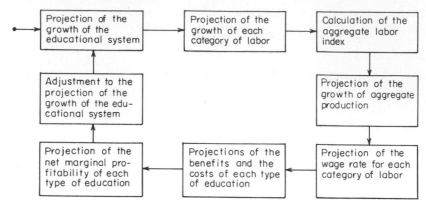

Figure 12.4

count rate, these results can be used to modify the enrollment projection. Those branches of the educational system with rates of return greater than the social discount rate should be increased, and those with rates of return less than it should be reduced. The initial projections can thus be adjusted iteratively so that their rates of return are equal to the discount rate over the whole of the planning horizon. When this point is reached, the supply and the social demand for each type of labor are in balance, and the educational system is attaining its optimal growth path. Figure 12.4 represents the process schematically.

The remaining sections of this paper describe each of the stages in more detail with reference to an application of the methodology to education in Colombia.

II. The Educational System

In Colombia, primary education lasts 5 years; secondary education 6; and higher education up to 5 or 6.[4] Two kinds of information are required for the projection of the growth of each level of education: (1) the basic parameters, such as dropout rates and student-teacher ratios; and (2) the projection of the enrollment in the first grade[5] of each educational level for each year of the planning period.

The first task is to transform, for each educational level, the basic parameters into what will be referred to as an "impact table," a table which shows all the repercussions of increasing the enrollment in the first grade of that educational level by 100 students in year n. In order to shorten the exposition, the construction of the impact table will be described here in detail for Colombian secondary education only. The procedures for primary and higher education are similar; their descriptions are omitted (but can be found in Dougherty 1969: appendix 3).

The basic parameters needed for the analysis are (1) the student-teacher ratio, (2) the composition of the teaching staff according to educational level, (3) the

4. That is, if a student does not repeat any year. In fact, repeating rates are high, so that, for example, the average time taken to complete primary education is approximately 6 years.

5. The word "year" will be replaced by the word "grade" when referring to instruction within any educational level. For example, the first year of secondary education will be referred to as the first grade of secondary education.

Table 12.2. Calculation of the Number of University Trained Teachers Required by Secondary Education in 1978 (thousands)

Year	Number of students entering first grade of secondary school	Requirements in 1978 of university trained teachers
1969	164	0
1970	180	0
1971	198	0.1
1972	218	0.4
1973	240	1.8
1974	264	2.7
1975	290	3.9
1976	319	5.6
1977	351	7.7
1978	386	11.7
1979	424	
1980	467	
Total		33.9

capital cost of providing a place for one student, and (4) the dropout and repeating rates for each grade.

With these basic data the effects of enrolling 100 students in the first grade of secondary education in year n are calculated. The number of teachers required by the students is estimated using the student-teacher ratio, and this is divided between teachers with higher education and those with secondary education only. The capital stock associated with the students is also calculated.

The next step is to calculate the position at the beginning of year $n + 1$. By this time most of the students will be entering second grade. Some will be repeating first grade. The remainder will have dropped out. The total enrollment will be smaller than 100 by the number that have dropped out, and the number of teachers and the amount of capital required will have been reduced proportionately. The investment in the second year will be equal to the depreciation on the capital stock during the first year, less the reduction in the capital stock due to the dropout of a fraction of the students and, hence, is likely to be negative. The fraction of the students that dropped out during the previous year represents a potential addition to category 4 (see Section III) of the labor force.[6]

The process is repeated for each succeeding year. In year $n + 6$ the first graduates appear—those students that have neither dropped out nor repeated. In the next few years more graduates appear, these being students who have repeated one or more grades. By the eighth year after the initial enrollment, most of the students have dropped out or graduated and will have been assigned either to category 4 or 5 of the labor force.

The results of these calculations are gathered together in the impact table (Table 12.3) With this table it is possible to calculate the effect on the secondary school

6. For the purposes of this paper the Colombian labor force is classified into seven categories according to educational level. For the definitions of these categories, see Section III.

system and on the labor force of a projection of the number of students entering the first grade of secondary education from 1969 onward.

As an illustration take the enrollment projection shown in the second column of Table 12.2, which is based on the assumption that the present 10 percent annual growth rate is maintained.

The consequences of this projection for, say, the year 1978 can be calculated using the impact table. As an example, the total demand of the secondary school system for university trained teachers will be estimated. The number of university trained teachers needed by the cohort of students entering secondary education in 1978 will be $386/100 \times 3.04 = 11.7$ thousand. The number needed in 1978 by the cohort which entered in 1977 will be $351/100 \times 2.18 = 7.7$ thousand. Generalizing, the number needed by the cohort entering in the year $(1978 - n)$ will be equal to the amount of the enrollment in that year multiplied by $1/100$ of the coefficient for year $n + 1$ in the impact table. It can be seen from Table 12.2 that the closer a cohort is to 1978, the larger is its requirement of teachers. This is because the later its date of entry, the larger its initial size and the less it will have been reduced by desertion and graduation by 1978. The aggregate requirement of university trained teachers by secondary education in 1978 is shown as the total in Table 12.2. In the same way one may calculate the requirement of teachers with secondary education, the gross investment in fixed capital needed, the dropouts to labor category 4, the dropouts to labor category 5, and the number of graduates in 1978. Likewise all these quantities may be calculated for the secondary school system for every year from 1969 until the terminal year of the planning period. And by the same methodology, the consequences of enrollment projections for primary and higher education may be calculated. The next stage is to compute the combined effects of these enrollment projections on the supply of each category of labor.

III. The Labor Force

In the application to Colombia the labor force is divided into seven categories:

Category
1   illiterates
2   those with some primary education but not more than 3 complete years of it
3   those with more than 3 years of primary education but with no secondary education
4   those with some secondary education but no more than 4 complete years of it
5   those with more than 4 complete years of secondary education but no higher education
6   those with some higher education but not more than 3 complete years of it
7   those with more than 3 years of higher education

The projection for category 5 is described in detail here. Since the projections for the remaining categories are made in similar fashion, their descriptions are omitted (but can be found in Dougherty 1969: appendix 4). Category 5 contains five separate subcomponents:

a. Those workers remaining from the initial stock of the category in 1969, the year the calculations for Colombia begin. This subcomponent declines slowly as its members retire or die.

Table 12.3. Impact Table for Secondary Education: The Consequences of Enrolling 100 Students in the First Grade of Secondary Education in Year n

					Year				
	n	$n+1$	$n+2$	$n+3$	$n+4$	$n+5$	$n+6$	$n+7$	$n+8$
Total enrollment	100.0	71.7	57.6	44.7	33.4	24.8	6.3	1.0	0.1
Enrollment in first grade	100.0	5.0	0.3	0	0				
Enrollment in second grade		66.7	6.7	0.5					
Enrollment in third grade			50.6	7.6	0.8	0.1			
Enrollment in fourth grade				36.6	7.3	0.9	0.1		
Enrollment in fifth grade					25.3	6.3	1.0	0.1	
Enrollment in sixth grade						17.5	5.3	0.9	0.1
Secondary-school trained teachers	4.57	3.27	2.63	2.04	1.53	1.13	0.29	0.05	0.01
University trained teachers	3.04	2.18	1.75	1.36	1.02	0.76	0.19	0.03	0
Capital requirements (thousand 1958 pesos)	235.3	168.7	135.4	105.1	78.7	58.4	14.8	2.4	0.3
Depreciation on capital in previous year		7.1	5.1	4.1	3.2	2.4	1.8	0.4	0.1
Gross investment	235.3	−59.5	−28.2	−26.3	−23.3	−17.9	−41.9	−11.9	−2.0
Drop-outs from grades 1–4 in previous year		28.3	14.2	12.9	11.2	2.1	0.3		
Cumulative drop-outs from grades 1–4		28.3	42.5	55.3	66.6	68.6	68.9	68.9	68.9
Drop-outs from grades 5–6 in previous year						6.5	1.6	0.3	0
Cumulative drop-outs from grades 5–6						6.5	8.2	8.4	8.4
Graduates at end of previous year							16.7	5.0	0.9
Cumulative graduates							16.7	21.7	22.5

Table 12.4. Example Projection of the Growth of Labor Category 5 (thousands)

Year	Residue from initial stock	Primary school teachers	Secondary school teachers	Cumulative drop-outs from secondary school	Cumulative graduates from secondary school not continuing to higher education	Total
1970	272.0	- 53.7	-28.0	20.4	7.2	232.4
1975	266.0	- 92.4	-37.7	82.5	17.6	236.1
1980	257.0	-114.9	-61.5	160.9	17.6	259.0
1985	242.0	-142.9	-99.1	289.5	17.6	307.1

b. Primary school teachers. Using the projected enrollment in primary education and the student-teacher ratio for that level, one can calculate the requirement of teaching staff. This figure forms a negative contribution to the labor force available for the rest of the economy.

c. Secondary school teachers. In the same way one can calculate the number of secondary school graduates who will be withdrawn from the potential labor force in order to teach secondary school.

d. Dropouts from secondary school. Using the projections of enrollment in secondary education and Table 12.3, one can calculate the number of students who drop out from the last two grades of secondary education and who are therefore assigned to category 5.

e. Graduates from secondary school who do not enter higher education. Using the projection of secondary school students and Table 12.3, one can estimate the number of graduates from secondary school for each year. From the projection of graduates one subtracts the projection of the enrollment in the first year of higher education and the remainder are assigned to category 5.

Subcomponents d and e represent potential additions to category 5 in the sense that they are estimates of students who leave the school system qualified to enter that labor category. However, a significant proportion, mostly women, for one reason or other will not actually enter the labor force. The figures for these two subcomponents are therefore multiplied by an adjustment factor calculated from data obtained in the 1964 census. Similar adjustment factors are calculated for the other six labor categories.

Table 12.4 shows a typical projection made for category 5. Although the projection has to be calculated for each year, it is sufficient to show here the results at 5-year intervals. It should be emphasized that each of the subcomponents b through e is dependent upon the particular projections of the enrollments in the different levels of the educational system.

The projections for the other six categories of labor are made in the same way. These are now combined by the use of a constant elasticity of substitution (CES) function in order to arrive at an aggregate measure of the labor force which takes into account the educational level of the workers as well as their number.

IV. The Aggregate Labor Index

International cross-section data indicate that most countries are experiencing two major long-term changes in their economies: (1) the structure of the labor force is changing as the proportion of the more highly educated categories increases; (2) and the structure of relative wages is contracting. These two processes work together in a complementary fashion to secure the absorption into the labor force of those students leaving the educational system. If techniques of production change readily in response to small changes in relative wages, then one can expect relative wages to change slowly. If, on the other hand, techniques are rigid, then the structure of wages may have to change considerably in order for the supply of new workers to be absorbed. If the rigidity is extreme, the increase in the relative supply of some type of worker may not be entirely absorbed at any acceptable wage, and the result would be unemployment.

A useful concept for the analysis of this interaction is the elasticity of substitution between factors of production. In the case of a process using only two factors, the elasticity of substitution is defined as the rate at which the relative use of two factors changes, divided by the rate at which the ratio of their marginal products changes, measured along a production isoquant. The concept has been generalized to cover more than two factors of production in several different ways, of which the most widely used is due to Allen (1938: 503–509). The higher the elasticity of substitution, the smaller the fall in the relative price of a factor that is required to induce the absorption of a given increase in the relative supply of that factor into production. When the elasticity is infinite, any quantity of the factor can be absorbed without requiring a fall in its relative price. When the elasticity is unity, the relative price of the factor must fall at the same rate as the relative supply is increased. When the elasticity is zero, the production process is of the Leontief fixed coefficients form. And, in this case, it is impossible to eliminate a surplus of the factor however much the price changes.

It is important to notice that the elasticity of substitution is a time-dependent concept. In the short run it is difficult to adapt techniques of production, and hence an increase in the relative supply of a factor is likely to cause a temporary surplus and a significant fall in its price. The long-run price elasticity of demand, however, may well be appreciably greater than the short-run elasticity. The initial fall in the relative price will induce a modification of the production process toward greater relative use of the factor. The increase in the relative demand for the factor may then restore the relative price part of the way toward its former level. Thus the factor could possess both a low short-run elasticity and a high long-run elasticity of substitution.

The same comment applies to the case in which the relative supply of a factor is being continually increased. The result will be a continuous decline in the relative price of the factor. The relationship between the rate of decline of the relative price and the rate of increase of the relative supply can be expected to be sensitively dependent upon the magnitude of the latter. A small rate of increase in the relative supply might cause virtually no change in the relative price. A slightly larger rate of increase might cause an equal rate of decline in the relative price. A substantial rate of increase might not be capable of being absorbed at all and might lead to a drastic rate of decline in the relative price.

In view of these comments one might expect the elasticity of substitution between different types of labor to be high, since the ratio of the annual increase of each type of labor to its existing stock is quite small and the rates of relative increase, even smaller. It is therefore not surprising that the empirical results quoted in Section **I** indicate that the elasticities of substitution between different types of labor are large, even when the number of types of labor distinguished is small.

Table 12.5. Example Projections of the Seven Categories of the Labor Force and of the Aggregate Labor Index, Sample Years[a]

Year	Category							
	1	2	3	4	5	6	7	L
1970	1481.0	2808.4	1321.8	504.7	232.4	30.6	43.7	380.2
1975	1378.0	3852.9	1442.9	877.9	236.1	68.3	96.6	499.1
1980	1258.0	4291.5	1968.2	1477.9	259.0	119.8	200.0	663.6
1985	1118.0	4424.3	2281.2	2463.4	307.1	195.3	316.6	849.2

[a] See Section V.

The aggregate labor index is calculated using the straightforward CES function

$$L = (a_1 C_1^\theta + \cdots + a_7 C_7^\theta)^{1/\theta} \qquad (12.1)$$

where

$\theta = (\sigma - 1)/\sigma$

σ = elasticity of substitution

C_i = number of workers in labor category i

and the a_i are constants.

For Colombia the a_i are calculated using 1964 census data and information on relative wage rates (see Section V). There is at present no reliable estimate for σ, and so the calculation of the labor index is made for a range of reasonable values of this parameter. There exist more sophisticated forms of the CES function, notably the two-level version introduced by Sato (1967), which permits a partial relaxation of the assumption of a single elasticity of substitution between any two types of labor.[7] However, in the Colombian case, given the data limitations, it has appeared advisable to keep the form of the index as simple as possible. (The appendix to this chapter discusses further problems in the use of this aggregate labor index.)

Table 12.5 shows some projections of the categories of the labor force for some of the years of the planning period (based on underlying projections of the enrollment in the different branches of the educational system), and the aggregate labor index calculated on the assumption that the elasticity of substitution is equal to 6.

V. The Projection of Wages

Section IV described the estimation of an aggregate index for labor over the planning period. The next step is to use this index in order to project the marginal productivity of each category of labor using equation (12.2). (Some of the implications of this equation are discussed in the appendix to this chapter.)

$$w_i = \frac{dY}{dC_i} = \frac{\partial Y}{\partial L} \cdot \frac{dL}{dC_i} \qquad (12.2)$$

where

w_i = marginal product of labor category i

Y = aggregate output

7. Bowles (1968) has estimated such a function using three types of labor and subaggregating two of them.

The term dL/dC_i can be calculated by differentiating equation (12.1). The projection of the value over time of the term $\partial Y/\partial L$ is less straightforward. One may expect it to be a decreasing function of L and an increasing function of the supplies of other factors of production, for example, capital. One may also expect it to be an increasing function of time, *ceteris paribus*, as a result of the effects of what may loosely be termed "technical progress."

In order to project the value of the term $\partial Y/\partial L$, it is therefore essential to construct some sort of aggregate production function. An attempt was made to estimate for Colombia the coefficients of a Cobb-Douglas function using regression analysis. This was abandoned when it was found that an exponential time trend by itself would explain 99.6 percent of the variance in production over an observation period of 13 years and that it was highly collinear with the other independent variables used.

With some reluctance the function[8]

$$Y = AL^{\beta}e^{\lambda t} \tag{12.3}$$

has been used instead. The term $e^{\lambda t}$ is intended to cover all sources of growth of output other than labor, λ being the total rate of growth due to these sources. It is not possible to predict with any confidence the value of λ for Colombia, and hence all the calculations have been repeated for a range of values for this parameter. The results obtained in each case are therefore conditional on the particular value of λ associated with them. The higher the value of λ, the faster is the projected growth of GDP and thus of the demand for labor, and hence the greater is the need for improving the educational level of the labor force and the greater is the rate of return to education.

The marginal product of each category of labor can now be calculated using equations (12.1), (12.2), and (12.3).

$$w_i = a_i \beta Y C_i^{\theta-1} L^{-\theta} \quad (i = 1, \ldots, 7) \tag{12.4}$$

where all the symbols are as defined above.

The values of the parameters a_i were estimated by using equation (12.4) and the values of the w_i and the C_i in 1964.

$$w_i = \frac{a_i \beta Y C_i^{\theta-1}}{\displaystyle\sum_j a_j C_j^{\theta}} \quad (i = 1, \ldots, 7)$$

$$w_i \sum_j a_j C_j^{\theta} = a_i \beta Y C_i^{\theta-1} \quad (i = 1, \ldots, 7)$$

These equations are homogeneous in the a_i and therefore possess an infinite number of solutions if consistent, and no solution at all if not consistent. Consistency is proved by multiplying equation i by C_i and summing:

$$\sum_i \left(w_i C_i \sum_j a_j C_j^{\theta} \right) = \sum_i a_i \beta Y C_i^{\theta}$$

since

$$L^{\theta} \sum_i w_i C_i = L^{\theta} \beta Y$$

Table 12.6 shows the projection of the wage rates for the different categories, using the projection of their numbers shown in Table 12.5 and $\sigma = 6$ and $\lambda = 0.04$.

8. The average share of labor in GDP in recent years, 0.55, has been used to estimate β.

Table 12.6. Example Projection of the Wage Rates for the Seven Labor Categories, Sample Years (thousand pesos per year)

Year	Category						
	1	2	3	4	5	6	7
1970	1.74	2.50	3.74	6.11	14.38	18.54	24.88
1975	1.99	2.68	4.17	6.30	16.22	18.33	24.66
1980	2.27	2.96	4.46	6.51	17.99	18.81	24.61
1985	2.64	3.36	4.95	6.81	19.92	19.75	25.96

In Table 12.5 labor category 6 is projected to grow sixfold over the period 1970–1985, and as a result by the latter date its shadow wage would fall below that of category 5. In reality one would expect the declining profitability of 3 years of higher education to encourage potential students either to opt for professional studies leading to category 7 instead of technical studies, or not to enter higher education at all but to go straight into the labor force on graduating from secondary school.

VI. Calculating the Rate of Return to Education

The value of education has many components, some of them "economic," like the increase in the productivity and the occupational mobility of an individual, some of them "noneconomic," like his cultural enrichment and the satisfaction he derives from the improvement in his social status. Of these only the increase in the marginal product of an individual is readily susceptible to measurement,[9] and for this reason the analysis below is confined to this subcomponent.[10]

Section II described how one can calculate the impact of a cohort of 100 students entering the first grade of each level of the educational system. The calculations were described in detail for secondary education. The impact was estimated in real terms: the number of teachers required, the number of graduates produced, the number of drop-outs generated, the stock of capital required. Using these figures alone, it is impossible to evaluate the worth of the educational system. They must be converted to social-value terms by multiplying them by the relevant shadow prices calculated in Section V.

This yields a series of benefits and costs for each year from the date of entry of the cohort into secondary school until the retirement of the last of its members from the labor force. The rate of return is then that rate of discount for which the net present value of the series is zero.[11]

9. And this only at the expense of assuming that the marginal product of an individual is equal to his wage. For lack of a better alternative, this assumption is used here.

10. The omission of the other components therefore constitutes a downward bias in the calculation of the value of education in this study. A bias in the other direction should also be noted. In most countries a positive correlation exists between the innate ability of an individual and the education he receives. Thus to some extent salary differentials ascribed to education are in fact due to differences in ability. However, it appears that in Colombia this correlation is relatively weak, and no attempt is made here to adjust for it.

11. In principle such a discount rate may not exist; if it does exist, it may not be unique. The latter problem was not encountered in the calculations for Colombia; when the former occurred, the economic interpretation was clear.

There are five sources of cost:

1. *Opportunity cost to society of withdrawing 100 primary graduates from the labor force and putting them into secondary education.* The actual deduction from labor category 3 (the category to which primary graduates would be assigned if they entered the labor force instead of enrolling in secondary education) is less than 100 because a large proportion would not have entered the labor force in any case. The estimated participation rate for labor category 3 is 56.4 percent, and this figure is used in the estimation of the cost. Hence the opportunity cost in year u of enrolling 100 primary graduates in secondary school in year t $(u \geq t)$ is 56.4 $\times$ the wage of a category 3 worker in year u.

2. *Cost of secondary-school educated teachers.* In Section II it was shown that the number of teachers with secondary-school training required by a cohort of 100 students entering secondary school in year t would be 4.57 in year t, 3.27 in year $t + 1$, and 2.63, 2.04, 1.53, 1.13, 0.29, 0.05, 0.01 in years $t + 2$ through $t + 8$. The decline in the number of teachers required during the first 6 years is due to the reduction in the size of the cohort caused by desertion. In the seventh year the number is reduced still further with the graduation of those students who have gone through secondary school without dropping out or repeating a grade. By the ninth year all but a fraction of hardy triple-repeaters have left secondary school, and the number of teachers required is negligible. The social cost of these teachers in year u is equal to the number required in that year multiplied by the wage for that year for the labor category 5, to which these teachers belong.

3. *Cost of university educated teachers.* The calculation of the cost of university educated teachers is made in the same manner as that of the secondary-school educated teachers. In this case the shadow price used to value them is the marginal product of the labor category 7, the category to which workers with this level of education belong.

4. *Overheads.* In addition to teachers' salaries there is a certain amount of expenditure on administration, maintenance, and materials. It is assumed that this will continue to bear the historically observed relationship to expenditure on salaries.

5. *Capital costs.* The cost of fixed capital is calculated on an implicit cash flow basis. The stock of capital required by a cohort of 100 students entering secondary school in year t is calculated and registered as an expenditure in year t. By year $t + 1$ part of the cohort has dropped out, and the amount of capital required has diminished. The reduction in capital is then registered as a receipt for year $t + 1$, after deducting from it a charge for depreciation. In the succeeding years the rest of the capital will be returned as the cohort is reduced by further desertion and then, in years $t + 6$ onward, graduation. The cost of capital is thus a series consisting of one large expenditure followed by a number of small receipts whose total is less than the expenditure by the total of depreciation charges. The net discounted cost is thus an increasing function of the discount rate used.

The benefit derived from entering a cohort of 100 students in secondary school is the value of their earnings after they have left that level of education. During the first four grades 68.9 members of the cohort will drop out and will therefore be assigned to labor category 4. During the last two grades 8.4 will drop out and will be assigned to category 5. The remaining 22.7 will graduate, and their value will again be the marginal product of category 5. (Some of the students who graduate will proceed to higher education and have their marginal products increased further; but this fact is not relevant to the estimation of the benefits of the secondary school system.)

Table 12.7 shows the present discounted values of each of the series of costs and benefits of entering 100 students in the first grade of secondary education in 1969, using the example wage projections in Table 12.6 and two different discount rates. With a discount rate of 5 percent the net discounted value per student is 52,782 (constant 1958 pesos); with a discount rate of 20 percent the net value falls to 342 pesos. It can therefore be seen that in this example calculation, the rate of return to entering an additional student in the first grade of secondary education is just over 20 percent.

These calculations can be repeated for students enrolling in the first grade of secondary school in 1970 and in subsequent years. The rate of return to secondary education will change from year to year, reflecting principally the changes in the shadow wages for categories 3, 4, and 5 of the labor force, these being the most important shadow prices used in estimating the benefits and the costs associated with this educational level.

Similarly these calculations may be made for the other branches of the educational system. Table 12.8 shows typical estimates of the rate of return to enrolling an additional student in primary, secondary, and higher education for 1969, 1975, 1980, and 1985.

From Table 12.7 it may be observed that the direct cost of secondary education, that is, the salaries of teachers, overheads, and the cost of fixed capital, is considerably smaller than the discounted values of the earnings of the workers withdrawn from category 3 and of the weighted earnings of those who graduate or drop out from secondary school. It should therefore be evident that the estimate of the rate of return

Table 12.7. Present Discounted Value of the Costs and Benefits of Entering 100 Students in the First Grade of Secondary Education in 1969— Example Calculation[a] (thousand constant 1958 pesos)

	Discount rate	
	5 percent	20 percent
Costs		
Lifetime earnings of category 3 workers	4832.1	1169.3
Secondary-school educated teachers	208.1	168.4
University educated teachers	235.7	192.4
Overheads	259.2	210.7
Capital cost	55.9	114.6
Total	5591.0	1855.4
Benefits		
Earnings of 68.9 drop-outs to category 4	3675.4	879.0
Earnings of 8.4 drop-outs to category 5	2025.5	309.9
Earnings of 22.7 graduates	5168.3	700.7
Total	10869.2	1889.6
Net value	5278.2	34.2

[a] Assumptions: $\sigma = 6$, $\lambda = 0.04$, enrollments grow at historical rates.

Table 12.8. Rate of Return to the Additional Enrollment of One Student in Primary, Secondary, and Higher Education, Selected Years—Example Calculation[a]

Year	Primary	Secondary	Higher
1969	21.1	20.7	7.4
1975	20.7	20.3	5.2
1980	20.5	19.5	3.4
1985	19.8	17.8	0.9

[a] Assumptions: $\sigma = 6$, $\lambda = 0.04$, enrollments grow at historical rates.

to secondary education is at least as sensitive to the assumptions used for projecting the earnings streams as to those used for calculating the direct cost. In the case of higher education the discounted values of the earnings are very much greater than the direct cost, and the rate of return is not much affected by substantial changes in the latter. In the case of primary education the direct cost is more important.

VII. Optimizing the Growth of the Educational System

In the example calculation in Section VI the rate of return to entering an additional student into the first grade of secondary school in 1969 is just over 20 percent. This fact implies that if the social discount rate were 20 percent or less, it would profit society to increase the entry for that year above the number shown in the original projection. This would have the effect of increasing the supply of categories 4 and 5 labor in the future and, hence, of reducing the shadow wages of those categories. At the same time the number of primary school graduates entering labor category 3 in that year would be decreased, causing a slight rise in the shadow wage of that category. Both these effects would tend to reduce the difference between the shadow wages of categories 4 and 5 and the shadow wage of category 3, with the result that the marginal rate of return to secondary education would decline. As long as the rate of return to adding an additional student to the enrollment in the first grade is greater than the social discount rate, the enrollment ought to be increased. If it should happen that the rate of return is less than the social discount rate, this would imply that society is taking a loss on educating the marginal students, and the enrollment should be cut back.

Ideally the enrollment should be adjusted so that the rate of return to secondary education is equal to the social discount rate. This observation applies to every year in the projection of secondary school enrollment. The enrollment for each year of the planning period should be adjusted so that the rate of return to enrolling an additional student in the first grade becomes equal to the social discount rate for each year.

Similarly, the projection of enrollment in primary and higher education should be adjusted until the marginal rates of return to those levels of education become equal to the social discount for each year. Since the rates of return to the three levels of education are dependent on the projected enrollment of each (through their common dependence on the structure of wage rates), the adjustment of the three enrollments must be done simultaneously or by using an iterative process.

When the adjustments are completed and the rate of return to each educational level is equal to the discount rate for each year, the educational system has achieved its optimal growth path. It should be emphasized that the optimal growth path thus calculated is conditional on the assumptions made about the key parameters, in particular the social discount rate and the elasticity of substitution.

It is possible that the optimal projections may show unrealistic rates of growth for some of the branches, at least for the first few years. When this is the case, it is necessary to examine the factors limiting growth and to estimate the maximum rate. The revised optimal projections then should show for each branch for each year either a rate of return equal to the social discount rate or constrained maximum growth in enrollment over the previous year. As will be seen in Section VIII, this proved to be the case for secondary education in Colombia; an upper bound of 15 percent per year was imposed upon its growth rate, and this bound should be attained for at least the next 10 years unless the elasticity of substitution is very low or the social discount rate is very high.

VIII. Results for Colombia

The first part of this section reports results based on the assumption that secondary and higher education continue to maintain their recent growth rates of 10 percent and 11 percent per year, respectively. The projection for primary education is made on the assumption that universal primary education is achieved by 1985. (For a description of the projection, see Dougherty 1969: appendix 3.) The second part of the section describes the results of following the procedure outlined in Section VII for optimizing the projection of enrollments in secondary and higher education.

Results Based on Present Trends

The estimates of the rates of return to the different levels of education in Colombia are dependent on the assumptions concerning a number of parameters whose values are open to debate. In view of this fact a reference analysis was executed, using plausible values for these parameters, and then a series of sensitivity analyses were made varying each of the parameters in turn.

In the reference analysis σ, the elasticity of substitution, was set at 6; λ, the rate of growth of GDP due to factors of production other than labor, was set at 4 percent per year; and β, the share of labor in GDP, was set at 0.55. The illustrations of the stages in the analysis given in Sections II through VI all assume that the parameters take their reference values. Table 12.4 shows the construction of the projection of labor category 5, with the hypothesis that present enrollment trends in secondary and higher education are maintained. Table 12.5 shows the projections for the other six categories with the same assumption and the projection of the labor index using the reference value of 6 for the elasticity of substitution. Table 12.6 gives the projection of wages corresponding to the projections of the labor categories in Table 12.5 on the assumption that λ takes its reference value of 4 percent per year. Table 12.7 shows the calculation of the rate of return to secondary education, and Table 12.8 shows the rates of return to each of the three levels of education for selected years. In Figure 12.5 these rates of return are plotted over time together with the results of three sensitivity analysis experiments described below.

The parameter which is the most obvious candidate for sensitivity analysis is the elasticity of substitution. Table 12.9 shows the rates of return for each of the levels for the years 1969, 1975, 1980, and 1985 for different values of this parameter. The results for the years 1969 and 1980 have already been plotted in Figures 12.2 and 12.3.

Other important parameters are λ and β, both of which appear in the production function, equation (12.3). Sensitivity analysis showed that for each 1 percent increase in λ, the rates of return to each level of education would increase by between 1.4 percent and 1.6 percent. It was not easy to estimate β from the official Colombian statistics. Its value was calculated to be 0.55, but it is possible that the true value may be lower. Reducing the estimate to 0.45 had the effect of decreasing the rates of return to primary and secondary education by 1 percent and of decreasing the rate of return to higher education by 0.7 percent.

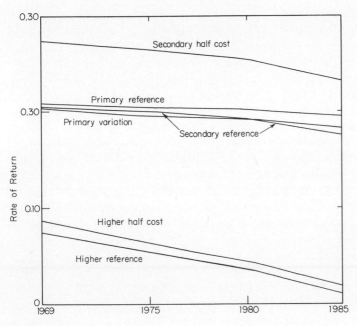

Figure 12.5

Table 12.9. The Rates of Return as Functions of σ

	Primary				Secondary				Higher			
σ	1969	1975	1980	1985	1969	1975	1980	1985	1969	1975	1980	1985
2					18.8	17.3	14.4	8.8	a	a	a	a
4	19.6	19.0	18.5	17.1	20.2	19.5	18.3	15.9	2.7	a	a	a
6	21.1	20.7	20.5	19.8	20.7	20.3	19.5	17.8	7.4	5.2	3.4	0.9
8	21.7	21.4	21.2	20.7	21.0	20.7	20.1	18.7	8.9	7.3	5.9	4.0
10	22.0	21.7	21.6	21.1	21.1	20.9	20.5	19.3	9.7	8.4	7.3	5.6
∞	23.0	22.9	22.7	22.3	21.8	21.8	21.9	21.5	12.5	12.2	11.9	10.9

[a] A negative rate of return. No rate of return existed for primary education when $\sigma = 2$. The present discounted value of the series of benefits and costs was negative for all values of the discount rate.

The results of three other experiments are shown together in Figure 12.5. The primary variation curve shows the effect over time on the rate of return to primary education of increasing substantially the projection of the enrollment in the first grade. The projection assumes that all 7-year-olds are enrolled in first grade and that their number grows exponentially at a rate of 3.2 percent per year from a base of 700,000 in 1969. An adjustment is made for the backlog of students who in the past failed to enter school at age 7. It is assumed that the additional enrollment in first grade due to this source is 300,000 in 1969 and declines over the next 10 years at a rate of 30,000 per year. In the variation on the enrollment projection the figure of 700,000 was raised to 750,000, its growth rate remained the same, and the additional enrollment due to the backlog was assumed to be 400,000 in 1969, decreasing at a rate of 40,000 per year. The effect on the rate of return is to reduce it but not significantly.

The other two variations assumed that the costs of, first, secondary and, then, higher education were halved. In both of these levels the typical unit is too small. In secondary education the average number of students per school is just over 100. That inevitably means that, given the high drop-out rates, the number of students per grade, and therefore the student-teacher ratio, in grades 4 through 6 are unreasonably small. In higher education the failure of the universities to organize a division of labor among themselves has led to excessive duplication of undersized departments, again meaning unnecessarily high costs and probably a loss of quality as well.

The effect of halving the costs is much more pronounced for secondary education—whose rate of return rises from 20.7 percent to 27.7 percent for 1969—than for higher education—whose rate of return rises from 7.4 percent to 8.6 percent for the same year. This asymmetry reflects the fact that the direct costs of education are smaller, relative to the discounted values of the relevant earnings streams, for higher than for secondary education. It is also partly due to the fact that the rate of return itself is much higher for the latter.

The results of the experiments show that the rates of return to primary and secondary education are high and the rate to higher education is low, assuming that secondary and higher education maintain their present growth rates of 10 percent and 11 percent, respectively, and that enrollment in primary education accelerates so that universal primary education is attained by 1985. Under any plausible set of assumptions, the rates of return to primary and secondary education are both around 20 percent and will remain near that level for the next 15 years. By contrast, unless one assumes a very high elasticity of substitution, the rate of return to higher education is well below 10 percent and can be expected to fall substantially over time. If one assumes as low a value for the elasticity as 4, the rate of return is less than 3 percent in 1969 and rapidly becomes negative.

These conclusions suggest that secondary education should grow faster than its present rate and higher education, more slowly.

Optimizing the Enrollment Growth Rates

For the calculations discussed below the projection of the enrollment in primary education was kept fixed. Colombia would have difficulty increasing the enrollment at a rate faster than that foreseen by the program; and, since the rate of return to primary education remains above the highest social discount rate considered here, it should not be allowed to grow more slowly.

**Table 12.10. Optimal Solution: Social Discount Rate Set at 10 Percent
(parameters at reference values)**

	Growth rates (percents)		
	1969–1978	1979–1988	1989–2008
Secondary	15	max[a]	max[a]
Higher	2	5	5

	Rates of return (percent)		
Year	Primary	Secondary	Higher
1969	22.0	19.4	10.3
1975	22.7	17.1	9.9
1980	23.4	14.8	9.9
1985	24.3	13.0	9.9

[a] Until 1982 this was 15 percent per year. After 1982 this was the growth rate of primary school graduates which, according to the primary school projection, is 5.1 percent in 1982 and falls to the population growth rate of 3.2 percent per year by 1990.

In principle, as outlined in Section VII, the optimization process of the enrollment growth rates for secondary and higher education should have been executed on a year-to-year basis over the 40-year planning period. This would have required a search for the optimal values of 80 variables and, given the complexity of the analysis, was not practicable even with the aid of a large computer. In order to simplify the problem, the planning period was divided into three parts—1969–1978, 1979–1988, 1989–2008—and it was assumed that within each part the growth rate of each level of education would be constant.[12] Further, an upper bound of 15 percent per year was put on the growth rate of both levels in the belief that this would be the maximum administratively feasible.

With this drastic reduction in the complexity of the task, it was possible to search for the solutions on a trial-and-error basis. The solutions thus obtained are suboptimal but have the advantage of suppressing the unevenness that year-to-year optimization might have yielded.

The solution using the reference values for the key parameters and a discount rate of 10 percent is shown in Table 12.10. Secondary education grew at the maximum rate until 1982, when the number of students entering secondary school became equal to the number of primary school graduates the previous year. After 1982 the growth of secondary education was limited to the growth of the supply of primary school graduates.

The descent in the rate of return to secondary education is caused by the rapid increase in the supply of category 5 of the labor force, due more to the reduction in the absorption of secondary school graduates by higher education than to the increase in the rate of their formation.

12. The third subperiod was made twice as long as the other two on the ground that the results for those years would be of less interest.

It was assumed that higher education should have a nonnegative growth rate. If the social discount rate is raised to 15 percent, the lower bound of zero growth is attained. The rate of return is 11.6 percent in 1969, and by 1985 it still will not have reached 15 percent. Secondary education grows at its maximum rate for the first period and then should show slightly slower growth[13] for the few years until it reaches the primary graduate supply constraint.

If the elasticity of substitution is lowered to 4 and the social discount rate set at 10 percent, the growth rate of higher education should be approximately 2 percent in each period. Secondary education should be at its maximum growth rate until it becomes equal to the supply of primary graduates.

Finally, the optimal rate of growth was calculated for higher education, assuming that direct costs could be cut to half their present levels. With the elasticity of substitution equal to 6 and a social discount rate of 10 percent, the optimal growth rate would be roughly 5 percent for each period. This is hardly different from the solution shown in Table 12.10 and indicates again that direct costs are relatively unimportant in the evaluation of higher education.

IX. Conclusions

The extension to the rate of return approach described in this paper has made it possible to calculate in quantitative terms optimal enrollment projections for Colombia. Since the methodology thus provides an alternative to the manpower requirements approach to educational planning, it may be worthwhile to point out the essential differences between the two.

The manpower requirements approach, in its usual fixed coefficients form, implies that there is a zero elasticity of substitution between different categories of labor. The rate of growth of the demand for each type of labor can thus be calculated given the rate of growth of output of each industry and the rate of increase of productivity within it. Given the projection of aggregate demand for each kind of labor, one can derive the need for education. No attempt is made to value this need or to place costs on the manpower bottlenecks or surpluses that would arise if the actual growth of the educational system is different from the required growth. There is therefore no way in which one may evaluate the return to the investment of real resources in education.[14]

The present technique assumes that there is sufficient substitutability between different types of labor for their supplies to be absorbed by the labor market. The projection of the educational system determines the supplies, and the demands are equated to them by movements of relative wage rates. The concept of "manpower requirements" thus loses most of its significance. This, of course, does not imply that any projection of the growth of the educational system is as good as another. The technique takes into account explicitly the diminishing returns effect of the growth of the educational system on its own profitability, and this feedback can be used to calculate the optimal enrollment projections and the derived optimal supply projections for the different kinds of labor.

---

13. The exact rate of growth was not calculated.
14. It could be done if the analysis were imbedded in an optimizing model, for example, a linear programming model. But to my knowledge this has never been done. I am indebted to Robert Repetto for this point.

The results for Colombia show that, for the next 10 years at least, the country should accelerate the rates of growth of primary and secondary education and, unless the social discount rate used is very low, should cut back the growth of higher education. Even if the forced march towards universal primary education were implemented, the rate of return to primary school would remain around 20 percent for the next 15 years. Similarly, even if secondary education were to grow at 15 percent per year for the next 10 years, and even if one makes the pessimistic assumptions that the present inefficient student-teacher ratio and the high drop-out rates are not improved, the rate of return would remain around 20 percent for the next 15 years. If it were possible for secondary education to grow at a faster rate without reducing the quality of instruction, this would certainly be justified. Eventually, of course, the growth of secondary education would be limited by the supply of primary school graduates.

On the other hand, the rate of return to higher education is low. If the present growth rate of 11 percent per year were maintained, the rate of return would be less than 10 percent now and would fall over time, probably approaching zero by 1985. If the present mix of courses remains unchanged, higher education should grow at no more than 5 percent per year for the next 10 years if one assumes a social discount rate of 10 percent; it should not grow at all if one assumes a social discount rate of 15 percent. If one were to assume a social discount rate as low as 5 percent, the present growth rate would be justified until 1975 but should be reduced substantially after that date.

It should be remembered that the calculations for higher education were made on the assumption that the present mix of courses will not change. Doubtless, many of the courses yield much higher rates of return than that for higher education as a whole. If these courses were identified and future growth restricted to them, then the university system would be justified in growing faster than suggested in the preceding paragraph.

Finally, it should be emphasized that the analysis here has been confined to the narrowly economic aspects of education. The policy-maker should modify the recommendations above, taking into account the social and political aspects of education, particularly its role in the redistribution of income and in increasing social mobility. Nonetheless, it is unlikely that the basic findings of this paper (that primary and secondary education should be expanded as fast as possible for at least the next 10 years) would be changed by such considerations.

Appendix to Chapter 12
Some Problems with the Use of the
Aggregate Labor Index

In the analysis two strong implicit assumptions have been made:

1. separability between labor and all other factors of production in the aggregate production function
2. separability between the different categories of labor within the aggregate labor index

The first assumption is implied by the form of the aggregate production function and the second, by the use of a simple CES function in order to calculate the labor index.

Neither of these assumptions is realistic. The first implies that each category of labor has the same elasticity of substitution with all the factors of production responsible jointly for the term $e^{\lambda t}$ in the production function. In particular it implies that the amount of capital per worker influences the demand for labor as a whole but does not otherwise have any special effect on the demand for an individual category. There is, however, reason to believe that a correlation exists between the capital intensity and the demand for more educated types of labor. The greater the capital intensity, it may be argued, the greater is the sophistication of the technology being used and hence the greater the demand for specialists. The reason for this relationship is the fact that those countries with the greatest stocks of physical capital per capita have been the industrial pioneers and have been responsible for the application of new scientific discoveries to industrial processes. Those countries have also had relatively highly educated labor forces, largely as a result of social pressures; and in consequence the new industrial processes have tended to be designed to make use of the skills available. Hence one may expect a supply-induced joint use of capital and skilled labor in advanced countries to imply a complementary demand for them in less developed countries.[15]

The assumption of separability between different categories of labor within the CES function implies that the demand for any given category of labor is a function of the supplies of the other categories but not of the structure of those supplies. However, it is unlikely that the elasticity of substitution is independent of the quantities used. It is even more unlikely that the elasticity is the same for each pair of categories. One would expect it to be an increasing function of the closeness of their educational levels. The use of a two-level CES function would partially overcome this problem, but data for deciding upon groupings of categories and for estimating the elasticity of substitution within each group are lacking in Colombia.

The use of equations (12.1) and (12.3) in the analysis, therefore, reflects a present inability to find superior functions rather than an unawareness of the influences of complementarities on the future structure of wage rates. Empirical research in this area is still in its infancy and is likely to progress slowly because time series on wage rates by level of education, essential for such research, are scarce.

---

15. The existence of such complementarity, together with relatively fast growth of the more educated categories of labor, would lead to an upward bias in the estimates of the elasticity of substitution between labor categories. This may partially account for the very high elasticities found by Samuel Bowles and Marcelo Selowsky. In fact it would not be surprising if "greater than infinity" estimates of the elasticity were encountered.

Part IV
Empirical Bases
for Development Programs

Introduction to Part IV

Christopher Sims
and Carl Gotsch

Perhaps the most serious limitation to improving planning methods has been the relative neglect of their empirical foundations. While this neglect is partly due to a lack of historical series for most economic variables, much better use can be made of the statistical information that is now available. Even though very simple formulations of economic relations may have been justified 10 years ago by the lack of time series, it is no longer necessary to describe the economic structure in such simplified terms.

The five studies in this section illustrate the type of fruitful interaction between planners and econometricians that is now possible. These studies cover a variety of structural relations and growth processes: the determinants of savings, price, and income effects on consumer demand; substitution among different types of labor; disequilibrium in factor markets; and the measurement of sources of growth in developing economies. Some studies try to discover the best formulation of a given structural relationship, such as a demand or production function; others try to explain development phenomena in particular countries or through cross-country comparisons.

Econometric analysis is useful in both designing planning models and applying them to particular countries. Its results help to determine which structural relations limit development and to test the effects of omitting others that are less important. For example, Bruno's analysis of the sources of growth in Israel tests the common assumption of planners that capital formation is one of the most important determinants of growth in developing countries. While this assumption has been challenged for advanced countries, Bruno shows that it is valid for Israel, where more than half of the rapid growth of the past 15 years is attributable to capital formation. Bowles, on the other hand, shows that increases in education add little to the explanation of rapid postwar growth in Greece.

In the absence of long time series for statistical estimation, the econometrics of development relies heavily on cross-section analysis. Both Landau's study of savings and Weisskoff's study of consumption are based on intercountry data, supplemented with relatively short time series for individual countries. Their results provide a check on the estimates used in planning models, which of necessity rely on the more limited data for a given country. They also indicate other variables that should be included in behavioral relations when data permit. This work suggests that it is often better to use an estimate of an income or price effect based on cross-country data than to follow the usual practice of omitting such variables when time series are insufficient.

These studies also illustrate the usefulness of interaction between econometricians and planners in the area of development. Without pressure from policy-oriented economists, econometricians studying development may end up estimating and testing convenient or elegant models which are uninteresting for practical purposes, ignoring some of the messy problems which matter most. Bruno's paper attacks the messy but important question of how to deal with deviations from the neoclassical theory of functional income distribution. Landau addresses the question—of long-standing interest to planners but never before taken up in an econometric savings study—of how domestic saving may interact with the trade balance.

Although planners and econometricians purport to be dealing with the same phenomena, one is struck by the differences in approach between these five studies and the planning models of earlier chapters. The level of aggregation selected by the planners is primarily determined by the nature of the problem and the instrument variables that the government controls. The latter considerations lead to the use of interindustry models of 20 to 100 sectors or more in order to reflect differences in production and trade among sectors. Empirical work on individual aspects of the economic structure, on the other hand, must be guided by the data available. Weisskoff and Selowsky, for example, are led to a more aggregated treatment of consumption and labor use than would be desirable in a planning model.

Because of the practical necessity of including large numbers of variables in a planning model and of actually doing computations involving the whole system, planners have in general been slower than the econometricians to experiment with a variety of functional forms and with variables (such as prices) which may enter behavioral relationships in computationally inconvenient ways. The comparison between Tendulkar's "planner's" treatment of savings and Landau's econometric treatment illustrates this contrast in style. Hopefully the continuing progress in computational capacities will help to make econometric work on specification—like Weisskoff's use of price variables in demand relations and Landau's improved form of the savings function—more directly useful to planners.

Although some of the differences in formulation reflect the decision orientation of planning models and the data orientation of econometrics, there are other areas in which the econometrician's perspective could be incorporated to advantage in the planning framework. Three of the five studies in this section are probabilistic in the sense that they take formal account of some kinds of uncertainty. Decision-making would be improved if planners would quantify their uncertainty about parameter values by means of probability distributions instead of relying on intuitive sensitivity analysis.

Several other studies in this volume reflect the benefits of parallel work by planners and econometricians. For example, Dougherty's educational planning model (Chapter 12) owes much of its formulation and emphasis on the elasticity of substitution between different levels of schooling to work by Selowsky (Chapter 17) and Bowles. Not only was Dougherty's decision to specify production relations by a CES function influenced by the empirical work, but the choice of parameters was dictated as well. Similarly, Chenery and Raduchel (Chapter 2) utilize Weisskoff's results to specify more realistically the opportunities for substitution in consumption. The Chenery-Raduchel chapter in particular is an example of the kind of more flexible planning model structure which should facilitate interaction between econometricians and planners.

In the future, it is likely that there will be the same kind of convergence between the formulations of planners and econometricians for developing countries that is already discernible in advanced countries. The typical input-output relations on which planning models are based are of the same order of simplicity as the early Keynesian formulations of the short-run determinants of income. Once these began to be used as a basis for policy decisions, they were greatly refined and extended. One can hope that the demands of decision-makers will also provide a spur to econometric analysis and theoretical refinement in the tools of long-term policy.

13 Saving Functions for Latin America

Luis Landau

The relation between saving rates and income levels is one of the most critical aspects of development planning. Despite the theoretical and statistical attention that it has received, however, there is little agreement as to the causes of variation in saving levels either among countries or over time. There is also considerable debate as to how domestic saving is affected by an inflow of foreign capital, which is another critical feature of planning models.

This study represents the results of econometric investigation of both these questions based on postwar experience in Latin America. Several theories of development have been drawn on to formulate a set of expectations about the nature of the effect of rising income. These properties are then tested in several econometric formulations, using both cross-section and time series data. A similar procedure has been followed in using the two-gap hypothesis to test the effect of external capital on saving rates.

Saving rates are the result of many interrelated changes that take place as economies develop—in the structure of production, the type of income received, the inequality of income distribution, and so on. Many of these structural changes are quite significant at low income levels but are of decreasing importance at higher levels of development. The nature of the development process suggests a nonlinear function in which saving levels rise with per capita income at low levels of development but are less affected at higher levels. All of the findings of this study are consistent with this general conception.

I. An Aggregate Saving Function

Although most theories pertain to individual components of public or private saving, there is considerable evidence of substitution among various types of saving.[1] This likelihood, together with the impossibility of securing a comparable breakdown of saving on a disaggregated basis, leads to an analysis of the aggregate gross national saving rather than its separate components. The substantial variation in aggregate saving as a ratio to GNP existing in Latin America is shown in Table 13.1 and in Figure 13.1.

---

1. This thesis is argued by Abramovitz (1952: 151), Goode (1961: 305–322), Harrod (1963: 47–48), Hansen (1965: 143–155), and Krishnamurty (1968).

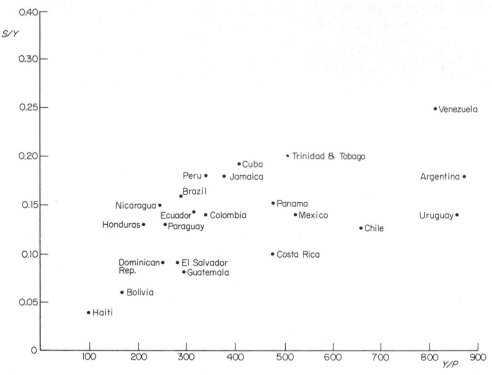

Figure 13.1 Latin American countries: 1963 saving ratio (current prices) on Y/P (U.S. dollars).

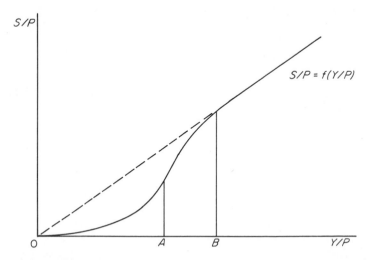

Figure 13.2

On the basis of the following discussion, an aggregate saving function having the shape shown in Figure 13.2 is hypothesized. That functional relationship is based mainly on the expected behavior of private saving, assuming that the other components of gross domestic saving, that is, government saving and depreciation, do not vary in such a way as to modify significantly the aggregate function.

Table 13.1. Latin America, 1963: Aggregate Saving Ratios and Levels of Income
(in 1960 US$)

	Saving ratio[a]	Income per capita[b]
Argentina	0.18	868
Uruguay	0.14	853
Venezuela	0.25	809
Chile	0.11	658
Mexico	0.14	518
Panama	0.15	474
Costa Rica	0.10	471
Cuba[c]	0.19	400
Peru	0.18	338
Colombia	0.15	336
Ecuador	0.14	304
Guatemala	0.08	291
Brazil	0.16	289
El Salvador	0.09	280
Paraguay	0.13	255
Dominican Republic	0.09	253
Nicaragua	0.15	243
Honduras	0.13	208
Bolivia	0.06	165
Haiti	0.04	94

[a]Ratio of gross national saving to gross national product, from United Nations (1967b: 779-782, table 2).

[b]U.S. Dollars converted at purchasing power parities, based on Braithwaite (1967: 107-142).

[c] 1962. Ratio of gross domestic saving to gross domestic product. Income per capita is an estimation.

Most empirical studies of the relationship between the share of government saving in national product and the levels of income per capita show no significant pattern.[2] The share of depreciation in GNP, on the other hand, should increase with economic development, because the proportion of depreciable to nondepreciable capital goes up and the average life of capital goods declines with economic development.[3] This deduction has been confirmed empirically.[4]

In the case of private saving, several well-known models of economic development and at least one theory of saving are consistent with the function postulated here. The relevant aspects of those theories are sketched below.

2. See, for example, Martin and Lewis (1956: 203–244); Williamson (1961: 43–56); Thorn (1967: 19–54) and Kuznets (1962).

3. The average life of capital goods diminishes as economic development proceeds because the proportion of equipment relative to buildings goes up. Also, with economic progress, technologies change more rapidly, and obsolescence becomes more important. See Kuznets (1955: appendix B).

4. International comparisons conducted by Kuznets (1966: table 8.1, line 85) show the proportion of "capital consumption" in gross national product to have been, on the average, 6.6 percent for countries with product per capita below US$199; 7.2 percent for countries with product between US$200 and US$574; and 8.0 percent for countries whose product exceeds US$575 per inhabitant.

Hirschman's Model

In his *Strategy of Economic Development* (1958) Hirschman criticizes the view that in poor countries incomes may be so low as to leave no possibility for saving after allowing for subsistence consumption. He argues that even in the lowest income countries, there is a potential for saving which is not realized either because of the inadequacy of channels to transform savings into productive investment or because of a lack of investment opportunities. As a result, in underdeveloped countries ". . . frustrated savings exist whenever the total supply of savings is highly responsive to the appearance of new investment opportunities" (1958: 37–40). With economic development, new opportunities for investment appear, and the ratio of saving to income increases rapidly until it reaches its potential level; at that level the saving ratio is stabilized.

The implications for the saving-income level relations are: (1) a positive association among poor countries and (2) a weaker association or even independence among the more advanced nations.

Lewis' Model

Lewis (1954) assigns a crucial role to an increase in the saving proportion in the process of economic development. His model is applicable to countries with surplus labor and excludes, as he points out (p. 401) "some parts of . . . Latin America" where there may be shortages of male labor. Lewis assumes that practically all saving in underdeveloped countries is done by economic units whose income originates in profits or rent: backward countries save little, not "because they are so poor . . . [but] because their capitalist sector is so small; . . . if they had a larger capitalist sector, profits would be a greater part of their national income, and saving and investment would also be relatively larger." (The "capitalist" sector can be either private or the state.)

Because of this direct connection between saving and profits, it becomes necessary to analyze the latter to explain the changes in saving ratios. In the Lewis model the share of profits in the national income grows as long as unlimited supplies of labor are available at a constant—subsistence—real wage rate, assuming that some part of the profits is reinvested in productive capacity. As economic development proceeds, there will be pressures generated within the system to raise real wages as surplus labor is reduced, and thus the increase in the share of capitalists' profits in the national income is slowed down. When the labor surplus disappears, this model no longer holds. A neoclassical model presumably becomes applicable, in which the saving ratio is dependent on the rate of interest and other factors but not on the level of development.

This model also has clear implications for the relationship between saving ratios and the level of development (or income per capita): for the poorer countries, the saving ratio increases as the capitalist sector grows (and as the level of income per capita goes up); for more developed countries, there is little reason to expect a positive association between the two magnitudes.[5]

5. Fei and Ranis (1964: 21–36) provide a more complete formulation of the implication of "surplus economy" development models for saving behavior in their formalization and analysis of Nurkse's "hidden rural savings."

Income Distribution and Saving

It is sometimes asserted that greater inequality in the size distribution of income should result in higher saving ratios for a country because the higher income groups are believed to have higher (marginal and average) saving propensities.[6] Time series studies do not offer much support for this hypothesis,[7] but the question cannot be analyzed in international comparisons until comparable measures of inequality become available for more countries.

To the extent that this hypothesis has any validity, its empirical implications are consistent with the saving function proposed here. The scattered evidence available suggests that in the early stages of economic development there is a widening in the inequality of the distribution of income by size but that this process is reversed and the inequality reduced as development continues.[8] It follows that the impact on saving ratios should be: (1) a positive association with the level of income among the less advanced countries, whose income distributions are becoming more unequal; and (2) either negative or no association with income per capita among the more advanced countries, which are slowly narrowing the differentials in levels of income.[9]

Life Cycle Theories

Life cycle theories of saving have been extended by Modigliani (1965) to international comparisons of saving ratios. In simple form, the relevant aspects of the theory consist of the accumulation of savings during the (young) productive years of an individual or of a household in order to provide for the anticipated needs after retirement ("hump saving," in Harrod's terminology). One implication of the theory is that the aggregate saving/income ratio is independent of the level of income per capita but is a function of the rates of growth of the population and of total income. Modigliani (1965) found that a cross-section of thirty-six countries[10] yielded results consistent with this implication.

It would seem, however, that in underdeveloped countries this motive for accumulation should be less important than in the more advanced societies: the proportion of retired individuals in the total population is smaller, and the family provides for the needs of older people who are unable to earn their subsistence.[11]

The life cycle theories of saving thus imply that among underdeveloped countries the proportion saved increases *paripassu* with the level of income per capita, but among more advanced nations the proportion is determined by other factors.

The preceding discussion leads to the hypothesis that the functional long-run association between gross national saving and the level of real national income, both expressed in per capita terms, should have four specific characteristics.

6. But these are not the implications of the relative income hypothesis (Duesenberry 1949: 41).
7. Lubell (1947); Bronfenbrenner, Yamane, and Lee (1955); Abou Ali (1965); Bergan (1967: 160–212); Maneschi and Reynolds (1966).
8. Kuznets (1966: 206–217, 423–426) and (1963: part II).
9. It does not seem likely that saving ratios should decline as countries become more advanced as a result of this reduction in inequality.
10. Included in the sample were countries of all levels of development: all the Western, highly industrialized nations as well as some very poor, underdeveloped countries.
11. Modigliani (1965: part III) recognized the inapplicability of the life cycle model to underdeveloped countries: "The life cycle model does not purport to represent a universal theory of individual and aggregate saving formation and wealth holding, but is instead basically designed to apply to private capitalistic economies in which at least the bulk of income, consumption, and accumulation transactions occur through markets."

1. At very low levels of income (Y) total saving (S) should be close to zero.

2. When income increases from the subsistence level, total saving should rise at an increasing rate, as the process of development progresses. The rate of growth of S should soon exceed that of Y.

3. With further advances in economic development, the rate of growth of S should begin to slow down. This retardation in the growth of the saving ratio can be explained by the maturing of the capitalist sector and other characteristics of the transactions to an advanced society. The retardation in the rate of growth of S is likely to continue until the saving ratio (S/Y) ceases to increase.

4. Beyond this degree of development, the level of income per capita should no longer be an important determinant of saving ratios.

The actual values of the saving ratio once it reaches an equilibrium will, of course, be different for each country; the following factors are likely to have some relevance:

    a. the extent of government participation in the economy
    b. the relative importance of social security, health insurance, and similar institutional arrangements
    c. the presence of inflation and its degree; organization and features of the financial markets
    d. the age structure of the population and other demographic characteristics
    e. the rate of growth of the economy
    f. the production functions of the different productive sectors, the shares of agriculture, manufacturing, and the other sectors
    g. the "openness" of the economy and extent of fluctuations in export proceeds

The solid line in Figure 13.2 illustrates a saving function having the characteristics just described. The horizontal axis measures gross national product per capita (Y/P), and the vertical axis shows gross national saving per capita (S/P).

It is possible that saving could be negative for low values of Y/P, depending on whether the nation has access to foreign credits or aid. The slope of the line increases between (Y/P) = 0 and (Y/P) = A, corresponding to the situation outlined in characteristic 2 above. At A there is an inflection point, and the slope of the line declines between A and B in accordance with characteristic 3. Beyond B the function becomes a straight line, corresponding to a constant saving/income ratio.[12] (The dotted line shows that if it were extrapolated toward the left, this straight line would pass near the origin.) The income elasticity of the saving function is greater than unity to the left of B, and it is about unity to the right.

Figure 13.3 illustrates the corresponding relationship between the saving ratio S/Y and the level of income per capita, labeled in a manner comparable with Figure 13.2. The value at which S/Y levels off in Figure 13.2 corresponds to the slope of the dotted line in Figure 13.2. B marks the same level of Y/P in both figures, but there is no clear counterpart to A in Figure 13.3.

II. Statistical Tests

The statistical tests described in this section are based on national accounts time series of Latin American countries covering generally the period 1950–1966.

---

12. It must be stressed that the function of Figure 13.2 assumes that other variables that may affect saving are being held constant. The constancy of the saving ratio to the right of $Y/P = B$ depends crucially on this assumption, as the discussion characteristic 4 above indicated.

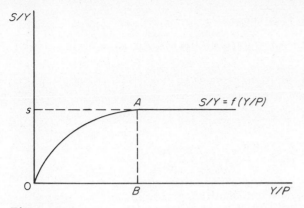

Figure 13.3

The purpose of these tests is to show that in this sample there is a relationship between saving ratios and levels of income per capita approximating that shown in Figure 13.3; that is, saving ratios are an increasing function of income, with the 1963 elasticity of the function diminishing as incomes increase.

Cross-Section Analysis

First we regress the aggregate saving ratio S/Y on the logarithm of income per capita log (Y/P) in cross-sections of countries, taken for the years 1956, 1961, and 1963 and for averages of the 3-year periods 1950–1952 and 1958–1960.[13]

13. The underlying data for equations (13.1)–(13.4) were derived from time series in constant prices in 1950 US$, obtained from unpublished worksheets of the U. N. Economic Commission for Latin America; S and Y were deflated separately, after adjusting for the effect of changes in the terms of trade, and are thus estimates of "real" S and "real" Y. In this data, sharp changes in, say, capital goods prices relative to the GDP deflator could change S/Y even though current dollars S/Y remains unchanged. The per capita income figures were converted to 1950 US$ without very extensive corrections for purchasing power parities in the exchange rates. Equations (13.5)–(13.10) are based on the data shown in Table 13.1; the ratio S/Y was obtained from series in current prices, local currencies; Y/P was converted to 1960 US$ using purchasing power parities obtained from S. N. Braithwaite (1967: 107–142 and table 4). For equations (13.11)–(13.18) the underlying data comes from unpublished worksheets of the Inter American Committee of the Alliance for Progress (CIAP); S and Y are expressed in constant prices—generally based on 1960—also converted from local currencies to 1960 US$ using the Braithwaite parities.

The 1963 data, which use current-dollar S/Y and Y/P at purchasing power parity exchange rates, is preferable for our purposes. Hence it is encouraging that r^2 is highest for the 1963 data. Due to limitations of time, some of the subsequent experimentation with functional forms was limited to the conceptually better 1963 sample.

For all equations (13.1)–(13.18) the t ratio (ratio of the regression parameter to its estimated standard error) is shown in parentheses.

For equations (13.8), (13.9), and (13.11)–(13.14), the classification of the countries into "richer" and "poorer" was done by ordering them according to their levels of GNP per capita and observing that there was a gap in the ranked list of per capita incomes. For equations (13.11)–(13.14) the per capita income values used in the classification were for the year 1960, and the gap was around the level of 1960 US$300/year. The five richer countries included are: Argentina, Chile, Mexico, Uruguay and Venezuela. The twelve poor countries are: Brazil, Colombia, Costa Rica, Dominican Republic, Ecuador, El Salvador, Guatemala, Honduras, Nicaragua, Panama, Paraguay and Peru. For equations (13.8) and (13.9)—1963 values—the gap moved up to around 1960 US$400 and two more countries—Costa Rica and Mexico—joined the group of richer countries. Cuba was added to equation (13.8), Haiti and Bolivia to equation (13.9).

Twenty Latin American Countries

1950–1952: $S/Y = -0.1334 + 0.052699 \log (Y/P)$ $r^2 = 0.340$ (13.1)
$$(3.1)$$

1956: $S/Y = -0.1809 + 0.058914 \log (Y/P)$ $r^2 = 0.343$ (13.2)
$$(3.1)$$

1958–1960: $S/Y = -0.1673 + 0.053631 \log (Y/P)$ $r^2 = 0.318$ (13.3)
$$(3.0)$$

1961: $S/Y = -0.1450 + 0.049786 \log (Y/P)$ $r^2 = 0.255$ (13.4)
$$(2.5)$$

1963: $S/Y = -0.1893 + 0.055018 \log (Y/P)$ $r^2 = 0.410$ (13.5)
$$(3.5)$$

All the slope coefficients are seen to be statistically significant,[14] and the parameters imply reasonable values for the saving ratios:

Implied Saving Ratios: Equations (13.1)–(13.5)

Year	$Y/P = \$100$	$Y/P = \$1000$
1950–1952	10.9	23.0
1956	9.0	22.6
1958–1960	7.9	20.3
1961	8.4	19.9
1963	6.4	19.0

The implied saving ratios corresponding to the high level of income are seen to decline over time, and the saving ratios for the low level of income go down, up, and down again. This behavior is consistent with the following explanation.

Suppose that the semilog equations do not capture all the nonlinearity in the function, so that equations (13.1)–(13.5) are linear approximations to a curve such as the one shown on Figure 13.4. If the observations in the sample have been moving along (and around) this curve as time passed and income levels increased, then linear approximations such as lines a, b, and c may indeed result in diminishing saving ratios estimates for high income levels and in a mixed pattern for low levels of income.

In an attempt to capture better the shape of the function and at the same time to confront directly the alternative hypothesis of linear versus nonlinear relationship between S/Y and Y/P, we now introduce regressions—for a cross section of our countries, year 1963—having as explanatory variable both Y/P and a nonlinear transformation of Y/P:

Twenty Countries, 1963

$$S/Y = -0.131781 - 0.000138Y/P + 0.009269 \log (Y/P)^2 \quad R^2 = 0.422 \quad (13.6)$$
$$(0.9) \qquad\qquad (1.7)$$

$$S/Y = -0.34977 \; - 0.000087Y/P + 0.088475 \log (Y/P) \quad R^2 = 0.426 \quad (13.7)$$
$$(0.7) \qquad\qquad (1.7)$$

14. It seems almost unnecessary to point out here the great limitations of interpreting tests of significance when so little is known about the underlying distributions of the variables. Significance tests are at the 5 percent level, unless otherwise indicated.

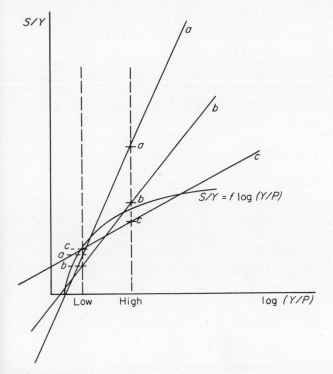

Figure 13.4

The estimates of the slope coefficients of the nonlinear terms in equations (13.6) and (13.7) are significant at 10 percent; the linear variable Y/P is not significant, thus providing support for the hypothesis of nonlinearity.

Another way of testing the shape proposed in Figure 13.3 is by partitioning the observations into two groups of "richer" and "poorer" countries and regressing S/Y on Y/P within each group. According to our hypothesis, the fitted line for the poorer countries should be steeper and more significant than the line for the richer nations. Our results confirm this expectation:

Eight Richer Countries, 1963

$$S/Y = 0.1042 + 0.000084Y/P \quad r^2 = 0.1111 \tag{13.8}$$
$$(0.9)$$

Twelve Poorer Countries, 1963

$$S/Y = 0.0124 + 0.00041Y/P \quad r^2 = 0.491 \tag{13.9}$$
$$(3.1)$$

The line segments of poorer and richer countries can be pooled by introducing a new variable Y^*

$$Y^* = Y/P - 400 \quad \text{for } Y/P > \$400$$
$$= 0 \quad \text{for } Y/P < \$400$$

The addition of Y^* allows the two line segments to bend but not to break at $Y/P = \$400$ and, hence, gives a fairly good approximation to the Figure 13.3 shape.

Twenty Countries, 1963

$$S/Y = 0.03392 + 0.000307Y/P - 0.000273Y^*$$
$$\quad\quad\quad (2.5) \quad\quad\quad\quad (1.6) \quad R^2 = 0.413 \quad\quad\quad (13.10)$$

Y^* is significant at 10 percent; and it has the correct negative sign, which indicates that for higher values of Y/P the deviations of S/Y from a straight line are negative.

The preceding tests offered some indirect evidence of the long-run changes in marginal propensities to save (MPS) in response to changes in the level of income. A more direct test is now introduced. It consists in the fitting, to time series of S and Y for each Latin American country, of a regression line of the type $S = a + bY$, where b is taken to be the MPS of that country.[15] The MPS's thus obtained are then regressed on Y/P in the expectation of approximating linearly the shape of Figure 13.2. Time series of S and Y were obtained for 17 countries and generally cover the period 1950–1966.

Five Richer Latin American Countries, 1950–1966

$$\text{MPS} = 0.2469 - 0.000184Y/P \quad r^2 = 0.03 \quad\quad\quad (13.11)$$
$$\quad\quad\quad (0.3)$$

Twelve Poorer Latin American Countries, 1950–1966

$$\text{MPS} = -0.0937 + 0.00067Y/P \quad\quad\quad r^2 = 0.588$$
$$\quad\quad\quad (3.8) \quad\quad F(1,10) = 14.3 \quad\quad\quad (13.12)$$

The fit for the poorer countries is remarkably good, as evidenced by the t ratio of the slope coefficient and the F-test of the significance of the equation as a whole.[16] The values of the parameters are reasonable; they imply, for example, that for a country whose average income per capita is US\$300 (at purchasing power parities, prices of 1960) the marginal propensity to save should be 0.107 and when $Y/P = $ US\$400, MPS $= 0.174$.

The lack of any significant association evidenced by equation (13.11) suggests that the five richer countries may have moved to the right of point B (Figure 13.2) and their MPS's are now independent of the level of income.

There is another direct test of the applicability of the function depicted in Figure 13.2 to Latin American countries. It was already seen that, if a straight line were fitted to a set of yearly observations of S and Y for a country whose saving behavior agreed with our hypothesis, the slope of that line would depend on the range of income levels of the country during the years observed. Moving from lower to higher levels of income, the line would become steeper at first; then less steep; and finally, for levels of income higher than B, the slope would cease to change in response to increases in the level of income.

---

15. This is clearly a rough approximation, since the relationship between S and Y is not believed to be linear over long periods of time. The failure to deflate S and Y by population is also expected to introduce some bias.

16. The critical values of $F(1,10)$ are 4.96 and 10.04 at the 5 percent and 1 percent levels of significance.

It follows from the same model that for the poorer countries—those that are to the left of the inflection point A—there should be a negative association between the value of the standardized constant term (a) and the level of income per capita. For the richer countries, on the contrary, the association between a and Y/P should be positive or nonexistent depending on whether the country in question has, on the average, been to the left or right, respectively, of point B in Figure 13.2. Once again the results provide good support for the hypothesis

Five Richer Latin American Countries, 1950–1966

$$a = -1.2632 + 0.00223Y/P \quad r^2 = 0.120 \tag{13.13}$$
$$(0.64)$$
$$a = 1.747 - 0.055Y/P \quad r^2 = 0.517 \tag{13.14}$$
$$(3.27)$$

Pooling of Time Series

The time series of Latin American countries which provided the estimates of constant terms and slopes used in the tests of equations (13.11)–(13.14) can be used in a more direct statistical test of the function presented in Figure 13.3. This new test consists of pooling all the observations into one large sample and then fitting a line that approximates the hypothesized shape.

The enlarged sample is composed of time series covering approximately the period 1950–1966 for 18 countries:

Argentina	Ecuador
Uruguay	Guatemala
Venezuela	Brazil
Chile	El Salvador
Mexico	Paraguay
Panama	Dominican Republic
Costa Rica	Nicaragua
Peru	Honduras
Colombia	Bolivia

(Bolivia has now been added to the other 17 countries; thus there are a total of 307 observations on S/Y and Y/P.)

The differences in saving ratios are due to a variety of specific factors in addition to the levels of income, as was evidenced by the low coefficients of correlation of the preceding equations. When several observations for each country are pooled into one regression, it becomes desirable to make some adjustment in order to hold those specific factors constant and to isolate the relationship between S/Y and Y/P. The procedure followed here is to assume that the intercountry differences in saving ratios that are not explained by income levels can be represented by an upward or downward shift in the function, whereas the functional relationship between S/Y and Y/P (slopes) is identical for each country.

Given this assumption it is possible to regress S/Y on Y/P, introducing into the relation a set of additional variables X_i—dummy variables—that allow each country's constant term to take on a different value.[17] One such dummy variable is intro-

17. For a discussion of the method followed, see Johnston (1963: 221–228) and Goldberger (1964: 218–227).

duced for each country in the sample, minus one (the omitted country is called the "reference country"). The general constant term computed for the regression as a whole can be interpreted as an estimate of the constant term of the reference country, and the values taken by the X_i are added to the general constant to obtain an estimate of each country's constant. The t ratios of the X_i can be used to test the significance of the difference between the constant term of each country i and the constant of the reference country.

Our theory suggests that the relationship between S/Y and Y/P is nonlinear when a wide range of levels of income is considered. Since we are now interested in fitting one relationship to all the countries in the pooled sample, it is desirable to transform the data or look for a specification of the model so that it is still possible to employ a linear method of estimation. We start by trying a semilogarithmic transformation:

$$S/Y = -0.1605 + 0.05065 \log (Y/P) \quad R^2 = 0.703 \qquad (13.15)$$
$$(3.1)$$

The constant term shown corresponds to Argentina. The dummy variables for the other countries in the sample are shown below. The countries are listed by decreasing income per capita.

	Dummy variable	t ratio
Uruguay	−0.0295	(2.8)
Venezuela	.0942	(8.6)
Chile	− .0048	(0.4)
Mexico	− .0211	(1.5)
Panama	− .0363	(2.5)
Costa Rica	− .0449	(3.2)
Peru	.0722	(3.9)
Colombia	.0636	(3.4)
Ecuador	.0080	(0.4)
Guatemala	− .0480	(2.4)
Brazil	.0370	(1.7)
El Salvador	− .0274	(1.3)
Paraguay	.0038	(0.2)
Dominican Rep.	.0383	(1.7)
Nicaragua	.0145	(.6)
Honduras	.0126	(.5
Bolivia	− .0211	(.7)

In a relationship of the type $S/Y = a + b \log (Y/P)$, the slope at any income level is given by

$$\frac{d(S/Y)}{d(Y/P)} = \frac{b}{(Y/P)}$$

so the slopes are seen to be the same for each country and not affected by the size of the constant term. The level of income at which there is zero saving is given by $(Y/P) = \exp (-a/b)$.

As just indicated, the coefficient of log (Y/P) is an estimate of the average within-country effect of log (Y/P) on S/Y, because the dummy variables have been allowed to take care of the differences between country means. Equations (13.1)–(13.5) on the other hand, have the same functional shape but are a measure of the between-countries relationships. It becomes interesting, then, to compare the slope estimates of the within- and between-countries equations and find out whether they are different.

The estimated between-countries slopes are

Year	Variable	t ratio
1950–1952	0.0527	(3.1)
1956	.0589	(3.1)
1958–1960	.0536	(3.0)
1961	.0498	(2.5)
1963	.0550	(3.5)

The unweighted average equals 0.0540.

The coefficients are seen to be remarkably close to the pooled result. On the average they differ by only 6 percent and in no case by more than 14 percent, that is, they are well within one-half of one standard error. This can be taken as the indication that the cross-section and the time series relationships are the same.

This is a good point at which to take note of an argument which has sometimes been advanced against this interpretation of the cross-section results. A standard prediction of neoclassical growth theory is that a higher saving ratio will, in the very long run, lead to a higher level for a country's growth path. This theory is in agreement with the sort of relation found in all our cross-section results, but it implies reversed causality in their interpretation. The growth theory explanation of the cross-section results does not, however, predict that the income-saving ratio relation should be similar in relatively short country time series to what is observed in international cross-section. Hence the agreement between our cross-section and time series results confirms the causal interpretation—income controlling saving ratio—which we have been giving our results.

Returning now to equation (13.15), we find it to be quite satisfactory; the slope coefficient, as well as the explanatory power, are significant at the 1 percent level, and the estimated values of the parameters are reasonable. There is one aspect of the equation that is not completely in line with the expectation. The reasoning underlying the functions depicted in Figures 13.2 and 13.3 assumes that beyond a certain level of income, B, the saving ratio ceases to increase as a result of increases in that income level. In other words, the function moves toward some asymptotic value in Figure 13.3. Equation (13.15), on the contrary, continues to rise indefinitely as income goes up.

We attempt to overcome this shortcoming by introducing a new term into the relationship: the square of log (Y/P):

$$S/Y = a + b \log (Y/P) + c[\log (Y/P)]^2$$

where the coefficient c is expected to be negative in order to ensure a flattening of the curve. One problem with this approach is the high correlation between log (Y/P)

and $[\log (Y/P)^2]$—$r = 0.9993$ with 307 observations—which is certain to introduce colinearity and reduce the significance of the estimates:

$$S/Y = -0.8349 + 0.28260 \log (Y/P) - 0.01957[\log (Y/P)]^2 \quad R^2 = 0.704 \quad (13.16)$$
$$\quad\quad\quad (1.0) \quad\quad\quad\quad\quad\quad (0.9)$$

Here again the constant term shown corresponds to Argentina, and the following values must be added in order to obtain the estimated constant terms of other countries:

	Dummy variable	t ratio
Uruguay	−0.0290	(2.8)
Venezuela	.0909	(7.9)
Chile	− .0114	(0.8)
Mexico	− .0324	(1.7)
Panama	− .0477	(2.4)
Costa Rica	− .0564	(2.9)
Peru	.0601	(2.6)
Colombia	.0510	(2.1)
Ecuador	− .0033	(0.1)
Guatemala	− .0596	(2.4)
Brazil	.0264	(1.1)
El Salvador	− .0388	(1.6)
Paraguay	− .0069	(0.3)
Dominican Rep.	.0284	(1.1)
Nicaragua	.0053	(0.2)
Honduras	.0068	(0.3)
Bolivia	− .0217	(0.8)

The new term has the expected negative sign. Given the estimated values of (13.16), the function reaches a maximum at a value of Y/P around US$1000 (1960 prices) and then declines. The relevant range for our purpose is, of course, to the left of that maximum. For values of Y/P in excess of US$1000, the saving ratio is assumed to remain constant, at a level that will differ among countries in line with the values taken by the dummy variables. The coefficient of $\log (Y/P)$ is higher than it was in equation (13.15), indicating that in (13.16) the saving ratio rises more steeply at lower values of Y/P as well as it reaches a plateau sooner when Y/P increases.

The explanatory power of the equation is unchanged, and the low t ratios are reasonable in view of the extremely high correlation between the two explanatory variables.

Finally we introduce alternative specifications of equation (13.16) that have the advantage of offering a direct test of the hypothesis of nonlinearity, as well as a new opportunity to verify the equality of the time-series and cross-section coefficients. We look first at the simple linear equation:

Pooling of Time Series, 307 observations

$$S/Y = 0.1017 + 0.0000934Y/P \quad R^2 = 0.699 \quad\quad (13.17)$$
$$\quad\quad\quad (2.4)$$

Where the constant term shown corresponds to Argentina, and the following values must be added in order to obtain the estimates of the constant terms of the other countries:

	Dummy variable	t ratio
Uruguay	−0.0298	(2.9)
Venezuela	.0967	(8.5)
Chile	.0000	(0.0)
Mexico	− .0157	(0.9)
Panama	− .0316	(1.8)
Costa Rica	− .0395	(2.3)
Peru	.0724	(3.3)
Colombia	.0641	(2.9)
Ecuador	.0051	(0.2)
Guatemala	.0501	(2.1)
Brazil	.0328	(1.4)
El Salvador	.0297	(1.3)
Paraguay	− .0006	(0.0)
Dominican Rep.	.0328	(1.3)
Nicaragua	.0080	(0.3)
Honduras	.0008	(0.0)
Bolivia	− .0370	(1.3)

The next step is to introduce a nonlinear transformation, given by the square of the logarithm of Y/P:

$$S/Y = -0.1187 - 0.000149Y/P + 0.00937[\log (Y/P)]^2 \quad R^2 = 0.704 \quad (13.18)$$
$$(1.2) \qquad\qquad (2.1)$$

The constant term once more corresponds to Argentina, to which the following values are added to give the constant terms for other countries:

	Dummy variable	t ratio
Uruguay	−0.0288	(2.8)
Venezuela	.0893	(7.6)
Chile	− .0142	(1.0)
Mexico	− .0354	(1.8)
Panama	− .0504	(2.5)
Costa Rica	− .0593	(3.0)
Peru	.0586	(2.5)
Colombia	.0495	(2.1)
Ecuador	− .0043	(0.2)
Guatemala	− .0607	(2.5)
Brazil	.0254	(1.0)
El Salvador	− .0399	(1.7)
Paraguay	− .0078	(0.3)
Dominican Rep.	.0275	(1.1)
Nicaragua	.0042	(0.2)
Honduras	.0054	(0.2)
Bolivia	− .0243	(0.9)

A *t* test reveals the nonlinear variable to be significant at 5 percent, a very good result considering the high correlation between Y/P and $[\log (Y/P)]^2$—($r = 0.9859$ with 307 pairs of observations). The overall fit improves, and the coefficient of determination corrected for degrees of freedom ($\bar{R}^2$) increases from 0.679 in equation (13.17) to 0.684 in equation (13.18). The hypothesis of nonlinearity is thus upheld once more.

The slope coefficients of (13.18) are not statistically different from those in (13.6). In fact they are as close as 1 percent of each other in the case of the nonlinear slope coefficient (the only coefficient statistically significant) and only less than 8 percent apart for the coefficient of S/Y. The equality of the cross-section and time series coefficients is also confirmed.

III. Saving and Two-Gap Models

A recent contribution to the literature on economic development is the type of planning model that has come to be known as the Chenery-Strout or two-gap model.[18] An important feature of two-gap models is the recognition that the rate of growth of the GDP of a country can be limited by one of two factors[19]: (1) the availability of imports and (2) the capacity to generate domestic saving to finance the required investment. In the short run—until the necessary corrective measures can be taken and they can bring about the desired changes in the productive structure—the coefficients relating the necessary imports and investment to the level of economic activity are relatively inflexible.

Assuming then that the attainment of a target level of income requires a minimum flow of imports of goods and services as well as a minimum level of investment, the "trade gap" is given by the excess of required imports over possible exports; similarly, the "saving gap" represents the amount by which potential savings fall short of the investment needs. In an historical sense the two gaps are identical: the net inflow of foreign capital—that is, the excess of imports over exports—is equal to the excess of investment over saving and to the excess of resources used by the economy over the resources supplied by it.[20] On an ex ante basis, however, the two gaps can be different in the short run. The difference in the ex ante magnitudes is a reflection of disequilibrium in the economy, a disequilibrium which may persist over several years because it can take a long time for the productive structure of a developing country to adjust fully to changes in the international markets that it faces. In a changing world, it is quite possible that the intentions to save, invest, import, and export are not mutually consistent, since they are made by different individuals.

The process of adjustment that results in the ex post equality of the two gaps may follow a variety of patterns depending on each combination of circumstances and on the peculiar institutional characteristics of a country: (1) a corporation may desist from its plans to expand capacity and retain earnings in view of unforeseen import restrictions on capital equipment; (2) a devaluation of the currency may lead to a greater expenditure on imported food staples, thus reducing the saving of lower income groups of the population; (3) a large inflow of foreign capital may lower the exchange rate and stimulate "nonessential" imports, and so on. In the first two

18. See especially Chenery and Bruno (1962) and Chenery and Strout (1966).
19. Assuming that there are no shortages of "skills" for the contemplated rates of growth.
20. See Johnson (1967: 53).

examples, ex post savings may be reduced as a consequence of a large trade gap; in the third case, ex post imports exceed the ex ante required level, presumably in connection with a saving gap which is filled by foreign capital.

In order to reach the target level of income, the larger of the two ex ante gaps must be filled by foreign capital. After the equilibrating adjustments take place, the smaller gap will increase so that ex post the two gaps will be identical. Since the smaller, non-binding gap is the one assumed to bear the weights of adjusting, the two variables whose ex post levels will differ more from their ex ante values are those connected with this gap. The ex post levels of the other two variables should be similar to the ex ante values provided the capital inflows are just sufficient to fill the binding gap. For example, when the trade gap is binding and foreign capital is forthcoming to provide the necessary foreign exchange, realized saving may fall short of its potential level or new investment may go into less profitable projects, thus increasing the level of investment and the incremental capital-output ratio over the minimum necessary levels. Conversely, when the inflows of foreign capital are just enough to provide for the deficiency of national saving but exceed the foreign exchange gap, ex post imports may exceed the minimum levels required for the realized level of income. In the case when exportable commodities can be used for domestic consumption in significant proportions or when factors employed in the production of exports can be employed as inputs in internally oriented activities, actual exports may be lower than the intended levels.

In an analysis of the economic structure of a developing country, it is useful to identify whether one of the constraints was actually binding during all or part of a certain historical period. If such is the case, then it follows that the observed propensities to save and to import, and possibly the recorded incremental capital-output ratios, do not reflect the potential and more efficient values of these parameters.

The necessity for the two gaps to be equal ex post was discussed as early as 1720 by Isaac Gervaise in his exposition of the "absorption approach" to balance of payments analysis (see Nurkse 1961: 189). The possibility that realized saving might be below the potential level as a consequence of inflows of foreign capital has been recognized by several authors: the different models of H. Johnson (1967: 53–55); Little and Clifford (1966: 143–144); Linder (1967: 42–71); Ohlin (1966: 76–80); Mosak (1967: 53); Higgins (1955: 310); and Maizels (1968: 51–72) all reason along lines not very much different from those followed by two-gap models. Kafka (1967: 216–220) stresses mainly the impact of foreign capital on domestic saving through changes in the marginal efficiency of investment and in the local rate of interest. Gurley (1968: 107) mentions the possibility that foreign capital could help to keep the magnitude of the financial system of a developing country below its optimum size, with unfavorable consequences for domestic saving and investment. We can also mention here M. Anisur Rahman (1967) who suggested a psychological explanation of the negative impact of foreign capital on domestic saving. (The psychological explanation is discussed in note 24.)

In the remainder of this chapter we propose a method for identifying the binding constraint in the recent past experience of a developing country, and for estimating the potential marginal propensities to save and to import. The basic ideas were first developed in Landau (1966) and further elaborated and subjected to some statistical tests in CIAP (1968).

Algebraic Statement of Two-Gap Model

We present first in a simplified manner those aspects of the two-gap models that are relevant for our objective.

Variables
Y = gross national product
C = aggregate consumption expenditure (government included)
I = aggregate gross domestic capital formation (government included)
X = exports of goods and services
M = imports of goods and services (including net factor payments)
S = gross national saving
F = net foreign capital inflows (including use of international reserves)
Z = Other variables belonging in the production function (physical and human capital, and so on)

For convenience we shall denote the ex ante saving gap as G_s and the *ex ante* trade gap, G_t.

We start with three identities from the national accounts (every equation is for the period t):

$$Y \equiv C + I + X - M \tag{13.19}$$

$$Y \equiv C + S \tag{13.20}$$

$$F \equiv I - S \tag{13.21}$$

From the three identities (13.19), (13.20), and (13.21), it follows that:

$$F \equiv M - X \tag{13.21a}$$

The production function is:

$$Y = f(I,Z) \tag{13.22}$$

The *ex post* saving function:

$$S = a_1 + b_1Y + \alpha_1F \tag{13.23}$$

And the *ex post* import function:

$$M = a_2 + b_2Y + \alpha_2F \tag{13.24}$$

Two variables are determined exogenously:

$$X = \bar{X} \tag{13.25}$$

$$Z = \bar{Z} \tag{13.26}$$

We shall explain presently that:

$$\alpha_1 = 0 \text{ when } I - (a_1 + b_1Y) > M - X \tag{13.23a}$$

$$\alpha_2 = 0 \text{ when } (a_2 + b_2Y) - X > I - S \tag{13.24a}$$

Binding Trade Gap

We consider here the case of the binding trade gap: when the ex ante deficiency of foreign exchange exceeds the excess of required investment over potential saving for a given level of income. We assume that the inflows of foreign capital are positive and for an amount just equal to the trade gap. In this case actual imports are the same as *ex ante* imports, which are given by:

$$M = a_2 + b_2 Y \qquad (13.24b)$$

and $\alpha_2 = 0$ in (13.24).

It is necessary to distinguish three cases.

1. when G_s is zero; that is, when ex ante saving equals the necessary investment, and G_t is positive
2. when G_s is positive (though smaller than G_t)
3. when G_s is negative

In the first case, ex ante saving, which is given by:

$$S = a_1 + b_1 Y \qquad (13.23b)$$

is equal to the required investment. But since we have assumed that there is enough foreign capital flowing in to fill the trade gap, and since ex post the two gaps must be equal, there must be a fall in saving below the ex ante value, an increase in investment, or both. We shall assume that realized investment is always equal to the ex ante level, that is, the minimum required for the attained level of income. Therefore all the adjustment is done by saving:

$$S = a_1 + b_1 Y - F \qquad (13.23c)$$

Ex post saving is seen to fall short of the potential levels by an amount equal to F. F is a complete substitute for saving.

If such a situation prevailed over a period of several years in a country, then when fitting to the observed data a function such as (13.23)—assuming now that (13.23) also incorporates a stochastic component—we should obtain an estimate of α_1 that is close to unity, with a negative sign. The estimate of b_1 would be an approximation to the potential marginal propensity to save. An attempt to fit (13.24) should yield an estimate of α_2 close to zero. A positive α_2 would be an indication that actual imports exceeded the required level or that the realized Y was below the potential level, given M.

In the second case the ex ante saving gap G_s is positive but less than the trade gap G_t:

$$I - (a_1 + b_1 Y) < M - X$$

Assuming once more that investment does not participate in the process of adjustment of the two gaps, realized saving will be below potential saving by an amount equal to the excess of the ex ante trade gap over the ex ante saving gap. If G_s is large, then F will be mostly a complement to domestic saving, the necessary downward adjustment in saving is small. The extent to which F acts as a substitute for S goes from zero—when G_s is as large as G_t—to the full value of F when there is no ex ante saving gap. In equation (13.23), α_1 will lie between minus unity and zero:

$$\alpha_1 = - \frac{G_t - G_s}{G_t} \qquad (13.27)$$

If this case ($G_s < G_t$) had persisted for several years, the application of least squares to (13.23) would yield an estimate of some weighted average of α_1. Under our assumptions, F would be equal to G_t, so we should be able to estimate the magnitude of an average ex ante saving gap. An estimate of the potential MPS would again be given by b_1. The interpretation of α_2 in (13.24) remains the same as in the first case.

The third case is that of a negative G_s. The only change with respect to the preceding case is that now α_1 will be less than minus unity.

Binding Saving Gap

When the saving gap is binding, foreign capital is no longer a substitute for domestic saving but a complement. Ex ante and ex post saving are equal, and $\alpha_1 = 0$. F is now equal to G_s. Since G_t is smaller, imports must go up or exports down from their ex ante levels, so that the identities (13.21) and (13.21a) are preserved. Actual exports may fall short of the potential if

1. the goods or services exported can be consumed domestically in a significant proportion or
2. some inputs required for producing those exports can be employed in the production of goods for the internal market

Imports will exceed the minimum required levels in the presence of foreign capital inflows: α_2 will be positive. The value of α_2 will be smaller, the greater the downward adjustment in exports. In the case when the inputs of the export sector are highly specialized and the domestic use of exportable products is relatively low and price-inelastic, the value of α_2 should be close to $(G_s - G_t)/G_s$, indicating that part of the foreign capital goes to increase imports.[21]

Alternating Gaps

Typically, the exports of Latin American countries are subject to important fluctuations which are largely due to exogenous influences. It is possible that in years of high exports, G_s will be binding; when exports are low in relation to their trend, G_t is the more likely effective constraint. In the presence of alternating saving and trade gaps, the diagnosis becomes more difficult. If, over a period time, one of the two gaps has been predominantly binding, we may obtain some evidence of this by regressing equations (13.23) and (13.24).[22]

A value of $\hat{\alpha}_1$ close to -1, together with a value of $\hat{\alpha}_2$ not significantly different from 0, would be an indication of a trade gap having prevailed in that period. In this case, potential saving would be given by $a_1 + b_1 Y$. If $\hat{\alpha}_1$ turns out to be close to zero and $\hat{\alpha}_2$ is significantly positive, it is apparent that the saving gap has been binding, and observed saving propensities are probably close to the potential levels. When $\hat{\alpha}_1$ is significantly negative (but its absolute value less than unity) and $\hat{\alpha}_2$ is significantly positive, we are facing a case of alternating binding constraints, without a clear dominance of either gap. In this situation it might be possible to obtain some idea of the potential saving ratios. Suppose we found in those years when exports were highest with respect to their trend that saving ratios were also high: those would be years of a binding saving gap and observed saving ratios would be the same as the potential ones.

21. The derivation is similar to the one leading to (13.27). In the special situation when G_t is zero and the export sector is highly specialized, with low substitutability for domestic use, α_2 should be close to unity. Venezuela seems to be in such a situation.

22. We are ignoring here the problems of a simultaneous system. It would be desirable to estimate the model simultaneously.

Estimates of Parameters Obtained from Time Series

In the three preceding discussions we described ways in which the estimated parameters obtained by regressing equations (13.23) and (13.24) on time series of a country can be interpreted in order to identify a binding constraint as well as potential saving and import propensities. In Table 13.2 we present the estimates of α_1 and α_2 obtained from time series in constant prices for eighteen countries, extending over the approximate period 1950–1966.[23]

One reassuring thing about the values in the table is that they all fall within the expected range: α_1 always lies between -1 and 0, except for three cases in which it is positive (but not statistically different from zero); α_2 is always positive and less than unity, again with a few insignificant exceptions.

From the table it is possible to identify eight cases of binding trade gaps: Bolivia, Chile, Colombia, Dominican Republic, Guatemala, Nicaragua, Panama, and Uruguay. In all these cases α_1 is significantly negative and lies between -0.5 and -1, whereas α_2 is not significantly different from zero. Two of these countries, Dominican Republic and Uruguay, had outflows of capital (negative F) during 11 and 4 years, respectively; the two-gap model may not be applicable to these countries.

Four countries for which the saving gap appears to have been binding are Brazil, Paraguay, Peru, and Venezuela. In all of them, α_1 is not statistically different from zero and α_2 is significantly positive. Venezuela appears to be a country in which the ex ante trade gap was zero and the export sector is relatively isolated from the rest of the economy, in accordance with the discussion in note 21, since α_2 is close to unity. Such a characterization of Venezuela is intuitively appealing. It should be observed, however, that both Brazil and Venezuela had outflows of foreign capital in 5 different years; this fact, inconsistent with the two-gap model, creates doubts about the validity of including them in the analysis.

The remaining six countries appear to have alternated between the two situations; both α_1 and α_2 are different from zero, although their absolute values are smaller than the corresponding values of α_1 and α_2 for countries in the preceding two groups.

Within these six countries, Costa Rica appears to have been, on the average, more limited by trade than saving gaps, because α_1 is larger in absolute value (and statistically more significant) than α_2. Honduras, on the other hand, seems to have been affected more often by saving gaps; for both $|\alpha_2| > |\alpha_1|$ and the t ratio of α_2 is larger than that of α_1. For Argentina, Ecuador, El Salvador, and Mexico, the tests do not discriminate which constraint was more binding on the average. It would appear that they have been more closely balanced between the two gaps than the other countries. Here again, Argentina may not qualify for this type of analysis, because in 8 years, including the last 4 observed, F was negative.

It should be interesting to conclude this discussion by comparing the diagnosis just made with that presented in Chenery and Strout (1965: table 7). By following a different procedure, based mainly on observations of certain indicators, Chenery

---

23. In most cases,
$$M = a_3 + b_3C + c_3I + \alpha_2F \text{ (plus a random element)} \qquad (13.28)$$

was substituted for (13.24), as it was found to give a better fit. It should be observed that, contrary to the practice followed throughout this chapter, the figures shown in parentheses in Table 13.2 are standard errors rather than t ratios.

Table 13.2. Partial Derivatives of Saving and Imports with Respect to Foreign Capital Inflows[a] (time series in constant prices, 1950-1966; 1960 US $)

	Savings,[b] $\partial S/\partial F = \alpha_1$	Imports,[c] $\partial M/\partial F = \alpha_2$
Argentina	- 0.3366	0.2770
	(0.195)	(0.117)
Bolivia[d]	- 0.8211	0.1565
	(0.166)	(0.182)
Brazil	0.1688	0.4387
	(0.164)	(0.250)
Chile	- 0.7459	0.2852
	(0.250)	(0.15)
Colombia	- 0.7757	0.2522
	(0.216)	(0.170)
Costa Rica	- 0.6276	0.4947
	(0.07)	(0.126)
Dominican Republic	- 0.5609	0.3297
	(0.1769)	(0.279)
Ecuador	- 0.4515	0.5329
	(0.1419)	(0.170)
El Salvador[d]	- 0.6030	0.5644
	(0.110)	(0.070)
Guatemala	- 0.5051	- 0.0950
	(0.156)	(0.090)
Honduras[d]	- 0.4921)	0.7512
	(0.200)	(0.260)
Mexico[d]	- 0.6345	0.4194
	(0.272)	(0.140)
Nicaragua	- 0.5630	0.1237
	(0.130)	(0.150)
Panama[d]	- 0.9298	- 0.0460
	(0.240)	(0.360)
Paraguay[d]	0.0065	0.7543
	(0.09)	(0.170)
Peru[d]	0.1481	0.6417
	(0.2687)	(0.150)
Uruguay	- 0.5254	- 0.1000
	(0.125)	(0.200)
Venezuela	- 0.2006	1.0094
	(0.160)	(0.220)

Notation: S = Gross national savings; M = Imports; Y = GNP; C = Total consumption; I = Gross investment; F = Net foreign capital movements.
[a] Standard errors shown in brackets.
[b] Equation fitted: $S = a_1 + b_1 Y + \alpha_1 F$.
[c] Equation fitted: $M = a_2 + b_2 I + c_2 C + \alpha_2 F$.
[d] Equation fitted for imports: $M = a_2 + b_2 Y + \alpha_2 F$.

and Strout identify tentatively the growth limits in the period 1957–1962 for several countries, of which eight are from Latin America. Peru is classified as "savings limited"; Bolivia, Brazil, Chile, Colombia, Costa Rica, and Guatemala are "import limited"; and Mexico is "closely balanced." Only for Brazil do the two classifications disagree, but then we saw that Brazil may not qualify for this analysis in view of the 5 years when F was negative.

The simplified model just presented predicts that α_1 can take on values between -1 and 0, the latter value being evidence of a binding saving gap. By pooling all the time series utilized in Table 13.2, and using dummy variables once more for the constant terms of each country, we can obtain an estimated α_1 for Latin America, in the period 1950–1966:

Eighteen Latin American Countries, 307 observations
Time Series 1950–1966 (constant prices)

$$S/Y = a + 0.04716 \log (Y/P) - 0.5345 \, F/Y \quad R^2 = 0.80 \qquad (13.29)$$
$$ (3.5) (11.8)$$

The two parameters have reasonable values. The magnitude of $\hat{\alpha}_1$ indicates that the trade limitation has been important in this period, a finding that confirms the observations of several investigators, as indicated by Chenery and Strout (1968), Ohlin (1966), CIAP (1968), and, with a different model, by M. Mamalakis (1966).[24]

24. M. Anisur Rahman (1968) has criticized our interpretation that the two-gap model may explain the negative correlation between capital inflows and national saving. He suggests a possible psychological explanation: that governments of developing countries "may voluntarily relax domestic savings effort when more foreign aid is available than otherwise." We have attempted elsewhere to test the applicability of Rahman's hypothesis to the 10 Latin American countries for which disaggregated time series were available (Landau, 1969). Of the 10 countries, we find that possibly two behave in a manner that may be consistent with his explanation (Costa Rica and Colombia). We find no evidence in support of the applicability of Rahman's hypothesis to the other 8 countries.

14 Demand Elasticities for a Developing Economy: An International Comparison of Consumption Patterns*

Richard Weisskoff

I. Introduction

Despite the central importance of price in the theory of household behavior, few empirical studies of consumption succeed in measuring the effects of price changes on expenditure patterns. The most commonly employed consumption relationship states that expenditure on a particular good is simply a function of per capita income. Although some attempts have been made to account for price effects in predictions of consumption in industrial economies—as in Houthakker and Taylor (1966) and Almon (1966)—the omission of price elasticities of demand for consumption is carried farther with less apology, and perhaps less empirical justification, in studies of developing economies. In this chapter, we shall explore the relationship between expenditure patterns and changes in relative prices for a sample of developing countries.

The philosophy which underlies the suppression of the price variable maintains that at low-income levels, there is little opportunity for substitution between broad groups of commodities, especially within short periods of time. This view is built into planning models by fixing either or both the average or incremental proportions of consumption among sectors. These proportions are based on demand elasticities which are derived from budget studies or borrowed from other countries.[1] Greater flexibility has also been introduced in certain models by allowing variation around expenditure proportions.[2] However, recent empirical research has lent support to the hypothesis that the income elasticity of demand for broad groups of commodities may be constant over a range of income. It has therefore been suggested that planning models attempt to distribute private consumption as a logarithmic rather than linear

* This research was supported by the Harvard Transport Research Program, also by the Harvard Project for Quantitative Research in Economic Development through funds provided by the Agency for International Development under Contract CSD-1543. The views expressed in this paper do not necessarily reflect the views of AID.

I am indebted to Francine Blau Weisskoff and to M. S. Feldstein, H. S. Houthakker, G. Kraft, G. H. Orcutt, D. Schydlowsky, C. Sims, and T. E. Weisskopf for suggestions. However, I am solely responsible for the conclusions of this study.

1. See Eckaus and Parikh (1968: 1–12, and tables 3-24, 5-12) and T. E. Weisskopf (1969: 3.18) on India; A. R. Khan (1967: 57) and MacEwan (1968: 62–64) on Pakistan; L. Westphal (1970) on Korea; Bruno (1962: 153) on Israel; Nugent (1966: 70–72) on Greece; and P. B. Clark (1967: 76–85) on Nigeria.

2. See Sandee (1960: 35–37), who allows for ±13 percent variation, while Bruno (1966: 330–332) introduces ±10 percent variation around the Engel curves.

function of the income level.[3] Despite these refinements, the direct impact of price changes on consumption is still ignored.

The unresponsiveness of consumer demand to changes in relative prices in planning models is similar to the position implicit in the "structuralist" view of growth. The structuralist position argues that a moderate increase in per capita income and a high income elasticity of demand and low price elasticity of demand combine with rather rigid supply conditions to explain the continually rising relative prices and persistent excess demand in sectors such as food, transportation, and electricity. A per capita income growth of 2 percent and income elasticity of 0.6 for food are generally cited.[4]

The rising relative price in a sector, it is argued, fails to reduce the pressure of excess demand: first, because of the difficulty of substitution between categories of expenditure (price inelasticity); and second, because of the overwhelming positive effect of rising incomes. A low price elasticity of demand is further invoked to demonstrate that inflation causes heavy losses of real income to the urban worker who, to maintain a constant quantity of food purchases, must spend a larger share of his budget on food. Finally, a rising price also fails to evoke a positive response on the supply side due to the monopolistic or feudal elements among the producing units, especially in the agrarian sector.

The structuralist emphasis on excess consumer demand contrasts with the Marxist view of weak effective demand. The insufficient "actual market demand," which is primarily determined by the unequal distribution of income, differs substantially from the "actual social needs" of the working class which Marx believed to be rather elastic with respect to both income and price.[5] Weak consumer demand is held to be widespread, and this aggregate "disproportionality" between the low growth of demand for consumption goods and the high growth of capacity to produce consumption goods forms the basis of the Marxist theory of crises and stagnation.

Growth models in the classical, non-Marxian tradition stress the high elasticity of effective market demand, specifically with respect to price. It is the prompt response to changing prices which explains the flexibility embodied in the classical vision. A price rise due to an increase in demand signals higher profits and results ultimately in the expansion of output. For example, an initial shift in the supply of domestic food due to an increase in agricultural exports leads to an increase in food prices, the decline in domestic food demand, and, if resources are mobile, to the eventual expansion of the home food supply.[6] Technical progress, on the other hand, can be expected to yield an increasing supply of certain consumer products at lower equilibrium prices despite the increase in demand resulting from rising incomes and

3. Houthakker (1957) summarizes the empirical evidence which suggests constant elasticity of demand for categories of consumption expenditure. See Chenery (1960: 627) for a general statement of nonlinear demand and Carter (1967a, 1967b) for a nonlinear model.

4. See Felix (1961: 87); Grunwald (1961: 108–115); also Hirschman's remarks on structuralism in Baer and Kerstenetzky (1964: 455).

5. "The quantity demanded by these wants (social wants) is very elastic and changing." "Actual social need" is defined as ". . . that quantity which would be demanded if the money prices of the commodities, or other conditions concerning the money or living of the buyers, were different." Marx, *Capital*, III: 233–234, quoted in P. Sweezy (1956: 50; and see 183–184).

6. ". . . but till it [increased food supply] be obtained, the high price is absolutely necessary to proportion the consumption to the supply . . . [The higher price] is the means by which the demand of the home purchasers is diminished" (Ricardo 1965: 203). Note that this is the converse of the structuralist chain.

lower prices.[7] Finally, the classical model speculates that the short-run income elasticity of demand for food is low and may itself be a function of family size.[8]

There are a few examples in the current growth literature on empirical models which capture the flexibility of the classical spirit. Chenery and Raduchel (Chapter 2 in this volume) and Chenery and Uzawa (1958) explore a 4-sector programming model which includes prices as an explicit variable in determining consumption. Johansen's model (1960, 1964) of Norwegian growth employs an extensive set of price and expenditure elasticities based on Frisch's scheme (1959) for deriving demand coefficients. Other, less ambitious models make some attempt to include price effects on demand.[9]

We would expect simulation models of growth to be free from the linearity imposed by the optimizing framework and also to more readily incorporate price adjustments. Holland and Gillespie (1963: 55) briefly explore the sensitivity of the balance of payments and the general price level to different expenditure and price elasticities in a simulation of the Venezuelan economy. The simulation project of the Colombian economy by Roberts and Kresge (1968: 40) omits price elasticities, but the model does stress the importance of user price in the detailed analysis of transport flows.[10]

Perhaps a major reason for the omission of price coefficients in these empirical models is that few attempts have been made to estimate price and expenditure elasticities directly from time series data. Watanabe (1962), using United Nations data, has estimated expenditure elasticities of a "cross-country" sample by converting each of 24 country observations into German purchasing power equivalents calculated by the Statistiches Bundesamt (1960). Houthakker (1965a) estimates "short-run" elasticities by pooling annual observations from time series of 13 OECD countries and "long-run" elasticities by pooling country averages. Several of his estimates, however, yield positive price elasticities. Russell (1967) relates the different country expenditure elasticities to income level, relative prices, and a social class dummy. At the conclusion of this chapter, estimates from the above sources will be compared with the results obtained in the following sections.

To summarize the preceding survey, we note that several approaches to growth theory maintain specifically that the price elasticity of demand is unimportant or close to zero. This position of the unresponsiveness of demand to price which is held by programmers and structuralists contrasts with the view of a significantly negative price elasticity suggested in the classical system and incorporated into some simulation models.

The object of the present investigation is to estimate expenditure and price elasticities of demand for several broad consumer categories among a group of developing or low-income countries. Do the empirical findings support the view that price flexibility is unimportant in determining patterns of consumption expenditure?

---

7. "Diminish the cost of production of hats, and their price will ultimately fall to their new natural price, although the demand should be doubled, trebled, or quadrupled" (Ricardo 1965: 260).

8. "The increased wages are not always expended on food, but are first made to contribute to other enjoyments of the labourer" (Ricardo 1965: 103). See also Stigler (1954).

9. See Fox (1953) and his comments in Adelman and Thorbecke (1966: 319–321); Harberger (1964: 342); Tinbergen (1957); and Bos and Koyck (1961).

10. It was in the quest for empirical estimates of price elasticities to be used in the Colombian model that this study was first undertaken.

II. The Model

The basic expenditure relationship appears in exponential form:[11]

$$C_{ijt} = a_i E_{jt}^{\beta_{1i}} P_{ijt}^{\beta_{2i}} N_{jt}^{\beta_{3i}} e^{\delta_i t} u_{ijt} \tag{14.1}$$

where

C_{ijt} = consumption expenditure on commodity i ($i = 1, \ldots, 6$) in country j ($j = 1, \ldots, 15$) at time t ($t = 1, \ldots, 8, \ldots, 17$) at constant market prices

a_i = constant for each commodity i

E_{jt} = total expenditure in country j at time t, evaluated at constant market prices

P_{ijt} = relative price of commodity i in country j in time t

$$= \frac{\dfrac{\text{expenditure on } i \text{ in } j \text{ at } t \text{ (at current prices)}}{\text{expenditure on } i \text{ in } j \text{ at } t \text{ (at constant prices)}}}{\dfrac{\text{total expenditure in } j \text{ at } t \text{ (at current prices)}}{\text{total expenditure in } j \text{ at } t \text{ (at constant prices)}}}$$

N_{jt} = population in country j at time t

u_{ijt} = error term, log normally distributed, mean of unity and constant variance

β_{1i} = elasticity of expenditure on commodity i with respect to total expenditure

β_{2i} = elasticity of expenditure on commodity i with respect to its own price

β_{3i} = elasticity of expenditure on commodity i with respect to population

δ_i = trend coefficient of expenditure on commodity i

In double logarithmic form, the demand equation appears as:

$$\log C_{ijt} = \alpha_i + \beta_{1i} \log E_{jt} + \beta_{2i} \log P_{ijt} + \beta_{3i} \log N_{jt} + \delta_i t + \epsilon_{ijt} \tag{14.2}$$

where ϵ_{ijt} is the error term normally distributed with mean zero and constant variance.

By taking first differences of the annual observations, and then subtracting from each annual observation the mean of the first differences calculated from the country series, we derive equation (14.3), which represents the "within-countries" expression:

$$\Delta \log C_{ijt} - \overline{\Delta \log C_{ij}} = \beta_{1wi}[\Delta \log E_{jt} - \overline{\Delta \log E_j}] + \beta_{2wi}[\Delta \log P_{ijt} - \overline{\Delta \log P_{ij}}]$$
$$+ \beta_{3wi}[\Delta \log N_{jt} - \overline{\Delta \log N_j}] + \epsilon'_{ijt} \quad i = 1, \ldots, 6$$
$$j = 1, \ldots, 15$$
$$t = 1, \ldots, 7, \ldots, 16 \tag{14.3}$$

where the first differences appear as Δ; the country means, as barred terms; and ϵ'_{ijt} is the disturbance term assumed to be normally distributed with zero mean and constant variance.

The within-countries equation (3) states that the consumption of specific commodities is a function of total expenditure, relative price, and population, as expressed in terms of the deviations of the growth rates of the variables around their mean growth rates.[12]

---

11. See Houthakker (1960a) for discussion of defects and advantages of this form.
12. See Houthakker (1965a: 279). First differencing causes the loss of the intercept α_i, in equation (14.2), and the subtraction of the country means removes the trend term, δ_i.

The country means themselves are taken as the observations in the "between-countries" model:

$$\overline{\Delta \log C_{ij}} = \beta_{1bi}\overline{\Delta \log E_j} + \beta_{2bi}\overline{\Delta \log P_{ij}} + \beta_{3bi}\overline{\Delta \log N_j} + \delta_i + \epsilon_{ij}''$$

$$i = 1, \ldots, 6$$
$$j = 1, \ldots, 15 \quad (14.4)$$

where ϵ_{ij}'' is the error term which is assumed to be normally distributed with mean zero and variance inversely proportional to the number of observations in each country series. The elasticities are assumed to be constant over time as well as constant over the range of income. The trend, δ_i, appears in the between-countries model, but the equation has also been fitted without such a trend, setting $\delta_i = 0$.

Equation (14.3) may be taken to measure the short-run influence of total expenditure and price on consumption, while equation (14.4) captures the longer run effects. The long run, in this case, refers to a 7- to 17-year span in the postwar period.

The Population Variable

Only under special conditions is the elasticity of total expenditure (β_1) the same as the elasticity of per capita expenditure which is commonly used in demand analysis. Equation (14.1) above can be converted to per capita terms:

$$\frac{C}{N} = \left(\frac{E}{N}\right)^{\beta_1} P^{\beta_2} N^{(\beta_3 + \beta_1 - 1)} \quad (14.5)$$

If $\beta_3 + \beta_1 = 1$, then the estimates of β_1 are equivalent in the per capita and total expenditure formulation. If $\beta_3 + \beta_1 \neq 1$, then we are testing the hypothesis that population itself influences consumption other than through its effect on income per person. Indeed, in countries where the distribution of income is highly skewed, we expect that per capita expenditure is an artificial concept. The effective causes of changes in consumption may be changes in the aggregate level of income and in the distribution of that income.

If $\beta_3 + \beta_1$ is significantly less than one, then an increasing population leads to a decrease in per capita consumption expenditure. This is expected if economies of scale in utilization can be realized (as in durables and housing) or if the variable is a proxy for changes in age composition. If $\beta_3 + \beta_1$ is significantly greater than unity in the cases of transport and services, then the rise in consumption per person may be due to increasing congestion or to a greater level of mobility. Increasing population, in this case, acts as a proxy for changes in the degree of urbanization or population density.[13]

13. More can be said against the use of population estimates to obtain per capita expenditure. First, although the United Nations *Demographic Yearbook, 1966,* has reduced the number of discontinuities in the country series by replacing "out-of-line" estimates with "smoothed" or consistent series, there are still serious doubts about the reliability of the annual estimates. See United Nations (1967a: 22–23, 120–131). Thus the use of per capita variables would introduce an additional source of error into the series.

In the case of the Nigerian population statistics, P. B. Clark (1967: 76–85), comments on his own consumption research: "A better specification of the function might have been to use per capita income in place of gross domestic product. However, the last two Nigerian population censuses were rejected . . . making it impossible to find an agreed estimate of Nigeria's population."

Second, national consumption expenditure may refer to a different proportion of the population from the population estimates. Especially in those countries which have large rural populations, the

III. The Data

The two major difficulties in estimating price elasticities are, first, that few developing countries have sufficiently long expenditure and price series for the postwar period and, second, that official exchange rates bear little relation to the true purchasing power parity of the currency.

We overcome the first problem of short time series by pooling data from a number of countries to yield a sample of considerable size. By pooling observations of different countries and years, we postulate that there is a common underlying expenditure pattern that will emerge despite national and institutional differences. Later in our analysis we shall attempt to identify the influence of these "national" differences.

We avoid the second problem of converting the different national currencies to a common unit by adopting a ratio form for all observations or, in logarithmic form, by using first differences in equations (14.3) and (14.4).

Time series of annual private consumption expenditure for detailed categories of goods in many countries are reported by the United Nations (1967b: tables 7a, 7b). Our sample is limited to those 15 low-income countries which report consumption expenditure in both current and constant prices. United Nations worksheets were made available to supplement the published series. The sample consists of the countries listed in Table 14.1. Population for each annual observation was obtained from United Nations (1967a: table 4).[14]

The categories in the United Nations expenditure accounts have been aggregated into the commodity groups listed in Table 14.2.

IV. Results

The least squares regression estimates of the elasticities of equations (14.3) and (14.4) are presented in Table 14.3. The within-countries coefficients have been estimated from the unweighted pool of 149 observations drawn from 15 countries, while the between-countries coefficients are estimated from the pool of country means. In the between-countries equations, each country mean was weighted by the square root of the number of first-differenced observations from which the country average was constructed. The population variable is added for both equations on lines 3 and 4. Professor Houthakker's results for similar models using OECD per capita data are presented on lines 5 and 6. His intercept form is added on line 7 with the constant in place of the population coefficient. Intercepts were introduced in the

---

consumption expenditure of the nonmarket economy may be grossly underestimated. S. N. Braithwaite (1967b: 29), writes about the Latin American accounts: ". . . real income figures expressed in per capita terms reflect not only the errors of the national accounts data but also the inadequacies of the demographic statistics. For many countries in the region, no recent census has been conducted, and the annual figures given are extrapolations based on trends which may or may not be indicative of current growth rates . . . A further problem arises through basing per capita estimates on demographic figures which include a sizable population at the margin of, or completely outside, the market economy, e.g., in Brazil, Ecuador, Central America, etc. When this is the case, the per capita income figures tend to be low in comparison with a country where virtually all inhabitants contribute to or participate in economic activity."

14. The International Labour Office (1966: 661–665, table 28) gives the percentage of the family budget spent on food, housing, clothing, and miscellaneous for many countries. However, the consumer price indices given for selected cities in the various countries in chap. vii do not necessarily correspond to the expenditure categories of table 28.

Table 14.1. Countries Used in the Sample

Code	Country	No. of observations	Years	Base year
6	Nigeria	7	1951-1957	1957
7	Federation of Rhodesia and Nyasaland[a]	10	1954-1963	1954
9	South Africa[a]	17	1950-1966	1958
23	Jamaica	7	1959-1965	1960
24	Puerto Rico	16	1950-1965	1963
27	Honduras	11	1954-1964	1948
34	Ecuador	15	1950-1964	1960
42	Peru	9	1950-1958	1954
45	Dominican Republic	15	1950-1964	1960
51	Thailand	10	1957-1966	1962
53	Ceylon	8	1958-1965	1958
54	Korea	14	1953-1966	1965
56	Israel	13	1952-1964	1952
67	Taiwan	8	1958-1965	1964
71	Greece	8	1958-1965	1958
87	Ireland	12	1953-1964	1958

[a]South Africa has been included only in the country studies and is excluded from the pooled sample. Consumption accounts for the Federation of Rhodesia and Nyasaland, which has since split into Zambia, Malawi, and Southern Rhodesia, exclude African rural household expenditure. See United Nations (1967b: 261).

three variable between-countries equations for the developing country sample, but not one was found to be significant. Almost all the expenditure and price elasticities in Table 14.3 are of the theoretically admissible sign, and most are significantly different from zero. Measures of the goodness of fit (correlation coefficients corrected for degrees of freedom) and the standard errors of estimate for these equations follow in Table 14.4.[15]

Are the differences between the elasticities derived from equation (14.3) and those from equation (14.4) statistically significant? We obtain a "total" residual sum of squares by pooling the between- *and* within-countries observations in one total equation. A residual sum of squares due to the different regression coefficients is calculated by subtracting the residual sum of squares of the within- and between-countries from the residual sum of squares of the total regression. The mean square of the within-countries equation is then compared to the mean square due to the different regressions by the F-statistic.

The results are shown in Table 14.5 and indicate that in the cases of food, rent, and

15. Note that the use of implicit price deflators as relative prices may lead to a negative bias in the estimates of the price elasticities. If the consumption of food, for example, is misstated in constant prices but is approximately correct in current prices, then the regression of the dependent variable expressed in constant prices will yield spurious negative correlation with the price deflator. If, however, the food consumption is correct in constant prices but is misstated in current prices, then the price deflator will be high. Since consumption in current prices is nowhere expressed in the equation, error in this latter direction will not offset bias due to any misstatement of consumption in constant terms. See Houthakker (1965a: 280, n. 5).

Also, since we are regressing consumption of particular commodities on total expenditure, which includes that commodity, we expect a positive bias in the expenditure coefficient for those commodities which are a large share of the market basket.

Table 14.2. Commodity Groups Used in this Study

United Nations expenditure accounts categories	Commodity groups
Food Beverages Tobacco	Food
Rent and water charges Fuel and light Household operation	Rent
Personal care and health expenses Recreation and entertainment Miscellaneous services (includes financial services; education and research; other services)	Services
Clothing and other personal effects	Clothing
Transport and communications[a]	Transport
Furniture, furnishings, and household equipment Passenger cars[a]	Durables
Sum of all the above	Total expenditure

[a] The transport category is composed of four items: (a) personal transport equipment; (b) operation of personal transport equipment; (c) purchased transport; and (d) communication. No breakdowns for these items are entered in the published accounts or on the questionnaires, except "passenger cars" in the case of South Africa. See United Nations (1964: 39-41) for further detailed classification of private consumption expenditure.

durables, the elasticities of the within-countries equation are significantly different from the between-countries model.

In comparing the coefficients (Table 14.3) of the within- and between-countries models, we note that only in the case of food is the between-countries expenditure elasticity less than the within-countries coefficient.[16] The rest of the former's expenditure elasticities, especially for rent, clothing, and durables, are greater than the latter's coefficients. This evidence is contrary to Houthakker's hypothesis and findings that the between-countries expenditure elasticity for durables should be lower in the long run than the within-countries elasticity due to a negative stock adjustment effect. On the other hand, Houthakker finds that the former's elasticities for perishable goods, such as food and services, are higher because of the positive effect of habit formation over time.[17]

The dynamic stock adjustment and habit-formation effects appear to operate in the opposite directions for the sample of developing countries. This may be explained by, first, noting that the purchases of durables and housing may be the major form

16. Since the within-countries expenditure coefficients for food are not significantly greater than one, these results should not significantly affect our faith in Engel's law.
17. The explanation appears in Houthakker (1965a: 282–283) and also in Houthakker and Taylor (1966: 8ff).

Table 14.3. Expenditure and Price Elasticities for Pooled Countries

Model	Food Exp.	Food Price	Food Popul.	Rent Exp.	Rent Price	Rent Popul.	Services Exp.	Services Price
(1) Within countries[a]	1.1095	-0.8743		0.4202	-0.3090		0.9974	-0.644
(2) Between countries[b] $\delta_i = 0$	0.8258	-0.4612		0.9454	-0.3213		1.1884	-1.110
(3) Between countries[b] $\delta_i = 0$	0.6413	-0.6404	0.4135	0.7375	-0.2506	0.4427	1.1178	-1.105
(4) Within countries[a]	1.1074	-0.8750	0.0170[c]	0.3930	-0.3103	0.3278	0.9935	-0.643
(5) Within countries[d] (Houthakker, 1965a)	0.351	-0.161		0.029[e]	-0.114		0.755	-0.388
(6) Between countries[f] (Houthakker, 1965a) $\delta_i = 0$	0.744	0.234[e]		1.545	-0.362		0.934	0.455
(7) Between countries[f] (Houthakker, 1965a) with intercept	1.145	0.277	-0.0044[g]	0.753	-0.257	0.0069[e,g]	1.035	0.424

[a] Observations are unweighted.
[b] Observations are weighted by square root of the number of observations in country series.
[c] Not significant at 95 percent level.
[d] Observations are weighted by the square root of population.
[e] Probably not significant at 95 percent level; no t-statistic given.
[f] Observations are weighted by the square root of the product of population and the number of observation in the country series.
[g] Coefficient of intercept.

of personal saving, especially under inflationary conditions. Expenditure on these items can be expected to increase over time as the public comes to rely on this form of accumulation or "hedging," and habit-forming behavior might accurately describe the consumption of durables.[18]

Second, although our model postulates a constant expenditure elasticity over the entire range of countries, there is evidence suggesting that the coefficients themselves are functions of per capita income (Russell 1967: 581). In this case, we might find a lower between- than within-countries elasticity of demand for food, even though the habit-formation model may still be appropriate.

Comparison with European Patterns

How do the absolute values of our estimates for developing economies compare to Houthakker's European elasticities (see Table 14.3)? Only food rent, and clothing are strictly comparable, since our "transport" group draws on expenditure from both the services and durables categories. In comparing the within-countries equations (Table 14.3, lines 4 and 5), we find that for food and rent (necessities, since $\beta_1 < 1$), the developing group yields higher income and price elasticities, while the European

18. In our sample, Korea, Taiwan, and Peru experienced high annual rates of inflation; Thailand and Ceylon experienced "mild" inflation of less than 5 percent per year; and Ecuador, Honduras, Dominican Republic, and Puerto Rico demonstrate price stability. See Dorrance, in Baer and Kerstenetzky (1964: tables 11–13).

Grunwald notes for the Chilean case, in Hirschman (1961: 100), that "nearly all the sectors of the community hedged through the building up of inventories. This applied also to consumer groups, who bought consumer goods for storage rather than for use."

pul.	Clothing			Transport			Durables incl. cars		
	Exp.	Price	Popul.	Exp.	Price	Popul.	Exp.	Price	Popul.
	0.8123	-0.5760		1.3139	-0.4099		0.7993	-0.5037	
	1.0218	-0.8536		1.5884	-0.5972[c]		1.1383	-0.6601[c]	
512[c]	1.2148	-0.9332	-0.4485[c]	1.2864	-0.5379[c]	0.6339[c]	1.6352	-0.9839	-1.1972
441[c]	0.7875	-0.5514	0.2568[c]	1.2738	-0.4062	0.4652[c]	0.9277	-0.5461	-1.3163
	1.574	-0.282					3.919	-0.502	
	0.713	-0.052					1.946	-1.371[e]	
011[e,g]	1.050	-0.476	-0.0064[g]				1.831	-1.397	0.0012[e,g]

sample (United States included) reveals higher expenditure elasticities for clothing and durables. The higher European between-countries elasticities (Table 14.3, lines 3 and 6) for rent may be due to greater market responsiveness in the developed countries. Durables expenditure coefficients for the between-countries form in both samples are similar and greater than unity.

Population

Does population exert an independent influence? In Table 14.6, we test the null hypothesis that population influences consumption only through per capita expenditure, as expressed in equation (14.5). For the within-countries model, we note that the population coefficient $(\beta_1 + \beta_3 - 1)$ is significantly negative for rent and durables, indicating that in the short run, a rise in population (holding per capita expenditure constant) leads to a decrease in per capita consumption. This result is explained by the hypothesis that significant economies of scale in utilization are realized in the consumption of these goods; they are, in a limited, short-run sense, "common goods." Alternatively, a rapidly growing population is on the whole younger and demands less per person of these commodities.

The change from negative to positive in the population elasticity for the rent coefficient in the between-countries model reflects rising housing standards and the liquidation of serious short-term overcrowding characteristic of urban areas in developing countries. The short- and long-run population coefficients for transport are significantly positive and probably reflect an increasingly mobile and urbanized society.

Table 14.4. Goodness of Fit and Standard Error of Estimate Within- and Between-Countries Models with Two and Three Variables[a]

Model	Food	Rent	Service	Clothing	Transport	Durables
(1) Within countries	0.9390	0.2142	0.5189	0.3295	0.4089	0.1575
	(0.0265)	(0.0367)	(0.0415)	(0.0666)	(0.0789)	(0.0863)
(2) Between countries[b]	0.8285	0.5355	0.5365	0.7817	0.3973	0.4992
	(0.0272)	(0.0445)	(0.0538)	(0.0521)	(0.1039)	(0.0831)
(3) Between countries (incl. β_3)[b]	0.8887	0.5776	0.4999	0.7915	0.3888	0.6561
	(0.0219)	(0.0425)	(0.0559)	(0.0509)	(0.1046)	(0.0689)
(4) Within countries (incl. β_3)	0.9356	0.2268	0.5157	0.3273	0.4108	0.2071
	(0.0266)	(0.0364)	(0.0416)	(0.0667)	(0.0787)	(0.0837)

[a]The top number in each group is the coefficient of multiple correlation (R^2) corrected for degrees of freedom. The standard error of estimate for each equation appears beneath in parentheses.
[b]Observations weighted by square root of number of annual observations.

Weighting Schemes

In a double logarithmic regression equation, the assumption that the error term is distributed with constant variance is likely to be less of a problem than is usual in international cross-section studies. There will be no heteroscedasticity problem in the equations fitted here if the size of deviations of consumption from the predicted values tends to be a constant proportion of total consumption across different country sizes in each consumption category.

It may be natural, however, to suppose that widely deviant behavior is more likely for small country statistics than for large country statistics. For example, suppose that the standard deviation about the true worldwide relationship of C_i, measured consumption of the ith individual in any country, is given by $E_i\sigma$, where E_i is the ith individual's total expenditure. Then for a country of population N, made up of individuals with expenditure E_0, the standard error about the true relationship of total consumption is $E_0\sigma \sqrt{N}$. Total consumption itself is, roughly, $E_0^\beta N$, where β is the expenditure elasticity for the category of consumption being dealt with. Hence the standard error of the log of total consumption is approximately $E_0\sigma \sqrt{N}/E_0^\beta N = E_0^{(1-\beta)}/\sqrt{N}$. To get an idea of the effects of this sort of assumption, then, it should be enough to ignore the $E_0^{(1-\beta)}$ term and weight observations by $1/\sqrt{N}$. In our sample, this would give the small countries (Jamaica, Puerto Rico, Honduras, Israel) four times the weight of the large countries.[19]

If we regard the transitory component of income as proportional to the level of

19. Houthakker (1965a: 279) uses per capita consumption expenditure and therefore weights directly by population. Furthermore, Houthakker (1965b: 213) cautions against the undue importance that would be given to numerous small country observations, in the absence of population weights: "That weighting is necessary can also be seen by supposing we had separate figures for each of the fifty states of the U.S.; these would swamp any unweighted mean, but have no particular effect on a weighted mean." Houthakker applies the weights directly to the matrix of sums of squares and cross products rather than directly to the observations.
It should also be noted that weighting per capita expenditure directly by the root of population is equivalent to weighting total expenditure by the inverse of the root of population except for its effect on the price variable.

income, then we would expect the variance of the error of consumption expenditure in the wealthier countries to be larger. Each observation should then be weighted by the square root of the inverse of per capita income. In this scheme, the observations of the poorer countries, regardless of population size, would receive greater importance in the sample.[20]

Houthakker (1965b) employs weights in estimating a direct linear relationship between personal savings and income. However, the application of direct rather than inverted population weights to a double logarithmic function, as in Houthakker (1965a), loses meaning unless we argue that the variance of the error of the growth rate of consumption (the first-differenced logs, which are the variables in our equation) are inversely proportional to country size.[21]

How much do the different weighting schemes influence the estimated parameters? The results of five different weights are presented in Table 14.7. In the first scheme (line 2), it was decided to limit each country series to six central observations rather than "overrepresent" countries with longer annual series.[22] There are no notable differences in the estimates, except in the case of transport price elasticity.

20. Kuznets (1962: 26–27) uses unweighted per capita expenditure to estimate expenditure elasticities, although he does not fit a double logarithmic function.

21. It may make more sense to hypothesize that the variance of the error of the growth rate of durables expenditure, for example, is proportional to the actual growth rate of total expenditure, while the variance of the error of the growth rate of food expenditure may be inversely related to the growth rate of total expenditure. Estimates of the variance of the error of the growth rates can be obtained from the original data and may suggest other hypotheses.

22. To limit the six observations to the same actual years would have eliminated four countries from the sample, since all series do not cover the same period. See Section III for description of the data.

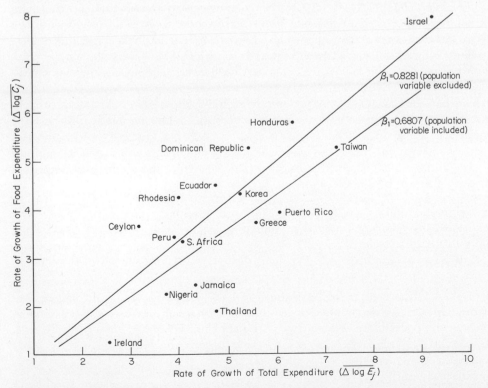

Figure 14.1   International Engel's curve for food expenditure.

Table 14.5. Residual Sum of Squares and Analysis of Covariance for Two and Three Variable Equations of Within- and Between-Countries Models

	d.f.[a]	Food		Rent		Services
		2	3	2	3	2
Residual sum of squares						
(1) Total	162/161	0.12341	0.12353	0.26440	0.23126	0.29675
(2) Within countries	147/146	0.10323	0.10330	0.19799	0.19344	0.25317
(3) Between countries	13/12	0.00692	0.00575	0.02574	0.02167	0.03762
(4) Due to different regressions[b]	2/3	0.01326	0.02774	0.04068	0.01615	0.00596
Mean square						
(5) Separate groups[c]	160/158	0.00069	0.00069	0.00140	0.00136	0.00182
(6) Due to different regressions[d]	2/3	0.00663	0.00924	0.02034	0.00538	0.00298
(7) F-ratio[e]		9.64[g]	13.39[g]	14.55[g]	3.95[f]	1.64

[a]Means "degrees of freedom" in this and other tables in Chapter 14.
[b]Line 1 - (line 2 + line 3).
[c](Line 2 + line 3) ÷ (d.f. for line 2 + line 3).
[d]Line 4 ÷ d.f. for line 4.
[e]Line 6 ÷ line 5.
[f]Significant at 95 percent level.
[g]Significant at 99.5 percent level.

The results of weighting by the inverse of the square root of population are presented on line 4, and the results of weighting directly by the square root of population are presented on line 3. Compared to the unweighted results (line 1), the price elasticities are reduced in absolute terms across most categories. The expenditure elasticities, however, do not appear to be very different from the unweighted case. In the between-countries model as well, the weighting of the observations by population (lines 6 and 7) does not appear to alter coefficients, although no further significance tests were performed.

The between-countries observations, it should be remembered, are themselves derived by averaging the annual country observations. On the assumption that the variance of the error of each of these means is inversely proportional to the number of country observations,[23] each observation is weighted by the square root of the number of observations available for that country (line 8). Again, the coefficients themselves do not appear to be altered by the weights.

The constancy of the regression coefficients is to be expected if the least squares fit to the original data is relatively good and the underlying relationship stable. The application of ordinary least squares to the unweighted data, despite the hypothesized, heteroscedastic error term, results in estimates which are inefficient but nevertheless unbiased.

The influence of weights on the between-countries Engel's curves can be seen in Figures 14.1 (unweighted food expenditure) and 14.2 (weighted by the square root of the number of observations per country). The scale of measurement is extended, and the observations are "rearranged" along the same basic ray. Taiwan and Greece, for example (which have short series), slide toward the origin (relative to other

23. We maintain that the variance of the disturbance of each observation is constant across countries and time.

Clothing		Transport		Durables	
2	3	2	3	2	3
0.69927	0.69707	1.05502	1.02782	1.19815	1.15775
0.65202	0.64953	0.91510	0.90428	1.09481	1.022283
0.03528	0.03108	0.14033	0.13129	0.08977	0.056966
0.01197	0.01646		0.00225	0.01557	0.07851
0.00430	0.00431	0.00660	0.00665	0.00740	0.00683
0.00598	0.00548		0.00075	0.00778	0.02617
1.39	1.27		0.11	1.05	3.83[f]

countries) while the Dominican Republic, Honduras, Puerto Rico, Ecuador, and Korea gain in relative importance.

The expenditure functions for durables are plotted in Figures 14.3 (unweighted) and 14.4 (weighted by the number of observations). Note the change in relative positions of Ireland (which has a long series) and Nigeria (short series). Taiwan and Greece are also reordered relative to the surrounding country observations. Although use of generalized least squares in the between-countries model leaves the regression coefficients still highly significant, tests of other hypotheses are marginally affected.[24]

Country Results

In the following sections, we examine the patterns for individual countries and for various regional groups.

Individual country elasticities are presented in Table 14.8 (South Africa is now included). Measures of goodness of fit appear in Table 14.9.

Glancing first at the arrays of expenditure elasticities, we note that all the significant coefficients are of the correct sign and plausible magnitude. The expenditure elasticities for food are, for the most part, close to unity or noticeably lower in the

24. Firstly, on the basis of an F-test, we concluded (Table 14.3) that the between-countries elasticities for food, rent, and durables, were significantly different from the within-countries elasticities. If we had used the residuals of the unweighted between-countries regressions, then only the rent coefficients would have been significantly different. We would have then concluded that there is no major difference in the short- and long-run elasticities, which is plausible given the shortness of the country series.

Secondly, in our analysis of the impact of population on per capita consumption, we concluded (Table 14.4) that population exerts a significant independent influence only on the consumption of transport and durables in the between-countries model. When the unweighted results are used to test this hypothesis, the independent influence of population is significant in the consumption of rent, services, and clothing as well.

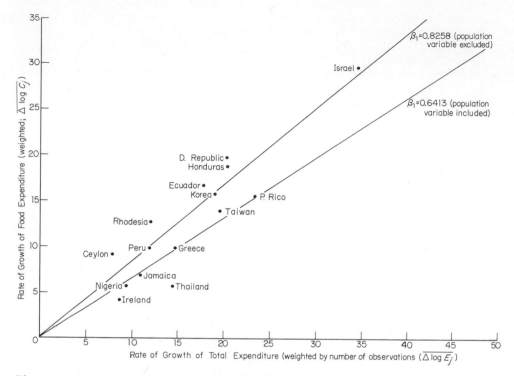

Figure 14.2   Weighted Engel's curve for expenditure.

higher income countries (South Africa, Puerto Rico, Israel, Ireland). Although the "pooled" clothing and service elasticities are less than unity, eight countries indicate higher than unity coefficients for these goods. Expenditure elasticities for transport are greater than unity in five countries and more than twice unity in six others. Expenditure elasticities for durables are unusually high ($\beta_1 > 2$) in seven countries.

It is more difficult to discern patterns in the absolute value of the price elasticities. Four of the significant food price elasticities and six transport price elasticities are greater than unity. Rent coefficients are lower, but this might reflect a "frozen" price variable, due to rent controls in many countries. Six significant service price elasticities are less than one, while only two are greater than unity.

Although these country coefficients should not be given too much importance due to the shortness of the individual time series, the overall significance of the price elasticities does seem to support the hypothesis that relative price is an important variable in determining expenditure patterns in low-income countries.

The variety of country expenditure elasticities for food is sketched in Figure 14.5. Each country slope passes through the cell mean. Note that the mean rate of growth of total expenditure appears on the horizontal axis, not the mean level of income.

The analysis of covariance of the country residuals (Table 14.10) indicates that in three cases we fail to reject the hypothesis that there are no significant differences between the individual country elasticities taken as a group. In the cases of rent, services, and durables, we conclude that pooling of country data is justifiable on the basis of the homogeneous country relationships. For the three other commodities, however, we can reject the null hypothesis. In the cases of food, clothing, and transportation, the heterogeneity of the underlying country functions leads us to question the reliability of the overall coefficients.

Suggesting Causes of Heterogeneity: Sequential Testing

How can the heterogeneity in the underlying country consumption functions be explained for food, clothing, and transport? We suspect that other variables in addition to total expenditure, price, and population have been omitted in the overall, pooled function and that these variables are responsible for the differences in country patterns. In the absence of specific annual values for these omitted variables, we shall divide the sample of countries into groups which are likely, on an a priori basis, to reveal the influence of these variables. The differences between elasticities esti-

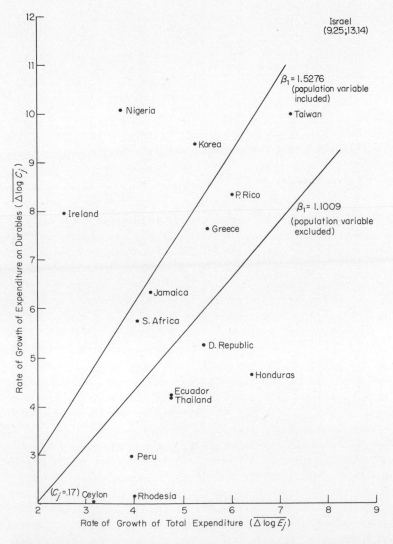

Figure 14.3   International Engel's curve for expenditure on durables.

Table 14.6. The Impact of Population as an Independent Variable

	Food	Rent	Services	Clothing	Transport	Durables
Within-countries						
Population coefficient[a]	0.1244	-0.2792	0.0376	0.0443	0.7390	-1.3886
(Standard error)	(0.1082)	(0.0469)	(0.0640)	(0.0883)	(0.0108)	(0.0917)
t-ratio (147 d.f.)[d]	1.1497	5.9531[b]	0.5875	0.5017	68.4259[b]	15.1429[b]
Between-countries						
Population coefficient	0.0548	0.1802	0.2690	-0.2337	0.9203	-0.5620
(Standard error)	(0.2383)	(0.2672)	(0.3153)	(0.3143)	(0.3950)	(0.3243)
t-ratio (12 d.f.)[d]	0.2300	0.6744	0.8532	0.7435	2.3299[b]	1.7319[c]

[a] $(\beta_1 + \beta_3 - 1.)$

[b] Significant at 97.5 percent level.

[c] Significant at 90 percent level.

[d] t-test where $t = \beta_1 + \beta_3 - 1/[\text{var}\,(\beta_1 + \beta_3)]^{1/2}$ and var $(\beta_1 + \beta_3) = \text{var}\,\beta_1 + \text{var}\,\beta_3 + 2\,\text{cov}\,\beta_1\beta_3$.

Table 14.7. Demand Elasticities: Results of Different Weighting Schemes (two variables, population excluded)

	Food		Rent		Services		Clothing		Transport		Durables	
	Exp.	Price	Exp.	Price	Exp.	Price	Exp.	Price	Exp.	Price	Exp.	Price
Within countries												
(1) No weights	1.1095	-0.8743	0.4202	-0.3090	0.9974	-0.6443	0.8123	-0.5760	1.3139	-0.4099	0.7993	-0.5037
(2) No weights 6 obs./country	0.9637	-0.9671	0.4619	-0.4591	0.8501	-0.6896	0.8649	-0.7101	1.5623	-0.8620	0.8274	-0.6279
(3) Weight $N^{1/2}$	1.1442	-0.8829	0.3725	-0.2972	0.7591	-0.5141	0.7126	-0.6234	0.9384	0.0001[a]	0.3705	-0.1779
(4) Weight $1/N^{1/2}$	1.2550	-0.8321			1.2967	-0.4627	1.0019	-0.2653	1.7421	-0.1534	0.5797	
Between countries												
(5) No weights	0.8281	-0.5440	0.9527	0.4803	1.2068	-1.2399	1.0306	-0.8336	1.5805	-0.4845[a]	1.1009	-0.7988
(6) Weight $N^{1/2}$	0.8611	-0.7474	0.9400	-0.5606	1.2532	-1.3705	1.0357	-0.7163	1.7206	-0.0383[a]	1.0933	-0.9206
(7) Weight $1/N^{1/2}$	0.8126	-0.2692[a]	0.9504	-0.4356	1.1785	-1.0090	1.0183	-0.9870	1.5131	-0.8544[a]	1.1104	-0.6620
(8) Weight $n^{1/2}$	0.8258	-0.4612	0.9454	-0.3213	1.1884	-1.1108	1.0218	-0.8536	1.5884	-0.5972[a]	1.1383	-0.6101[a]

Note: N = population; n = number of observations.
[a]Insignificant at 90 percent level.

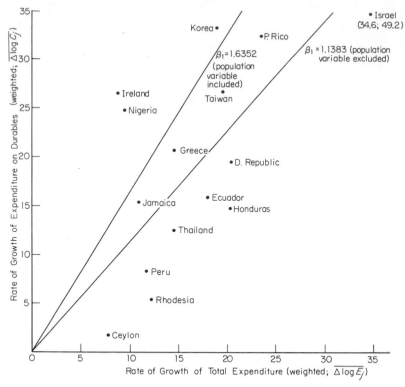

Figure 14.4   Weighted Engel's curve for expenditure on durables.

mated in this way will then be tested against the null hypothesis that both sets of coefficients are similar.

If we reject the null hypothesis of homogeneity between the two sets of coefficients, then we proceed to test whether each of the two groups is itself homogeneous. If we fail to reject the null hypothesis that there are no differences within each group, then we can conclude that by stratifying, we have successfully identified two sets of countries grouped in a meaningful way. If only one of the groups proves to be homogeneous, then we have still identified at least one meaningful division of the sample.

However, after dividing the pool into two groups, we may fail to reject the null hypothesis that there are no differences between the two sets. In this case, we may decide that the a priori division does not reveal any particular quality about the grouping, and it may be argued that there is no point to continue testing for the homogeneity within each of the two groups. Nevertheless, even if the differences between divisions are not significant, we shall proceed to test the homogeneity of each division separately. If one division proves to be homogeneous, then we have in effect acquired additional information defining a subset or "pocket" of similar countries which demonstrates homogenous expenditure behavior.

There is one further possibility to be examined. In the cases of rent, services, and durables in Table 14.10, we conclude that there are no significant differences within the pooled 16 country sample when all are treated symmetrically. Why should we further divide the sample into groups and test for differences between these groups?

Table 14.8. Elasticities for Individual Countries, Within-Countries Model[a]

Country	Size Weight[b]	Food Exp.	Food Price	Rent Exp.	Rent Price	Services Exp.	Services Price	Clothing Exp.	Clothing Price	Transport Exp.	Transport Price	Durables Exp.	Durables Price
Pooled		1.1074[c]	-0.8750[c]	0.3930[c]	-0.3103[c]	0.9935[c]	-0.6438[c]	0.7875[c]	-0.5514[c]	1.2738[c]	-0.4062[c]	0.9277[c]	-0.5461[c]
Nigeria	178	0.9439	0.9583	0.4336[d]	-0.4396	-0.1701	0.0800	1.5063	-0.1904	-0.9658	-0.8367	4.9506	-1.4209
Rhodesia	77	0.7373	-0.1279	0.6529[c]	-0.9104[c]	0.8162	-1.4700	1.1317[c]	0.0221	0.9330[e]	-1.6167[e]	2.2486[c]	-3.5763[c]
South Africa	124	0.5883[c]	0.0176	0.2005[c]	-0.1037[e]	0.5007[c]	0.1759	1.5481[c]	-0.8579[c]	2.2025[c]	-0.6495	3.6395[c]	0.1245
Jamaica	41	0.6901[e]	-1.2277	0.0896	-1.7766[c]	2.1909[c]	-1.3035[c]	1.3920[e]	-3.9917[c]	0.7870	-1.9928[c]	1.4384[d]	-1.4819[c]
Puerto Rico	48	0.4677[c]	-0.2488	0.3334	-0.3848[c]	1.7432[c]	-0.7758[c]	1.2887	1.6139	2.0037[c]	0.1852	2.5648[c]	-0.9667[c]
Honduras	42	0.9181[c]	0.3725	0.0130	0.1325	0.8327[e]	0.2545	2.1241[c]	1.0653[e]	2.2930[c]	-1.3270[c]	0.0557	-0.7230[c]
Ecuador	63	1.4138[c]	7.8312	0.3529	32.2778	0.3852	9.1967	0.3491	-12.1794	5.1198[c]	-24.5210	-0.0770	23.4744[e]
Peru	97	0.9868[c]	-1.0117[c]	1.1313[e]	-0.5782	1.0886[c]	-1.0648[c]	-0.1473	-3.5277[e]	0.8987[c]	-0.9305[c]	0.6969[c]	-0.8174[c]
Dom. Republic	53	0.9367[c]	-6.4505	1.2411[c]	6.0726	1.0220[c]	0.6571	0.6493	0.2014	1.4175[e]	4.0013	1.1892	-0.5557
Thailand	167	0.8350[c]	-1.0270[c]	0.1732[c]	-0.1251[c]	1.0589[c]	-0.9435[c]	2.8886[c]	-3.1748[c]	1.5590[c]	-0.8587[c]	0.3933	-0.6888
Ceylon	102	0.9338[c]	-2.3840[c]	-0.1541	5.7324	0.6894	-2.2737	2.6197[c]	0.2597	1.6175[c]	-2.4805[e]	0.2818	4.9572
Korea	158	0.9319[c]	-0.1625	0.2595	-0.3565[c]	1.7206[c]	-0.3399[e]	1.1954	0.2165	2.6211[c]	-0.2168[c]	2.0040[e]	0.2882
Israel	45	0.2482	-1.0662[c]	0.0921	0.0521	1.1562[c]	-0.8333[c]	0.1257	0.3348	1.1238[e]	1.0258	2.4714[c]	0.0248
Taiwan	106	1.1900[c]	-0.0367	0.1624	0.1442	0.1044	0.2024	0.6773[c]	0.1413	5.7243[c]	-0.5850[c]	0.7852	-0.3505
Greece	92	1.1761[c]	0.4124	0.2858	-0.3204	0.3929[d]	-0.9350[e]	3.0535[e]	0.8278	1.4724[c]	0.4139	5.7952[c]	-4.0567[c]
Ireland	53	0.6166[c]	0.1568[e]	0.7007[c]	-0.2491[c]	1.2452[c]	-0.3339[c]	1.6106[c]	0.2323			2.6048[c]	0.1371

[a] Population coefficients are omitted in this table. South Africa excluded in pooled category.
[b] Weights are not used in these estimates. Weight is the square root of mean population.
[c] Indicates significance at 95 percent level.
[d] Population variable is excluded from this equation.
[e] Indicates significance at 90 percent level.

Table 14.9. Goodness of Fit and Standard Error of Estimate: Elasticities for Individual Countries, Within-Countries Model[a]

	Code	Food	Rent	Services	Clothing	Transport	Durables
Pooled[b]		0.9356 (0.0266)	0.2268 (0.0364)	0.5157 (0.0416)	0.3273 (0.0667)	0.4108 (0.0787)	0.2071 (0.0837)
Nigeria	6	0.6351 (0.0185)	(0.0725)[c]	(0.0716)	0.3428 (0.1393)	(0.0536)	(0.2701)
Rhodesia	7	0.5808 (0.0182)	0.5707 (0.0213)	0.3171 (0.0456)	0.7876 (0.0201)	0.3268 (0.0502)	0.7016 (0.0665)
South Africa	9	0.4469 (0.0111)	0.2540 (0.0055)	0.4093 (0.0108)	0.5069 (0.0306)	0.6211 (0.0364)	0.5959 (0.0555)
Jamaica	23	0.4570 (0.0261)	0.6334 (0.0361)	0.8902 (0.0143)	0.5845 (0.0547)	0.5453 (0.0696)	0.4543[c] (0.0797)
Puerto Rico	24	0.2709 (0.0262)	0.6765 (0.0128)	0.5588 (0.0483)	0.4176 (0.0355)	0.3688 (0.0507)	0.5180 (0.0414)
Honduras	27	0.9519 (0.0166)	0.7648 (0.0246)	0.8298 (0.0553)	0.7126 (0.0599)	0.8512 (0.0648)	0.1706 (0.0734)
Ecuador	34	0.6827 (0.0172)	(0.0506)	(0.0333)	0.5453 (0.0234)	(0.1378)	(0.0705)
Peru	42	0.9999 (0.0002)	0.5402 (0.0289)	0.9842 (0.0071)	(0.0890)	0.9793 (0.0072)	0.8125 (0.0212)
Dominican Republic	45	0.0767 (0.0354)	0.0015 (0.0564)	0.0485 (0.0423)	(0.0619)	(0.0909)	(0.0843)

Table 14.9 (*continued*)

	Code	Food	Rent	Services	Clothing	Transport	Durables
Thailand	51	0.9990	0.5831	0.5417	0.7954	0.7450	0.0012
		(0.0127)	(0.0038)	(0.0254)	(0.0373)	(0.0852)	(0.0712)
Ceylon	53	0.9698		0.1588	0.9179	0.0611	
		(0.0071)	(0.0388)	(0.0321)	(0.0378)	(0.0793)	(0.1642)
Korea	54	0.3307	0.1408	0.2195	0.3545	0.4708	0.1198
		(0.0268)	(0.0532)	(0.0676)	(0.0766)	(0.0750)	(0.1047)
Israel	56	0.7931		0.5439	0.3470	0.4760	0.5417
		(0.0125)	(0.0157)	(0.0192)	(0.0698)	(0.0590)	(0.0537)
Taiwan	67	0.8091			0.6993	0.9713	
		(0.0152)	(0.0758)	(0.0523)	(0.0254)	(0.02171)	(0.0452)
Greece	71	0.0358	0.3525	0.2176	0.2119	0.4436	0.8250
		(0.0202)	(0.0143)	(0.0286)[c]	(0.0476)	(0.0188)	(0.0267)
Ireland	87	0.7932	0.7778	0.8427	0.3253		0.4818
		(0.0081)	(0.0137)	(0.0153)	(0.0471)		(0.0534)

[a] The top number in each group is the coefficient of multiple correlation (R^2) corrected for d.f. The standard error of estimate for each equation appears beneath in parentheses. The population variable was included in each equation as in Table 14.8.

[b] Excludes South Africa.

[c] Population variable excluded from this equation.

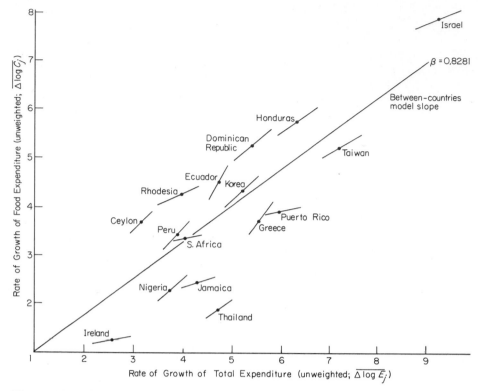

Figure 14.5   Engel's curves for food expenditure by country.

The testing of a more specific, alternative hypothesis of differences by groups may allow us to reject the null hypothesis of homogeneity, even though the same null hypothesis had not been rejected earlier against a broader alternative. Further findings of significant differences between groups provide us with information about homogeneous subdivisions or "uniform swirls" within the sample, which are submerged in the broader currents of the averaging process.

Suggesting Causes of Heterogeneity: Life-Style and Geographical Patterns

Three major divisions within the 16 country sample will be carried out. The first division, according to "life-style" groups, separates those countries exposed to greater "European" influence from the typical "developing" nation. The former include Rhodesia (since rural African consumption is excluded in the accounts), South Africa, Israel, Greece, and Ireland. These countries also have the highest levels of per capita consumption. The second major division of the pooled sample is made according to continent. The geographical distribution of observations is so uneven, however, that only two continental patterns, for Latin America (62 observations) and Asia (36 observations), could be isolated. The third classification of the countries is formed by pooling "island" and "continental" countries.

In Table 14.11, the coefficients for the different groups of countries are presented for the three-variable model. The measure of the goodness of fit and the corresponding standard error follow in Table 14.12. The sequential steps for testing the life-style grouping are presented in Tables 14.13 through 14.15. In Table 14.13, we are testing

Table 14.10. Analysis of Covariance on Within-Countries Regressions for Individual Countries and Pooled (test for homogeneity of regression coefficients of three-variable model)

	d.f.	Food	Rent	Services	Clothing	Transport	Durables
Residual sum of squares							
(1) Pooled[a]	162	0.11290	0.19506	0.25920	0.66770	0.93571	1.12950
(2) Individual countries	117	0.04697	0.15183	0.18535	0.35936	0.58060	0.81140
(3) Due to different regressions	45	0.06592	0.04322	0.07384	0.30833	0.35511	0.31809
Mean square							
(4) Individual countries		0.00040	0.00129	0.00158	0.00307	0.00496	0.00693
(5) Due to different regressions		0.00146	0.00096	0.00164	0.00685	0.00789	0.00706
(6) F-ratio (45, 117 d.f.)[b]		3.651[c]	0.740	1.036	2.231[c]	1.591[d]	1.019

[a] Includes South Africa.
[b] Line 5 ÷ line 4.
[c] Significant at 99.5 percent level.
[d] Significant at 95 percent level.

Table 14.11. Elasticities for Regional Groups of Within-Countries Model[a] (for three variables; population excluded from this table)

Groups	Food		Rent		Services		Clothing		Transport		Durables	
	Exp.	Price	Exp.	Price	Exp.	Price	Exp.	Price	Exp.	Price	Exp.	Price
(a) Pooled[b]	1.0985	-0.8699	0.3877	-0.3071	0.9749	-0.6277	0.8052	-0.5569	1.2936	-0.4074	0.9791	-0.5089
Life-style groups												
(b) Developing	1.1964	-0.8591	0.3205	-0.3085	0.9717	-0.6459	0.6416	-0.5156	1.3101	-0.3955	0.8075	-0.6353
(c) European[b]	0.7045	-0.1024	0.5058	-0.2331	0.9328	-0.3814	1.3499	1.0275[c]	0.9800	-1.0123	2.7082	-0.0475[c]
Continental groups												
(d) Latin American	0.9305	-0.2269[c]	0.4972	-0.3210[c]	1.0336	-0.8264	0.9429	-0.0341[c]	1.9544	-0.6831[c]	0.7474	-0.6228
(e) Asian	1.0668	-0.9273	0.2791[c]	-0.2796	0.6183	-0.4317	0.6356[c]	-0.5098	1.0746	-0.3561	0.5798[c]	-0.5158[c]
Boundary groups												
(f) Island	0.8072	-0.2399[c]	0.4289[c]	-0.3671	1.0828	-0.7034	1.5027	-0.4660[c]	1.8708	-0.8591	1.7887	-0.6005
(g) Continental[d]	1.1946	-0.8676	0.3687	-0.2887	0.9705	-0.6230	0.6309	-0.5612	1.1717	-0.3868	0.7410	-0.5522

[a] *Boxed-in coefficients* in line (a) indicate that hypothesis of pooled sample homogeneity is not rejected at 95 percent level of significance; *boxed-in coefficients* in other lines indicate that hypothesis of sample homogeneity is not rejected at 95 percent level of significance provided that pooled sample homogeneity of line (a) was rejected at 95 percent level; *brackets* surrounding pair of coefficients indicate hypothesis of homogeneity between the two samples is rejected at the 95 percent level of significance; *underlined coefficients* indicate that hypothesis of sample homogeneity is not rejected at 95 percent level provided that pooled sample homogeneity of line (a) was also not rejected at 95 percent level.

[b] European countries are 7, 9, 56, 71, 87.

[c] Insignificant at 99 percent level.

[d] Excludes South Africa.

Table 14.12. Goodness of Fit and Standard Errors: Elasticities for Regional Groups of Within-Countries Model (corrected R-squared for three-variable model)

Groups	d.f.	Food	Rent	Services	Clothing	Transport	Durables
(a) Pooled[a]	162	0.9298 (0.0264)	0.2275 (0.0347)	0.5079 (0.0400)	0.3307 (0.0642)	0.4138 (0.0760)	0.2002 (0.0835)
Life-style							
(b) Developing	107	0.9470 (0.0279)	0.2196 (0.0406)	0.4980 (0.0464)	0.3594 (0.0693)	0.4078 (0.0884)	0.2107 (0.0855)
(c) European 7, 9, 56, 71, 87	52	0.6224 (0.0134)	0.5877 (0.0135)	0.5556 (0.0227)	0.3263 (0.0487)	0.4500 (0.0417)	0.5657 (0.0576)
Continental							
(d) Latin American 24, 27, 34, 42, 45	59	0.7166 (0.0228)	0.2503 (0.0384)	0.6884 (0.0414)	0.3157 (0.0563)	0.4496 (0.0817)	0.1935 (0.0619)
(e) Asian 51, 53, 54, 67	33	0.9761 (0.0314)	0.1181 (0.0413)	0.2632 (0.0465)	0.1614 (0.0859)	0.3618 (0.1049)	0.0893 (0.0977)
Boundary							
(f) Island	57	0.5023 (0.0231)	0.1616 (0.0391)	0.4726 (0.0364)	0.3271 (0.0571)	0.3468 (0.0699)	0.2575 (0.0739)
(g) Continental[b]	86	0.9627 (0.0257)	0.2414 (0.0353)	0.5175 (0.0455)	0.3511 (0.0712)	0.4448 (0.0836)	0.2106 (0.0882)

[a] Includes South Africa.
[b] Excludes South Africa.

Table 14.13.   Analysis of Covariance: Elasticities for Life-Style Groups (three variable regressions)

	d.f.	Food	Rent	Services	Clothing	Transport	Durables
Residual sum of squares							
(1) Total[a]	162	0.11290	0.19506	0.25920	0.66770	0.93571	1.12950
(2) Developing	107	0.08328	0.17637	0.23036	0.51386	0.83615	0.78219
(3) European	52	0.00933	0.00947	0.02679	0.12332	0.09042	0.17252
(4) Due to different regressions	3	0.02028	0.00921	0.00203	0.03051	0.00913	0.17478
Mean square							
(5) Separate regressions[b]		0.00058	0.00117	0.00162	0.00401	0.00583	0.00600
(6) Due to different regressions		0.00676	0.00307	0.00067	0.01017	0.00304	0.05826
(7) F-ratio (3, 159 d.f.)[c]		11.62[d]	2.63[e]	0.41	2.54[e]	0.52	9.70[d]

[a] Includes South Africa.
[b] (Lines 2 + 3) ÷ Σ d.f. of lines 2 + 3.
[c] Line 6 ÷ line 5.
[d] Significant at 99.5 percent level.
[e] Significant at 90 percent level.

for significant differences between the coefficients estimated from the developing-country sample against the coefficients estimated from the European sample. In Table 14.14, we proceed to test for homogeneity within the developing-country sample, and in Table 14.15, we test for homogeneity within the European-country sample. The sequence of these tests has also been performed for the two other sub-divisions, and the values of the respective F-tests appear in Table 14.16. The findings of these sequential tests are summarized in Table 14.11 by means of brackets, boxes, and underlines of the original coefficients.

Proceeding first in the case of the first major subdivision between developing and European countries, we conclude from the highly significant F-ratios in Table 14.13 that we have identified differences between the coefficients for foods and durables. This is also shown in Table 14.11 by means of brackets around the food and durables coefficients for the life-style groups. Differences between the group coefficients for rent and clothing are significant only at the 90 percent level. We conclude from this test that the developing countries exhibit higher expenditure and price elasticities for food, while the European sample exhibit higher expenditure elasticity for durables and, marginally, for rent and clothing than in the developing countries.

However, can we be sure that each of these groups itself is homogeneous? From the values of the F-ratio given in line 6 of Table 14.14, we reject the null hypothesis and decide that there are differences within the developing-countries subgroup in the cases of food, clothing, and transport. Thus, we conclude that, first, the stratification into a developing-countries sample still leaves the heterogeneity in the consumption of food and clothing of the overall sample unexplained. Second, the test suggests that this grouping is inappropriate for the estimation of the transport equation.

Turning to tests for the homogeneity for the European sample, we find quite different results (Table 14.15). First, we conclude that the null hypothesis of homogeneity within the sample of European countries (for any commodity) cannot be rejected. The European classification has captured some of the heterogeneity of the overall pool, especially in the cases of food and clothing. Third, the finding of homogeneity for the transport function contrasts with the finding of heterogeneity of the developing-country subgroup (Table 14.14). We conclude that it is the underlying inconsistency of the transport pattern among the developing countries that may cause the overall heterogeneity for the general 16 country sample.

The significance of differences in the coefficients between continental groups is tested by means of the F-values presented in Table 14.16; the results are summarized by means of brackets and boxes around the relevant coefficients in Table 14.11. We conclude that the elasticities for food in Latin America are significantly lower and more homogeneous than the elasticities estimated from Asian data. The rent elasticities are also significantly higher and homogeneous, while the elasticities for clothing and transport, although not significantly different from their Asian counterparts, do not lead us to reject the null hypothesis that there are no differences between the Latin American countries.

The outcome of the final classification of the countries into a group of islands and continental countries is summarized in lines f and g of Table 14.16 and indicated in Table 14.11, lines f and g. We conclude, first, that the food elasticities for the islands are significantly lower than the elasticities for the continental countries and form a homogeneous subsample. Second, in the case of the transport elasticities, we cannot reject the null hypothesis that there are no differences within each of the

Table 14.14. Analysis of Covariance: Elasticities for Life-Style Groups; Test of Homogeneity for Developing-Countries[a] Subgroup

	d.f.	Food	Rent	Services	Clothing	Transport	Durables
Residual sum of squares							
(1) Developing	107	0.08328	0.17637	0.23036	0.51386	0.83615	0.78219
(2) Individual countries	77	0.03983	0.15121	0.16522	0.27411	0.51551	0.69273
(3) Due to different regressions	30	0.04345	0.02516	0.06514	0.23975	0.32064	0.08946
Mean square							
(4) Individual countries		0.000517	0.001964	0.00214	0.00356	0.00669	0.00900
(5) Due to different regressions		0.001448	0.000839	0.00217	0.00799	0.01069	0.00298
(6) F-ratio (30, 77)[b]		2.80[c]	0.43	1.01	2.24[c]	1.60[d]	0.33

[a] Developing countries include 6, 23, 24, 27, 34, 42, 45, 51, 53, 54, 67.
[b] Line 5 ÷ line 6.
[c] Significant at 99.5 percent level.
[d] Significant at 95 percent level.

Table 14.15. Analysis of Covariance: Life-Style Groups; Test of Homogeneity for European-Countries[a] Subgroup

	d.f.	Food	Rent	Services	Clothing	Transport	Durables
Residual sum of squares							
(1) European	52	0.00933	0.00947	0.02679	0.12332	0.09042	0.17252
(2) Individual countries	40	0.00715	0.00765	0.02246	0.08526	0.06509	0.11819
(3) Due to different regressions	12	0.00218	0.00182	0.00433	0.03806	0.02533	0.05433
Mean square							
(4) Individual countries		0.0001788	0.000191	0.000562	0.002132	0.00163	0.00295
(5) Due to different regressions		0.0001817	0.000152	0.000361	0.003172	0.00211	0.00453
(6) F-ratio (12, 40)[b]		1.02	0.80	0.64	1.49	1.29	1.54

[a] 7, 9, 56, 71, 87.
[b] Line 5 ÷ line 4.

Table 14.16. Summary of Analysis of Covariance: *F*-Ratios for Homogeneity Tests within each Regional Group

Groups	d.f.	Food	Rent	Services	Clothing	Transport	Durables
(a) Pooled[a]	(45,117)	3.65[b]	0.74	1.04	2.23[b]	1.59[c]	1.02
Life-style	(3,159)	11.62[b]	2.63[d]	0.41	2.54[d]	0.52	9.70[b]
(b) Developing	(30,77)	2.80[b]	0.43	1.01	2.24[b]	1.60[c]	0.33
(c) European	(12,40)	1.02	0.80	0.64	1.49	1.29	1.54
Continental	(3,92)	9.72[b]	6.41[b]	2.03		0.58	
(d) Latin American	(12,47)	0.45	0.68	0.76	1.65	0.32	0.54
(e) Asian	(9,24)	6.68[b]		0.28	5.95[b]	4.90[b]	0.61
Boundary	(3,143)	8.80[b]			2.13[d]	1.32	2.07
(f) Island	(15,42)	0.51	0.62	0.44	2.84[c]	1.94[d]	0.60
(g) Continental[e]	(24,62)	4.88[b]	0.60	1.22	1.83[c]	1.31	0.78

[a] Includes South Africa.
[b] Significant at 99.5 percent level.
[c] Significant at 95 percent level.
[d] Significant at 90 percent level.
[e] Excludes South Africa.

two subdivisions. However, the differences between these two sets of transport coefficients are not significant.

It is difficult to explain the consumption patterns between these last two groups of countries. Continental countries (Nigeria, Rhodesia, Honduras, Ecuador, Peru, Thailand, Korea, Greece, and Israel, which perhaps may be shifted to the island group) typically are self-sufficient providers of food and hence may experience more variation in their food prices which are subject to local rather than international fluctuations. Islands (Jamaica, Puerto Rico, Dominican Republic, Ceylon, Taiwan, Ireland) import larger portions of their food supply at stable and perhaps lower relative prices. The continental countries are typically rural and less densely populated. Therefore, we expect rural food consumption to increase faster with rising incomes than food consumption on the islands.[25] The greater urban concentration and density of the islands may also be a factor in explaining the higher expenditure elasticities for clothing and durables.[26] Further speculation on these phenomena is left to the reader.[27]

V. Conclusions

To summarize some of the empirical findings in this study, we have found, first, that pooling time series data for 15 developing countries yields significant estimates of expenditure and price elasticities for six categories of goods; these estimates distinguish different consumption patterns between the short run (annual) and the long run (7–15 years).

Expenditure Elasticities

In the short run, as indicated in the within-countries model, the expenditure elasticities for food and transport are greater than unity ($\beta_{1w} = 1.11$, $\beta_{5w} = 1.27$), while the elasticities for rent (0.39), services (0.99), clothing (0.79), and durables (0.93) are all less than unity. In the long run, as indicated in the between-countries model, food (0.64) and rent (0.74) may be classified as necessities, while services (1.12), clothing (1.21), transport (1.29), and durables (1.64) are luxuries with elasticities greater than unity (see Table 14.3).

The expenditure elasticities for both rent and durables increase from the short to the long run (Table 14.3). This may be due to the effect of positive habit formation and the increasing use of these goods as forms of saving. The fall in expenditure elasticity for food over time may indicate a growing "satisfaction" with consumption levels of this good.

The partitioning of our own sample into European and developing countries (Tables 14.11, 14.13) indicates significantly lower expenditure elasticities for food and

25. Edmundo Flores (1959) suggests this in the case of Mexico.
26. Budget studies for Sudan, India, and Mexico suggest higher income elasticities in rural areas for food, clothing, and miscellaneous goods but lower income elasticities for housing and transport than in the urban areas. The evidence, however, is by no means unanimous. See articles by J. Roy, G. G. Laha, Ashok Rudra, and Bina Roy in Indian Statistical Institute (1960: 13, 14, 33, 64); also National Council of Applied Economic Research, *Long-Term Projections of Demand and Supply of Selected Agricultural Commodities*, New Delhi (1962: 209, 213).
27. See Barrie (1914).

higher elasticities for durables and, marginally, for clothing among the European group in the short run. When we compare our pooled results to Houthakker's all-European coefficients (Table 14.3), we note a similar short-run effect: a lower elasticity for food and a higher elasticity for clothing in the European countries. We conclude that the level of income itself is an important factor in determining demand elasticities.

It was also found that the more densely populated, urbanized islands in the sample yield a lower expenditure elasticity for food and marginally higher elasticity for clothing than the land-extensive countries (Tables 14.11, 14.16).

Price Elasticities

Our findings emphasize the importance of price elasticities in determining expenditure patterns in developing countries. For every commodity, the price elasticity of demand is significantly different from zero (Table 14.3). Only the long-run demand elasticity for services is greater than unity ($\beta_{2b} = -1.11$). The price elasticities rise in absolute value from the short to the long run for clothing (-0.55 to -0.93), transport (-0.41 to -0.54), and durables (-0.55 to -0.98), while the price elasticity for food declines from -0.88 in the short run to -0.64 in the long run.

In many individual countries (Tables 14.8, 14.9, 14.10), the demand for food, transport, and clothing is extremely elastic with respect to price. We expect that even slight declines in relative price of these goods will result in large surges of demand for these commodities.

Price Elasticities and the Structuralist Model

Our estimates indicate that substitution does occur between all the broad groups of commodities. The findings give little support to the structuralist contention that price adjustments are unlikely to reduce excess demand. The pooled results indicate that if per capita expenditure increases 2 percent in one year, then a 2.5 percent rise in the relative price of food will leave per capita demand for food unchanged. Using our long-run estimates, we conclude that over a longer period, little rise in per capita demand for food will occur if the percentage increase in per capita expenditure is matched by an equal percentage increase in relative price. Even in the case of the higher expenditure elasticity for transport, the short-run increase in demand which results from a 2 percent rise in expenditure can be offset by a rise in relative price of 6 percent, assuming constant population.

Although the estimates of price elasticities found in this study are *not* consistent with the extremely low values hypothesized by the structuralists, our coefficients do support an alternative explanation of the persistent excess demand for consumer goods, which is the central phenomenon of structuralist attention.

Our explanation is based on a behavior of government policy that may attempt to freeze certain prices, especially food and transport prices, in an effort to maintain the value of workers' real wages. This well-intended action, guided perhaps by the structuralist assumption of near-zero price elasticity and supported by the subsidized imports in the case of foodstuffs, leads rather to a decline in the relative price of these goods, if the prices of other commodities are permitted to rise. This fall in relative price strengthens the demand for the price-frozen commodities, and reinforces, rather than offsets, the elastic demand due to rising incomes.

Population

The elasticities estimated in this study measure the influence of a change in per capita total expenditure and price on per capita consumption of the commodity. We have shown, moreover, that population growth has an independent and significant influence on per capita consumption (Table 14.6). In the short run, population growth leads to a decrease in per capita consumption of durables and rent, indicating both a more intensive utilization and the influence of a younger age distribution. In the long run, population growth exerts a positive impact on rent and transport expenditures, indicating rising standards in the case of rent and increased mobility in the case of transport.

Heterogeneity of Underlying Country Patterns

In analyzing the results of the individual country data (Table 14.8), we found initially that the overall pooled functions proved to be an acceptable summary representation of the underlying country patterns for expenditure on rent, services, and durables (Table 14.10). We conclude that rather than rely on statistically unacceptable estimates of elasticities for an individual country, we are justified in pooling multinational data and in "borrowing" elasticities for these commodities from these pooled results in the absence of more extensive country information. However, the significant differences between demand elasticities estimated from various subgroups of countries suggest that other factors have been omitted from the expenditure relationship. We have hypothesized that the absolute level of income, country size, population density, and "national" tastes account for the heterogeneous demand patterns and that the various groupings of countries are acting as proxies for the effects of these variables.

In the cases of food, clothing, and transport we found that the overall pooled sample was composed of subgroups which differed significantly for one another. In attempting to identify these subgroupings of countries, we found that each of the separate divisions of the European, Latin American, and island-nations yielded elasticities which are lower in value than the pooled elasticities and that also indicate acceptable within-group homogeneity. In the cases of clothing and transport, the grouping of European and Latin American countries and the island-continental division for transport alone also resulted in samples which indicate sufficient underlying homogeneity to justify borrowing these elasticities in the absence of specific country information.

Comparisons to Other Consumption Studies

Are our elasticities comparable to the results of other international studies? The reader may contrast these pooled results with elasticities calculated from other studies of time series and budget data (Table 14.17). In Table 14.18, we summarize the array of information gathered in Table 14.17. If we assume that our long-run between-countries coefficients are drawn from a normally distributed sample of "universal" elasticities, then we expect other estimates of the same parameters also to fall within an established interval. In lines 1 and 2 of Table 14.18, we set 99 percent confidence intervals around the between-countries parameters. Using a simple arithmetic mean to summarize the expenditure elasticities of the three *other* inter-

Table 14.17. Comparison of Elasticities from Many Sources*

	(1) Food		(2) Rent		(3) Services		(4) Clothing		(5) Transport		(6) Durables	
	Exp.	Price	Exp.	Price	Exp.	Price	Exp.	Price	Exp.	Price	Exp.	Price
Between countries (Table 14.1)	0.64	-0.64	0.74	-0.25	1.12	-1.11	1.21	-0.93	1.29	-0.54	1.64	-0.98
(1) All	0.75[a]		1.04[a]		1.36[a]		1.22[a]				1.81[a]	
(2) All	0.6[a]		0.8[a]		1.81		1.24[a]					
(3) All	0.49[a]		1.19[a]				1.25[a]					
	1.17											
Within countries (Table 14.1)	1.11	-0.88	0.39	-0.31	0.99	-0.64	0.79	-0.55	1.27	-0.41	0.93	-0.55
(4) Peru	0.75[a]	0.26	0.96[a]	0.45			1.15[a]	-0.51[b]			1.80[a]	0.05
(5) Sweden	0.39	-0.12[a]	0.11	-0.04[a]	1.33[a]	-0.61[b]			3.34	-2.20	1.47[a]	-0.62[b]
					0.43	-0.04						
					0.81	-0.50						
(6) Norway	0.79[a]	-0.54[a]	0.89[a]	-0.50[a]	1.18[b]	-0.68[b]	1.01[b]	-0.62[b]	2.04[a]	-1.07[a]	1.81[a]	-0.96[a]
(7) Greece	0.73[a]	-0.56[a]	1.67	-0.86	1.20[b]	-0.73[b]	0.93[b]	-0.54[b]			1.34[b]	-0.70[b]
(8) Greece	0.73[a]	-0.34[a]	1.67	-0.12[a]	-1.28	-0.94[a]	1.17[a]	-0.88[a]			1.80[a]	-1.13[a]
(9) Greece	0.54[a]	0.41			1.36[a]	-0.94[a]	1.13[b]	0.83	2.76		1.47[a]	
(10) Greece	1.18[b]	-0.39[a]	0.29[b]	-0.32[b]	0.39		3.05	-0.24	1.47[b]	-0.41[b]	5.80	-4.06
(11) Ireland	0.73[a]	0.16	0.93[a]	-0.25[b]	1.06[b]	-0.56[b]	0.76[b]	0.23			2.40	-0.63[b]
(12) Ireland	0.62[a]		0.70[a]	-0.25[b]	1.26	-0.33[a]	1.61[a]				2.60	-0.13
(13) Chile (1962)	0.73[a]	-1.07[a]										
(14) Chile (1965): Santiago only	0.45[a]	-0.45[a]			1.30[a]	-1.30[a]	1.11[b]	-0.99[a]			1.40[a]	-1.21[a]
(15) Nigeria (1966)	0.94[b]		0.85[a]				0.97[b]		1.67[b]		4.43	
(16) Argentina (1963) budgets	0.50[a]		0.75[a]		1.87		0.98[b]		0.89[b]		2.13[a]	
(17) Sudan (Urban budgets)	0.76[a]		1.02[a]				1.09[b]		2.55			
(Rural budgets)	0.84[a]		0.75[a]				1.14[b]		1.54[b]			
(18) India (1960) (Urban budgets)	0.86[a]				1.44[a]		1.39[a]					
(Rural budgets)	0.82[a]				1.72		1.38[a]					
(19) Pakistan (budgets)	0.8[a]		0.8[a]		1.5[a]		1.2[a]					
(20) Israel	0.25	-1.07[a]	0.09				0.13		1.12[b]	-1.03[a]	2.47	-0.02
(21) Israel – Time series	0.64[a]	-0.63[a]			1.16[b]	-0.83[b]						

Table 14.17 (continued)

	Food		Rent		Services		Clothing		Transport		Durables	
	Exp.	Price	Exp.	Price	Exp.	Price	Exp.	Price	Exp.	Price	Exp.	Price
(22a) Israel (All budgets)	0.52[a]		0.98[a]		1.84		1.10[b]				2.04[a]	
(b) Asian origin 56/57	0.58		0.77		2.00		1.53[a]				1.51[a]	
(c) European origin	0.52		0.78		1.22		1.42[a]				2.31[a]	
(23a) Israel (All budgets)	0.51[a]		0.77[a]		1.32[a]		1.37[a]				1.41[b]	
(b) Asian origin 59/60	0.58		0.57		2.09		1.31				1.73[a]	
(c) European origin	0.46		0.86		0.98		1.32				1.00[b]	
(d) Israeli origin	0.55		0.61		2.13		1.77				0.32	
(24) Other budgets												
(a) Sweden	0.53[a]						1.15[a]					
(b) Greece	0.70[a]						1.40[a]					
(c) Ireland	0.62[a]						1.39[a]					
(25) Mexico												
(All budgets, 1963)	0.81[a]		1.20[a]				0.69[b]				2.11[a]	
Urban	0.81		1.13				0.69				1.80	
Rural	0.83		1.06				0.66				3.85	

* Where expenditure categories in the studies listed have differed substantially from those of this paper, the titles of the categories have been listed in the accompanying notes with the numbers of columns in which they are displayed.

[a] Value falls in 99 percent confidence interval around between countries estimates. See Table 14.18, lines 1 and 2, for intervals.

[b] Value falls in 99 percent confidence interval around within countries estimates. See Table 14.18, lines 4 and 5, for intervals.

Sources: Row (1) Watanabe (1962). (2) Houthakker (1957). (3) Kuznets (1962: 27): (1) food; also alcoholic beverages and tobacco; (2) housing; (3) other; (4) clothing. (4) M. Gilbert, reported in Watanabe (1962). (5) Parks (1969: tables 7 and 8, line 3): (1) agriculture; (2) housing; (3) commerce, domestic services, public services; (6) manufacturing. (6) Johansen (1964: tables 6.3.2:1 and 6.4.2:1): (2) dwelling; (4) textiles; (5) land transport; (6) wood. (7) Goldberger (1966: table 5). (8) Houthakker (1965a: 286). (9) Nugent (1966: appendix C, table 4.34): (1) agriculture; (4) clothing and footwear; (5) transport equipment; (6) manufacturing. (10) Table 14.9. (11) Goldberger (1966). (12) Table 14.9. (13) D'Acuna (1964). (14) Dillon and Powell (1965: 34). (15) Clark (1967: table III-16): (1) food, drink; (2) house rent; (4) craft weave; (5) transportation; (6) metal furniture. (16) OAS (1963: chap. VI). From budget studies. Coefficients are income, not expenditure, elasticities. (17) FAO (1960: 60–61). (18) Roy and Laha (1960: tables 1 and 2). (19) Md. I. Khan (1963) and Rahman (1963: 237). (20) Table 14.9. (21) Mundlak (1964: table 37). Coefficients are income elasticities. (22,a) From Liviatan (1964: table 1): (1) total food; (2) maintenance (of household); (3) health, education, and literary expenditures; (4) clothing and footwear; (6) durables. (22,b and c)—budgets classified by continent of origin of immigrant household heads—from Liviatan (1964: tables 18 and 28): the first for food, the second for (2) maintenance; (3) education only; (4) clothing, excluding footwear; (6) durables. (23) Landsberger (1965: appendix A, tables 2 and 3): (1) total food; (2) housing maintenance; (3) education only; (4) clothing, excluding footwear; (6) durables. (24, a) From Wold and Jureen (1952: 25). (24, b and c) From Goreux (1959: 36–37). (25) Banco de Mexico (1966: Table 32): (1) food, drink, tobacco; (2) housing, light, and other services; (4) clothing and footwear; (6) vehicles, furniture, and household appliances.

Table 14.18. Summary Comparison of Elasticities: Averages of Many Sources Compared to Confidence Limits Around Pooled Estimates[a]

	Food		Rent		Services		Clothing		Transport		Durables	
	Exp.	Price	Exp.	Price	Exp.	Price	Exp.	Price	Exp.	Price	Exp.	Price
Between-countries limits (this report)												
(1) Upper limit	0.86	-1.30	1.18	-0.77	1.68	-2.59	1.73	-1.60	2.36	-2.60	2.33	-2.20
(2) Lower limit	0.42	0	0.30	0	0.55	0	0.70	-0.26	0.22	0	0.94	0
(3) Average value of table 14.16, lines 1-3:[b]	0.61		1.01		1.59		1.24				1.81	
Within-countries limits (this report)												
(4) Upper limit	1.27	-0.96	0.59	-0.46	1.22	-0.84	1.14	-0.80	1.68	-0.58	1.38	-0.85
(5) Lower limit	0.94	-0.79	0.19	-0.16	0.77	-0.44	0.44	-0.31	0.87	-0.24	0.48	-0.24
Average value												
(6) Time series[b,c]	0.69	-0.68	1.21	-0.71	1.23	-1.26	1.29	-0.64	2.87		2.33	-1.42
(7) Budget studies[b,d]	0.69		0.90		1.82		1.31		1.66		2.43	

[a] Confidence limits are set at 99 percent.
[b] Unweighted arithmetic means.
[c] From Table 14.17, lines 4, 7, 8, 9, 11, 13, 14, 15, 21.
[d] From Table 14.17, lines 16, 17, 18, 19, 22, 23, 24b, 24c, 25.

national comparisons (Table 14.18, line 3), we conclude that the estimates of these studies are drawn from the same universe of intertemporal and international consumption patterns. Those individual estimates which fall within the interval are indicated by superscript [a] in Table 14.17.

We also establish confidence intervals around the within-countries parameters (Table 14.18, lines 4 and 5) and compare them to the unweighted averages of the elasticities from individual time series and budget studies (lines 6 and 7). In only two cases of the 12 coefficients can we conclude that these individual elasticities are drawn from the same universe as our within-countries coefficients.

It is interesting that most of the average expenditure elasticities and all of the average price elasticities calculated from the independent studies (Table 14.18, lines 6 and 7) do fall in the confidence interval of our *between*-countries model. We conclude that the individual studies, presented in detail in Table 14.17, measure patterns that are similar to our long-run, between-countries results, rather than our annual, within-countries patterns.

What then can be made of the within-countries parameters? How realistic are the estimates if most of the independent country studies fail to corroborate these patterns? On the contrary, these short-run patterns are quite useful, for they reflect the immediate effects on consumption expenditure which a single country might expect to experience as the result of its annual prices or incomes policy.

15 Estimation of
Factor Contribution to Growth
Under Structural Disequilibrium*

Michael Bruno

I. Introduction

Suppose we have time series data on output capital and labor inputs and on factor shares in a rapidly industrializing economy, and we want to measure the contribution of various factors to growth. Would it be correct to weight capital and labor by their observed average income shares in order to assess the growth of productivity or technical progress over time?[1] This would imply that we are assuming competitive equilibrium in both product and factor markets, constant returns to scale, and also a specific form of production function (usually Cobb-Douglas).

Intuitively one feels that there are many cases where such simplifications might give us biased results. The use of the expression "structural disequilibrium" when talking of "developing" economies has become a rather hackneyed phrase of which everyone is aware, yet rarely can the monster be forced into the straitjacket of quantitative theory and measurement.[2] However, an attempt to tackle the empirical problem, at least partially, can be based on the modern approach to production function estimation which views production and distribution as a whole, by incorporating both the technical relations and the equilibrium side-conditions in one testable model.[3]

Arrow, Chenery, Minhas, and Solow (1961)—hereafter called ACMS—have taught us that if one starts from an empirical relation between output per unit of labor V/L and the real wage w and assumes equilibrium in the labor and product markets, one can work out the implied general family of production functions (of any degree of homogeneity) which can then be put to an independent empirical test. Also, authors such as Hoch (1962) and Mundlak (1963) have shown systematic ways of

* Reprinted from the *International Economic Review*, February, 1968, n, 49–62 by permission of the publisher. This study was first started while I was completing my Ph.D. studies at Stanford University in the summer of 1962, and a paper based on the preliminary results was presented at the European meeting of the Econometric Society in Copenhagen, July 1963. The present paper applies the previous theoretical framework to a revised and updated set of data and uses a more direct nonlinear estimation procedure. I am indebted to K. J. Arrow, P. J. Dhrymes, F. M. Fisher, Z. Griliches, and L. R. Klein for helpful comments on the earlier work and to Christopher Dougherty of Harvard University for computer programming.

1. We are referring here mainly to the method used by Abramovitz (1956), J. Kendrick (1961), and Denison (1962) for the United States. Our strictures will also refer, however, to the use of the statistically preferable method introduced by Solow (1957).

2. A notable exception is the introduction of linear programming concepts and techniques in planning. None of that, however, has been used in the quantitative explanation of growth.

3. The pioneering step in this field was taken by Marschak and Andrews (1944).

estimating a production model in a form which allows for a test and modification of the equilibrium conditions themselves.[4]

Our main concern in this study will be to try to use the ACMS approach for a case where neither the capital nor the labor market can be assumed to be in equilibrium, by setting up an empirically testable model in which the extent of displacement from equilibrium is given explicit measure. Our own empirical investigation ties in better with the linear relationship between V/L and w than with the logarithmic (CES function) case with which ACMS have been mainly concerned.[5] This implies another family of production functions which in itself has some interesting aspects. Our main emphasis, however, is on taking account of disequilibrium.

The theoretical framework is discussed in detail in Section II and is then applied, in Section III, to the growth of manufacturing and the total private economy of Israel during 1953–1964. The model turns out to give a plausible rationalization of some interesting growth and distribution phenomena which would not make sense on the basis of a more "naive" set of assumptions.

II. Disequilibrium and the Constant-Marginal-Shares Model

Suppose that the following empirical linear relation between output per unit of labor ($V/L = y$) and the real wage w is observed:[6]

$$\frac{V}{L} = cw + d \tag{15.1}$$

where $c > 0$. This relationship implies that *marginal* factor shares are *constant*. As for the *average* labor share wL/V, this will be falling, constant, or rising, according to whether d is negative, zero, or positive, respectively. As we shall note below, c and d, the share parameters, may depend on both technical or institutional conditions.

Suppose now that in this economy or industry there exists an aggregate production function, to be specified below, describing technical relations between output V, labor L, capital K and time t. We also assume that the marginal labor product $\partial V/\partial L$ derived from this function is linearly related to the real wage in the following general form:

$$\frac{\partial V}{\partial L} = pw + q \tag{15.2}$$

p and q, which can usually not be observed directly, are assumed to be fixed institutional or behavioral parameters. The special case $p = 1$ and $q = 0$ corresponds to competitive equilibrium in the factor and product markets. More about this relationship in the case $p \neq 1$ and/or $q \neq 0$ will be said below.

We can now look for the general form of production function that would give rise to an empirical relationship (15.1) via a postulated institutional wage adjustment equation (15.2). Using a method very much like that used by ACMS, we can derive

4. Hoch and Mundlak have confined themselves to cross-section estimation of an a priori specified Cobb-Douglas function.

5. The linear case assuming equilibrium was worked out by ACMS but not included in the published paper (1961).

6. As is customary in all of these discussions, we take the real wage to be measured in terms of output as numeraire.

the general mathematical form of such function by eliminating w from equations (15.1) and (15.2) and solving the resulting differential equation.

For convenience we now introduce two new parameters, α and m, to which the previous parameters (p,q,c,d) are assumed to relate through the following transformation:

$$c = \frac{p}{1 - \alpha}, \qquad d = \frac{q + m\alpha}{1 - \alpha} \qquad (15.3)$$

where we assume $\alpha \neq 1$. We get the following partial differential equation from (15.1), (15.2) and (15.3):

$$\frac{\partial V}{\partial L} = (1 - \alpha) \frac{V}{L} - m\alpha \qquad (15.4)$$

(α and m will be assumed to be fixed technical constants—see below.) (15.4) has the general one-parameter family of solutions[7]

$$V = C(K,t)L^{1-\alpha} - mL \qquad (15.5)$$

or

$$\frac{V}{L} = C(K,t)L^{-\alpha} - m \qquad (15.5a)$$

The parameter or constant of integration C has here been written as a function of variables that are assumed to play a role in the underlying production relationship but do not appear explicitly in (15.4). Clearly not every function of the form (15.5) can be a genuine production function. The form in which K can appear in $C(K,t)$ is restricted by such conditions as nonnegative and diminishing marginal factor productivities. Similarly the form in which t appears is determined by the specification of technical progress. If we stick to constant returns to scale and exponential technical progress then we must choose $C(K,t) = Ae^{\lambda t}K^{\alpha}$ where A is a constant, so that the function in this specific form becomes[8]

$$V = Ae^{\lambda t}K^{\alpha}L^{1-\alpha} - mL \qquad (15.6)$$

or

$$y = Ae^{\lambda t}x^{\alpha} - m \qquad (15.6a)$$

where $y = V/L$ and $x = K/L$. If $0 \leq \alpha < 1$, then we must have $A > 0$. Also there is some restriction on the range of x in the form $x \geq x_0$ to ensure nonnegativity of y.[9]

We can now turn our model around and start, so to say, from the other end. Suppose the economy (or industry) produces according to the general technical relationship (15.6), with the above restrictions. Suppose also that the wage-marginal productivity adjustment relationship takes the general form (15.2). In that case we would expect to find the linear empirical relationship (15.1) to hold,[10] where the parameters

---

7. As in ACMS, this is obtained directly if we recall that $\partial V/\partial L = L\, \partial y/\partial L + y$ where $y = V/L$, so (15.4) becomes $L\, \partial y/\partial L + \alpha y + m\alpha = 0$.

8. More general increasing or decreasing returns functions can be represented by $ae^{\lambda t}K^{\beta}$.

9. If $\alpha < 0$ we must have $A < 0$ and $m < 0$. The case $\alpha = 1$ must be excluded here. Solving (15.4) with $\alpha = 1$ would give rise to a different form of production function. For practical considerations this limiting case can be ignored.

10. We must keep in mind that (15.1) is consistent with a more general form of (15.5), as previously indicated, but we ignore this possibility here. In our empirical investigations we have also used alternative formulations with increasing returns as suggested in note 8, but in time series analysis it is virtually impossible to distinguish between time and scale effects.

c and d can now be interpreted on the basis of (15.3) to be functions of the technical parameters, α, m and λ and the institutional parameters p and q. Moreover, by fitting a two-equations model (15.1) and (15.6) to observations on the variables V, K, L and w we can estimate all of these parameters simultaneously and perform significance tests on them. Before we turn to the question of empirical implementation, however, let us go back to discuss some of the underlying economic relationships. We start with the production function (15.6).

The following properties of the family of functions (15.6) may be noted:

1. The case $m = 0$ in (15.6) shows that the simple Cobb-Douglas function appears as a special case of this constant-marginal-shares (CMS) family just as it appears as a special case of the CES family (when the elasticity of substitution is unity). In general (15.6) can be looked upon as a weighted sum (or difference) of Cobb-Douglas and a constant-proportions production function.

2. The elasticity of substitution implied by (15.6) is given by the following expression:

$$\sigma = \frac{y'(y - xy')}{xyy''} = 1 - \left(\frac{\alpha m}{1 - \alpha}\right)\frac{1}{y} \tag{15.7}$$

When $0 < \alpha < 1$ we have the following properties of σ: when $m > 0$, the elasticity of substitution is always less than 1, and monotonically approaches 1 from below, as y increases. Similarly, when $m < 0$, the elasticity of substitution is always greater than 1 and monotonically approaches 1 from above, as y increases. This could also be seen from direct inspection of the form of the production function (15.6). It has the ordinary Cobb-Douglas function as its asymptote. For large x (as the economy "develops") its production function behaves more and more like the Cobb-Douglas term of equation (15.6).

3. Since the shift factor multiplies only the first term of the function, technical progress will be neutral only asymptotically, as x or t or both become large. Otherwise its effect is to increase or decrease the ratio of marginal productivities $(\partial V/\partial L)/(\partial V/\partial K)$ for any given x according to whether the intercept m is positive or negative.[11]

The case $m > 0$ in which technical progress starts off being "capital saving" $[(\partial V/\partial L)/(\partial V/\partial K)$ increases with $t]$ seems to be the relevant one for our own empirical study (see Section III). One way of looking at it might be that of the labor force undergoing some process of "learning" with time in a way that increases their marginal product in relation to that of capital. This may very well be a more realistic description for an economy in the early stages of rapid industrialization than the ordinary "neutrality" assumption (which would here correspond to the case $m = 0$). On the other hand, as t increases and m/y becomes small this discrepancy from neutrality becomes small, which again may be a realistic aspect of this crude version of "learning."

Next we turn to a discussion of the assumptions underlying the behavior of the factor markets.

Although in the very long run equilibration of wages and marginal productivities could reasonably be assumed, we have strong reason to believe that in some situations this assumption would lead to wrong results and must at least be put to empirical test.

The conflict in economies which are relatively abundant in manpower, between

---

11. An alternative formulation with a neutral shift factor multiplying the whole production function would be relevant if the original relation (15.1) had taken the form $y = cw + e^{\lambda t}d$.

rapid industrialization requiring high investments per capita and the maximization of employment, is a familiar one. To suggest a low level of real wages as a means of absorbing more labor in industry is easier said than done. In many developing economies the transfer of workers from the countryside into town and industry involves a considerable boost to the remuneration of labor which is more than is warranted by the increase in labor productivity.[12] Partly this is due to the high overhead costs of urbanization (housing and public utilities, higher costs of living, a more pronounced demonstration effect, and so on). In part this is no doubt due to the strengthening of organized trade unions that goes with it.

In the case of Israel, which we shall investigate in the next section, strong trade unions were probably the main determinant of wages during the 1950s.[13] Here the problem of employment did not take the form of a transfer of workers from agriculture (which had to be developed alongside industry) but rather that of absorbing a mass influx of new immigrants in productive employment.

If real wages are rigid and cannot be brought down to marginal productivity of labor, one way of increasing employment is to bring the marginal productivity of labor up to the wage rate and invest as much as one can from domestic savings and foreign aid. If investment funds are limited, and they usually are, supplementary ways must be found to induce a high rate of employment. Where enterprises are state-owned this is no problem, since employment can be made a policy variable. In economies where private initiative plays an important role, entrepreneurs must be induced to employ labor beyond the point where the marginal productivity of labor equals the wage rate. One way of doing this is through the mechanism of government-financed development loans. The government subsidizes industry by means of low interest rates on its loans and makes the increase of employment in development areas one of the conditions for the granting of such loans. It may also subsidize the price of labor by other means, for example, through funds designed to encourage "training on the job."[14] At the same time one should not rule out the possibility that, with time, closer cooperation between labor and government might itself contribute towards the closing of such a gap between the market and the shadow price of labor.[15]

The simplest form in which one can specify the existence of a discrepancy between the marginal productivity of labor and the wage rate is to assume that it is linear in nature, as is done in (15.2).[16] As mentioned before, the case $p = 1$, $q = 0$, is that

12. Such assumption usually underlies much of the "dual economy" discussion. See, for example, Jorgenson (1961).

13. There is a problem here when it comes to statistical estimation in that trade unions can usually enforce only the nominal wage, and not the real wage rate. We have to assume that the prices of the product are set independently of the current period wage rate, that is, on the basis of past costs, or in close relationship with exogenously given import prices (unless we assume that they are government controlled). This is not always an entirely realistic assumption, since wages may affect current prices on both the cost and the demand side. The proper treatment would be to bring the market for the product explicitly into the model. However, there is a limit to what can be done at a first level of abstraction, especially when the number of empirical observations is limited.

14. In some cases it may pay the entrepreneur to produce for a time with high wage, low marginal productivity labor, even in the absence of government subsidy, provided he can expect to be compensated by correspondingly higher profits in the future, say, through a resulting greater rise in "total productivity." In such a case his behavior could be described in terms of maximizing profits over a longer period.

15. Since wages are rigid in absolute terms, this would take the form of a slower *rate of increase* of wages over time until marginal productivity catches up with the wage rate.

16. The linearity assumption fits in best in the present model. In the literature one finds the use of disturbance terms for the Cobb-Douglas function which are additive in logs (see Hoch 1962; Mundlak 1963).

of simple profit maximization under perfect competition. Another special case $p = 1$, $q < 0$ comes close to the empirical situation to be analyzed in the next section. In such a case there is a constant positive discrepancy between the wage rate and marginal productivity whose relative importance becomes smaller and smaller as the wage rate and marginal productivity grow over time.[17] We note that if $q = 0$ and $p \neq 1$ (or, in fact, $p > 1$) we would have a simple case of imperfectly competitive equilibrium in the labor market. This can be seen by writing $p = 1 + 1/\epsilon_s$ where ϵ_s is the elasticity of supply of labor. It is the existence of an intercept $q \neq 0$ which makes (2) a "disequilibrium" relationship. We can thus call q the disequilibrium parameter. The disequilibrium in the labor market clearly implies a corresponding disequilibrium in the opposite direction in the capital market. We have

$$\frac{\partial V}{\partial K} - r = -\frac{1}{x}\left(\frac{\partial V}{\partial L} - w\right) \tag{15.8}$$

where r is the rate of return and x the capital-labor ratio, as before. If $p = 1$ and $q < 0$ the difference $\partial V/\partial K - r$ is positive and monotonically decreasing as x increases.

Turning, therefore, to the market for capital, it is clearly implicit in the above discussion that we are dealing with an economy in which funds for investment are more or less rationed, and there is little in the way of a price-regulated market for capital. It does not matter whether this takes the form of an ultimate limitation imposed by availability of foreign exchange (with which machinery has to be bought), or whether the effective bottleneck is the supply of savings, with the government financing development through inflationary but controlled credit expansion. In any actual situation in a developing economy one would probably find a mixture of both. It suffices for our purposes to assume that there is no market in which capital can be acquired at will and with everybody scrambling to equate the marginal productivity of capital to a going rental rate.[18] The rate of interest which the government or a foreign agency would charge for a development loan is way below the real or shadow rate, as measured by the long-run marginal productivity of the same. Funds on a black market are impossible to come by or else they are forbiddingly expensive, with the price reflecting a private risk factor which exaggerates the social cost involved.

Let us now turn to the problem of statistical estimation. Unfortunately there is no way of fitting the model consisting of (15.1) and (15.6) in a form which would always be completely free of simultaneous equations bias. Even if we ignore the problem of the exogeneity of w mentioned earlier and express the model in "reduced form," the resulting expression in terms of w and K does not lend itself to direct estimation.[19] Instead we must fit the model by applying single equation least squares. We consider the following forms

$$\frac{V}{L} = cw + d \tag{15.1}$$

17. $(w + q)/w \to 1$ as $w \to \infty$. The speed of convergence in this case is a slow one, and one could argue for attempting other functional forms.

18. In a different empirical and theoretical setting we could use the same production model to incorporate some measure of the rental rate on capital, which is then assumed to be given whereupon capital becomes an endogenous variable, as we have done with respect to labor. We would, in that case, use an equilibrium condition for the marginal efficiency of capital and the rental rate.

19. For example, we could write $L/K = A^{1/\alpha}e^{\lambda t}(cw + d - m)^{-1/\alpha}$. This can only be fitted by trial and error (since we do not know m). However, we cannot obtain significance tests on x and m from fitting this expression.

or

$$w = \frac{1}{c}\frac{V}{L} - \frac{d}{c} \qquad\qquad (15.1a)^{20}$$

and

$$V = Ae^{\lambda t}K^{\alpha}L^{1-\alpha} - mL \qquad\qquad (15.6)$$

or

$$\frac{V}{L} = Ae^{\lambda t}\left(\frac{K}{L}\right)^{\alpha} - m \qquad\qquad (15.6b)$$

and we obtain p and q from

$$p = (1 - \alpha)c, \qquad q = (1 - \alpha)d - \alpha m \qquad\qquad (15.3a)$$

For equation (15.6) or (15.6b) a direct nonlinear estimation procedure must be used to obtain nonlinear confidence intervals for λ, α, and m. Since there exists no theory of confidence region estimation for nonlinear systems, we cannot give "true" confidence intervals for the implied parameters p and q. Nonetheless we can give approximate bounds for these parameters by using the confidence intervals derived for the parameters α and m and for c and d, and substituting these in (15.3).[21] As is shown in the next section's example, crude as our method has to be at this stage, it does give very reasonable results in a case where the more simple minded competitive model, or the Cobb-Douglas function, fail.

III. Factor Remuneration and Factor Contribution to Growth in Israel, 1953–1964

Table 15.1 sets out the main ingredients for a production function, input and output data, in terms of average rates of growth. Figures are given for both a subsector manufacturing and the total private economy during the period 1953–1964 and the subperiod 1958–1964.

One approach to the measurement of productivity is to use the Abramovitz (1956) and J. Kendrick (1961) output per unit of input measure of total productivity. The latter method was applied by Gaathon (1961) in a study of Israel's growth during the period 1950–1959.[22] A variant of the method was also used by Patinkin (1960). The trouble with this type of analysis, however, is the restrictiveness of the assumptions that have to be made to justify its use. In particular, the assumption of perfect competition in the labor market is needed to justify the use of distributive shares as relative weights of labor and capital inputs. Inspection of the distributive shares data shows that the share of labor has gone down more or less systematically over the period in question.[23] An associated puzzling feature is a systematic increase in the average gross rate of return on capital.[24]

Various attempts at explaining the data by fitting V/L to w and the implied production relationships under assumptions of perfect competition, and likewise attempts

20. To use (15.1a) rather than (15.1) as an alternative is relevant, in principle, if we think of a model for the whole economy with K/L as exogenous and w as endogenous. In our own experience this made very little difference, however.

21. We are specifically interested in "testing" $p \neq 1$, $q \neq 0$.

22. Gaathon has recently updated his figures for the capital stock, employment, and output to 1964; I am indebted to him for letting me use some of his unpublished data in the present study.

23. From 71.5 to 65.8 percent in manufacturing and from 69.7 to 66.1 percent for the private economy as a whole. (These can be worked out from Table A15.1 by applying the formula wL/V.)

24. 17.6 to 21.0 percent in manufacturing and 15.0 to 19.5 in the total economy. (Apply the formula $(V - wL)/K$ to Table A15.1.)

Table 15.1. Rate of Growth of Output, Factor Inputs, and Wages 1953-1964

	Manufacturing			Total private economy[a]		
	Level	Average growth rates		Level	Average growth rates	
	1964	1953-1964	1958-1964	1964	1953-1964	1958-1964
Employment, L (thousand man-years)	225	6.5	7.4	723	4.2	4.8
Capital stock, K (I. L. million, 1955 prices) (beginning-of-the-year stock)	1974	12.0	13.0	6418	10.8	10.6
Gross domestic product, V (I. L. million, 1955 prices)	1215	12.0	13.4	3686	12.3	12.2
Real wage rate, w (I. L. per man-year, 1955 prices)	3561	4.4	5.1	3373	7.3	6.9

[a] The total private economy is defined to exclude the current operations of the government and other public and nonprofit institutions, as well as the dwelling sector. It does, however, include productive enterprises owned by these sectors.

Source: The primary source for most of the data in Tables 15.1 and A15.1 is Gaathon (1961). See the appendix to this chapter for complete source information and for the appropriate definitions used.

to fit simple Cobb-Douglas functions have all failed to give any sensible results, or else produced internal contradictions.[25] In both the private economy and manufacturing a straight attempt to fit a Cobb-Douglas function [that is, equation (15.6) or (15.6b) with $m = 0$] gives α values of around 1 or higher (that is, $\partial V/\partial L$ zero or negative) and zero technical progress, with large standard errors of the coefficients. The alternative approach starting from the relation (15.1) and fitting the implied production function under the assumption of perfect competition gave significantly contradicting answers for α.[26] It is on this basis that we were led to modify the model along the lines of the previous discussion. We shall briefly indicate the resulting estimates of coefficients. Starting with the *total private economy*, fitting equation (15.1) by simple least squares, we obtain

$$c = 1.566 \qquad\qquad d = -0.164$$
$$[1.400, 1.672] \qquad\quad [-0.240, -0.098]$$

The figures in brackets denote lower and upper 5 percent confidence bounds (approximately two standard errors).[27] We note that the intercept d is negative and significantly so.

25. We have also tried the CES model, various increasing returns specifications, and lagged capital input assumptions.

26. In the case $p = 1$ and $q = 0$, we have from (15.3) $1 - \alpha = 1/c$, $m = d/(c - 1)$. Our preliminary "test" consisted of fitting (15.6) in the form log $(V + mL)$ on t and log K using the estimated value of m and then performing a significance test on the resulting estimate of $1 - \alpha$, comparing it with the independent estimate $1/c$. This experiment was repeated using the lower and upper confidence bounds on the hypothesized value of $m = d/(c - 1)$.

27. Since we deal with time series, all our R^2 values come out extremely high (around 0.99); there seems no point to produce these here.

Direct fitting of the production function (15.6b) by nonlinear regression gives[28]

$$A = 1.952 \qquad \lambda = 0.0228$$
$$[1.907, 1.998] \qquad [-0.0140\,^*, 0.0248]$$
$$\alpha = 0.403 \qquad m = 1.510$$
$$[0.208\,^*, 0.413] \qquad [1.387, 1.633]$$

Turning now to the interpretation of our model in terms of the institutional coefficients p and q of (15.2), we get upon substitution in (15.3a)[29]

$$p = 0.935 \qquad q = -0.707$$
$$[0.822, 1.324\,^*] \qquad [-0.864, -0.340\,^*]$$

We thus find that both our more general specification of the production function ($m \neq 0$) and the disequilibrium relationship (15.2) are well justified by the data. The "imperfection" parameter p is not significantly different from 1, but the disequilibrium parameter q is significantly negative. In the production function we have a considerably high positive intercept m.

That our results are not just a matter of coincidence or aggregation is further seen when we consider the very similar results for the more homogenous subsector, manufacturing. Using the same procedure we obtain

$$c = 1.750 \qquad d = -0.750$$
$$[1.566, 1.954] \qquad [-0.916, -0.584]$$
$$A = 2.237 \qquad \lambda = 0.0127$$
$$[2.198, 2.277] \qquad [-0.0122\,^*, 0.0143]$$
$$\alpha = 0.441 \qquad m = 1.667$$
$$[0.383\,^*, 0.477] \qquad [1.553, 1.782]$$
$$p = 0.978 \qquad q = -1.154$$
$$[0.855, 1.206\,^*] \qquad [-1.362, -0.918\,^*]$$

We note that the production parameters α and m are very close to the aggregate results, technical progress probably somewhat smaller than the average and the disequilibrium parameter considerably higher in absolute value.

Consider now the general implications of our model for the analysis of factor contribution to growth. If we denote the two factor elasticities by E_1 and E_2, respectively,

---

28. We have used the IBM Share Distribution Program set up by D. W. Marquardt (1964). A description of the maximum neighborhood algorithm used is also given in Marquardt (1963). The lower and upper values are the nonlinear 5 percent confidence bounds given by the program. These are calculated on the assumption that the error-variance ratio is distributed like the F-statistic. The program uses a limit process to work out upper and lower bounds for each coefficient, given the critical level for the residual variance. The two bounds marked by an asterisk indicate cases in which this method did not give proper convergence, and these two lower bounds are most probably biased downwards. We have no way of correcting these. However, our main results are not affected by this ambiguity.

29. A remark made earlier (see page 365) is appropriate here. The bounds on p and q that we have indicated here are not true confidence intervals in a statistical sense, since they have been obtained from straight substitution of the lower and upper bounds of the underlying coefficients. However, if anything, these bounds are probably biased in an outward direction, since this computation implicitly assumed full correlation between the component parameters (that is, that they attain their bounds simultaneously). The bounds marked with asterisks are those that are affected by the corresponding lower bound on α.

and use the usual dot representation for time derivatives, we have[30]

$$\frac{\dot{V}}{V} = \frac{1}{V}\frac{\partial V}{\partial t} + E_1 \frac{\dot{L}}{L} + E_2 \frac{\dot{K}}{K} \tag{15.9}$$

where

$$\frac{1}{V}\frac{\partial V}{\partial t} = \lambda\left(1 + \frac{m}{y}\right), \qquad E_1 = 1 - \alpha\left(1 + \frac{m}{y}\right), \qquad E_2 = 1 - E_1$$

Since $m > 0$ the role of the "total productivity" factor decreases over time, as y increases. Of a GDP growth rate of about 12 percent in both sectors, this factor explained between one third (1953) to a quarter (1964) in the total economy and only about one sixth of the growth in manufacturing. When the capital-output ratio is more or less constant, the relative contribution of capital is approximately equal to E_2. Its estimated contribution to growth amounted to between 60–50 percent in the total and was even somewhat higher in manufacturing. These figures should be compared with the contribution of capital that is implied, under a "naive" model, by the share estimator (30–35 percent). Also these results are in sharp contrast to the usual empirical findings for the United States and Western Europe. They should help to restore our faith in capital formation as a major contribution to the development process.

The same results can be used to compute the difference between the marginal productivity of capital and the actual rate of return, along the lines of equation (15.8) above. This calculation points to a gradual reduction in this discrepancy to about half of its original value by 1964. While the actual rate of return had been increasing, the marginal productivity shows a slight decrease. For the private sector as a whole, its estimated value moved from about 33 percent to 29 percent in gross terms;[31] the figures for manufacturing are somewhat higher.

A note of caution: To say that labor got more than its marginal product is not to imply that private owners of capital got less than the marginal productivity of their own capital. The capital stock in manufacturing and in the economy as a whole throughout the period was only partly financed by private entrepreneurial capital, the order of magnitude being roughly $1:2$; the rest was financed by government development loans on which the effective rate o f interest was as low as 3–5 percent. The effective rate of return on entrepreneurs' own capital thus reached above 30 percent and corresponds well with the implied marginal productivity of capital.[32] It thus seems as if the government (or foreign tax payers) subsidized capital and paid the difference in the form of higher wage income. This situation is gradually changing, as the government is slowly withdrawing from its role as the major source of investment finance. Rising private investments from abroad instead of previous unrequited transfers and greater resort to a newly developing domestic capital market have in more recent years begun to take the place of previous strict rationing of capital through government control. This is the obverse of the narrowing of the gap between the "market" and shadow prices of this factor.

Before concluding let us make a few additional comments on the choice and formu-

30. See Solow (1957).
31. About 5–7 percent have to be subtracted for depreciation.
32. In terms of the capital formation account, the bulk of net investment in the economy was financed by capital imports through the public sector of which only a small part was obtained on commercial terms.

lation of our model. First it should be noted that our limited number of observations also limits our ability to isolate only one particular model and state it as the *only* one consistent with the data. For example, as already mentioned, an increasing returns specification can be incorporated into equation (15.6).[33] Next, one could attempt to rationalize the data in terms of a disequilibrium relationship introduced into the CES model[34] The main point is that we have not found an alternative production model which could rationalize the data without assuming disequilibrium, nor did the alternatives give better or as good statistical fits.

We have devoted our attention to a relaxation of equilibrium assumptions in the factor markets, not saying anything about the product market. It was implicitly assumed to be in perfectly competitive equilibrium. In principle the model could be extended to cover the case where the product market is, say, imperfectly competitive. We would then have to bring in additional variables for which we do not have empirical data now. One can, however, safely say that the existence of imperfect competition in the product market would even strengthen our previous results. This can be seen in the following way: Suppose that the labor market were perfectly competitive, but not the product market. Denoting the demand elasticity for the product by η (positive), we would have

$$ w = \frac{\partial V}{\partial L}\left(1 - \frac{1}{\eta}\right) < \frac{\partial V}{\partial L} \qquad \eta = -\frac{P\partial V}{V\partial P} $$

where

P = product price

that is, we would expect the marginal productivity of labor to be *higher* than the wage rate.

A much weaker aspect of our model is the fact that it was set up in terms of a very heterogenous factor called labor services. If labor had been split up into different categories, the individual estimates of marginal productivities might have been rather different. It is known, for instance, that certain categories of skilled and even semiskilled labor have become more and more of a scarce factor in manufacturing towards the end of the period, and it is quite possible that in their case wages have tended even more towards equality with marginal productivities, whereas for the less skilled types of labor the gap still remains larger than that observed for labor as a whole.

---

33. We have tried $V = AK^{\beta}L^{1-\alpha} - mL$ (the observations are too limited to allow for both non-homogeneity and technical progress). The results are qualitatively similar, only the "share" of capital now increases. Obviously, with time series there is no way of distinguishing between scale and time effects.

34. The resulting estimates, not reproduced here, again point to similar qualitative conclusions but are on the whole less satisfactory from a statistical point of view.

Appendix to Chapter 15

Table A15.1. Data for Israel Manufacturing (M) and Total Private Economy (P)

Year	Wage rate w (I.L. per man-year, 1955 prices)		Capital stock K (I.L. million, 1955 prices)		Employment L (thousand man-years)		Gross domestic product V (I.L. million, 1955 prices)	
	M	P	M	P	M	P	M	P
1953	2,216	1,560	566.5	2,078.0	112.4	460.8	348.6	1,031.1
1954	2,251	1,731	629.5	2,319.3	120.6	471.0	385.5	1,222.4
1955	2,393	1,979	699.1	2,546.9	125.4	472.8	429.4	1,386.0
1956	2,518	2,100	767.5	2,818.9	130.0	494.4	467.8	1,521.8
1957	2,471	2,167	861.9	3,158.0	138.8	520.7	501.4	1,689.5
1958	2,650	2,264	949.6	3,503.1	146.7	544.3	571.2	1,850.3
1959	2,865	2,454	1,071.5	3,875.7	153.5	567.0	655.0	2,091.5
1960	3,007	2,571	1,231.8	4,287.7	162.2	585.8	733.7	2,274.4
1961	3,135	2,691	1,370.5	4,768.4	178.7	617.6	848.7	2,494.8
1962	3,120	2,958	1,541.5	5,252.1	193.9	644.1	930.0	2,885.7
1963	3,343	3,164	1,774.4	5,851.0	208.9	688.3	1,066.0	3,287.3
1964	3,561	3,373	1,974.2	6,417.6	224.7	722.9	1,215.2	3,686.4

Sources and Definitions: Wage rate w: Average compensation of employees, including social benefits, per standard man-year (based on 1958). Source of data: Central Bureau of Statistics (CBS) and Bank of Israel (BOI) Annual Reports. Capital stock K: Gross figure, net of discards. Does not include inventory or land. Figures for 1952-1959: Gaathon (1961: Table A-6, appendix A. 1960-1964); Gaathon, Working Papers. (Figures also processed in BOI Reports 1961-64). Employment L: Standard man-years (based on 1958). Figures for number of employees from Gaathon (1961), CBS, and BOI Reports 1957-1964. Correction for hours worked based on CBS Statistical Abstracts. Gross domestic product V: Figures based on CBS. Price deflators for M from Gaathon (1961), and BOI Reports 1957-1964.

16 Growth Effects
of Changes in Labor Quality
and Quantity, Greece: 1951–1961*

Samuel Bowles

I. Introduction

The Greek economy experienced rapid growth over the decade of the 1950s. GDP (in constant prices) grew at over 5 percent per annum for the period 1951–1961, a rate higher than most countries on which we have data, and one which is particularly striking when expressed in per capita terms, due to the low rate of population increase.

The purpose of this paper is to measure the contribution of changes in the quality of the labor force to this rapid growth. One embarks on a study of this type with a firmly (if recently) established preconception. Based on the work of E. Denison, T. W. Schultz, A. Harberger, and M. Selowsky, as well as on estimates of rates of return on educational expenditures in poor countries, it is expected that the growth contribution of the improved educational level of the labor force should be quite considerable. The results for Greece presented below do not fall into this general pattern; the growth contribution of changes in the educational composition of the employed labor force is very small.

It should be stressed at the beginning that given the limitations of the conceptual tools and the data used in this study, the results should be treated with the greatest skepticism. Nonetheless, it is hoped that with the aid of the sensitivity analysis in Appendix B, to this chapter some plausible ranges of estimates can be developed to provide a rough indication of the contribution of changes in labor quality and quantity to Greek growth over the 1950s.

II. Estimating the Factor Contribution to Growth

The approach outlined below is to view growth as a consequence of increases in the productive services of factors. The limited nature of the inquiry should be stressed at the outset. Institutional changes, alterations in the structure of final demand,

* The research for this study was initiated during the summer of 1966 as part of the Harvard Development Advisory Service Project at the Center of Planning and Economic Research in Athens. I am grateful to the members of the Center for their help and to Emmanuel Potiriadis and Constantine Stratigopoulos for assistance in data collection. My thanks also to Jim Huntsberger and particularly to Jun Onaka, who performed most of the computational work and suggested a number of significant improvements.

371

innovation, and other phenomena central to the growth process are considered only indirectly as they affect the augmentation of factor supplies.

We seek to identify and measure the contribution to growth of increases in the quantity and quality of capital and labor. We begin by describing the aggregate production process:

$$Y = f(K,L) \tag{16.1}$$

where

Y = GDP

K = a measure of the input of capital, including land

L = a measure of labor input

As we are concerned with the change in GDP over time, we write:

$$\frac{dY}{dt} = \frac{dK}{dt} f_K + \frac{dL}{dt} f_L + r \tag{16.2}$$

or, letting the dot over a symbol indicate its time derivative, and rearranging,

$$\frac{\dot{Y}}{Y} = \frac{\dot{K}}{K}\left(\frac{Kf_K}{Y}\right) + \frac{\dot{L}}{L}\left(\frac{Lf_L}{Y}\right) + \frac{r}{Y} \tag{16.3}$$

where r is the combined growth contribution of inputs not explicitly taken account of in the measures of capital and labor used, and f_K and f_L represent the social marginal products of capital and labor, respectively. The terms Kf_K/Y, and Lf_L/Y, are the elasticities of output with respect to the capital and labor input, respectively, or the percentage change in Y associated with a 1 percent change in K or L.

If the time unit for the analysis is the year, we can write the expression (3) in terms of annual rates of growth:

$$\gamma_Y = \gamma_K S_K + \gamma_L S_L + \frac{r}{Y} \tag{16.4}$$

where γ_Y, γ_L, γ_K are the annual rates of growth of Y, L and K, respectively, that is

$$\gamma_Y = \frac{\dot{Y}}{Y}, \ \gamma_L = \frac{\dot{L}}{L} \ \text{ and } \ \gamma_K = \frac{\dot{K}}{K}$$

In this study we shall consider growth over a 10-year period. Thus γ_K, γ_L, and γ_Y represent average annual rates of growth of capital, labor, and GDP.[1]

In order to use expression (4) for the analysis of growth over a long period of time, we must make some special assumptions about the shape of the aggregate production function, namely, that the elasticity of output with respect to labor and capital remains constant over the range of variations being considered.

We define the following sources of growth:

1. the contribution of capital, $G^K = \gamma_K S_K$
2. the contribution of labor, $G^L = \gamma_L S_L$

3. the unexplained residual, $R = \dfrac{r}{Y}$

We turn now to the contribution of education to growth. There is apparently no agreed upon method for the estimation of the growth contribution of education.

---

1. We are unable to work with each of the 10 annual equations corresponding to (16.4) because labor force data are available for only the terminal and base years.

The methods used by T. W. Schultz (1961), E. Denison (1962), Z. Griliches and D. Jorgenson (1967), A. Harberger and M. Selowsky (1966), and others differ, in some cases, significantly.[2] Schultz and Harberger and Selowsky used the estimate of the internal rate of return on educational expenditures as the basis of their estimates, while Denison developed an index of the quality of the labor force as affected by education (see Bowman [1964]). The method used below is similar to that adopted by Denison.

In this model education contributes to growth only by being embodied in workers; it is thus different from the Schultz approach, which makes education a factor of production in its own right and in which the education contribution and the labor force contribution are formally separate. The method used here directs attention away from the possibly important areas in which education contributes directly to growth without embodiment in the worker, for example, in the production of economically useful knowledge as a by-product of an educational process.[3]

The approach used here is based on the notion that the amount of labor input in the economy is a function of both the numbers (N) and the average quality (Q) of the workers, or

$$L = L(N,Q) \tag{16.5}$$

One form of equation (16.5) comes immediately to mind; we may say that

$$L = N_1 w_1 + N_2 w_2 + \cdots + N_n W_n \tag{16.6}$$

where

N_i = the number of laborers of type i ($i = 1, \ldots, n$).

$w_i = \dfrac{f_{Li}}{f_{Lo}}$ = the ratio of the marginal product of labor of type i to the marginal product of an arbitrarily chosen category of labor, o, or the marginal rate of substitution in production between labor of type i and type o.

The index of labor quality, average labor input per employed worker, is then written

$$Q = \frac{\sum\limits_i N_i w_i}{\sum\limits_i N_i} \tag{16.7}$$

from which it follows that,

$$L = QN \tag{16.8}$$

Equation (16.7) is the form used by Denison and Griliches.[4] It implies a constant marginal rate of substitution in production between different types of labor. "Labor" can be considered a single, homogeneous factor. A 1 percent increase in the quality of labor has the same effect on output as a 1 percent increase in labor numbers.

2. For discussion of the methods of Schultz and Denison, see Mary Jean Bowman (1964).

3. While treating education as a separate factor formally allows the consideration of growth effects not embodied in labor, in actual empirical practice the rates of return to education are generally estimated on the basis of relative earnings of labor with different educational qualifications, thus confining attention solely to the labor-embodied growth contribution.

4. If the aggregate production function can be written

$$Y = AK^{S_K}L^{S_L}$$

substitution gives us $Y = AK^{S_K}(N_1 w_1 + \cdots + N_n w_n)^{S_L}$.

We may now estimate the contribution of labor quality increases to economic growth. Recall that the growth contribution of labor is

$$G^L = \gamma_L S_L \tag{16.9}$$

Since

$$L = QN$$

we know that

$$\gamma_L = \gamma_N + \gamma_Q \tag{16.10}$$

Substituting (16.10) into (16.9), we arrive at the following definitions:

$G^L = (\gamma_N + \gamma_Q)S_L =$ the growth contribution of labor adjusted for quality (16.11)
$G^N = \gamma_N S_L =$ the growth contribution of increase in labor numbers (16.12)
$G^Q = \gamma_Q S_L =$ the growth contribution of increase in labor quality (16.13)
$$G^L = G^N + G^Q \tag{16.14}$$

Turning to the increase in average labor quality, we consider only two dimensions of the quality of the labor force: sex and education. The change in average labor quality is equal to the effects of changes in the sex and education composition of the labor force plus an interaction term.

Define

$$L^s = N_m w_m + N_f w_f \tag{16.15}$$

and

$$L^e = \sum_j N_j w_j \tag{16.16}$$

where L^s and L^e are the indices of labor input adjusted respectively for sex and education. The letter subscripts, m and f, indicate sex and subscript j, various levels of education.

The labor quality index, Q, can now be decomposed. Let

$$Q^s = \frac{L^s}{N} = \text{average quality of labor force, adjusted for sex}$$

$$Q^e = \frac{L^e}{N} = \text{average quality of labor force adjusted for educational level}$$

We now rewrite equation (16.7)

$$Q = \frac{\sum_j N_{mj} w_{mj} + \sum_j N_{fj} w_{fj}}{N}$$

where the double subscripts indicate the sex and the educational level. Let

$$Q = Q^e Q^s Q^{es} \tag{16.17}$$

where Q^{es} represents the effects of interaction between sex and education.

Thus

$$\gamma_Q = \gamma_e + \gamma_s + \gamma_{es} \tag{16.18}$$

where γ_Q, γ_e, and γ_s represent the average annual rate of growth of labor quality and the average annual rates of growth of labor quality adjusted separately for changes in the educational composition and the sex composition of the labor force, respectively.[5] The remaining term, γ_{es}, is the average annual rate of growth of the education-sex interaction effect, computed as a residual.

We now define the growth contribution of changes in the sex and educational composition of the labor force. The growth contribution of quality change in the labor force can be written

$$G^Q = \gamma_Q S_L = \gamma_s S_L + \gamma_e S_L + (\gamma_Q - \gamma_s - \gamma_e)S_L \qquad (16.19)$$

from which we define:

$$G^s = S_L \gamma_s \qquad (16.20)$$

which is the growth contribution of changes in the sex composition of the labor force;

$$G^e = S_L \gamma_e \qquad (16.21)$$

which is the growth contribution of changes in the educational composition of the labor force;

$$G^{es} = S_L \gamma_{es} \qquad (16.22)$$

which is the growth contribution of age-sex interaction effects; from which it follows that,

$$G^Q = G^s + G^e + G^{es} \qquad (16.23)$$

The education-sex interaction may arise if the relative earnings among labor characterized by different educational levels differ between sexes, or what is equivalent, if the relative earnings of the two sexes differ among educational levels. Thus, for example, if the level of education or the size of the male labor force is increasing faster than the female and if the effect of schooling on productivity is greater for males than females, the education-sex interaction effect will be positive.

The term G^e, representing the contribution of increases in the educational level of the labor force to economic growth, is *not* an estimate of the contribution of education to growth. First, no account is taken of the opportunity costs of resources devoted to education. Second, it measures only the growth effects of *increases* in labor quality, while a major proportion of the educational effort is devoted to equipping new workers with educational attainments equal to those possessed by retiring workers in order to maintain the average educational level of the labor force.

In his essay in this volume, Marcelo Selowsky has suggested a method of estimating the contribution of education to growth which arises through the role of schooling in maintaining the educational level of the labor force. In order to estimate this quantity, we must decompose the contribution of labor to growth into two components: the contribution of increases in labor, assuming the new workers have no schooling; and the additional contribution of increases in labor due to the fact that the average level of schooling in the work force is maintained. Thus, following Selowsky,

$$G_L = \gamma_L S_L = \gamma_L(S_E + S_P) = \gamma_L S_E + \gamma_L S_P$$

where
    G_L = the growth contribution of increases in labor numbers
    S_L = total labor earnings as a fraction of gross domestic product
    γ_L = the rate of growth of labor numbers

5. Namely, $\gamma_Q = \dot{Q}/Q$, $\gamma_e = \dot{Q}^e/Q^e$, and $\gamma_s = \dot{Q}^s/Q^s$.

S_P = the share of gross domestic product paid to the pure unschooled labor component in each worker in the labor force

S_E = the share of gross domestic product paid to labor above and beyond that paid to pure unschooled labor

The first term on the right, $\gamma_L S_E$, is the contribution of education to growth through maintaining the average level of schooling in the labor force. The second term on the right, $\gamma_L S_P$, is the contribution to growth of the increase in pure labor.[6]

We turn now to the estimation of the growth contribution of labor force quality and quantity.

III. Sources of Growth: The Quality and Quantity of Labor

Our estimates of the contribution of changes in the quality and quantity of workers are based on an estimate of the elasticity of output with respect to labor, estimates of the relative marginal products of labor categorized by education and sex, and data on the size and composition of the 1951 and 1961 labor force according to years of schooling and sex.

Proceeding on the assumption that the wage represents the marginal productivity of the worker, we have used the wage share of gross domestic product, 0.78, as an estimate of S_L, the elasticity of output with respect to labor.[7] The data underlying the estimate of the wage share are presented in Appendix A to this chapter.

The data on the rate of growth and changing composition of the labor force are based on the 1951 and 1961 censuses. Because the 1951 population, but not the labor force, is classified in the census by educational level, estimates of participation rates by detailed age, sex, and education categories for 1961 were used in conjunction with the 1951 population data to arrive at an estimate of the size and composition of the 1951 labor force. Table 16.1 presents the average annual rates of growth of each category of labor over the decade. The basic data used in this chapter appear in Appendix A to this chapter. The main characteristics of the labor force growth over the period are a very slow rate of growth of employment among males (less than 1 percent per annum), no growth in the number of females employed, and an increase in the average educational level of the labor force, particularly among females.

The slow growth of the Greek labor force over the period 1951–1961 was a result of a low rate of population growth and a declining fraction of the population employed.[8] In Table 16.2 the growth contribution of the increase in the number of persons employed is decomposed into the contribution of population increase and the change in the fraction of population employed.[9]

6. The distinction between the earnings of pure labor and of schooling is necessarily somewhat arbitrary. For a further explication of these concepts, see Marcelo Selowsky (Chapter 17 in this volume).

7. The wage share, wL/Y, is assumed to be a good approximation of $f_L L/Y$ (or S_L) in equation (16.3).

8. The fraction of total population economically active in Greece in 1961 was lower than any other European country. See Economic Commission for Europe (1963: 5).

9. Because the 1951 employment figures were estimated on the basis of 1961 participation rates for each subcategory of labor by age, sex, and kind of education, there may have been shifts in the actual employment ratio which have not been observed here. Changes in the overall rate are, of course, consistent with constant individual rates by age, sex, and education as the overall rates probably change primarily through changes in the age, sex, or educational composition of the labor force.

Table 16.1. Average Annual Rates of Growth of Labor, 1951-1961

| Sex | Highest level of schooling completed | | | | |
	Not finished primary	Primary	Secondary	Higher	All
Female	-0.0295	0.0554	0.0581	0.0539	-0.00116
Male	-0.0335	0.0445	0.0446	0.0394	0.00925
All	-0.0318	0.0470	0.0478	0.0421	0.00582

Source: 1951 and 1961 Population Census and S. Bowles (1968: Appendix 1).

The total contribution of the increase in labor number G^n represents less than 9 percent of the rate of growth. The fall in the fraction of population employed, accounting for a negative growth contribution of 5.4 percent of the observed growth, is explained in part by the emigration of large numbers from age groups characterized by high labor force participation rates. The most drastic reductions in the labor force occur at the school-age categories and reflect the expansion of education.[10]

The expansion of education can be viewed as having three effects on the amount of labor input in the economy: the withdrawal of young people from the labor force for schooling; the transfer of labor to a higher educational category characterized by a different labor force participation rate or a different level of unemployment; and the increase in productivity due to additional years of schooling. Thus the effect of increased education in reducing the size of the 1961 labor force was accompanied by an offsetting increase in the average quality of labor associated with increased

10. The impact of increased schooling on the fraction employed was probably greatest for women, both because education expanded more rapidly among women than men and because the effect of increasing education on labor force participation appears to be negative for women, at least up to the level of higher education. See Samuel Bowles (1967).

Table 16.2. The Growth Contributions of Population Increases and Change in the Fraction of Population Employed[a]

| | Average annual rate of change | Growth contribution | |
		In absolute terms	As a fraction of observed growth
Population[b]	0.00944	0.00739	0.140
Fraction of population employed	-0.00362	-0.00284	-0.054
Numbers employed[c]	0.00582	0.00455	0.086
Gross domestic product[d]	0.0527		

[a] These estimates are based on $N = PR$ when P represents total population and R, the fraction of the population employed. Thus we have $\gamma_N = \gamma_P + \gamma_R$ when γ_P and γ_R represent the average annual rate of growth of P and R, and $G^N = \gamma_N S_L = \gamma_P S_L + \gamma_R S_L = G^P + G^R$.
    [b] National Statistical Service of Greece (1966: 19).
    [c] These are the estimated figures obtained through the participation rates based on 1961 population figures. The census figure for 1961 employed labor force was 3,424,500. National Statistical Service of Greece, vol. II (1966: 27).
    [d] Expressed in 1954 drachmae, from Ministry of Coordination, *National Accounts of Greece*, various years.

years of schooling.[11] At the same time, changes in the sex composition of the labor force affected the average labor force quality.

In order to estimate the growth contribution of increases in the educational level of the labor force, as well as changes in its sex composition, we construct sex- and education-weighted labor input indices. The relative marginal productivity weights for labor by sex and educational level used in the construction of the labor quality index are based on a survey of earnings, by years of schooling, sex, and age for the year 1960, of over 1000 workers in private establishments in the Athens area.[12] The use of earnings data as the basis for marginal productivity calculations is based on the assumption that the relative earnings of each category of labor correspond to the relative marginal products.[13] While this assumption is undoubtedly violated in the Greek case, Appendix B to this chapter shows that significant changes in the marginal productivity ratios yield comparatively minor changes in the crucial estimates.

In view of the fact that the attributes of an individual which are positively correlated with higher earnings (for example, intelligence, energy, social class background) are also positively correlated with the likelihood of one's getting an education; the observed earnings differentials among labor classified by years of schooling are only partly attributable to educational differences. In order to take account of this problem, the arbitrary assumption is made that 60 percent of the differences in earnings among categories of labor are to be explained by differences in educational attainment and the weights in Table 16.3 are arrived at.[14] The estimated growth contributions are not sensitive to plausible alternative assumptions.[15]

Even using the corrected weights, too much growth may still be attributed to formal education if there is a positive relation between the years an individual has been in school and the amount of on-the-job training received.[16] The higher earnings associated with additional years of education may be partly explained by the fact that a larger amount of resources is devoted to on-the-job training and other forms

11. Obviously the students withdrawn from work for schooling in 1961 were not contributing to increased labor quality in that year. But the steady growth of education over the decade which led to increases in the educational level of the labor force also led to withdrawals in 1961.

12. This survey was directed by Harvey Leibenstein and was carried out by A. Kalergi and the statistical staff of the Center of Planning and Economic Research in Athens. I am indebted to Harvey Leibenstein for allowing me to use these data.

13. In the construction of the quality of labor index we do not require that the wage equal the value of the marginal product; proportionality of wages and marginal products is sufficient. However, the use of the wage share as an estimate of the elasticity of output with respect to labor requires equality of wages and marginal products.

14. I have no plausible explanation for the lower earnings in the group with 6–11 years of education compared to those with 0–5 years. Harvey Leibenstein is preparing a detailed study of returns to education in Greece on the basis of these and other data, and I have therefore not offered any comprehensive discussion of the relative earnings of labor with different educational qualifications. The absolute level of earnings in the Athens area is undoubtedly higher than the national average. However, we have no reason to suspect that the relative earnings are distorted. The observed earnings may represent an understatement of actual earnings of the group with the highest level of education because of various nonwage payments to this group and the greater ease with which they can understate their earnings. Any plausible correction to take account of this possibility will not significantly alter the results. See Appendix B to this chapter.

15. Denison used the 60 percent assumption in his study of United States growth. Recent work in the United States has suggested that his estimate was in the right general area. However, currently available studies for the United States on this question are far from conclusive. We have no comparable studies for Greece.

16. On the basis of the United States data as reported in Mincer (1962), we would expect this to be the case.

Table 16.3. Relative Marginal Productivity Weights by Sex and Schooling[a]

| Sex | Highest level of schooling completed | | | | |
	Not finished primary	Primary	Secondary	Higher	All
Female	0.80	0.73	0.98	1.35	0.75
Male	1.01	1.00	1.30	1.93	1.00
All	0.98	1.00	1.30	1.94	

Source: The sample described in the text has been reweighted by age, sex, and education to represent the Greek labor force in 1960.

[a] Based on the assumption that 60 percent of earnings differences between workers of different educational backgrounds is attributable to educational differences.

of human capital formation for individuals with relatively more schooling. On the other hand, the use of personal earnings as the basis for the estimate of the effect of education on output may understate the education contribution since it obscures those productive effects of education which are diffused over factors other than the worker in question. Moreover, a considerable amount of economically useful learning takes place outside the school and is not closely correlated with the years of schooling. Thus the decision to use the years of schooling as a measure of education, and earnings as a measure of its productivity, may well have relegated some of the growth effects of education (broadly construed) to the residual.

A further possible bias arises because the definition of total quality adjusted labor services (equation 6) is based on the use of constant relative earnings of labor classified by sex and education. Use of this definition of total labor services in the study of growth implies an infinite elasticity of substitution among all types of labor. Assuming that substitutability among labor inputs is less than infinite, and given that the categories of labor with relatively more schooling were less abundant in 1951 than at the end of the period, we may expect that the use of relative earnings from a survey in 1960 would understate the relative marginal productivity of schooling in the early part of the decade. Our procedure may thus result in downward biased estimates of the contribution of increased schooling to economic growth.

In order to determine the magnitude of this bias, I experimented with an alternative form of the definition of total labor services, one which allows for less-than-infinite elasticities of substitution among labor inputs. The alternative form is a two-level constant elasticity of substitution function in which labor with three different levels of schooling is aggregated to form the quantity total labor services. A detailed description of the international cross-section estimates of the elasticity of substitution among the types of labor I used is available in Bowles (1970). Those estimates yielded the following empirical form of the aggregation function defining total labor services:

$$L = [0.7995(0.3651L_2 + 0.6349L_3)^{0.8806} + 0.2005L_1^{0.8806}]^{1/0.8806}$$

where

L_1 is the total quantity of labor with 0–7 years of schooling
L_2 is the total quantity of labor with 8–11 years of schooling
L_3 is the total quantity of labor with 12 or more years of schooling

Table 16.4. Growth Contribution of Changes in Labor Quality and Quantity

	Average annual growth rate	Contribution to growth as a fraction of observed growth
Number employed		
Pure unschooled labor		0.081
Maintenance of average schooling level		0.005
Total	0.00582	0.086
Labor quality		
Sex composition	0.00062	0.009
Educational composition	0.00186	0.028
Interaction between sex and education	-0.00099	-0.015
Total	0.00149	0.022
Total labor adjusted for quality	0.00731	0.108

Sources: See Tables 16.3, A16.1, and A16.2.

Implicit in this function is an estimated elasticity of substitution between L_2 and L_3 of infinity. That between L_1 and the composite factor formed by L_2 and L_3 is 8.

The estimated contribution of increased schooling to growth based on this function was virtually identical to what is reported below. The estimated elasticities underlying the alternative labor aggregation function are, by any standard, high. However, Marcelo Selowsky has shown that even with considerably lower elasticities of substitution among labor inputs, changes in the relative earnings of different types of labor are likely to be comparatively minor over a period as short as a decade.[17] Apparently the bias resulting from the assumption of infinite elasticities of substitution among labor inputs is small. Because the constant elasticity of substitution function is defined for only three categories of labor, I have proceeded with the more disaggregated labor aggregation function based on the assumption of infinite elasticities (equation 6) and the relative productivity weights in Table 16.3.

Combining the relative productivity weights with the labor force data by sex and education, we arrive at the indices of quality and quantity change in the labor force and the estimated growth contributions which appear in Table 16.4.[18]

The contribution of increased labor services adjusted for changes in sex and education composition is 10.8 percent of the observed rate of growth. The 2.2 percent difference between the adjusted and unadjusted growth contribution of labor is composed of slightly less than 3 percent contribution of education; a contribution of sex changes of about 1 percent; and interaction effects between education, sex, and labor numbers accounting for roughly −1.5 percent. The negative effect of education

17. See Selowsky (Chap. 17, this volume).
18. Calculation of the contribution of education to growth through maintaining the average level of schooling in the labor force is based on the following decomposition of labor's share in gross domestic product. Pure unschooled labor was represented by the lowest schooling category, those who had not completed primary school or had no schooling. The adjusted earnings of all labor above the earnings of this group were represented as earnings due to schooling. The data in Tables 16.3 and A16.1 yielded a figure of 6 percent for the share of gross domestic product earned by education above the minimum schooling category. This figure is slightly less than one-tenth of the total labor share.

and sex interaction is more than one-third of the positive effects of sex and education taken together and is accounted for by the more rapid rate of growth of the male labor force coupled with the fact that the increment in earnings for additional education is proportionally greater for females than males.

The total growth contribution of education—both in maintaining and increasing the level of schooling in the labor force—is 0.033 of the observed rate of growth. This very small growth contribution is due to the low rate of labor force growth and to the small share of total labor earnings attributable to education above the lowest schooling category.

IV. Summary and Conclusions

Summary estimates of the contribution of increases in labor numbers and in the educational level of the labor force to economic growth in the Greek economy appear in Table 16.5, along with comparable estimates for eight other European countries, the United States, and Chile. The estimates for the United States and Europe are based on an approach very similar to that adopted here.[19] The Harberger-Selowsky estimates (1966) for Chile are derived from a model similar to this one except that human capital is considered a separate factor of production. The contribution of the increased schooling of the labor force to growth was remarkably small in Greece, considerably smaller than all other countries in Table 16.5, except Germany, where increased education apparently contributed a miniscule 2 percent to the rate of growth.

The very small growth contribution of increased schooling in the Greek labor force may be explained by two related facts. The first is that transformation of the educational composition of the labor force has not been particularly marked; the second

19. The estimates for Europe and the United States are from Denison (1967).

Table 16.5. Growth Contributions of Changes in Labor Quality and Quantity Expressed as a Fraction of the Observed Rate of Growth in 11 Countries

	Increase in educational level of labor force	Increase in employment
Greece (1951–1961)	0.03	0.09
United States	0.15	0.13
Belgium	0.13	0.20
Denmark	0.04	0.02
France	0.06	0.02
Germany	0.02	0.21
Netherlands	0.05	0.16
Norway	0.07	0.04
United Kingdom	0.13	0.22
Italy	0.07	0.07
Chile (1941–1962)	0.15	0.23

Source: Data on all countries except Greece and Chile are from E. F. Denison with Jean-Pierre Poullier (1967). Data refer to the period 1950–1962. For Chile, see A. Harberger and M. Selowsky (1966). For Greece, see Table 16.4.

is that with the exception of university education, the increase in productivity associated with additional years of schooling appears to be relatively small.[20] The estimated growth contribution of increases in the educational level of the labor force should be considered in the light of the quality of the available data and the restrictive nature of the underlying conceptual model of the relationship between education and labor quality.

Even if the estimates do provide a meaningful measure of the growth contribution of labor quality increases through increased schooling, it should be emphasized that while the failure of an educational system to contribute significantly to economic growth may be viewed by economists as unusual or surprising, it cannot be regarded as a general indictment of the system or of the content of the courses offered. The apparently small economic contribution of Greek education may be the result of a perfectly rational decision to use the school primarily as a vehicle to transmit the nation's cultural heritage to the new generation and to inculcate other values thought to be socially important. Or it may simply reflect the fact that a relatively small quantity of resources was devoted to education over this period.[21] This point is clearly illustrated by the results of prescriptive, rather than descriptive, models of Greek education. Application of a programming model to the Greek educational sector over a planning horizon extending from 1961 to 1975 indicated that given an economically rational allocation of educational resources, schooling can make a major contribution to growth.[22]

The complexity of the growth process defies adequate comprehension using a static, single-equation factor accumulation model: most of the interesting questions are left unasked. What do we learn, then, from estimates of the growth contribution of labor quality and quantity in the Greek economy? The method is primarily diagnostic rather than prescriptive. In conjunction with comparable studies for other economies, it can be used to identify some deviant characteristics of Greek growth. The results may indicate areas for further studies, but they cannot by themselves prescribe changes in patterns of resource allocation.

20. Harvey Leibenstein's forthcoming work indicates very low rates of return for some types of Greek education.

21. In 1961 total educational expenditure constituted 2.1 percent of the Greek gross national product compared to over 4 percent in the United States, the Netherlands, and Sweden and over 3 percent in the United Kingdom, France, Italy, and Denmark. The only OECD member country with a lower percentage of GNP devoted to education was Spain. OECD (1965: 70).

22. See Bowles (1969: chap. 5).

Appendix A to Chapter 16
Basic Data, Sources, and Methods

Table A16.1. **Estimated Employment:** **Labor Force by Sex and Education, 1951-1961[a]**

Educational group (j)	Years of schooling	1951		1961	
		M	F	M	F
1	0-5	1,163,500	834,353	831,927	621,153
2	6-11	785,899	221,241	1,226,928	385,215
3	12-15	125,360	35,626	195,918	63,690
4	16+	54,366	11,910	80,597	20,423
Total		2,129,125	1,103,130	2,335,370	1,090,481

[a] The 1951 and 1961 labor force estimates are based on the 1951 and 1961 censuses of population and estimates of the fraction employed in each population cell by age, sex, and education as reported in Samuel Bowles (1968), available on request. A very small number who did not report their age or education have been omitted.

Table A16.2. Wage Share, 1961

	Figures in current million drs.
GDP[a]	87,916
Wages and salaries of workers outside of agriculture[b]	34,908
Wages and salaries imputed to	
agricultural labor[c]	17,669
self-employed[d]	16,211
Total actual and imputed wages	68,788
The wage share[e]	0.78

[a] GDP is in current drachmae, excluding ships.

[b] Data from Ministry of Coordination, *National Accounts of Greece*, vol. 14 (p. 45).

[c] The labor remuneration in agriculture is based on data for labor earnings in agriculture in 1960 and the assumption that the labor share agriculture in 1961 was the same as in 1960, namely, 0.62. I am grateful to Dr. Anna Kokkova for supplying data on labor earnings in agriculture in 1960.

[d] The estimate of the remuneration of the self-employed is based on the number of self-employed in 1961 and 1958 data on relative earnings of the self-employed vis-à-vis wage and salary earners. Cf. Geronimakis (1962: 12, table 5). Remuneration for labor services was assumed to constitute 75 percent of the earnings of the self-employed.

[e] Total actual and imputed wage divided by GDP.

Appendix B to Chapter 16
Sensitivity of the Results to Errors

Much of the data used in this study is subject to considerable error. For this reason I offer the following do-it-yourself skeptic's kit.

It can be seen from equation (16.3) that a 1 percentage error in the estimate of the wage share yields a 1 percent change in the estimated growth contribution of labor (either unadjusted or quality weighted). Advocates of a wage share different from 0.78 are invited to read off their preferred-estimates from Figures 16.1 and 16.2.

The estimate of the growth contribution of increases in the educational level of the labor force depends crucially on the fraction of earnings differences between labor of different educational levels assumed to be due to differences in education itself as opposed to differences in motivation, social advantage, and other attributes

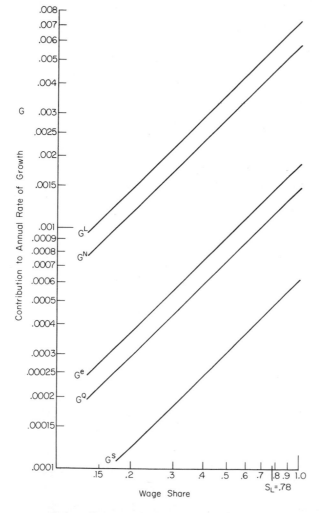

Figure 16.1 Growth contributions of labor input indices as a function of the wage share.

positively associated with both earnings and level of education. In the study we have assumed α, the fraction of income differences attributable to education, to be 0.6. The nature of the dependence of estimates of the growth contribution of education on the assumed value of α can be viewed via the relation $Q^e = Q^e(\alpha)$: the education-weighted quality of labor index as a function of α.

Figure 16.2 shows the effect on the estimated contribution of education to growth of assuming alternative values of α. An α greater than 1 implies that productivity differences attributable to educational differences are even greater than observed earnings differences. This might be the case, for example, if there existed a divergence between the marginal product of labor and the wage differences such that the ratio, f_L/W, rose with increasing years of education or if the probability of going on in school was negatively associated with personal attributes associated positively with higher earnings.

It can be seen that even with implausibly large values for α, the growth contribution of education remains relatively small.

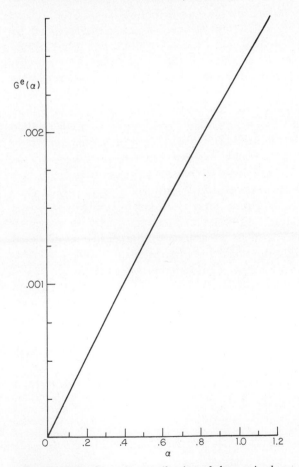

Figure 16.2 Growth contribution of change in the educational composition of the labor force as a function of α.

17 Labor Input Substitution in the Study of Sources of Growth and Educational Planning*

Marcelo Selowsky

Knowledge of the elasticity of substitution among labor inputs classified by schooling is important in any study that requires information on relative wages by schooling for periods far removed from the present. Information on past relative wages by schooling is necessary for studying the past contribution of education to economic growth. Future relative wages by schooling are required for evaluating the benefits of investing in schooling, and therefore they become relevant in the analysis of educational planning.

Earlier studies on sources of growth and cost benefit analysis of investment in schooling have used present relative wages by schooling as the measure of the relative contribution of each type of the labor input to output.[1] This procedure implicitly assumes that either relative wages by schooling are independent of changes in the educational composition of the labor force or those changes have not been important in the past and are not expected to be important in the future.

For many countries, the educational distribution of the labor force has experienced major changes over time, yet for almost all of them, time series data on wages by schooling are not available.[2] Therefore, unless we assume that labor groups classified by schooling are perfect substitutes (the elasticity of substitution among them is infinite), we would expect those wages to have changed through time.

On the other hand, many underdeveloped countries face investment decisions in education that are not "marginal," that is, they will substantially change the future educational distribution of the labor force. The use of present relative wages to evaluate the benefits of those investments implicitly assumes that relative earnings by schooling will remain constant, that is, labor categories classified by schooling

* This study is based on Economic Development Report 116, Center for International Affairs, Harvard University (November 1968) and on "On the Measurement of Education's Contribution to Growth," *Quarterly Journal of Economics*, Vol. 83, August 1969, by permission of the publisher. Portions of this research were supported by the Development Advisory Service and Project for Quantitative Research in Economic Development, Harvard University, through funds provided by the Agency for International Development under contract CSD-1543.

I am indebted to Arnold C. Harberger, Samuel Bowles, and Christopher Dougherty for valuable comments on an earlier version.

1. For the analysis of sources of growth, see E. Denison (1967). Cost benefit analyses to invest in education using internal rate of return approach are found in G. Becker (1964); M. Carnoy (1963); W. L. Hansen (1963); and Selowsky (1967). For an optimizing model using present relative wages as arguments of the maximand, see Bowles (Chapter 11, this volume).

2. To my knowledge the United States is the only country for which time series on earnings by schooling are available.

are perfect substitutes. The purpose of this study is to analyze the sensitivity of the estimates of the past contribution of education to growth as well as the estimates of rates of return to education to this assumption of constant relative wages by schooling over time.

To analyze the first problem, I have studied two countries, Chile and Mexico, which have experienced major changes in the educational distribution of the labor force in the last 25 years.

To study the second problem, I have used the case of Colombia, whose government faces investment decisions in education which will significantly alter the future educational composition of the labor force.

I. Past Relative Wages and the Measurement of Education's Contribution to Growth

The Analytical Framework

Let us begin by specifying a production function of the following form:

$$Y = F[K, L_0, L_1, \ldots, L_n] \tag{17.1}$$

where Y is aggregate output; K is the flow of services of the physical capital stock; and $L_0, L_1, \ldots, L_n$ are man-hour inputs of members of the labor force with 0, 1, $\ldots$, n years of schooling, respectively.

Differentiating (1) with respect to time, we get:

$$\dot{Y} = f_K \dot{K} + f_{L_0} \dot{L}_0 + f_{L_1} \dot{L}_1 \cdots f_{L_n} \dot{L}_n \tag{17.2}$$

where the dots indicate time derivatives and the f's are partial derivatives. If we assume that wages reflect marginal productivities, we can rewrite (17.2) as:

$$\dot{Y} = f_K \dot{K} + \sum_i w_i \dot{L}_i \tag{17.3}$$

where w_i is the real wage of individuals with i years of schooling. Define $L = \sum_i L_i$, so that $\dot{L} = \Sigma_i \dot{L}_i$. Equation (17.3) then can be written as:

$$\dot{Y} = f_K \dot{K} + w_0 \dot{L} + \sum_i (w_i - w_0) \dot{L}_i \tag{17.4}$$

where $f_K \dot{K}$ is the contribution of physical capital to growth; $w_0 \dot{L}$ is the contribution of "bodies," that is, of the "uneducated" component of all members of the labor force, and $\sum_i (w_i - w_0) \dot{L}_i$ is the contribution of education.[3]

The contribution of education can be disaggregated into two components. Define $a_i = L_i/L$. Then $\Sigma_i \dot{a}_i = 0$, and we get:

$$\sum_i (w_i - w_0) \dot{L}_i = \dot{L} \sum_i (w_i - w_0) a_i + L \sum_i w_i \dot{a}_i \tag{17.5}$$

---

3. This term is obviously an understatement of the true contribution so long as education creates external economies not captured by wage differentials and an overstatement if ability is correlated with years of schooling.

$L \sum_i w_i \dot{a}_i$ is the contribution to growth of changes in the relative distribution of workers by years of schooling. $\dot{L} \sum_i (w_i - w_0)a_i$ is the contribution to output stemming from the educational effort entailed in maintaining constant the relative distribution of the labor force by years of schooling. We shall call this term the contribution of the "maintenance" component. Equation (17.4) can be written as:

$$\dot{Y} = f_K \dot{K} + \left[w_0 + \sum_i (w_i - w_0)a_i \right] \dot{L} + L \sum_i w_i \dot{a}_i \qquad (17.6)$$

The average wage $\bar{w}$ is $\sum_i w_i a_i$. Equation (17.6) can therefore be written as:

$$\frac{\dot{Y}}{Y} = \alpha_K \frac{\dot{K}}{K} + (\alpha_B + \alpha_E) \frac{\dot{L}}{L} + \alpha_L \frac{\dot{Q}}{Q} + R \qquad (17.7)$$

where

$\alpha_B = w_0 L/Y$	the share of bodies in total output
$\alpha_E = (\bar{w} - w_0)L/Y$	the share of educational inputs in total output
$\alpha_B + \alpha_E = \alpha_L$	the share of labor in total output
$\dot{Q}/Q = \sum_i (w_i/\bar{w}) \dot{a}_i$	the relative change in an index of the quality of the labor force
R	is a residual summarizing the contribution of other forces to the growth rate

From equation (17.7) we can see that the total contribution of education to the growth rate is $\alpha_E \dot{L}/L + \alpha_L \dot{Q}/Q$, where $\alpha_E \dot{L}/L$ is the contribution of the maintenance factor and $\alpha_L \dot{Q}/Q$ is the contribution of increases in the quality of the labor force due to education.

From the previous discussion we can see that the weights of the changes in the schooling distribution of the labor force are relative wages by schooling at a given moment of time. For the countries we are interested in, only one-year data on earnings are available. (This information is presented in Table 17.1.)

One way of solving this problem is simply to use these one year figures for all the other years; this has been the method used in all the country studies in which such information on relative wages was missing (see Denison 1967). As we mentioned earlier, this method would give a correct measurement only if relative wages were

Table 17.1. One-Year Data on Earnings, 1964

Chile		Mexico	
Years of schooling	Relative wages ($w_i/\bar{w}$)	Years of schooling	Relative wages ($w_i/\bar{w}$)
0-2	0.451	0-1	0.574
3-5	0.609	2-3	0.770
6-7	0.759	4-5	1.022
8-10	1.084	6	1.343
11	1.428	7-9	1.810
12	1.976	10-11	2.392
13-16	6.632	12-14	3.567
17+	11.288	15+	7.080

Sources: Carnoy (1963); Selowsky (1967: Tables 6 and 14).

constant over time and therefore independent of changes in the input mix. Our purpose is to analyze how sensitive the results are to this assumption on constant relative wages; for this purpose we want to explore how the relative wages of the missing years would have looked given the input endowment of that time and some assumptions concerning the production function of the economy.

In order to do this, we generate relative wages by schooling as a function of the input mix of other dates, taking as a starting value the single-year data available. For this we must assume certain properties of the production function, and the problem is to find a function that is easy to work with empirically and also consistent with the available empirical evidence.

The rough evidence provided by the available data is the following:

1. Time series data on most countries show a rather constant share of the total labor input even in view of strong changes in the capital-labor ratio.
2. Time series and intercountry data show a low sensitivity of relative wages by schooling to changes in the educational distribution of the labor force and to changes in the overall capital-labor ratio (Bowles 1969; Griliches 1968). This phenomenon could be the result of a number of factors:

a. a relatively high elasticity of substitution among labor categories classified by schooling
b. a labor-saving technical progress "less biased" against more educated labor
c. physical capital being significantly more complementary with more-educated labor than with less-educated labor
d. A higher intensity in the use of educated labor in the commodities of higher income elasticity

In this study, we want to reproduce this low sensitivity of relative wages through a production function that is able to use the limited information in existence.

Empirical evidence about factors b, c, and d (outlined above) is almost non-existent (Bowles 1969; Griliches 1968: 46–51): the few attempts made to explain this low sensitivity have used factor a as the empirical relationship thus, perhaps, implicitly attributing part of the effect of b, c, and d to the elasticity of substitution. We shall use relation a because of its simplicity, but we explicitly recognize that it may serve as a proxy for relations b through d.

Given the two pieces of information (1 and a), what we need is a production function that both allows for unitary elasticity of substitution between capital and the aggregate labor input and leaves unconstrained the value of the elasticity of substitution among labor inputs classified by schooling. If we restrict this last elasticity to a constant value, this function can be written as a combination of a Cobb-Douglas and a CES production function:

$$Y = K^{\alpha}(L^*)^{1-\alpha} \qquad (17.8)$$

where Y and K are aggregate output and the services of the capital stock and where L^* is the labor input index, itself a CES function of different types of labor classified by years of schooling.

$$L^* = \left(\sum_i d_i L_i^{\rho}\right)^{1/\rho} \qquad (17.9)$$

where

L_i = labor category with i years of schooling

d_i = distribution parameter of the ith kind of labor

$\rho = \sigma_L - 1/\sigma_L$

where σ_L is the (constant) elasticity of substitution among the various categories of labor.

The marginal product of any labor category i, which we assume equal to the observed wage rate w_i, is:

$$\frac{\partial Y}{\partial L_i} = K^\alpha (1 - \alpha) d_i L_i^{\rho-1} \left[\sum_i d_i L_i^\rho \right]^{(1-\alpha/\rho)-1} \tag{17.10}$$

$$\frac{\partial Y}{\partial L_i} = (1 - \alpha) d_i Y L_i^{\rho-1} \left[\sum_i d_i L_i^\rho \right]^{-1} \tag{17.11}$$

$$\frac{\partial Y}{\partial L_i} = (1 - \alpha) d_i \frac{Y}{L_i} \left[\frac{L_i}{L^*} \right]^\rho = w_i \tag{17.12}$$

The average wage in the labor force, $\bar{w}$, is equal to:

$$\bar{w} = \frac{w_{L^*} L^*}{L} = (1 - \alpha) \frac{Y}{L} \tag{17.13}$$

where w_{L^*} is the marginal product of the labor index L^* and L is the total labor force. The expression we are interested in, or the relative wage of any category L_i, is:

$$\frac{w_i}{\bar{w}} = d_i \frac{\sum\limits_i L_i}{L_i} \left[\frac{L_i}{L^*} \right]^\rho \tag{17.14}$$

If we know the parameters d_i and assume alternative values of ρ (and therefore the elasticity of substitution among labor groups), we can determine for any year the relative wages of any category L_i as a function of the educational distribution of the labor force of that year.[4]

---

4. The values of d_i are obtained through the 1-year data on earnings and on the educational distribution of the labor force. For this purpose, we can substitute (17.9) into (17.12), so we have for any w_j

$$w_j = \frac{(1 - \alpha) d_j Y L_j^{\rho-1}}{\sum\limits_i d_i L_i^\rho} \qquad d_j = \frac{w_j \sum\limits_i d_i L_i^\rho}{(1 - \alpha) Y L_j^{\rho-1}}$$

The ratio of d_j to any d_i is

$$\frac{d_j}{d_i} = \frac{w_j L_j^{1-\rho}}{w_i L_i^{1-\rho}}$$

summing across i, and using the restriction $\Sigma_i d_i = 1$, we get

$$d_j = \frac{w_j L_j^{1-\rho}}{\sum\limits_i w_i L_i^{1-\rho}}$$

It is important to notice that the estimated parameters d_j are a function of the assumed values of ρ, namely, of the elasticity of substitution among the different categories of labor.

Table 17.2. Chile: Educational Distribution of the Labor Force (percents)

Years of schooling	1940	1945	1950	1955	1960	1964
0-2	53.48	48.87	43.28	37.01	28.08	20.64
3-5	11.74	17.31	22.05	25.65	29.65	32.12
6-7	12.19	12.85	14.43	17.16	20.95	24.51
8-10	14.34	13.21	12.61	12.05	12.26	12.68
11	3.10	2.71	2.40	2.27	2.19	2.27
12	2.42	2.47	2.89	3.47	4.30	4.93
13-16	1.72	1.58	1.34	1.29	1.26	1.36
17 or more	1.01	1.00	1.00	1.10	1.31	1.49

Source: Selowsky (1967).

Empirical Evaluation

Using equation (17.14) and the educational distribution of the labor force shown in Tables 17.2 and 17.3, it is possible to derive time series data on relative wages for Chile and Mexico. Figure 17.1 shows the behavior of relative wages as a function of time and different values of σ_L; the relative wages we selected correspond to those categories (classified by schooling) of the labor force who, over time, experienced strong increases as a fraction of the total labor force.[5] We can observe that these relative wages increase when we go back in time and those groups become relatively scarce, the increase being stronger, the lower the value of σ_L.

Table 17.3. Mexico: Educational Distribution of the Labor Force (percents)

Years of schooling	1940	1945	1950	1955	1960	1964
0-1	60.80	59.09	55.57	49.62	43.49	38.05
2-3	9.59	12.50	16.43	21.10	25.32	27.95
4-5	11.29	11.12	11.01	11.11	11.11	11.02
6	11.59	10.85	10.49	11.01	12.04	13.20
7-9	2.92	3.03	3.21	3.79	4.39	5.60
10-11	1.49	1.29	1.23	1.18	1.28	1.53
12-14	1.16	1.06	1.04	1.13	1.24	1.40
15 or more	1.16	1.06	1.02	1.06	1.13	1.25

Source: Selowsky (1967).

Having determined relative wages through time and given (for practical purposes constant) the value of total labor share ($\alpha_L = 0.50$ for Chile and $\alpha_L = 0.41$ for Mexico), it is possible to estimate α_E or the share of educational inputs.[6] These values are presented for both countries in Table 17.4.

5. The complete data on relative wages under different assumptions on σ_L appear in Selowsky (1968b).

6. For the case of Mexico we used the wage of L_1 as the value for w_0. In the case of Chile we had for 1964, independent estimates of w_0. Therefore, $(w_0/\bar{w})$ at any period t was estimated through the equation

$$\left[\frac{w_0}{\bar{w}}\right]_t = \left[\frac{w_0}{w_1}\right]_{1964} \left[\frac{w_1}{\bar{w}}\right]_t$$

where $(w_1/\bar{w})_t$ is the relative wage of category L_1 in period t.

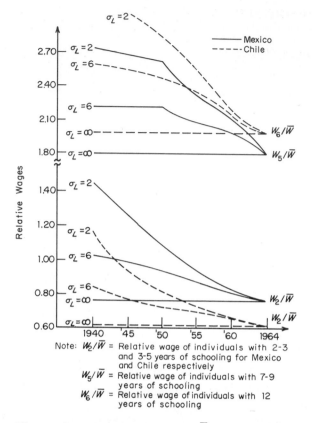

Figure 17.1 Relative wages $(W_i/\overline{W})$ as a function of the elasticity of substitution.

From Table 17.4 we can see the influence of different assumptions on σ_L on the value of α_E. Given that α_L is constant, the behavior of α_E through time is only a function of $w_0/\overline{w}$, or the proportion of the average wage represented by the payments to bodies. The lower the value of σ_L, the stronger will be the decline in this ratio when, going back in time, people without education become relatively more abundant.[7] In other words, the share of the educational inputs embodied in the labor force is higher, the smaller the value of σ_L—the reason being that these inputs receive a relatively higher price when they become relatively more scarce.

Table 17.5 presents the annual rate of growth of the labor quality index $(\dot{Q}/Q)$ due to changes in its educational composition using the relative wages generated under different assumptions on σ_L.

The use of $\sigma_L = 2$ instead of $\sigma_L = \infty$ (or the constant relative wage assumption) increases the average growth of quality by factors of 2.2 and 2.0 for Chile and Mexico, respectively (period 1940–1964). The reason is that with lower values of σ_L the rela-

7. For extremely high values of σ_L, it is possible to have the opposite case. The reason is that $w_0/\overline{w} = w_0 \Big/ \sum_i a_i w_i$ could increase under roughly constant relative wages (w_0/w_i) and declines in $\overline{w}$ due to a deterioration of the average schooling of the labor force.

Table 17.4. Share of Educational Capital on GNP $(a_E)^a$

Elasticity of substitution (σ_L)	1940-1945	1945-1950	1950-1955	1955-1960	1960-1964
Chile					
2	0.36	0.35	0.35	0.34	0.32
4	0.32	0.31	0.31	0.31	0.30
6	0.30	0.30	0.30	0.30	0.30
10	0.29	0.29	0.29	0.29	0.30
∞	0.27	0.27	0.27	0.28	0.28
Mexico					
2	0.21	0.21	0.20	0.19	0.18
4	0.18	0.18	0.18	0.18	0.18
6	0.17	0.17	0.16	0.16	0.17
10	0.16	0.16	0.16	0.16	0.17
∞	0.15	0.15	0.15	0.16	0.16

[a] Beginning-of-the-period relative wages $(w_0/\bar{w})$ were used to obtain a_E.

tive wages of more educated individuals tend to increase when we go back in time (they become relatively more scarce), and those wages themselves are the weights for the changes in the proportion that those groups represent in the labor force. In other words, the positive $\dot{a}_i$'s (which, in general, are those for the higher educational categories) are weighted by relatively higher wages in the past when the past wage data are generated on the assumption of a lower elasticity of substitution.

In the case of Chile, the growth of the quality index increases from −0.18 to 0.58 percent for 1940–1945 and from 1.35 to 1.65 percent for 1960–1964 when $\sigma_L = 2$ is used instead of $\sigma_L = \infty$; in the case of Mexico, this increase is from −0.26 to 0.10 percent for 1940–1945 and from 1.15 to 1.37 percent for 1960–1964.

We would like now to compare cross-country differences in both the trend and magnitude of education's contribution to growth. Tables 17.6, 17.7, and 17.8 show the contribution of education to the growth rate for Chile, Mexico, and the United

Table 17.5. $\dot{Q}/Q$: Annual Growth Rate of the Labor Quality Index Due to Education (percents)

Elasticity of substitution (σ_L)	1940-1945	1945-1950	1950-1955	1955-1960	1960-1964	1940-1964
Chile						
2	0.58	0.58	1.12	1.66	1.65	1.10
4	0.16	0.26	0.88	1.42	1.53	0.82
6	0.04	0.15	0.78	1.34	1.50	0.73
10	-0.07	0.06	0.72	1.27	1.47	0.66
∞	-0.18	-0.06	0.52	1.04	1.35	0.50
Mexico						
2	0.10	0.48	1.00	1.00	1.37	0.77
4	-0.10	0.24	0.78	0.86	1.30	0.59
6	-0.16	0.18	0.70	0.82	1.25	0.53
10	-0.22	0.12	0.65	0.78	1.23	0.48
∞	-0.26	0.04	0.50	0.66	1.15	0.39

Table 17.6. Chile: Contribution of Education to the Annual Growth Rate (in percentages)

σ_L	Source	Period					Average
		1940-1945	1945-1950	1950-1955	1955-1960	1960-1964	1940-1964[a]
2	$a_L(Q'/Q)$	0.29	0.29	0.56	0.83	0.82	0.54(14.5)
	$a_E(L'/L)$	0.65	0.63	0.56	0.49	0.53	0.57(15.3)
	Total	0.94	0.92	1.12	1.32	1.35	1.11(29.8)
4	$a_L(Q'/Q)$	0.08	0.13	0.44	0.71	0.77	0.41(11.0)
	$a_E(L'/L)$	0.58	0.56	0.50	0.45	0.50	0.52(14.0)
	Total	0.66	0.69	0.94	1.16	1.27	0.93(25.0)
6	$a_L(Q'/Q)$	0.02	0.07	0.39	0.67	0.75	0.36(9.7)
	$a_E(L'/L)$	0.54	0.54	0.48	0.44	0.50	0.50(13.5)
	Total	0.56	0.61	0.87	1.11	1.25	0.86(23.2)
10	$a_L(Q'/Q)$	-0.04	0.03	0.36	0.64	0.74	0.33(9.2)
	$a_E(L'/L)$	0.52	0.52	0.46	0.42	0.50	0.48(12.8)
	Total	0.48	0.55	0.82	1.06	1.24	0.81(22.0)
∞	$a_L(Q'/Q)$	-0.09	-0.03	0.26	0.52	0.67	0.25(6.8)
	$a_E(L'/L)$	0.48	0.48	0.43	0.41	0.45	0.45(12.1)
	Total	0.39	0.45	0.69	0.93	1.12	0.70(18.9)

[a] Values in parentheses show the percentage contribution to the growth rate.

States, respectively. It is interesting to note that this contribution has remained roughly constant for the United States (except for 1957–1959), the percentage contribution having varied only because of different growth rates of output in the different periods. On the other hand, the main characteristic of the Chilean and Mexican cases is the rising trend of this contribution. The important features of this increased contribution are discussed below.

1. The rising trend stems from the $\alpha_L \dot{Q}/Q$ component and therefore from $\dot{Q}/Q$,

Table 17.7. Mexico: Contribution of Education to the Annual Growth Rate (in percentages)

σ_L	Source	Period					Average
		1940-1945	1945-1950	1950-1955	1955-1960	1960-1964	1940-1964[a]
2	$a_L(Q'/Q)$	0.04	0.20	0.41	0.41	0.56	0.32(5.0)
	$a_E(L'/L)$	0.43	0.55	0.48	0.54	0.59	0.52(8.1)
	Total	0.47	0.75	0.89	0.95	1.15	0.84(13.1)
4	$a_L(Q'/Q)$	-0.04	0.10	0.32	0.35	0.53	0.24(3.7)
	$a_E(L'/L)$	0.37	0.47	0.43	0.51	0.59	0.47(7.3)
	Total	0.33	0.57	0.75	0.86	1.12	0.71(11.0)
6	$a_L(Q'/Q)$	-0.07	0.07	0.29	0.34	0.51	0.22(3.4)
	$a_E(L'/L)$	0.33	0.42	0.38	0.48	0.56	0.43(6.7)
	Total	0.26	0.49	0.67	0.82	1.07	0.65(10.1)
10	$a_L(Q'/Q)$	-0.09	0.05	0.27	0.32	0.50	0.20(3.0)
	$a_E(L'/L)$	0.33	0.42	0.38	0.46	0.56	0.42(6.6)
	Total	0.24	0.47	0.65	0.78	1.06	0.62(9.6)
∞	$a_L(Q'/Q)$	-0.11	0.02	0.21	0.27	0.47	0.16(2.5)
	$a_E(L'/L)$	0.31	0.39	0.36	0.46	0.53	0.41(6.4)
	Total	0.20	0.41	0.57	0.73	1.00	0.57(8.9)

[a] Values in parentheses show the percentage contribution to the growth rate.

Table 17.8. United States: Contribution of Education to the Yearly Growth Rate[a] (percents)

Source	1940-1948	1948-1952	1952-1957	1957-1959	1959-1962	1962-1965	1940-1965
(1) $\dot{Q}/Q$	0.78	0.62	0.59	1.20	0.79	0.62	0.73
(2) a_L	0.68	0.72	0.72	0.72	0.74	0.74	0.71
(3) $a_L(\dot{Q}/Q)$	0.53(11.8)	0.45(8.8)	0.42(15.0)	0.86(33.1)	0.58(16.1)	0.53(10.4)	0.52(12.9)
(4) a_E	0.34	0.34	0.40	0.42	0.37	0.44	0.37
(5) $\dot{L}/L$							0.90
(6) $a_E(\dot{L}/L)$							0.33(8.0)
Total[b]							0.85(20.9)

Sources: Line (1): Jorgenson and Griliches (1967). (2) and (5): U.S. Department of Commerce (1966). (4): For w_0 the average earnings of individuals with 0-4 years of schooling has been used.
[a] Values in parentheses show the percentage contribution to the growth rate.
[b] Line 3 plus line 6.

or the growth rate of the index of quality of the labor force. The increase of $\dot{Q}/Q$ over time is mainly due to the rate of acceleration of the number of people with high levels of schooling with respect to the total labor force.[8]

2. The rate of increase in $\dot{Q}/Q$ is higher, the higher the value of σ_L. The reason is that under a higher σ_L the relative wages of the groups with higher schooling have a lower decline when their relative number increases. Given that those relative wages represent the weights for the (positive) $\dot{a}_i$'s of those groups, a higher σ_L will tend to increase $\dot{Q}/Q$ over time.[9]

On the other hand, a rough constancy of $\dot{Q}/Q$ and of relative wages for the United States implies no acceleration in the number of people with higher education relative to the total labor force. This is the main explanation of a constant value of $\alpha_L\dot{Q}/Q$ for the United States as compared with an increase value for Chile and Mexico.

From Tables 17.6 and 17.7 we can see that the total contribution of education is a function of different assumptions concerning σ_L. In the case of Chile, this contribution (expressed as a percentage of the growth rate) increases for the overall period 1940–1964 by 63 percent (from 18.9 to 29.8 percent) when $\sigma_L = 2$ is used instead of $\sigma_L = \infty$. For Mexico and for the same period, this increase is equal to 47 percent. Again we can see that the difference in the contribution that comes from different assumptions about σ_L is larger, the further in the past is the period we look at.

These results imply that the use of one (recent) year data on relative wages (the $\sigma_L = \infty$ assumption) could understate substantially the contribution of education to growth depending on how much lower the real value of σ_L is. In other words, the contribution of education obtained with (recent) constant relative wages would represent a lower limit of this magnitude.

8. This can be analyzed by differentiating $\dot{Q}/Q$ with respect to time. Denoting $\dot{Q}/Q$ by q, $w_i/\bar{w}$ by v_i, and differentiating with respect to time, we get

$$\dot{q} = \sum_i v_i\dot{a}_i + \sum_i v_i\ddot{a}_i \qquad (17.1a)$$

The first term of the right-hand side of (17.1a) shows the effect of changes in relative wages and the second one, the rate of acceleration of the percentage distribution of the labor force by years of schooling.

9. See equation (17.1a), note 8 above.

II. Future Relative Wages and Their Effect on the Rate of Return to Education

For the purpose of determining priorities of investment in formal education, some measures of the benefits of schooling are required. Given our state of knowledge, we adopt the same technique as in the analysis of sources of growth: we assume that wage differentials by schooling reflect the increment in labor productivity due to additional schooling.

The most familiar approach to determining investment priorities in education is the estimation of internal rates of return by various levels of schooling. For this purpose cross-section wages, sometimes adjusted by an overall time trend, are used in the construction of age-earning profiles that are required to compute the benefits and costs of achieving a given level of schooling.

The use of present relative wages in the calculation of rates of return is appropriate only to the extent that those relative wages will not change over time. However, if the educational distribution of the labor force changes due to the expansion of the school system itself, we would expect those relative wages to change over time, this change being a function of the elasticity of substitution among labor categories classified by schooling. This means that rates of return to schooling cannot be computed independently from the investment programs in education in the present or the ones planned for the future. Every investment program through time implies a specific rate of return over time or the one resulting from the relative wages generated under this particular program.

The purpose of this section is to analyze the effect of alternative projections of the labor force classified by schooling—resulting from different expansions of the school system—on:

1. The actual rate of return to investment in different levels of schooling
2. the behavior of those rates of return over time

The purpose of the second exercise is to obtain an idea of the magnitude of the decreasing returns to invest in education over time and its sensitivity to alternative projections of the school system.

The Case of Colombia

In estimating the rate of return to education in Colombia, we have analyzed only the urban sector.[10] The main reason is the lack of data on earnings by schooling in the agriculture sector. Second, given the low quality of the educational inputs used in this sector (teachers, educational equipment, and so on), we believe its cost data on schooling is not relevant for a future policy of investment in education.

For estimating rates of return in the urban sector, we have used wages of workers and self-employed workers in Bogota which were provided for the period 1963–1966 by the unemployment surveys of the Center for Economic Development Studies of the University of the Andes (CEDE).

The cost data, which include teachers' salaries, depreciation of the educational equipment, and schooling materials, were obtained mainly through the government records on the annual operating costs of the public sector of the school system.[11]

In order to determine future wages by schooling, we have to project through time

---

10. The urban sector excludes agriculture and mining.
11. The basic data are reported in Selowsky (1968a).

Table 17.9. Colombia: Labor Input Categories

Category	Hourly wage[a] (1963-1966)	Level
L_1	0.88	illiterate or no schooling
L_2	1.41	1-3 years, primary schooling
L_3	3.57	4-5 years, primary schooling
L_4	5.93	1-4 years, high school
L_5[b]	14.26	5-6 years, high school; 1-2 years, university education
L_6	23.28	3-6 years, university education

[a] In pesos of 1966.
[b] Also includes specialized secondary education.

the supply and demand for each category of the labor force, classified by schooling. For this purpose, we have classified the labor input into six categories: the criterion used was to include in each category all schooling levels with relatively similar wages. The categories used are given in Table 17.9:

For the purpose of projecting the demand for each category, we must again assume some properties of the aggregate production function of the urban sector of Colombia: we have used the same kind of production function as we used in the preceding section, namely, one that allows for a unitary elasticity of substitution between capital and labor and leaves unconstrained the (constant) elasticity of substitution among different types of labor classified by schooling. This production function has the property that the relative wage of any category w_i/w_j is only a function of the relative supply of that category, L_i/L_j.

In projecting the future supply of each category, we used two alternatives. The first one, of pessimistic nature, assumes that the educational distribution of the labor force will remain constant and equal to the one obtained through the population census of 1964. Given that the growth rate of the urban labor force was projected at 3.5 percent, this implies that each category of the labor force will also increase at 3.5 percent per year. The second alternative was based on the trend observed in the period 1951–1964 (intercensus period) and projects the growth rates of the different categories as:

$$\begin{array}{ll} L_2 & 3.5 \text{ percent} \\ L_3 & 4.0 \text{ percent} \\ L_4 & 4.0 \text{ percent} \\ L_5 & 5.8 \text{ percent} \\ L_6 & 5.8 \text{ percent} \end{array}$$

Category L_1—illiterates and individuals with no schooling—was obtained residually as the difference between the total labor force (projected to grow at 3.5 percent) and the sum of categories L_2 to L_6. This projection implies a strong decline in the

Table 17.10. Colombia: Educational Distribution of the Labor Force (percents)

Category	Projection A 1970-1985	Projection B 1970	1975	1980	1985
L_1	12.70	10.00	7.58	4.97	2.17
L_2	33.28	33.28	33.28	33.28	33.28
L_3	31.44	32.36	33.15	33.96	34.79
L_4	12.65	13.02	13.34	13.67	14.00
L_5	7.75	8.85	9.87	11.02	12.30
L_6	2.18	2.49	2.78	3.10	3.46

absolute number of illiterates and individuals with no schooling, a result that will seem highly implausible. However (as we shall see later), the purpose of this projection is to overstate the change in relative wages over time to see how much difference it makes to the rate of return to education: given our production function, this change in relative wages can come about only as a result of changes in the educational distribution of the labor force.

Table 17.10 presents the educational distribution of the labor force under two projections A and B. With projection A, this distribution is constant and equal to the one of 1964. With projection B, we have tried to overstate the changes in this distribution by strongly increasing the relative abundance of the groups of relatively higher levels of schooling.

For determining any future wage w_i, we use equation (17.12). For this purpose we have projected the growth rate of output in the urban sector of Colombia at 5 percent and equal to the one observed in the decade 1956–1966. The values of d_i were estimated using the 1963–1966 wage information and the 1964 educational distribution of the labor force provided by the population census. The expression $(1 - \alpha)$ is simply the relative share of the labor input in the aggregate product of the urban sector of Colombia.

Under projection A the educational distribution of the labor force remains constant, and, given the production function used, we obtain constant relative wages through time. The effect of a 5 percent growth rate of output is to increase all wages by 1.4 percent per year independently of the elasticity of substitution among labor groups.

Table 17.11 shows the annual growth rate of the real wages obtained with projection B and two alternative values of the elasticity of substitution. We can see that the relative wages of the more educated groups of the labor force tend to decline, the reason being that those groups become relatively more abundant through time. The wage of L_1 has the highest growth rate, given that its relative supply diminishes strongly over time. By increasing the value of σ_L from 3 to 6, relative wages become less sensitive to changes in the educational distribution and therefore experience a less different annual growth rate.[12]

12. Recall that σ_L is defined as

$$\sigma_L = - \frac{d \log (L_i/L_j)}{d \log (w_i/w_j)}$$

Table 17.11. Colombia: Annual Growth Rate of the Hourly Wage under Projection B (percents)

| Category | $\sigma_L = 3$ | | | | $\sigma_L = 6$ | | | |
	1964-1970	1970-1975	1975-1980	1980-1985	1964-1970	1970-1975	1975-1980	1980-1985
L_1	2.1	2.6	3.7	6.4	1.2	1.5	2.0	3.3
L_2	0.8	0.7	0.7	0.7	0.6	0.6	0.5	0.5
L_3	0.6	0.6	0.6	0.6	0.5	0.5	0.4	0.4
L_4	0.6	0.6	0.6	0.6	0.5	0.5	0.4	0.4
L_5	0.1	0.1	0	0	0.2	0.2	0.2	0.1
L_6	0.1	0.1	0	0	0.2	0.2	0.2	0.1

Estimating the Rates of Return

With the help of the initial cost data and the growth rate of wages over time, it is possible to estimate the rate of return to schooling for the base year 1964. For this purpose it was assumed that the wage data generated by the 1963–1966 samples were determined by the 1964 educational distribution of the labor force obtained through the population census in Colombia.

Figure 17.2 presents the resulting rates of return with projections A and B together with a value of $\sigma_L = 3$. With projection A, the rates of return were 30 percent, 23 percent, and 7 percent for primary, high school, and university, respectively. When evaluating those rates with projection B, we obtained values equal to 28 percent, 20 percent, and 6 percent, respectively. The reason for this decline is that, under projection B, the relative wages of the less educated groups go up during the lifetime of the educational project. This implies, for each project, an increase in the foregone income and a relative decline in the wage differential by schooling.

When analyzing the second problem—the change of the rates of return over time—we observe a constant rate when using projection A and (except for university) a declining rate when using projection B.

The reason for a constant rate under projection A is the constancy of relative wages over time. One of the characteristics of an educational project is that almost all of its cost components are also payments to the labor input, namely, foregone income and teacher salaries; in other words, the benefits and costs of this kind of project could be classified as payments to different categories of the labor input classified by schooling. Constant relative wages over time imply that the costs and benefits grow through time at the same rate (1.4 percent per year), which means a constant rate of return over time.

This can be shown as follows: the internal rate of return *in 1964* of increasing the level of schooling of an individual from a to b years of schooling is r_0, the discount rate that equates:

$$\sum_{i=1}^{b-a} (w_i^a + \beta w_i^c)(1 + r_0)^{-i} = \sum_{i=b-a+1}^{\infty} (w_i^b - w_i^a)(1 + r_0)^{-i} \qquad (17.15)$$

where the left-hand side represents the present discounted cost of schooling—foregone income plus teacher salaries—and the right-hand side, the present discounted value of the benefits or the wage differential. The terms w_i^a, w_i^b, w_i^c represent the yearly wages of individuals with a, b, and c years of schooling in the ith year of the 1964 project. Individuals with c years of schooling are used as teachers in the $(b - a)$ years of this schooling level with a student-teacher ratio equal to $1/\beta$. When evaluating this same project at any year $1964 + T$, we have:

$$\sum_{i=1}^{b-a} [w_i^a(1 + \lambda_a)^T + \beta w_i^c(1 + \lambda_c)^T](1 + r_T)^{-i}$$

$$= \sum_{i=b-a+1}^{\infty} [w_i^b(1 + \lambda_b)^T - w_i^a(1 + \lambda_a)^T](1 + r_T)^{-i} \qquad (17.16)$$

where λ_a, λ_b, and λ_c is the (constant) annual growth rate of wages w^a, w^b, and w^c. The term r_T is the internal rate of return at year $1964 + T$. If relative wages remain

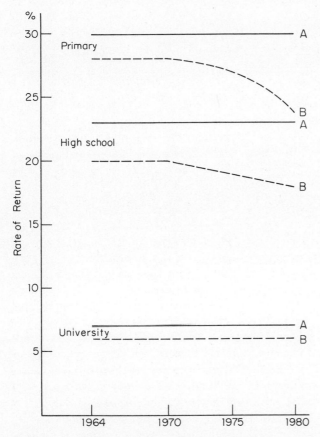

Figure 17.2 The internal rate of return through time: projections A and B ($\sigma_L = 3$).

constant over time, then $\lambda_a = \lambda_b = \lambda_c$ (equal to 1.4 percent in our case) which implies $r_0 = r_T$.

With projection B, the rates of return, except for university education, tend to decline over time. Increasing relative wages of the less educated groups through time imply lower rates of return when we evaluate an educational project in the future.

By looking at Figure 17.2, we can see that the decline in the rates of return over time is stronger for the lower levels of schooling. This can be analyzed with the help of equation (17.16) by assuming that the λ's are constant over time. We then have three cases.

Primary Education

In analyzing primary education, λ_a, λ_b, and λ_c are the annual growth rates of wages of illiterates, primary graduates, and high school graduates, respectively. The reason for including the last group is that high school graduates are used as teachers in primary schools.

By looking at Table 17.11 ($\sigma_L = 3$), we can see that $\lambda_a > \lambda_b$, and that λ_c is almost nil. A positive λ_a implies an increase in costs due to foregone income, and a positive $\lambda_a - \lambda_b$ implies a decline in the relative benefits: both effects explain the decline of r over time.

High School Education

In this case, λ_a and $\lambda_b = \lambda_c$ are the growth rate of wages of primary and high school graduates, respectively; the reason for $\lambda_b = \lambda_c$ is that high school graduates are used as teachers in high school education.

Given that $\lambda_b = \lambda_c$ is negligible, the only effect is the one of a positive λ_a. This implies an increase in costs due to an increased foregone income and a decline in the benefits due to a relatively lower wage differential. The reason for a lower decline in r than in the case of primary education is that λ_a is much higher in the case of primary schooling. By looking at Table 17.11 we can see that the growth rate of the wage of illiterates is approximately between 3.5 and 10 times the growth rate of the primary graduates' wage, the exact value being a function of the period chosen.

University Education

The constancy of the rate of return to university education is explained by the fact that all of the relevant λ's are almost zero (see Table 17.11). In other words, projection B implies almost no growth in the real wages of high school and university graduates, which results in a constant r and equal to the 1964 one.

III. Interpretation of the Results and Conclusions

The bias involved in valuing the product of education for periods far away from the present at current relative wages can be analyzed in view of the small amount of available empirical evidence on σ_L. Samuel Bowles (1969), working with inter-country data and with three classifications of the labor input, found values of σ_L for the two pairs of labor equal to 6 and 12. On the other hand, Christopher Dougherty (Chapter 12, this volume), using United States time-series data and eight classifications of labor, found a value equal to 3.63 (the value of $1/\sigma_L$ was 0.276 and its standard error 0.045).

By using $\sigma_L = 4$ instead of $\sigma_L = \infty$ (or the constant relative wage assumption), the contribution of education to past growth increases, for the period 1940–1945, by 69 percent and 65 percent for Chile and Mexico, respectively. For the period 1960–1964 this contribution increases by 13 percent and 12 percent, respectively.

In analyzing the contribution of investment in schooling to future output, we find a decline in the rates of return when using $\sigma_L = 3$ instead of the constant relative wage assumption. For the case of Colombia, this decline is 6, 5, and 1 percentage points between 1964 and 1980 for primary, high school, and university education, respectively. However, for the period 1964–1975 this decline is only 3 and 4 percentage points for primary and high school education, respectively.

These results would imply that the use of present relative wages by schooling, either in the measurement of education's contribution to past growth or future output, can be justified provided the periods studied are not significantly far away from the present. In the light of the values of σ_L used and the past and projected changes in the educational distribution of the labor force of the countries studied, this period is roughly a decade.

The above results would justify the use of a linear maximand of (constant) present relative wages in short-run optimizing models of investment in education. In this kind of framework the determination of optimum magnitudes of investment comes from the "supply side" or the short-run constraints implied by the educational production function and the available amounts of educational inputs. This has been the method followed by Bowles (1969) in his 8- and 15-year optimizing models for Nigeria and Greece, respectively.

On the other hand, optimizing models of a longer run should take explicitly into account the changes in relative wages generated by the expansion of the educational system itself. In this case, the determination of optimum amounts of investment will be also a function of the diminishing returns generated by the demand for educated labor.

Finally, it is useful to recall that in our exercise σ_L was used as a single simple device relating changes in relative wages to changes in the educational distribution of the labor force. However, as long as this relationship is affected by the factors b to d enumerated on p. 389, the estimated values of σ_L are affected by all those elements not included explicitly, namely, changes in the composition of output, different complementary between physical capital and each type of labor, and so on.

Ideally, any projection of future relative wages by schooling should be a function of these variables taken separately. This is particularly true if we expect differences in the trends of changes in the sectorial composition of output, capital accumulation, and so forth. Unfortunately, the existing amount of information does not allow us to take explicitly into account these possible relationships.

References

Abou Ali, M. S. A., 1965. "Effects of Income Distribution on Saving-Income Ratios, with Special Reference to Underdeveloped Countries." Ph.D. dissertation, Harvard University.

Abramovitz, M., 1952. "Economics of Growth," in B. F. Haley (ed.), *A Survey of Contemporary Economics*, American Economic Association, Homewood, Ill.: Irwin.

———— et al. (eds.), 1959. *The Allocation of Economic Resources*. Stanford: Stanford University Press.

———— 1956. "Resource and Output Trends in the U.S. since 1870," *American Economic Review*, May 1956, *46*, 5–23.

Adelman, I., and F. L. Adelman, 1959. "The Dynamic Properties of the Klein-Goldberger Model," *Econometrica*, Oct. 1959, *27*, 596–625.

———— and E. Thorbecke (eds.), 1966. *The Theory and Design of Economic Development*. Baltimore: Johns Hopkins Press.

Adler, J. H., and P. W. Kuznets (eds.), 1967. *Capital Movements and Economic Development*. New York: Macmillan Co.

Agarwala, A. N., and S. P. Singh (eds.), 1954. *The Economics of Underdevelopment*. London: Oxford University Press.

Allen, R. G. D., 1938. *Mathematical Analysis for Economists*. New York: Macmillan Co.

Almon, Clopper, Jr., 1966. *The American Economy to 1975*. New York: Harper & Row.

Archibald, G. C., 1964. *Investment and Technical Change in Greek Manufacturing*. Lecture Series 15. Athens: International Pub. Service.

Arrow, K. J., L. Hurwicz, and H. Uzawa (eds.), 1958. *Studies in Linear and Non-Linear Programming*. Stanford: Stanford University Press.

———— H. Chenery, B. Minhas, and R. Solow, 1961. "Capital-Labor Substitution and Economic Efficiency," *Review of Economics and Statistics*, August 1961, *43*, 225–250.

———— and M. Kurz, 1970. *Public Investment, the Rate of Return, and Optimal Fiscal Policy*. Baltimore: Johns Hopkins Press.

Baer, W., and I. Kerstenetzky (eds.), 1964. *Inflation and Growth in Latin America*. Homewood, Ill.: Irwin.

———— and F. T. Sparrow, 1966. "Experiments with Linear and Piece-Wise Linear Dynamic Programming Models," in Adelman and Thorbecke (eds.), *The Theory and Design of Economic Development*.

Barr, J. L., and A. S. Manne, 1967. "Numerical Experiments with Finite Horizon Planning Models," *Indian Economic Review*, April 1967, *2*, 1–31.

Barrie, J. M., 1914. *The Admirable Crichton*. London: Hodder & Stoughton.

Banco de Mexico, Oficina de Estudios sobre Proyecciones Agrícolas, 1963. *Encuesta sobre ingresos y gastos familiares en México*. Mexico, D.F., March 1966.

Becker, G., 1964. *Human Capital*. New York: National Bureau of Economic Research.

Bergan, A., 1967. "Personal Income Distribution and Personal Savings in Pakistan," *Pakistan Development Review*, Summer 1967, *7*, 160–212.

Bergsman, J., and A. S. Manne, 1966. "An Almost-Consistent Intertemporal Model for India's Fourth and Fifth Plans," in Adelman and Thorbecke (eds.), *The Theory and Design of Economic Development*.

Bhagwati, J., 1964. "The Pure Theory of International Trade," *Economic Journal*, March 1964, *74*, 1–84.

Bos, H. C., and L. M. Koyck, 1961. "The Appraisal of Road Construction Projects: A Practical Example," *Review of Economics and Statistics*, Feb. 1961, *43*, 13–20.

Bowles, S., 1964. "A Planning Model for the Efficient Allocation of Resources in Education." Mimeographed. Cambridge, Mass.: Harvard University.

———— 1965. "The Efficient Allocation of Resources in Education: A Planning Model with Applications to Northern Nigeria." Ph.D. dissertation, Harvard University.

———— 1967. "Changes in the Structure of Employment in Greece by Age, Sex and Education, 1951–1961." Mimeographed. Cambridge, Mass.: Harvard University.

———— 1968. "The Aggregation of Labor Inputs in the Study of Growth and Planning: Experiments with a Two-Level CES Function," Economic Development Report No. 122, Project for Quantitative Research in Economic Development, Harvard University.

———— 1969. *Planning Educational Systems for Economic Growth*. Cambridge, Mass.: Harvard University Press.

———— 1970. "Aggregation of Labor Inputs in the Economics of Growth and Planning: Experiments with a Two-Level CES Function," *Journal of Political Economy*, Jan.–Feb. 1970, *78*, 68–81.

Bowman, M. J., 1964. "Schultz, Denison and the Contribution of 'Eds' to National Income Growth," *Journal of Political Economy*, Oct. 1964, *72*, 450–464.

Braithwaite, S. N., 1967a. "The Measurement of Latin American Real Income in U. S. Dollars," *Economic Bulletin for Latin America*, Oct. 1967, *12*, 107–142.

———— 1967b. "Comparison of Latin American Real Incomes," Tenth General Conference of the International Association for Research in Income and Wealth.

Bronfenbrenner, M., T. Yamane, and C. H. Lee, 1955. "A Study in Redistribution and Consumption," *Review of Economics and Statistics*, May 1955, *37*, 149–59.

Brown, A., et al., 1964. "Output Manpower and Industrial Skills in the United Kingdom," in OECD, Study Group in the Economics of Education, *The Residual Factor and Economic Growth*, 240–263. Paris: Organisation for Economic Cooperation and Development.

Bruno, M., 1962. *Interdependence, Resource Use and Structural Change in Israel*. Jerusalem: Bank of Israel.

———— 1966. "A Programming Model for Israel," in Adelman and Thorbecke (eds.), *The Theory and Design of Economic Development*.

———— 1966a. "Experiments with a Multi-Sectoral Programming Model," in Adelman and Thorbecke, *The Theory and Design of Economic Development*.

———— 1966b. "Estimation of Factor Contribution to Growth Under Structural Disequilibrium." Mimeographed. Jerusalem: Bank of Israel and Hebrew University.

———— 1967a. "Optimal Accumulation in Discrete Capital Models," in Shell, K. (ed.), *Essays on the Theory of Optimal Economic Growth*. Cambridge, Mass.: M.I.T. Press.

———— 1967b. "Optimal Patterns of Trade and Development," *The Review of Economics and Statistics*, Nov. 1967, *49*, 545–554.

———— 1967c. "The Optimal Selection of Export-Promoting and Import-Substituting Projects," in United Nations, *Planning the External Sector: Techniques, Problems and Policies*, Report on First International Seminar on Development Planning, Document No. ST/TAO/SER C/91.

———— 1969. "Fundamental Duality Relations in the Pure Theory of Capital and Growth," *Review of Economic Studies*, Jan. 1969.

────── M. Fraenkel, and C. Dougherty, 1968. *Dynamic Input-Output, Trade and Development.* Mimeographed. Jerusalem: Bank of Israel and Hebrew University.

Bryson, A. E., and Y. Ho, 1969. *Applied Optimal Control.* Waltham, Mass.: Blaisdell Publishing Co.

Burt, O., 1966. "Economic Control of Groundwater Reserves," *Journal of Farm Economics,* August 1966. *48*(3) Part 1: 632–647.

Carnoy, M., 1963. "The Costs and Returns to Schooling in Mexico." Ph.D. dissertation, University of Chicago.

Carter, A. P., and A. Brody (eds.), 1969. *Applications of Input-Output Analysis.* Amsterdam: North Holland.

Carter, N. G., 1967a. "A New Look at the Sandee Model," in Shell (ed.), *Essays on the Theory of Optimal Economic Growth.*

────── 1967b. "On the Use of a Non-Linear Criterion Function in Development Programming Models." Ph.D. dissertation, M.I.T.

Chakravarty, S., 1962. "Optimum Savings with a Finite Planning Horizon," *International Economic Review,* Sept. 1962, *3*, 338–355.

────── 1965. "Optimal Programme of Capital Accumulation in a Multi-Sector Economy," *Econometrica,* July 1965, *33*, 557–570.

────── and L. Lefeber, 1965. "An Optimizing Planning Model," *Economic Weekly,* Feb. 1965, *17* (5, 6, and 7), 237–252.

Chenery, H. B., 1952. "Overcapacity and the Acceleration Principle," *Econometrica,* Jan. 1952, *20*, 1–28.

────── 1959. "The Interdependence of Investment Decisions," in M. Abramovitz et al. (eds.), *The Allocation of Economic Resources.*

────── 1960. "Patterns of Industrial Growth," *American Economic Review,* Sept. 1960, *50*, 624–654.

────── 1961. "Comparative Advantage and Development Policy," *American Economic Review,* March 1961, *51*, 18–51.

────── 1963. "Foreign Assistance and Economic Development," paper presented to the Econometric Society, December 1963.

────── 1965. "Comparative Advantage and Development Policy," in *Surveys of Economic Theory,* vol. II. London: St. Martin's Press.

────── and M. Bruno, 1962. "Development Alternatives in an Open Economy: The Case of Israel," *Economic Journal,* March 1962, *72*, 79–103.

────── and P. G. Clark, 1959. *Interindustry Economics.* New York: John Wiley.

────── and P. Eckstein, 1967. "Development Alternatives for Latin America," Economic Development Report No. 29, Project for Quantitative Research in Economic Development, Harvard University.

────── and K. Kretschmer, 1956. "Resource Allocation for Economic Development," *Econometrica,* Oct. 1956, *24*, 365–399.

────── and A. MacEwan, 1966. "Optimal Patterns of Growth and Aid: The Case of Pakistan," in Adelman and Thorbecke (eds.), *The Theory and Design of Economic Development.*

────── and A. Strout, 1966. "Foreign Assistance and Economic Development," *American Economic Review,* Sept. 1966, *56*, 679–733.

────── and A. Strout, 1968. " 'Reply' to a Comment by Fei and Ranis," *American Economic Review,* Sept. 1968, *58*, 915.

────── and Lance Taylor, 1966. "Intercountry and Intertemporal Patterns of Industrial Growth," Memorandum No. 15, Center for International Affairs, Harvard University.

────── and L. Taylor, 1968. "Development Patterns: Among Countries and Over Time," *Review of Economics and Statistics,* Nov. 1968, *50*, 391–416.

────── and H. Uzawa, 1958. "Non-Linear Programming in Economic Development," in K. J. Arrow, L. Hurwicz, and H. Uzawa (eds.), *Studies in Linear and Non-Linear Programming.*

———— and L. E. Westphal, 1967. "Economies of Scale and Investment over Time," Memorandum No. 16, Project for Quantitative Research in Economic Development, Harvard University.

Christ, C. F., 1956. "Aggregate Econometric Models," *American Economic Review*, June 1956, *46*, 385–408.

———— et al., 1963. *Measurement in Economics*. Stanford: Stanford University Press.

CIAP, 1968. *La Brecha Externa de la América Latina, 1968–1973*. Comité Inter-Americano de la Alianza para el Progreso (Pan American Union), Washington, D.C.

Clark, P. B., 1967. "A Study of Optimal Import Substitution Strategies for Nigeria." Ph.D. dissertation, M.I.T.

Coale, A. J., and E. M. Hoover, 1958. *Population Growth and Economic Development in Low-Income Countries*. Princeton, N.J.: Princeton University Press.

Cohen, B. I., 1966. "Foreign Exchange Constraints in Economic Development and Efficient Aid Allocation: A Comment," *Economic Journal*, March 1966, *76*, 168–170.

Coutsomaris, G., 1963. *The Morphology of Greek Industry*. Athens: Center of Planning and Economic Research.

Dantzig, G. B., 1963. *Linear Programming and Extensions*. Princeton, N.J.: Princeton University Press.

Davis, R. E., D. A. Kendrick, and M. Weitzman, 1967. "A Branch and Bound Algorithm for Zero-One Mixed Integer Programming Problems," Memorandum No. 69, Project for Quantitative Research in Economic Development, Harvard University.

Denison, E. F., 1962. *The Sources of Economic Growth in the U.S. and the Alternatives before Us*, Supplementary Paper 13, Committee for Economic Development, New York.

———— with Jean-Pierre Poullier, 1967. *Why Growth Rates Differ: Postwar Experience in Nine Western Countries*. Washington, D.C.: The Brookings Institution.

Dillon, J. L., and A. A. Powell, 1965. "Un Modelo Econométrico de la Demanda al Detalle en Santiage de Chile," *Cuadernos de Economía*, Sept. 1965, *2*, 7.

Dorfman, R., P. A. Samuelson, and R. M. Solow, 1958. *Linear Programming and Economic Analysis*. New York: McGraw-Hill.

Dorrance, G. S., 1963. "The Effect of Inflation on Economic Development," *IMF Staff Papers*, March 1963, *10*, 1–47.

Dougherty, C. R. S., 1969. "The Optimal Allocation of Investment in Education," Economic Development Report No. 129, Harvard University.

Duesenberry, J. S., 1949. *Income, Saving, and the Theory of Consumer Behavior*. Cambridge, Mass.: Harvard University Press.

———— and H. Kistin, 1953. "The Role of Demand in the Economic Structure," in W. Leontief et al. (eds.), *Studies in the Structure of the American Economy*.

Eckaus, R. S., 1964. "Economic Criteria for Education and Training," *Review of Economics and Statistics*, May 1964, *46*, 181–190.

———— and K. S. Parikh, 1968. *Planning for Growth: Multisectoral Intertemporal Models Applied to India*. Cambridge, Mass.: M.I.T. Press.

Economic Commission for Europe, 1963. *Some Factors in the Economic Growth of Europe During the 1950's*. Geneva: United Nations.

Ellis, H. S., in collaboration with D. Psilos, R. Westebbe, and C. Nicalaou, 1964. *Industrial Capital in Greek Development*. Athens: Center of Planning and Economic Research.

Everett, H., 1964. "Generalized Language Multiplier Method for Solving Problems of Optimum Allocation of Resources," *Operations Research*, *2*, 543–567.

Falcon, W. P., 1964. "Farmer Response to Price in an Underdeveloped Area: A Case Study of West Pakistan," *American Economic Review*, May 1964, *54*, 580–91.

———— and C. H. Gotsch, 1966. "Relative Price Response, Economic Efficiency and Technological Change: A Study of Punjab Agriculture," Economic Development Report No. 11, Project for Quantitative Research in Economic Development and the Development Advisory Service, Harvard University.

——— and G. F. Papanek (eds.), 1971. *Development Policy II: The Pakistan Experience.* Cambridge, Mass.: Harvard University Press.

Fei, J. C. H., and G. Ranis, 1964. *Development of the Labor Surplus Economy.* Homewood, Ill.: Irwin.

——— 1968. "Foreign Assistance and Economic Development: Comment," *American Economic Review,* Sept. 1968, *58,* 897–912.

Feldstein, M. S., 1964. "The Social Time Preference Discount Rate in Cost Benefit Analysis," *Economic Journal,* June 1964, *74,* 360–379.

Felix, D., 1961. "An Alternative View of the 'Monetarist'-'Structuralist' Controversy," in A. O. Hirschman (ed.), *Latin American Issues.*

Fletcher, R., and M. J. D. Powell, 1963. "A Rapidly Convergent Descent Method of Minimization," *The Computer Journal,* 1963, *6,* 163–168.

——— and C. M. Reeves, 1964. "Function Minimization for Conjugate Gradients," *British Computer Journal,* July 1964, *7,* 149–154.

Flores, E., 1959. "Significance of Land Use Changes in the Economic Development of Mexico," *Land Economics,* May 1959, *35,* 115–124.

Food and Agriculture Organization, 1960. "Analysis of Family Budget Data of Wadi Halfa (Sudan)." Mimeographed. Rome.

Fox, K. A., 1953. *The Analysis of Demand for Farm Products.* U.S. Department of Agriculture Technical Bulletin 1081, Washington, D.C.

Friedman, S. I., 1968, "An Algorithm for Dynamic Programming of Economic Growth," Technical Report No. 28, Center for Research in Management Science, University of California, Berkeley.

Frisch, R., 1959. "A Complete Scheme for Computing All Direct and Cross Demand Elasticities in a Model with Many Sectors," *Econometrica,* 1959, *27,* 177–196.

——— 1961. *A Survey of Types of Economic Forecasting and Programming and a Brief Description of the Oslo Channel Model.* Oslo, Norway: Institute of Economics, University of Oslo.

Gaathon, A. L., 1961. *Capital Stock, Employment and Output in Israel, 1950–1959.* Jerusalem: Bank of Israel.

García-D'Acuna, E., 1964. "Inflation in Chile, A Quantitative Analysis." Ph.D. dissertation, M.I.T.

Geronimakis, S., 1962. *Distribution of National Income and Employment in Greece* (in Greek). Athens.

Gervaise, I., 1720. *System or Theory of the Trade of the World.* London: H. Woodfall.

Gilbert, R., 1964. "The Works Programme in East Pakistan," *International Labour Review,* March 1964, *89.*

Goldberger, A. S., 1964. *Econometric Theory.* New York: John Wiley.

——— 1966. "International Comparison of Consumption Patterns: An Application of Stone's Linear Expenditure System." Mimeographed. University of Wisconsin.

Goode, R., 1961. "Taxation of Saving and Consumption in Underdeveloped Countries," *National Tax Journal,* Dec. 1961, *14.*

Goreux, L. M., 1959. *Income Elasticity of the Demand for Food.* Rome: Food and Agriculture Organization.

Gotsch, C. H., 1966a. "Aggregate Water Response Curves: Some Inconclusive Evidence." Mimeographed. Harvard University.

——— 1966b. "Technological Change and Private Investment in Agriculture: A Case Study of the Pakistan Punjab." Ph.D. dissertation, Harvard University.

Griliches, Z., 1963. "The Sources of Measured Productivity Growth: United States Agriculture, 1940–1960," *Journal of Political Economy,* August 1963, *71,* 331–346.

——— 1968. "Notes on the Role of Education in Production Function and Growth Accounting." Paper presented at the Conference on Education and Income of the Conference on Research in Income and Wealth, Madison, Wisconsin.

——— and D. W. Jorgenson, 1967. "The Explanation of Productivity Change," *Review of Economic Studies*, July 1967, *34*, 249–284.

Grunwald, J., 1961. "The 'Structuralist' School of Price Stability and Development: The Chilean Case," in A. O. Hirschman (ed.), *Latin American Issues*.

Gurley, J. G., 1968. "Hacia una Teoría de las Estructuras Financieras y el Desarrollo Económico," in *Estructura Financiera y Desarrollo Económico*. Buenos Aires: Di Tella.

Haberler, G., and R. M. Stern (eds.), 1961. *Equilibrium and Growth in the World Economy, 1954–1961*. Cambridge, Mass: Harvard University Press.

Haldi, J., 1960. "Economies of Scale in Economic Development," Memorandum No. E-7, Stanford Project for Quantitative Research in Economic Development, Stanford University.

——— and D. Whitcomb, 1967. "Economies of Scale in Industrial Plants," *Journal of Political Economy*, August 1967, *75*, 373–385.

Halkin, H., 1966. "A Maximum Principle of the Pontryagin Type for Systems Described by Non-linear Difference Equations," *SIAM Journal on Control*, 1966, 90–111.

Hansen, B., 1965. "Tax Policy and Mobilization of Saving," in A. T. Peacock and G. Hauser (eds.), *Government Finance and Economic Development*.

Hansen, W. L., 1963. "Total and Private Rates of Return to Investment in Schooling," *Journal of Political Economy*, April 1963, *71*, 128–140.

Harberger, A. C., 1964. "Some Notes on Inflation," in Baer and Kerstenetzky (eds.), *Inflation and Growth in Latin America*.

——— and M. Selowsky, 1966. "Key Factors in the Economic Growth of Chile: An Analysis of the Sources of Past Growth and of Prospects for 1965–70." Mimeographed. Chicago: University of Chicago.

Harrod, R. F., 1963. *Towards a Dynamic Economics*. London: Macmillan & Co.

Harza Engineering Co. International and C. H. Gotsch, 1967. "A Sample Survey of Private Tubewells and Farms, Gujranwala Area." West Pakistan Water and Power Development Authority, Lahore, April 1967.

Heady, E. O., and W. Chandler, 1958. *Linear Programming Methods*. Ames, Iowa: Iowa State College Press.

Higgins, G. H., 1955. "Financing Development of Underdeveloped Areas" in *International Conciliation*, March 1955, No. 502.

Hirschman, A. O., 1958. *The Strategy of Economic Development*. New Haven: Yale University Press.

——— 1961. *Latin American Issues*. New York: Twentieth Century Fund.

Hoch, I., 1962. "Estimation of Production Function Parameters Considering Time-Series and Cross-Section Data," *Econometrica*, Jan. 1962, *30*, 34–53.

Holland, E. P. and R. W. Gillespie, 1963. *Experiments on a Simulated Underdeveloped Economy: Development Plans and Balance of Payment Policies*. Cambridge, Mass.: M.I.T. Press.

Hopkins, D. S. P., 1969. "Sufficient Conditions for Optimality in Infinite Horizon Linear Economic Models," Technical Report No. 69-3, Operations Research House, Stanford University.

Houthakker, H. S., 1957. "An International Comparison of Household Expenditure Patterns, Commemorating the Centenary of Engel's Law," *Econometrica*. Oct. 1957, *25*, 532–551.

——— 1960a. "Additive Preferences," *Econometrica*, April 1960, *28*, 244–257.

——— 1960b. "The Influence of Prices and Income on Household Expenditure," *Bulletin of the International Statistical Institute*, 1960, *37*, 1–16.

——— 1961. "An International Comparison of Personal Savings," *Bulletin of the International Statistical Institute*, 1961, *38*, 56–69.

——— 1965a. "New Evidence on Demand Elasticities," *Econometrica*, April 1965, *33*, 277–288.

——— 1965b. "On Some Determinants of Saving in Developed and Underdeveloped

Countries," in E. A. G. Robinson (ed.), *Problems of Economic Development*, Proceedings of a Conference by the International Economic Association. New York: St. Martins.

—— and L. D. Taylor, 1966. *Consumer Demand in the United States, 1929–1970.* Cambridge, Mass.: Harvard University Press.

Indian Perspective Planning Division, 1964. Planning Commission, *Notes on Perspective of Development, India, 1960–61 to 1975–76.* New Delhi.

Indian Perspective Planning Division, 1966. Planning Commission, *Draft Fourth Plan, Material and Financial Balances: 1964–65, 1970–71, and 1975–76.* New Delhi.

Indian Statistical Institute, 1960. *Studies on Consumer Behavior.* Calcutta.

International Bank for Reconstruction and Development (IBRD), 1966. *Programme for the Development of Irrigation and Agriculture in West Pakistan: Vol. 10. Annexure 14, Watercourse Studies.* London: Gibb and Partners.

International Labour Office, 1966. *Yearbook of Labour Statistics 1965.* Geneva.

Johansen, L., 1960. *A Multi-Sectoral Study of Economic Growth.* Amsterdam: North-Holland.

—— assisted by T. Lindholt, 1964. "Savings and Growth in Long-Term Programming Models. Numerical Examples with a Nonlinear Objective Function." Mimeographed. Oslo, Norway: Oslo Institute of Economics.

—— H. Alstadheim, and A. Langsether, 1968. "Explorations in Long-Term Projections for the Norwegian Economy," *The Economics of Planning*, 1968, *8*, 343–373.

Johnson, H. G., 1967. *Economic Policies Toward Less-Developed Countries.* New York: Praeger.

Johnston, J., 1963. *Econometric Methods.* New York: McGraw-Hill.

Jorgenson, D. W., 1961. "The Development of the Dual Economy," *Economic Journal*, June 1961, *71*, 309–334.

—— and Z. Griliches, 1967. "The Explanation of Productivity Change," *Review of Economic Studies*, July 1967, *34*, 249–283.

Kafka, A., 1967. "Economic Effects of Capital Imports," in Adler and Kuznets (eds.), *Capital Movements and Economic Development.*

Kendrick, D., 1967. *A Programming Investment in the Processes Industries.* Cambridge, Mass.: M.I.T. Press.

—— and L. Taylor, 1969. "A Dynamic Nonlinear Planning Model for Korea," in I. Adelman (ed.), *Practical Approaches to Development.* Baltimore: Johns Hopkins Press.

—— and L. Taylor, 1970. "Numerical Solution of Nonlinear Planning Models," *Econometrica*, May 1970, *38*, 453–467.

Kendrick, J. W., 1961. *Productivity Trends in the United States*, National Bureau of Economic Research No. 71, General Series. Princeton, N.J.: Princeton University Press.

Khan, A. R., 1967. "A Multisectoral Programming Model for Regional Planning in Pakistan," *Pakistan Development Review*, Spring 1967, *7*, 29–65.

Khan, M. I., 1963. "A Note on Consumption Patterns in Rural Areas of East Pakistan," *Pakistan Development Review*, Autumn 1963, *3*, 399–413.

Koutsoyanni-Kokkova, A., 1964. *Production Functions in Greek Manufacturing* (in Greek). Athens: Center of Planning and Economic Research.

Kreugel, R., and D. Mertens, 1966. *Fixed Capital Stock and Future Investment Requirements in Greek Manufacturing.* Athens: Center of Planning and Economic Research.

Krishna, R., 1963. "Farm Supply Response in India-Pakistan: A Case Study of the Punjab Region," *Economic Journal*, Sept. 1963, *73*, 477–487.

Krishnamurty, K., 1968. "Savings and Taxation in Developing Countries: An Empirical Study," Economics Department Working Paper No. 23, IBRD, Washington, D.C.

Krivine, D. (ed.), 1967. *Fiscal and Monetary Problems in Developing States*, New York: Praeger.

Kuznets, S. 1955. "International Differences in Capital Formation and Financing," in *Capital Formation and Economic Growth*, Special Conference Series No. 6, NBER Princeton, N.J.: Princeton University Press.

—— 1960. "Quantitative Aspects of the Economic Growth of Nations: II. Capital Formation Proportions, International Comparisons for Recent Years," *Economic Development and Cultural Change*, July 1960, *8*.

—— 1962. "Quantitative Aspects of the Economic Growth of Nations: VII. The Share and Structure of Consumption," *Economic Development and Cultural Change*, Jan. 1962, *10*, 1–92.

—— 1963. "Quantitative Aspects of the Economic Growth of Nations: VIII. Distribution of Income by Size," *Economic Development and Cultural Change*, Jan. 1963, *2*.

—— 1966. *Modern Economic Growth*. New Haven: Yale University Press.

Landau, L., 1966. "Determinants of Savings in Latin America," Report No. 13, Project for Quantitative Research in Economic Development, Mimeographed, Harvard University.

—— 1969. "Differences in Saving Ratios Among Latin American Countries." Ph.D. dissertation, Harvard University.

Landsberger, M., 1965. "Changes in Israeli Consumption Patterns during the Period 1956–57 to 1959–60," in *Bank of Israel Bulletin*, No. 23, Jerusalem, Adar B, 5725.

Lange, O. R., and F. M. Taylor, 1969. *On the Economic Theory of Socialism*. New York: Kelley.

Lasdon, E. S., S. K. Mitter, and A. D. Warren, 1967. "The Conjugate Gradient Method for Optimal Control Problems," *IEEE Transactions on Automatic Control*. April 1967, *12*, 132–138.

Lee, J., 1967. "Improving Aggregation Validity," presented at the Conference on Implications of Structural and Market Changes on Farm Management and Marketing Research, sponsored by the Center for Agriculture and Economic Development, Iowa State. Chicago.

Lefeber, L., 1968. "Planning in a Surplus Labor Economy," *American Economic Review*, June 1968, *88*, 343–373.

Leibenstein, H., 1967. "Rates of Return to Education in Greece," presented at the Development Advisory Service Conference, Sorrento, Italy, September.

Leontief, W. W., 1954. "Domestic Production and Foreign Trade: The American Capital Position Re-examined," *Economia Internazionale*, 1954, *7*, 9–38.

—— 1956. "Factor Proportions and the Structure of American Trade: Further Theoretical and Empirical Analysis," *Review of Economics and Statistics*, Nov. 1956, *38*, 386–407.

—— et al. (eds.), 1953. *Studies in the Structure of the American Economy*. New York: Oxford University Press.

Lewis, J. P., 1962. *Quiet Crisis in India*. Washington, D.C.: The Brookings Institution.

Lewis, W. A., 1954. "Economic Development with Unlimited Supplies of Labor," in Agarwala and Singh (eds.), *The Economics of Underdevelopment*.

Linder, S. B., 1967. *Trade and Trade Policy for Development*. New York: Praeger.

Little, I. M. D., 1960. "The Strategy of Indian Development," *National Institute Economic Review*, May 1960.

—— and J. M. Clifford, 1966. *International Aid*. Chicago: Aldine.

Liviatan, N. 1964. *Consumption Patterns in Israel*. Falk Project for Economic Research in Israel, Jerusalem.

Lubell, H., 1947. "Effects of Income Redistribution on Consumers' Expenditures," *American Economic Review*, March 1947, *37*, 157–169.

MacEwan, A., 1968. "Development Alternatives in Pakistan." Ph.D. dissertation, Harvard University.

—— 1971. *Development Alternatives in Pakistan*. Cambridge, Mass.: Harvard University Press.

McKinnon, R. I., 1964. "Foreign Exchange Constraints in Economic Development and Efficient Aid Allocation," *Economic Journal*, June 1964, *74*, 388–409.

—— 1966. " 'Rejoinder' to B. I. Cohen," *Economic Journal*, March 1966, *76*, 170–171.

Maizels, A., 1968. *Exports and Economic Growth of Developing Countries*. Cambridge: Cambridge University Press.

Mamalakis, M., 1966. "The Export Sector, Stages of Economic Development, and the Saving-Investment Process in Latin America," Center Discussion Paper No. 17, Economic Growth Center, Yale University.

Maneschi, A., 1966. "Optimal Savings with Finite Planning Horizon: A Note," *International Economic Review*, January 1966, *7*, 109–118.

——— and C. W. Reynolds, 1966. "The Effect of Import Substitution on Foreign Exchange Needs, Savings Rates, and Growth in Latin America," Discussion Paper No. 18, Economic Growth Center, Yale University.

Manne, A. S., 1963. "Key Sectors of the Mexican Economy, 1960–1970," in Manne and Markowitz (eds.), *Studies in Process Analysis*.

——— 1966a. "Key Sectors of the Mexican Economy, 1962–1972," in Adelman and Thorbecke (eds.), *The Theory and Design of Economic Development*.

——— 1966b. *Investment for Capacity Expansion*. London: Allen & Unwin.

——— (ed.), 1967 *Investments for Capacity Expansion: Size, Location, and Time Phasing*. Cambridge, Mass.: M.I.T. Press.

——— 1968. "Sufficient Conditions for Optimality in an Infinite Horizon Development Plan," Technical Report No. 68-7, Department of Operations Research, Stanford University.

——— and H. M. Markowitz (eds.), 1963 *Studies in Process Analysis*. New York: John Wiley.

——— and A. Rudra, 1965. "A Consistency Model of India's Fourth Plan," *Sankhya: The Indian Journal of Statistics*, Dec. 1965, series B, *27*, 57–144.

——— and T. E. Weisskopf, 1969. "A Dynamic Multi-Sectoral Model for India: 1967–1975," in Carter and Brody (eds.), *Applications of Input-Output Analysis*.

Marglin, S., 1967. "Industrial Development in the Labor Surplus Economy." Mimeographed. Harvard University.

Markowitz, H. M., and A. S. Manne, 1957. "On the Solution of Discrete Programming Problems," *Econometrica*, 1957, *25*, 84–95.

Marquardt, D. W., 1963. "An Algorithm for Least Squares Estimation of Non-Linear Parameters," *Journal of Society of Industrial and Applied Mathematics*, 1963, *11*.

——— 1964. "Least Square Estimation of Nonlinear Parameters," March, 3094, revision of S. D. No. 1428.

Marschak, J., and W. H. Andrews, 1944. "Random Simultaneous Equations and the Theory of Production," *Econometrica*, July–Oct. 1944, *12*, 143–205.

Martin, A. M., and W. A. Lewis, 1956. "Patterns of Public Revenue and Expenditure," The Manchester School of Economic and Social Studies, Sept. 1956. *24*, 203–244.

Mera, K., 1968. "An Empirical Determination of a Dynamic Utility Function," *Review of Economics and Statistics*, Feb. 1968, *50*, 117–122.

Millikan, M., 1966. "Comment," in Adelman and Thorbecke (eds.), *The Theory and Design of Economic Development*.

Mincer, J., 1962. "On-the-Job Training: Costs, Returns, and Some Implications," *Journal of Political Economy* (supplement), Oct. 1962, *70*, 50–79.

Ministry of Coordination, *National Accounts of Greece* (various years). Athens.

Modigliani, F., 1965. "The Life Cycle Hypothesis of Saving," presented at the First Congress of the Econometric Society, Rome.

——— n.d. "Tests of the Long Run Determinants of the Saving Ratio Based on International Comparisons," unpublished paper.

Mohammad, G., 1963. "Some Physical and Economic Determinants of Cotton Production in West Pakistan," *Pakistan Development Review*, Winter 1963, *3*, 491–526.

——— 1965. "Private Tubewell Development and Cropping Patterns in West Pakistan," *Pakistan Development Review*, Spring 1965, *5*, 1–53.

Moore, F. T., 1959. "Economies of Scale: Some Statistical Evidence," *Quarterly Journal of Economics*, May 1959, *73*, 232–245.

Mosak, J. L., 1967. "Priorities in the Use of Funds," in D. Krivine (ed.), *Fiscal and Monetary Problems in Developing States*.

Mundlak, Y., 1963. "Estimation of Production and Behavioral Functions from a Combination of Cross-Section and Time-Series Data," in C. F. Christ et al. (eds.), *Measurement in Economics*.

———— 1964. *Long-Term Projections of Supply and Demand for Agricultural Products in Israel*. Falk Project for Economic Research in Israel, Jerusalem.

National Council of Applied Economic Research, 1962. *Long-term Projections of Demand and Supply of Selected Agricultural Commodities*. New Delhi: India.

National Statistical Service of Greece, 1961. *Census, 1961*. Athens: National Printing Office.

———— 1966. *Statistical Yearbook of Greece 1965*. Athens: National Printing Office.

Nerlove, M., 1958. "Distributed Lags and Demand Analysis for Agricultural and Other Commodities," *Agricultural Handbook*, 141. Washington, D.C.: U.S. Department of Agriculture.

Nugent, J. B., 1966. *Programming the Optimal Development of the Greek Economy, 1954–1961*. Athens: Center of Planning and Economic Research.

Nurkse, R., 1961. "Home Investment and External Balance," in Haberler (ed.), *Equilibrium and Growth in the World Economy*.

Ohlin, G., 1966. *Foreign Aid Policies Reconsidered*. Paris: OECD.

OAS, 1963. "Estudio sobre política fiscal en la Argentina." Mimeographed. Buenos Aires: Organization of American States.

OECD, 1964. *Statistics of National Accounts, 1950–1961*. Paris: Organisation for Economic Cooperation and Development.

———— 1965. *The Mediterranean Regional Project, Country Reports: Greece*. Paris: Organisation for Economic Cooperation and Development.

Pakistan Institute of Development Economics, 1967. *Population Projections for Pakistan 1960–2000*. Mimeographed. Karachi.

Pakistan Planning Commission, 1965. *The Third Five Year Plan (1965–1970)*. Karachi.

Papandreou, A., 1962. *A Strategy for Greek Economic Development*. Athens: Center of Planning and Economic Research.

Parks, R. W., 1969. "Systems of Demand Equations: An Empirical Comparison of Alternative Functional Forms," *Econometrica*, Oct. 1969, 37(4): 629–650.

Patinkin, D., 1960. *The Israel Economy: The First Decade*. Falk Project for Economic Research in Israel, Jerusalem.

Peacock, A. T., and G. Hauser (eds.), 1965. *Government Finance and Economic Development*. Paris: OECD.

Phelps, E. S., 1965. "Second Essay on the Golden Rule of Accumulation," *American Economic Review*, Sept. 1965, 55, 793–814.

———— and R. A. Pollak, 1968. "On Second-Best National Saving and Game-Equilibrium Growth," *Review of Economic Studies*, April 1968, 35, 185–200.

Porwit, K., 1966. *Central Planning, Evaluation of Variants*, tr. J. Stadler. New York: Pergamon Press.

Prais, S. J., and H. S. Houthakker, 1955. *The Analysis of Family Budgets*. Cambridge: Cambridge University Press.

Radner, Roy, 1963. *Notes on the Theory of Economic Research*. Athens: Center of Planning and Economic Research.

———— 1966. "Optimal Growth in a Linear-Logarithmic Economy," *International Economic Review*, Jan. 1966, 7, 1–33.

———— and S. Friedman, 1965. "An Algorithm for Dynamic Programming of Economic Growth," Working Paper 99, Center for Research in Management Science, University of California, Berkeley.

Raduchel, W. J., 1969. "Dealing with Substitution in Planning Models," Project for Quantitative Research in Economic Development, Harvard University. Mimeographed.

———— 1970. "Technical Supplement to Substitution in Planning Models," Project for Quantitative Research in Economic Development, Harvard University.

Rahman, A. N. M. Azuzur, 1963. "Expenditure Elasticities in Rural West Pakistan," *Pakistan Development Review*, Summer 1963, 3, 232–249.

Rahman, M. Anisur, 1967. "The Welfare Economics of Foreign Aid," *Pakistan Development Review*, Summer 1967, 7.

————— 1968. "Foreign Capital and Domestic Savings: A Test of Haavelmo's Hypothesis with Cross-Country Data," *Review of Economics and Statistics*, Feb. 1968, *50*, 137–138.

Ramseyer, C. F., 1954. "Comparative Investment Costs for Different Steelmaking Processes. A Study of the Iron and Steel Industry in Latin America," vol. II, *Proceedings of the Export Working Group held at Bogota, Colombia* (E/CN. 12/293/Rev. 1).

Ricardo, D., 1965. *The Principles of Political Economy and Taxation.* New York: Everyman's Library.

Roberts, P. O., and D. T. Kresge, 1968. *Models for Transport System Simulation*, chap. 2, "The Macroeconomic Model." Washington, D.C.: The Brookings Institution.

Roy, J., and R. G. Laha, 1960. "Preliminary Estimates of Relative Increase in Consumer Demand in Rural and Urban India," *Studies on Consumer Behavior.* Calcutta: Indian Statistical Institute.

Russell, R. R., 1967. "International Disparities in Income Elasticities," *Review of Economics and Statistics*, Nov. 1967, *49*, 579–582.

Samuelson, P. A., 1947. *Foundations of Economic Analysis.* Cambridge, Mass.: Harvard University Press.

————— 1951. *Activity Analysis of Production and Allocation*, T. C. Koopmans (ed.). New York: John Wiley.

————— 1965. "A Catenary Turnpike Theorem Involving Consumption and the Golden Rule," *American Economic Review*, June 1965, *55*, 486–496.

————— and R. Solow, 1956. "A Complete Capital Model Involving Heterogeneous Capital Goods," *Quarterly Journal of Economics*, Nov. 1956, *70*, 537–562.

Sandee, J., 1960. *A Demonstration Planning Model for India.* New York: Asia Publishing House.

Sato, K., 1967. "A Two-Level Constant-Elasticity-of-Substitution Production Function," *Review of Economic Studies*, April 1967, *34*, 201–218.

Schultz, T. W., 1961. "Education and Economic Growth," in National Society for the Study of Education (eds.), *Social Forces Influencing American Education.* Chicago.

Scitovsky, T., 1954. "Two Concepts of External Economies," *Journal of Political Economy*, April 1954, *62*, 143–151.

Selowsky, M., 1967. "Education and Economic Growth: Some International Comparisons," Report No. 83, Project for Quantitative Research in Economic Development, Harvard University. Mimeographed.

————— 1968a. "The Effect of Unemployment and Growth on the Rate of Return to Education: The Case of Colombia," Report No. 116, Project for Quantitative Research in Economic Development, Harvard University. Mimeographed.

————— 1968b. "Labor Input Substitution and the Measurement of Education's Contribution to Growth," Report No. 119, Project for Quantitative Research in Economic Development, Harvard University. Mimeographed.

Sen, A. K., 1960. *Choice of Techniques.* Oxford: Oxford University Press.

————— 1961. "On Optimising the Rate of Saving," *Economic Journal*, Sept.1961 ,*71*, 479–496.

Shell, K., 1967. *Essays on the Theory of Optimal Economic Growth.* Cambridge: M.I.T. Press.

Solow, R. M., 1957. "Technological Change and the Aggregate Production Function," *Review of Economics and Statistics*, August 1957, *39*, 312–320.

————— 1959. "Competitive Valuation in a Dynamic Input-Output System," *Econometrica*, Jan. 1959, *27*, 30–53.

Srinivasan, T. N., M. R. Saluja, and V. C. Sabherwal, 1965. *Studies in the Structure of the Indian Economy, 1975–76*, Discussion Paper No. 4. New Delhi: Indian Statistical Institute.

Statistisches Bundesamt Wiesbaden, 1960. "Internationaler Vergleich der Preise für die Lebenshaltung," *Preise Löhne Wirschaftsrechnungen*, Reihe 10.

Stern, J. J., 1971. "Growth, Development, and Regional Equity in Pakistan," in Falcon and Papanek (eds.), *Development Policy II: The Pakistan Experience.*

Stigler, G. J. 1954. "The Early History of Empirical Studies of Consumer Behavior," *Journal of Political Economy*, April 1954, *62*, 95–113.

Stone, R., 1954. "Linear Expenditure Systems and Demand Analysis: An Application to the Pattern of British Demand," *Economic Journal*, Sept. 1954, *64*, 511–527.

—— 1965. "A Model of the Educational System," *Minerva*, Winter 1965, *3*, 172–187.

Suits, D., 1964. *An Econometric Model of the Greek Economy*. Athens: Center of Planning and Economic Research.

Sweezy, P., 1956. *The Theory of Capitalist Development*. New York: Monthly Review.

Tendulkar, S. D., 1968. "Some Experiments in a Multi-Sectoral Programming Model for India." Ph.D. dissertation, Harvard University.

Theil, H., 1961. *Economic Forecasts and Policy*, 2d ed. Amsterdam: North-Holland.

Thorn, R. S., 1967. "The Evolution of Public Finances during Economic Development," The Manchester School of Economic and Social Studies, Jan. 1967, Vol. 35.

Tinbergen, J., 1956. *Economic Policy: Principles and Design*. Amsterdam. North-Holland.

—— 1957. "The Appraisal of Road Construction: Two Calculation Schemes," *Review of Economics and Statistics*, August 1957, *39*, 241–249.

——. 1960. "Optimum Savings and Utility Maximization over Time," *Econometrica*, April 1960, *28*, 481–489.

—— and H. Correa, 1962. "Quantitative Adaptation of Education to Accelerated Growth," *Kyklos*, 1962, *15*, 776–785.

United Nations, 1964. Department of Economic and Social Affairs, *A System of National Accounts and Supporting Tables*, Studies in Methods, Series F, No. 2, Rev. 2. New York.

—— 1967a. Department of Economic and Social Affairs, *Demographic Yearbook, 1966*. New York.

—— 1967b. Department of Economic and Social Affairs, *Yearbook of National Accounts Statistics, 1966* (and other years). New York.

—— 1967c. *Economic Survey of Asia and the Far East, 1966*. New York, Sales No. 67, II, F.1.

U.S. Department of Commerce, 1966. *Long-Term Economic Growth, 1860–1965*. Washington, D.C.

Vanek, J., 1964. *Future Foreign Resource Requirements of Colombia*. Washington, D.C.: AID.

—— 1967. *Estimating Foreign Resource Needs for Economic Development: Theory, Method, and a Case Study of Colombia*. New York: McGraw-Hill.

Vietorisz, T., and A. S. Manne, 1963. "Chemical Processes, Plant Location, and Economies of Scale," in Manne and Markowitz (eds.), *Studies in Process Analysis*. New York.

Watanabe, T., 1962. "A Note on the International Comparison of Private Consumption Expenditure," *Weltwirtschaftliches Archiv*, 1962, *88*, 145–149.

Weisbrod, B., 1964. *The External Benefits of Public Education, an Economic Analysis*. Princeton, N.J.: Princeton University Industrial Relations Section.

Weisskopf, T. E., 1967. "A Programming Model for Import Substitution in India," *Sankhya: The Indian Journal of Statistics*, December 1967, *29*, series B, 257–306.

—— 1969. "Alternative Patterns of Import Substitution in India," Economic Development Report No. 127, Project for Quantitative Research in Economic Development, Harvard University. Mimeographed.

West Pakistan Water and Power Development Authority, 1965. *Salinity Control and Reclamation Project No. 4: Upper Rechna Doab*. Denver, Colo.: Tipton and Kalmach.

—— 1966. *Salinity Control and Reclamation Project No. 1: A Technical and Economic Appraisal*. Harza Engineering Co. International.

Westphal, L. E., 1969a. "Planning the Timing and Scale of Investment in Lumpy Projects," Discussion Paper No. 8, Development Research Project, Princeton University.

—— 1969b. "Multi-Sectoral Project Analysis Using Mixed Integer Programming," Report No. 101 (rev.), Project for Quantitative Research in Economic Development, Harvard University. Mimeographed.

—— 1970. *Planning Investment with Economies of Scale*. Amsterdam: North-Holland.

White House, Dept. of Interior, Panel on Waterlogging and Salinity in West Pakistan, 1964.

Report on Land and Water Development in the Indus Plain. Washington, D.C. U.S. Govt. Printing Office.

Williamson, J. G., 1961. "Public Expenditure and Revenue: an International Comparison," The Manchester School of Economic and Social Studies, January 1961, Vol. 29, 43–56.

Wold, H., and L. Jureen, 1952. *Demand Analysis.* New York: John Wiley.

Yaron, Dan, 1966. *Economic Criteria for Water Resource Development and Allocation*, Supplement A. Rehovot, Israel: Hebrew University.

Index

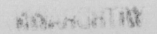